Secondary School Literacy Instruction

THE CONTENT AREAS

TENTH EDITION

Betty D. Roe
Professor Emerita, Tennessee Technological University, Cookeville

Barbara D. Stoodt-Hill
Retired, John Tyler Community College and Old Dominion University

Paul C. Burns
Late of University of Tennessee at Knoxville

 **WADSWORTH**
CENGAGE Learning™

Australia • Brazil • Japan • Korea • Mexico • Singapore • Spain • United Kingdom • United States

WADSWORTH
CENGAGE Learning™

**Secondary School Literacy Instruction:
The Content Areas, Tenth Edition**
Betty D. Roe, Barbara Stoodt-Hill,
and Paul C. Burns

Publisher: Linda Schreiber

Development Editor: Lisa Kalner Williams

Editorial Assistant: Linda Stewart

Media Editor: Ashley Cronin

Content Project Management:
 Pre-Press PMG

Creative Director: Rob Hugel

Art Director: Maria Epes

Manufacturing Buyer: Brian Pieragostini

Marketing Manager: Kara Kindstrom
 Parsons

Marketing Associate: Dmitri Pfeiffer

Rights Acquisitions Account Manager,
 Text: Don Schlotman

Rights Acquisitions Account Manager,
 Image: Leitha Etheridge-Sims

Production Service: Pre-Press PMG

Copy Editor: Pre-Press PMG

Cover Designer: Irene Morris

Cover image: © Getty Images

For product information and technology assistance, contact us at
Cengage Learning Customer & Sales Support, 1-800-354-9706.

For permission to use material from this text or product,
submit all requests online at **www.cengage.com/permissions.**
Further permissions questions can be e-mailed to
permissionrequest@cengage.com.

Library of Congress Control Number: 2010922387

ISBN-13: 978-0-495-80950-0

ISBN-10: 0-495-80950-0

Wadsworth
20 Davis Drive
Belmont, CA 94002–3098
USA

Cengage Learning is a leading provider of customized learning solutions with office locations around the globe, including Singapore, the United Kingdom, Australia, Mexico, Brazil, and Japan. Locate your local office at: **www.cengage.com/global.**

Cengage Learning products are represented in Canada by Nelson Education, Ltd.

To learn more about Wadsworth, visit **www.cengage.com/Wadsworth**

Purchase any of our products at your local college store or at our preferred online store **www.cengagebrain.com.**

Printed in the United States of America
1 2 3 4 5 6 7 8 13 12 11 10

BRIEF CONTENTS

PART 1   Contexts of Literacy Instruction in a Technological Age / 1

    1   Content Area Literacy in a Changing World / 3

    2   Integrating Technology in Content Area Literacy Instruction / 27

PART 2   Instruction and Assessment of All Learners / 61

    3   Content Literacy Assessment / 63

PART 3   Strategies for Learning: Constructing Meaning and Studying / 109

    4   A Conceptual Approach to Developing Meaningful Vocabulary / 111

    5   The Process of Constructing Meaning in Texts / 145

    6   Strategies for Constructing Meaning in Texts / 175

    7   Location and Organization of Information / 205

    8   Reading–Study Strategies for Textbook Use / 227

PART 4   Applying Literacy Instruction in the Content Areas / 263

    9   Writing in the Content Areas / 265

    10   Literature-Based and Thematic Approaches to Content Area Teaching / 313

    11   Reading in the Content Areas: I / 343

    12   Reading in the Content Areas: II / 384

Glossary / 419

References / 425

Name Index / 443

Subject Index / 447

CONTENTS

Preface / xv

PART 1 Contexts of Literacy Instruction in a Technological Age / 1

1 Content Area Literacy in a Changing World / 3

MEETING THE CHALLENGE / 4

Literacy Demands on Secondary School Students / 5

Legislation Related to Secondary School Literacy / 7

Reading Instruction in the Content Area Curriculum / 8

What is Reading? / 8

Personnel Responsible for Secondary School Literacy Instruction / 11

Aspects of a Secondary School Literacy Program / 14

Some Misconceptions about Teaching Reading / 15

Some Misconceptions about Teaching Writing / 17

Literacy Performance and Standards / 17

Literacy Performance / 17

Range of Students in Content Area Classrooms / 21

MEETING THE CHALLENGE / 22

2 Integrating Technology in Content Area Literacy Instruction / 27

Media Literacy / 29

FOCUS ON ENGLISH LANGUAGE LEARNERS / 30

FOCUS ON STRUGGLING READERS / 32

Computers / 33

Word-Processing and Desktop-Publishing Programs / 33

Writing Development Software / 34

Collaboration Software / 34

Databases and Spreadsheets / 35

Using the Internet / 35

**TeachSource
Video Case**
Middle School Reading
Instruction: Integrating
Technology 37

MEETING THE CHALLENGE / 37

    Electronic Communications / 39

MEETING THE CHALLENGE / 40

MEETING THE CHALLENGE / 43

    Electronic Books and Reference Works / 45

    Computer-Assisted Instruction (CAI) / 46

Multimedia Applications / 47

Building on Past Experiences with Technology / 50

    Overhead Projectors / 50

    Televisions / 50

    Audio Recordings / 51

    Video Recordings / 52

Technology for Students with Special Needs or Disabilities / 53

Evaluating Literacy Applications of Technology / 54

Advantages of Technology in the Classroom / 56

Perspective on Technology Use for Literacy Learning Tomorrow / 57

**TeachSource
Video Case**
Multimedia Literacy:
Integrating Technology
into the Middle School
Curriculum 48

PART 2   Instruction and Assessment of All Learners / 61

3   Content Literacy Assessment / 63

Norm-Referenced Tests / 64

    Criteria for Choosing Norm-Referenced Tests / 65

    Norm-Referenced Tests of Reading Achievement / 65

    Concerns about Traditional Standardized Reading Tests / 66

Criterion-Referenced Tests / 67

Classroom-Based Assessments / 68

    Assessments of Background Knowledge / 69

MEETING THE CHALLENGE / 70

    Group Reading Inventories / 72

    Written Skill Inventories / 76

    Informal Reading Inventories / 80

    Cloze Tests / 83

    Gamelike Activities / 85

    Observation / 85

    Interviews and Conferences / 87

    Performance Samples / 87

Portfolio Assessment / 90

    Contents / 91

**TeachSource
Video Case**
Formative Assessment:
High School History
Class 69

**TeachSource
Video Case**
Grading: Strategies and
Approaches 86

**TeachSource
Video Case**
Performance
Assessment: Student
Presentations in a High
School English Class 87

Purpose / 92

Selection and Evaluation / 93

Self-Assessment / 94

Attitude Measures / 95

Interest Assessments / 95

Using Computer Applications for Assessment / 96

Assessing the Readability of Printed Materials / 98

Readability Formulas / 99

Other Methods of Readability Assessment / 101

FOCUS ON STRUGGLING READERS / 103

FOCUS ON ENGLISH LANGUAGE LEARNERS / 104

PART 3 Strategies for Learning: Constructing Meaning and Studying / 109

4 A Conceptual Approach to Developing Meaningful Vocabulary / 111

Word Knowledge / 112

Conceptual Knowledge / 113

MEETING THE CHALLENGE / 113

How do Students Learn Word Meanings and Concepts? / 114

Direct Systematic Instruction / 114

Targeted Vocabulary Instruction / 115

Identifying Categories of Vocabulary / 115

Selecting Words for Direct Instruction / 116

Context Clue Strategies / 118

Kinds of Context Clues / 120

Offer Opportunities to Develop and Expand Meanings / 121

Assess Students' Progress in Developing Vocabulary / 122

FOCUS ON ENGLISH LANGUAGE LEARNERS / 122

FOCUS ON STRUGGLING READERS / 123

MEETING THE CHALLENGE / 125

Background Building / 126

Discussion / 126

Conceptual Relationships / 126

Conceptual Reinforcement Instructional Activities / 129

Visual Organizers / 134

Additional Strategies for Students' Vocabulary Learning / 135

Using Reference Books / 136

Expanding Meaning / 138

    Word Walls / 139

    Mnemonic Strategies / 140

    Computer Software and the Internet / 141

MEETING THE CHALLENGE / 142

5   The Process of Constructing Meaning in Texts / 145

Reading Activities of Adolescents / 146

    Reading Comprehension / 146

Active Readers / 148

    The Context for Active Readers / 148

MEETING THE CHALLENGE / 149

    Self-Questioning / 150

    Question/Answer Relationships (QARs) / 150

Linguistic and Cognitive Components of Comprehension / 151

    Cognitive Flexibility and the Situational Context / 153

    The Situational Context / 154

Schema Theory / 155

    Schemata Types and Relationships / 155

    Building Schemata / 156

    Activating Schemata / 156

Reader-Response Theory / 157

    The Textual Context of Reading Comprehension / 158

FOCUS ON STRUGGLING READERS / 169

FOCUS ON ENGLISH LANGUAGE LEARNERS / 171

6   Strategies for Constructing Meaning in Texts / 175

Good Readers / 175

    Cognitive Processing / 177

    Thinking and Questioning / 177

    Effective Questioning / 177

MEETING THE CHALLENGE / 178

Types of Thinking and Reading / 180

    Literal Thinking and Reading / 180

    Inferential Thinking and Reading / 181

    Critical Thinking and Reading / 182

    Creative Thinking and Reading / 186

Authentic Reading Tasks / 188

MEETING THE CHALLENGE / 188

Strategies to Increase Comprehension / 191

Scaffolds for Comprehension / 192

Directed Reading-Thinking Activity (DRTA) / 192

Discussion / 194

Know–Want to Know–Learned (K-W-L) / 194

Problem-Solving Approach / 194

Reciprocal Teaching / 196

Writing Strategies / 196

Visualization Strategies / 197

Enhancing Comprehension Before, During, and After Reading / 197

Study Guides / 197

Directed Reading Lessons / 199

FOCUS ON STRUGGLING READERS / 200

FOCUS ON ENGLISH LANGUAGE LEARNERS / 202

7   Location and Organization of Information / 205

Location Skills / 206

Libraries and Media Centers / 206

Locating Information in Books / 207

Special Reference Books / 210

Motivational Activities / 212

MEETING THE CHALLENGE / 212

Using Computer Databases / 213

Using the Internet / 214

Organizational Skills / 215

Outlining / 216

Summarizing / 218

Note Taking / 219

FOCUS ON STRUGGLING READERS / 223

FOCUS ON ENGLISH LANGUAGE LEARNERS / 224

8   Reading–Study Strategies for Textbook Use / 227

Preparation for Study / 228

Importance of a Study Method / 228

Teaching Procedures / 230

Specific Study Methods / 232

Study Methods for Expository Texts / 232

A Study Method for Mathematics / 234

**TeachSource
Video Case**
Metacognition: Helping
Students Become
Strategic Learners 229

Reading to Follow Directions / 235

Graphic Aids / 236

    Maps / 238

MEETING THE CHALLENGE / 241

    Graphs / 241

    Tables / 246

    Charts and Diagrams / 246

    Pictures and Cartoons / 248

Adjusting Rate to Fit Purpose and Materials / 252

    Factors Affecting Rate / 253

    Techniques for Increasing Rate and Flexibility / 253

Fluency / 256

Retention / 256

Test Taking / 258

FOCUS ON STRUGGLING READERS / 260

FOCUS ON ENGLISH LANGUAGE LEARNERS / 261

PART 4 Applying Literacy Instruction in the Content Areas / 263

9 Writing in the Content Areas / 265

The Relationships Among Reading, Writing, and Thinking / 266

    The Nature of Writing / 266

    Values of Writing in the Content Areas / 266

    The Relationship Between Reading and Writing in Content Area Classes / 267

    Techniques of Combining Reading and Writing Effectively / 267

The Process Approach to Writing in the Content Areas / 269

    Prewriting / 270

    Writing a Draft / 272

    Revising / 275

    Editing / 276

    Publishing / 277

MEETING THE CHALLENGE / 278

Types of Writing-to-Learn Activities in the Content Areas / 280

    Language Experience Writings / 281

    Poetry / 282

    Content Journals / 283

**TeachSource
Video Case**
Developing Student
Self-Esteem: Peer
Editing Process 271

MEETING THE CHALLENGE / 289

    Dialogue Journals / 293

    Written Conversations / 294

    RAFT Assignments / 294

    Research Reports / 294

MEETING THE CHALLENGE / 297

    Laboratory Reports / 304

    Photo Essays / 304

    Pen Pals / 305

    Internet Writing Projects and Activities / 305

    Mentoring Projects / 306

FOCUS ON STRUGGLING READERS / 307

FOCUS ON ENGLISH LANGUAGE LEARNERS / 309

10   Literature-Based and Thematic Approaches to Content Area Teaching / 313

Values and Uses of Literature in the Secondary School Curriculum / 313

    Young Adult Literature / 314

    Picture Books / 316

    Comic Books and Graphic Novels / 317

    Read-Alouds / 318

Literature Instruction / 320

    Mini-Lessons / 320

    Use of Reading Guides / 321

    Electronic Discussions / 322

    Whole-Class Novel Study / 322

    Literature Response Groups (Literature Circles) / 323

    Sustained Silent Reading (SSR) / 323

    Readers' Theater / 324

    Directed Reading Lessons / 324

MEETING THE CHALLENGE / 326

Activities to Encourage Students' Response to Literature / 326

    Written Responses / 326

    Oral Responses / 327

Developing Thematic Teaching Units / 327

    Introduction of the Unit / 328

    Development of the Unit / 330

**TeachSource
Video Case**
Performance
Assessment: Student
Presentations in a High
School English Class 327

Organization of Findings / 331

Culmination Activities / 331

Sample Unit Ideas / 331

MEETING THE CHALLENGE / 334

FOCUS ON STRUGGLING READERS / 340

FOCUS ON ENGLISH LANGUAGE LEARNERS / 340

11   Reading in the Content Areas: I / 343

Introduction to Reading Content Material / 344

Discourse / 344

Content Teaching and Learning that Works / 344

Reading and Critical Literacy / 345

Content Strategies and Assignments / 345

Authentic Reading Assignments / 346

Content Text Structures / 346

Organizational Patterns in Content Texts / 346

MEETING THE CHALLENGE / 347

Social Studies Content / 348

Critical Thinking in Social Studies / 348

Writing Patterns / 349

Exercises for Social Studies Instruction / 353

Science and Health Content / 355

Authentic Learning Experiences / 356

Writing Patterns / 357

Mathematics Content / 363

Literacy in Mathematics / 363

Reading Mathematics / 364

Writing Patterns / 365

Teaching Mathematics Content / 369

English (Language Arts) Content / 370

Vocabulary Development / 370

Literature / 373

Genre and Multigenre Studies / 375

Grammar and Composition / 375

Foreign Languages / 377

FOCUS ON STRUGGLING READERS / 380

FOCUS ON ENGLISH LANGUAGE LEARNERS / 381

**TeachSource
Video Case**
Integrating Technology
to Improve Student
Learning: A High
School Science
Simulation 362

12   Reading in the Content Areas: II / 384

Literacy for Career-Related Education / 385

Aspects of Vocational Literacy / 386

Technical and Specialized Terminology / 386

Following Directions / 388

Technology / 390

Graphic Materials / 390

Reading Rate / 390

Problem Solving / 392

Writing / 392

Utilizing Motivation / 393

The Textbook as a Reference / 393

Reading Strategies / 394

Applications of Literacy Strategies / 396

Technical Education / 396

Business Education / 396

MEETING THE CHALLENGE / 400

Human Environmental Science (Human Ecology) / 401

Agriculture / 405

Physical Education / 405

Art / 408

Music / 409

FOCUS ON STRUGGLING READERS / 415

FOCUS ON ENGLISH LANGUAGE LEARNERS / 416

Glossary / 419

References / 425

Name Index / 443

Subject Index / 447

PREFACE

Secondary school teachers use textbooks, trade books, and electronic reference sources extensively to convey content area information to their students. Content area teachers often discover, however, that their students are not maximizing their learning potential and do not read at levels necessary for understanding the types of material the teachers would like to use. These students also often do not use appropriate reading and study strategies or writing-to-learn strategies. In view of the current push nationwide to establish literacy standards for secondary school students, this situation is particularly frustrating to teachers who do not know how to help their students learn literacy strategies to support learning of content area material. Teachers and administrators may feel unprepared to find solutions for students' literacy problems, especially as more and more English language learners and students who have special needs are being included in regular classrooms.

This book offers all content area teachers detailed and practical explanations of reading, writing, and study strategies that students need to allow them to acquire and use new information that is available in electronic and traditional print media. Techniques for assessing student performance and for teaching needed strategies in a broad range of disciplines are included. Teachers using these techniques help their students become more efficient, effective readers of their content materials and facilitate their students' learning of the subject matter content.

Audience and Purpose

Secondary School Literary Instruction: The Content Areas, Tenth Edition, has been written primarily for preservice teachers preparing for secondary school certification in teacher education programs and for experienced secondary school teachers who want to help their students read content assignments with more understanding. Neither group is likely to have substantial background knowledge in literacy instruction. This book has thus been written at an introductory level, with the needs and concerns of these teachers in mind. The text also contains information that is useful for reading specialists who work cooperatively with content teachers in helping secondary students with reading difficulties and for secondary school administrators who must know about the reading needs of secondary school students if they are to set school policies appropriately.

This book provides a strategy-based approach to content reading. Much secondary content area material is written at a high difficulty level, and students are required to read extensively. Teachers who know how to teach the reading and study skills strategies appropriate to their content areas enhance their students' success in the classroom.

Revisions in This Edition

The tenth edition of *Secondary School Literacy Instruction: The Content Areas* has been thoroughly updated and revised. The chapter on assessment has been moved closer to the beginning of the book to reflect the need to assess students' knowledge and capabilities in order to focus instruction on students' needs. There are many new examples from content area materials and applications of instructional applications throughout the book. Several new "Meeting the Challenge" features show how teachers in secondary schools have applied the ideas presented in this book. These vignettes can make the information in the chapters easier to understand because they are placed in the context of real situations.

Chapter 1, "Content Area Literacy In A Changing World," has new material on current literacy practices of adolescents, including their extensive use of the Internet; authentic and motivational activities; and sample reading suggestions for various content areas. It presents updates on NAEP results and educational standards; cultural and linguistic diversity, with special emphasis on English language learners; and students with disabilities.

Chapter 2, "Integrating Technology In Content Area Literacy Instruction," is extensively updated. Media literacy, including use of information communication technology, is given thorough treatment. New and updated material is presented on cautions about the influence of advertising, stereotypes, and misinformation in the media; critical evaluation of websites and television shows and commercials; influence of electronic games on critical literacy skills; collaborative writing software; navigating the Internet; using wikis, blogs, social networking sites, online book clubs, and chat rooms; podcasts and videoconferencing; computerized reading management programs, and electronic books. Some new suggestions are given for simulation software for content area use, and new examples of multimedia lessons and projects are presented. Activities involved with producing content area videos are described. Additional attention is given to technology for students with special needs or disabilities.

Chapter 3, "Content Literacy Assessment," has been moved close to the beginning of the book to emphasize the importance of basing instruction on assessment. New material about formative assessment and summative assessment, issues related to high-stakes tests, rubrics, retellings, think-alouds, and portfolios has been added. The discussion of computer applications to assessment has been expanded to discuss Computer Adaptive Testing, web-based testing, simulation-based assessments, digital portfolios, and the need for assessing online reading comprehension. The material on assessing English language learners has been expanded. There is a new example of a group reading inventory.

Chapter 4, "A Conceptual Approach to Developing Meaningful Vocabulary," has been extensively updated. It emphasizes the critical relationship between vocabulary and comprehension and focuses on the relationship between vocabulary and conceptual development, which is important to knowing words. An instructional approach is developed that emphasizes strategies for direct instruction of targeted key words in content textbooks. The importance of academic vocabulary is stressed, and more information on use of the thesaurus and of word walls has been added. Several new examples have been included in this edition.

Chapter 5, "The Process of Constructing Meaning in Texts," introduces strategies for comprehending new literacies that offer new opportunities for learning. This chapter focuses on learning to read multiple types of content for complex purposes, as well as adjusting knowledge and cognitive strategies to the situation. More information is provided on the relationships among vocabulary, comprehension, and fluency and on active reading, metacognition, and helping English language learners. Several new examples have been included in this chapter.

Chapter 6, "Strategies for Constructing Meaning in Text," focuses on developing a repertoire of research-based strategies that readers can apply before, during, and after reading to enhance comprehension of text material. The goal of teaching and modeling these strategies is to guide students to understand deeply and apply knowledge and information. Emphasis is given to explicit teaching of comprehension strategies. Sections on questioning, including self-questioning by the students and new examples of questions based on literature selections, and critical thinking and reading have been expanded. Several new examples have been included in this chapter.

Chapter 7, "Location And Organization Of Information," and Chapter 8, "Reading-Study Strategies For Textbook Use," present useful strategies for all content areas. Both chapters have been thoroughly updated. Chapter 7 contains a new section on annotating text and new information on summarizing and working with English language learners. It also has a new I-Chart example. Chapter 8 includes new material on preparation for study and three new examples.

Four chapters that focus more specifically on instruction in content area classes follow. Chapter 9, "Writing in the Content Areas," has new material on motivation for writing, writing for different audiences and in different genres, preparation for writing position papers, zines as types of publication products, character web pages, writing tweets that book characters might have written, language experience writing, poetry writing, producing classic comic books based on literature selections that are being studied, formats for research reports, Internet writing projects and activities, instant messaging, and computer slide-show activities. The sections on working with struggling readers and English language learners have been expanded. There are also several new examples and two new "Meeting the Challenge" features.

Chapter 10, "Literature-Based And Thematic Approaches To Content Area Teaching," has many new suggestions of young adult literature to use for various purposes in content classes. It includes new material on use of graphic novels and comic books, drama presentations to aid comprehension, children's books to build enjoyment, online discussions of literature, book clubs, literature response groups, and sustained silent reading; motivation to read; preview techniques; understanding characterization; authentic writing, including writing fan fiction; and instructional units. There is more information on working with struggling readers and English language learners.

Chapter 11, "Reading in the Content Areas: I," addresses the importance of literacy in understanding and learning from content area texts. The demands of multiple literacies and multimedia are increasing in all content area classes; therefore, teaching strategies are introduced that guide students in understanding both content and related materials. There is more information on academic literacy, question-answer relationships, the K-W-L procedure, critical thinking, content text characteristics, scientific discourse forms, and mathematics instruction. Many new examples from student texts and examples of instructional activities are included in this edition.

Chapter 12, "Reading in the Content Areas: II," addresses reading in career-oriented and performance-based content areas. The importance of literacy in these subjects is increasing due to the growth of interest in career-oriented and technical education. Instruction in these areas emphasizes the relationship between literacy and performance and hands-on work. A major goal of this chapter is preparing students to communicate with technology and to update their knowledge of their content areas. This chapter contains new material on laws related to career and technical education and new content area examples.

Features of the Text

This text presents a balance of theory and applications related to secondary school literacy. It provides unique emphasis on the content areas, with practical strategies and illustrations of content materials from all secondary school subject areas. In all chapters, extensive use is made of actual secondary school material to explicitly bring theory into practice. A major strength of this book is the guidance it provides teachers in helping students improve their reading performance through the application of reading and study skills. To help the reader gain a more complete understanding of content, each text chapter contains the following features:

Overview. This section provides a brief description of the most important concepts and themes of each chapter. Readers can use the overview to create a mental set for reading the chapter.

Purpose-Setting Questions. Purpose-setting questions focus readers' attention on the important aspects of chapter content.

Meeting the Challenge Vignettes. These vignettes illustrate how teachers have used the ideas discussed in the chapter to meet their teaching challenges. The vignettes put the concepts from the chapter into realistic contexts for readers and help answer the question that content teachers often ask: how will I use this information on reading in my future classroom teaching?

Focus on English Language Learners and Focus on Struggling Readers. These features highlight the important applications for students with special needs in separate, easy-to-locate sections in each chapter.

TeachSource Video Cases. Video cases that correlate to chapter content have been highlighted in the margins for quick reference. The special icon with case title in the margin denotes the video that students can access on the Internet to watch the corresponding teaching strategies in practice. Available on this text's book-specific website, Cengage Learning's Education CourseMate, these 4–6 minute videos bring topics in the text to life by presenting actual classroom scenarios. Students can access these videos by registering their access code at www.cengage.com/login.

Margin Questions. These questions focus attention on important terminology and concepts in the material.

Content Area Marginal Icons. These icons easily alert content area teachers to material specific to their content areas.

Summary. The summary pulls together the main ideas of the chapter. Readers can use the summary to review chapter material and to reinforce chapter content.

Discussion Questions. Instructors can use these higher-level essay questions as homework assignments or as the basis of class discussion.

Enrichment Activities. Application activities that go beyond chapter content provide students with opportunities to practice what they have learned in each chapter. These range from ideas for research papers to creating lesson plans and using strategies.

Glossary. The glossary helps readers unfamiliar with specialized literacy terminology understand key terms.

Teaching and Learning Supplements

The *instructor's manual* offers learning objectives, suggested teaching and learning strategies, and instructional materials for each chapter. Appropriate performance-based assessment activities are also included. Model syllabi that could be used for a course in secondary school reading instruction and a study skills learning activity packet are also provided in this manual.

Test items are available on the *PowerLecture with Examview CD*. Sets of examination items provided for chapters include multiple choice, true/false, essay questions, case study questions, and performance-based assessment questions.

For instructors, PowerLecture is a one-stop digital library and presentation tool that includes preassembled Microsoft® PowerPoint® lecture slides and the full Instructor's Manual and Test Bank. PowerLecture includes ExamView® testing software with all the test items from the printed Test Bank in electronic format, enabling you to create customized tests in print or online, and all of your media resources in one place including an image library with graphics from the book itself and the TeachSource Video Cases.

Education CourseMate (www.cengage.com/login) brings course concepts to life with interactive learning, study, and exam preparation tools that support the printed textbook. This website provides links to related resources, glossary flashcards, tutorial quizzes, and additional study tools and resources for students, as well as access to the TeachSource Video Cases related to each chapter. For instructors, the instructor's manual, testbank files for your course management system, and PowerPoint slides are available for download. Text-specific content is available within your course management system with WebTutor™ Toolbox for WebCT™ or Blackboard®.

Acknowledgments

We are indebted to many people for their assistance in the preparation of our manuscript. Although we would like to acknowledge the many teachers and students whose inspiration was instrumental in the development of this book, it is impossible to name them all. Particular appreciation is due Barbara Bridges, Melissa Comer, Dick Heyler, Barbara Vaughn, Larry Lynn, Katherine M. Dooley, Lance Jasitt, Meagan Jasitt, Rory Lewelyn, Annette Littrell, Cathy McCurdy, and Jill Ramsey. Grateful recognition is also given to our editors, Lisa Kalner Williams and Jared Sterzer, and the following reviewers whose constructive advice and criticism helped greatly in the writing and revision of the manuscript:

John D. Beach, St. John's University
Karen Moroz, Concordia University
Diane Steiner, Chestnut Hill College
Jacqueline Tilles, Wayne State University
Marcia Walker, Trevecca Nazarene University
Lynette Zuroff, Carroll College

In addition, appreciation is expressed for those who have granted permission to use sample materials or citations from their works.

Betty D. Roe, *Professor Emerita, Tennessee Technological University, Cookeville*
Barbara Stoodt-Hill, Retired, *John Tyler Community College and Old Dominion University*

Contexts of Literacy Instruction in a Technological Age

CHAPTER 1
Content Area Literacy in a Changing World

CHAPTER 2
Integrating Technology in Content Area Literacy Instruction

Content Area Literacy in a Changing World

Overview

This chapter opens by identifying literacy demands on secondary school students and by looking at literacy instruction needs in content areas. Then it provides an overview of the nature of reading and the strategy and skill areas involved, the personnel responsible for secondary school literacy instruction, and the five aspects of a secondary school literacy program. Misconceptions about literacy instruction are examined next. Finally, we discuss current concerns about literacy performance and the resulting development of standards, taking into consideration the diversity of students found within content area classrooms.

Purpose-Setting Questions

As you read this chapter, try to answer these questions:

1. What occurs during the reading process?
2. What literacy demands do secondary school students face?
3. What school personnel are responsible for literacy instruction?
4. What are some faulty assumptions about developing literacy in secondary schools?
5. What are some concerns about the literacy performance of secondary school students?
6. How have new standards for literacy learning affected secondary school instruction?
7. What is the range of students in content area classrooms?

MEETING THE CHALLENGE

"My students aren't doing their reading assignments for my class," a new secondary school teacher complained to a colleague. "I don't know whether they *can't* or just *won't* read the material. Either way, my lessons haven't been going smoothly."

"First, you need to find out if they *can* read the material," the colleague replied. "Do you know how to construct a cloze test or a group reading inventory?"

"No. Are they hard to do?" the new teacher responded.

"Cloze tests are easier to construct. However, you may feel that you get more specific information from the inventory," the colleague answered.

"Will you show me how to make these assessments?" asked the new teacher. "And will you help me interpret the results?"

"I'll lend you a book that describes them," the colleague said. "I got it for a college methods course. I'm sorry that I don't have more time to help, but you might ask the reading teacher for some assistance, too."

"I didn't think of that," the new teacher admitted. "Thanks for your advice."

After studying the book's description of the two assessment measures, the teacher chose to prepare and administer a cloze test to the students. The results surprised her. Only a small number of the students appeared to be capable of reading the text independently. The majority could read it with teacher assistance, but some could not read it with understanding, even with teacher assistance.

"Thank goodness for the independent-level group," she thought, "but what can I do to help the others?"

She returned to her colleague with her new question. He replied, "Check out that book some more. It suggests strategies that help prepare students for reading, guide them through reading, and direct them in analysis after reading. It describes study methods and ideas for study guides and other instructional activities for those students who can learn from the text with help. It suggests alternative materials and strategies for the other, less capable readers, but I still think you should talk to the reading teacher about this as well."

The new teacher examined more sections of the recommended book and gained ideas from it. Then she went to the reading teacher in her school and asked, "Where can I locate lower-level reading material for the students who can't read this text?"

"Enlist the help of the media specialist," she was told. "Also make some transcripts of class discussions that can be duplicated and used as reading material for these students."

Reading specialists can help classroom teachers learn how to help their students read content materials with understanding.

zhang bo/iStockphoto.com

"Oh, yes. I remember that idea," she said. "The book called it 'use of language experience materials.' What would you suggest that I do to prepare the ones who can read the text with help for successful reading?"

"For *all* your students, try developing the new vocabulary through semantic webs or semantic feature analysis. Provide purposes for their reading that involve higher-level thinking. Perhaps use anticipation guides," the reading teacher said.

"The book explains all those activities," she said. "I guess I had better get busy."

"If you need help when you get into the process, call me," the reading teacher said. "I'll be glad to lend a hand with specifics."

"It's sure good to have some direction for this," the teacher sighed. "Who would have thought I'd be so concerned about *reading*? I'm a *science* teacher."

SCIENCE AND HEALTH

Although the scenario in the "Meeting the Challenge" vignette is not based on the experience of a single teacher, the situation it depicts is a common one. Teachers who have not had courses in secondary reading methods often find themselves in this situation.

This text is designed to help teachers know what to do about their students' literacy problems and whom to ask for assistance when they need it. All the techniques and activities mentioned in the scenario and many others are explained in detail in later chapters. "Meeting the Challenge" sections in the remainder of this book are based on the experiences of individual teachers in various school settings, as are the features that focus on struggling readers and English language learners.

Literacy Demands on Secondary School Students

How will the levels of literacy that your secondary school students have affect their content area learning?

The term **literacy** refers to the ability to comprehend and produce written language in order to operate effectively in a particular social context. Moje (2008, p. 103) reports that recent surveys of literacy practices among adolescents in a midwestern U.S. city reveal that they read "books, websites, music lyrics, and magazines several times per week," as well as the reading for school.

Secondary school students have to read content textbooks and supplementary materials (including trade books, magazines, and newspapers) in school and for homework outside of school. This may include reading text on a computer or e-book reader. Some of the material is likely to be highly technical in nature. Students also need to write in-class and homework papers and to write responses to test questions, study questions, and assigned readings. However, they have even more varied literacy needs in their activities outside school.

Even if students avoid purely recreational reading, they need to read signs found in their environment, recipes, menus, manuals for operating equipment, instructions for assembling items, job applications, television schedules, transportation schedules, road maps, labels on food or medicine, newspapers, public notices, advertisements, bank statements, bills, and many other functional materials. Failure to read some of these materials with adequate understanding can result in their committing traffic violations, becoming lost, having unpleasant reactions to food or medicine, being ejected from unauthorized areas, missing desirable television programs, failing to make connections with needed transportation, losing employment opportunities, and other undesirable outcomes.

Secondary students may also need to write letters to family and friends, instructions to people who are doing things for them (such as feeding their pets), notes to themselves about tasks to be completed, phone messages for other members of their households, responses to a multitude of forms, and many other literacy tasks. Mistakes in these activities can have negative results. For example, an inaccurately written phone message may cause someone to fail to pick up a young child at school on time. Our culture places a high value on literacy, and we are inundated with reading and writing demands in order to carry out everyday tasks.

The job market also affects students' literacy needs. The number of low-literacy jobs continually decreases, and even jobs considered to be low in literacy demands may require the ability to read materials such as manuals for operating equipment. Many literacy demands of schools and the workplace are different, although vocational classes often have similar literacy demands to those of the workplace. In both the workplace and vocational classes students must locate information for immediate use and infer information to solve problems. They generally use texts in a non-linear fashion, searching for isolated information to solve immediate problems or enhance projects (Darvin, 2006; Gerber and Finn, 1998).

Workers and vocational students need to be able to understand schematics, diagrams and other graphic aids, comprehend legal documents and safety codes, categorize information, and skim and scan to locate information. They have to integrate information from books, trade magazines, and the Internet with hands-on experiences. These skills are often not emphasized in secondary school instruction (Darvin, 2006; Gerber and Finn, 1998). The reading and writing of a variety of types of documents—memos, manuals, catalogs, letters, reports, graphs, charts, and instructions—are also necessary literacy skills for the workplace. Workers need to monitor their understanding of the material that they read and take notes on important points.

Vocational classes often employ as many texts as are used in academic classes. The texts are generally used differently in the two types of classes, however.

Good literacy skills are especially important to students who plan to attend college. Educators have realized for years that reading at grade level is not good enough for these students because students entering college are expected to be able to read at higher than twelfth-grade level, as determined by traditional reading tests.

Today's teenagers spend much time on the Internet, where there are large collections of books online. However, students do not often report reading books online. They do engage in many literacy practices: e-mailing, tweeting, instant messaging, visiting social networking sites on the Internet and maintaining their own networking pages, participating in online chat rooms, blogging, constructing webpages, and reading comics and graphic novels. They learn from these experiences because they find them pleasurable.

Pleasurable learning often provides internal motivation. Teachers can build on these out-of-school literacy practices by allowing the students to produce materials related to the curriculum (Baines, 2009; Hughes-Hassell and Rodge, 2007; Lenhart, Madden, and Hitlin, 2005; Wolk, 2008). It can be beneficial for the teacher to assess students' preferred reading materials and instructional modes in order to enhance student motivation (Pitcher, et al., 2007). Then students can participate in lessons that are related to their interests and talents, causing them to focus their attention on the content involved (Bartholomew, 2008).

High school students don't do a great deal of reading from their textbooks, and they may balk at completing traditional writing assignments. In a survey of high-school student engagement by Indiana University's Center for Evaluation and Education Policy, 43 percent of students reported spending an hour or less doing written homework in a week, and 55 percent said they spent an hour or less reading and studying for school in a week (Azzam, 2008).

Smith and Wilhelm's research (2004) shows that boys may reject literacy activities in school because they lack competence in them, and they generally pursue activities in which they are competent. They may, however, engage in literacy activities at home in areas in which they feel competent, for example, blogging and designing webpages. Some complained about the difficult language of school texts, especially those laden with description, and reading in unfamiliar genres. Several indicated that teachers should do more to support their learning of strategies needed to interpret these materials. Alvermann, Huddleston, and Hagood (2004) believe that teachers should instruct students in a way that encourages them to make connections between personal literacies, such as reading comics or watching World Wrestling Federation matches, with school literacies, such as textbook reading.

Early adolescents can be engaged successfully in authentic activities that are used "as vehicles for learning key skills and knowledge processes" (Ryan, 2008, p. 191). These projects are cross-curricular and community-based, and they encompass substantive issues and employ multiliteracies. These multiliteracies include visual, spatial, audio, gestural, and linguistic ways of communicating. Students are directly taught academic skills and then given responsibility for their own learning. They work in focus groups that have tasks that contribute to the overall project. The groups have mentors from the school or community (Ryan, 2008).

Legislation Related to Secondary School Literacy

Currently, federal legislation has entered the picture for all of our students. *No Child Left Behind* legislation emphasizes the importance of continuous reading instruction and learning of vocabulary and comprehension strategies, echoing the beliefs of secondary literacy educators. The legislation also promotes assessment-based, individually appropriate reading instruction and many opportunities to use a wide variety of texts, other practices that literacy educators support. Its recommendations fail to address many of the issues in adolescent literacy, however.

Secondary teachers need to acquire strategies to involve parents as partners in the adolescents' education and design interventions for struggling adolescent readers (Conley and Hinchman, 2004).

Reading Instruction in the Content Area Curriculum

What is Reading?

How would you define reading?

Reading is described in different ways by different people. Despite continuing disagreement about the precise nature of the reading process, there are points of general agreement among reading authorities. One such point is that comprehension of written material is the purpose of reading instruction. In fact, we consider *reading comprehension* and *reading* to be synonymous because when understanding breaks down, reading actually has not occurred.

During the reading process, there is an interplay between the reader's preexisting knowledge and the written content. Competent reading is an active process in which the reader calls on experience, language, and schemata (theoretical constructs of knowledge related to experiences) to anticipate and understand the author's written language. Therefore, readers both bring meaning to print and take meaning from print. It is, as Rosenblatt (1989) and Goodman (in Aaron et al., 1990) would say, transactive.

The nature of the reading process alters as students mature. In the early stages of reading, word identification requires a reader's concentration. Eventually, however, readers are able to use their reading ability for pleasure, appreciation, knowledge acquisition, and functional purposes. Thus, reading competence has many faces. Competent readers locate materials and ideas that enable them to fulfill particular purposes, which may be to follow directions, to complete job applications, or to appreciate Shakespeare's plays. In addition, competent readers adjust their reading style as they move from narrative to expository content. Finally, they read with various types of understanding—literal, interpretive, critical, and creative.

The terms *literal, interpretive (inferential), critical,* and *creative* refer to the types of thinking that are commonly associated with reading comprehension. *Literal understanding* refers to the reader's recognizing or remembering ideas and information that are explicitly stated in printed material. *Interpretive comprehension* occurs when the reader synthesizes ideas and information from printed material with knowledge, experience, and imagination to form hypotheses. Interpretive comprehension requires that the reader use ideas and information that are not stated on the printed page; that is, the reader must "read between the lines," use deductive reasoning, and make assumptions based on the facts given. *Critical comprehension (evaluation)* requires that the reader make judgments about the content of a reading selection by comparing it with external criteria. The reader may have developed these criteria through experience, through reference to resource materials, or through access to information provided by authorities on the subject. *Creative understanding (reading beyond the lines)* has to do with the reader's emotional responses to printed material (appreciation) and his or her ability to produce new ideas based on the reading experience. Creative understanding is built on literal, inferential, and critical understanding. A reader's intellectual understanding provides a foundation for his or her emotional reaction. For example, a reader may respond to an author's style or may identify with a certain character, a story incident, or the author's use of symbolism.

Good readers exercise comprehension monitoring (metacognitive) strategies as they read. They constantly ask if the material they are reading makes sense, and if not, what they should do to remedy their lack of understanding.

Reading Orally

Because there are times when students must read orally to convey information to others, oral reading fluency is important. **Fluency** involves reading with expression, appropriate phrasing, and accuracy. Rasinski and Hoffman (2003) report that the National Assessment of Educational Progress showed that oral reading fluency was positively related to overall reading achievement.

Good ways to work on fluency with secondary-level students are readers' theater (discussed in Chapter 10) and the method of repeated readings (discussed in Chapter 5). Research supports instruction in oral reading fluency for older students who are not fluent readers (Rasinski and Hoffman, 2003).

Word Identification

Word identification skills and strategies include sight-word recognition, contextual analysis, morphemic or structural analysis, phonic analysis, and use of the dictionary's respellings to determine pronunciation. The goal of word identification instruction is to develop students' independence in identifying words.

Sight words are words students have memorized and are able to identify immediately. Secondary students usually have a good store of sight words that help them read content materials with understanding. Each time a content teacher introduces a new technical or specialized term that is important to understanding the content area, the teacher hopes to turn the new word into a sight word for the students. The study of the subject would be inefficient if many of the important words had to be analyzed carefully each time they were encountered before recognition occurred. The content teacher can help impress new words on the students' memories and thus turn them into sight words by writing them on the board, pronouncing them, and discussing them with the students. Knowledge of sight words also enables students to use contextual analysis.

Contextual analysis is the use of the context in which an unknown word occurs (the surrounding words and sentences) to identify the word. Contextual analysis skills are powerful tools for secondary students to use in reading content area materials, and content area teachers will benefit from helping students become aware of the usefulness of context in word identification. Contextual analysis not only plays a role in word identification, but also is an important tool for determining word meaning.

Morphemic or structural analysis entails the use of word parts, such as affixes, root words, syllables, and smaller words that are joined to form compound words, to help

Do students need to be able to use all of the different word identification skills and strategies? Why or why not?

in the identification of unfamiliar words. Morphemic analysis is extremely helpful in understanding content area words because in many cases certain prefixes, suffixes, and root words appear repeatedly in the related technical terms of a discipline.

Phonic analysis involves breaking words into basic sound elements and blending these sounds together to produce spoken words. Phonic analysis is not taught by the content area teacher but lies in the province of the special reading teacher.

Use of the dictionary's respellings to determine pronunciation is an important skill for students to master. Many students need lessons in using the dictionary's pronunciation key to help them decode the respellings.

Comprehension

Reading comprehension is an interactive process of meaning construction. The reader's background knowledge structures (schemata), the information in the text, and the context in which the reading takes place all interact to produce comprehension. Schemata related to the reading material must be activated if students are to comprehend material as fully as possible.

Students must understand word meanings before reading comprehension can occur. Many of the words that content readers encounter represent labels for key concepts in the content areas. A reader learns word meanings through experience, word association, discussion, concept development, contextual analysis, morphemic analysis, and use of a dictionary and a thesaurus. Content teachers can help students comprehend content materials by teaching the meanings of key vocabulary terms. Morphemic analysis, analogy exercises, semantic feature analysis, word sorts, and word webs (or semantic webs or arrays) are all good vocabulary development activities. These activities are explained in detail in Chapter 4.

To read with comprehension, readers must also be able to perceive the internal organization of reading materials, understand the various writing patterns used to structure content materials, and understand the material at the appropriate cognitive levels. Expository writing patterns may include cause–effect, comparison–contrast, sequence of events, or one or more of a variety of other organizations. For narrative materials, knowledge of story grammar (or story structure) is important. Readers understand content better when they are able to follow the particular writing pattern and organization used. Content area teachers need to be familiar with the types of writing patterns encountered frequently in their particular disciplines so that they can help students to understand these patterns.

When reading, students must comprehend material literally, interpretively, critically, and creatively, as each type of comprehension is appropriate. Modeling, discussion, a problem-solving approach to reading, comprehension monitoring, visualization strategies, judicious use of questioning techniques, use of writing to learn, use of study guides, and directed reading lessons serve as vehicles for developing these types of understanding. Chapters 5 and 6 address comprehension instruction, and Chapter 9 covers use of writing to learn.

Content reading requires flexible use of reading rate. The concept of rate can be examined best as it relates to comprehension. Rate is governed by purpose for reading, type of comprehension desired, familiarity with content, and type of content. Content area teachers need to help students learn to vary their reading rates to fit

Why is reading comprehension a central concern of the content area teacher?

particular instructional materials and different purposes for reading. Chapter 8 discusses reading rate.

Study Skills

How can poor study skills affect content area learning?

In secondary school, students are expected to become more independent in applying their reading skills and strategies in work-study situations. **Study skills** include the application of reading skills and strategies to the learning of written content area material. There are three basic types of study skills: locating information through reading; understanding and remembering content; and organizing information once it has been located and read. Content area teachers need to help students learn to use these study skills efficiently so that they can study the content assignments more effectively. Teaching study skills in the situations in which they are expected to be used is more effective than teaching them in isolation. Examples of location and study skills can be found in Chapters 7 and 8, and applications of these skills to particular content areas are discussed in Chapters 11 and 12.

Personnel Responsible for Secondary School Literacy Instruction

The personnel responsible for various portions of the program include content area teachers, special reading teachers, reading consultants, principals and other administrators, and librarians or media center specialists.

Content Area Teachers

How does the content area teacher's responsibility for his or her students' reading skills differ from that of the special reading teacher?

The content area teacher's responsibility is to help students *read* their textbooks and supplementary materials more effectively in order to *learn* the content more effectively. **Content area teachers** need to know what reading skills are necessary for successful reading of the materials in their particular disciplines, and they need to be capable of assisting students in applying these skills as they complete their content area assignments. In other words, they need to teach disciplinary literacy, literacy that "builds an understanding of how knowledge is produced in the disciplines" (Moje, 2008). In many cases, such as in teaching technical vocabulary, reading instruction and content instruction are identical.

Content teachers often find that mini-lessons in a particular reading strategy will pay large dividends in the students' understanding of an assignment. Content area teachers do not have the *primary* responsibility for teaching reading strategies. The responsibility for helping students with significantly impaired reading abilities belongs to a **special reading teacher**. However, content teachers do have to adjust assignments for these students.

Content area teachers need to know the reading skills that secondary students require in order to read content materials in their disciplines effectively; assessment measures that can help them identify students who cannot read the standard assignments, students who can read the assignments only with much assistance, and those who can read the assignments with ease; ways to help students learn specific skills and strategies needed for their content areas; study aids and procedures that can help students achieve success in content area reading; and effective ways to differentiate assignments for students reading at different levels of proficiency. They also need to be able to identify specific learning problems that should be referred to a specialist for help, and they need to be willing to cooperate with other school personnel, such as the special reading teacher, to help students reach their full potential in content reading.

Even though some content area teachers are initially hesitant about reading strategy instruction, they often change their attitudes when they learn useful strategies, such as those presented in this text. Hesitancy about assisting students to improve their writing proficiency in related content areas may also exist for teachers who have not been taught the appropriate strategies. There are many strategies that can be helpful to teachers in the area of writing as well. Content area teachers can use writing to accomplish content objectives while helping students become more effective communicators by using strategies described in Chapter 9. Graves (2004) believes, as we do, that teachers are more important to student learning than are teaching methods. However, having a working knowledge of effective methods makes a good teacher even better.

Special Reading Teacher

What kinds of interactions do the special reading teacher and the content area teacher need to have?

Special reading teachers generally work directly with students on reading skills. They also administer and interpret reading assessments, plan and teach reading classes, and work with other school personnel who have responsibilities in the reading program. They may model teaching strategies for classroom teachers, observe the classroom teachers' instruction and students' responses and provide feedback, help teachers learn how to provide individualized instruction and deal with large classes, show teachers how to choose appropriate strategies for various groups, and/or act as a liaison among various teachers and departments (Henwood, 1999/ 2000). After a review of research on the role of the reading specialist, Quatroche, Bean, and Hamilton (2001, p. 292) stated that "a major role seems to be the assessment and instruction of students with difficulties."

Reading Consultant

What are the main differences between the job of the reading consultant and that of the special reading teacher?

The reading consultant works with administrators and other school personnel to develop and coordinate schoolwide reading programs. The reading consultant may work from the central office with more than one school. This person is freed from classroom teaching and instruction of special reading classes.

These educators often assist in planning comprehensive reading programs; keep school personnel informed about the philosophy, procedures, and materials for the programs; evaluate reading programs and materials; provide in-service training; and provide resources for other personnel.

Principal or Administrator

A prerequisite for a good secondary literacy program is administrative direction. The administrator should know about literacy and students, provide a good teaching/learning environment, work with teachers in creating an appropriate organizational plan for instruction, see that appropriate instructional and assessment tools are available, make sure that all components of a secondary school literacy program are included in the school's plan, communicate with parents about literacy concerns, and hire capable personnel.

Librarian or Media Center Specialist

The librarian or media center specialist provides assistance to the special reading teacher and the content area teacher alike by locating books and other printed materials on different subjects and at different reading levels, by making available multimedia aids that can be used for motivation and background building, and by providing students with instruction in location strategies related to the library or media center, such as doing online computer searches for information or searching electronic or printed reference books. The librarian may set up special displays of printed materials or may create specialized bibliographies or lists of Internet addresses on specific subjects at the request of the teachers, and he or she also may provide students with direct assistance in finding and using appropriate materials. Recreational reading may be fostered by the librarian's book talks or attractive book displays on topics with high levels of interest to students.

Teamwork

All of the personnel responsible for the secondary school literacy program need to work together as a team. The content area teacher is definitely a part of this team. The content teacher is concerned with proficiency in literacy largely because it can either enhance or adversely affect the learning of content.

Content area teachers may ask for the reading consultant's assistance in identifying approaches that will best meet the special reading needs of their students. They may send students who are reading far below the level of the instructional materials assigned for the grade to the special reading teacher for assessment and remedial instruction, or the special reading teacher may come into the content classrooms to provide assistance. Content teachers should work closely with the special reading teacher in planning reading assignments for students who are receiving remedial assistance; they should consult with the special reading teacher about what instructional materials will meet the reading needs of their students; and they may ask the special reading teacher to teach lessons in some aspects of reading. They may also cooperate with tutors for some students with special needs.

Content area teachers should expect to work hand in hand with the librarian or media center specialist when assembling materials for teaching units and when teaching library skills. Content magazines, print and electronic reference materials, and recreational reading materials should be a part of the library's yearly budget allocation, and it should be the content teachers who recommend appropriate materials.

Other content area teachers may team with the English teachers for projects that require writing skills that their students have not mastered. The English teachers can teach the writing skills and evaluate the resultant writing products, and the other teachers can evaluate the level of learning achieved in the specific content area subject matter.

The content area teacher should be able to approach the principal for funding for instructional materials that are needed to meet the diverse reading and writing needs of the students in content classes. The principal should also help with organizational arrangements, such as special grouping practices that will enhance the content area literacy program.

Aspects of a Secondary School Literacy Program

In an excellent secondary school literacy program all school personnel cooperate to advance effective reading and writing skills, and all students are offered literacy instruction according to their needs. Such instruction may be offered in special reading classes, special writing labs, or English classes, but it is also a priority in all content area classes. The literacy program must include the following components:

Why is developmental reading instruction needed in secondary school?

1. *Developmental reading* is taught to students who are progressing satisfactorily in acquiring reading proficiency. Students are helped to develop further comprehension skills and strategies, vocabulary knowledge, rate of reading, and study skills in reading classes.

How does reading in content area materials pose special problems for students?

2. *Content area reading* is taught to all students. The students in content classes are helped to comprehend specific subject matter. Within each content area—English, mathematics, social studies, science, and so forth—reading materials with which students can experience reading success must be used. Such materials may include multilevel texts, materials from library sources with levels of reading difficulty that correspond with the students' abilities, interactive computer programs, videos, and audio recordings. The main focus of this book is on content area literacy.

Why should content teachers be concerned with recreational reading?

3. *Recreational reading* is encouraged. The recreational reading component is an important, although frequently neglected, aspect of the comprehensive literacy program since the ultimate goal of reading instruction is to develop good lifelong reading habits. Although English teachers and reading specialists have particularly strong reasons for motivating students to read for pleasure, content area teachers should encourage recreational reading for three major reasons:
   - The content area teacher may have a special rapport with some students who do not like to read and with whom no other secondary teacher has established this special relationship.
   - A certain content area may be the only one that holds a student's interest at a particular time. For example, a physical education teacher might be able to motivate a particular boy or girl to read extracurricular books on sports.
   - Particular subject matter becomes more "real" as a reader experiences events through imaginative literature. For example, the topic of the Civil Rights movement, which might take up only one section of a chapter in a social studies textbook, will be more meaningful to a student who reads *The Land* by Mildred D. Taylor, which offers a glimpse of an African American's

PHYSICAL EDUCATION

SOCIAL STUDIES

experience in obtaining land for his family shortly after the Civil War, and other books in the saga of this family, including *Roll of Thunder, Hear My Cry*, and ending with *The Gold Cadillac*, which is set in 1950. Good nonfiction selections can also add interest to the study of history. Teachers may want to recommend *Eyes on the Prize: America's Civil Rights Years, 1954–1965* by Juan Williams for American history, or for world history study they may recommend *Alive in the Killing Fields* by Nawuth Keat with Martha E. Kendall for an easy-to-read story of a Khmer Rouge survivor. Teachers of agriculture can use literature to sustain student interest; for example, Henry Billings's *All Down the Valley* is an interesting story of the Tennessee Valley Authority (TVA). Teachers of composition may find Lois Duncan's *Chapters: My Growth as a Writer* useful. Extra effort by each content area teacher to find interesting supplementary reading material may lead to enduring reading habits and tastes in the students.

AGRICULTURE

ENGLISH/ LANGUAGE ARTS

4. *Writing instruction* is provided to facilitate completion of meaningful and purposeful content area assignments that involve writing. Some content teachers may team with English teachers to accomplish both literacy and content area goals.

5. *Instruction for struggling readers* is important for students who are experiencing difficulties. Students who are performing at one year below their grade levels or less are usually served by the regular classroom teacher through in-class adjustments to assignments and materials. Students who are further behind usually need to work on basic word recognition and comprehension strategies and skills. Good comprehenders, in general, tend to use more strategies and be more flexible in their use than do poor comprehenders (Kletzien, 1991), so developing strategies and the ability to use them is very important to these students. As their fluency improves, the students can learn how to apply general study skills. This part of the program is directed primarily by the special reading teacher, often in a separate class.

   San Diego's Morse High School has offered a successful multidimensional reading course to those ninth- and tenth-graders who are reading at the seventh-grade level or below. The course includes vocabulary building through dictation of natural language and through reading. Students are encouraged to read both in school and at home, and teachers read aloud to them and "think aloud" about their reading strategies. Students induce phonetic and structural principles as they examine banks of words they have collected. Teachers also provide explicit reading comprehension instruction (Showers et al., 1998).

Some Misconceptions about Teaching Reading

Several misconceptions about the teaching of reading should be recognized.

1. *Teaching reading is a concern only in the elementary school.* In many school systems, formal reading instruction ends at the fifth or sixth grade. Schools with this approach fail to take into account that learning to read is a continuing process. People learn to read over a long period of time, attempting more

advanced reading materials as they master easier ones. Even after encountering all the reading skills through classroom instruction, readers continue to refine their use of them, just as athletes first learn the techniques of a sport and then practice and refine their abilities over time.

2. *Teaching reading in the content areas is separate and distinct from teaching subject matter.* Content teachers' efforts to teach students how to use the printed materials that they assign are important to content acquisition. When a teacher employs printed materials to teach a content area, that teacher is using reading as a teaching aid. Teaching reading in subject matter areas is a complementary learning process, inseparable from the particular subject matter, because it makes the content accessible.

3. *Reading needs in the secondary school can be met through remedial work alone.* Some schools fail to make an essential distinction between *developmental reading*, which is designed to meet the needs of all students, and *corrective reading* and *remedial reading*, which provide specific assistance to struggling readers. Not only should developmental (as well as remedial) classes be made available, but also within each class the content teacher can promote developmental reading by helping students learn the concepts and vocabulary of that content area, and teachers can enhance their students' reading comprehension by assisting them in interpreting and evaluating the text material. Corrective reading assistance can also be given within each class, as needed.

    Teachers can help students develop better reading study skills and other specialized skills associated with their particular content areas. For example, reading written directions with understanding is a necessary skill in every secondary classroom. Students must also be able to read to discover main ideas, details, and inferences. Even more important than absorbing the vast amount of printed material that they encounter every day is secondary school students' development of critical reading ability. Before they leave secondary school, students should know how to distinguish fact from opinion, truth from half-truth, information from emotion.

4. *A reading specialist or an English teacher should be responsible for the teaching of reading.* Reading specialists have distinct responsibilities in secondary literacy programs, but the results of their efforts are negligible without the help of content area teachers. Responsibility for teaching reading cannot be delegated solely to English teachers. Reading as a tool for learning is no more important in English class than it is in most other classes, and English teachers do not necessarily have any better preparation for teaching reading skills and strategies than do other teachers, although they generally have been prepared to teach writing skills and strategies. All content teachers have a responsibility to teach the language and organization of their particular content areas, and to do so they must help students read that content.

**ENGLISH/
LANGUAGE
ARTS**

5. *The teaching of reading and the teaching of literature are one and the same.* Reading skills are important to the study of literature, as they are to the study of every content area. It should be understood, however, that teaching literature should

not consist merely of having students read stories and then giving them vocabulary drills and exercises to find details and main ideas. It is also dangerous to assume that a student will improve content reading skills by practicing with only literature selections, for reading in other content areas involves primarily expository, rather than narrative, selections and requires integration of information gained from graphic aids, such as pictures, maps, graphs, charts, and diagrams, with the written text.

Some Misconceptions about Teaching Writing

1. *Students learn what they need to know about how to write in elementary school. After that they just use writing as a basic tool in other subjects.* People who believe this fail to recognize the developmental nature of writing competency. Teachers know that older students need assistance to learn more advanced and complex reading skills for necessary reading activities in secondary school after mastering basic word recognition and comprehension skills. After mastering the basics of sentence structure and writing conventions, these students also need help to learn more advanced writing techniques in order to meet ever more demanding writing tasks as they work in different content area studies.

2. *Writing skills are only important to secondary school students in English class.* Although writing receives attention in English classes, both as direct instruction in writing and as writing for the purpose of analysis of literature, writing is important in every class. Clarity of expression in writing is particularly important. Scientists must be able to write coherent and precise reports on experiments and observations of phenomena, and science students need to be able to perform such tasks, as well. Almost all classes require written projects or reports to demonstrate learning both from class and from outside research. Learning cannot be adequately demonstrated if the writing is inexact, unfocused, or unclear. Failure to observe writing conventions and standard spellings and failure to use clear sentence constructions may completely mask the learning that has taken place. If the report or project represents a typical real-world task, it has not been successful if it would not be acceptable in a real-world situation, such as a business meeting.

Literacy Performance and Standards

There is widespread concern in the United States about the literacy skills of secondary students. This concern has manifested itself in much testing.

Literacy Performance

The wide range in literacy achievement among secondary school students presents their teachers with a difficult problem. For example, in a group classified as seventh-graders, there may be boys and girls whose literacy skills equal those of many tenth- or eleventh-graders. Some twelfth-graders may have a fifth- or sixth-grade reading ability, whereas others may read at the level of college seniors. The same differences are found in the area of writing. Not only do secondary schools have students with a wide range of reading and writing abilities, they also often have large numbers of struggling readers. Thus, teachers in these schools should know that a student's grade placement may not reflect his or her literacy levels. Teaching literacy skills and strategies in the secondary schools includes strengthening the performance of students who are reading and writing well for their grade placements *and* giving more basic assistance to students who are reading and writing at levels significantly below their grade placements.

The National Assessment of Educational Progress (NAEP) is a study to determine competence in a number of learning areas, including reading and writing. NAEP assessments involve nationally representative samples of students in the fourth, eighth, and twelfth grades. Overall assessment results are analyzed by placement on a single subject-matter proficiency scale, showing the kinds of tasks the students can perform at different achievement levels.

Currently, the NAEP reports results in terms of three achievement levels. Those students scoring at the *basic* level showed partial mastery of the knowledge and skills fundamental for proficient work at each grade. Those scoring at the *proficient* level exhibited solid academic performance and demonstrated competence with challenging material, including application and analysis of the particular subject-area knowledge. Students who scored at the *advanced* level displayed superior performance at each grade according, to the *Nation's Report Card* (NAEP, 2009).

The NAEP writing assessment asked students to perform narrative, informative, and persuasive writing tasks. For both eighth- and twelfth-graders, average writing scores and the percentages of students performing at or above the basic level increased from their levels on previous assessments, but the average writing scores and percentages performing at or above the proficient level showed no change from the 2002 assessment (Salahu-Din, Persky, and Miller, 2008).

In the 2007 assessment, reading abilities were evaluated "in the contexts of literary experience, gaining information, and performing a task" (Lee, Grigg, and Donahue, 2007, p. 2). Reading skills improved for fourth- and eighth-graders, with most improvement among lower- and middle-performing students. Results for twelfth-graders (tested in 2005) did not show improvement over 2002 results; they were not significantly different from the 2002 results (Grigg, Donahue, and Dion, 2007).

Such test results continue to spur demands for the development of standards related to classroom knowledge or performance. Many states have developed standards for literacy of students at specific grade levels, specifying minimum competencies that students must acquire. Students may have to pass a minimum competency test in order to receive a high school diploma.

Professional organizations have also sought to develop standards to improve instruction in various areas of the curriculum, such as language, mathematics, science, and social studies. The Teachers of English to Speakers of Other Languages (TESOL) developed a set of standards for English as a Second Language (ESL) instruction that can complement content area standards (Reiss, 2008). The International

Society for Technology in Education's National Educational Standards (ISTE NETS) are standards for teacher educators, designed to ensure that their students learn to handle important technological challenges. The ISTE website also delineates standards that students should meet in order to knowledgeably use computers and the Internet (Forcier and Descy, 2008). Not long after the *No Child Left Behind Act* became law, "U.S. Secretary of Education Rod Paige introduced the 'Enhancing Education Through Technology' (ED TECH) initiative" to emphasize new goals in technology (Forcier and Descy, 2008, pp. 101, 103).

Specific to the main focus of this text, the National Council of Teachers of English and the International Reading Association cooperatively developed a set of standards for the English language arts for kindergarten through twelfth grade. (See Figure 1.1.) The *Standards for the English Language Arts* (National Council of Teachers of English and International Reading Association, 1996) can be used as a guide for discussion about learning and evaluation, but it is not intended to be the basis of a national core curriculum that specifies definitive, grade-level performance standards. Instead, it specifies a range of areas in the English language arts in which students must be proficient, rather than providing performance standards that specify levels of achievement (Faust and Kieffer, 1998; Smagorinsky, 1999).

FIGURE 1.1

Standards for the English Language Arts **(Sponsored by NCTE and IRA)**

Source: *Standards for the English Language Arts*, by International Reading Association and the National Council of Teachers of English. Copyright 1996 by the International Reading Association and the National Council of Teachers of English. Reprinted with permission.

The vision guiding these standards is that all students must have the opportunities and resources to develop the language skills they need to pursue life's goals and to participate fully as informed, productive members of society. These standards assume that literacy growth begins before children enter school as they experience and experiment with literacy activities—reading and writing, and associating spoken words with their graphic representations. Recognizing this fact, these standards encourage the development of curriculum and instruction that make productive use of the emerging literacy abilities that children bring to school. Furthermore, the standards provide ample room for the innovation and creativity essential to teaching and learning. They are not prescriptions for particular curriculum or instruction.

Although we present these standards as a list, we want to emphasize that they are not distinct and separable; they are, in fact, interrelated and should be considered as a whole.

1. Students read a wide range of print and nonprint texts to build an understanding of texts, of themselves, and of the cultures of the United States and the world; to acquire new information; to respond to the needs and demands of society and the workplace; and for personal fulfillment. Among these texts are fiction and nonfiction, classic and contemporary works.

2. Students read a wide range of literature from many periods in many genres to build an understanding of the many dimensions (e.g., philosophical, ethical, aesthetic) of human experience.

3. Students apply a wide range of strategies to comprehend, interpret, evaluate, and appreciate texts. They draw on their prior experience, their interactions with other

readers and writers, their knowledge of word meaning and of other texts, and their understanding of textual features (e.g., sound-letter correspondence, sentence structure, context, graphics).

4. Students adjust their use of spoken, written, and visual language (e.g., conventions, style, vocabulary) to communicate effectively with a variety of audiences and for different purposes.

5. Students employ a wide range of strategies as they write and use different writing process elements appropriately to communicate with different audiences for a variety of purposes.

6. Students apply knowledge of language structure, language conventions (e.g., spelling and punctuation), media techniques, figurative language, and genre to create, critique, and discuss print and nonprint texts.

7. Students conduct research on issues and interests by generating ideas and questions, and by posing problems. They gather, evaluate, and synthesize data from a variety of sources (e.g., print and nonprint texts, artifacts, people) to communicate their discoveries in ways that suit their purpose and audience.

8. Students use a variety of technological and information resources (e.g., libraries, databases, computer networks, video) to gather and synthesize information and to create and communicate knowledge.

9. Students develop an understanding of and respect for diversity in language use, patterns, and dialects across cultures, ethnic groups, geographic regions, and social roles.

10. Students whose first language is not English make use of their first language to develop competency in the English language arts and to develop understanding of content across the curriculum.

11. Students participate as knowledgeable, reflective, creative, and critical members of a variety of literacy communities.

12. Students use spoken, written, and visual language to accomplish their own purposes (e.g., for learning, enjoyment, persuasion, and the exchange of information).

Competency tests to assess the students' mastery of material and skills mandated by standards have been developed at the state level in some states and at the local level in others. Instructional objectives commonly included on these tests are identifying main ideas and details, finding sequence and cause-and-effect patterns, making inferences, following written directions, using an index and table of contents, using a dictionary, extracting information from graphic aids, and interpreting and completing common forms. Many secondary schools use commercially available standardized reading tests, some of which focus specifically on survival reading skills or basic skills. In some cases, students who fail the tests must take remedial classes.

Some educators feel that standardized curricula, brought about because of minimum competency testing requirements, impair their ability to match learning objectives to particular student needs. They believe that individual differences in students' development of skills and knowledge are overlooked when these minimum competency tests are given, because all students do not master the same material or skills at the same rate. They worry about covering all the skills with all the students, even though some students have not mastered the skills already presented.

Others worry that standardized tests that focus on speed discriminate against some students who work more slowly than others. They also may not adequately reflect important areas of learning, because isolated factors are easier to test, and generally such tests do not attempt to test for creativity and higher-order thinking skills.

The Association for Supervision and Curriculum Development endorses the position that making important decisions based on a single test score is not wise. Multiple sources of assessment data, such as teacher observation, student work samples, and tests, collected over a period of time, are essential to informed decision making (Seltz, 2008).

Range of Students in Content Area Classrooms

Teachers are faced with a wide range of students in their classrooms. Federal laws have mandated inclusion of many students with both physical and learning disabilities in regular content area classrooms, and many students from low socioeconomic backgrounds have had limited experiences and opportunities, putting them at risk for failure. While dealing with students who are at risk, teachers still must accommodate the needs of the gifted and talented students, who may become bored and unproductive if they are not presented with higher-level challenging experiences. Lastly, adding more complexity to the situation, the cultural and linguistic diversity of the population of the United States has greatly increased in recent years, and the country's racial and ethnic makeup is more diverse than U.S. Census data indicate. There are at least 276 ethnic groups in the United States (Garcia, 2002; Gollnick and Chinn, 2002; Ajayi, 2009).

Language and Cultural Diversity

In recent years, **English language learners (ELLs)** who have limited English proficiency have been rapidly increasing in numbers in U.S. classrooms. Judging the ability of ELLs to handle the language needed in content areas by their oral language communication in social discourse is misleading. Academic language presents far more cognitively complex material than the language of everyday life. Academic language must be explicitly taught to these students, and it takes years to master (Reiss, 2008).

Secondary school teachers must be prepared to teach the students from the different cultural, linguistic, and educational backgrounds who have been included in regular classrooms. However, many of these teachers have not been prepared to do so effectively. To accomplish this difficult task, they must determine which language demands in their subject areas offer the most challenges to ELLs. Just exposing the students to English is not enough to help them reach grade-level proficiency. Secondary school textbooks and classroom activities and presentations contain complex language and present many abstract concepts for students to comprehend. Therefore, help with grammatical, morphological, and phonological aspects of English and with the language of classroom discourse is important to students' mastery of the content presented. Scaffolded instruction (instruction that provides support to students) can give them improved access to content material, and supports can be discarded as students master the language and material. The scaffolds offered make success more likely for the students and build students' self-confidence and motivation (Reiss, 2008).

Providing both oral and written directions for assignments may be beneficial for ELLs who have culturally different learning approaches from those of the dominant classroom culture (Gibbons, 2002; Harper and de Jong, 2004). Instruction involving multiliteracies can be beneficial to ELLs in learning about text types and promoting alternative ways of reading and composing. This instruction makes information available to ELLs in multiple ways, including print, oral language, graphics, and pictures (Ajayi, 2009). Individual tutoring may also help these students with academic assignments, as is described in this chapter's "Meeting the Challenge."

MEETING THE CHALLENGE

Lance Jasitt has served as a literacy tutor of children of Mexican and Guatemalan immigrants to Tennessee for two years. During his tutoring experiences with high school Hispanic ELLs, Lance has focused on providing comprehensible, but challenging, input for English language instruction to his tutees. New vocabulary, fresh concepts, and content can be assimilated and applied with a confidence that ultimately results in independent learning when comprehension is the focus of instruction.

Particularly in the content areas of science and social studies, Lance finds a scarcity of bilingual resources for supporting comprehensible input for Spanish-speaking ELLs. Other factors that limit the acquisition of content area knowledge and access to supplemental resources for many Hispanic ELLs are family economic restrictions, the limited formal education of their parents, and lack of familiarity and experience with the educational system.

SCIENCE AND HEALTH

Maria is a ninth-grade ELL from Mexico who enrolled in a middle-Tennessee high school during the middle of the 2003–2004 academic year. Although she could read Spanish, her ability to comprehend English text was limited. One weekend she brought home a health sciences research assignment that involved drafting a one-page paper on the topic of cerebral palsy. She had no significant background knowledge about either the topic or the research process. Compounding her academic dilemma, she did not have access to resources necessary to meet the project requisites and her family did not own a personal computer.

Lance determined that in order to write a paper on cerebral palsy, Maria would have to enhance her schema for that topic through comprehensible input. Lance and Maria traveled to the Tennessee Technological University library and found Spanish language references (i.e., online *Wikipedia* encyclopedia and *Infotrac ¡Informe!* database of Spanish periodical articles) to build background for Maria. After she read briefly about her topic in Spanish, she was able to synthesize some basic English reference articles and write a short paper. She could read and understand her report and retell key facts orally.

The tutoring that Maria received was integrated with her content area assignments and scaffolded her learning process. Maria was able to complete her report and acquire important content knowledge, in addition to locating new research tools and resources for future homework and projects.

Students who speak languages other than English often come from diverse cultural backgrounds. Those whose cultural backgrounds differ from that of the dominant culture encounter information outside their background knowledge but that the general population is assumed to know. They may need to build new schemata to understand concepts that authors expect to be a part of their background knowledge. For example, students may lack knowledge about famous U.S. leaders that is assumed in textbooks. Another area that is commonly problematic for readers is use of figurative expressions in American English. Because of these types of problems, students may comprehend better when they read materials about their own cultures. Teachers and media specialists can work together to identify literature, videos, and Internet resources for these students.

Students whose families speak little or no English often have no help with schoolwork at home. Moreover, their families may need the assistance of an interpreter to understand the educational system and the schooling process.

A caring environment fosters literacy learning for all students, especially at-risk students. One way that teachers can exhibit a caring attitude is to work at understanding and responding with sensitivity to their students' cultures (Sanacore, 2004).

Armon and Ortega (2008) report a program in which college students were paired with Latino children to work with them as they wrote and illustrated autobiographical pieces. The college students received instruction on the writing genre and started their own illustrated autobiographical writing and a print-making process for the illustrations. They shared their own writing with their partners and then taught the processes they had used to the partners. They used bilingual children's literature for models of such writing. The children wrote and illustrated two or three vignettes that reflected their self-identities. They were allowed to choose the use of Spanish or English or write using hybrid language. Some instruction was given in both Spanish and English, sometimes requiring the pairs to cluster with other pairs to include both languages. The writing instruction included using a process writing approach. (See Chapter 9 for more about this approach.) The college students learned about culturally relevant teaching approaches in an authentic setting.

Reilly (2008) found that middle-school ELLs performed better on the New Jersey state assessment in language arts when they participated in a project in which they drew pictures and created poetry about U.S. immigration after hearing books on the topic read to them, discussing the books, and viewing visual aids (a map, pictures, and a film). This improved performance happened although the test preparation time was decreased in order to include this special project. Arts integration with literacy instruction is a strategy that teachers should consider trying.

Students with Educational Challenges

Increasing numbers of challenged learners, who were once taught in special education classes, are now enrolled in regular classrooms through **inclusion** programs. This component of diversity arises largely from the special needs of individuals who have mental, physical, sensory, communication, and learning challenges or who are emotionally or behaviorally challenged (Kirk, Gallagher, and Anastasiow, 2003).

Exceptional students differ from average students in a variety of ways. "These differences must occur to such an extent that the child requires a modification of school practices, or special educational services, to develop to maximum capacity" (Kirk, Gallagher, and Anastasiow, 2003, p. 2). Some have multiple handicapping conditions.

What is the purpose of the IDEA?

Secondary school students with disabilities have often received a portion of their education in public school classrooms since the Education for All Handicapped Children Act (EHA) was reaffirmed in 1983 with the passage of legislation that extended it to focus on secondary education, parent training, and preschool children. The EHA has been renamed the **Individuals with Disabilities Education Act (IDEA)** and updated several times since then. This legislation ensures the right to a free and appropriate public education to all students from age five to twenty-one who have disabilities (Office of Innovation and Improvement, 2004; Watson, n.d.).

Why is participation in regular classrooms increasing for special education students?

In recent decades, advocates for students with learning problems have actively pursued increased integration of students with disabilities into the regular classroom. The Regular Education Initiative (REI) calls for **full inclusion** of disabled students in the regular classroom, thus increasing the likelihood that many students with disabilities will receive all or a significant portion of their instruction in the regular classroom. In such programs, the special education teacher collaborates with the classroom teacher about the student's goals, achievement, and appropriate instruction. Then the classroom teacher integrates the student with special needs entirely into the regular classroom (Mastropieri and Scruggs, 2000).

What is the purpose of an IEP?

Each student identified as handicapped must have an **individualized education plan (IEP)**, which includes a description of the student's problem, the program's long-term goals and its short-term objectives, the special education services needed for the student, and the criteria for assessing the effectiveness of the services. Classroom teachers serve on the committees that develop IEPs for students who are eligible for special education services, but not every content teacher will be on the IEP committee. Content teachers who do not serve on the IEP committee for a student can learn about the student's IEP requirements through collaboration with special education personnel.

Students with disabilities often benefit from intensive, individualized instruction and explicit teaching of skills. Their needs may include academic, adaptive, and/or functional life skills (Hardman, Drew, and Egan, 2008).

At-Risk Students

What reasons can you suggest to explain the relationship between socioeconomic status and school achievement?

Students enter school expecting to learn to read and write, but failing over and over again may cause them to give up. **Socioeconomic status** is the single best predictor of students' reading achievement. Through no fault of their own, many students of low socioeconomic status are at risk of failing to learn and of failing to complete high school. Other risk factors commonly associated with school dropouts include low achievement, retention in grade, behavior problems, poor attendance, and attendance at schools with large numbers of poor students (Slavin, 1989; Polloway, Patton, and Serna, 2001). These students may be from any racial, ethnic, and linguistic background (Mastropieri and Scruggs, 2000).

Summary

Secondary school students today face a wide array of literacy demands. Secondary school teachers must decide how to help these students handle the literacy demands they face in their content area classes. A variety of reading skills is necessary for effective content area learning. The content area teacher is responsible for helping students apply these skills, and necessary writing skills, in content area assignments. Other educators—special reading teachers, reading consultants, administrators, and librarians or media center specialists—are responsible for other aspects of the secondary school literacy program.

Secondary school literacy programs include five components: developmental reading instruction, content area reading instruction, recreational reading, writing instruction, and instruction for struggling readers. Content area teachers are responsible for content area reading and writing and for encouraging recreational reading, but they should also cooperate with other literacy professionals who deal with the other components.

There are a number of misconceptions about the teaching of reading at the secondary school level. These misconceptions include the ideas that (1) teaching reading is a concern only in the elementary school; (2) teaching reading in the content areas is separate and distinct from teaching subject matter; (3) reading needs can be met through remedial work alone; (4) a reading specialist or an English teacher should be totally responsible for the teaching of reading; and (5) the teaching of reading and the teaching of literature are one and the same.

There are two basic misconceptions about the teaching of writing at the secondary school level: that students learn all that they need to know about *how* to write in the elementary school, and that writing skills are only important to secondary students in English class.

Currently there is much concern about secondary school students' reading and writing performance, and various groups have developed standards for judging this performance. Teachers face this concern about performance while encountering a wide range of students in their classrooms. Many of these students exhibit language diversity and disabilities of various types and come from backgrounds that leave them at risk for failure in literacy tasks, whereas others are gifted and talented students with a need to be challenged with higher-level material.

Discussion Questions

1. Which of the misconceptions about teaching reading listed in the chapter seem most evident in your school situation?
2. Do you see evidence of the two misconceptions about writing instruction in your school situation? What can you do to refute these beliefs?
3. Do you believe that it is possible to increase learning in the content areas by providing appropriate help to students in their study of printed materials? Give as many examples as possible to support your position.
4. What factors account for many secondary school graduates' inability to read well enough to cope with basic reading requirements? Give reasons for your answer.
5. What factors account for the wide range of reading and writing ability of secondary school students? Defend your answer.
6. What particular problems do English language learners face in content area classrooms?
7. What new literacy experiences can be integrated into content area instruction to provide student motivation and enhance student communication skills?
8. How would you integrate literacy learning and the arts?
9. What are the differences between vocational reading and reading in academic subjects, if any?

Enrichment Activities

1. What do you think are the most important things about reading that a content area teacher should know? Interview a content area teacher about this question. Compare the teacher's response with your own views.
2. Keep a log of your literacy activities for a week. What do your findings suggest about reading and writing to meet the daily needs of young adults?
*3. Visit a secondary classroom. Try to identify the range of reading and writing abilities. Compare your impressions with those of the teacher.
*4. Administer the survey in "Assessing Adolescents' Motivation to Read" *Journal of Adolescent & Adult Literacy* 50 (February 2007): 378–396 to a classroom of adolescent students. Write an analysis of your findings.

---

*These activities are designed for in-service teachers, student teachers, and practicum students.

Resources including the TeachSource Video Cases can be found on the website for this book. Cengage Learning's CourseMate brings course concepts to life with interactive learning, study, and exam preparation tools that support the printed textbook. Go to www.cengage.com/login to register your access code.

CHAPTER 2

Integrating Technology in Content Area Literacy Instruction

Overview

Many students today are immersed in technology daily, so much so that they are often referred to as *digital natives* (Considine, Horton, and Moorman, 2009; National Council of Teachers of English, 2008; Prensky, 2005/2006). They have been surrounded by information communication technology (ICT) for their entire lives. They encounter it in store checkout lanes, as well as in popular video games. They communicate by e-mail and text messaging and listen to digital music. They play computer games incessantly. They use videos from which to learn new skills, rather than using instructional books. They get their news from television and the Internet, instead of from a newspaper. They communicate with cell phones that also serve as digital cameras, rather than by writing traditional letters. Many of these phones allow access to e-mail, text messaging, and surfing the Internet. In short, many students are familiar with technology outside of school and are comfortable with it as a tool and information source. However, although they are surrounded by texts, images, and sounds, some students fail to interpret these messages correctly. In fact, "extensive use of ICT often creates a false sense of competency, as well as the misperception among many adults that contemporary youth are 'media savvy'"(Considine, Horton, and Moorman, 2009, p. 472). Many are, but many are not, and may not realize their lack of understanding. If they are not helped to analyze media content critically, they are "open to manipulation and misinformation" (p. 476).

According to Lenhardt, Madden, Rankin McGill, and Smith (2007), 90 percent of Americans aged twelve to seventeen use the Internet. Many of them read and construct media texts outside of school as they participate in online social networks (Knobel and Wilber, 2009; Richardson, 2009).

Unfortunately, some students have only superficial contact with technology outside of school. They may not have computers in their homes, so they need exposure to technology use in school, because technology will be an integral part of their lives when they enter the work force. They need to expand their grasp of literacy to include informed use of technology and interpretation and production of multiple forms of representation—receiving and transmitting information with multiple symbol systems, such as visual symbols and images, color, shapes, and so on (Kist, 2002; Ohler, 2009; Smolin and Lawless, 2003). As Love (2004/2005, p. 304) points out, "Meaning is being made in ways that are becoming more multimodal because the way language is used is continually being reshaped by new forms of communication media." The Alliance for a Media Literate America and the Association for Media Literacy emphasize the importance of integrating media literacy across the curriculum (Considine, Horton, and Moorman, 2009).

Lawrence, McNeal, and Yildiz (2009) found that many of the high school students in a summer program designed to promote reading, writing, and technology skills did not initially know how to use spell check in *Microsoft PowerPoint,* change fonts and space sentences in *Microsoft Word,* save to a USB drive, upload digital pictures to the computer, or use *Microsoft Excel.* With instruction from the teachers and assistance from more proficient peers, they were able to use technology effectively at the end of the program.

Classrooms of today often reflect a technological environment, but many classrooms have limited computer access for the number of students being served. In some cases, the schools are not as thoroughly equipped as are many of the students' homes. Another problem is that some educators did not grow up in a technological environment and did not have training that covered some of the newer technologies. As a result, available equipment may lie unused or underused in classrooms, laboratories, or media centers, a situation that is not acceptable in current educational settings.

Educators must learn how to harness technology for the benefit of their instructional programs. Any type of technology in a classroom should be used to advance the learning of the students and/or facilitate the job of the teacher. Each decision to use technology should be made because that particular technological application will be more effective for the task at hand than would other approaches.

Today's world demands that students acquire a high degree of media literacy. Literacy learning naturally accommodates the use of technology. Teachers find that everything from overhead projectors, television, and audio recordings to computers, videos, and multimedia has an application to the literacy curriculum. Internet use is particularly important in today's world. Literacy instruction must embrace consumption of media content online, as well as creation of such content through blogs or on social networking sites, for as they perform these activities, students "are filtering information, building personas, identifying audiences, and formulating arguments" (Beach and Doerr-Stevens, 2009, p. 467), all important literacy skills.

As is true in other curricular areas, standards for technology have been developed by professional organizations and other entities. The International Society for Technology in Education (ISTE) has developed National Educational Technology Standards (NETS) for students and teachers (http://www.iste.org/AM/Template.cfm?Section=NETS).

Purpose-Setting Questions

As you read this chapter, try to answer these questions:

1. What is media literacy, and why is it currently of concern?
2. How can media use help English language learners (ELLs)?
3. How can media use help struggling readers?
4. How can word-processing and desktop-publishing programs benefit literacy instruction?

5. What are some valuable aspects of using the Internet for literacy learning?

6. How can teachers make use of blogs, wikis, and podcasts?

7. Does social networking have a place in an educational program?

8. What are the types of computer-assisted instruction, and what purpose does each type serve?

9. What are some valid applications of overhead projectors, televisions, audio recordings, and video recordings in literacy learning?

10. What multimedia applications might be used in literacy instruction?

Media Literacy

Why is media literacy an important component of content area instruction?

Media literacy is the ability to comprehend, evaluate, and produce material for both print and nonprint media, including the ability to interpret and develop electronic messages that include images, sounds, movements, and animations (Considine, Horton, and Moorman, 2009; Grabe and Grabe, 2007; Forcier and Descy, 2008). According to Scharrer (2002/2003), it involves critical analysis of what students watch and read and the effects the material may have on the viewers and readers, so that students can become critical viewers. Other media literacy concerns include critical thinking about how the messages from different media are created and learning how to produce media messages. Some educators are particularly concerned about negative effects of media violence, propaganda, and sexual content on viewers.

Ohler (2009) points out that applying the techniques of media persuasion is an important part of media literacy and that the development of media messages requires students to reflect about reading of media. Media literacy is needed so that students can see how media techniques influence thinking. Online reading requires critical analysis of the accuracy, quality, and value of the material read. So much material is available that students must be able to filter it through a critical lens. Otherwise, they may become bogged down in material that is unreliable or irrelevant for their purposes (Wolf and Barzillai, 2009). Many of them may be unduly influenced by advertising and stereotypes that they find in the media (Considine, Horton, and Moorman, 2009). They also may be distracted by advertisements and follow Web links to advertisements and other material, causing them to jump from place to place and to move away from their intended tasks (Weigel and Gardner, 2009).

Wolf and Barzillai (2009, p. 36) point out that "from a cognitive neuroscience perspective, the digital culture's reinforcement of rapid attentional shifts and multiple sources of distraction can short-circuit the development of the slower, more cognitively demanding comprehension processes that go into the formation of deep reading and deep thinking." However, they add that online reading tutors and programs with embedded strategy prompts, think-alouds, and feedback in the material may encourage the needed strategic thinking and that WebQuests may help, as well.

Students come to media literacy, as to all literacy experiences, with varying backgrounds of experiences. Many have done extensive viewing, but much of it has been uncritical absorption of the material with which they have been presented. Scharrer (2002/2003) believes that sustained instruction in media literacy has a chance to reduce the negative effects some media have on adolescents. Knowing how advertising uses propaganda, being aware of how fake but realistic-looking violence is used for sensationalism, and distinguishing how different types of people are portrayed, often in stereotyped ways, are all part of becoming critical viewers, as well as critical readers. Realizing that anyone can post material on the Internet and that much of the material is unedited and may be false can make students more careful in choosing information for personal or school use. Critical reading skills must be applied to all electronic media as well as to print media that students encounter. Chapter 6 discusses critical thinking and reading in more detail.

Many of today's secondary school students have developed some of their media literacy through playing electronic games. Many of these games involve complex thinking in order to solve problems, and students learn some critical literacy skills as a by-product. They have to make decisions, and they learn about consequences when they take risks. They learn to evaluate the trade-offs they must make between risk and possible benefits (Gee and Levine, 2009). According to a recent survey, fifteen- to nineteen-year-old Americans play games or use a computer forty-two minutes per day on weekdays and one hour per day on weekends and holidays. Unfortunately, this compares to ten minutes spent reading for pleasure daily (U.S. Bureau of Labor Statistics, 2008). In addition to acquiring some critical reading skills through playing video games, teens learn to perform multiple tasks at the same time and to respond rapidly when confronted with new information. They interpret words, pictures, sounds, and actions as part of their play. Some games also offer new worthwhile experiences and content that can be applied to life experiences. The line between learning and playing becomes blurred during a game. When playing, the gamers interact and create within the game environment, which may be more engaging to them than reading books, and even students who are believed to have short attention spans often persevere with the games for extended periods (Gee, 2003; Norton-Meier, 2005).

Some of the technology that students must master in order to attain media and technological literacy include digital imaging technologies, such as *PowerPoint*'s slide-show feature; research on the Internet to locate information for classes; web-page construction; blogging; developing wikis; interaction on social media, such as MySpace, Facebook, and YouTube; texting and use of e-mail. Acquiring these skills will prepare students to construct meaning with and obtain meaning from a variety of texts (Ohler, 2009).

FOCUS ON   *English Language Learners*

Media Use to Help English Language Learners (ELLs)

English language learner (ELL) programs need well-designed bilingual instruction to afford students full English literacy (Grant and Wong, 2003). Technology and electronic literacy transform learning for ELLs (Matthews, 2000; Seal, 2003). For example, research shows the importance of extensive reading in second-language instruction (Jacobs and Gallo, 2002), and Black (2005) points out advantages to ELLs of participation in an online "fanfiction" community. (Fanfiction is discussed in the section on electronic communications later in this chapter.) The Internet, computer software, and electronic books offer extensive opportunities for second language learning.

Text-to-speech (TTS) software helps ELLs learn to read and comprehend (Balajthy, 2005). The goal of TTS is presenting electronic book (e-book) files with electronic voice synthesis software to provide oral reading of electronic text files. Students using this software see the visual text and hear the auditory version of the text at the same time. Currently marketed TTS word processors include such programs as *OutLoud* (Don Johnston) and *IntelliTalk3* (IntelliTools). Balajthy (2005) identifies the following related software: *Read-Please 2003* and *HelpRead* are available as free downloads from the Internet, and they provide simple text-to-speech. The *CAST eReader* and *TextHelp* are not free, nor are *Kurzweil 3000* and *WordSmith*; however, they offer more options in their software.

Websites such as the following offer digitized materials that can be used with TTS software. This is not an exhaustive list, since additional materials are developed constantly:

The World Fact Book by the U.S. Central Intelligence Agency (http://www.cia.gov/library/publications/the-world-factbook/) is one source.

The Electronic Text Center at the University of Virginia (http://etext.lib.virginia.edu/collections/languages/) includes an extensive collection of materials by African American, Native American, and women writers.

The Internet Public Library for Teens includes TeenSpace for adolescents (http://www.ipl.org/div/teen/aplus/toc.htm), a site that offers a step-by-step approach to research and writing.

Text-to-speech materials provide instructional support for echo reading, which involves reading a print text aloud in unison with a teacher or classmate. Text-to-speech materials and taped books can serve the same function as a teacher or classmate up to a point. However, teachers must also provide instructional support to develop student understanding.

ELL students can build background for understanding content assignments by consulting sites such as those of the Library of Congress (includes recorded information), Smithsonian Institution (includes recorded information), and the World Wide Web Virtual Library (includes many subjects and cultures). Teachers can find lists of Internet sites that will assist them and their students at http://www.eduref.org/. This webpage has an index of materials for different educational levels and specific populations. Teaching ideas, activities, and units can be found at http://www.thegateway.org/browse/makes/. Teachers can find dictionaries and translations available on various other websites.

FOCUS ON *Struggling Readers*

Media Use to Help Struggling Readers

The Internet provides a variety of sites that will help struggling readers acquire word meanings that will enhance their comprehension. Teachers can use search engines to find online dictionaries and thesauruses. For example, the Bibliomania website (http://www.bibliomania.com/) contains an up-to-date list of useful sites.

Struggling readers will benefit from many of the same resources that help ELLs. They too need extensive practice reading; however, struggling readers are not transferring knowledge of reading and language from their native languages. Struggling readers also need the support provided by electronic books, the Internet, and computer programs (Matthews, 2000). Electronic books (e-books), talking books, and books on CDs are valuable sources of reading material. These books include the actual text, as well as supplementary information selected to provide assistance and increase comprehension. This information may include graphics, video, and sound.

Some readers struggle because of physical challenges. Visually challenged learners may benefit from text-to-speech software, such as the programs previously cited as helpful for ELLs.

Struggling readers need reading practice that contributes to their developing accurate, fluent, high-comprehension-level reading ability. However, struggling readers need to read books that are "just right" (Allington, 2001). "Just right" books are those written at a level where they can read successfully. Teachers can use informal reading inventories to identify the students' correct reading levels (see Chapter 2). After identifying the appropriate reading level, teachers can consult websites such as Leveled Books (http://www.Leveled-books.com/) and the Barahona Center (http://www2.csusm.edu/csb/) at California State University–San Marcos, which provides information about recommended books in Spanish. Project LITT: Literacy Instruction through Technology, which was based at San Diego State University and funded through the U.S. Department of Education, focused on the use of technology to improve the reading skills of students with learning disabilities (Johnson, 2001). The following are just a sampling of the riches on the Internet that are available to teachers: the University of Pennsylvania's On-Line Books (http://onlinebooks.library.upenn.edu/) website is a searchable digital library, and the Andy Holt Virtual Library (Docu-Stack 2) (http://www.utm.edu/vlibrary/docust2.shtml) provides links to numerous websites featuring free online books.

Computers

Computers are the key to success in most walks of life. Not only are computers found in businesses for communications, record keeping, and accounting, they also are found in the cash registers of stores and restaurants, in household appliances, and in children's toys and games, and they are used in homes for e-mail, game playing, music sources, information sources, entertainment distribution, and social networking. They have many potential functions in literacy education.

Digital literacy is a subset of media literacy. Valmont (2003, p. 92) points out that digital literacy "includes the active interpretation of nonverbal symbolic systems that authors include in electronic messages" and "the construction of sounds, images, graphics, photos, videos, animations, and movements to add nonverbal components to electronic messages."

Word-Processing and Desktop-Publishing Programs

What are some advantages of having students use word-processing programs to write creative works or research reports?

**ENGLISH/
LANGUAGE
ARTS**

The writing of student papers, both creative efforts and research reports, is an obvious application of computers to literacy education. The ease of revision and editing that **word-processing programs** provide makes students more likely to reconsider content, organization, wording, and mechanical aspects of their papers and to make changes after a draft has been completed. Spelling checkers and grammar checkers alert students to spellings and syntactic constructions that they may need to change. They then have to make their own decisions about the correctness of their material and the best ways to change it. These programs do not merely serve as crutches; they stimulate thought about the writing and initiate decision making. This revision and editing process often results in better-written products and offers a learning experience as students see the benefits of trying different organizations and approaches. Word-processing programs often include a dictionary and a thesaurus. The dictionary can be used to decide if the chosen word has the correct meaning for the context. The thesaurus can be used to choose a synonym when a word has been overused in a selection or to pick a word with just the right connotations. More on word processing is found in Chapter 9.

What are some applications of desktop-publishing programs that could be useful in your content area?

Desktop-publishing programs allow for integration of text and graphics. Generally, users can flow text around graphics, choose from a variety of styles and sizes of type, format text into columns, and set up special formats (such as greeting cards, business cards, and banners). Creating posters, flyers, and class newsletters and magazines are the most common uses of desktop publishing for literacy and content development.

At one time, there was a clear-cut delineation between word-processing software and desktop-publishing software. Today's deluxe word-processing programs, such as *Microsoft Word*, contain many features that once were available only from desktop-publishing programs, including the ability to combine text and graphics, use different fonts, and set up text in columns. Therefore, creative writing, class reports, newsletters, and magazines may all be produced with the same software. Microsoft Word and many other word-processing programs also offer a function that converts word-processed documents to webpage formats suitable for posting on the World Wide Web.

**ENGLISH/
LANGUAGE
ARTS**

Writing Development Software

Some electronic outliners are available to help students organize the content of a paper by enabling them to put ideas in outline format. When an outline has been created, the student can easily add or delete items, as the program reconfigures the material to fit the new content (Geisert and Futrell, 2000). Concept maps, or semantic maps, are often developed as a result of brainstorming as a prewriting activity. *Inspiration®*, an outlining and diagramming program, is useful for creating semantic maps. A projection device or large monitor can be used with the computer to allow the class to see the development of the map. Symbols can be dragged around the screen to organize them. New symbols can be inserted as labels for categories that are formed as the material is organized. More ideas or categories can be added, graphics can indicate the importance or order of ideas on the map, and specific instructions can be added to the map. Such mapping allows students to record information from multiple sources on a single map to aid in synthesizing information. It is also possible to link items on the map, clarifying the relationships among the terms. *Inspiration* can have multiple layers of smaller maps that are hidden until the user accesses them, keeping the screen from becoming crowded and confusing.

Write It Right is a program that is "designed to analyze student writing and help the writer correct errors. Some error correction programs, such as *StyleWriter*, provide not only feedback and support, but also guidance designed to make your students better writers" (Recesso and Orrill, 2008, p. 243).

Writer's Studio offers process-writing instruction appropriate for students in grades seven and eight. This program incorporates the writing process (prewriting, drafting, revising, proofreading, and publishing) and includes graphic organizers (cluster maps, story maps, sequencers, and checklists). *Microsoft Word* and similar word-processing programs are useful during the drafting and revising stages.

Collaboration Software

What are some types of collaboration software?

Using collaborative writing software, such as *Writeboard* (http://writeboard.com/), multiple people can work on a single document, adding material as it is located, and editing the document when the need occurs. It is possible to tell which changes were made by which students and to retrieve previous versions, if the need arises (Recesso and Orrill, 2008).

One type of collaboration software is the multiplayer video game. Since 2000, many video games are Internet-based multiplayer games, often known as MMORPGs (massively multiplayer online role-playing games). As players become immersed in these online games, they seek and form relationships, both cooperative and antagonistic, with others sitting at keyboards all over the world. Entire social communities (often taking the form of "guilds" of players) are created, and they have many of the same characteristics as social organizations and relationships formed face to face. It is common for players to begin to view others as extensions of the avatars or icons that the others have chosen to represent themselves. These MMORPGs require a type of social and cultural literacy within a technological medium.

Databases and Spreadsheets

What are some applications of database programs in your content area?

SOCIAL STUDIES   **SCIENCE AND HEALTH**

ENGLISH/ LANGUAGE ARTS

A database is an organized collection of data. **Database programs** make possible a search of the database by the computer. The information in a database is filed so that it can be retrieved by category. Many commercial, governmental, and educational databases are available for students to use in their research, and students can form their own databases of information that they collect when doing personal research. Students in U.S. history classes might develop databases of facts related to various wars; students in biology classes, databases of the characteristics of certain species; students in English classes, databases of characteristics of particular literature selections; and so on. Creating databases helps students decide what data are relevant to particular topics, and they learn to analyze and synthesize large amounts of information. Many libraries catalog their holdings in a computer database that students can search by author, title, or subject. More on databases is found in Chapter 7.

Spreadsheets also organize data into a pattern, using a grid of rows and columns. They are ordinarily used to store and manipulate numerical data. Spreadsheet programs often make it possible for data to be presented in chart and graph form. The reading and production of meaningful charts and graphs are important parts of literacy in today's society. Science, economics, and business math teachers may choose to have students use and interpret spreadsheets.

For what content areas are spreadsheets most useful?

SCIENCE AND HEALTH   **SOCIAL STUDIES**

MATHEMATICS

Using the Internet

Material on the Internet is made up of hypertext and hypermedia. **Hypertext** refers to nonsequential text. Hypertext links allow computer users to access documents in an order chosen by the user. Highlighted words and symbols serve as links to other texts, which can be accessed by clicking on the highlighted elements. **Hypermedia** refers to nonsequentially linked text, graphics, motions, and sounds. This nonsequential linkage makes accessing information for research quicker and easier than it would be if each individual location had to be separately addressed. It also presents a problem in terms of navigating among different texts, even for some students who do quite well in following the linear text in books. Students must learn to select links in a reasonable order to create their individual paths through information, and they must understand the relationships among the ideas and intertextual referents as they navigate the nonlinear paths (Alvermann, 2008; Grabe and Grabe, 2007; McNabb, 2005/2006; Schmar-Dobler, 2003). Many students are quite comfortable using the Internet. They can search for information to use in research papers and other class assignments. Some students, however, will need to be taught appropriate search strategies.

Much text found on Internet sites is expository. Students need to have skills and strategies for reading expository text in order to get the most from such sites.

A great deal of information is available on the Internet about any topic that is studied in school. One problem, however, is that not all of the information is accurate. To use the Internet as a research source, students have to learn to check the credentials of the authors of information found on the Internet, to double-check information with print or other sources when possible, and to look for documentation of information presented. Anonymous information, accompanied by no documentation, must be approached skeptically. Some websites are known to be reputable, such as those of the Smithsonian Institution (http://www.si.edu/), the Library of Congress (http://www.loc.gov/), and *National Geographic* (http://www.nationalgeographic.com/), and can be used with confidence as sources. In some instances, the teacher may wish to supply the students with a list of sites to use in their research. The teacher may wish to bookmark acceptable sites on the classroom computers and ask the students to use these sites for their research. This action eliminates some of the higher-order thinking needed to evaluate sites, but it can be a major time saver in a classroom in which time or computer availability is limited, and it can help to lessen the danger of students' accessing unacceptable sites (Forbes, 2004). Many schools have installed filter software, such as *Cyber Patrol* to restrict access to undesirable sites.

Uniform Resource Locators (URLs) are Internet addresses. The URLs for the websites mentioned in the previous paragraph are shown in parentheses. One of the problems with specifying sites on the Web to students or in a book such as this one is that a site may be relocated or removed. Unlike books, whose contents never change from one reading to another, the text on the Internet can change constantly. A website that a student visits today may not be there tomorrow, or it may contain additional or different information tomorrow.

Finding information on the Internet is facilitated by a Web browser, such as Mozilla Firefox or Microsoft Internet Explorer. In addition, there are many search engines, such as Google and Yahoo!, and metasearch engines, such as Dogpile, that will provide the user with the results from several search engines with a single request. These tools allow users to conduct keyword searches. (Chapter 7 further discusses locating information on the Internet.) A group or individual doing a research project might complete the first two sections of a K-W-L about the topic and use the "W" (Want to Know) column to generate keywords to guide an Internet search. The results of the search would go in the "L" (Learned) column.

Students who locate websites with search engines must then evaluate the sites for unbiased, accurate, up-to-date, and relevant information. That may entail checking the author's credentials, if possible. Some sites have information about the author posted. Students may also have to check information found on the site in other sources, including print sources. It helps if the students understand the difference between paid and unpaid listings in search engines and know how the paid sites are indicated. Students who do not use these techniques in analyzing websites may submit papers that contain information from sites that are completely bogus, as well as ones that are just slanted or have some poorly researched information (David, 2009). The Internet Reciprocal Teaching Strategies for Critically Evaluating Websites (http://ctell1.uconn.edu/somers/quag.htm) presents a procedure that students can use in learning to evaluate websites.

**ENGLISH/
LANGUAGE
ARTS**

A teacher of a secondary English class might want to search the Web for an appropriate site where students can publish work and get critiques. These sites must be carefully chosen, but they can be very effective.

ENGLISH/
LANGUAGE
ARTS

**TeachSource
Video Case**
Middle School Reading
Instruction: Integrating
Technology

Online discussion groups can be implemented with students in English classes in a number of ways. Participants can e-mail their fellow students about classwork or read classmates' papers and write comments. English language learners can benefit from online discussion groups because they are motivational and interactive in nature. Students practice their writing skills, share experiences, and learn from others (Cote Parra, 2000). Love (2002) cautions that teachers' success with online discussions depends on the clarity with which they define the purposes of the discussions and communicate these purposes to their students.

Using the Internet allows the development of virtual learning communities that reach beyond cultural, geographic, generational, and institutional boundaries. The next "Meeting the Challenge" describes one such community.

MEETING THE CHALLENGE

SCIENCE AND
HEALTH

SOCIAL
STUDIES

ENGLISH/
LANGUAGE
ARTS

Larry Lynn, a teacher in Cumberland County, Tennessee, enrolled three of his classes in the International Telecomputing Consortium's World Class project. World Class is an online forum for the discussion of real problems by students, teachers, and field experts. Citizen's Energy, an energy company, brought in experts from across the country to answer questions posed by students during the project. Larry's classes were in contact with students worldwide, including students from China, Brazil, Ethiopia, Germany, and the United States. During the project, the students learned about alternative energy sources.

Larry had this to say about the project:

Each week during the project we would receive e-mail with a lot of information for us to read and respond to. I would print the e-mail, and my classes would read the mail and discuss it in their groups. When they had arrived at a consensus about the answers to any questions that were asked, I would let them e-mail their answers to World Class so that the other participants could view them. We did the same thing with their responses. We would also pose questions to experts in the field of discussion and receive their answers by e-mail.

During the time that we were involved in World Class, we were able to send e-mail directly to some of the participating schools. My students really enjoyed this part because they could learn firsthand about the cultures and circumstances in which others live.

I encouraged my students to be open-minded about what they were reading and learning. They realized that everyone does not have the same things they do. Also, they enjoyed analyzing the grammar of the students from other countries. It was good practice without a textbook! Sometimes my students would have to try to understand what the other students were trying to say. Most of the participating teachers did not correct their students' grammar when they were sending their e-mail. I explained to my students that English was not the native language of these students, and my students treated their foreign peers with respect.

It was a very interesting project for my students and for me. You have to be willing to give some of your class time to something other than what's in the book to do this kind of activity, but I believe it is worth the time and trouble.

SCIENCE AND HEALTH

NASA sponsors Online Interactive Projects (http://quest.arc.nasa.gov/) that involve students in authentic scientific explorations through television broadcasts, videos, online interaction, and workbooks.

Homepages

What kinds of information might a student or a class put on a homepage?

Many classrooms or individual students now have their own **homepages** on the Web. Although a discussion of homepage development is beyond the scope of this section, students can learn to use HTML to code the material for their own homepages. Knowledge of HTML is not essential to the development of webpages, however. Students may be able to use a special function of their word-processing program to convert their word-processed text to HTML or other Web formats, or they can use a Web editor or builder, such as Microsoft's *FrontPage* or Macromedia's *Dreamweaver*, that is designed to aid in webpage publishing. Text, graphics, photographs, and animations may be included. Classes may develop webpages to display class newspapers, students' creative writing or written reports, students' artwork, and so on. The importance of careful composition, proofreading, and editing becomes evident when writing is to be displayed to the world on the Internet. Webpages produced by students should be examined for accurate and appropriate information, correct grammar and mechanics, interesting presentation, readable and attractive page layout, useful links, and appropriate graphics. In producing webpages, students learn to use size, color, screen placement, symbols, and more, along with print, to convey ideas (Alvermann 2008).

Wikis

Wikis provide the ultimate collaborative writing experience. They are websites that do not require knowledge of HTML. They allow users to edit content—adding, removing, or changing information. Because anyone can make a change to a wiki, however, there is a danger of inaccurate information being posted. Although the changes to wikis are usually not reviewed before they are posted, most of them are easy to edit when misinformation is discovered, and there are often archives of revision histories that allow the restoration of accurate information that has been removed.

Wikipedia is probably the best known example of a wiki. According to Badke (2009, p. 54), "it has become the most frequently used encyclopedia in the world." Students must learn the difference between Wikipedia and an encyclopedia that has been commercially prepared, complete with reviews and editing of material before it is published. Wikipedia may be a good place to start some investigations of a topic, but it should not be considered the ultimate source.

Google has launched a website called Knol (http://knol.google.com/k) that is similar to Wikipedia. Most Knol articles are expected to have bylines. Readers can rate articles or comment on them. They also may write articles on the same subjects to show differing views.

How could you use wikis in your classroom curriculum?

Wikis have many possible applications in classrooms. Students in William Bishop's Spanish class have used wikis to create reports related to class studies, such

FOREIGN
LANGUAGES

SOCIAL
STUDIES

ENGLISH/
LANGUAGE
ARTS

as profiles of Spanish speaking-countries. Viki Davis, a computer sciences teacher in Georgia, has won an award for her class's "The Flat Classroom Project," which addressed globalization, outsourcing, and virtual communication (Davis, 2007). Other students have used wikis to post drafts of writing and receive comments and suggestions from others about revision (Morgan and Smith, 2008). The prospects are endless.

As is true with websites in general, material on wikis should be read critically. All information should be verified by other means.

WebQuests

According to Recesso and Orrill (2008, p. 316), a **WebQuest** is an "inquiry-based instructional approach in which students use Web resources to accomplish a defined task." These activities are useful in thematic units and interdisciplinary activities. Bernie Dodge developed the model for WebQuests, which have clearly identified purposes and lead students to assume roles in order to solve problems from a variety of perspectives. The model for a WebQuest includes these parts: introduction, task, resource list, description of the process, evaluation rubric, and conclusion. The task primarily involves use of Web resources, but books and other media may also be used. Students may take on roles such as consumers, merchants, and manufacturers as they work through various research tasks. In the process students collect and evaluate information, make connections between concepts and integrate information from various sources (Coiro, 2003; Dodge, 2007; Ikpeze and Boyd, 2007).

Online Think-Alouds

Think-alouds are generally activities during which a reader reads aloud from a text, stopping periodically to describe thoughts about the content being read and strategies being used to understand it. Teachers often model this process for students to help them acquire comprehension and research skills. (See Chapters 4, 6, and 10 for more on think-alouds.) Students may be asked to think aloud in class to allow the teacher a view of the students' thinking processes. Online think-alouds work in the same way, except the teacher models using a projected Internet location. Teachers can model search strategies, use of links to clarify word meanings or to provide elaborations or additional information, or use of different procedures to contact people who can provide clarification (for example, the author of the site) Kymes (2005).

Electronic Communications

E-mail, subscriptions to electronic mailing lists (called *listserves*), posting to electronic bulletin boards (newsgroups), podcasts, blogs (Web logs), social networking sites (Facebook and MySpace, for example) and electronic videoconferencing are all ways of communicating by way of the Internet.

E-mail

SOCIAL STUDIES

ENGLISH/ LANGUAGE ARTS

E-mail has many potential benefits for the classroom. Students can e-mail students in schools in other parts of the world to discuss such things as current study topics, current events, differences in their schools and environments, and the literature they are reading. Students may also e-mail experts in various fields to get answers to questions for class studies. Secondary school students can e-mail college students in methods courses to discuss matters related to the content of their curricula. A number of e-mail connections have been set up between college students and public school students to discuss books that both are reading (Roe and Smith, 1996; Roe and Smith, 1997; Sullivan, 1998) or for other types of conversation or instruction (Stivers, 1996). The next "Meeting the Challenge" describes the project that Roe and Smith developed and implemented at Tennessee Technological University (TTU).

MEETING THE CHALLENGE

E-mail exchanges about literature can promote analysis of the literature selections.

Guy Cali/PhotoLibrary

A section of Betty Roe's undergraduate reading methods students, plus some graduate students in reading and language arts methods courses, were paired with the seventh-graders in Barbara Vaughn's and Melinda Beaty's homerooms. Both the university students and the seventh-graders read the book *Bridge to Terabithia* on a predetermined schedule and exchanged e-mail messages about the reading on a weekly basis. They discussed literary elements of the book and connections that they could see between the book and their lives. Both groups also viewed a video based on the book; then, in an e-mail exchange, the partners compared and contrasted the book and the video. The seventh-graders produced a multimedia presentation based on the book to show the university students. At the end of the project, the partners met on the university campus and discussed the experience.

The seventh-grade students, the university students, the two seventh-grade teachers, and the university professor all felt the project was beneficial and enjoyable. One seventh-grader wrote to Betty Roe, "Dear Dr. Roe, I liked reading the book. I thought it was a good learning experience. I liked the feeling that I'm not the only one who sometimes doesn't understand something that I read. She helped me understand it. It was like she was my sister. I talked to her all the time. Your friend, Angie Adkins." The two seventh-grade teachers wrote, "Reading *Bridge to Terabithia* and e-mailing their thoughts concerning the book improved our seventh-graders' reading, writing, and communicative skills. Our students were very enthusiastic about the project and really enjoyed the trip to TTU to meet their e-mail partners. We have found our students continuing to communicate with their partners even though, technically, the project is concluded for this semester. We also noticed a marked improvement in some students' self-expression. Over time, the letters became longer and more focused on the book's contents. This positive association with older students, responsible for the same work, enhanced our seventh-graders' self-esteem. Some students felt that they were 'almost doing college work.'" University student Stacy Webb said, "I think it gives students a sense of responsibility and promotes the idea of discussing and enjoying what they read. It was also helpful for me in the sense that I was able to practice responding and interacting with the kind of students I will be teaching one day." Noel Roberts, another university student, said, "I read *Bridge to Terabithia* through the eyes of a child." The university students appeared to enjoy the e-mail interactions. The multimedia presentation developed by the seventh-graders was extremely well done, and the university students were impressed.

The project was so successful that it was continued for years, with many professors, public school teachers and students, and university students involved. The students read and discussed a variety of books, some assigned and some self-selected.

**ENGLISH/
LANGUAGE
ARTS**

Some secondary school students e-mail "fanfiction" pieces to friends and acquaintances whom they have met electronically. *Fanfiction* is developed by using media texts, such as cartoons (particularly Japanese *anime* cartoons) and video games, as the starting point for writing creative stories. The Japanese cartoons are written in many genres, including fantasy, romance, and science fiction. Some students post their fanfiction on websites for like-minded adolescents to read. The fanfiction that is produced often integrates visual, linguistic, and audio designs in one text. Chandler-Olcott and Mahar (2003, pp. 562–563) say that "fanfictions make intertextuality visible because they rely on readers' ability to see relationships between the fan-writer's stories and the original media sources." They result in hybrid texts that integrate different discourses and genres, a process that definitely involves creativity (Chandler-Olcott and Mahar, 2003). The fact that many students choose this activity as a recreational one emphasizes the fact that students will work on writing skills with the right motivation. Teachers should consider how they can tap into the abilities that are displayed by writers of fanfiction for use in school-related pursuits.

Electronic Mailing Lists

Electronic mailing lists send out messages to a group of readers interested in the same topic. Readers "subscribe" to a particular list, and, thereafter, every member in the list receives all communications sent to the list until they choose to "unsubscribe" to stop the flow of mail. Although the subscriber may be interested in the topic, the volume of mail generated by some mailing lists is often too difficult to handle. It must be read and deleted on a regular basis, generally daily. Mailing lists of interest may be subscribed to for only the period of time when a topic is being studied.

Teachers may wish to do a scan of the mail from the mailing list and delete any messages containing inappropriate language. Then they may ask students to examine the remaining messages and to delete irrelevant ones and print and annotate any that appear to contain inaccurate material, as well as ones that appear to have truly useful material. The class should check out both types for accuracy. This evaluation is a good critical reading activity.

Electronic Bulletin Boards, Newsgroups, Conferences, and Forums

Electronic bulletin boards, or **newsgroups, conferences,** or **forums,** have messages "posted" to a network location. Interested readers can read these messages electronically if they know the address of the newsgroup. Messages may be posted and read by people from all over the world (Grabe and Grabe, 2007). One way to locate newsgroups is to go to Google groups (http://groups.google.com), which has links to many newsgroups that could be of interest. This website should be used with supervision, because some of the newsgroups listed contain inappropriate material. Like mailing lists, newsgroups should be used with caution.

"An *electronic threaded discussion group* is a group of people who exchange messages about topics of common interest. A thread is a chain of postings on a single topic" (Grisham and Wolsey, 2006, p. 851). The postings to a threaded discussion are not done in real time, but take place when it is convenient to the user. The lack of time pressure allows the students to write thoughtfully considered posts. In one eighth-grade class, the students discussed literature through threaded discussions after the teacher had stressed the need to use academic language in their contributions. The teacher also participated to provide a model by encouraging students to respond and by replying to their messages. Teacher-modeling of *netiquette* (net etiquette) and use of the computers and software was facilitated by using a data projector. The students' postings to the group discussion were more thoughtful than ones in a paper journal that was only read by the teacher. Teacher participation, providing encouragement for using appropriate strategies, helped to increase the complexity of the students' responses.

ENGLISH/
LANGUAGE
ARTS

Blogs

One Web-based communication activity that is popular with secondary school students is the **blog (web log)**. Littrell (2005, p. 7) defines *blog* in the following manner: "Web log; Web-based journal. A blog takes the form of an online diary but allows the user to personalize the appearance, add hyperlinks to other websites, add multimedia components such as audio or video, and invite comments from readers." Blogs usually contain personal comments, reflections, and links to other websites. They can informally expose students to new vocabulary, concepts, and points of view as they read main entries and comments (Davis and McGrail, 2009; Winer, 2002). Because the blogs are maintained over a period of time and most are updated frequently, their authors are involved in ongoing writing—a goal of secondary literacy programs (Richardson, 2004). Blogs give adolescents motivation to write, an audience for their ideas and accomplishments and a place to collaborate with others, and they can give teachers a place to post assignments and other material (Curry and Ford, 2002; Davis and McGrail, 2009; Littrell, 2005; Zawlinski, 2009).

ENGLISH/
LANGUAGE
ARTS

Blogs can be the venue for online debates on real issues that are of concern to the students. These debates may take extended periods of time. The students can adopt roles and voice their opinions on a chosen issue, based on the roles that they are playing. They may create links to other participants' posts or other material on the Web as they present their arguments. Downloads of images may also be utilized. Participants can work collaboratively with people who hold like positions to make recommendations. An appropriate agency, such as the school board, resolves the debates. These role-play debates help students learn collaborative argument processes (Beach and Doerr-Stevens, 2009).

How do blogs differ from wikis?

**ENGLISH/
LANGUAGE
ARTS**

Blogs have been successfully used for informal online discussions of American literature in a high school English class (West, 2008). They have also been used for literature discussions between urban students and preservice teachers. One administrator paired students in her school with teacher education students from a nearby college. The preservice teachers set up blogs and posted introductions to their student partners that made use of text, photos, and audio recordings. Their partners responded with their own introductions and their choices of books to read. The partners then read and blogged about the chosen books over a period of a month (Anderson and Balajthy, 2009). This is a variation of the e-mail partnerships discussed earlier in this chapter.

Free hosting services, such as Blogger and LiveJournal, and ease of use and maintenance make blogging attractive to both secondary school students and adults. The next "Meeting the Challenge" vignette tells of a way that blogging may be useful in an English classroom.

MEETING THE CHALLENGE

**ENGLISH/
LANGUAGE
ARTS**

To examine the possible uses of blogs for writing, Annette Littrell involved ten eighth-grade girls in using both blogs and traditional literature response journals. The students were initially interviewed to determine their existing uses of technology and journaling.

Over the course of eight weeks, they read two books by Joan Bauer, while alternating their methods of literature response in two-week intervals between blogging and traditional journaling. Both the frequency with which the students made journal entries and the average length of the entries were monitored.

At the end of the eight weeks, the students were interviewed again and asked to elaborate on their journaling experiences. During these interviews, 90 percent of the students reported that they preferred using a blog over the traditional journal.

In reviewing the project, Annette found that the students wrote an average of 50 percent more often when using their blogs and wrote 30 percent longer entries than they did when using the traditional journal. Although adolescent girls are generally viewed as more resistant to the adoption of technology than are boys, the use of blogs appeared to motivate them to write. All of the participants categorized using the blog as "easy," while 70 percent also found it "fun." Students who participated in the study reported that they enjoyed customizing the appearance of the blog and that they enjoyed having a place to write that was free from criticism. Thirty percent of the participants mentioned the positive feelings they received from publishing their work for an audience.

Podcasts

**ENGLISH/
LANGUAGE
ARTS**

Podcasts involve preparing audiofiles and making them available on the Internet, like radio programs (Deubel, 2007). These files can be listened to on the computer or downloaded to an MP3 player. Podcasts of students reading their writing may be posted on student blogs, thereby incorporating two senses, hearing and seeing, to help them revise their writing (Davis and McGrail, 2009), when the texts of the podcasts are also located on the blog.

Social Networking Sites

Social networking sites, such as MySpace, Facebook, and YouTube, are extremely popular with adolescents, who use these sites to communicate with friends. They create profiles, upload photos, form groups, send messages and write on each others' "walls." In the case of YouTube, they both create and upload videos and download videos to enjoy. Many of the videos are unedited video footage, but others are remixes of music, digital images, voice and sound effects, print, and animations that require a great deal of technical competency (Knobel and Lankshear, 2008). These products are acts of composition as much as formal essays are. However, they recognize authorship as "neither a solitary nor completely original enterprise" (Alvermann, 2008, p. 17). They create something new from combining material from a variety of other sources. Restrictions on use of social networking sites in schools prevent teachers from using content that students care strongly about to help them see their strengths in communication and to show them ways to improve the effectiveness of their communication. Considine, Horton, and Moorman (2009, p. 473) feel that restricting access deprives adolescents of "the adult supervision and guidance that many of them would benefit from during their online encounters."

Does social networking
have valid educational
applications?

Some schools are trying to incorporate high-interest student Internet use. For example, the eighth-grade curriculum in one middle school focuses on use of the Internet. As a part of their studies, the students analyze social networking, learning purposes of sites like Facebook, as well as how they work and the dangers involved with participation (Mustacchi, 2008).

Chat Rooms

**ENGLISH/
LANGUAGE
ARTS**

Chat rooms are virtual spaces in which users can meet in real time and have conversations by entering their comments on the keyboard and sending them to be posted in the chat room (Lever-Duffy and McDonald, 2008). They are most often used for social purposes, but teachers are beginning to use them as instructional tools as well. Groenke (2008) had her preservice English teachers and a group of middle-school students log onto Web Pen Pals (http://www.webpenpals.org) for the purpose of discussing the young adult novel *Nothing But the Truth*. In this environment, the participants could make comments or ask questions at any time, and they had the option of changing the topic, as they would in face-to-face interactions. Therefore, the flow could be nonlinear and fast paced. Abbreviations and emoticons could be used to provide speed and nuances to the comments. The methods students had a chance to interact with adolescents, practice facilitating a literature discussion, and practice taking a critical literacy stance in the discussion. This interaction revealed some areas in which their methods of facilitating critical literacy discussions needed to be further developed.

In chat rooms the conversations often overlap, and the lack of linear flow may make them particularly hard to follow. The immediacy of the exchanges may make up for this disadvantage, but many teachers find threaded discussions better suited to instructional activities.

Online Book Clubs

ENGLISH/
LANGUAGE
ARTS

Scharber (2009) points out the values of **online book clubs** in which the students read a book before the club begins its activities. The teacher or librarian can post a new question each day on an online forum and the participants can log on when it is convenient for them to answer the question, read what other participants have said, and make any other book-related comments that they want to make. Moodle (http://www.moodle.org) "is free, open-source classroom management software that provides the security . . . to host safe, interactive online book clubs" (Scharber, 2009, p. 434). This software provides forums for asynchronous discussions and real-time chats, as well as links to relevant websites. It also provides profile spaces for the registered users, who can upload images and other material. Participants in a single book club could come from anywhere in the world (Scharber, 2009).

Videoconferencing

Videoconferencing is not used extensively in classrooms at present, but the future may offer more opportunities for students to hold conferences over the Internet with someone who can be seen on a computer's monitor and heard through its speakers. The improvements in videoconferencing software and hardware and the availability of broadband Internet access are making videoconferencing more accessible to schools (Recesso and Orrill, 2008).

What are some ideas for using videoconferencing in your content area?

Videoconferencing allows students to interview authors, scientists, historians, mathematicians, business people, and others who can shed light on a current area of study. The students can compile interview questions; conduct the interview, taking notes; and write up a report of the findings, which they then may integrate into a larger project's report. Maring's Cyber Mentoring projects at Washington State University, in which preservice education students interacted with K–12 students, have involved the successful use of videoconferencing (Maring, 2002).

Electronic Books and Reference Works

ENGLISH/
LANGUAGE
ARTS

Electronic books (e-books), available online or on CD or DVD, have text and illustrations, as traditional books do, but they also may include animation, sound, video, and hyperlinks to enhance the reading experience. Some of them have editing tools that allow readers to insert or delete text; highlight, underline, or mark out text; add notes or voice comments; modify the format; and search for keywords or specific pages. Students may be able to purchase both literature selections and textbooks in electronic form. Some users find reading a book on the computer distracting, because they are so accustomed to multiprocessing while on the computer. Reading books on the computer also restricts the opportunity to read in spare moments (Larson, 2008).

Dictionaries, thesauruses, encyclopedias, atlases, and specialized reference books are available in electronic format, as well. More on electronic reference works is found in Chapter 7.

Computer-Assisted Instruction (CAI)

What types of computer-assisted instructional programs exist, and what is the value of each type?

Computer-assisted instructional programs are generally of four types: (1) drill-and-practice, which offer practice on skills that teachers have already taught; (2) tutorial, which offer actual instruction; (3) simulations, which set up situations that simulate reality and give students the opportunity to use decision-making and problem-solving skills; and (4) educational games, which take a variety of formats to give students experiences related to educational goals. All of these types of programs may be used to enhance the instructional program, but some programs are not pedagogically sound, so they must be evaluated carefully before they are used with students. CAI programs need to be focused on legitimate educational objectives; appropriate for the maturity levels of the students; user friendly; and manageable, timewise, in the classroom.

**ENGLISH/
LANGUAGE
ARTS**

Many drill-and-practice, tutorial, and game programs focus on such skills as vocabulary development, parts of speech, punctuation, and spelling. A frequently used computerized reading management program is the Accelerated Reader (Renaissance). This is a reading practice and assessment program that involves no actual reading instruction. It is designed to motivate students to read more books. The books in the program are ranked by reading difficulty level. Students read books and take computer-generated, multiple-choice tests to earn points and incentives. The tests generally cover literal-level comprehension. For struggling readers and English-language learners, the program has recorded voice quizzes and Spanish quizzes. Although the program producers emphasize that it is not a complete reading program and should not be used to take the place of instruction (Renaissance Learning, 2006), some educators have used it for this purpose. Renaissance Learning points out that the program emphasizes the importance of adequate *teacher-guided* independent reading and the use of information from the tests to guide instruction.

Schmidt (2008) worries that the program, as often implemented, encourages students to consume books quickly and move on to others after taking a test, without taking time to discuss or savor the reading experience, and that students limit their book choices to books included in the program, because they are the ones available to earn points for class. Likewise, Thompson, Madhuri, and Taylor (2008) studied a small group of high school students who expressed dislike of being "forced" to read, concern about the limited selection of multicultural books and books with a high readability level at their school, and dislike of having to take the tests and having it affect their grades. Renaissance Learning emphasizes that use of the program for grading purposes is not appropriate, so misuse of the program had some effect on the student responses.

Simulation programs for any content area are good to encourage critical reading and thinking and problem solving, areas in which students have not shown proficiency on the National Assessment of Educational Progress. Although it is beyond the scope of this text to identify software for each application, a few examples are described here.

SOCIAL STUDIES

Making History: The Calm and the Storm is appropriate for history classes. *The Calm and the Storm* is the first program in a series called Making History. In this simulation video-game program, the players "act as world leaders, make momentous decisions, and discover the consequences" (Brumfield, 2005, p. 28). The series is designed to help students learn history by taking on leadership roles in different nations during World War II. The students compete against other "national leaders" and the program's scoring considers the players' performance against actual historical events. They make major decisions related to the economy, the military, and foreign and domestic issues. They may even perform better than the real leaders did historically. The game involves analysis of situations, synthesis of information, recognition of cause and effect, detection of bias, and negotiation—all necessary language skills (Brumfield, 2005).

SOCIAL STUDIES

SimCity, a simulation game, involves students in zoning land, setting tax rates, and building infrastructure for a city. They learn social studies vocabulary, such as *zone, commercial,* and *industrial,* as they play. Other simulations that work well for social studies are *Rise of Nations* and *Civilization* (Gee and Levine, 2009). *Quest Atlantis* at the University of Indiana (http://atlantis.crlt.indiana.edu/) "offers a 3D virtual multiuser environment in which students use scientific information and tools to solve problems collaboratively" (Gee and Levine, 2009, p. 51). In such a situation, students can learn science and communication skills. Fourth through eighth graders in North Carolina schools have had growth in reading skills when using *Quest Atlantis,* especially the disadvantaged and poor-performing students. Some middle-schoolers made amazing gains in a year (Prabhu, 2008). Transfer of learning to achievement on standardized tests has been found by researchers (Barab, *et al.,* 2007).

SCIENCE AND HEALTH   **ENGLISH/ LANGUAGE ARTS**

What are the main advantages to use of simulation programs?

Simulations for other content areas include *Operation Frog* for science, which simulates a dissection, and the *Math Shop* Series for math, which has the students solve problems in everyday situations related to customer services provided for stores. Any one of a wide variety of interactive fiction story programs can be used as recreational reading in an English class.

MATHEMATICS

Multimedia Applications

What is meant by multimedia?

Multimedia refers to the mixing of different media. A multimedia presentation may include text, photographs, line drawings, video clips, sounds, and animated figures. The sounds and images may be drawn from videotapes, CDs, DVDs, audiotapes, and the Internet. Images may be scanned in from printed documents. Multimedia computer systems allow teachers to combine text, graphics, animation, music, voice, and full-motion video that are controlled by a computer. These systems have interactive capabilities. Multimedia encyclopedias are common in schools today, and they allow students to read text, see video clips, hear audio clips, or see still pictures related to the subject being accessed.

Students can develop their own multimedia presentations with special software, as the students in the e-mail project in the previous "Meeting the Challenge" did. Such a presentation takes much organization, composition, and critical reading and thinking. It is truly a good literacy activity.

**TeachSource
Video Case**
Multimedia Literacy:
Integrating Technology
into the Middle School
Curriculum

Considine, Horton, and Moorman (2009) describe a multimedia lesson that explores the story of the *R.M.S. Titanic* through still images, sounds, music, video, and print, and develops skills set forth in state and national standards for English Language Arts and Social Studies. The lesson includes a song; an editorial cartoon from the *San Francisco Examiner*; an eyewitness newspaper story from a survivor, a documentary clip from the Discovery Channel, a short film clip from the motion picture *Titanic*; a pop-up book filled with artifacts and primary documents, including photographs, letters, ads, and more; an Internet search for resources; and an obituary of a survivor from the *New York Times*. These materials make possible discussion of point of view, comparisons and contrasts of accounts, and techniques for successful Internet searches, as well as understanding of the facts about the actual event.

Hutchison (2009) described a project in which the students read Karen Hesse's *Into the Dust* and with partners used *Moviemaker* to produce documentaries that related to living during the Great Depression in various locations or to the Dust Bowl. They used Internet sources to locate information and develop their movies with a script and related images.

SCIENCE AND
HEALTH

The JASON Project, a nonprofit subsidiary of National Geographic Society connects students with scientists through a standards-based multimedia curriculum designed to motivate students to learn science. *Operation: Monster Storms* is a weather curriculum unit that runs for nine weeks. Scientists from NASA, NOAA, and National Geographic work with the students and teachers to help them learn about weather events. In addition to print materials, there are online "video, podcasts, digital labs, chats, journals, bulletin boards, and teacher tools for lesson planning, alignment, assessments, reporting and classroom management" (Recesso and Orrill, 2008, p. 225). Students read research articles and participate in hands-on laboratory activities and a field assignment. Students are challenged to create and upload a scientifically based video weather report for global peer review, a highly motivational activity that involves advanced literacy skills (Recesso and Orrill, 2008).

MUSIC   ENGLISH/
LANGUAGE
ARTS

Copeland and Goering (2003) taught the Faustian theme of selling one's soul to the devil for personal gain through use of music, film, and literature. This theme has been the nucleus of books such as Goethe's *Faust*, Nolan's *Born Blue*, and Gantos's *Hole in My Life*. It has also been the theme in music such as Liszt's *Faust*

Symphony, Gounod's opera *Faust*, and the Charlie Daniels Band's "The Devil Went Down to Georgia." Movies such as *O Brother, Where Art Thou?* contain the theme, as do *Damn Yankees, The Devil and Daniel Webster*, and *Bedazzled*. Several blues musicians, including Robert Johnson, were said to have sold their souls to the devil for outstanding musical talent.

In the unit that Copeland and Goering (2003) taught, the students brainstormed, used a process writing approach, wrote based on a model, did research and produced visual aids about a blues artist's life, and viewed and analyzed films. Their culminating activity was a project in which they used "the devil's pact legend to bring a contemporary ethical, social, or political issue into sharp (and often entertaining) focus" (p. 111). They could choose to create a hypertext and graphics presentation, write blues song lyrics, videotape a movie, or write a short story. This project helped the students connect popular culture with classical and literary content.

Teachers can help students to locate and interpret common textual elements in various media, as well as to challenge the authority of the texts through critical analysis. Textual information, verbal and audio input, and visual images are all used, along with background experiences, to construct meaning through viewing audiovisual media, just as printed words, sentences, and longer selections are examined in light of background experiences to construct meaning from print. Students can use media logs to record the time they spend with various media and to answer guiding questions about the content of each medium (Watts Pailliotet et al., 2000). See Figure 2.1 for guiding questions to ask about media in order to critically analyze their appropriateness.

FIGURE 2.1

Guiding Questions for Critical Media Literacy

What type of medium is this? Is it effective for communicating this material? Does it take advantage of the capabilities of the technology?

Is the material up-to-date? Does it contain misperceptions based on datedness?

Does it contain stereotypes of people or groups? What people are represented?

What images, sound, and motions are used? Are they effective?

Who developed this medium? Are they qualified to communicate accurately about the subject? Do they have obvious biases about the topic or project a particular values orientation?

Is there documentation of the information presented? How is the documentation handled?

Who is the target audience? How can you tell? Is it appropriate for this audience? Will the audience understand the vocabulary and images used?

Does this presentation make personal connections and evoke particular feelings in the user?

Is the material accessible to people with physical or mental challenges?

Building on Past Experiences with Technology

Bruce (2001) pointed out that it is important to understand the antecedents of current technologies and to be able to evaluate current technologies in light of knowledge gained from past technologies. Sometimes older technologies are more appropriate and efficient to use for a particular purpose than are newer technologies. Teachers should consider the needs of the lessons and carefully choose technology to assist each lesson.

Overhead Projectors

The use of transparencies displayed on overhead projectors has for many years benefited those who needed to display complex diagrams and illustrations. Many artistically challenged teachers have bought sets of well-prepared transparencies to help them illustrate their classroom explanations of various topics. Commercial transparencies have the advantage of providing high-quality images, but they may not include all of the concepts that the teacher would like to present (Lever-Duffy and McDonald, 2008). Transparencies can be made out of material that teachers have word processed or illustrated themselves at a more leisurely pace than is possible when trying to produce materials in class. Many computer programs, such as *Microsoft PowerPoint*, allow teachers to design transparencies with a variety of fonts, colors, and appropriate graphics. Teachers can also obtain many inexpensive or free graphics from the Internet and from CD-ROMs of clip art.

ENGLISH/ LANGUAGE ARTS

Overhead transparencies may be used to advance literacy learning in a number of ways. When describing the stages in developing a written product, for example, the teacher can use a series of transparencies with overlays that show each succeeding step as he or she describes it. Transparencies can allow the teacher to record ideas for writing that result from a brainstorming session held prior to writing. Students can then organize the recorded ideas, and volunteers can put their organizational arrangements on transparencies for sharing. Transparencies can allow teachers to display students' work for class analysis of accuracy, clarity, and organization of ideas. Student permission for use of the work should be obtained in advance, or the teacher could use work from classes other than the one in question, with identifying labels deleted, in order to highlight problems that are common to the current class.

Transparencies can be used before reading about any topic to record semantic maps or webs of prior knowledge about the topic or entries for a K-W-L chart. After reading, they can be used to elaborate the chart and fill in the last stage of the K-W-L chart. (See Chapter 4 for an example of a semantic map or web and Chapter 6 for a discussion of K-W-L charts.)

Televisions

Televisions also have many uses. Public broadcasting programs may fit in with the curricula of teachers in many different disciplines. Video recording programs to show students later for educational purposes is often a possibility, when pertinent programs are not broadcast during class hours. However, teachers must be careful to adhere to copyright laws. Visual literacy skills must be used to analyze material in television broadcasts.

Many schools currently have cable television connections, and some cable operators offer schools special programming and teachers' guides. Sometimes television programs contain historic or scientific information that can fit into unit study. Students who watch television to obtain this information will need to use their note-taking skills to record what they learn to add to the information gathered from other sources. Newscasts or news specials may highlight a class topic—an ongoing military action somewhere in the world, a current election campaign, or a new archaeological discovery, for example. Critical analysis of the information presented could take the form of reports that compare the information obtained from this source with information gathered from primary sources, such as military personnel, participants in the campaign, or archaeologists, and current print media, such as newspapers or newsmagazines.

SOCIAL STUDIES

SCIENCE AND HEALTH

Sometimes movies that are based on books that are being studied in the class are available. In this case, students may also take notes in order to compare and contrast the story in the book and the story as presented in the movie. Movies based on literature selections that the students have not read may be viewed and critiqued, and students may be encouraged to read these selections for extra credit or for personal enjoyment and to report back to the class on the experience.

ENGLISH/ LANGUAGE ARTS

Broadcast video can provide "high-impact, high-quality video production that can dramatically demonstrate content" (Lever-Duffy and McDonald, 2008, p. 337) to students. Teachers would be wise to help them view critically. Such instruction can help them with recreational viewing as well as informational viewing. Many of the negative messages that teachers hope students will learn to recognize and evaluate are seen during recreational viewing.

Some educators use media literacy as a bridge to print literacy. Like print presentations, television and video presentations are developed with particular audiences in mind, and they can be divided into a number of recognizable genres. Secondary school students readily identify the audiences for which television programs and movies have been developed, and they recognize such genres as soap operas, mysteries, sitcoms, and documentaries. This knowledge can be a stepping stone in teaching about how to determine the audiences for whom the authors are writing, authors' purposes, techniques used to accomplish purposes or focus on particular audiences, and common characteristics of a particular genre. Electronic and print media have many commonalities and connections that should be explored in the classroom (Williams, 2003).

In one seventh-grade curriculum, television shows and commercials are analyzed for sexism, violence, and other attributes. Students create thirty-second television commercials for school-related activities using Apple's *iMovie*. They also create a television newscast, with field reporters and anchors who are chosen through screen tests. The products are aired on the school district's cable channel (Mustacchi, 2008).

Audio Recordings

Audio recordings can be used to provide prerecorded information on a topic, but they are probably most useful when they are used to record group discussions or class lectures for later review and note taking, interviews with primary sources for use in

SCIENCE AND
HEALTH

ENGLISH/
LANGUAGE
ARTS

writing reports, or findings from experiments being done in science class. Students can use them to record themselves practicing oral reports that they must give in class, so that they can play the recordings back and critique their performances. Much material that lends itself to audio recording now is being video recorded instead.

Having students listen to a challenging audio-recorded book before reading the book as a part of a class activity can lead to better comprehension of the material when it is covered in class. Struggling readers may benefit from listening to a recording of an unabridged book while following along in the book to help them increase their sight vocabularies and comprehend the material better as they hear it read with proper phrasing and inflections. Recordings of content area text materials, done by the teacher or by a gifted reader, could be used in the same way. If a student reader makes recordings for this purpose, the teacher must check the recordings before using them for instruction.

Audio recordings of oral presentations may make good material to place in portfolios for assessment purposes. Written explanations about how the presentation was developed and what the student learned from the experience can add to the usefulness of such recordings.

Video Recordings

ENGLISH/
LANGUAGE
ARTS

SCIENCE AND
HEALTH

Videos on many topics can be used to enhance learning in those areas. They can be used to illustrate text materials for less proficient readers or for students with limited experiential backgrounds; for example, they may be used to help bring a literary selection to life for students or to make a process (such as pasteurization) that is discussed in their text more comprehensible. Showing videos can provide students with much support for comprehending texts, while at the same time being motivational and enjoyable (Hibbing and Rankin-Erickson, 2003). Videos on a multitude of topics are available for purchase, for rental from video stores, or from libraries. Students can view these videos, take notes, and use the information for classroom discussion, reports, and projects. Videos based on literature selections are often available for use in English classrooms. Students can compare and contrast the video presentations with the books. When the students described in the "Meeting the Challenge" on page 44 did this comparison, they decided that the book was much more effective than the video. Several studies have indicated that viewing a related video before reading a book has a positive effect on comprehension of the text (Lapp, Flood, and Fisher, 1999).

Videos are available on most topics of study. Content area teachers can use movies to set the stage for reading in textbooks. For example, they could view *1776* when studying the American Revolution. Documentaries are particularly useful in science, social studies, and health classes.

In these days of relatively inexpensive media production resources, such as camcorders and editing equipment, teachers have involved students in making videos. The process of producing videos not only helps students learn to communicate in another medium, but also helps them to see how the producers of these videos have put together sound, action, and images to communicate ideas to them.

SCIENCE AND
HEALTH

SOCIAL
STUDIES

**SOCIAL
STUDIES**

Middle-school students in Mabry, Alabama, develop two- to three-minute videos on topics such as immigration and homelessness (http://mabryonline.org/archives/mtv/). These videos are judged largely by people in communications and media businesses. Awards are given in categories such as "best cinematography, best sound, best documentary, best dramatic comedy, and best teaching and learning film" (Prensky, 2008). These students are learning while engaging in highly motivational tasks.

In another class, the teacher had students produce digital videos to help them explore topics multimodally. Students worked in pairs to choose topics, research them, and create videos using *Video Studio Editor 8*. The research included reading books on their topics, conducting Web searches for articles and images (sometimes printing out the articles to read more carefully later), organizing their material, writing narratives to accompany their visual material, and recording and importing their narratives to go with the visual images. This process thoroughly integrated inquiry learning with technology learning.

Authoring with Video (AWV) is recommended by Strassman and O'Connell (2007/2008) for motivating student writing and revision and producing material to share with their classmates or post to a website or blog. With AWV, students take short video clips without audio and write narration scripts to accompany the videos. They can use *MAGpie*, which is free software, to add the narration script as captions for the video.

Students can also make their own videos of class presentations or field trip activities. They can prepare special video presentations for which they write scripts and practice polished presentations, such as simulated newscasts.

Technology for Students with Special Needs or Disabilities

In inclusive classrooms, students with disabilities face challenges in completing many of the writing requirements. Assistive technology for students with disabilities includes special computer input devices (including touch screens, joysticks, specially designed keyboards with overlays, and voice recognition software) and image magnifiers (Forcier and Descy, 2008).

Barbetta and Spears-Bunion (2007) have found use of technology can help these students in a number of ways. For example, digitizing text can make the adjustment of font size, style, and color and changing of background color possible. The Zoom functions on computers allow text that is displayed on screen to be magnified up to forty times its original size, another help for students with visual difficulties. Cursor size can also be increased (Forcier and Descy, 2008). Highlighting digital text (such as key words or main ideas) or adding illustrations can also be done to simplify the reading task. Text-to-Speech software can convert digital text to auditory text, spoken with a selected voice gender, pitch, and speed. Some programs track the spoken words with highlighted text, reinforcing visual and auditory connections. This is also particularly helpful for students with visual disabilities or learning disabilities (Hasselbring and Bausch, 2005/2006). Some books are available in digital format.

Project Gutenberg (http://www.gutenberg.org/) has thousands of works that are in the public domain and can be downloaded for noncommercial use, and the Library of Congress (http://lcweb.loc.gov/) has nonfiction materials available (Barbetta and Spears-Bunion, 2007).

Students with physical disabilities can be helped with speech-recognition technology, in which students speak into a microphone and the words appear on the computer screen. Some programs read aloud text as students enter it into a word-processing program, allowing them to edit their work more easily. The programs can also read back a specified portion of the text at a time (Barbetta and Spears-Bunion, 2007).

Students with physical disabilities and learning disabilities particularly can benefit from word-prediction technology. The student types the beginning of a word, and the software predicts the word, allowing the students to choose from a list of predicted words, thereby speeding up the writing process and lessening fatigue (Hasselbring and Bausch, 2005/2006).

Coencas (2007), a secondary school language arts teacher, uses scenes from movies to work on the visual and auditory skills of special education students who struggle with the printed word. Through the movies, he helps these students build confidence in their ability to discuss the components of a narrative critically. Movies from different genres can be used to examine literary elements and to evaluate acting, editing, cinematography, special effects, and other elements of the medium. The activity can give them the understanding and vocabulary to speak knowledgeably about a movie with others, inside and outside of class.

ENGLISH/ LANGUAGE ARTS   **SOCIAL STUDIES**

Coencas (2007) uses the film *Twelve Angry Men* as a platform to discuss such things as point of view, theme, plot, characterization, and symbolism, depending on the needs of particular groups of students. The movie also exposes students to social studies vocabulary such as *prosecutors* and *juries* and provides them with visual context for these terms. Showing segments of the movie followed by pertinent questions can lead the students to analyze the different elements involved and provoke their interest and contributions. Students are given choices of questions to answer for homework and are allowed to volunteer to answer at the next class meeting. Coencas combines the reading of Shakespeare's *Romeo and Juliet* with an opening clip from a movie version of the play and *West Side Story,* the musical based on the play. The students compare the two adaptations of the play they are reading. They also do Internet research on movie versions of the play. They write two papers, one based on critical reviews of the play by others, and one a personal review of one version that they have viewed. He breaks down the process into small steps that these special needs students can handle. This process is a confidence builder for these students.

Evaluating Literacy Applications of Technology

Why is it important to evaluate websites carefully?

Teachers have the job of evaluating literacy applications of technology. They should decide if each application addresses content that is needed, motivates the students to learn the content, clarifies the material for the students, and lends itself to use in the classroom. They also need to ask if the application is easy to implement, instructionally sound, cost-effective, and more effective than other ways to accomplish the task (Roe, Smith, and Burns, 2009). Evaluation of computer software involves asking other questions as well. Roe, Smith, and Burns (2009, p. 481) present a set of questions to ask when evaluating computer software. Some are specific to computer-assisted instructional software, but most are applicable to any software that is to be used in the school. These questions are found in Figure 2.2. Websites also must be evaluated. Questions to ask to evaluate websites are found in Figure 2.3.

FIGURE 2.2

Evaluating Computer Software

Source: Betty D. Roe, Sandy H. Smith, and Paul C. Burns, *Teaching Reading in Today's Elementary Schools* (Boston: Houghton Mifflin, 2009). Used with permission.

When evaluating computer software, ask the following questions:

1. Is the program compatible with the available hardware and operating system?

2. Does the program meet a curricular need better than another approach would?

3. Is the program well documented?
    a. Are the objectives of the program clearly presented?
    b. Are steps for initiating and running the program clearly stated?
    c. Are hardware requirements for the program clearly specified, and is this hardware available?
    d. Are time requirements for program use described, and are they reasonable for classroom use? (If a program can be saved at any time and re-entered at the same place, some of the problems with time are alleviated.)

4. Is the program user-friendly?

5. Is there a management system that keeps up with a student's performance on the program, if that would be appropriate?

6. Are the screens well designed and readable?

7. Is the program essentially crash-proof?

8. Is feedback about performance offered to the students? Is the feedback appropriate for them?

9. Do the students have control over the
    a. speed of the program presentation?
    b. level of difficulty of the program?
    c. degree of prompting offered by the program (including seeing instructions for use)?
    d. sequence of presentation of material?

10. Is the program highly interactive, requiring more of the student than just page-turning?

11. Is sound used appropriately, if at all? Can the sound be turned off without destroying the effectiveness of the program?

12. Is color used effectively, if at all?

13. Is the program adaptable for a variety of levels of students? Are your students within this range?

14. Is the material free of stereotypes and bias?

15. Is there a way that the teacher can modify the program for a particular class, set of data, or student? Is this procedure protected against student tampering?

16. Is information presented in the program accurate and presented clearly and in grammatically correct form?

FIGURE 2.3

Website Evaluation Questions

Source: Betty D. Roe, "Using Technology for Content Area Literacy." *In Linking Literacy and Technology: A Guide for K–8 Classrooms.* Shelley B. Wepner, William J. Valmont, and Richard Thurlow, Eds. Newark, Del.: International Reading Association, 2000, p. 155. Reprinted with permission of the International Reading Association. All rights reserved.

When you are evaluating websites, you must consider the reliability of the sources of the material, accuracy of the content, clarity of the material presented, and purposes of the sites. Ask yourself the following questions when judging a website:

1. Can you determine who has developed the site? (If not, you may not want to place undue confidence in its contents.) If so, is the developer a reliable source for the information you are seeking? (A noted authority on the topic or an agency of the government would be considered reliable. Someone you have not heard of before may need to be investigated.)

2. Is there enough information given on the site developer that qualifications can be checked? (If not, be cautious.)

3. Are sources provided for information displayed on the site, so the user can cross-check information? (If they are, this is a definite plus.)

4. Does any of the information conflict with reliable sources that you have consulted? (If some of the information is in question, all of it is suspect.)

5. Is the layout of the site busy and confusing, making information difficult to evaluate? (Disorganization, particularly, is a bad sign.)

6. Is site navigation easy? (Sloppy navigational methods sometimes indicate a lack of attention to detail.)

7. Is the presented material grammatically correct, and is it free from errors in spelling and mechanics? (If it is not, the clarity is badly affected.)

8. Is the site free of advertising? (If not, look for possible bias of information presented, based on the advertising present.)

9. If currency of information is important, can you tell when the page was developed and last updated? (If not, be careful in accepting the information. If currency is not a factor—for example, for a Civil War site on which the material is not likely to become dated—this will not be a major concern.)

Advantages of Technology in the Classroom

McGrath (1998) found that technology use resulted in increased student motivation, increased cooperation and collaboration among students, more in-depth conversations between teachers and students and among students, more equity between students and teachers, more student persistence in solving problems, improved communication skills, and more opportunities for interdisciplinary activities. She also indicated that use of computers allowed for more effective work with diverse students. Many other educators have echoed these sentiments, and activities cited in this chapter support these ideas as well.

Students also are becoming familiar with technologies that are increasingly important to them in the world of work and even in home activities. Students who use technology in the classroom enter life activities better prepared to face the challenges they present.

Perspective on Technology Use for Literacy Learning Tomorrow

The incredible pace of emergence of new technology provides challenges for teachers, who must understand the new technologies and incorporate the ones that have educational applications into the curriculum in a meaningful fashion, as a part of the overall curriculum, not as add-ons. Schools usually cannot keep up with the cutting-edge applications, but they will continually be advancing to higher levels of applications. It is impossible to know what new technologies will evolve into educational tools. Virtual reality applications are already making some advances, and there are more and more options for the development of multimedia projects. Web-based courses, already in use in many locations, are likely to spread in the future.

Although many students have advanced media skills, others need instruction in media use. Teachers may enlist the assistance of technology-adept students to teach their peers complex media access and creation techniques. Time spent familiarizing students with new media will pay dividends in the works that they are capable of producing as a result of content area learning (Sefton-Green, 2001). There is a high level of uncertainty in many Web-based activities, encouraging collaborative learning and problem solving, with the teacher and student both working to solve problems. Adolescents may be comfortable with computer-mediated learning because they can make mistakes privately in an environment that allows them time to experiment and reflect on their work (Kapitzke et al., 2000–2001).

Today there are many resources for teachers to help them learn about and have successful experiences with today's literacy learner. The technology section of most large bookstores and the magazine racks in a variety of stores provide many publications that will explain emerging technologies at various levels of sophistication. Professional organizations, such as the International Reading Association (IRA) (http://www.reading.org) and the National Council of Teachers of English (NCTE) (http://www.ncte.org), which offer increasing numbers of sessions on technology at their conferences and conventions each year, are good resources. The locations of these conferences and conventions vary from year to year, so one may be within easy reach in the near future. The ISTE Conference is managed by the International Society for Technology in Education (ISTE), and ED-MEDIA: World Conference on Educational Media and Hypermedia is an Association for the Advancement of Computing Education (AACE) conference.

Many professional journals include articles about integrating technology into literacy instruction and instruction in content areas. For example, *The Reading Teacher* (focus on elementary and middle school) and the *Journal of Adolescent & Adult Literacy* (focus on middle school through adult) are IRA journals; *Language Arts* (focus on elementary and middle school) and *English Journal* (focus on middle school through senior high) are NCTE journals. ISTE has many helpful publications, including *Learning & Leading with Technology*, *Journal of Research on Technology in Education*, and *Journal of Computing in Teacher Education*. AACE has several journals also, including *Journal of Interactive Learning Research* and *Journal of Educational Multimedia and Hypermedia*.

Summary

Teachers in today's schools have a wide variety of technological applications available for use in their content area instruction. These applications include digital technologies, such as computer-based activities. Many multimedia applications are possible, often through computer technology. In particular, ways to use the resources of the Internet in the classroom abound. Classroom applications also include older technologies, such as overhead projectors, televisions, and audio recorders.

Teachers must be able to evaluate the technological applications available to them because they are of varying quality. Some are appropriate for particular curricular uses, and some have little instructional value. Careful evaluation of the applications facilitates their wise integration into the curriculum.

There are many advantages to using technology for content area literacy, both in classroom instruction and in preparing students for the world of work. These advantages are evident in working with a wide variety of students, including struggling readers and English language learners.

The use of technology in schools is increasing rapidly, with new applications becoming more widely available and more affordable. Teachers must strive to keep up-to-date in order to optimize their instruction.

Discussion Questions

1. How can word-processing, desktop-publishing, writing development, and conference and collaboration software be used in writing instruction?
2. What are some applications of databases and spreadsheets in literacy learning?
3. What literacy skills are involved in using the Internet for research?
4. What are some cautions about using the Internet for gathering information?
5. What values can classroom webpages, blogs, wikis, and podcasts have in content area learning?
6. What are the benefits of e-mail for literacy learning?
7. What types of computer-assisted instructional programs involve the highest levels of literacy activities? Why do you think so?
8. How can videos be used to enhance literacy learning?
9. For what purposes would multimedia presentations be useful in a literacy classroom?
10. What are some uses of technology that are effective for English language learners?
11. What are some uses of technology that are effective for struggling readers?
12. What are valid applications for overhead projectors, televisions, and audiotapes in literacy learning?

Enrichment Activities

1. Develop a set of transparencies or a multimedia presentation to teach vocabulary from a content area chapter.

*2. Video or audio record presentations made by your students and play them back to allow students to critically analyze their own presentations.

*3. Develop and teach a procedure for conducting an Internet search for information on a research topic.

*4. Set up an e-mail exchange between your students and the students in another school about a topic of study.

5. Develop a multimedia presentation to teach students a reading strategy.

6. Maintain a blog about the literacy activities that you could use in a content area of your choice.

7. Evaluate a website that has the potential to be used as reading material for a particular content area lesson.

---

*These activities are designed for in-service teachers, student teachers, and practicum students.

Resources including the TeachSource Video Cases can be found on the website for this book. Cengage Learning's CourseMate brings course concepts to life with interactive learning, study, and exam preparation tools that support the printed textbook. Go to www.cengage.com/login to register your access code.

PART

2

Instruction and Assessment of All Learners

CHAPTER 3
Content Literacy Assessment

CHAPTER 3

Content Literacy Assessment

Overview

A major purpose of this chapter is to assist the content area teacher in determining if students possess the literacy and study skills necessary to deal successfully with course materials. To perform this evaluation, the content teacher must be aware of the literacy and study skills appropriate to the particular subject. Assessment involves collecting data from multiple sources in order both to guide instructional decisions and to obtain a valid evaluation of students' capabilities for accountability and to assign grades or compare schools and districts (Chappuis and Chappuis, 2007/2008; Edwards, Turner, and Mokhtari, 2008; Tomlinson, 2007/2008). Teachers must recognize that students' performances on particular tasks are influenced by the tasks themselves, the background the students bring to the tasks, the students' ability related to task requirements, the students' interest in the task, and the contexts in which the tasks take place.

When assessment is data collection designed to help teachers determine problem areas and make instructional decisions, it is **formative assessment** (*Encarta Dictionary*, 2009). Formative assessment is an ongoing process and involves more than testing. It includes assessment aimed at making informed adjustments to instruction, and it has been shown to improve student learning. Popham (2009, p. 85) describes it as "a *test-supported process* instead of a test." Formative assessment is particularly important in triggering needed interventions for struggling students and in allowing students to track their own progress (Stiggins and Dufour, 2009). When an assessment is used to show levels of performance for purposes of grading, accountability, and comparisons of schools and is administered at the end of a teaching cycle, the assessment is a **summative assessment**. Useful assessment of either type is directly linked to instruction (Chappuis and Chappuis, 2007/2008; Invernizzi, Landrum, Howell, and Warley, 2005; Tomlinson, 2007/2008).

Some assessments focus more on processes (strategies used to understand text or revise written work) than on products (specific knowledge the student has acquired). Students are asked to produce or do something meaningful. The activity generally involves higher-level thinking and solving of real-life problems. Because of the difficulties of developing norm-referenced measures that will reveal such processes, many of these assessment procedures are informal and classroom based and appear much like regular classroom instruction.

Many types of assessment are needed to obtain a complete picture of students' abilities. Performance assessments help teachers determine how well their students can apply information, but multiple-choice tests may be a more efficient way to determine how well the students have learned the basic facts and concepts. For this reason, teachers need to be familiar with a variety of assessment tools and the implications of assessment data for instructional planning (Guskey, 2003).

Often content area instructional material is not written at its designated grade level. Teachers need to know whether their students can read at the level on which the textbook is written. To discover this, they need to know what the reading level of the book actually is. Additionally, teachers need to understand the factors that influence readability and how to use readability formulas and other measures for determining the difficulty of materials.

After an assessment, teachers need to give students feedback on their performance. Self-assessment by students is also important. This activity makes students more aware of their strengths and weaknesses (Edwards, Turner, and Mokhtari, 2008).

In this chapter we discuss norm-referenced tests; criterion-referenced tests; informal, classroom-based tests; portfolio assessment; assessment of the readability of printed materials; and computer applications to assessment.

Purpose-Setting Questions

As you read this chapter, try to answer these questions:

1. What are the functions of norm-referenced tests?
2. What are criterion-referenced tests?
3. What are some classroom-based assessments of reading and writing achievement, and how can the results of each be used to help teachers plan instructional programs?
4. What is meant by portfolio assessment?
5. How are computers being applied in the area of assessment?
6. How is an understanding of the readability levels of textbook materials important to a teacher?
7. What assessment approaches are particularly appropriate for struggling readers and English language learners?

Norm-Referenced Tests

What types of information can norm-referenced tests give teachers?

Content teachers may administer and interpret certain types of **norm-referenced tests**, especially survey achievement tests, to check student performance in a wide range of literacy areas: reading, writing, language, reference skills, and others. Test results indicate the relative achievement of the groups tested in these areas. Teachers can compare a student's performance on a subtest in one subject with his or her performance on other subtests in a test battery to discover a pattern of strengths and weaknesses. Teachers also can learn how a student's performance on a test compares with his or her earlier or later performance on the same test, but scores from two different kinds of norm-referenced tests on the same topic (e.g., reading or writing) are not likely to be comparable. Standardized testing on a statewide basis has become a major focus for standards-based instruction.

Criteria for Choosing Norm-Referenced Tests

Why are the validity and reliability of norm-referenced tests important?

A norm-referenced test should meet certain criteria. Its norms should be based on a population similar to the population being tested, and it should have high levels of **validity** and **reliability**. A valid norm-referenced reading test represents a balanced and adequate sampling of the instructional outcomes (e.g., knowledge and skills) that it is intended to cover. In addition to measuring the skills it claims to measure (validity) and having subtests that are long enough to yield reasonably accurate scores, a test should not result in a chance score with students obtaining high scores by luck or guessing (reliability). The reliability of a test refers to the degree to which the test gives consistent results.

A test is inappropriate if the sample population used to establish norms is significantly different from the class or group to be tested. A description of the norming population is usually contained in the test manual.

Norm-Referenced Tests of Reading Achievement

Norm-referenced reading tests yield objective data about reading performance. They are designed so that each response to a test item is subject to only one interpretation. The types of norm-referenced reading tests that content teachers are most likely to hear about are **survey tests** and **diagnostic tests**.

What is the difference in the information obtained from a survey test and that obtained from a diagnostic test?

Reading survey tests measure general achievement in reading. The results can show how well students are performing in relation to others who have taken the test. Looking at scores of all students in a class gives an indication of the range of reading achievement in the class.

A single score on a survey test represents the student's overall reading achievement and does not reveal how the student will perform on specific reading tasks. However, some reading survey tests designed for secondary school students have separate sections that yield scores on vocabulary, comprehension, and reading rate. A wise teacher is not only concerned with a student's total achievement score, but also wants to determine if the student is equally strong in all areas tested.

Diagnostic reading tests are used most frequently by special teachers of reading, however, content teachers need some basic information about this type of test in order to discuss test results with special reading teachers. Diagnostic reading tests help to locate specific strengths and weaknesses of readers. Such tests often include subtests for comprehension, vocabulary, word identification skills, and rate of reading. Reading specialists usually administer diagnostic reading tests because they have the required experience and training.

Concerns about Traditional Standardized Reading Tests

Traditional standardized tests treat reading as if it were simply skill mastery of a variety of skills (a product) rather than a constructive, strategic process in which readers make use of their prior knowledge and techniques for unlocking meaning in the text in order to understand its message (a process). There are concerns among educators that high-stakes standardized testing can have a negative effect on both teachers and students. High-stakes testing is testing that can result in severe penalties for failure, such as denial of graduation. As a result, there is sometimes data manipulation and cheating, as well as reduction of instruction to isolated bits of information, because of the added pressure to pass the test (Nichols and Berliner, 2008). Warren and Grodsky (2009) studied current high school exit exams and concluded that they "fail to improve either academic achievement or early labor market outcomes" (p. 648). However, the political pressure to have "objective" measures of literacy achievement makes it unlikely that such testing will disappear anytime soon. To add to concerns, some research has suggested that the states' high stakes tests are not measuring the same reading abilities that the National Assessment of Educational Progress (NAEP) measures, although the state standards indicate that they are attempting to do so. The NAEP, which uses more open-ended items, appears to require more thoughtful responses than the state tests, which lean heavily on literal recall questions. Teachers should "encourage their students to engage thoughtfully with text and attend to the ways that details support thoughtful conclusions" in order to prepare them to do well on both many of the state tests and the national assessment (Applegate, Applegate, McGeehan, Pinto, and Kong, 2009, p. 381).

Many students have trouble with these high-stakes standardized tests because of the reading difficulty involved. Hornof (2008) addressed this problem by treating standardized tests as a separate genre of reading. She taught her students strategies that they could use in reading standardized tests, just as she did with other genres. Among other activities, she analyzed the state assessment test, found out what the students knew about it, defined useful test-specific words (such as *passage* and *summary*), had students examine sample tests that the state had released, and modeled the strategies that should be used to take the tests. Her students were able to apply the strategies that she taught when they took the test.

Another concern about current tests is that these assessments do not deal with the evaluation of online reading comprehension and learning on the Internet (Mokhtari, Kymes, and Edwards, 2008/2009). This area of comprehension has become more vital in recent years.

The use of high-stakes tests based on world-class standards is intended to cause students to work harder and learn more, but the students will do so only if they *believe* that they will succeed with more effort. If they have a history of failure, the tests may instead be discouraging to them. With the current mandate to teachers to "leave no child behind" in meeting state standards, students who believe that they cannot attain these standards may give up. Teachers must build learning environments to convince students that they can succeed if they persevere (Stiggins, 2004).

Although the goals for assessment should ideally be (1) tied to the teaching and learning that is going on within the classroom, (2) set by the teachers and students involved, and (3) flexible enough to be adjusted to changes that occur in the classroom, with the predominance of high-stakes testing for accountability, many teachers "teach to the test" to ensure adequate performance from their students (Higgins, Miller, and Wegmann, 2006; Tierney, 1998). Monitoring of students' reading and writing activities, keeping anecdotal records and holding conferences with students, and having students produce portfolios and keep journals are seen by Tierney (1998) as better ways to assess student performance. Invernizzi and others (2005, p. 612) believe that "test developers sometimes limit or avoid the use of more authentic, qualitative, or subjective measures, the reliability of which is difficult to establish, in favor of more contrived, quantitative, objective measures that can be more easily constructed to be reliable."

Well-constructed informal tests based on important curricular goals should be given the most credibility by the educational establishment (Tierney, 1998). Process-oriented comprehension measures will not tell teachers what their students have learned about a text passage or compare their students' reading achievement to the achievement of other students. They will, however, allow teachers to learn which strategies their students use to comprehend text. This information helps teachers plan instruction to increase the students' comprehension strategies (Wittrock, 1987).

Criterion-Referenced Tests

What is the difference between norm-referenced tests and criterion-referenced tests?

Whereas norm-referenced tests compare the test taker's performance with that of others, **criterion-referenced tests** (CRTs) check the test taker against a performance criterion, which is a predetermined standard. Thus an objective for a criterion-referenced test might read, "Given ten paragraphs at the ninth-grade reading level, the student can identify the main idea in eight of them." In short, a CRT indicates whether or not the test taker has mastered a particular objective or skill rather than how well his or her performance compares with that of others. A norm-referenced test, on the other hand, may indicate that the student can identify the main idea of a paragraph better than 90 percent of the test takers in his or her age group.

The results of criterion-referenced tests can be used as instructional prescriptions; that is, if a student cannot perform the task of identifying the main idea in specified paragraphs, the need for instruction in that area is apparent. These tests are therefore useful in day-to-day decisions about instruction. Teachers often prefer criterion-referenced tests for this reason (Invernizzi et al., 2005). Criterion-referenced tests may be either commercially produced or teacher-constructed tests and may have objective written items or classroom-based performance tasks.

However, there are a number of unresolved issues related to criterion-referenced tests. For example, the level of success demanded is one issue. Often the passing level is set arbitrarily at 80 or 90 percent, but there is no agreement as to the nature of mastery or how to measure it. Additionally, many criterion-referenced tests give the appearance that hundreds of discrete reading skills must be mastered separately, overlooking the fact that the skills are highly interactive and must be integrated with one another if effective reading is to occur. Some question exists about whether CRTs can measure complex domains such as critical/creative reading skills, reading appreciation, or attitude toward reading.

Both criterion-referenced tests and norm-referenced tests will likely continue to be important reading assessment tools, serving different purposes. Content teachers may make frequent use of certain CRTs. They may construct these measures themselves, choosing items from banks of criterion-referenced test items that are available for all subject areas from some state educational departments or other educational sources, or they may construct their own items.

Traditionally, content teachers have used their own criterion-referenced measures to assess the results of instruction. In such cases, definite instructional objectives are tested, and there is a definite standard of judgment or criterion for "passing." Example 3.1 shows an instructional objective that is measured by five items on a test prepared by a teacher. The criterion for demonstrating mastery of this objective is set at four out of five; that is, the student must answer four out of five items correctly to show mastery.

Note that each question in Example 3.1 is related to the objective. The criterion level for "passing" must be determined by the teacher. Results give the teacher precise information concerning what each student can and cannot do; therefore, the test results can be used to improve classroom instruction.

EXAMPLE 3.1 **Criterion-Referenced Test**

Objective: Utilize the information found on the content pages of the almanac.

Directions: Find answers to the following:

1. Who was the fifteenth president of the United States?
2. Who holds the world record for high diving?
3. What was the Academy Award winner for the Best Picture of 2007?
4. What are the names of the Kentucky Derby winner of 2008 and the jockey who rode the horse to victory?
5. Where is the deepest lake in the United States?

Classroom-Based Assessments

The term *classroom-based assessments* refers here to informal, primarily teacher-constructed assessments used daily in classrooms. Informal tests (tests not standardized against a specific norm or objective) are valuable aids to teachers in planning instruction. Most of them are constructed by teachers themselves. Other informal measures, such as observations, interviews/conferences, performance samples, and portfolio assessments provide much information. At present such measures are necessary in order for a teacher to assess outcomes of currently endorsed instructional procedures in reading because most current norm-referenced tests are not designed to do so. Teachers' feedback to students on class work, homework, and tests gives students strategies for improvement. Students must receive an opportunity to work on improvement and scaffolding to assist them in their endeavors.

Teachers are expected to teach in a way that meets local, state, and even national standards related to their subject areas. Whenever possible, teachers should align both their teaching procedures and their informal evaluations with the standards that they are expected to follow.

Informal tests are important in formative assessment. They allow teachers to assess students' understanding of what has been taught and adjust future instruction based upon the results of the assessment. Formative assessment involves teachers and students communicating about mastery of concepts and skills. This communication lays a foundation for differentiated instruction (Brookhart, Moss, and Long, 2008).

Following formative assessment, teachers can change the type of presentation of concepts that were not learned initially and use different learning activities that engage students with different learning styles. In some cases, a student needs individual tutoring. This may be offered by the teacher or by peer tutors. In other cases, different material may be needed for some students. Computer-assisted instruction may also help (see Chapter 2). Without adjustment of instruction, formative assessments are not helpful (Guskey, 2007/2008).

Formative assessments give teachers timely information for instructional implementation. They also allow the teacher to provide students with ongoing feedback on specific strengths and needs, so that students can adjust their approaches to the material. Students need feedback that is immediate, specific, understandable, and usable. The feedback may be written or oral, and it may include a demonstration by the teacher. Interactive discussions often provide the best feedback (Brookhart, 2007/2008).

Many informal tests of reading achievement can be useful to the teacher in revealing student reading achievement. Six of these measures are discussed in the sections that follow: (1) assessments of background knowledge, (2) group reading inventories, (3) written skill inventories, (4) informal reading inventories, (5) cloze tests, and (6) gamelike activities. Creative teachers often adapt assessment techniques to their specific teaching situations. See the next "Meeting the Challenge" for an example.

Assessments of Background Knowledge

Since the background knowledge of the students plays a vital role in their comprehension of reading material (see Chapters 5 and 6), it is wise to assess background knowledge about a topic before asking students to read about that topic. When prior knowledge of the topics covered in the reading passages is lacking because students with diverse home backgrounds and mental capabilities have acquired different sets of background information, teachers should develop the missing concepts before assigning the reading. Students with varying backgrounds will often have difficulties with concepts in different content fields.

Background knowledge may be assessed in several ways. Oral methods of assessment may be better for less advanced students because they may actually know more than their writing skills allow them to express.

Some common ways to assess prior knowledge are brainstorming, word association, preliminary questioning by the teacher, and informal discussion. When students tell or write down all the facts they know about a topic before reading, they are *brainstorming*. This technique is more successful with older skilled readers than with younger students and less skilled older readers, who do not appear to be able to retrieve their knowledge as easily. *Word association* involves having the students tell everything they can think of about selected words that are subtopics of the main topic, one at a time. This technique may provide more information about prior knowledge than does brainstorming. The teacher may engage in *preliminary questioning* about subtopics of the main topic to probe prior knowledge, but this approach requires expertise in question formulation and time for the preparation of questions. This technique offers the largest amount of information of the four types of assessments, and it provides the largest number of facts per minute of administration time. *Informal discussion* of the students' prior experiences with a topic often yields less information than the other three approaches, but is preferable to no assessment.

MEETING THE CHALLENGE

ENGLISH/ LANGUAGE ARTS

Creative teachers have always found ways to adapt assessment techniques to their particular teaching situations. Katherine Dooley, an English teacher in a rural high school, worked out classroom-based assessment techniques to meet her students' needs. Here is her account of her experience:

In my first year of teaching, I quickly learned my expectations for a unit often could not be evaluated in one fifty-minute period; therefore, I divided tests into objective and subjective (essay-type) questions and gave the test over two days or allowed students to work on the essay part at home. When I returned the tests, I noticed lots of smiles (something I thought was strange because the grades were average at best). Our discussion of the test turned into an evaluation of my evaluation of them. They loved the two-part test. Almost everyone had made a grade they were pleased with on at least one part of the test. Instead of receiving one mediocre grade, they had one great grade, and that made them feel good.

The Shakespeare unit formed a new challenge. Shakespeare is my favorite, and more than anything I wanted to transfer my love of the Bard to them. In our pre-unit discussion, I discovered their negative feelings toward Shakespeare would make that difficult. In assessment, I was locked into several things by virtue of unwritten department policy. They would have to take an objective test, take a test about quotations, write an essay, and memorize the Macbeth dagger soliloquy; however, those things alone would only compound their dislike of Shakespeare. I wanted them to play with the play, and I knew a group of my students had been videotaping their parties and club meetings since elementary school. The solution was the fact that my students were video babies. I added a video assignment to their growing list and prepared for the groaning, complaining, and whining. But they were not upset about the workload as much as

Assessment methods may include performance measures.

bjones27/iStock Photo

the instructions for the video project: "Videotape something related to Macbeth (act out scenes or do a newscast or ???). It should be at least seven minutes long." They begged for more directions; I refused. I wanted them to be creative, but I was secretly petrified that the project was going to bomb. A week before the due date, they became excited and secretive. One group refused to let me near them when they were discussing the video. Students guarded their groups' ideas for sports stories and funny commercials.

This project was the biggest success of the year. The videos, most of which were newscasts, were loaded with lines from the play and complex puns. My favorite was a live remote from the local Taco Bell where Fleance (one of my students in lovely purple tights) was "making a run for the border" after the murder of Banquo. Students told me this was the most fun they had had all year; parents, many of whom worked the camera or did makeup, called and sent gifts saying they "had a blast" helping with this assignment. After we watched all the videos, we voted, dressed up, and gave out the Doolies (huge pieces of minerals) for best actor, actress, cinematography, and picture. In their mandatory acceptance speeches, some thanked parents, some made political or social statements, but all said they would never forget Macbeth. I don't think they realized it, but that was the whole idea!

Langer (1981) developed the PreReading Plan (PReP) technique to help teachers to assess students' background knowledge about a content area topic and to activate their prior knowledge about the topic before they are asked to read the material. The PReP is a discussion activity for a small group of students, in which the teacher selects a key word, phrase, or picture about the topic to start the discussion. First, the teacher has the students brainstorm about the presented stimulus by saying something like, "What do you think of when you hear (the particular word or phrase) or see (the selected picture)?" The responses are recorded on the board. Then the students explain what made them think of the responses they gave, which develops an awareness of the networks of ideas they have in their experiential backgrounds and exposes them to the associations that their classmates have made. Finally, the teacher asks students if they have any new ideas about the word, phrase, or picture related to the topic of the content passage before they begin to read the text. The opportunity to elaborate on their prior knowledge often results in more refined responses, because students can use input from others to help in shaping responses.

After the PReP discussion ends, the teacher can analyze the responses to discover the students' probable ability to recall the content material after they have read it. Students who have much prior knowledge about the topic usually respond with superordinate concepts, definitions, analogies, and comparisons with other concepts. Those with some prior knowledge generally respond with examples or attributes of the concept. Those with little prior knowledge usually make low-level associations, offering word parts (prefixes, suffixes, and/or root words) or sound-alike words or sharing irrelevant personal experiences. Initial responses may fall into one category, and responses during the final elaboration may fall into a higher category of knowledge, showing that the process may activate knowledge as well as assess it. Langer states that responses that show much or some prior knowledge indicate that the students will be able to read the text with sufficient understanding. Responses that show little prior knowledge indicate that the students need direct instruction related to relevant concepts before they are asked to read the material.

Group Reading Inventories

What kind of information can a group reading inventory yield?

The content teacher may administer a **group reading inventory** (GRI) before asking students to use a particular text for study. A GRI of content material involves having students read a passage of 1,000 to 2,000 words from their textbooks and then asking them certain types of questions. The teacher should stay closer to 1,000 words to cut down on administration time, but use enough words to allow the formation at least three questions of each type. This procedure can give some indication of how well students will be able to read a particular textbook. Content books to be studied should be written on a student's instructional or independent reading level (instructional for material to be worked on in class with the teacher's assistance; independent for material to be used by the students outside of class); trade and supplementary books should be on a student's independent level, since they are generally used for outside reading assignments. Therefore, by using a group reading inventory, the content teacher can decide whether or not to use material from a particular book for in-class or homework assignments and can decide which materials are inappropriate for use with particular students at any time.

The selection used in an inventory should be material that the students have not read previously. The teacher introduces the selection and directs the students to read it for the purpose of answering certain kinds of questions. Students may note beginning and ending times for their reading. Later, a words-per-minute score can be computed by dividing the time into the total number of words in the passage. After reading, the student closes the book and answers a series of questions of such types as the following:

1. Vocabulary (word meaning, word recognition, context, synonyms, antonyms, affixes)

2. Literal comprehension (stated main ideas, significant details)

3. Higher-order comprehension (inferential and evaluative)

A sample GRI from a secondary-level journalism textbook is provided in Example 3.2.

EXAMPLE 3.2	**Sample Group Reading Inventory**

Name _____ Date _____

Motivation Statement: Why must journalists conduct themselves ethically?

Selection: Everyday Ethics

Ethics are the moral principles that govern the appropriate conduct for individuals and organizations. Journalists must always conduct themselves ethically. What are the elements of ethical conduct in journalism?

When you read an article in a newspaper or on a Web site, or when you see a story reported on your local television station, you most likely assume it is true. There's nothing more important to a news organization than accuracy, which means getting all the facts right and always seeking the truth. Consistent accuracy gives the journalist and the news organization credibility, a reputation for being right. Credible news organizations and their employees strive to be fair and independent; that is, free from the influence of government, businesses or individuals.

Good journalists live in fear of making mistakes, and they work very hard to avoid them. Mistakes do happen, however, so news organizations make an effort to correct them as soon as possible. The willingness to correct mistakes is another mark of credibility.

There are many day-to-day situations in which journalists have to make ethical decisions. Some people try to influence reporters, or persuade the journalists to write favorably about certain people or businesses. Some ethical decisions are small, such as whether they should let a community leader pay for the lunch they have together. Some are larger, such as whether they should take a free trip offered by the resort about which they will write a travel story. The Society of Professional Journalists has a broad Code of Ethics, but opinions may differ on how to handle some specific situations.

Not so many years ago, a columnist at the *San Francisco Chronicle* turned down a free trip she won in a random drawing at a trade show hosted by the British consul. She had put her business card into a bowl with others, not realizing at first that it was for a drawing. When she won the trip, worth about $20,000, she turned it down immediately. To her, accepting the trip would have compromised her credibility. What if in the future she would have to write about the airline? Would she look free of influence? It also would have violated her own newspaper's policy against accepting gifts of any kind.

Not everyone thought the journalist made the right decision. The British consul was definitely surprised, though another winner was drawn immediately. The columnist's action even made the news. She might not have made news if she had turned down dinner or free tickets to a concert. But it's the same thing. Issues concerning influence arrive in packages big and small. Good journalists must say no to them all.

Integrity

Journalists frequently face situations that test their integrity, that quality of possessing an inner sense of knowing right from wrong and adhering to high moral principles or professional standards. Often journalists have to decide the honorable way to handle a source, or the right way to deal with information they get from a source.

Suppose you agree to keep confidential a source who supplies you some good information. Back at the office, however, your editor says the information cannot run without attribution. Do you go back to the source and ask that person to go on the record? Do you publish the source and explain later that it was the boss's decision? Your natural instinct is probably to go back to the source and ask that person to go on the record because that's the right thing to do. Your integrity is guiding your decision making.

What about the information from your source? Suppose you see a few facts that you question. Do you run the information anyway because you got it from an on the record source? Do you take the time to verify those facts that raised questions for you? Verifying facts, no matter who presents them, is always a good idea.

Some reporters say that their reputation is the most important professional asset they have. Reputable reporters always try to do the right thing. They don't misrepresent themselves or break the law to get a story. They treat their colleagues, the public and their sources—the people from whom they get information—fairly and respectfully. They live and work with integrity.

Journalists who act with integrity are honest in their reporting, and they are honest with readers and viewers about where they get their information. This principle of honesty is the reason many news organizations discourage or ban the use of anonymous sources except in extraordinary cases. Anonymous sources are sources who don't want to be named. News organizations now encourage transparency, which means writing into the story where the information came from and allowing the public to decide for itself whether to believe the story.

Imagine you are a reporter for your high school newspaper and you find out from the principal's son, a fellow student, that his mother will be moved to another high school at the end of the semester. Because the son was not supposed to tell anyone this news, he wants to be anonymous, or unnamed in the story. He says you should call him "a source close to the principal."

That would not be permitted by many news organizations. However, a good reporter may still go after the story by trying to get the information on the record, meaning that the source understands that his or her name will be published. Some ways to do that would be:

(1) Directly ask the principal if she is leaving at semester's end, or **(2)** ask the superintendent of schools if the principal will be moved. If the information comes from one of those credible, named, transparent sources, the truth of the story is verified and readers can see where it originated.

Impartiality

Journalists are expected to keep their distance from the people and organizations they cover so that they can be impartial when they write about them. Impartial means being objective, putting aside personal opinions, and not accepting gifts, meals, trips or anything else that could be seen as seeking to influence the news. It also means avoiding any conflict of interest.

An example of conflict of interest would be reporters who write about companies in which they own stock, or an organization to which they belong, or even the schools their children attend.

Journalists often are sent free books, CDs, movies and other material by sources who would like the journalist to write about them. Are these items gifts that attempt to influence the reporters? Not usually. Most news organizations allow reporters to use and keep material that is clearly intended for mass press consumption, though some organizations strongly encourage employees to give such material to libraries or charitable organizations when their use for a story is complete. Critics and reporters on entertainment and sports beats often are offered tickets to games, concerts, theaters, or movies. Some organizations require that reporters buy tickets to any event they cover so there is no question about the impartiality of their reporting. Others allow reporters to attend screenings intended only for press, or use seats set aside for press that would not be sold to the public. This is the case for sports reporters who sit in a press box to cover a game. If ever in doubt about accepting anything from a source or the source's representatives, a reporter should discuss it with editors.

Source: Lorrie Lynch. *Exploring Journalism and the Media*. Mason, Oh.: South-Western Cengage Learning, 2009, pp. 30–34.

Inventory Questions

Directions: Write a short answer to each question.

Vocabulary
1. What are *ethics*?
2. What is *integrity*?
3. What is a synonym for *impartial*?
4. What does the *im-* in *impartial* mean?
5. Who are *anonymous sources*?
6. What does the word *transparency* mean in this selection?
7. What does it mean to speak "on the record"?

Literal Comprehension
1. What gives a journalist *credibility*?
2. What quality do we say journalists with high moral principles or professional standards have?
3. What ethical problem do reporters have when they write about companies in which they own stock?

Higher-Order Comprehension

1. Why might you refuse a free meal in a restaurant that you will be describing in an article?
2. How ethical is it to print information that was given to you "off the record," revealing the name of the source?
3. Why is it a good idea to verify facts, even if you have a quotable source?
4. Are the rules of ethical behavior clear-cut, giving journalists definite guides to all the decisions they will face? What does the selection say that makes you believe that?

Materials are suitable for instructional purposes if the student can comprehend 75 percent of what he or she reads, as indicated by performance on well-constructed comprehension questions. If students can comprehend 75 percent of what they read, their comprehension will probably increase if teachers introduce specialized vocabulary words, help with comprehension, teach a study method, and provide specific purposes for reading. Of course, students have many different reading levels, depending on their interests and the background information they possess on any specific topic. Thus, a GRI must be applied to the text in each specific content area. When the student comprehends 90 to 100 percent of what he or she reads, the material can be classified as being on his or her *independent* reading level, indicating that the student can read it without assistance. A student who comprehends 75 to 90 percent is reading at an instructional level, and can handle the material with teacher assistance, or scaffolding. When the student comprehends 50 percent or less of what he or she reads, the material is on his or her *frustration* level. Students who comprehend 50 to 75 percent are likely at their frustration levels, but some of them (especially those at 70 percent or above) may be able to function at an instructional level if they are given enough teacher assistance.

Written Skill Inventories

Content teachers may want to know if students have developed the specific reading skills necessary to understand textbooks and other printed materials in their particular content areas. When teachers are preparing to teach particular chapters or units that involve reading content area materials, they should be aware of the nature of the assigned reading material. Teachers can prepare and administer skill inventories based on textbook chapters or units, modeling them after the skill inventories presented in this section. On the basis of the results, the teachers will become more aware of what activities are needed to prepare students to read and to understand the assigned materials.

Skill inventories may serve as a part of the total assessment program; that is, part of a test by a science teacher may require students to read a table or graph that appears in the text; questions about interpretation of a map that appears in the text

SCIENCE AND HEALTH

SOCIAL STUDIES **MATHEMATICS**

might be used as part of a social science teacher's chapter or unit test; symbol knowledge and diagram-reading ability might be included in a mathematics teacher's test; questions on vocabulary words may be used to check understanding of the special terms in a content chapter or unit; assignments in outlining or note taking or adjusting reading rate to purpose and degree of difficulty may be included in tests by all content teachers. The ultimate purpose of skill inventories is that students master and comprehend the content found in their textbooks and in other printed materials used in the classroom. The following skills are common to all content areas:

1. Understanding and using parts of textbooks (table of contents, index, list of illustrations, appendixes, bibliography, glossary)

2. Interpreting maps, tables, charts, graphs, diagrams, cartoons

3. Comprehending specialized vocabulary

4. Using reference materials (encyclopedias, dictionaries, supplemental reference books)

5. Recognizing special symbols, formulas, and abbreviations

6. Locating information related to a content topic on the Internet, using a search engine

Other necessary general skills are using study methods, outlining, taking notes, and reading at a flexible rate. Of course, general comprehension skills are involved in all content areas, as suggested in the GRI.

The following items may be used to prepare skill assessments:

1. *Parts of textbooks.* Have students make use of different elements in their textbooks, such as preface, index, glossary, and appendixes.

2. *Maps, tables, charts, graphs, diagrams, cartoons.* Using examples from the students' textbooks, ask students to answer questions you have prepared.

3. *Specialized vocabulary, symbols, and abbreviations.* Use words from the glossaries of textbooks or supplemental materials and symbols and abbreviations that are frequently found in your content area.

4. *Reference materials.* Using the reference materials that are available for your content area, develop questions to see if students know the various reference sources and how to use them.

5. *Computers.* Ask students to locate pertinent websites related to a specific content topic.

Examples 3.3 through 3.6 provide some sample reading skill tests.

A skills chart can be developed for recording the instructional needs of students. A skills chart has a list of skills down the left side of a page and a list of students' names across the top of the page. The teacher places a check mark beside a skill under the name of a student who successfully achieves the skill. A glance at the

| EXAMPLE 3.3 | Finding Information in a Textbook—Skill Inventory |

Directions: Use your textbook to answer the following questions:

1. What is the title of your book?
2. When was it published? How did you find out? Where did you look?
3. Who wrote the book?
4. What are the titles of the first three chapters? Where did you look to find out?
5. How are the chapters arranged or grouped? How did you find out?
6. On what page does Chapter 4 begin? How did you find out?
7. Find the meaning of the term _____. Where did you look to find out?
8. What does the map on page _____ tell you?
9. On what page does the book explain the construction of a _____? Where did you find out?
10. What index entries are given for _____? Where did you look to find the index? How is it arranged?

| EXAMPLE 3.4 | Reading Graphs—Skills Inventory |

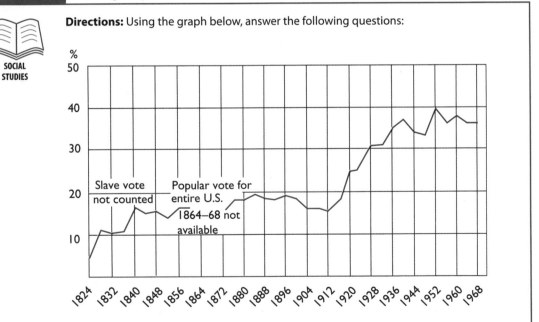

SOCIAL STUDIES

Directions: Using the graph below, answer the following questions:

Percentage of the total population voting in presidential elections

Source: Historical Statistics and Statistical Abstract.

Questions

1. Was there a steady growth of voters from 1824 to 1860? Why do you think so?
2. Around what year was there a sudden increase in popular votes cast in presidential elections?
3. Does the graph show the percentage of voting-age citizens participating in presidential elections?
4. For what years are complete data not provided? What may have caused this?

| EXAMPLE 3.5 | Using Reference Sources—Skill Inventory |

ENGLISH/
LANGUAGE
ARTS

Directions: Find the following words in a dictionary, and list the guide words and page number on which each falls:

Word	Guide Words	Page Number
anachronism		
epigram		
foreshadowing		
irony		
soliloquy		

Directions: Answer the following questions about reference materials:

1. How does the information in a dictionary differ from that in an encyclopedia?
2. How does information in a dictionary differ from that in a thesaurus?
3. What are guide words?
4. What is meant by cross-reference?
5. What is the purpose of the bibliographies at the ends of articles?
6. Where is the index located in a reference book?

| EXAMPLE 3.6 | Vocabulary—Skill Inventory |

SOCIAL
STUDIES

Directions: Study the terms listed below that were taken from a secondary history book. Use your knowledge of meanings of any of the word parts to help you understand the meanings of the whole words.

vaccination
pasteurization
evolution
genetics
sociology
psychology

Directions: Answer the following questions about the terms above:

1. What are the root words of the following words: *vaccination*, *pasteurization*, *evolution*, and *genetics*?
2. If you know the meanings of the root words, use these meanings to help you determine the meanings of the new words.
3. How is the word *pasteurization* different from the others? Does knowing the root word for this word help you? Why or why not?
4. Does being familiar with common suffixes help you figure out the meanings of these words?
5. What are the combining forms that make up the words *sociology* and *psychology*? If you know the meanings of these combining forms, use them to help you determine the meanings of the new words. Notice how knowing the meaning of one combining form can help you with two different words.

Directions: Define the italicized words.

1. When a person has been given a *vaccination*, an injection of a solution of weakened germs, he or she may be protected from contracting the disease.
2. The process of *pasteurization* of milk was invented by Louis Pasteur when he realized that bacteria could be killed by heat.
3. The *evolution* of living things over time could result in one species slowly evolving into another, according to Darwin.
4. Genes carry the traits that are passed from parents to their children. Mendel did work that established the foundation of the science of *genetics*.
5. When searching for a set of laws under which human society operates, Comte invented the term *sociology* to describe his scientific study.
6. Those who wish to learn more about the mind and behavior may wish to major in *psychology*.

chart shows which students need special help in developing a required skill. If most students need help with a particular skill, the teacher may plan a total-class instructional session around that skill. If only certain students lack a skill, the teacher may set up a small skill group to help students who need it. Skill groups are temporary groups in that they are dissolved when the members have mastered the skill. A skills file (collection of materials, equipment, and supplies) may provide the needed practice activities for some students.

Informal Reading Inventories

What information can informal reading inventories provide for teachers?

Commercial **informal reading inventories** (IRIs), which are compilations of graded reading selections with questions prepared to test the reader's comprehension, are used to gauge students' reading levels. These types of inventories are often administered by the special or remedial reading teacher to students identified as problem readers, but they can also be used by regular classroom teachers for special situations. According to

Bader and Wiesendanger (1989, p. 403), "If we examine the definitions of *informal* (not prescribed or fixed) and *inventory* (appraisal) we realize that the intention behind these devices is to provide a window on the reading process. The reader's confidence, willingness to risk error, ability to make semantically and syntactically sound substitutions, fluency, perception of organization, and a host of other understandings and abilities can be observed." They further point out that it may be inappropriate to expect reliability coefficients for alternative forms of informal reading inventories because of "the effect of content on attention, understanding, and recall" (p. 403). Professional judgment is needed to make decisions when greater prior knowledge about or interest in the content of a particular passage results in unusually high performance on that passage or when limited prior knowledge or interest in the content of a passage results in unusually low performance on that passage.

A chief purpose of these inventories is to identify the independent, instructional, and frustration reading levels of the student, as well as the listening comprehension level. The listening comprehension score is based on the percentage of questions answered correctly for a passage read to the student.

Such inventories are valuable in that they not only provide an overall estimate of the student's reading ability, but they also make possible identification of the specific strengths and weaknesses of the reader. They are helpful in determining what books a student can read independently and how difficult assigned reading can be if it is to be used as instructional material. The listening comprehension level lets the teacher know the difficulty of material that a student is capable of understanding, if there are no decoding problems.

Although a reading specialist might give a student an entire series of inventory selections and locate all four of these levels, the content teacher may give only a few levels to find approximate instructional or independent levels or may give a similar inventory based on selections from textbooks used in a particular class to find out if students can benefit from using those books. Developing such material is time consuming, because choosing representative passages and constructing a well-designed set of about ten comprehension questions that cover a variety of skills for each passage are necessary for a useful assessment.

The following chart shows criteria for finding the various reading levels of the students:

Level	Word Recognition		Comprehension
Independent	99%	and	90%
Instructional	95%	and	75%
Frustration	<90%	or	<50%
Listening Comprehension			>75%

Various writers in the field suggest slightly differing percentages relative to independent, instructional, frustration, and listening comprehension levels. The set of criteria given here for the reading levels is basically the one proposed by Johnson, Kress, and Pikulski (1987). An example of a published informal reading inventory selection is found in Example 3.7.

EXAMPLE 3.7   **Informal Reading Inventory Selection**

TEACHER 11

FORM A

◆11 PASSAGE◆

INTRODUCTORY STATEMENT: Read this story to find out some things Johnny Appleseed did.

There is some disagreement concerning the way in which Johnny went about planting apple trees in the wild frontier country. Some say that he scattered the seed as he went along the edges of marshes or natural clearings in the thick, almost tropical forests, others that he distributed the seeds among the settlers themselves to plant, and still others claim that in the damp land surrounding the marshes he established nurseries where he kept the seedlings until they were big enough to transplant. My Great-Aunt Mattie said that her father, who lived in a rather grand way for a frontier settler, had boxes of apples brought each year from Maryland until his own trees began to bear, and then he always saved the seeds, drying them on the shelf above the kitchen fireplace, to be put later into a box and kept for Johnny Appleseed when he came on one of his overnight visits.

Johnny scattered fennel seed all through our Ohio country, for when the trees were first cleared and the land plowed up, the mosquitoes increased and malaria spread from family to family. Johnny regarded a tea brewed of fennel leaves as a specific against what the settlers called "fever and ague," and he seeded the plant along trails and fence rows over all Ohio.

Source: "Johnny Appleseed and Aunt Mattie," by Louis Bromfield, in *Pleasant Valley* (New York: Harper and Row, 1945).

SCORING AID
Word Recognition
%–Miscues
99–3
95–12
90–22
85–33
Comprehension
%–Errors
100–0
90–1
80–2
70–3
60–4
50–5
40–6
30–7
20–8
10–9
0–10
217 Words
(for Word Recognition)
217 Words
(for Rate)
WPM
13020

COMPREHENSION QUESTIONS

____ main idea   1. What is the main idea of this story?
(Johnny Appleseed planted apple trees and fennel seed.)

____ detail   2. In what kind of country did Johnny plant trees?
(wild frontier country; marshes; thick forests)

____ vocabulary   3. What does the word "distributed" mean?
(handed out to different people)

____ vocabulary   4. What are the nurseries mentioned in the story? (places where trees, shrubs, and vines are grown until they are large enough to transplant)

____ inference   5. Was Great-Aunt Mattie's father rich or poor? (rich)
What in the story caused you to answer that way?
(He lived in a grand way for a frontier settler and had boxes of apples brought from Maryland until his own trees began to bear.)

____ detail   6. What did Great-Aunt Mattie's father save for Johnny?
(seeds from his apples)

____ sequence   7. Name, in order, the two things Great-Aunt Mattie's father did with the seeds. (He dried them on the shelf above the kitchen fireplace and then put them in a box.)

____ cause and effect/inference   8. What caused the spread of malaria through Ohio? (The increase in mosquitoes when the trees were first cleared and the land plowed up.)

____ inference   9. What did the settlers call malaria? (fever and ague)

____ inference   10. What did Johnny believe would help malaria sufferers?
(a tea brewed of fennel leaves)

Source: Betty D. Roe, *Roe/Burns Informal Reading Inventory: Preprimer to Twelfth Grade*, 8th ed. Copyright © 2011 by Cengage Learning. Reprinted by permission of Cengage Learning.

Some teachers may just want to choose passages for the texts being used in their classes, to decide if the students can read them independently or if they need teacher scaffolding.

Cloze Tests

An alternative method of assessment that can provide information similar to that provided by the informal reading inventory is the **cloze test** (Bormuth, 1968a and 1968b; Taylor, 1956). This test is easy to construct, administer, and score. For these reasons, content area teachers are likely to find the cloze test procedure attractive for classroom use.

How is a cloze test administered?

For a cloze test, the student is asked to read selections of increasing levels of difficulty and to supply words that have been deleted from the passage. A sample cloze passage is given in Example 3.8.

EXAMPLE 3.8	Sample Cloze Passage

SCIENCE AND HEALTH

People rely on many different measures to control and prevent floods. Most of these measures _____ both advantages and disadvantages.
(1)

_____ way that people can _____ the impact of flooding _____ to
(2)   (3)   (4)
restore natural flood _____ that human activity has _____. In areas where
(5)   (6)
vegetation _____ been removed, replanting helps _____ control runoff. Re-
(7)   (8)
planting is _____ important at the headwater _____ of a river's drainage
(9)   (10)
_____. Such measures cannot prevent _____, however.
(11)   (12)

Dams are often _____ to control and prevent _____. When dams are built
(13)   (14)
_____ rivers, reservoirs can store _____ runoff. One example is _____
(15)   (16)   (17)
Tennessee River system where _____ 50 dams have been _____. Some of
(18)   (19)
the risks _____ with dams are that _____ can break, causing floods _____
(20)   (21)   (22)
may be more destructive _____ natural flooding. Dams also _____ sedi-
(23)   (24)
ment, which upsets the _____ between erosion and deposition _____. Less
(25)   (26)
deposition means more _____ of a floodplain, which _____ flooding. Dams
(27)   (28)
become less _____ at controlling floods once _____ fill up with sediment.
(29)   (30)
_____ can also damage river _____.
(31)   (32)

Artificial levees, such as _____ stacked on top of _____ river's natural
(33)   (34)
levees, are _____ method of flood control. _____ principle behind using arti-
(35)   (36)
ficial _____ is that a deeper _____ will hold more water. _____ problem
(37)   (38)   (39)
occurs, however, when _____ water level rises within _____ deeper channel.
(40)   (41)

As the _____ height increases, so does _____ velocity, creating a powerful
        (42)   (43)
_____ force that can break _____ levees downstream, sometimes causing
   (44)   (45)
_____ damage than might have _____ if the river had _____ allowed to
   (46)   (47)   (48)
overflow the _____ levee onto the floodplain.
                    (49)
        _____ the lower Mississippi, spillways control flooding.
           (50)

Answers:
1. have, 2. One, 3. lessen, 4. is, 5. protections, 6. altered, 7. has, 8. to, 9.
most, 10. regions, 11. basin, 12. floods, 13. used, 14. floods, 15. across, 16.
excess, 17. the, 18. about, 19. built, 20. associated, 21. they, 22. that, 23. than,
24. trap, 25. balance, 26. downstream, 27. erosion, 28. worsens, 29. effective,
30. they, 31. They, 32. ecosystems, 33. sandbags, 34. a, 35. another, 36. The,
37. levees, 38. river, 39. A, 40. the, 41. this, 42. river's, 43. its, 44. erosive, 45.
through, 46. more, 47. occurred, 48. been, 49. natural, 50. On

Source: Text from Nancy E. Spaulding and Samuel N. Namowitz, *Earth Science*, page 292. Copyright © 2005 by McDougal Littell Inc., a division of Houghton Mifflin. All rights reserved. Reprinted by permission of McDougal Littell Inc., a division of Houghton Mifflin Company.

Following are the steps used for constructing, administering, and scoring the cloze test:

1. Select a set of materials typical of those used in your classroom; from each level of these materials, select a passage of about 250 words. The chosen passages should be ones the students have not read previously.

2. Leave the first sentence intact, and then delete every fifth word until you have about fifty deletions. Replace the deleted words with blanks of uniform length.

3. Ask the student to fill in each blank with the exact word that has been deleted. Allow time to complete the test.

4. Count the number of correct responses. Do not count spelling mistakes as wrong answers; do not count synonyms as correct answers.

5. Convert the number of correct responses into a percentage.

The following criteria may be used in determining levels when cloze tests are used:

Accuracy	*Reading Level*	*Assignments*
57% or greater	Independent reading level	Material that student can read alone
44–57%	Instructional reading level	Material that student can read with instructional assistance
Below 44%	Frustration level	Material not suitable for the student

A student who achieves a percentage of accuracy at or above the instructional level is asked to complete the next higher-level cloze test until that student reaches his or her highest instructional level.

Students should be given an explanation of the purpose of the procedure and a few practice passages to complete before a cloze test is used for assessment. Students need to be encouraged to use the information contained in the material surrounding each blank to make a decision about the correct word to place in the blank; otherwise they may simply guess without considering all of the available clues. Some students exhibit anxiety with this form of test, but practice may help alleviate this anxiety.

Although use of the traditional fifth-word deletion pattern is most common, some educators use a tenth-word deletion pattern, as suggested by Burron and Claybaugh (1974) for content area materials. This pattern is intended to compensate for the denseness of concepts and technical language in content materials.

Teachers who wish to discover the ability of their students to use semantic and syntactic context clues effectively may wish to administer the cloze test and accept as answers synonyms and reasonable responses that make sense in the passage. To obtain information about students' use of particular types of context clues, a teacher may wish to delete specific categories of words (for example, only nouns or only adjectives) in specific contexts, rather than every *n*th word. Of course, such modifications would make determination of reading levels according to the criteria indicated in this section inappropriate, but they would allow the teachers to see how the students process language as they read.

Cloze tests place heavy demands on short-term memory, because the reader must remember the words surrounding the blanks while searching for information in the selection to help in filling in the blanks. Therefore, because of the short-term memory demands, some students may not score as well on a cloze test as they would on another type of test.

Gamelike Activities

Some teachers use games to test students informally on the content just covered. Some base the games on the formats of popular television shows like *Jeopardy!* or competitions like *College Bowl*. Others use self-created game formats. Such activities take advantage of the students' attraction to fast-moving video games, and they offer students immediate knowledge of results to reinforce appropriate responses.

Observation

Systematic daily observation of students' reading performances can provide teachers with clues for planning effective instruction. Most decision making in the classroom is done by teachers as they observe classroom activities. Teachers, then, need to know how to look for patterns of behavior and to keep records related to the patterns observed. Without a written record of observations, teachers are likely to forget much of what they have seen or to remember it inaccurately. Various record-keeping devices that teachers use with observation, such as checklists, logs, and anecdotal records, can help them systematize observation and document findings.

Johnston and Costello (2005, p. 257) point out that "literacy assessment should reflect and encourage resilience—a disposition to focus on learning when the going gets tough, to quickly recover from setbacks, and to adapt." Teachers can best assess resilience through documented narratives of observed behaviors (Carr and Claxton, 2002; Johnston, 2004).

Teachers should try to observe students reading in a variety of settings in order to develop a complete picture of reading behaviors. Every reading activity the students engage in provides assessment data that teachers can record and analyze. Over a period of days or weeks, patterns of student development will become evident, providing a basis for instructional assistance. Teachers do need to be cautious about conclusions drawn from their observations because many biases can creep in. For example, people often base assessments on early evidence and ignore later evidence if they think that they are observing a stable characteristic, and they are more likely to think a poor paper is worse than it is if they see it just after a good one (MacGinitie, 1993).

The teacher should keep questions such as the following in mind during observation of each student:

1. Does the student approach the assignment with enthusiasm?

2. Does he or she apply an appropriate study method?

3. Can he or she find answers to questions of a literal type (i.e., detail questions)?

4. Does he or she understand ideas beneath the surface level (answering inferential- and critical-level questions)?

5. Can he or she ascertain the meanings of new or unfamiliar words? What word-recognition skills does the student use?

6. Can he or she use locational skills in books?

7. Can he or she use reference skills for various reference sources?

8. Is he or she reading at different rates for different materials and purposes?

In addition, when a student gives an oral report or reads orally, the teacher has the opportunity to observe the following:

Oral Report	*Oral Reading*
Pronunciation	Methods of word attack
General vocabulary	Word-recognition problems
Specialized vocabulary	Rate of reading
Sentence structure	Phrasing
Organization of ideas	Peer reactions
Interests	

**TeachSource
Video Case**
Grading: Strategies and
Approaches

Observations can be more valid assessment tools than standardized tests because they involve actual reading tasks, not artificial situations. Use of observation over an extended period allows patterns of performance in real reading situations to become evident. This makes the assessment more reliable than a single test can be.

Interviews and Conferences

Interviews and teacher-student conferences can yield much information about literacy skill. Interviews are particularly good for collecting information about interests and attitudes. They are also useful for discovering why students have chosen particular strategies in their reading and writing activities. Teacher-student conferences about portfolios are discussed later in this chapter, and teacher-student conferences about students' writing pieces are discussed in Chapter 9.

Performance Samples

Performance samples can be written, oral, multimedia, or live action activities.

**TeachSource
Video Case**
Performance
Assessment: Student
Presentations in a High
School English Class

Rubrics

Rubrics can be developed to evaluate oral and written retellings as well as other oral and written responses to reading, performances (such as reader's theater and drama presentations), and multimedia presentations. Rubrics provide a set of criteria for each quality level of performance for a given assignment. They clarify teacher expectations for students and help students see their strengths and weaknesses. Students may participate in the development of rubrics to be used in assessment. When they do this, they have clear expectations for the assessment (Andrade, 2007/2008). (The students in the TeachSource Video Case Performance Assessment: Student Presentations in a High School English Class helped create a rubric.) A rubric for a written retelling might resemble the one in Example 3.9. A rubric is a scoring plan "that defines the level of accomplishment you desire for products (poems, essays, drawings, maps), complex cognitive processes (skills in acquiring, organizing, and using knowledge), use of procedures (physical movements, use of specialized equipment, oral presentations), and attitudes and social skills (habits of mind, cooperative group work)" (Tombari and Borich, 1999, p. 65).

Wilson (2007, p. 62) does not use rubrics to grade writing because "the categories of the rubric represented only a sliver of [her] values about writing: voice, wording, sentence fluency, conventions, content, organization, and presentation didn't begin to articulate the things [she] valued such as promise, thinking through writing, or risk-taking." She does not feel that standardized criteria can capture the nuances of the writing that her students produce, and she believes that the use of rubrics narrows her concept of good writing. She instead writes her reactions and questions as feedback to a student as she grades a paper. Rubrics can't question the writer or point out particularly well-chosen wording. They focus on form, not communication of intended ideas.

| EXAMPLE 3.9 | Rubric for Evaluating Written Retelling of Nonfiction |

Score Level	Content
3	Includes all main ideas and at least one supporting detail for each one. Includes both literal and implied information (if appropriate). Includes no inaccurate content.
2	Includes at least one main idea with one or more supporting details. Includes only literal information even when implied information is appropriate. Includes no inaccurate content.
1	Includes only a main idea with no supporting details or only details without a main idea statement. Includes no inaccurate content.
0	Includes inaccurate content.
	Organization
3	Follows author's organization in retelling, with all parts included.
2	Generally follows author's organization, but omits or misplaces one part.
1	Attempts author's organization, but omits multiple parts.
0	Does not follow author's organization.
	Conventions Used
3	Uses standard English, correct spelling, and correct punctuation and capitalization consistently.
2	Generally uses standard English and mechanics, but has more than one deviation.
1	Has numerous deviations from some language aspects of standard English and mechanics, but shows control of other aspects.
0	Shows little evidence of standard English or correct mechanics of writing.

Retellings

What value does retelling have as an assessment technique?

Written work done for authentic purposes can be evaluated for effectiveness and sometimes can also be analyzed for ideas, organization, voice, style, and mechanics. Similarly, teachers may ask students to react in writing to narrative passages to discover whether they are attending to the surface-level plot, underlying themes, or character development. This can be a form of written **retelling** of the story, which has the advantage over oral retelling of not requiring the individual attention of the teacher during the retelling. This written retelling can be a valuable piece to include in a student's portfolio. Later retellings can be added to demonstrate progress.

Assessing comprehension of material read by having students retell a selection in response to the reading can be effective, but retelling is time-consuming, and it may be difficult for struggling readers. Teachers should model how to retell a story or selection by including in a retelling the elements that they expect the students to include in their retellings. Students should know what elements are on the scoring rubric that the teachers are using and should be given opportunities to practice retellings before this technique is used for assessing their comprehension (Hansen, 2004).

Readers construct a text in their minds as they read a particular selection. The texts constructed by better readers are more complete and accurate than those constructed by less skilled ones. The retelling technique shows what the students consider important in the text and how they organize that information, rather than showing if the students remember what the adults doing the testing consider important. A selection to be retold should be read silently and then retold to the teacher without interruption. When the retelling is completed, the teacher may request elaboration on some points, for the students may know more about the material than they can produce in a free recall situation (Blachowicz and Ogle, 2008). Teachers should listen for such things as identification of major characters, characteristics of the characters, the story setting (where and when it takes place), the story's problem and solution, and an accurate sequence of events in retellings of narrative texts. They should listen for main ideas and important supporting details in expository texts (Hansen, 2004; Richek, List, and Lerner, 1989). The retellings are a type of window to the reading comprehension process that goes on within a student and can be highly valuable in selected settings. Morrow (1989) cautions that retelling is difficult for students and suggests that teachers offer students guidance and practice with retelling before it is used for evaluation. She also stresses that students should be told before they read a story that they will be expected to retell it, and they should be given a purpose for the reading that is congruent with the information that the teacher is looking for in the evaluation.

MATHEMATICS

Cutler and Monroe (2006) studied the use of oral retellings as a problem solving strategy for word problems in sixth-grade mathematics classes. The students were taught to use oral retellings as a strategy for solving story problems. After offering instruction in the retelling strategy, they analyzed student retellings for problem representation, strategy development, and language. They tested students by having them read the problems, retell them, and then solve them. The instruction in oral retellings did not result in significantly better overall success in problem solution or in significantly fewer computational and operational errors. It did appear to have a positive effect on the students' accuracy in selecting needed operations for problem solving. In addition, Monroe, Black and Buhler (2007) did not find that third graders improved their problem solving for story problems after receiving formal instruction in oral retelling.

Retellings can be evaluated by counting the number of idea units included (probably weighted for importance) and checking for appropriate sequence. Retellings can also be checked to determine such things as inclusion of literal and implied information, attempts to connect background knowledge to text information or to apply information to the real world, affective involvement with the text, appropriate language use, and control of the mechanics of spoken or written language (Morrow, 1989). Checklists can be used to facilitate evaluation (McKenna and Stahl, 2008).

Think-Alouds

How are think-alouds used to assess reading comprehension and strategy use?

When students think aloud about what they are reading, teachers can observe the strategies that they use to make sense out of text and can adjust their instruction appropriately. Teachers should model the process before using it for assessment

(Israel, 2007). Teachers should be aware that think-alouds may be difficult for students with weak verbal skills (Blachowicz and Ogle, 2008). Wade and Adams (1990) describe the use of a think-aloud procedure for comprehension assessment. With this procedure, students read short segments of passages in which they cannot be certain what the topic is until they have read the last segment. After reading each segment, they think aloud about the passage's meaning, generating hypotheses about the meaning from the clues in the segment just read. At the completion of the passage, the reader retells the complete passage. The activity can be recorded for later analysis as to how the reader generated hypotheses, supported them with text information, related information to background experiences, integrated new information with existing knowledge, and so on. Such recordings can be included in students' portfolios.

Use of the think-aloud procedure can reveal students who are good comprehenders, those who overly rely on bottom-up (text-based) or top-down (knowledge-based) processing, and those who fail to integrate information in the different segments of the passage. Knowing these approaches to reading can help the teacher plan appropriate instruction, such as focusing on developing or activating prior knowledge to help students understand the text; helping them understand the function of background knowledge in comprehension; helping them link information from various sentences to form a unified, coherent idea; helping them develop flexibility in interpretations; and helping them learn to use metacognitive skills.

Analysis of Video Recordings

Video recordings of a variety of learning events—oral reports, creative dramas, skits, debates, and group discussions, for example—can provide excellent performance samples. Video recordings made over a period of time filled with like activities can show growth in various areas, as well as continuing weaknesses.

Cloze Procedure

The cloze procedure, described earlier, is a type of process assessment because readers have to respond *while* they are working on figuring out the text. The readers use the semantic and syntactic clues in the supplied text to construct a meaningful whole text.

Portfolio Assessment

Use of **portfolios** of students' work can be an effective way of accomplishing authentic classroom-based assessment of literacy skills, as well as skills and knowledge in other content areas. Portfolios allow teachers to examine real products of instruction, rather than a limited sample found on a test. In addition, portfolios can serve as an integral part of classroom instruction as the teacher and student confer about the contents and what the contents say about the student's literacy. Portfolios can be important, not only for teacher assessment, but also for self-assessment by the students, and they can aid the development of metacognition (Serafini, 2000/2001). Stansberry and Kymes (2007) fear that, with such current concern about the standardized testing of students, portfolio assessment may receive less consideration by busy educators.

Contents

What types of items belong in a literacy portfolio?

A portfolio can show achievement at a particular point in time or improvement over time. The purpose of the portfolio affects decisions about its contents. Barrett (2007, p. 436) says that "an educational portfolio contains work that a learner has collected, reflected upon, selected, and presented to show growth and change over time." Such a portfolio is intended to monitor ongoing learning and is a continuous activity to document and promote student learning. Students can use them to assess their own progress, and teachers can use them to decide upon needed instruction and show parents evidence of progress over time. A portfolio that is essentially a snapshot of a student's current abilities is more likely to be used for accountability purposes. It would be used to document student learning for grading or reporting to administrators and policy makers. It could also be used to showcase skills to parents and others.

Each student's literacy portfolio should include materials showing that student's accomplishments as a reader and a writer. These materials can vary widely, depending on the function that the portfolio assessment is intended to serve. Some examples of materials that might be included in traditional portfolios follow:

1. Writing samples judged to be the student's best efforts—either current samples or those chosen for the portfolio at regular intervals in order to show progress.

2. All prewriting materials and drafts for a piece that has been developed through to the publication stage, to show the process that was followed.

3. Recordings of a student's best oral reading (done with prior preparation), either current samples or those collected at regular intervals to show progress.

4. Written responses to literature that has been read and discussed in class (which can be analyzed for inclusion of information on theme, characters, setting, problem, events, solution, application, and personal response).

5. Journal entries that show analysis of literacy skills or that show interest or engagement in literacy activities.

6. Functional writing samples (letters, lists, etc.).

7. Reading logs that show the number and variety of books read in various time periods.

8. Videos of group reading discussions, audience reading activities, reading/writing conferences, or literacy-based projects (creative dramatizations, readers' theater presentations, etc.).

9. Photographs of completed literacy-based projects, with attached captions or explanations.

10. Examples of writing-to-learn in content area activities. (See Chapter 9 for examples.)

11. Informal tests.

12. Checklists or anecdotal records made from observations by the teacher.

13. Questionnaires on attitudes toward reading and writing and on reading interests.

14. Digital recordings of webpages or multimedia presentations developed.

15. The student's written explanation of portfolio contents, rationale for inclusion, and assessment of personal literacy achievements based on this evidence.

Purpose

Teachers or administrators must decide the purpose for the portfolios and the criteria for inclusion of materials. If the portfolios are to be used by the administration or outside agencies, this decision making may be entirely out of the hands of teachers and students. If the portfolios are for the teacher to use in making instructional decisions or in keeping parents informed of the student's progress or for the teacher and student to use in observing and documenting the student's progress and literacy abilities, the student may make many or all of the decisions alone or in collaboration with the teacher. If the portfolios are primarily for evaluation or documentation for outside individuals, including parents and administrators, the teacher may take a more active role in the decision making than if the portfolios are only for classroom instructional purposes.

Teachers must be clear about the skills and strategies they want to assess and must require that the portfolios include a variety of products that demonstrate the use of these skills and strategies. Portfolios "can measure growth and development of competence in cognitive areas such as knowledge construction (e.g., knowledge organization), cognitive strategies (analysis, interpretation, planning, organizing, revising), procedural skills (clear communication, editing, drawing, speaking, building), and metacognition (self-monitoring, self-reflection). They can also provide evidence of certain dispositions—or habits of mind—such as flexibility, adaptability, acceptance of criticism, persistence, collaboration, and desire for mastery" (Tombari and Borich, 1999, p. 170). Teachers must ensure that the instruction in their classes involves the skills and strategies needed for the construction of the portfolio.

Teachers may want students to keep separate portfolios for different purposes. The types of materials selected depend on the purpose of the portfolio. For example, one portfolio might focus on a student's best work in a variety of areas, whereas another portfolio might focus on the range of genres the student has experienced and experimented with in reading and writing. Still another portfolio might show the process used in developing written pieces or in evaluating reading selections. Some teachers may want evidence of all these varying literacy aspects in the same portfolio, which magnifies the importance of the organization of the material.

Selection and Evaluation

Why is it important to guide students in their selection of portfolio materials?

Ideally, the students will participate in the selection and evaluation of materials for their portfolios. They may need guidance, however, as to the criteria for inclusion because otherwise they may either put everything or very little into their portfolios. Including too much may obscure the information that is most helpful. Including too little may not offer sufficient input for decision making. They also need to know what scoring criteria will be used—what is being judged and the standards for acceptable materials. The scoring criteria need to be clear and specific. Students may participate in developing these criteria. Collaborating with teachers to choose portfolio items that represent their progress over time and their current levels of achievement can help students to feel ownership of the learning process. Reflection about their learning activities not only leads them to choose assessment items, but also helps them understand their strengths and weaknesses. It helps them understand what they need to do in the future as well (Wolf and Siu-Runyan, 1996).

Students should have the opportunity to organize their portfolios in ways that help them best display their literacy products and processes. Labeling the materials and indicating what criterion or criteria they meet can enhance clarity. Students may be asked to rank their products from best to worst, arrange pieces chronologically to show a picture of literacy activities for the period, choose pieces to show a range of genres in their reading and writing experiences, or describe the development of a long-term project.

Graves (1992a and b) asks students to decide which pieces have particular value to them by asking them to label pieces that they found hard to write, that made them realize that they were learning something about the writing or the content they were writing about, that helped the reader picture the written ideas, that needed reworking, and so on. Students' written rationales for including items in their portfolios are crucial elements in their portfolios (Barrett, 2007).

A portfolio can indicate the student's work habits, preferences, literacy strengths and weaknesses, attitudes, and range of reading and writing activities (Simmons, 1992). The use of portfolios encourages analytic grading and the recognition that humans have multiple abilities and skills.

Portfolio conferences can be opportunities for the teacher to learn more about the process behind the development of the portfolio materials. The students should explain why they included what they did and what these items show about them as literate people. The students can tell what they have learned, using the portfolio pieces as documentation, and then the teacher and students can plan future activities to work on any evident weaknesses or gaps in literacy achievement (Milliken, 1992; Rief, 1992).

Portfolios may contain both hard copies of written products and electronic works, such as videos or copies of webpages. Electronic portfolios can include graphics, photographs, text, and audio and video segments. (See section "Computer Applications to Assessment" later in this chapter for more on digital portfolios.)

Self-Assessment

Students need to be helped to monitor their own literacy learning, rather than depending exclusively on teacher monitoring. Teachers can facilitate this by asking students questions about how literacy tasks are going and how they can tell. This type of questioning lets them know that they are capable of evaluating their performance. Activities such as having students rank several examples of their own writing and asking them to tell the basis for the ranking encourages self-assessment (Johnston, 2005). If students are to self-assess, they must have knowledge of criteria that must be met for success.

Self-assessment may also take place during whole-class or small-group discussion, as students discuss the strengths and weaknesses of their writing or the extent to which they understood the reading materials. Peer conferences about reading and writing can also be the basis for self-analysis. Involving students in self-assessment makes them partners in evaluation (Fryar, 2003; Van Kraayenoord, 2003).

Self-assessment techniques include the following:

1. *Discussion.* Self-assessment may focus on a single topic, such as word recognition, meaning of vocabulary, comprehension, study strategies, or problems in reading a particular textbook. With guiding questions from the teacher, the students can discuss, orally or in writing, their strengths and weaknesses in regard to the particular topic.

2. *Structured interview or conference.* The teacher may ask such questions as the following:
   a. How do you figure out the pronunciation or meaning of an unknown word?
   b. What steps are you taking to develop your vocabulary?
   c. What do you do to get the main ideas from your reading?
   d. Do you use the same rate of reading in most of your assignments?
   e. What method of study do you use most?
   f. How do you organize your material to remember it?
   g. What special reference books have you used lately in the writing of a report?
   h. How do you handle graphic aids that appear in the reading material?
   i. How do you study for a test?
   j. What could you do to become an even better reader?

3. *Self-rating checklist.* Checklists can focus on particular skills, such as reading to follow directions, or a broad range of skills. Students rate themselves.

4. *Learning logs.* Students keep learning logs to document daily progress and learning.

5. *Written reflections about work.* Portfolios should include students' written analyses of the materials included.

6. *Rubrics.* Rubrics can be used by students to assess the quality of their own performances and guide them in making appropriate revisions (Andrade, 2007/2008).

Self-evaluation can lead to the use of metacognitive strategies when students are reading. They ask themselves if they understand the material, and if not, what they can do to understand it better.

Attitude Measures

Students' affective responses to reading selections influence whether or not the students will become willing readers. Additionally, attitude is a factor in determining if students will read in specific content area textbooks or other content-related materials. Therefore, a measure of students' attitudes toward reading experiences in general and in specific content areas is an important aspect of the total assessment program. Reading takes many forms and means many different things to different students. One student might enjoy reading the sports page but be bored or even dislike reading a library book to complete an English assignment, whereas another student might prefer the library book.

Observation, interviewing, techniques in which reading is compared with another activity, sentence completion activities, questionnaires, summated rating scales (which involve having students respond to statements on a Likert-type scale), and semantic differentials (which involve having students choose descriptive adjectives to rate the items) have all commonly been used to assess attitudes in the United States. Multiple measures are recommended because single measures may give an incomplete picture (Alexander and Cobb, 1992).

Whether or not a student likes reading depends on what he or she is reading and for what purpose. Therefore, perhaps the most valid measure of a student's attitude toward reading is his or her oral or written responses to individual selections.

Students are not expected to respond positively to all their reading experiences, but if the majority of their responses indicate negative attitudes toward reading, something is amiss. A profile of individual scores may be kept as an ongoing assessment of each student's attitude toward reading. Content teachers should be concerned about the attitudes of students toward reading material; students who have negative attitudes may not comprehend well and will probably need additional motivation for reading. An assessment of this type carried out near the beginning of the school term should be valuable to content teachers.

Interest Assessments

In reading, as in other areas, interest is often the key that unlocks effort. Consequently, study of students' reading and other interests is an important part of the teaching process. Teachers should plan ways to motivate students and show how a subject is related to their personal lives.

Content area teachers need to know the *specific* interests of each student in order to capitalize on them in recommending reading materials. One of the ways to learn a student's reading interests is through observation in daily classes. The teacher can note the books the student chooses to read, the degree of concentration and enjoyment with which he or she reads them, his or her eagerness to talk about them, and the desire expressed to read more books of similar nature or more books by the same author.

More detailed information about reading interests may be obtained from an interest inventory. A sample inventory is presented in Example 3.10.

EXAMPLE 3.10   **Reading Interests Inventory**

Name _____ Grade _____ Age _____

Reading Interests

1. How often do you go to the public library?
2. What are your favorite books that you own?
3. What things do you like to read about most?
4. Which comic books do you read?
5. Which magazines do you read?
6. What are some books you have enjoyed?
7. Have you read any good graphic novels?
8. What parts of the newspaper do you read most frequently?
9. Do you like to read in your spare time? Why, or why not?
10. What websites do you visit to get the latest news?

Using Computer Applications for Assessment

Of the computer applications mentioned in this section, which ones appear to be most useful to content teachers

Computer technology has been applied to the area of assessment. The most appealing possibility to many educators may be on-computer testing, but most tests given on the computer are limited in form to objective questions that have definite single answers, limiting the scope of testing and the quality of items possible.

More commonly used are programs that enable teachers to construct multiple-choice, true/false, fill-in-the-blanks, and essay questions, store them, and allow various tests to be formed from different arrangements of the items. Additionally, when mark-sensitive answer sheets are used for responding to objective items, some tests can be computer scored when the answers are read by a special scanner or optical card reader.

Some computer-based assessment software, using a computer technology called Computer Adaptive Testing (CAT), is available for school computers. "In CAT, a student is administered a sequence of questions on the computer that is individually tailored to quickly zero in on the student's ability level," moving on to harder questions when initial questions are correctly answered (Balajthy, 2007, p. 242). Easier questions are administered if the initial questions are not answered correctly. This process allows the student's ability level to be located without administering many questions that are too easy or too difficult (Balajthy, 2007).

There are also some tests that are web-based. This allows them to be scored immediately, giving teachers quick access to results. Scheduling the administration of these tests to large numbers of students at once is not practical at most schools, but the procedure is convenient for small group or individual administrations (Balajthy, 2007). One test, the Diagnostic Online Reading Assessment (DORA), is designed to assess a variety of reading skills for students in grades K-12 and to recommend reading resources. A Spanish version is available. The diagnostic profiles that are generated can help teachers differentiate instruction.

Simulation-based assessments measure "students' understanding of complex problems using multiple-choice formats that are automatically scored" (Silva, 2009, p. 634). *River City*, cited in Chapter 2, is one example.

Teachers may also have students maintain digital portfolios. These are adaptations of traditional portfolios which allow for the collection of a wider variety of materials (for example, audio, video, graphics, photographs, and text) in a compact format. Hypertext links can connect goals and standards to evidence of processes and outcomes of learning (Barrett, 2007; Goodson, 2007; Williams, 2007). Students may scan writing samples; prepare word-processed documents; link to webpages, blogs, wikis, videos, or podcasts that they have developed; and place these artifacts in a digital portfolio for their teacher to examine. Analysis of the artifacts and hyperlinking in these portfolios encourages metacognitive activity on the part of students. Digital portfolios can meet the goals of learning portfolios by providing a digital archive of the students' products over time; examples of the processes by which the products were attained; a blog that reflects on ongoing learning activities and reactions; and teacher evaluations with test grades and rubrics to assess learning products and processes (Barrett, 2007).

Educators at Timilty Middle School in Boston, Massachusetts, used bulletin-board technology for an electronic portfolio forum. All of the "papers, drafts, analyses, pictures, videos, and so forth" were visible to the students, their peers, and their teachers. Students have self-registered names and passwords that allow the system to track their posts and let them view one another's work and respond to it in a respectful manner. Their posts can include attached documents or image files and web links. After reading feedback from their peers, the students can revise their work. Teachers have control of the forum areas (Fahey, Lawrence, and Paratore, 2007).

The Internet is also a source of assessment tools. Several sites offer sample rubrics (Balajthy, 2007).

Online reading skills, as well as book-based reading skills need to be assessed, because online reading requires some different skills from book-based reading. Typical reading assessments are not designed to evaluate online reading ability (Coiro, 2009). In addition to needing to have appropriate vocabulary knowledge, ability to comprehend at literal and higher levels, and knowledge of text structure,

Why do online reading skills need different assessment measures from traditional print reading skills?

online readers must be able to navigate hypertext and hypermedia texts, use search engines, and evaluate websites.

Coiro (2009) suggests the use of online reading comprehension assessments (ORCAs), based on curricular units, in which students are engaged in several related information requests in an online quiz. They must use the Internet to "locate, critically evaluate, and synthesize the requested information or share ideas using such tools as e-mail, blogs, or wikis" (p. 60). Software such as Camtasia (http://www.techsmith.com/camtasia.asp) can allow the teacher to video record the students as they perform the tasks, and a tool like Survey Monkey (http://www.surveymonkey.com/) can compile the student responses.

Positive dispositions toward online reading are also important. They may be ascertained by having students fill out surveys of their attitudes toward online reading (Coiro, 2009).

Assessing the Readability of Printed Materials

What effect does readability of textbooks have on content area instruction?

Readability of printed materials is the reading difficulty of these materials. Selections that are very difficult to read are said to have high readability levels; those that are easy to read are said to have low readability levels.

Textbooks are sometimes written at higher levels of difficulty than the grade levels for which they are designed. Teachers need to know whether or not this is the case, because students will not learn content from textbooks that are too difficult for them to read with comprehension.

Since secondary school teachers frequently use textbooks for independent homework assignments and may expect students to read the complete textbooks, matching the textbooks assigned to students with the students' reading levels is particularly important. Just getting a book that fits the curriculum at a particular level will not necessarily result in an appropriate text. Teachers should check the readability of particular texts that they expect their students to read.

Textbook users often overlook the fact that different sections of the same textbook may have different readability levels, some topics may require more difficult language for their presentation, or different sections may be written by different authors with writing styles that vary in complexity or clarity. English teachers, in particular, should be aware of the wide differences in readability levels of selections in literature anthologies because different authors have written the materials.

Many factors influence the level of difficulty of printed materials. Some of these are vocabulary, sentence length, sentence complexity, abstract concepts, organization of ideas, inclusion of reading aids (such as underlining, boxing of information, and graphic aids), size and style of type, format, reader interest, and reader background. Concept load seems to be particularly important. If many new or technical concepts are introduced on each page or in each paragraph of text or if many of the concepts presented are abstract rather than concrete, the readability will be more difficult. Of the factors identified that influence the level of difficulty, two are directly related to the uniqueness of the reader: interest and background. A piece of literature may be of great interest to one student and yet have little appeal for another. A reader's areas of interest may be related to his or her background experience. This background enables readers to understand easily material for which they have experienced vocabulary and concepts either directly or vicariously. (See Chapter 5 for a discussion of background experience as one area in which students exhibit individual differences.) Although all the other factors named here affect difficulty, vocabulary and sentence length have been found by researchers to be the most important in predicting readability.

Readability Formulas

Various formulas have been developed to measure the readability of printed materials. Most contain measures of vocabulary and sentence difficulty. Teachers should be aware that these formulas have been developed for use with connected prose; their use with other types of text, such as mathematics calculations, is inappropriate and will result in inaccurate scores.

The Fry Readability Graph is a relatively quick readability measure (Fry, 1972). To use the graph, the teacher selects three 100-word samples and determines the average number of sentences and the average number of syllables per 100 words. (The number of sentences in a 100-word sample is determined to the nearest tenth of a sentence.) With these figures, it is possible to use the graph to determine the approximate grade level of the selection. The Fry Graph and the instructions for using it are reprinted in Figure 3.1. The Fry Graph reflects an instructional reading level, the level at which a student should be able to read with teacher assistance. The authors of this text have found that, in many cases, secondary classroom teachers are more comfortable with this method than with more complex formulas. For that reason, the Fry Readability Graph is presented here in detail.

Considering the number of factors that formulas fail to take into account, no formula can provide more than an approximation of level of difficulty. Determination of the relative difficulty levels of textbooks and other printed materials can be extremely valuable to a teacher, however. It has been demonstrated that estimating reading difficulty by using a formula produces much more consistent results than estimating without one.

If you are daunted by the prospect of counting syllables, words, sentences, and unfamiliar words required by many formulas and you have access to a computer and appropriate software, you can use your computer to save you time and effort in making calculations. A number of programs can analyze the readability levels of texts according to a variety of readability formulas. Some grammar and style checker programs, including those built into word-processing programs, run multiple formulas. These programs perform the calculations that teachers would ordinarily have to do manually. Teachers just have to enter the passages to be analyzed and read an on-screen menu that allows them to choose such things as which formulas to run. Some commercial sites, such as Amazon.com, offer readability statistics on some of the books they list.

Why should teachers use caution when interpreting readability scores?

FIGURE 3.1

Fry Readability
Graph

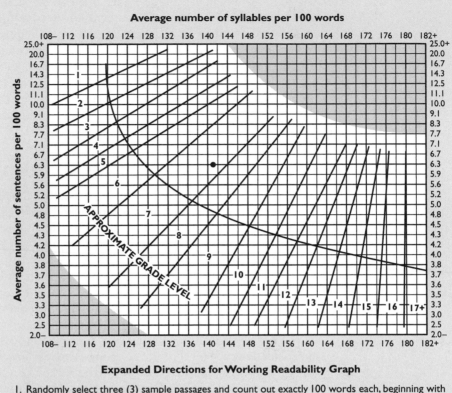

Expanded Directions for Working Readability Graph

1. Randomly select three (3) sample passages and count out exactly 100 words each, beginning with the beginning of a sentence. Do count proper nouns, initializations, and numerals.
2. Count the number of sentences in the hundred words, estimating length of the fraction of the last sentence to the nearest one-tenth.
3. Count the total number of syllables in the 100-word passage. If you don't have a hand counter available, an easy way is to simply put a mark above every syllable over one in each word, then when you get to the end of the passage, count the number of marks and add 100. Small calculators can also be used as counters by pushing numeral 1, then push the + sign for each word or syllable when counting.
4. Enter graph with *average* sentence length and *average* number of syllables; plot dot where the two lines intersect. Area where dot is plotted will give you the approximate grade level.
5. If a great deal of variability is found in syllable count or sentence count, putting more samples into the average is desirable.
6. A word is defined as a group of symbols with a space on either side; thus *Joe, IRA, 1945,* and *&* are each one word.
7. A syllable is defined as a phonetic syllable. Generally, there are as many syllables as vowel sounds. For example, *stopped* is one syllable and *wanted* is two syllables. When counting syllables for numerals and initializations, count one syllable for each symbol. For example, *1945* is four syllables, *IRA* is three syllables, and *&* is one syllable.

Note: This "extended graph" does not outmode or render the earlier (1968) version inoperative or inaccurate; it is an extension. (REPRODUCTION PERMITTED — NO COPYRIGHT)

Cautions and Controversies

All teachers should be familiar with at least one readability formula so that they can check the printed materials used in their classes. Then perhaps students will not be asked so frequently to read textbooks or supplementary materials that are too difficult for them. However, because of the limitations of the available formulas, teachers should always combine results obtained from the formulas with judgment based on personal experience with the materials and knowledge of the abstractness of the concepts presented, the organization and writing style of the author, the interests of the students in the class, the backgrounds of experience of the students, and other related factors such as size and style of type and format of the material. Because sampling procedures suggested by several formulas result in limited samples, teachers should be very cautious in accepting calculated grade levels as absolutes. They also should remember that textbooks vary in difficulty from section to section and should interpret samples with that in mind.

**SOCIAL
STUDIES**

Readability formulas do not have any measure for abstractness or unfamiliarity of concepts covered. Familiar words, such as *run* and *bank*, do not always have their familiar meanings in school materials. A social studies text might discuss a "run on the banks," which would present a less familiar situation than reading about "fast movement by a person on the shore of a stream," which may be the meaning of these words that comes to mind immediately.

Authors may organize materials clearly, or they may have very poor organization, and the clarity of their writing styles may vary immensely, with some choosing to construct sentences in less common ways and others choosing familiar sentence structures. Readability formulas contain no measures for organization, style, or the cohesive structure of a text (the interrelationships of ideas in the text).

Factors within individual students help determine the readability of particular material for those students. Material that is interesting to students is easier for them to read because they are more motivated to read it. Other people with similar reading skills may find the material uninteresting and, thus, much more difficult to read. Likewise, readers who have had much experience related to the topic will find the material easier to read than those who have had little experience related to it. No formula has the power to foresee the interests and backgrounds of particular readers.

Formulas also do not contain measures for mechanical features such as size and style of the font (i.e., the typeface) and the format of the printed material. Print that is too small or too large may adversely affect readability, and some font styles make reading the material more difficult than do other styles. Additionally, text that is crowded together, unrelieved by sufficient white space or illustrative material, can make reading more difficult.

Other Methods of Readability Assessment

There are means other than readability formulas of assessing the appropriateness of printed materials for specific students. Some of these are discussed next.

| EXAMPLE 3.11 | Readability Checklist |

1. _____ Is the vocabulary used appropriate for your students?
2. _____ Is the content presented appropriately for your students' prior knowledge and experiential backgrounds?
3. _____ Is there an effort to explicitly link new concepts to the students' prior knowledge or experiential backgrounds?
4. _____ Do concrete examples accompany the introduction of abstract concepts?
5. _____ Are new concepts introduced one at a time with sufficient examples?
6. _____ Are words defined clearly for the reading abilities of your students?
7. _____ Are the style and sentence structure appropriate for your class?
8. _____ Is the organization of the material clear, with main ideas clearly stated?
9. _____ Are important complex relationships (e.g., causality, conditionality, etc.) explicitly explained?
10. _____ Is the readability level indicated by a recognized readability formula appropriate for your students?
11. _____ Are aids to text organization (chapter introductions, summaries, headings, and subheadings; table of contents; glossary; and index) provided?
12. _____ Are there adequate graphic aids, such as maps, graphs, illustrations, to supplement prose descriptions of content area concepts?
13. _____ Are there both literal recall questions and higher order questions to check students' understanding?
14. _____ Are questions clear and unambiguous?
15. _____ Are interesting activities and applications included to increase student motivation?
16. _____ Does the book show how the information being learned is related to the students' real lives?
17. _____ Is the format (print size and style, use of illustrations, use of color, etc.) appealing to and appropriate for your students?

Checklists

A checklist approach has also been used to assess readability. A checklist can include many considerations not covered by readability formulas. Items similar to the ones in Example 3.11 may be included in a checklist to help teachers estimate the readability of materials for their classes.

User Involvement Techniques

Some techniques involve trying out representative portions of the material on prospective users. These techniques take into account reader interest, reader background, author's writing style and organization, and abstractness of concepts, and, except for the cloze test, they also may consider format and type size and style. Three of these techniques are cloze tests, group reading inventory selections, and informal reading inventory selections, all discussed earlier in this chapter.

Chance (1985) found the cloze procedure to be a quick and reliable way to determine the readability of specific material for individual students. He also verified that subject matter teachers find it easy to construct cloze tests and to use them for determining readability.

FOCUS ON *Struggling Readers*

Assessment for Struggling Readers

Background knowledge can often be more accurately assessed for struggling readers through oral, rather than written, means. Limited writing ability may result in inaccurate results from written responses.

A modification of the cloze test that appears to be appropriate for struggling readers is used by some educators. This is a "matching" cloze: students select from several (three to five, usually) words randomly ordered in the margin and copy the correct ones into the blank spaces for several consecutive sentences of the passage, continuing this procedure for other sections of the passage.

Brozo (1990) makes a case for interactive assessment for struggling readers that has multiple steps: a (1) diagnostic interview to collect background information about reading strategies and ability, interests, and attitudes; (2) determination of passage placement in an informal reading inventory with word lists; (3) activation and expansion of prior knowledge of the topic of the material to be read; (4) preteaching of vocabulary; (5) setting purposes for the reading; (6) having the student read silently first and then orally as his or her use of strategies is observed; (7) asking questions about strategies and modeling effective strategies as needed; and (8) having the student retell the material. The teacher may then probe for additional information through questions, allowing the student to look back through the passage to find answers. Comprehension is extended through activities that connect the student's prior knowledge with the new content. A number of techniques found in this text—for example, semantic mapping and anticipation guides—may be used in both the preparation for reading step and this final step. This procedure is obviously time consuming, but it has the potential for uncovering a student's actual ability to perform in-class work, rather than his or her ability to perform independently.

A dynamic form of assessment is also suggested for struggling readers by Kletzien and Bednar (1990). They suggest initial assessment and strategy analysis to establish the student's reading level and to determine his or her strategy knowledge and use. They also suggest an informal reading inventory for this purpose. The teacher observes the student's strategy application and questions the student about reading strategies used. Then the teacher plans a mediated learning mini-lesson to determine the reader's capacity for modifying his or her approach to reading. The teacher discusses the student's initial performance with him or her, stressing both strengths and limitations. Then the teacher chooses a strategy to teach, using independent-level materials. The student is taught how, when, and why the strategy can be used. The teacher models the strategy directly through a think-aloud procedure and then offers the student guided practice and independent practice. The teacher observes the student's attempts to learn the strategy. A postassessment and strategy analysis follows, using another form of the informal reading inventory that was used initially. Comparing the student's performance on the two assessment measures helps the teacher to determine his or her ability to integrate the targeted strategies into the reading process. This approach also takes quite a bit of time, although it yields useful information.

FOCUS ON   *English Language Learners*

Assessment for English Language Learners

Oral assessments of background knowledge are more helpful with ELLs than are written ones because the students' delayed instruction in writing may result in their being unable to adequately express themselves through writing. The "matching" cloze test and interactive and dynamic assessment that are explained in the "Focus on Struggling Readers" box are particularly appropriate for lower secondary school ELLs. ELLs have many challenges when undergoing testing. Giving them some scaffolding can make the task more manageable.

Multiple types of assessments are particularly important for ELLs because they give the students more ways to demonstrate their learning. Some ways that assessments may be adapted to help ELLs include reducing the number of items to complete, increasing the amount of time allowed (unless there is a requirement that the test must be timed), having a helper explain the task or provide simplified instructions, allowing the use of a dictionary, and allowing the students to draw responses or respond orally (Deschenes, Ebeling, and Sprague, 1994; Echevarría, Vogt, and Short, 2008).

The No Child Left Behind Act mandates the inclusion of ELLs in assessments of reading and language arts unless they have been in the country less than a year. Unfortunately, those who are not proficient in English are at a disadvantage because they process English more slowly than English-proficient students, and they may encounter unfamiliar cultural references and language. When teachers find it necessary to use standardized tests with ELLs, the tests can be adapted to help the student because, "[i]f language diversity is not considered during assessment and educational planning, a child may receive an inappropriate educational placement" (Hardman, Drew, and Egan, 2008, p. 121). Accommodations are allowed for ELLs who must take standardized assessments. Accommodations should support the ELLs' linguistic needs and should be made according to the needs of each student. For example, ELLs with beginning English language proficiency may need oral accommodations, such as oral translations, whereas those with higher language proficiency may be able to use dictionaries or dual-language tests. Another possible accommodation is extended time for taking the test. An ELL Accommodations Database of good practices for providing accommodations is available on the Internet (http://ells.ceee.gwu.edu) (Pennock-Roman, and Rivera, 2007; Willner, Rivera, Acosta, 2009).

Summary

Teachers at the secondary school level often need to interpret norm-referenced reading test results to learn about individual students' reading abilities and about the range of reading abilities within the classroom. Survey and diagnostic tests can both be useful.

Traditional achievement tests do not generally reflect current views of the reading process as a constructive strategic process in which readers make use of their prior knowledge and techniques for unlocking meaning in the text. Work is being done to develop standardized assessment procedures that reflect these views, however, and current tests do provide useful information.

Criterion-referenced tests, which check the test taker's performance against a performance criterion as a predetermined standard, can also be helpful to teachers. Results of criterion-referenced tests can be used as instructional prescriptions, making them useful in decisions about instruction.

Perhaps more useful to content teachers are informal tests, such as the group reading inventory (GRI), which gives an indication of how well students read a particular textbook; the informal reading inventory, which provides an overall estimate of a student's reading ability as well as a picture of some of his or her strengths and weaknesses; the cloze procedure, which provides the teacher with two types of information—an overall view of the student's reading ability and the appropriateness of text material for the student; and gamelike activities. The type of assessment measure used most frequently by secondary school content teachers is the skill inventory, which provides information about whether or not students have developed the specific reading skills necessary to understand content material in the teacher's particular area.

Since teacher judgment enters into decisions about the level of each student's performance, the classroom teacher must carefully observe students as they perform daily tasks with printed materials. Retellings, written responses to writing, and portfolios for students are all informal procedures that, along with more common informal testing procedures, can facilitate assessment. Many teachers make use of electronic portfolios.

Student attitudes toward the reading experiences in the content classroom are an important aspect of the overall assessment program. Besides observation and discussion, there are teacher-made devices, self-evaluation devices, and other instruments available to show attitude. Similarly, since student interest often encourages effort, interest inventories can help content teachers plan ways to motivate the students and capitalize on student interests when selecting and using materials.

In order to adjust reading assignments to fit all students, teachers need to know the difficulty levels of classroom reading materials so they can match the materials to the students' reading levels. Difficulty levels can be estimated by using readability formulas or other readability measures in conjunction with teacher judgment.

Discussion Questions

1. What do you consider to be the major strengths and weaknesses of each of the major assessment procedures discussed in this chapter?
2. In what ways may a group reading inventory be useful to a content area teacher? An informal reading inventory?
3. Which reading skill inventory do you think would be most helpful to you as a content area teacher? Why?
4. Why might secondary teachers find the cloze test easy to use?
5. Do you think a self-assessment checklist would help you learn more about a student's reading of a content area textbook? If so, prepare a self-rating checklist that would be most appropriate for your classroom. If not, explain why not.
6. How would you revise the reading interests inventory to be most appropriate for your specific content area?
7. What are some effective uses of portfolios for evaluating different literacy concerns?
8. What are some advantages of online assessments? What could be drawbacks to them?
9. Why should teachers be concerned about the readability of content area reading materials?
10. What are some assessment approaches especially suited to struggling readers and English language learners, and why are these particularly appropriate?

Enrichment Activities

*1. Prepare a group reading inventory, using content area reading materials. Administer your inventory to a student, record your results, and share the findings with the class.
2. Using a textbook of your choice, develop at least two sample questions on each of the book parts listed. (If a particular book part is not included in your text, select examples from supplemental materials.)

   a. Preface, Introduction, or Foreword
   b. Table of Contents

c. Index

d. Appendix

e. Glossary

f. Unit or Chapter Introduction and/or Summary

*3. Prepare a reading skills inventory for a content area textbook. Administer it to a student, record your results, and share the findings with the class.

*4. Secure a published informal reading inventory, and administer it to a student. Report the results to the class.

*5. Prepare a cloze test for a passage of content area reading material. Administer it to a student. Report the results to the class.

*6. Prepare an interest checklist on one topic of study in your content area. If feasible, administer it to a student.

*7. Assemble a portfolio that represents your own literacy skills and features. Describe the criteria you used for including items in your portfolio.

---

*These activities are designed for in-service teachers, student teachers, and practicum students.

Resources including the TeachSource Video Cases can be found on the website for this book. Cengage Learning's CourseMate brings course concepts to life with interactive learning, study, and exam preparation tools that support the printed textbook. Go to www.cengage.com/login to register your access code.

Strategies for Learning: Constructing Meaning and Studying

CHAPTER 4
A Conceptual Approach to Developing Meaningful Vocabulary

CHAPTER 5
The Process of Constructing Meaning in Texts

CHAPTER 6
Strategies for Constructing Meaning in Texts

CHAPTER 7
Location and Organization of Information

CHAPTER 8
Reading-Study Strategies for Textbook Use

A Conceptual Approach to Developing Meaningful Vocabulary

Overview

Content reading instruction focuses on increasing students' comprehension of content materials. Word knowledge is essential for successful comprehension (Berne and Blachowicz, 2008; Graves, 2009; Yopp and Yopp, 2007). Students who know the meanings of most of the words they read and hear can comprehend text better than those who do not (Spencer and Guillaume, 2006). The opposite is also true—students who do not know the words in a content text will find comprehension impossible (Yopp and Yopp, 2007). Word knowledge determines how we understand texts, define ourselves for others, and define the way we see the world (Bromley, 2007).

Words are our labels for concepts; they shape meaning in oral and written language. Word knowledge enables students to connect concepts and meaning with printed words (Bromley, 2007). Content concepts make up a large portion of words found in printed materials for middle and secondary students. Students will encounter more than 100,000 words during their school careers (Ruddell and Shearer, 2002). This is significant when we realize that the ability to apply word meanings is significantly related to reading comprehension, intelligence, thinking abilities, and academic achievement (Bromley, 2007).

A limited vocabulary creates significant reading difficulties for struggling readers. English language learners (ELLs) may have mastered the vocabulary and concepts in their primary language. Their challenge is to transfer this knowledge to English.

Berne and Blachowicz (2008) surveyed teachers' specific concerns about teaching word meanings and found that teachers prefer to work in collaborative situations in which they share knowledge of the best practices for developing vocabulary. Teachers also indicated that they would like to create systematic programs for vocabulary instruction. This chapter shares information on best practices and systematic instruction.

The key instructional focuses in this chapter are activation of student engagement with learning words and development of systematic direct teaching of targeted vocabulary, which results in greater learning (Biemiller, 2003). Strategies are included for cultivating students' word and conceptual knowledge.

Purpose-Setting Questions

As you read this chapter, try to answer these questions:

1. What is direct instruction?
2. What does it mean to know a word?
3. How are words and concepts related?
4. What strategies are important in vocabulary instruction?

Word Knowledge

What does it mean to know a word?

Knowing a word is having a core meaning for that word and recognizing how the meaning changes in different contexts. Readers need more than definitions for words, and more than the knowledge derived from context. Both context and definitions can be misleading. An instance of misleading context occurred when a sixth-grade student said that *dumb* was a synonym for *genius* because his mother called him a genius when he did something dumb. Experience with words expands students' range of meanings, so their knowledge grows from superficial to in-depth knowledge.

What are the dimensions of word knowledge?

Word knowledge has two dimensions: depth and breadth. Depth is determined by the amount an individual knows about a word, such as recognizing the word, attaching meaning to the word, and using the word. Word breadth refers to the ways that the individual can connect the word to other words. For example, seeing, hearing, smelling, and tasting are connected as forms of sensory data. Teaching students about the connections among words, such as antonyms and synonyms, expands their word knowledge. Morphemic analysis gives students other ways of making connections for meaning (Kieffer and Lesaux, 2007).

Why is acquiring word knowledge a long process?

"Acquiring knowledge of a word in the richest sense is a long process involving multiple exposures in many contexts," according to Yopp and Yopp (2007). English words are multidimensional; their meanings are learned gradually in small steps. Readers must understand that English words have multiple meanings that are determined by the context in which the words occur. Students have to use context to identify the meanings of words. For example, the word *credit* changes meanings in various contexts. Students understand the word *credit* when referring to a *credit* card or *credits* required for graduation. However, a *credit* report may be an unknown concept. An economics student will acquire an understanding of *credit* through a formal definition such as "the provision of money, goods, or services at the present, in exchange for the promise of future pay" (Lowe, Malouf, and Jacobson, 1997). Terms such as *credit* bureau, *credit* disclosure form, *credit* rating, *credit* references, *credit* union, and *creditor* may be encountered in a consumer economics class. In history class, students may read, "Abraham Lincoln is often *credited* with freeing the slaves," thus illustrating credit in yet another context.

SOCIAL STUDIES

In-depth word knowledge is usually acquired for those words that an individual uses frequently in reading, listening, speaking and writing. Students with special interests, studies, and hobbies often have extensive word knowledge related to these interests. An individual who is planning a nursing career develops a vocabulary including words such as *temperature*, *chart*, *IV* (intravenous), *ICU* (Intensive Care Unit), and so forth.

How can a student show that he or she knows a word?

To know a word well, one must know how to pronounce the word. The words and concepts that students learn and use as they listen and talk become the basis for reading and writing (Bromley, 2007). Furthermore, knowing how to pronounce words can motivate students to use them in their speaking and writing. If vocabulary terms are not taught directly, students may not acquire words they need to learn for content-area comprehension.

Conceptual Knowledge

How is vocabulary related to conceptual knowledge?

MATHEMATICS

How is conceptual knowledge related to schema theory?

Concepts are the categories into which our experiences are organized and our webs of ideas are created. Items in a category share similar characteristics. In the process of conceptualizing, we group objects, experiences, or information into categories based on common features. For example, the concept of measurement includes *meter*, *ounce*, *gram*, and *inch*. However, a word can have a number of different referents. The word *meter* can represent a machine that is used to measure amounts, a unit of measurement, or patterns of strong and weak beats in poetry. The context in which the word is found helps readers know whether the author is writing about a machine, a unit of measurement, or the rhythm of speech.

Conceptual knowledge is a component of schema theory. According to this theory, knowledge is composed of an organized, structured network of concepts and information, based on experiences. These networks of knowledge in memory structure our thoughts. Therefore, schemata (plural of schema) influence learning, as well as thinking. Sharing similar schemata, concepts, and vocabulary enables people to communicate without explaining every idea, event, or object. New schemata build on preceding ones; this cumulative pattern makes each experience important to those that follow.

When communication falters, it is probably because one person lacks the schemata basic to the discussion. This problem occurs with textbooks when a textbook author or a teacher incorrectly assumes that students have acquired certain concepts. An ELL teacher encountered a mismatch between the schemata of students who were new to the United States and teachers who were teaching English and the culture of the United States. The situation is described in the next "Meeting the Challenge."

MEETING THE CHALLENGE

The ELL teachers and student volunteers for the Crestwood Volunteer ELL Program planned a Thanksgiving feast to introduce the concept of Thanksgiving to students who had recently arrived from the Congo, Nepal, Iraq, and India.

Joann, the lead teacher, explained the menu planned for the feast. However, none of the students recognized turkey, cranberries, or mashed potatoes. The students did not want to eat foreign food, so Joann brought white potatoes and cranberries for tasting. Then she asked the students whether they had eaten chicken. All of the students had eaten chicken, so she explained that a turkey is a "big chicken." The students enjoyed the feast, including turkey, mashed potatoes, and sweet potatoes (yams), which they had eaten in their home countries. They passed on cranberries and pumpkin pie. Although they recognized pumpkins, *pumpkin pie* was a new concept.

How do Students Learn Word Meanings and Concepts?

Listening and reading develop students' **receptive vocabularies**, the words they recognize when they hear them or see them. Speaking and writing develop students' **expressive vocabularies**, the words they know well enough to use in speaking and writing. Receptive vocabularies are usually substantially larger than expressive vocabularies, because learners have to know a word rather well before using it. While students may recognize many words in their listening and/or reading vocabularies, their knowledge may be partial, lacking the richness of the in-depth word knowledge that they require for effective content learning. Appropriate teaching and learning strategies are essential to developing the word knowledge that students need to succeed.

Direct Systematic Instruction

What is direct systematic instruction?

Students who have parents with good vocabularies or read a lot have an advantage in developing rich vocabularies. Independent reading, listening to stories read aloud, and listening to enriched oral language stimulate students' growth in word knowledge. Furthermore, students learn the majority of new words after third grade through reading (Cunningham and Stanovich, 1998). Current students have many demands on their time, and many of them do not read enough to acquire the necessary vocabulary for comprehension. Fortunately, we can teach students word learning strategies. Direct, systematic, explicit, teacher-led instruction is effective, and makes a significant difference in students' overall vocabularies. This instruction is critical for many students (Beck, McKeown, and Kucan, 2002). Direct instruction in content area vocabulary is focused on targeted vocabulary related to content area concepts (Curtis and Longo, 2001). Teaching key vocabulary prepares students to comprehend textbook selections.

Kamil and Hiebert (2005) assert that educators need to design multifaceted classroom experiences to help students acquire new words. In other words, students need to have multifaceted experiences rather than simply to look up a list of words in the dictionary and write the definitions.

Direct vocabulary instruction focuses on the following objectives:

1. Direct teaching of targeted vocabulary selected by the teacher.

2. Teaching context clues and how to use them by demonstrating such use and having students practice it (Greenwood and Flanigan, 2007).

3. Teaching morphemic analysis and how to use it.

4. Developing students' strategies for solving unknown words.

5. Having students develop individual word collections.

6. Teaching students to use references such as dictionaries and thesauruses. These references can be misused, but students can learn to use them effectively with instruction.

How is targeted vocabulary instruction related to direct vocabulary instruction?

MATHEMATICS

Targeted Vocabulary Instruction

Alerting students to key words focuses their attention on these words, which helps the students' vocabularies grow and improves their comprehension. Targeted words include key vocabulary for chapters or sections of their content textbooks. For example, when introducing mathematics content, teachers can call students' attention to words such as *commutative*, *metric*, *symmetrical*, *pentagon*, and *hexagon*. After introducing key words and their meanings, teachers activate prior knowledge, thus connecting the new with the known. Research shows that new learning requires integration of new information with existing information (Bromley, 2007).

Identifying Categories of Vocabulary

What three categories of words do students learn?

SOCIAL STUDIES

SCIENCE AND HEALTH

In general, learners need three categories of words. The first is general vocabulary, consisting of common words that have generally accepted meanings. These words appear in both content reading materials and general reading materials with the same meaning. Words such as *student* and *teacher* are in this group because they have the same meaning wherever they appear. The second category, specialized vocabulary, consists of words having both general and specialized meanings. The word *mouth* is in this group. In general use, *mouth* refers to a facial feature. The word *mouth* also has a specialized meaning in social studies content, as in "mouth of a river." The last category is technical vocabulary, consisting of words representing specific concepts that are applicable to specific content subjects. These are often low frequency words, but they are important to understanding content material. *Photosynthesis* is an example of a technical word used in scientific content. The vocabulary in all of these categories appears not only in textbooks, but also in literature and reading materials that students encounter in daily life. Therefore, teachers can use real-life reading materials to enhance vocabulary development.

Students are likely to encounter many unknown, or partially known, words as they read. Teachers generally find it impossible to teach all unknown words that students may encounter in a single assignment. Consider this: If an assignment has twenty-five to thirty unfamiliar words and a teacher devotes one minute to each word, twenty-five to thirty minutes have been spent in vocabulary development, which cuts into other instructional time. Since time and energy constraints make it impossible to devote this amount of time to vocabulary instruction on a regular basis, teachers need to focus on words that are essential to comprehension of the major points in the selection.

Literary material presents a somewhat different vocabulary problem than does exposition, because literature includes more symbolic, abstract meanings. Literary text requires a higher level of student involvement than exposition. Students have to realize that knowing a single word can help them accomplish such things as visualizing a character, comprehending a character's motivation, perceiving a theme, and understanding an author's point of view. To achieve this, Chase and Duffelmeyer (1990) created a strategy, VOCAB-LIT, to teach the significant words, such as *ingratiating*, used to describe Brother Leon in Cormier's *The Chocolate War*. This type of word is one that, when fully understood, would reveal an important aspect of the novel. The students complete study sheets that require them to reflect on their personal levels of

ENGLISH/ LANGUAGE ARTS

word knowledge, write the sentence in which the word appears, make connections with content, look the word up in a reference, and discuss what they have learned about the word. After the students learn this strategy, they are each assigned a day for presenting a word to the group. This program has been quite successful.

How are word files created?

Having students create a file of words they are studying gives them a tool for learning words. The students can develop word cards similar to their study sheets. They should write the word's meaning, three contexts for the word, two or three synonyms, and a sentence using the word. Students can study these cards for quizzes and for exercises similar to "Possible Sentences," a learning strategy discussed later in this chapter. Word cards are especially useful for struggling readers and English language learners. They can carry the cards with them to study and to refer to when they are writing.

Academic vocabulary is a component of *academic literacy*. According to Lewis (2007), many students who are articulate outside of school lack the experiences, skills, attitudes, formal knowledge, thinking skills, comprehension, language and vocabulary that comprise academic literacy. Furthermore, struggling readers, English language learners, and a large population of other students in middle school, high school, and college lack the academic language for learning.

Academic vocabulary contributes to students' comprehension and communication about content texts that may be disconnected from their experiences. Terms such as *analysis, synthesis, cause and effect* and so forth represent thinking processes that are basic to comprehension. Academic literacy is basic to understanding content textbooks with difficult words that are dependent on the context of specific disciplines. (Academic literacy is discussed in Chapter 5.)

Selecting Words for Direct Instruction

How do teachers choose the words to teach?

SOCIAL STUDIES

Teachers should choose the words that students must understand to achieve the objectives of the lesson. The objectives may be in the text, or the teacher may have formulated objectives related to his or her own goals. Since time is a precious commodity in secondary classes, these targeted words must be selected carefully. For example, in a chapter of a middle school social studies text, the main ideas to develop pertain to Roman government, culture, and belief systems; therefore the key words are **government, culture,** and **belief systems**. The text identifies *acre, series, establish,* and *contain. Acre* is the only word that many students may not know. The other three words can be reviewed when they occur in the text. Although students may know a meaning for each of these words, the context can reveal additional meanings (Curtis and Longo, 2001). When teachers become acquainted with their students, they can anticipate the words students know and words that can be solved through use of context clues or another strategy, such as morphemic analysis.

Morphemic Analysis

What is the basis of morphemic analysis?

Morphemic analysis is based on using prefixes, suffixes, root words, and inflected endings. Prefixes are word parts added to the front of roots, and suffixes are word parts added to the end of roots. Morphological analysis enables students to identify words rapidly and accurately. It is based on identification of a root that carries the base meaning of the word. Affixes, such as prefixes and suffixes, change the base meaning. *Graph* is a root that means "write," as in *autograph*. Many of the roots used in content area writing are from Greek or Latin. Morphological analysis is especially valuable when used in combination with context clues, which help students determine the correct meaning of an affix. Many affixes have multiple meanings, so all meanings that occur frequently should be taught. For example, the suffix *ways* in the word *sideways* can mean "course," "direction," or "manner." When a multiple-meaning affix occurs, students can use context clues to determine which meaning is appropriate. Students can practice using morphological analysis through building new words by combining prefixes and suffixes with various root words. For instance, the word *construct* can be changed in a variety of ways, some of which are illustrated here:

construct	deconstructing	reconstruct
construction	deconstruct	reconstruction

SCIENCE AND HEALTH

To develop a student's morphological analysis skills, teachers can pose questions that will stimulate students to examine the structural aspects of words. Sample questions that might be used to develop vocabulary in a science class follow:

1. If *thermo* means "heat," what is a *thermostat*? A *thermometer*?

2. If *hydro* means "water," what do these words mean: *Dehydrate*? *Hydrophobia*? *Hydrometer*? How is *hydroplane* related to *hydrant*?

3. If *tele* means "far," what are the meanings of these words: *Telescope*? *Television*?

4. If *zoo* means "animal," what is the meaning of *zoology*? Who is a *zoologist*?

5. If *tome* is the act of cutting, what is an *appendectomy*?

6. If *micro* means "small," what is a *microscope*?

7. Why would you call *dynamite* and *dynamo* first cousins?

When teaching morphological analysis, the best beginning point is teaching prefixes which are most useful. Prefixes, such as *pre, tri, bi,* and *un*, are very useful. Struggling readers may benefit from instruction on prefixes, but they may find root words to be difficult. ELLs may be able to relate common word parts from their languages to some related words in English (Mountain, 2005).

Context and Word Knowledge

Contextual analysis involves inferring a word's meaning through reading surrounding text and using syntactic and semantic linguistic clues provided by preceding and succeeding words, phrases, and sentences. Context narrows a word's field of reference and helps specify its meaning. It also builds connections between known and new information. Context is most useful when students are fluent readers who automatically recognize most of the words in a sentence, because they can use the surrounding known words to determine the meanings of unknown words. Context can help students understand content text; however, context alone may not provide enough clues to word meaning.

SOCIAL STUDIES

How does context help develop word meaning?

Teachers facilitate students' learning by encouraging them to read backward and forward to locate clues and to generate hypotheses about word meaning; then students can test alternative possibilities to see if their predicted meaning makes sense. To refine word meaning, readers can use context clues in combination with the dictionary or glossary. For example, the word *rendezvous* appears in this passage: "Bourgoyne took four weeks to reach the Hudson. Still confident, he looked forward to the rendezvous" (Garcia et al., 2001, p. 197). The corresponding glossary provides this definition: "rendezvous (RAHN day voo) n. a meeting" (p. R56). The reader who combines these two sources of information learns that Bourgoyne was planning to meet someone or something. However, the authors of this text also helped the reader by explaining *rendezvous* in the text. The reader continued through the sentence: "Still confident, he looked forward to the rendezvous, or meeting, with St. Leger and Howe in Albany."

In content reading, students may read long selections that lack neat contextual explanations. For this reason, content teachers should teach important words in a text prior to assigning the text to students. The figure on page 119 shows a content text teacher's edition that illustrates this concept.

Context can help the reader select one of several possible meanings among the multiple meanings an English word may have. Students who read widely in material that includes challenging words will improve their vocabularies (Kuhn and Stahl, 2000). Unfortunately, the reverse is also true; students who do not read widely fail to acquire vocabulary, creating a self-defeating cycle. However, direct instruction can build the word knowledge that will permit these students to read widely and subsequently acquire more vocabulary through context, as well. Wide reading is very important for adolescents.

In material written expressly for students, such as textbooks, context clues may be contrived, neatly providing information about an unfamiliar word. However, some selections will not contain clear contextual explanations. After all, authors write to transmit ideas rather than to define vocabulary.

Context Clue Strategies

What do students have to learn about context clues?

Students do not automatically use context to comprehend text. They have to learn to look for and use **context clues**. Greenwood and Flanigan (2007) found that giving students context clue instruction and practice exercises enhanced vocabulary growth. The context in some sentences is thin, which means the sentence does not provide enough explicit context to reveal the meaning of an unknown word. The sentence *We had a frightening experience* does not provide the information needed to identify the word *frightening*. When planning instruction, teachers need to include both thin context sentences and revealing context sentences. Teachers can do think-alouds for students, revealing their thinking as they read a selection and call students' attention to context clues and how to use them.

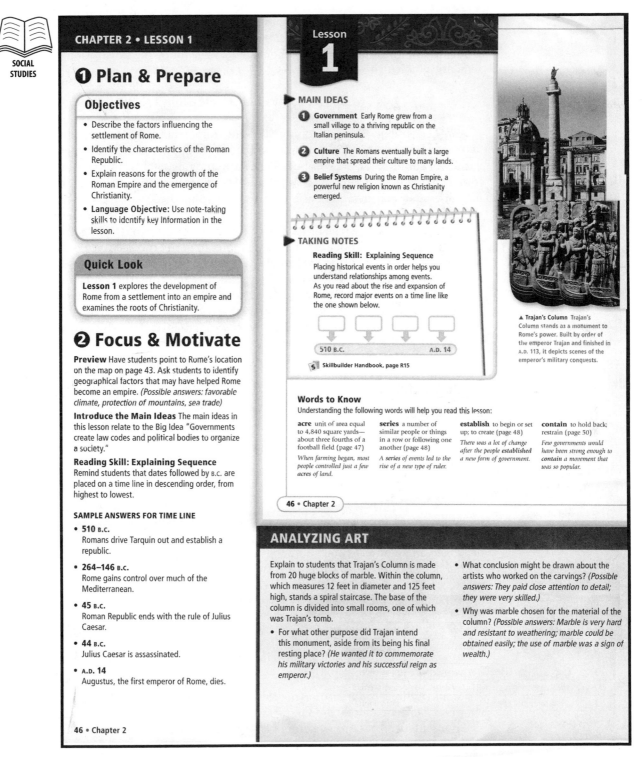

CHAPTER 2 • LESSON 1

SOCIAL STUDIES

❶ Plan & Prepare

Objectives

- Describe the factors influencing the settlement of Rome.
- Identify the characteristics of the Roman Republic.
- Explain reasons for the growth of the Roman Empire and the emergence of Christianity.
- **Language Objective:** Use note-taking skills to identify key information in the lesson.

Quick Look

Lesson 1 explores the development of Rome from a settlement into an empire and examines the roots of Christianity.

❷ Focus & Motivate

Preview Have students point to Rome's location on the map on page 43. Ask students to identify geographical factors that may have helped Rome become an empire. *(Possible answers: favorable climate, protection of mountains, sea trade)*

Introduce the Main Ideas The main ideas in this lesson relate to the Big Idea "Governments create law codes and political bodies to organize a society."

Reading Skill: Explaining Sequence Remind students that dates followed by B.C. are placed on a time line in descending order, from highest to lowest.

SAMPLE ANSWERS FOR TIME LINE

- **510 B.C.**
  Romans drive Tarquin out and establish a republic.

- **264–146 B.C.**
  Rome gains control over much of the Mediterranean.

- **45 B.C.**
  Roman Republic ends with the rule of Julius Caesar.

- **44 B.C.**
  Julius Caesar is assassinated.

- **A.D. 14**
  Augustus, the first emperor of Rome, dies.

46 • Chapter 2

Lesson **1**

▶ **MAIN IDEAS**

❶ **Government** Early Rome grew from a small village to a thriving republic on the Italian peninsula.

❷ **Culture** The Romans eventually built a large empire that spread their culture to many lands.

❸ **Belief Systems** During the Roman Empire, a powerful new religion known as Christianity emerged.

▶ **TAKING NOTES**

Reading Skill: Explaining Sequence
Placing historical events in order helps you understand relationships among events. As you read about the rise and expansion of Rome, record major events on a time line like the one shown below.

510 B.C.   A.D. 14

Ⓢ Skillbuilder Handbook, page R15

▲ **Trajan's Column** Trajan's Column stands as a monument to Rome's power. Built by order of the emperor Trajan and finished in A.D. 113, it depicts scenes of the emperor's military conquests.

Words to Know

Understanding the following words will help you read this lesson:

acre unit of area equal to 4,840 square yards— about three fourths of a football field (page 47)

When farming began, most people controlled just a few acres of land.

series a number of similar people or things in a row or following one another (page 48)

A series of events led to the rise of a new type of ruler.

establish to begin or set up; to create (page 48)

There was a lot of change after the people established a new form of government.

contain to hold back; restrain (page 50)

Few governments would have been strong enough to contain a movement that was so popular.

46 • Chapter 2

ANALYZING ART

Explain to students that Trajan's Column is made from 20 huge blocks of marble. Within the column, which measures 12 feet in diameter and 125 feet high, stands a spiral staircase. The base of the column is divided into small rooms, one of which was Trajan's tomb.

- For what other purpose did Trajan intend this monument, aside from its being his final resting place? *(He wanted it to commemorate his military victories and his successful reign as emperor.)*

- What conclusion might be drawn about the artists who worked on the carvings? *(Possible answers: They paid close attention to detail; they were very skilled.)*

- Why was marble chosen for the material of the column? *(Possible answers: Marble is very hard and resistant to weathering; marble could be obtained easily; the use of marble was a sign of wealth.)*

46 • Chapter 2

Source: From Middle School World History by Douglas Carnine, Carlos Cortes, Kenneth Curtis, and Anita Robinson. Copyright © 2006 used by permission of McDougal Littell Inc., a division of Houghton Mifflin Company.

Both Greenwood and Flanigan (2007), as well as Blachowicz and Fisher (2006), report success with semantic gradients for context clue instruction. Semantic gradients are words placed along a continuum. The following illustration shows a semantic gradient:

Frozen | Ice cold | Cold | Cool | Chilly | Nippy

Another strategy for developing students' understanding of context clues is "Possible Sentences." This strategy gives students opportunities to experience a variety of contexts for the vocabulary they are studying. Stahl and Kapinus (1991) found that "Possible Sentences" significantly improved students' recall of word meanings and their comprehension of text containing those words. With this technique the teacher supplies target words from a selection, and the students try to make sentences that are true or "possible," using two or more of the target words in each sentence. Then students read the textbook to verify the accuracy of the sentences they constructed, and they modify the sentences, if necessary. In a variation of this strategy, the instructor chooses target words and constructs sentences with these words. The sentence context should be "Possible" in some instances and "Impossible" in others. Students can suggest ways to change "Impossible" ones to make them "Possible." When working with struggling readers, this is a practice activity for students to use after they have studied the words and read content including those words. The following sentences illustrate this activity:

1. After lengthy consideration, Melissa made an (impetuous) decision.

2. My mother was (maudlin) after my father's death.

3. Kay was (euphoric) after her dog died.

Kinds of Context Clues

There are both syntactic context clues, derived from the grammatical functions of the unfamiliar word and other words in a sentence, and semantic context clues, derived from the meanings of the other words in a sentence. Sometimes context clues define or explain an unfamiliar word. Sometimes they provide a comparison or contrast of the unknown word with a word that is known or a synonym or antonym of the unfamiliar word. **Figurative language** provides context clues by making abstract and uncommon ideas more concrete. Types of figurative language include the following:

**ENGLISH/
LANGUAGE
ARTS**

1. *Personification.* Human or personal qualities are given to inanimate things or ideas. Katherine Paterson used personification in *Bridge to Terabithia:* "Through his top ear came the sound of the Timmonses' old Buick—'Wants oil,' his dad would say" (Paterson, 1987, p.7).

2. *Simile.* A direct comparison is made between things. The words *like, as . . . as,* and *so . . . as* are frequently used in making the comparisons in similes. An example of a sentence containing a simile is "The thunder reverberated like an entire corps of bass drums."

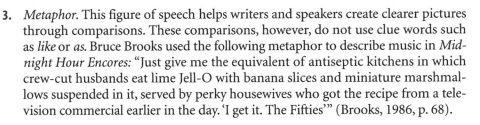

3. *Metaphor.* This figure of speech helps writers and speakers create clearer pictures through comparisons. These comparisons, however, do not use clue words such as *like* or *as.* Bruce Brooks used the following metaphor to describe music in *Midnight Hour Encores:* "Just give me the equivalent of antiseptic kitchens in which crew-cut husbands eat lime Jell-O with banana slices and miniature marshmallows suspended in it, served by perky housewives who got the recipe from a television commercial earlier in the day. 'I get it. The Fifties'" (Brooks, 1986, p. 68).

ENGLISH/
LANGUAGE
ARTS

4. *Hyperbole.* This is an exaggeration used for effect. Katherine Paterson used hyperbole to describe a girl in *Bridge to Terabithia*: "And the littlest one cried if you looked at her cross-eyed" (Paterson, 1987, p. 2).

5. *Euphemism.* Euphemism is used to express disagreeable or unpleasant facts indirectly. Death is often described as "passing away," "going to one's reward," or "going to the final rest."

ENGLISH/
LANGUAGE
ARTS

6. *Allusion.* Allusions are references to information believed to be common knowledge. Allusions are based on the assumption that the reader knows the characters or events, and this knowledge causes the reader to make associations that clarify a point. Mary E. Ryan used the following allusion in *The Trouble with Perfect:* "Brian started making ravenous gurgling sounds and lurching around the kitchen like the Hunchback of Wheaton" (Ryan, 1995, p. 9).

ENGLISH/
LANGUAGE
ARTS

Offer Opportunities to Develop and Expand Meanings

Why offer students opportunities to develop word meanings?

Multiple exposures to words give readers opportunities to move from an initial level of knowing to greater familiarity with the words and concepts. This familiarity enables learners to use the words to acquire additional words and concepts. The activities and strategies introduced throughout this chapter provide opportunities for multiple exposures to words and exploring words in multiple contexts.

Elaboration involves associations between words and meanings. Students who have many associations acquire richer vocabularies. Word knowledge is most effectively elaborated through meaningful, concrete experiences.

The initial level of elaboration is association, wherein the reader associates the term with other words that are often synonyms, which indicates that he or she has some sense of the word's meaning. The second level is comprehension; at this level, the reader recognizes the word and understands its meaning when encountering it in a reading context. Generative processing is the most sophisticated level of word understanding, one that reflects a deep level of cognitive processing. At this level, the reader is fluent enough to produce the target word in a novel context and can use the word to express thoughts in oral and written language. Association, comprehension, and generative processing involve active processing and transfer of knowledge. The latter section of this chapter includes a variety of association activities.

Comprehension activities for vocabulary expansion that are illustrated in this chapter include classification activities for science, **open and closed word sorts** for office procedures, and an open-ended sort for biology. Graphic organizers build comprehension, as does the Super Word Web in Figure 4.1.

FIGURE 4.1

Super Word Web

Source: Andrew Johnson and Jay Rasmussen, "Classifying and Super Word Web: Two Strategies to Improve Productive Vocabulary," *Journal of Adolescent and Adult Literacy* 42(3) (1998, November): 204–207. Reprinted with permission of Andrew Johnson and the International Reading Association. All rights reserved.

SWW is a technique designed to increase vocabulary development by expanding the breadth as well as the depth of students' word knowledge. This technique can be used in any subject area and implemented as either a pre-reading exercise, an advanced organizer, or a separate vocabulary lesson. While SWWs can be constructed individually, they are generally more effective when two or more students work together and share their ideas.

Procedures

Step 1: See the word in context.
Step 2: List three or four synonyms or defining phrases.
Step 3: List or draw three or four associations.

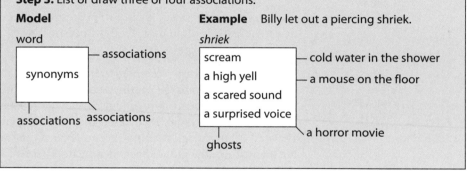

Model

Example   Billy let out a piercing shriek.

Assess Students' Progress in Developing Vocabulary

Consistent assessment of students' progress in learning the vocabulary that is presented in direct instruction lessons enables both teacher and students to recognize their progress. Assessments are often multiple-choice tests in which the students identify the synonym or phrase that best defines a word. Other simple assessments involve giving students lists of words and instructing them to respond with synonyms or antonyms for the target words, having them complete crossword puzzles containing the vocabulary terms, and having teams of students compete in a vocabulary-based quiz show. Students may also be asked to write meaningful sentences using the vocabulary. Each student should maintain a record of his or her vocabulary scores and the words missed.

FOCUS ON   *English Language Learners*

Vocabulary for ELLs

In a sense, English vocabulary may be easier to acquire for secondary ELLs who have previously learned to read in their first language than for those who have not done so. These ELLs are usually in a position to transfer their existing vocabulary knowledge to English. The linguistic resources that these students bring into the classroom provide a foundation for learning English (Greenwood and Flannigan, 2007). Their initial English lessons can focus on existing concepts and vocabulary. ELLs must be able to recognize opportunities for language transfer from their first language to English and be motivated to make the transfer.

Why do ELLs need academic vocabulary?

ELLs need *academic vocabulary*, which is the word knowledge that students need to understand and talk about texts that are valued in school. They need to understand academic vocabulary to ask questions and to follow directions (Flynt and Brozo, 2008). Understanding academic English permits ELLs to learn in content classrooms. ELLs need appropriate English skills to use for various contexts, audiences, and purposes, including those for instructional and other academic purposes.

Context in written language often presents problems for ELLs because their first language may have a different syntax from English. As they progress in reading and learning English, they need to learn how context functions in English. Many of the problems ELLs face in writing are due to the word order function of English. Many of the activities suggested later in this chapter are useful for teaching ELLs. Activities such as "Possible Sentences" and illustrated vocabulary cards are especially useful for ELLs because they help students explore English context.

The following list identifies important emphases the teacher must provide for ELL students:

1. Understand correct word meaning.

2. Use correct pronunciation.

3. Use correct spelling.

4. Use words correctly in context.

5. Use common English phrases correctly.

6. Understand academic vocabulary.

FOCUS ON *Struggling Readers*

Vocabulary for Struggling Readers

Many struggling readers populate the content classes in middle and secondary schools. These students may be able to read general materials, which may lead them to believe that they do not have a reading problem. However, they may not read well enough to understand and apply information in content texts and related materials. Many of these students read well below their grade placements. In fact, it is not uncommon to find such students reading at third- or fourth-grade level. Struggling readers often have weak vocabularies, and the gap between the vocabulary they need for success and the vocabulary they actually have widens as they go through school.

Struggling readers may have difficulty following directions, understanding teachers' questions, participating in class discussions, and taking tests. Adolescents usually do not experience academic vocabulary in out-of-school discourse. They may fail to understand the language of text, the Internet, and technology (Lewis, 2007).

Stoodt-Hill (2005) found that direct instruction is essential for struggling readers. These students may not acquire vocabulary incidentally, because they lack the foundational vocabulary to permit this. Teachers of struggling readers need to devote an adequate amount of instructional time to the task. This amount of time is greater than that needed in average classes. Struggling readers need at least ten to fifteen encounters with each word's meaning (Curtis and Longo, 2001). Teaching ten or twenty vocabulary words at a time is too many. Knowing five to seven words is more desirable for students than studying too many words and failing to learn any vocabulary. The next "Meeting the Challenge" feature illustrates this situation.

What characteristic is important to successful vocabulary programs for struggling readers?

Research indicates that the most successful vocabulary programs for struggling readers are based on direct teaching of word meanings. It also shows that struggling readers need many opportunities to generate contexts for the words they are learning (Stoodt-Hill, 2005). Understanding the various contexts in which a word makes sense is difficult for struggling readers (Stoodt-Hill, 2005). Activities such as "Possible Sentences" and making vocabulary word cards will help students enrich their understanding of vocabulary. The following guidelines for teaching struggling readers emerged from research (Curtis and Longo, 2001; Joseph, 2006; Stoodt-Hill, 2005):

Students need:

To have daily, direct instruction.

To have vocabulary presented with definitions in language that students understand.

To make connections to what is already known.

To have repeated encounters with the same words in various contexts.

To develop their own contexts for the vocabulary they are studying.

To develop strategies for acquiring a deeper knowledge of vocabulary, such as word maps, association activities, in-depth word study, sorts, classifications, and mnemonic instruction.

To have regular quizzes to assess their progress.

Activities for Struggling Readers

Many of the activities in this chapter are appropriate for struggling readers. When teaching vocabulary, teachers have learned to use material that they use in regular classrooms. Practice with especially prepared exercises that are unrelated to class materials does not help students learn. Strategies such as think-alouds, previewing the text, identifying main ideas, and using graphic organizers are best applied to classroom textbooks.

MEETING THE CHALLENGE

Tinsley Washington teaches developmental reading to students in grades nine through twelve in a county school system that serves a culturally diverse student population of city, suburban, and rural students. The school system recognized the students' significant vocabulary problems and adopted instructional materials that introduce ten words per week. Previously, it had adopted a vocabulary program that included memorizing the definitions of a required list of twenty words. These were generally words that the students had never encountered before. Simply memorizing the definitions did not give students the ability to use the words appropriately, and they quickly forgot the words.

Reduced list length is important because, although it may slow the acquisition of vocabulary some, when students actually know words, they can use them effectively enough that context becomes more helpful. Definitions and context are now the focus of lessons. Multiple-choice tests are included for assessment. The description below illustrates the challenges Tinsley encounters in teaching vocabulary.

Tinsley introduced a lesson to ninth-grade struggling readers that included these words: *delete*, *menace*, *impartial*, *morale*, *integrity*, *naive*, *legitimate*, *overt*, *lenient*, *undermine*. On a pretest, all of the students received a grade of zero. Then she introduced the words in the context provided by the text.

After organizing the students in groups of three, she instructed them to write sentences using the target words in appropriate contexts. The students loudly objected. Their argument was that they had never heard any of these words and they had no use for them because they would never use them in their daily writing or conversation. She explained the importance of vocabulary knowledge in learning and in employment, but the students remained unconvinced.

Tinsley decided that a new plan was essential. After considerable thought, she collected newspapers, magazines, speeches (from the Internet), and pages from content textbooks that the students would be required to read. Her next assignment required each student to read two selections from the collection and circle all of the unknown words. Through this assignment the students began to recognize that they needed to learn words in order to succeed. Tinsley started with the words they identified as unknown and expanded their word bank by having them examine more written materials and listen to television news, as well as to science and history television programs. After the students grew accustomed to recognizing unknown words and learning them, she was able to integrate words from the class text. The students continued to have problems with appropriate context because they did not understand the multiple meanings of many English words. However, they became more motivated as they saw the value of words in their lives. These students illustrate the difficulties that struggling secondary students face as they attempt to gain more education. In later sections, we introduce teaching and learning strategies to help students like these to succeed.

Teachers cannot teach all of the words that students will need to know for successful content-area learning, but direct instruction can be a springboard for independent vocabulary growth. The words learned through direct instruction create a foundation for acquiring additional words. Moreover, students can use the strategies learned in direct instruction for amassing a larger bank of word knowledge.

To build background and vocabulary for content-area reading, students need to see multiple relationships among words and concepts. Conceptual activities and mind maps contribute to the building of multiple relationships through instruction.

Background Building

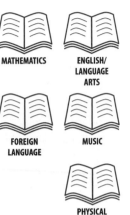

MATHEMATICS

ENGLISH/
LANGUAGE
ARTS

FOREIGN
LANGUAGE

MUSIC

PHYSICAL
EDUCATION

Vicarious experiences can support vocabulary development, but learning is more complete when it is attached to concrete experience. A student who encounters the term *intersect* in a mathematics text will understand it better because of his or her familiarity with street intersections. However, students cannot have direct experience with every concept they encounter in reading. Thus, teachers must help students build both direct and indirect experience through field trips, exhibits, dramatizations, videos, television, resource persons, and pictures. They can help students relate their own experiences to the passages they read. Computerized encyclopedias enable students to hear different languages, the sounds of musical instruments, and so forth, which enrich conceptual understanding. Moreover, the networking of concepts in multimedia materials enhances conceptual development. Of course, there are many multimedia programs that enhance learning in diverse areas of study. These programs often accompany both textbooks and trade books. The Internet provides a variety of programs to enhance learning.

Discussion

How does discussion relate to learning words?

Discussion helps students associate word pronunciation and meaning, as well as relate existing experiences and word knowledge to new vocabulary. For example, vocabulary instruction can proceed by asking students to think of and share ideas, synonyms, definitions, and associated words related to specified vocabulary terms. These words and ideas can be grouped in a chart, a computerized matrix, or a mind map.

Another strategy to help students see a word in a broader context is to have them answer questions like these: (1) What is it? (2) What is it like? (3) What are some examples? (4) What is the opposite? (5) What is your meaning for this word? These questions help students see relationships between familiar and less familiar terms and bring the meaning of an unknown term into focus.

The many instructional ideas we discuss in the following sections represent procedures and methods that teachers can build into their content area instruction. As with all vocabulary instruction, the overall goal is students' autonomy in learning, understanding, and using words. As teachers model and demonstrate the various word strategies and ways of figuring out word meanings and associations, the underlying goal is to help students internalize these strategies for eventual independent use in their reading.

Conceptual Relationships

How are conceptual relationships organized?

Conceptual relationships can be organized in various ways, such as class relations and examples and nonexamples. *Class relations* are hierarchical networks. For example, chromosomes are a part of the hereditary material in cells, and genes are

SCIENCE AND
HEALTH

SCIENCE AND
HEALTH

found within chromosomes. *Examples* demonstrate a concept, whereas *nonexamples* demonstrate what the concept is not; recognizing both can facilitate learning. For example, both dominant genes and recessive genes are examples of genes. Chromosomes are nonexamples of genes.

Learning ideas and their connections is more effective than learning lists of independent facts which can overwhelm students with the constant need to respond to each separate incident, object, or idea as unique. For example, developing a science concept for "organ" would include linking it to familiar ideas, as in "organs of the body such as the liver and the kidney," which is more effective than learning "The kidney is defined as. . . . The liver is. . . ." Recognizing the connections enhances understanding and memory.

Mind mapping is a way of pouring ideas onto paper. Through mapping, teachers and learners can enhance their thinking skills. Mind Mapping is a form of visual note taking and a way of showing connections among ideas, solving problems, and helping students remember and review. Mind mappers use a central image, key words, colors, codes, and symbols to put ideas on paper; all of these components make ideas more concrete and the connections more vivid. Mind maps are flexible and adaptable to many situations, such as learning words, showing comprehension, making plans, and studying for tests.

Mind maps have become very popular in business and industry which has led to an explosion of related websites. Simply entering the words "mind mapping" in your search engine will produce a plethora of information. Many sites offer free mapping and show students exactly how to create mind maps. Teachers can explore the list of sites and identify those that offer students good instructions. The mind map in Figure 4.2 on page 128 illustrates science vocabulary.

Conceptual relationships can be shown on **semantic maps** (or webs) that don't have the illustrations that are found in mind maps, but rely completely on printed words that are connected with lines. These maps are important in content area study because they develop conceptual understanding. Conceptual understanding evolves from four mental operations, which are emphasized in the reinforcement activities of this chapter. Reinforcement activities to build vocabulary should incorporate these mental operations:

1. Recognizing and generating critical attributes—both examples and nonexamples— of a concept.

2. Seeing relationships between the concept to be learned and what is already known.

3. Applying the concept to a variety of contexts.

4. Generating new contexts for the learned concept.

The **Frayer Model** (Frayer, Frederick, and Klausmeier, 1969) helps students develop a more complete understanding of the facets of a newly acquired concept. This model calls for the inclusion of examples, nonexamples, essential characteristics, and nonessential characteristics to extend learning. In developing a concept of *democratic government*, for example, students can identify governments that are not democratic,

FIGURE 4.2

Mind Map for Science Vocabulary

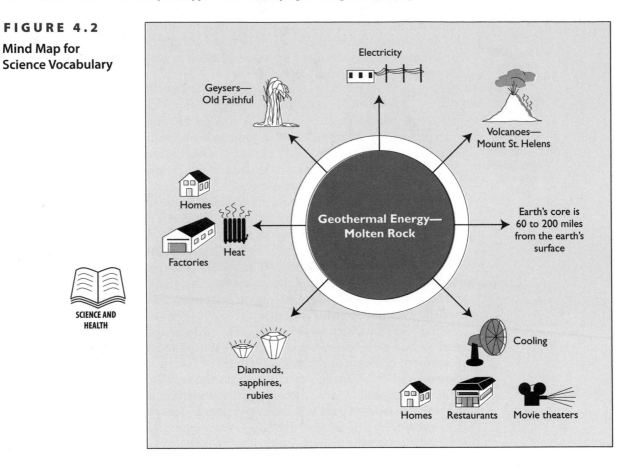

SCIENCE AND HEALTH

as well as ones that are democratic and can explain why a particular government is an example or nonexample. Schwartz and Raphael (1985) developed a word map based on identification of classification, attributes, and examples of the word under study. Example 4.1 illustrates an activity that emphasizes classification of examples.

EXAMPLE 4.1 | **Types of Taxes**

BUSINESS EDUCATION

Directions: Write examples of each type of taxes on the lines provided.

Direct Taxes	Indirect Taxes	Pay as You Go Tax
_____	_____	_____
_____	_____	_____
_____	_____	_____

Note: Example was developed for use with a section of the textbook *Economic Education for Consumers* by Roger Miller and Alan Stafford. South-Western/Cengage, 2010.

Conceptual Reinforcement Instructional Activities ▬▬▬▬

How do attribute relations relate to concept development?

Attribute relations provide an organizational network focusing on concept characteristics. Students use their existing concepts to learn new concepts and conceptual relationships. For example, students have knowledge about *horses*, which helps them understand a connected concept, *unicorns*, which may be encountered in a literature selection. Related concepts can be compared using **semantic feature analysis**. The attributes of the familiar words in a feature analysis give students a basis for comparison with the new words from their textbooks. For example, in the following semantic feature analysis (Example 4.2), students could begin with geometric figures. Then the teacher might develop the grid of vocabulary words and features, or attributes, related to them and let the students complete the grid by putting Xs in appropriate cells—the ones in which the rows for specific terms intersect with columns that represent features related to those terms—or the students and teacher could develop the grid together as the terms are discussed.

EXAMPLE 4.2   **Semantic Feature Analysis for Geometric Figures**

MATHEMATICS

	3 sides	All sides of equal length	2 sides of equal length	Contains a 90-degree angle
Isosceles triangle	x		x	
Scalene triangle	x			
Equilateral triangle	x	x		
Right triangle	x			x

Example 4.3 shows some questions that will help students think about conceptual relationships in exploring business concepts.

EXAMPLE 4.3   **Business Concepts**

BUSINESS EDUCATION

1. How does the author help you understand total quality management?

Deming began by studying how companies ensure that the products they produce are not defective. He came up with a mathematically based approach to quality control that became known as total quality management.

2. Why is it important to ensure quality control?

Total quality management (TQM) is a system of management based on involving all employees in a constant process of improving quality and productivity by improving how they work. This approach, which has been widely adopted by American businesses, focuses on totally satisfying both customers and employees.

Source: Leslie W. Rue and Lloyd L. Byars, *Business Management* (New York: Glencoe McGraw-Hill, 2001), p. 45. Reprinted by permission of Glencoe McGraw-Hill.

SOCIAL
STUDIES

Association activities can help students relate concepts to the words that represent them. We can learn unknown words by connecting them with known words that have similar meanings. Students can learn vocabulary for a field trip by viewing a video, listening to a speaker, or reading a text. Students preparing to visit a local courthouse may encounter such terms as *attorney*, *litigation*, *defendant*, and *prosecutor*. Teachers can introduce appropriate words on the board, pronounce them, and discuss their meanings, thus giving students opportunities to associate the visual forms of the words with the pronunciations and the meanings. In addition to discussion (which was introduced earlier in the chapter), association activities include matching exercises, in-depth word study, crossword puzzles, analogies, sorts, and graphic organizers, which can be used for prereading activities or for review. Example 4.4 is an association activity based on a world history text, Example 4.5 is based on a science chapter entitled "States of Matter," and Example 4.6 is based on a chapter on disease from a biology textbook.

EXAMPLE 4.4   History Association Activity

SOCIAL
STUDIES

Directions: Draw a line to connect the words in Column A with the words and phrases that are related in Column B.

A	*B*
Executive	Supreme Court
Legislative	President
Judicial	Senator
Lifetime appointment	Congressman
Four-year terms	
Two-year terms	
Six-year terms	

EXAMPLE 4.5   **Science Association Activity**

SCIENCE AND
HEALTH

Directions: Write *S* on the line beside a set of terms if they have the same meaning. Write *D* on the line if the terms have different meanings.

_____ tensile strength—can be pulled apart easily
_____ matter—gas
_____ malleability—lumpiness
_____ ductility—can be drawn into wires

EXAMPLE 4.6   **Science Association Activity**

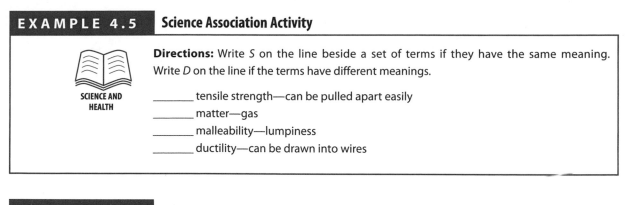

SCIENCE AND
HEALTH

Directions: Write each term from the list below on the line beside its meaning.

hypertension
hyperventilate
hyperthyroidism
hyperglycemic

_____ high blood pressure
_____ excessive production of glucose in the blood
_____ excessive production of thyroid hormones
_____ breathe fast and shallow

In-depth word study increases knowledge of word meanings through association. Students using this strategy study all aspects of a word, along with words that are related to it. The content teacher may identify specific words for such study or may ask students to identify words they feel they need to study in greater depth. Students can use their textbooks, a dictionary, and a thesaurus to obtain the necessary information. This activity is illustrated in Example 4.7, which is an in-depth word study of the word *economy*, selected from a social studies text.

EXAMPLE 4.7   **In-Depth Word Study**

SOCIAL
STUDIES

Economy: The management of the resources of a country, community, or business: the American economy.

Related Words and Meanings

Economy: (a second meaning) The careful or thrifty use or management of resources; freedom from waste; thrift.
Economics: The science of the production, distribution, and consumption of wealth.

Word Forms

economic, economical, economically, economics, economize, economization, economizer

Opposing Concepts that Relate to Economic Activities

liberal	frugal
generous	miserly
wasteful	thrifty
careless	prudent
spend	amass

MATHEMATICS

Analogies show a relationship or similarity between two words or ideas. Analogy activities are conceptual and associational, comparing two similar relationships. On one side of the analogy, the two objects or concepts are related in a particular way; on the other side, the objects are related in the same way. For example, in the analogy *triangle : three :: square : four*, the relationship is "geometric figure is to number of sides." An analogy has equal or balanced sides, like those in a mathematical equation.

Content teachers can demonstrate to students how analogies work and how to construct them. After learning how to form analogies, students can create their own. This kind of study is especially helpful for college-bound students, who will discover that analogies are popular items on college entrance examinations. Secondary school students are often unfamiliar with the format of analogies; therefore, teachers should explain that the colon (:) represents the words *is to*, and the double colon (::) represents the word *as*. The teacher can provide examples of analogies for the entire class to work through in preparation for analogy practice activities. When working through an analogy example, students should identify the relationship, complete the analogy, and explain their reasoning. Example 4.8 shows an analogy example prepared for a science textbook chapter.

E X A M P L E   4 . 8   **Science Analogy Exercise**

SCIENCE AND
HEALTH

Directions: Select the answer that completes each analogy. Identify the relationship expressed in the analogy, and be prepared to explain your answer.

1. water : dehydration :: vitamins : (mumps, deficiency diseases, jaundice, appendicitis)
2. taste buds : tongue :: villi : (mouth, stomach, small intestine, colon)
3. pepsin : protein :: ptyalin : (oils, fats, starch, sucrose)
4. liver : small intestine :: salivary glands : (mouth, stomach, small intestine, colon)
5. mouth : large intestine :: duodenum : (esophagus, jejunum, ileum, cecum)

6. protein : organic compound :: magnesium : (peptide, vitamin, mineral, salt)

7. pancreas : pancreatic fluid :: stomach : (water, saliva, gastric juices, intestinal fluid)

8. saliva : ptyalin :: pancreatic fluid : (trypsin, amylase, lipase, peptones)

Classification activities help students learn words and concepts by connecting new words with known concepts. When classifying, the student arranges items or information into a given set of categories. There are three steps: (1) identify the categories and their meanings, (2) read the items, and (3) group the items by similarities and association (Johnson and Rasmussen, 1998). To prepare for this activity, the teacher identifies focus words to introduce and writes familiar synonyms or associated words on cards. After being introduced, the new words become category headings, and the students classify the cards according to their relationships to the new words. A classification activity is illustrated in Example 4.9.

Sorts are a classification activity. The items in sorts are categorized according to common characteristics. Sorts may be closed-ended or open-ended. In closed-ended sorts, the common properties of the category are stated, and the students sort words into the categories. In open-ended sorts, no category is stated, and students have to identify the relationships among the concepts, group them together, and define the connection. Example 4.10 illustrates a closed-ended sort, and Example 4.11 illustrates an open-ended sort.

EXAMPLE 4.9 **Classification Activity for Science**

SCIENCE AND HEALTH

Directions: Read the target terms, and classify the terms in the word bank into the correct classifications. Then write a short paragraph that includes these terms on the back of this paper.

Target terms:

    Geothermal energy   *Fossil fuel*

Word bank:

    (Written on cards for students to sort.)

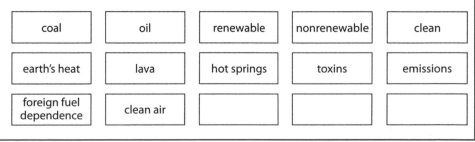

coal	oil	renewable	nonrenewable	clean
earth's heat	lava	hot springs	toxins	emissions
foreign fuel dependence	clean air			

EXAMPLE 4.10   **Closed-Ended Sort for Human Environmental Science (Human Ecology)**

HES/HUMAN ECOLOGY

Directions: Sort the list of words into the following categories: **Foods That Are High in Nutrients** and **Foods That Are Not High in Nutrients**. Be prepared to defend your choices.

chicken	eggs	biscuits	pears
potato chips	Chocolate candy	spinach	yogurt
sweet potatoes	asparagus	Cream sauces	All day suckers

EXAMPLE 4.11   **Open-Ended Sort for Office Procedures**

BUSINESS EDUCATION

Directions: Classify the following list of words into groups, and identify the common characteristic of each group.

sales invoice	multicopy
purchase order	purchase invoice
bills	horizontal spaces
sales order	binding space
credit memorandum	credit approval

Visual Organizers

Visual organizers can develop depth and breadth of word knowledge and are very useful as prereading activities with large or small groups (Johnson and Rasmussen, 1998). The new vocabulary is introduced and defined in advance. Figure 4.1, earlier in this chapter, showed a Super Word Web (SWW).

Graphic organizers or structured overviews can illustrate hierarchical and/or linear relationships among the key concepts in a content textbook, chapter, or unit. Graphic organizer use is based on Ausubel's (1978) theory that an orderly arrangement of concepts helps students learn them. A graphic organizer gives students a structure for incorporating new concepts with existing concepts, thus helping them anticipate the words and concepts in a content selection.

Hierarchical graphic organizers are used when the relationships portrayed fit into a subordinate–superordinate array. The social studies content in Example 4.12 fits into a hierarchical array. Barron (1969) recommended the following steps for developing structured overviews:

1. Identify the words (concepts) that are important for students to understand.

2. Arrange the words (concepts) into a structure that illustrates the interrelationships among them.

3. Add to the structure words (concepts) that the students understand in order to show the relationship between the specific learning task at hand and the discipline.

4. Analyze the overview. Are the major relationships shown clearly? Can the overview be simplified and still communicate the important relationships?

The relationships in a structured overview are usually arranged in the following manner:

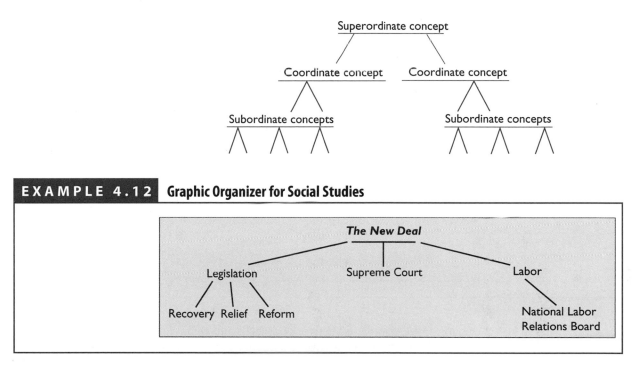

EXAMPLE 4.12 **Graphic Organizer for Social Studies**

The New Deal

Legislation — Supreme Court — Labor

Recovery Relief Reform

National Labor Relations Board

Additional Strategies for Students' Vocabulary Learning

The following additional strategies focus on giving students autonomy in acquiring word meanings. They include making webs, using reference books, expanding meanings, using word walls, using mnemonic strategies, and using computer programs and the Internet.

Students can create a web of words (a type of graphic organizer) structured upon a root. Webs may be developed by groups of students or by students working alone. Example 4.13 on page 136 illustrates a web for the root *migr*, and Example 4.14 on page 137 illustrates a word web for mathematics.

Learners find it easier to assimilate new information and to use prior knowledge when they have more connections and interconnections (Rosenshine, 1997).

EXAMPLE 4.13 **Web Graphic Organizer**

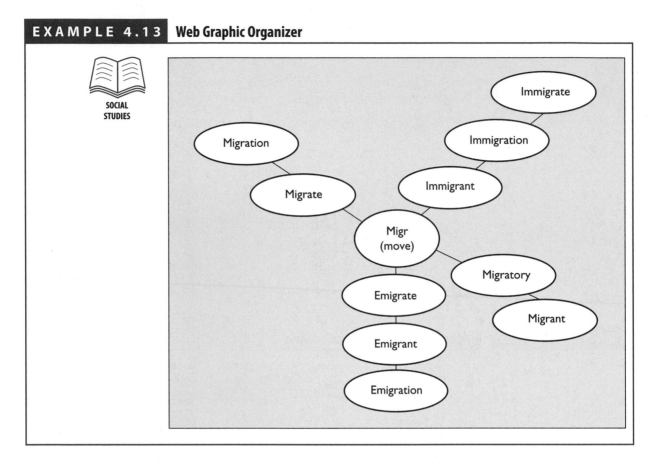

SOCIAL
STUDIES

Having a well-connected network of words and rich relationships among concepts makes information meaningful to students and gives them structures for enlarging their word knowledge. Example 4.15 on page 138 illustrates one approach to "Finding Connections" applied to earth science vocabulary.

Using Reference Books

Why is learning to use dictionaries and thesauruses essential to studying word meanings?

Reference books, such as dictionaries, thesauruses, and encyclopedias, either printed, computer-based, or Internet-based, are useful for developing word meanings. Students can use these reference books in conjunction with prior knowledge, context, and morphological analysis to build understanding. Teaching students how to use dictionaries and thesauruses is essential since many English words have multiple meanings and students have to choose the appropriate meaning for the context. Struggling readers and ELLs have particular difficulties choosing appropriate meanings. Here are suggestions related to use of reference materials:

1. Dictionaries are plentiful in print and on the Internet. Classrooms should have current printed dictionaries and make use of computer software or Internet

EXAMPLE 4.14   **Word Web for Mathematics**

MATHEMATICS

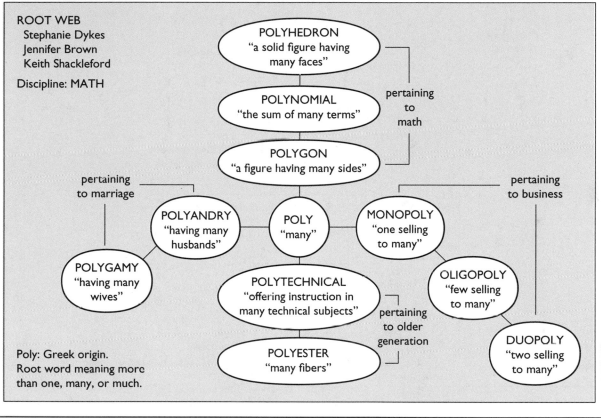

ROOT WEB
Stephanie Dykes
Jennifer Brown
Keith Shackleford

Discipline: MATH

POLYHEDRON
"a solid figure having many faces"

POLYNOMIAL
"the sum of many terms"

POLYGON
"a figure having many sides"

pertaining to math

pertaining to marriage

POLYANDRY
"having many husbands"

POLY
"many"

MONOPOLY
"one selling to many"

pertaining to business

POLYGAMY
"having many wives"

POLYTECHNICAL
"offering instruction in many technical subjects"

OLIGOPOLY
"few selling to many"

pertaining to older generation

POLYESTER
"many fibers"

DUOPOLY
"two selling to many"

Poly: Greek origin.
Root word meaning more than one, many, or much.

dictionaries, as well. To access dictionaries on the Internet, enter the address dictionaries_on_line.com, and a long list of dictionaries will appear; some of these are free and some have a charge.

2. Thesauruses are very useful for developing understanding of word meanings, particularly synonyms. Classrooms should have printed thesauruses. The dictionary style is preferable. Thesauruses are also widely available online.

Mountain (2008) recommends introducing the thesaurus by dividing the class into teams and asking students to brainstorm synonyms for an overused word, such as *secret*. After students make lists of the synonyms they have brainstormed, they are introduced to the thesaurus, where they find a treasure trove of synonyms. Thesaurus users expand their word meanings and they learn about shades of meaning, which is especially important for secondary students. Activities such as synonym tic-tac-toe, cross-synonym puzzles, and choosing the synonym to fit the context are illustrated in an article by Mountain (2008).

ENGLISH/
LANGUAGE
ARTS

| EXAMPLE 4.15 | Finding Connections: Earth Science Vocabulary |

SCIENCE AND HEALTH

Term (Key Concept)

Renewable Energy

Meaning (from text)

Energy resources that are replaced almost as fast as they are used.

Sentence (in which word occurred)

Water power, wind power, and solar energy are examples of renewable energy sources.

Examples

| 1. Hydroelectric power | 2. Windmills | 3. Sun |

Relate to preceding or succeeding unit, chapter, or lesson.

Nonrenewable energy sources in preceding unit means the opposite of renewable energy sources.

3. Identify only a few key words for dictionary study. It is perfectly legitimate for teachers to tell students the meanings of unknown words. Secondary students generally are more willing to use the dictionary when they need it if the teacher has not forced them to use it constantly.

Expanding Meaning

Readers have to integrate new words and concepts with existing knowledge in order to apply them in subsequent learning. Definitions alone provide only superficial word knowledge. Looking up words in a dictionary or memorizing definitions does not reliably increase reading comprehension (Joseph, 2006). Teachers who have tried this method alone will attest to its failure.

EXAMPLE 4.16   **Expanding Definitions**

1. Use the word in a sentence that shows its meaning.
   I am an *autonomous* person, who manages my own finances.
2. Give a synonym for the word.
   Autonomous—independent
3. Give an antonym for the word.
   Autonomous—dependent
4. State a classification for the word.
   Autonomy is a quality of character
5. Provide an example of the word. Either draw an illustration or locate a picture to illustrate it, if possible.
6. Compare the word with another word.
   Autonomy is like self-governing.

A strictly definitional approach to teaching word meanings fails for a variety of reasons. First, many definitions are not very clear or precise, as illustrated in the following examples:

Sedimentary: Of, containing, resembling, or derived from sediment.
Hogweed: Any of various coarse, weedy plants.

These definitions are accurate, but they would not help a person who did not already know the word meanings. Most of the words in a definition should be familiar to students if they are to understand the definition. In addition, using a form of the defined word in its definition further obscures the meaning, and this occurs in both of the preceding examples.

A second reason that strictly definitional approaches fail is that students may have difficulty choosing the correct definition for a particular context from the several definitions that are given in a dictionary or glossary. Third, many definitions do not give enough information to help students understand words for concepts with which they are unfamiliar. Fourth, definitions do not help learners use a new word. Research shows that students have difficulty writing meaningful sentences utilizing new words when given only definitions of those words (Miller and Gildea, 1987).

Definitions that students themselves generate help them relate new words to prior experiences. Thus, activities like the ones shown in Examples 4.16 and 4.17 are useful in developing students' understanding.

Word Walls

Word walls are effective instructional tools in secondary content classrooms (Harmon et al., 2009). Word walls expand content vocabulary knowledge. They help students develop word consciousness and motivation. Word walls give students multiple exposures to words and develop associative learning which

EXAMPLE 4.17   Content Concept Development for Business Management

	Concept word and definition	Classification	Example	Synonym	Antonym	Benefits
BUSINESS EDUCATION	*Networking:* talking to people who may offer you job leads, contacts, or other information	Career strategy	Talking with the school guidance counselor or business acquaintances	*connecting*	*disassociating*	Career planning Job leads Informed planning

relates new words to existing knowledge. Students like the fact that they have control over their learning.

Key words can be written on charts as they are introduced, and the charts can serve as reminders for students. One of the most important factors when introducing word walls is the interaction among students and teachers. Another major factor is the fact that teachers prepare students to think about four levels of word knowledge (Bauman et al., 2003). Interaction enables students to relate meaning to the words and develop individual ways of remembering words. Each individual can find something to serve as a reminder, such as a color or a symbol. This process can be especially effective for struggling readers.

ENGLISH/ LANGUAGE ARTS   MATHEMATICS

Students use word walls for studying, writing, completing assignments, and remembering. The words on word wall charts in content classes can be content specific. Mathematics teachers can use word walls to illustrate math symbols, while literacy teachers can introduce prefixes and suffixes, for example.

Mnemonic Strategies

Mnemonics is a memory-enhancing instructional strategy that involves teaching students to relate new information to existing knowledge. Research with mnemonic strategies verifies the value of these approaches (Mastropieri and Scruggs, 2000; Stoodt-Hill, 2005).

In the classroom, teachers can use these steps to create mnemonics for vocabulary words:

- Identify the word (e.g., "ostentatious").
- Define the word (e.g., "showy, elaborate").
- Write the word on a file card.
- Think of a key word. (Students discuss key words, but each chooses one that will trigger his or her memory.) Write this on the card.
- Draw a picture on the card to help memory. (Students may use stick figures, cartoon-like pictures, or magazine pictures.)

Example 4.18 shows mnemonic vocabulary cards prepared by students.

EXAMPLE 4.18 **Mnemonic Vocabulary Cards Prepared by Students**

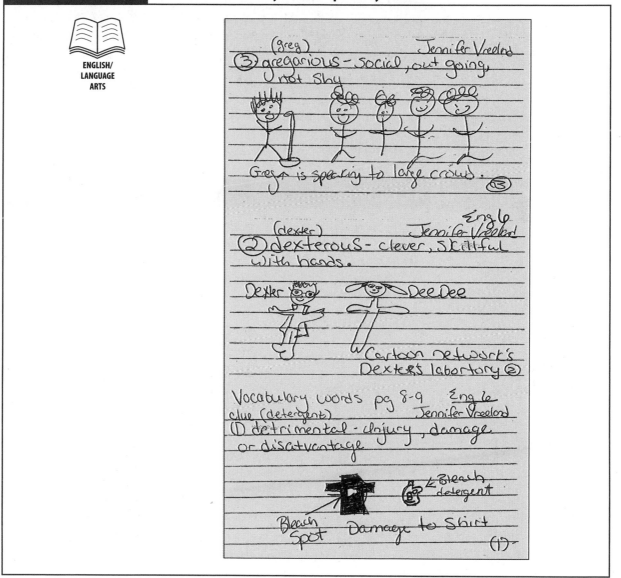

ENGLISH/
LANGUAGE
ARTS

Computer Software and the Internet

Computer programs that can help students to develop extensive word understanding are available. Such programs can be motivational learning tools for students, and students can use them independently. The most common types of computer software for vocabulary instruction are cloze passage programs; structural analysis programs; homonym, synonym, and antonym programs; computer dictionaries; and computer thesauruses. The specific software selected depends both on the type of computer available and on the instructional objectives. Software and computers are constantly being changed and upgraded; therefore, it is difficult to recommend specific materials. We do recommend that teachers read this chapter and Chapter 2 carefully to establish criteria for the vocabulary software they wish to use and that they evaluate available materials based on their own requirements.

The Internet offers a variety of excellent vocabulary websites. One such site is found at http://www.vocabulary.com. This is a dynamic site, so the activities it provides will vary from time to time. It is used in the next "Meeting the Challenge," which tells about Emily, who is an eighth-grade student in a Virginia middle school.

MEETING THE CHALLENGE

Emily was a student with average grades who was eager to improve them, so she asked her guidance counselor for assistance. The counselor arranged for testing, which revealed that Emily's vocabulary and fluency were limited. These limitations were influencing her achievement in social studies, science, and English. Unfortunately, the reading teacher reported a full schedule of students whose needs were greater. However, the reading teacher suggested that she go to the computer lab for assistance in accessing Vocabulary.com.

Emily was skeptical about using the computer, but she agreed to give it a try. With the instructor's assistance in the computer lab, she logged on to the site.

Level II, the middle-school level, seemed to be the right one for Emily. She started with fill-in-the-blank items based on the roots *ject, lect, leg, lig, pend, pent*. The meanings of these roots and the context provided in the puzzle were very helpful. After completing the blanks, she submitted the exercise to the site administrator; she received a page that showed her answers and the correct answers and a page of correct definitions with examples of the words used in sentences. Then she moved to a match-the-definition exercise with the same words, including *objective, pendant, diligently, perpendicular, intelligentsia, illegible, conjecture, legacy, pendulum, adjacent, projection*, and *appendage*. Synonym-and-antonym word encounters with the same set of words came up next, followed by a crossword puzzle based on these words. After completing these four meaningful exercises with a single set of words, Emily developed some confidence that significantly increased the following day, when she encountered two of these words in textbook assignments.

As Emily progressed, her content teachers became interested and encouraged other students to use the computer to expand their vocabularies. The teachers also discovered vocabulary activities for novels they were teaching as well as topical vocabularies that fit into their teaching plans.

Summary

Students who have large stores of word meanings comprehend content materials better than students who have limited vocabularies. Since many of the words used in content materials are labels for content-area concepts, concept development is also an important goal of content-area instruction. Knowing a word means understanding the concept it represents and the ability to use it in various contexts. Because content materials frequently contain a high proportion of unknown words, it is impossible for teachers to teach students every word they do not know. Therefore, teachers should focus on key vocabulary as well as on developing students' independent word-learning skills. Research shows that direct teaching of vocabulary increases students' word knowledge. Struggling readers and English language learners often have difficulty with academic English vocabulary and are especially responsive to direct instruction.

Discussion Questions

1. Why is word knowledge so important to comprehension?
2. What does it mean to know a word?
3. What are the weaknesses of a definitional approach to developing vocabulary?
4. Explain the meaning of *concepts* in your own words.
5. What are the strengths and weaknesses of context clues in deriving word meanings?
6. Why do you think practice is so important in developing students' ability to derive meaning from context?
7. What basic principles should teachers know in order to develop vocabulary with struggling readers?
8. Compare vocabulary instruction for English language learners with instruction for struggling readers.
9. Why is learning English vocabulary and concepts usually easier for ELLs who have a well-developed first language?
10. Why is direct instruction so helpful for students learning word meanings?

Enrichment Activities

1. Prepare a categorization activity, as illustrated in Examples 4.9 through 4.11, for a chapter from a content area textbook or nonfiction trade book of your choice.
*2. Prepare seven activities to develop vocabulary for a particular trade book or textbook.
3. Select a chapter in a content area book, and identify the vocabulary you would teach to a class. Plan ways to teach the chosen terms. Following is a list of content areas and the key terms that might be found in a chapter in each area:

> *Math:* kilometer, decimeter, millimeter, meter, centimeter
> *Music:* choreographer, prologue, prompter, score, overture, prelude, libretto, aria
> *Health:* bacteria, virus, protozoan, metazoan, fungus, carbuncle, psoriasis, shingles, scabies, eczema
> *Foreign language:* masculine, feminine, gender, predicate, cognate, singular
> *Art:* introspective, mural, appreciation, technique, expression, property, exhibition, contemporary, interpret

Psychology: learning curve, plateau, hierarchy, massed practice, feedback, frame, negative transfer, retention, overlearning

Government: delinquent, incorrigibility, omnibus, exigency, indeterminate, adjudicated, arbitrariness, interrogation, formulation, juvenile

4. Develop a procedure for in-depth study of a word.

*5. Make a graphic organizer for a selection in a content area textbook or a nonfiction trade book.

6. Prepare an analogy exercise sheet (similar to the one in Example 4.8) for a chapter or unit in a content area text.

*7. Visit Vocabulary.com and complete some of the exercises available.

*8. Plan a lesson for struggling readers using a text chapter from a content area text.

*9. Plan a lesson for English language learners (ELLs) using a text chapter from a content area text.

---

*These activities are designed for in-service teachers, student teachers, and practicum students.

Resources including the TeachSource Video Cases can be found on the website for this book. Cengage Learning's CourseMate brings course concepts to life with interactive learning, study, and exam preparation tools that support the printed textbook. Go to www.cengage.com/login to register your access code.

CHAPTER 5

The Process of Constructing Meaning in Texts

Overview

One has only to read "help wanted" advertising on the Internet, local job postings and the newspaper "want ads" to know that our economy has few jobs for people who lack higher levels of literacy. Moreover, the demand for a literate citizenry will dramatically increase in the future because fewer and fewer jobs will be available for those who lack advanced literacy development. Comprehension is a major aspect of literacy development. Students need to understand content whether they are reading electronic bulletin boards, e-mail messages, newsgroups, textbooks, or trade books or writing comprehensible text. They may be reading a social studies text, doing research on the Internet, and completing mathematics assignments on a computer.

Change is a defining element of life today. Comprehension needs have changed to meet the demands of the information and communication technologies that are emerging. New literacies build on and add to existing literacies, creating an ever-expanding collection of electronic communications. Secondary students need an ever-expanding collection of strategies for comprehending. New literacies offer new opportunities for learning. Gee (2004) believes in situating reading within a broad perspective that includes cognition, society, and culture.

Readers today face the challenge of comprehending multiple types of content in varying contexts for complex purposes. They also are expected to read more texts than previously. Successful comprehenders are active readers who read fluently. They use strategies to actively monitor their own cognitive processes (applying metacognitive ability). In this chapter, the first of two chapters that address the process of acquiring meaning and constructing knowledge, the goals are to develop readers' understanding of the comprehension process and to present strategies that students can implement as they read from various media. Chapter 6 focuses on comprehension strategies employed before, during, and after reading.

Purpose-Setting Questions

As you read this chapter, try to answer these questions:

1. How are multiple literacies related to content reading?
2. What do successful readers do when they read?
3. Why are good comprehenders active readers?
4. How important is metacognition in the comprehension process?

Reading Activities of Adolescents

Why are multiple literacies important?

The challenge of multiple literacies is illustrated by the literacy activities of an adolescent girl during one day:

- She searched the Internet to locate coupons for purchases she planned to make.

- She read the e-mail messages in her e-mail account and responded to them; then she added a status comment on her Facebook page and responded to a message in her inbox there.

- She used an Internet search engine to locate material for a science paper and then discussed the science paper with a classmate via instant messaging.

- She read class assignments in content textbooks and reference books and e-mailed questions regarding an assignment to her teacher's blog.

- She used the public library's computer to search for books, located the books, and checked them out.

Obviously, this incomplete list does not describe all of the reading a person would do in a day. Each area of reading and writing described here required different skills and strategies.

Reading Comprehension

What is reading comprehension?

Reading comprehension has been described in many ways, each of which contributes to our understanding of the process. Comprehension is a thinking process in which active readers construct meaning by interacting with text through the combination of prior knowledge, reasoning ability, experience, information in the text, perspective or point of view, and motivation to read the text (Pardo, 2004). Snow (2007) defines reading as "the process of simultaneously extracting and constructing meaning through interaction and involvement with written language." The reading process includes the *reader* who is comprehending, the *text* that must be comprehended, and the *activity or situation* in which the comprehension occurs. This definition focuses on the processing nature of reading comprehension which gives teachers more concrete ways of understanding the thinking processes involved in comprehension.

The Reader

How do readers interact with text?

Readers interact with the text content, using their vocabulary, experiences, world knowledge, skills, and schemata to understand. Schemata are mental organizations of personal experiences and world knowledge that provide a basis for interpretation, comprehension, and expectations of text. Schema theory is discussed in Chapter 4 and in later sections of this chapter.

The Text

How does the text influence comprehension?

The reader's language, experience, purpose (motivation), and vocabulary interact with the text to achieve comprehension. Readers comprehend better if the text is written in a style similar to their language usage and contains concepts that they can relate to their prior experiences. When too many of the factors in the text differ from the reader's background, the text is too difficult for the student to comprehend. Students' comprehension is influenced by their social, political, and cultural ideas. For example, students may reject the ideas and opinions expressed in the text, and that rejection can interfere with comprehension.

The Situation/Activity

How does the reading situation relate to comprehension?

The situation for reading includes the location (classroom, bus, home, etc.), the teacher and classmates (or other people present), and the sociocultural background of the students, as well as teacher and parental expectations. According to Lave and Wenger (1991), social interaction is an important component of situated learning. They believe that learners should become involved in a community of practice. The classroom organization (including whether there is or is not provision for individual assistance), classroom instruction, types of assignments, preparation for assignments, and the motivation and purposes for reading are all part of the reading situation (Ryan, 2008).

The elements related to the reader, the text, the situation, and purpose or motivation for reading all contribute to comprehension; but the *process* that occurs when students read integrates all of these influences to achieve understanding. When one component is weak or absent, students need help to comprehend. This is the point at which teachers introduce strategies that will assist in comprehension.

Fluency

What is reading fluency?

The emphasis on reading **fluency** is increasing because students have to read a greater number of texts than in the past, while being expected to comprehend at higher levels. Fluency helps readers comprehend at high levels. "Reading fluency is the ability to read accurately, quickly, effortlessly, and with appropriate expression and meaning" (Griffith and Rasinski, 2004, p. 24). Readers who have to decode words in a text cannot concentrate on understanding. On the other hand, readers who automatically read words can concentrate fully on the text meaning; thus, they are able to comprehend the text at higher levels than their less fluent counterparts.

Understanding vocabulary is an important component of comprehension. Walczyk and Griffith-Ross (2007) found that students who had memorized words (word callers) without understanding did not comprehend better in spite of reading the words rapidly. They emphasized that language comprehension was an important factor in fluency. Applegate and others (2009) researched the relationship between fluency and comprehension and concluded that they should be developed at the same time, not separately.

Active Readers

What is an active reader?

Active readers are engaged with the reading text and the reading purpose. They focus attention on the text and do not allow their thinking to wander from it. Active readers are motivated and thoughtful. They seek to understand. When the content makes sense, readers actively engage in the reading process because they have some ownership of the activity. When readers understand this relationship and the relevance of reading to their lives, they will invest greater energy and increase comprehension. Clarke and Whitney (2009) achieved this understanding through use of literature that expressed different points of view about a single incident, such as the assassination of Abraham Lincoln. James Cross Giblin's book *Good Brother, Bad Brother* is the story of the Booth brothers, John Wilkes and Edwin, one who was the assassin of Lincoln and the other who was an outstanding actor and a good person with different political beliefs from those of his brother.

Self-questioning and question/answer relationships (QARs) are useful active reading strategies that are discussed later in this chapter. Active readers also apply metacognitive skills to assess their own comprehension when they reflect on whether they understand the text.

The Context for Active Readers

What are the components of a reader's context?

The reader's context is composed of his or her attitudes, interests, purposes, prior knowledge, and skills. Reading comprehension is situated in the reader's world, including his or her world knowledge, as well as his or her social and cultural world. The contexts of comprehension include all of the activity that occurs around the reading transaction.

Teachers are a part of the classroom environment. They create contexts for active reading when they supply knowledge goals (purposes); real-world connections for text; choices about what, when, and how to read; and instruction in comprehension strategies. Students are invited into reading in a classroom where teachers value reading and provide books at various levels on a broad array of subjects. When students are asked to discuss a text, generate questions from the text, or identify the big idea, these activities form a context for them to interact with the text. The same reading assignment at another time or place might result in a different meaning (Pardo, 2004). The next "Meeting the Challenge" addresses concerns with the context of the text.

MEETING THE CHALLENGE

SOCIAL STUDIES

Sam Yung, a first-year teacher, faced early problems with his world history class. The opening unit in the text was on Rome. He discovered that the students read their assignments, but they could not sort out important details from unimportant ones and they could not recognize main ideas. This caused them to answer main idea questions with trivial details. He reviewed his objectives for this section of the textbook and identified three concepts or main topics that he planned to develop with the students. These main topics structured the chapter: Roman government, Roman culture, and Roman beliefs (religions). After reviewing his objectives, Sam thought about ways that he could help the students identify the main ideas and the details that supported each main idea. He recognized that he needed to work with the students in a way that would stimulate their thinking. First, using a paragraph from the text, he did a think-aloud that modeled his thinking as he identified the main idea and supporting details. This model helped his students understand ways they could think when identifying main ideas and supporting details. Then he explained the three major concepts developed in the chapter and related the paragraph to the concept of Roman government.

Group work can help with comprehension instruction.

Cleve Bryant/PhotoEdit

After his initial preparation, Sam divided the class into three groups. He assigned each group one of the concepts he planned to develop. Then he explained that the group members were to read the assignment and identify the important details related to their topic. The students wrote each detail on an index card and the group discussed each detail and its relationship to the concept. The members of each group were expected to agree regarding the important details that were related to their topic. When they completed reading and categorizing text information, group members served as experts on their topic and answered questions posed by the other groups. Finally, each group prepared a map of their main ideas and supporting details that they shared with the other groups. This process helped the students understand the relationship between main ideas and supporting details.

After completing the chapter, Sam decided to use this strategy with the next chapter to further the students' understanding of main ideas and supporting details and to give them additional practice in discerning these ideas and details.

Self-Questioning

What are the values of self-questioning?

Self-questioning is a means of encouraging active reading, and students can learn to control their own thought processes by employing this technique. Self-questioning refers to students asking themselves questions about a reading selection. Student-generated questions can focus their reading and result in deeper understanding. "Getting the facts is not enough to create understanding of the author's important ideas" (Buehl, 2009, p. 13). When students merely find answers, they miss the important ideas.

EXAMPLE 5.1 | **Self Questioning Examples**

SCIENCE AND HEALTH

The following questions are examples of questions based on Bloom's Taxonomy (1956) for a section of *Forensic Science*, a high school textbook by Anthony J. Bertino.

1. How is forensic science related to observation? (analysis)
2. What is the role of forensic scientists in the prosecution of crime? (application)
3. What types of evidence do pathologists study? (comprehension)
4. How are crimes solved? (synthesis)
5. How is deductive reasoning related to forensic science? (comprehension)
6. What is tunnel vision and how can it impede solving crimes? (comprehension)
7. Is this a good profession for me? Why or why not? (application)
8. What are the most important skills for forensic scientists? (knowledge)

Question/Answer Relationships (QARs)

What is the QAR strategy?

Question/answer relationships (**QARs**) provide another strategy that can be used to increase comprehension and active reading. This strategy focuses on the processes for generating answers to questions and on the relationships between questions and answers. Students are encouraged to think of sources for answers to questions. The following ideas are included to help teachers guide students when using this strategy:

1. First, the student looks in the text for the words used in the question and tries to identify these words in a sentence that answers the question. If he or she does this, the answer is "Right There," because the question is directly answered in the text.

2. Next, the student tries "Think and Search," which involves using information from one or more sentences or paragraphs to answer the question.

3. If the question does not have an answer in the text, it is considered "On My Own" and is answered from the reader's knowledge.

4. Still other questions, referred to as "Author and Me," are inferential questions that the reader answers by combining his or her knowledge with the information in the text.

When teaching students to use QARs, teachers should begin with short texts and work up to longer ones. Students should have immediate feedback on their responses. The goal is to have them become independent in applying the four relationships: Right There; Think and Search; On My Own; Author and Me. Example 5.2 illustrates the QAR strategy applied to mathematics.

EXAMPLE 5.2

QAR for Math (Developed by Stephanie Dykes, Jennifer Brown, and Keith Shackleford)

1. *Right There:* State the multiplicative identity.
    Answer: For any number a, a x 1 = 1 x a = a.

2. *Think and Search*:* Name the property illustrated by the following statement:
    If 8 + 1 = 9, then 9 = 8 + 1.
    Answer: symmetry
    *This is a Think and Search because the book gives a problem similar to it.

3. *Author and Me*:* Lincoln's Gettysburg address began "Four score and seven years ago, ..." Write an expression to represent four score and seven. How many years is that?
    Answer: 4(20) + 7 = 87 years
    *This is "Author and Me" because it involves the material in the section, but incorporates the learner's own experience. (score = 20)

4. *On My Own*:* If 4 quarters = $1.00 and $1.00 = 10 dimes, then 4 quarters = 10 dimes. Is this true? On your own, think of a money combination similar to the one above using any amount of money.
    Answer: may vary
    *This is "On My Own" because this problem could be done without even reading the textbook, yet it is related to the section.

Source: Based on material from Foster, Gell, Gordon, et al., *Algebra 1: Applications and Connections* (Lake Forest, Ill.: Glencoe, 1992), pp. 22–25.

MATHEMATICS

Linguistic and Cognitive Components of Comprehension ▬▬▬

What are the foundations for understanding content texts?

Language and cognitive competence are foundations for understanding content texts. **Literacy** involves the reader's language and thought that he or she engages in to make sense of and communicate ideas in a variety of situations. The student's underlying cognitive and linguistic skills are precursors of his or her ability to comprehend. A student comprehends most successfully when he or she reads meaningful materials that connect with his or her schemata, while studying for relevant purposes that link text with listening, speaking, and writing. Literacy above all involves communication. An understanding of both semantics and syntax is essential to comprehension. **Semantics** refers to word meaning. **Syntax** is concerned with the word order in sentences and paragraphs. Both semantics and syntax are important when a reader uses context clues to aid comprehension.

A content text presents the author's explanations, descriptions, and information. Authors use academic vocabulary and formal syntax to express the meaning they wish to convey. Textbook language is more formal than readers' conversational language. Moreover, the vocabulary in content texts is more technical, which imposes additional comprehension difficulties for some students.

Schema theory explains cognitive functions that undergird both comprehension and content reading instruction. Figure 5.1 shows some of the major aspects of readers' cognitive processing in comprehension.

What is metacognition?

Metacognition (metacomprehension) is thinking about one's own thinking and controlling one's own learning (Israel, 2007). Researchers generally agree that metacognition involves knowledge and self-regulation, as well as motivation. According to research, reading metacognition includes knowledge of (1) the self as a learner; (2) the demands of the reading task; and (3) the relationships among text, prior knowledge, reading strategies, and reading comprehension. When students are conscious of their own thinking and comprehension, and they are unable to comprehend, they try different strategies to fix their comprehension. Then they are taking responsibility for their own comprehension. Acquiring metacognitive skills helps students to become independent readers (Israel, 2007).

Cognitive strategies that are most useful in the metacognitive process include activating prior knowledge, establishing a purpose for reading, identifying important ideas, reading critically, and using reflection and self-questioning to evaluate understanding. The following scenario illustrates the metacognitive process.

Chris Thompson, a secondary-school math student, was assigned a unit about sampling that served as preparation for statistical analysis. He established prereading purpose questions to guide his reading. After reading the text, he reviewed these

MATHEMATICS

FIGURE 5.1

Major Aspects of Thinking in Comprehension

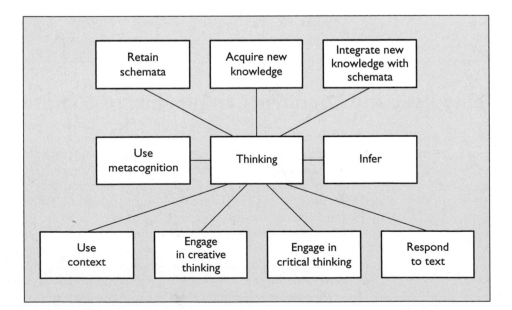

questions. This helped him realize that he understood the overall process of sampling, but could not define the terms *variance, population,* and *population parameter.* He recognized that he needed to reread specific portions of the text to locate and study the important terms.

Cognitive Flexibility and the Situational Context

What is cognitive flexibility?

SCIENCE AND HEALTH

Cognitive flexibility is the ability to adjust knowledge and cognitive strategies to meet new and unexpected situations. Cognitive flexibility is concerned with complex learning situations that go beyond what can be described by a simple application of schema theory (Bean, 2001; Jetton and Alexander, 2001). For example, an earth science instructor developed a schema for renewable energy with his class that was studying energy sources. He then decided to extend students' learning by exploring the multiple perspectives of the various groups that could be concerned with renewable energy sources and the impact of these sources on their lives, earning power, environment, and so forth. The students drew from a variety of schemata as they explored the issues that could arise from developing renewable energy sources. Example 5.3 shows the various multiple perspectives the students explored. This example makes it clear that a single schema could not account for the multiple inter-relationships examined. Cognitive flexibility is related to the **situational context**. (Darvin, 2006).

EXAMPLE 5.3   **Multiple Perspectives**

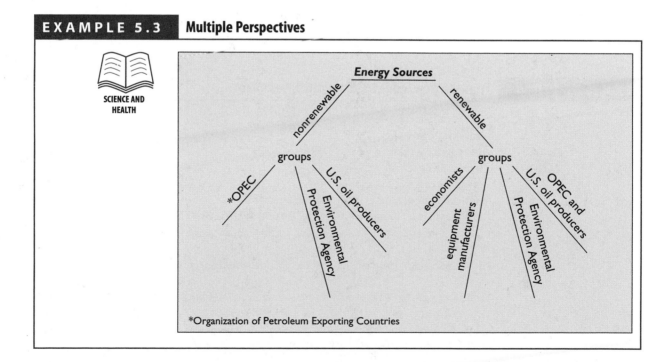

The Situational Context

What is a situational context?

SCIENCE AND HEALTH

What makes a reading purpose authentic?

Readers have a situational context for reading. Consider the differences in perspective among a physician, a pharmacist, and a patient reading a health text. Readers have to adjust their points of view to fit the purpose, to apply cognitive flexibility, and to activate schemata appropriate to the literary experience. Situational context involves the *stances* and *purposes*, that readers have for reading, writing, and learning. It gives form to the literacy experience as well as the mode for expressing a response (Rainville and Jones, 2008).

Authentic purposes help students recognize that content is meaningful and connected to their lives. When giving students a reading assignment or an inquiry task that involves reading and writing, teachers guide and focus readers' attention through identifying a **stance**, which is a point of view or perspective that integrates the text and the situational context. Reader stance influences the reader's response and comprehension. The two major stances are aesthetic and efferent (Rosenblatt, 1985). Aesthetic reading is that which leads to a pleasurable, interesting experience for its own sake. Efferent reading focuses on the meanings and ideas in the text.

Readers may interpret a text one way when reading for general understanding, but their interpretation may change when they apply ideas in real life because the context has changed. A reader's interpretation often changes after discussing a story with another student who has a different slant on a character or story incident. Research indicates that students' understanding changes over time, with readers relating ideas to a larger context and focusing on bigger ideas rather than the details that initially captured their interests. Considering various points of view and connections among ideas helps students organize main ideas and clarify their importance relative to details (Jetton and Alexander, 2001). Example 5.4 illustrates a point-of-view guide for American Government.

EXAMPLE 5.4   **Point-of-View Guide for American Government**

SOCIAL STUDIES

Topic: Social Security
Problems:
   Increased life span
   Increased benefits
   Solvency of funds questioned
   Borrowing from fund to meet current expenses
   Presidents and Congress using Social Security fund to offset budget deficits.

1. As a 70–year-old person, how would you feel about Social Security?

2. As a 55-year-old woman, how would you feel about Social Security?

3. As a 29-year-old employed man, how would you feel about Social Security?

Source: Guide developed for material in Susan Welch, John Gruhl, John Comer, and Susan Rigdon, *Understanding American Government* (Boston: Wadsworth Cengage Learning, 2009).

The situational context is also concerned with the group in which the instruction occurs, which may be a large group, a small group, an individual, or a pull-out group meeting outside of the classroom. Reading purposes and assignments often determine the nature of the group.

SOCIAL STUDIES

A situational context may address real-life or simulated circumstances that focus students' comprehension. The contexts should build students' motivation, curiosity, and insight. Then the students need literacy skills to acquire information or skills to solve problems that have meaning for them. A simulated situational context for social studies could have the student take the point-of-view of an individual who was elected to the House of Representatives. As a woman and parent of three children, she has a particular perspective. She needs to understand government, law, and the economic impacts of various proposals on various groups as she debates issues. The role of situation-based comprehension and its relationship to real-life learning will be further discussed in Chapter 6.

Schema Theory

What are schemata?

Schemata are mental networks of knowledge, information, and experiences stored in long-term memory. Learning occurs when we integrate new ideas with the ideas already stored in long-term memory. "This can occur through adding new information to preexisting schemata (assimilation), or discarding prior knowledge and replacing it with something different (accommodation)" (Lloyd, 1998, p. 185). As learning occurs, the categories within a schema are modified, and new ones are built.

The most efficient reading occurs when the schemata established in a reader's mind match the organization of the reading material. When stored knowledge relates to new information, readers can use both their schemata and the incoming information to predict language, organization, and ideas and to form hypotheses about the text. Then they read to confirm, discount, or revise their theories. Readers' schemata enable them to read actively and comprehend. Readers' predictions about text increase comprehension and fall into two categories: those based on content schemata and those based on textual schemata.

Schemata Types and Relationships

How are content schemata different from textual schemata?

Content schemata are based on world knowledge. We have only to contrast a sports-loving student's comprehension of the sports section of the newspaper with his or her understanding of a chapter of social studies to understand the significant role schemata play in comprehension. This student uses schemata developed from years of experience for a context, or frame of reference, just as a child development student who has had baby-sitting experiences with younger brothers and sisters has a context for understanding a child development text.

Textual schemata form the basis for multiple literacies. Readers' knowledge of and experience with different forms of written discourse prepare them to read a variety of content. Prior knowledge of the structural characteristics of written language enables readers to anticipate, follow, and organize it. Prior knowledge of and experience with textual features also enables students to find information within

ENGLISH/
LANGUAGE
ARTS

a text and to sort important ideas from unimportant ideas, which prepares them for success (Eckert, 2008). For example, a reader expects a textbook to have a particular form, and that form differs greatly from that of a novel. Readers expect the essential information in textbooks to be organized with headings, subheadings, theses, and main ideas, whereas fiction reveals its plot, characters, theme, and so forth throughout the story. Structural knowledge like this transfers to future literacy experiences.

Building Schemata

How can teachers help students build schemata?

ENGLISH/
LANGUAGE
ARTS

SOCIAL
STUDIES

Teachers can help students build schemata in a variety of ways, using activities such as discussion; drama; storytelling; oral reading of all types of literature; viewing television shows, videos, and Internet sites; examining models; and using computer software. Preteaching vocabulary, as discussed in Chapter 4, increases background experience and conceptual development. Multimedia presentations of related knowledge can build secondary students' interests, knowledge, textual schemata, multicultural schemata, and so on. For instance, in an eleventh-grade American literature course, teachers used folklore and family sayings such as those found in Benjamin Franklin's *Autobiography* and *Poor Richard's Almanac* to develop students' schemata for the U.S. colonial period. Then these students sought personal family materials, such as letters, diaries, and photographs, to build a sense of history (Renner and Carter, 1992).

Activating Schemata

What is the value of activating appropriate schemata?

When is a preview guide used?

When students activate appropriate schemata, they can anticipate the author's ideas and information and make inferences about content (filling in missing ideas and information). This process is necessary because an author cannot concretely explain all of his or her ideas. Teachers can help students activate schemata by posing questions or developing vocabulary, which also encourages students' active, engaged reading.

Many of the strategies and activities in this chapter are designed for activating students' schemata. For example, **reading guides**, especially **preview guides**, can help students relate what they are about to read to their own experiential backgrounds. In its simplest form, the preview guide may be a request to, for example, "list everything you already know about word processing." Another style of preview guide provides students with a list of statements to review and respond to before reading; after completing the assignment, students return to the guide to verify whether or not their statements are substantiated by the reading (resulting in a *reaction guide*). Students may also be asked to revise statements that were proved wrong by the text and to put question marks beside items that were not addressed in the reading. All three types of items are appropriate for class discussion; teachers can ask students to respond to items before reading and have them check their answers after reading. The highly structured preview guides are often called *anticipation guides*. One such guide is shown in Example 5.5. Another type of reading guide is presented in Example 5.6.

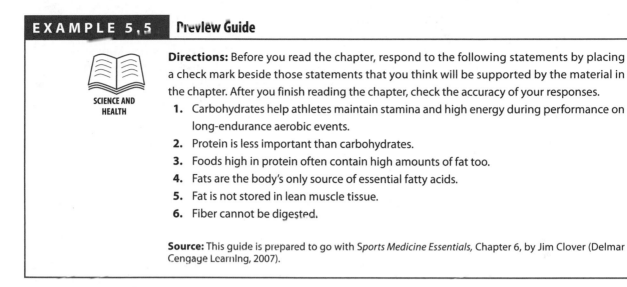

EXAMPLE 5.5	Preview Guide

SCIENCE AND HEALTH

Directions: Before you read the chapter, respond to the following statements by placing a check mark beside those statements that you think will be supported by the material in the chapter. After you finish reading the chapter, check the accuracy of your responses.

1. Carbohydrates help athletes maintain stamina and high energy during performance on long-endurance aerobic events.
2. Protein is less important than carbohydrates.
3. Foods high in protein often contain high amounts of fat too.
4. Fats are the body's only source of essential fatty acids.
5. Fat is not stored in lean muscle tissue.
6. Fiber cannot be digested.

Source: This guide is prepared to go with *Sports Medicine Essentials,* Chapter 6, by Jim Clover (Delmar Cengage Learning, 2007).

EXAMPLE 5.6	Social Science Guide

SOCIAL SCIENCE

Topic: Terrorism

Purpose Question: How does terrorism relate to me?

A What I already knew	B What I now know	C What I don't know
Terrorism is extending to many countries.	Terrorists are secretive; even those closest to them do not know what they are doing.	How much danger are we in?
England and the United States have both suffered from terrorism.	They use various bombs and tricks to kill and injure people.	Where in the United States are terrorists most likely to strike?
The ways that our lives have changed since 9/11.		What can I do?

Answer to Purpose Question: I have to be vigilant, because terrorists are a danger worldwide.

Reader-Response Theory

What are the types of reader response?

According to **reader-response theory,** a literary work is actualized only through a transaction between a reader and a text. Readers' responses related to a reading assignment or selection can range from total absorption to complete lack of interest. Response theory is based on a continuum that ranges from aesthetic response at one end and efferent response at the opposite end (Rosenblatt, 1978).

ART   **MUSIC**

ENGLISH/ LANGUAGE ARTS

Aesthetic response is characterized by readers' personal feelings about a story or text. This response may be expressed through art, music, drama, or composition. At the other end of the continuum, **efferent responses** focus on knowledge, information, and facts. Content teachers are usually most interested in the efferent response; however, they should encourage and respect both students' aesthetic and efferent responses.

Lloyd (1998) points out that a reaction log like the one shown in Example 5.7 provides a means of expressing both aesthetic and efferent responses. The comparison/ contrast guide shown in Example 5.8 illustrates efferent response.

EXAMPLE 5.7	**Reaction Log for Human Environmental Science**	

HES/HUMAN ECOLOGY

I learned	**My response**
How to find quality childcare.	I did not realize that babysitters had to be so knowledgeable.
The personal characteristics that a caregiver needs.	I liked babysitters who read to me.
The skills a caregiver needs.	I think a caregiver should be able to prepare food and feed a child.
The knowledge a caregiver needs.	I read in the newspaper that you should not put a baby on its stomach because of SIDS.

The Textual Context of Reading Comprehension

What aspects of text contribute to comprehension?

The quality of a text is important in the comprehension of both fiction and nonfiction. Both **text organization** and **text coherence** contribute to comprehension. For example, they would affect whether or not readers develop logical understandings of historical periods and historical topics.

Two major flaws are common in the content and presentation of texts. First, textbook authors often assume that students have a greater variety and depth of prior knowledge than is actually the case, providing an excellent argument for teachers to develop schemata in preparation for reading.

What is text coherence?

Second, the presentation in texts can lack **coherence**. Logical organization of the material can help students follow the ideas presented. Texts tend to present many facts with little explanation. This situation makes it difficult for readers to adjust their thinking to the organization of the selection and to follow the author's line of thought. Well-developed paragraphs are easier to understand, because each of them focuses on a single major topic, and a logical sequence of sentences is used in the structure. The sentences have coherence; they are related to the paragraph topic and to one another. In contrast, a poorly organized paragraph does not establish a focus, and the sentences frequently are not related to one another and are not presented in a logical order.

The following are examples of a well-developed paragraph and a poorly developed paragraph.

Paragraph A: Flowers are an important part of landscaping for a new home. They create a bright focal point in the landscaping and soften the harsh lines of the architecture. They also add value to a home.

Paragraph B: Flowers create a bright focal point in landscaping, and they soften the harsh lines of the architecture. They make nice bouquets for banquets. Flowers are an important part of landscaping for a new home. Flowers add value to a new home.

If you identified Paragraph A as the well-developed paragraph, which is easier to understand, you are correct. Notice that this paragraph sticks to the subject—the fact that flowers are an important part of landscaping for a new home. The ideas are presented in a logical order, and the sentences have coherence. No loosely related ideas are introduced to divert the reader's attention. On the other hand, Paragraph B lacks a clear focus.

Critics of textbook writing also suggest that good writing with active verbs, vivid anecdotes, lively quotations, and other literary devices contributes to readers' interest and recall (Wade and Adams, 1990; Wade et al., 1993). Moreover, the quality of readers' recall of main ideas and interesting details increases when the text includes a greater number of interesting, memorable details.

Considerate Text

What makes a text considerate or inconsiderate?

Effective readers use a variety of strategies and processes to construct text meaning. They understand the components and patterns of text structure, such as paragraphs. The initial sections of this chapter addressed the current emphasis on the reader's active role in comprehension. However, to read actively and responsibly, students also must understand the nature of *considerate* and *inconsiderate* text, so that they can compensate for text limitations.

Five characteristics account for the ease or difficulty students are likely to encounter when reading a text:

1. Organization and structure.

2. Whether the text addresses one concept at a time or tries to explain several at once.

3. The clarity and coherence of the explanations.

4. Whether the text is appropriate for the students' reading levels and the purpose.

5. Whether the information is accurate and consistent (Armbruster and Anderson, 1981).

Organizational Patterns

Students who recognize the various patterns of text structure perform better on recall, summarization, and other comprehension tasks than readers who do not. Text structures are organizational frameworks that students can learn to identify, giving the students a predictable means to interpret explanatory discourse. The common **organizational patterns** found in content textbooks and nonfiction and informational writing are illustrated in the following paragraphs.

What are the five common organizational patterns found in textbooks?

1. *Sequential or chronological order.* Paragraphs in sequential or chronological order present information in the order of its occurrence to clarify the ideas presented, as illustrated in the following example. Readers can use time or sequential order patterns to organize and remember this information. These words may signal this text organization: *after, before, begin, beyond, during, finally, first, next, now, second, then, third, until,* and *when.*

   > The gravel settles first, followed by the sand, and then the clay. Heavier particles settle first because they require the greatest water velocity to be moved. In step 3, the gravel does not move, but the clay becomes suspended (Spaulding and Namowitz, 2005).

SCIENCE AND HEALTH

2. *Comparison/contrast.* Authors use comparison/contrast to clarify certain points. Questions such as the following may help readers to understand this structure: What is the author's main idea? What similarities and/or differences does he or she use to illustrate the point? Student-constructed tables that list similarities and differences also enhance understanding. Some words that may signal the use of this pattern are *although, but, yet, nevertheless, meanwhile, however, on the other hand, otherwise, compared to, despite,* and *similarly.* The following paragraph illustrates the comparison/contrast pattern:

   > Past—As you have learned, the large deposits of gold throughout Africa brought great wealth and power to kingdoms in the west and south. Back then miners used picks and other light tools to dig gold from the land.
   >
   > Present—Gold remains a key resource of Africa; in fact Africa is a world leader in gold production. Modern miners in Africa and elsewhere use powerful drills to dig out gold thousands of feet underground (Carnine, Cortes, Curtis, and Robinson, 2006).

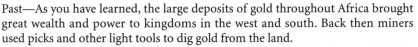

SOCIAL STUDIES

3. *Cause and effect.* Authors use this pattern to explain relationships among facts and ideas. Readers need to identify stated and implied causes and their related effects. The following words may signal the use of cause and effect: forms of the verb *cause,* as well as *because, since, so that, thus, therefore, if, consequently,* and *as a result.* An example of a cause-and-effect paragraph follows:

   > The area that experienced the Dust Bowl disaster had been largely grassland on which ranchers raised livestock during World War I. After that millions of acres were converted to wheat growing. Overcultivation and incorrect land use in the 1920s left the region vulnerable not only to the years of drought conditions, but

SOCIAL STUDIES

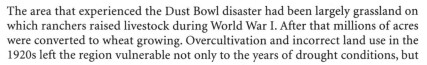

to strong winds that easily carried away the top soil (Arreola, Deal, Peterson, and Sanders, 2003).

4. *Definition or explanation.* This pattern explains a concept or defines terms that are essential to understanding in many content areas. An example of a definition or explanation pattern follows:

MATHEMATICS

> A box and whisper plot is a data display that divides data values into four parts. Ordered data are divided into a lower and an upper half by the median. The median of the lower half is the lower quartile. The median of the upper half is the upper quartile. The lower extreme is the least data value. The upper extreme is the greatest data value (Larson, Bosewell, Kanold, and Stiff, 2005).

5. *Enumeration or simple listing pattern.* Paragraphs in this pattern list items of information (such as facts or ideas), either in order of importance or simply in logical order. Clues to this pattern are the words *one, two, first, second, third, to begin, next, finally, most important, when, also, too,* and *then.* An example of the enumeration or simple listing pattern follows:

BUSINESS EDUCATION

> The Profit Motive
>
> The most important reason to run a business in a market economy is to earn a profit. Companies that do not earn a profit will not last. They can increase profit in three ways.
>
> 1. Reduce Costs They might find less expensive raw materials or buy machines that are more efficient at producing the product.
>
> 2. Change Price By changing prices, the company may increase profits. It could lower prices to gain more sales. Or, it could raise prices and earn a larger profit on each sale.
>
> 3. Increase Quantity of Products Sold Businesses often use advertising to encourage consumers to buy more of their products (Miller and Stafford, 2010, p. 24).

Instructional Activities for Teaching Organizational Patterns

What kinds of activities are useful for teaching organizational patterns?

Instruction should involve a communication approach and include speaking, listening, reading, and writing. The instruction should make use of the actual texts and materials that students have to read. Strategies for teaching text structure include use of preview guides, graphic organizers (also called *visual organizers*), and questions. Pattern guides are based on the organizational pattern of the text. If a text is organized according to a cause-and-effect pattern, for example, the guide would highlight causes and effects. Some possible focuses for pattern guides other than cause and effect are sequence, comparison/contrast, and categorization. Pattern guides activate a reader's schemata for the particular organizational patterns frequently found in various subject areas. Example 5.8 is a completed comparison/contrast guide for a selection from a world history text.

EXAMPLE 5.8 | Comparison/Contrast Guide

SOCIAL STUDIES

AGRICULTURE

Directions: Read the selection about the revolutions in food production and then fill in the chart below to help you compare the characteristics of the green revolution and the biorevolution. (Note: Chart has been filled in here for illustrative purposes.)

Green revolution	Biorevolution
Increased crop yields	Gene alteration
High-yield grain	Plants resistant to pests and disease
Doubled wheat production	Increased retention of flavor and freshness of tomatoes
Four rice crops a year required irrigation	Raised issues about negative consequences
Required chemicals for growth	

Revolutions in Food Production

One response to the problem of rapid population growth has been to boost food production. Two important examples of this effort are the **green revolution** and the **biorevolution.**

The Green Revolution In the 1950s, agricultural scientists began to look for ways to increase crop yields. Their success, known as the green revolution, has helped to boost food production greatly.

Scientists focused their efforts on producing high-yield varieties of grain. Their first great success occurred in Mexico in the 1950s. An American-led team developed high-yield wheat plants. Thanks to these new plants, Mexican farmers doubled their wheat production. In the 1960s, another American-backed team helped to develop a hybrid rice plant in the Philippines. It allowed rice farmers to harvest up to four rice crops every year. Soon, Asian governments were funding their own scientists to develop other hybrid plants to meet the needs of people in their nations.

Unfortunately, the techniques of the green revolution often call for much irrigation, or watering, of crops. Because many African nations have limited water supplies, they have not been able to make full use of the new seeds. This severely limits the usefulness of these methods in much of Africa, where there is little water.

In addition, the new hybrid varieties of plants require chemicals, such as fertilizers, herbicides, and pesticides, to help them grow. This requirement has caused a number of problems. First, the chemicals are expensive. Peasants usually cannot afford them. Second, the use of such chemicals often clashes with age-old methods of farming. Third, these chemicals pose a threat to the environment.

The Biorevolution In addition to the methods of the green revolution, genetic research has played a growing role in agricultural science in recent years. In this approach, scientists alter plant genes to produce new plants that are more productive and more resistant to pests and disease.

This biorevolution, or gene revolution, has led to some important developments. For example, one American company has developed a genetically altered tomato that ripens more slowly than other tomatoes. This means that the altered tomatoes keep much of their flavor and freshness longer. Similar work is being tried with other kinds of produce.

But the biorevolution has raised some troubling issues. Critics fear that altering genes may accidentally create new disease-causing organisms. Another fear is that plants produced by altering genes may become diseased more easily. As with the green revolution, science offers great opportunities in the search for more food, but results may also have negative consequences.

Source: Roger Beck, Linda Black, Larry Krieger, Phillip Naylor, and Dahiaibo Shabaka, *Modern World History: Patterns of Interaction*. Copyright © 1999 by McDougal Littell Inc., a division of Houghton Mifflin Company. All rights reserved. Used by permission of McDougal Littell Inc., a division of Houghton Mifflin Company.

Graphic, or visual, organizers and structured overviews are graphic arrangements of terms that apply to the important concepts in a reading selection (See Figure 5.2). They represent different kinds of thinking processes and text organizations that can be applied to listening, reading, and writing. These strategies also develop readiness for reading and writing. They help students to visualize what they are thinking and/or trying to understand. (See Chapter 4 for more on graphic organizers.) The following questions are guides for teachers to ask themselves when developing graphic organizers:

1. As I look at this content, what central facts, ideas, arguments, processes, or procedures do students need to comprehend? (This is related to purpose and/or objectives.)

2. What pattern or organization best holds the material together and makes it meaningful?

3. What kind of visual organizer will show students how to think their way through the content?

4. What problems or challenges can I pose that will force students to work through the steps of a thinking process?

Teachers can use these questions as they prepare graphic organizers for students to complete. The graphic organizers and questions in Figure 5.2 can be applied to most content area materials, and they are effective for main ideas and details, which are major tools for structuring information and knowledge.

Students can use computer graphic programs to create their own illustrations to show their thinking or the text organization. Our experiences indicate that students can be very creative when formulating their own graphic organizers. Student-created graphics are usually prepared as a follow-up or summary of reading content.

FIGURE 5.2

Graphic Organizers
for Text
Organizations

Items Compared	#1	#2
1st attribute		
2nd attribute		
3rd attribute		
4th attribute		

Guiding Questions
1. What is compared?
2. Why are these items compared?
3. What is the author's conclusion?
4. What is your conclusion?
   (Do you accept the author's
   conclusion? Why?)

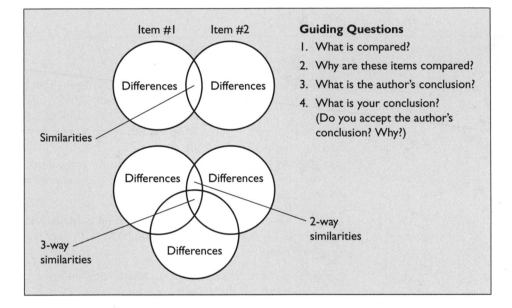

Guiding Questions
1. What is compared?
2. Why are these items compared?
3. What is the author's conclusion?
4. What is your conclusion?
   (Do you accept the author's
   conclusion? Why?)

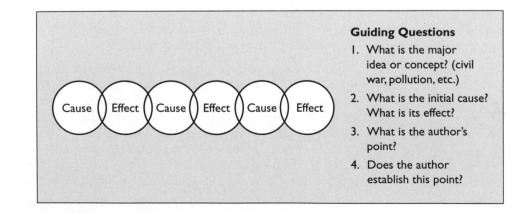

Guiding Questions
1. What is the major
   idea or concept? (civil
   war, pollution, etc.)
2. What is the initial cause?
   What is its effect?
3. What is the author's
   point?
4. Does the author
   establish this point?

FIGURE 5.2

Continued

SOCIAL
STUDIES

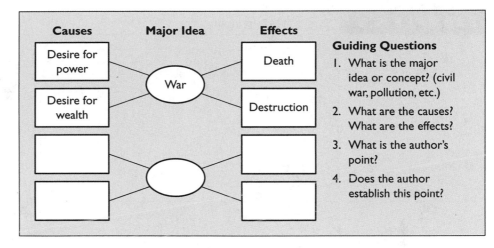

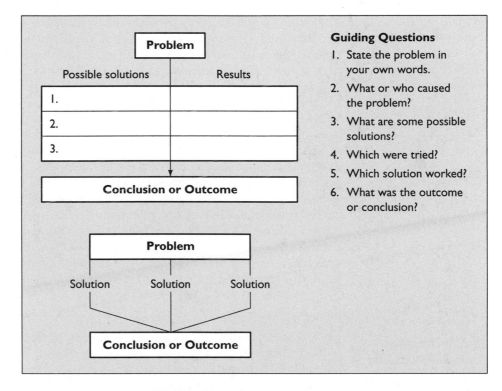

Teachers can model the development of overviews with visual presenters as the students watch each step and discuss it. Teachers can develop overviews on sentence strips by using bulletin boards and having the students organize the sentence strips. Then students can work in small groups, and finally individually, to develop overviews for their reading assignments. Example 5.9 shows a sample structured overview in the area of atomic structure.

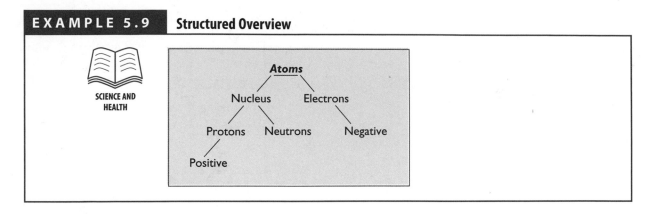

EXAMPLE 5.9 **Structured Overview**

SCIENCE AND HEALTH

Main Ideas and Details

Why is teaching identification of topics, main ideas, and details a high priority in reading programs?

The writing in most content area materials is structured around topics, main ideas, and details; therefore, teaching students to identify topics and main ideas of paragraphs and entire selections is a high priority in reading programs. Topics are frequently presented as titles, words, or phrases that label the subjects.

The main idea of a paragraph is the central idea that the author develops about the topic and supports with details throughout the paragraph. Details are the smaller pieces of information that are used to support this idea. See Figure 5.3 for the steps for finding the topic, main idea, and details in a paragraph.

Main ideas are interrelated with organizational patterns because they can be expressed in patterns such as cause and effect, comparison/contrast, sequential order, enumeration, and explanation. For example, a cause-and-effect pattern might have a main idea of "causes and effects of erosion." The details would be the specific causes and effects. Similarly, in a paragraph written with a comparison/contrast pattern, the details might be the contrasting points and the main idea the overall comparison.

Teachers need to go beyond simply presenting instructional strategies and must *show* students how to identify main ideas and details. Instructions requiring

FIGURE 5.3

Steps for Finding the Topic, Main Idea, and Details

A. **Identify the topic by asking who or what the paragraph is about.** Ask yourself, What general word or phrase identifies the subject? Remember that the topic is based on a broad idea such as sports, flowers, wars, cells (science), or communication.

B. **Identify the supporting details.** Search for details that seem important and the idea they point to. For example, details about sports might include facts about baseball, football, and basketball.

C. **Identify the main idea the author is communicating about the topic.** The author's main idea about sports could be that these sports all involve teamwork and competition.

students to generate the main idea of a selection or paragraph lead them to recall and understand content better than simply identifying the main idea from multiple-choice items. Therefore, students should practice writing the main idea in their own words. Students who learn to summarize main ideas improve their ability to answer questions and to identify important information. Students also need to identify and write both stated and unstated (implied) main ideas.

Main Idea and Detail Activities

Activities such as the following give students help with and practice in identifying and stating main ideas and supporting details:

1. Have students use categorization activities to separate important from unimportant details. For instance, students can write down the details they have identified in a paragraph and categorize them as either important or unimportant to the communication of the main idea. Having students state reasons that they classified details into either of these categories permits the teacher to clear up any misconceptions about the points the author stressed.

2. Model the procedure of finding main ideas for students before asking them to locate main ideas themselves.

3. Have students ask themselves these questions:
   - What is this sentence or paragraph about?
   - What do most of the key words seem to point to?
   - What words occur most frequently?
   - What do these frequently occurring words relate to?
   - What idea is related to most of the supporting details?
   - What sentence would best summarize the frequently occurring ideas?
   - Is the main idea stated or implied?
   - Where is the main idea located in the paragraph (at the beginning, in the middle, or at the end)?

4. Teach students to look for words and phrases that often indicate the main idea, for instance, *first, last, the most important factor, the significant fact.*

5. Prepare blank diagrams on which students can place main ideas and supporting ideas. Following is an example of a generic diagram.

Main Idea
Detail #1
Detail #2
Detail #3
Detail #4

6. Have students create their own diagrams for main ideas and supporting details.

7. Encourage students to write, in their own words, concise statements of main ideas.

Selection Organization of Expository Text

What is expository discourse?

Selections are longer units of discourse composed of series of paragraphs. In content reading, we are concerned largely with expository discourse. The organizational patterns presented earlier in this chapter (sequential, comparison/contrast, cause and effect, definition or explanation, and enumeration or simple listing pattern) are found in many selections, and they are frequently combined in structuring expository discourse. When these patterns are identified in longer selections, they can be interpreted in the same ways as in paragraphs. However, these common patterns become parts of a macrostructure in longer discourse.

Well-written expository content—such as a content textbook chapter—begins with an *introductory section*, which previews the subject. This introduction can be compared to an inverted triangle, because it starts with a broad, general idea of the topic and narrows the topic to a more specific point. This section may be developed in a variety of ways, such as comparison and cause and effect.

The second part of a selection is the *body*, which develops the ideas that have been stated in the introduction. Each of the paragraphs that make up the body usually has a main idea and details that relate to the topic presented in the introductory section. These paragraphs may be developed through any organizational pattern the author chooses.

The chapter or selection usually concludes with a *summary paragraph* that pulls together the ideas presented in the body. A triangle can be used to illustrate this section, which begins with a specific idea and broadens and becomes more general as it develops. The pattern of the summary is the reverse of that of the introductory section. Content teachers can illustrate organizational patterns with the table of contents, which is discussed in Chapter 7. Textbook headings, which are helpful in understanding, remembering, and locating information, are widely used in content textbooks and nonfiction trade books.

Selection Organization for Narrative Texts

Although narrative texts may have some paragraphs that are organized in some of the same ways as expository text, narrative selections are organized according to story grammars. The structure of narrative texts is a container for communicating a story. In stories, there are plots, characters, problems or conflicts, and themes that revolve around characters' goals and actions. Story grammar (*grammar* means "structural relationships"), is a mental representation of the parts of a typical story and the relationships among those parts.

What are the important elements in stories?

Students can identify the important elements in stories and relate these elements to one another by mapping them. Our discussion is based on the six major story elements posited by Mandler and Johnson (1977). These elements are setting, beginning, reaction, attempt, outcome, and ending. The *setting* introduces the main character and the time and place. A precipitating or initiating event occurs in the *beginning*, and the main character's response to the precipitating event is identified as the *reaction*. *Attempt* is concerned with the main character's efforts to attain his or her goal. The success or failure of the attempt is identified in the *outcome*. The *ending*, the last component of story structure, is the long-range consequence of

EXAMPLE 5.10	Story Grammar

ENGLISH/
LANGUAGE
ARTS

When My Name Was Keoko by Linda Sue Park

Setting	Korea during the Japanese occupation 1940–1945. Sun-hee and Tae-yul, a brother and sister, alternate as narrators of the story.
Beginning	The Japanese had imposed many restrictions on the Koreans. Then they announced that all Koreans must take Japanese names.
Reaction	Sun-hee and Tae-yul and their family find this very threatening to their identity. Members of the family react in different ways to protect their identities.
Attempt	Sun-hee keeps a journal where she can be herself rather than Keoko (her Japanese name). Tae-yul resents his father's compliance with the Japanese to choose a Japanese name.
Outcome	An uncle who publishes an underground newspaper is arrested and forced to become a Kamikaze pilot. Tae-yul becomes a pilot for the Japanese.
Ending	Sun-hee preserves her Korean self through her journal. Tae-yul understands his father at the end of the novel.

the action, the final response of a character, or an emphatic statement. A story may be composed of one story grammar, or it may include a series of story grammars. In an episodic story, each episode has a story grammar. Example 5.10 shows the story grammar for the young adult novel *When My Name Was Keoko* by Linda Sue Park.

Readers use their knowledge of fiction and nonfiction text structure to guide their expectations, understanding, recall, and production of text. When reading, listening, and writing, students use a structural outline of the major story and text components in their minds to make predictions and hypotheses about stories and information. These expectations focus students' attention on story events, help them understand the unfolding of time and sequence, and cue recall of text. When writing their own essays or analyses, students use knowledge of text structures to shape their discourse.

ENGLISH/
LANGUAGE
ARTS

FOCUS ON	*Struggling Readers*

Helping Struggling Readers Comprehend

Giving struggling students reading materials they can comprehend is fundamental to developing comprehension. Secondary classrooms include students who read anywhere from one to five (and possibly more) grades below or above their placement. The students reading below grade level may need alternate materials that are easier to read than texts that the rest of the class is reading. Teachers often need to locate interesting readable supplementary materials (Nelms, 2008). They can use readability formulas to measure the difficulty of text. Most of these formulas use vocabulary and sentence difficulty as elements. These formulas are discussed in Chapter 3.

Lack of academic literacy is a significant problem for struggling readers because academic literacy develops more slowly than general literacy. Many struggling readers' experiences and schemata differ from those needed for content textbooks and content teachers' instructions. Both reading and listening comprehension are often weak due to deficient word knowledge (See Chapter 4.) and below average oral language comprehension (Spear-Swerling, 2004). Teachers must pay particular attention when giving instructions to struggling readers to use language that students understand. Reading aloud to students is a means of helping them develop language comprehension. Struggling readers may lack knowledge of many reading comprehension strategies, or they may lack the ability to apply them. Struggling readers often have experiences and schemata that differ from textbook content. Figure 5.4 shows comprehension interventions for struggling readers that are supported by research (Ash, 2002, Samuels 2004; Spear-Swerling, 2004).

Finding topics, main ideas, and supporting details is a difficult task for struggling readers. They have to learn to sort important details from unimportant ones. This will lead them into writing summaries and paraphrasing. Paraphrasing requires the student to state important ideas in his or her own words. Teachers should help these students learn strategies through explicit instruction and scaffolding of reading. (See Chapter 6.) The comprehension strategies shown in this chapter and the other chapters of this book can be demonstrated, and teachers can use think-alouds to demonstrate the kind of thinking that occurs when reading silently.

FIGURE 5.4

Comprehension Interventions for Struggling Readers

ENGLISH/
LANGUAGE
ARTS

Comprehension Intervention

	Focus on main ideas; use prereading experiences.
Motivate/build interest	Activate/build schemata.
Vocabulary	Preteach vocabulary.
	Relate to concepts.
Purposes for reading	Provide questions to answer when reading.
Oral and shared reading	Students read with recorded textbook/coach.
Guided reading	Small group or partner (coach) reading.
Self-selected reading	Literature circles (see Chapter 10, "Literature Response Groups (Literature Circles)").

Struggling readers tend to avoid reading because they are not successful at it; unfortunately, they do not improve because they are not motivated to read. Internet activities (especially social networking) and computer programs motivate students and increase both vocabulary and comprehension.

Reading coaches also motivate struggling secondary readers. Bacon (2005) describes a program she designed to prepare her at- and above-grade readers to act as coaches for the struggling students in her classes. She found that the student coaches provided the intense, specific, and frequent instruction that struggling readers need; the program fostered a learning community. The reading coaches modeled comprehension strategies for the struggling readers in a cooperative learning environment. Teachers have found that coaches make a remarkable difference in the learning of struggling students.

FOCUS ON *English Language Learners*

Helping English Language Learners Comprehend

MUSIC

ART

Above all else, ELLs need assistance to read; they need to understand, learn from, and feel successful in reading (Graves and Fitzgerald, 2003). They bring world knowledge and schemata developed in their home language to aid them in comprehending English text. However, there are individual differences among ELLs because they bring different world knowledge and experience to learning language (Hernandez, 2003). Another difference depends on the native language of the learner; for example, English and Dutch are linguistically closer than English and German and the Romance languages.

There is a rich connection between language and cognition. Therefore, learning English vocabulary and English grammatical structure are foundations of the reading fluency needed for reading comprehension. Students tend to use English vocabulary in the syntactic patterns of their first language. Teachers can help ELLs by comparing their first and second languages, showing them the structures that are the same. This enables students to use English words to make complete and accurate sentences. DelliCarpini and Gulla (2009) recommend creating opportunities for ELLs to collaborate with fluent English-speaking students. Instructional materials should be meaningful and interesting to ELLs. ELLs may need schemata development and prereading preparation for the texts they are expected to read. They need meaningful opportunities to interact with classmates and will benefit from a peer coach or a peer tutor (Coppola, 2003). Hernandez (2003) suggests a strategic worksheet that ELLs could complete alone or with a partner. Figure 5.5 is adapted from an example in Hernandez (2003). DelliCarpini (2008) recommends using newspapers, music and art in ELL classes, because these materials are more interesting than many materials prepared for ELLs.

F I G U R E 5.5

A Guide for Developing the Reading Comprehension of ELLs and Partners

Directions: Write answers to the following questions:

1. Before reading, look at the following:

   Title and subtitles   Highlighted vocabulary   Illustrations, including graphs and charts

   What is the topic?

   _____

   _____

   Predict the main idea.

   _____

   _____

2. Read the first paragraph and the last paragraph and write what you have learned.

   _____

   _____

3. Ask yourself questions about the topic; if there are subheads, they can become questions. Write your questions here.

   _____

   _____

4. Begin reading and stop at the end of each section to summarize in a sentence or two. Write the sentences here.

   _____

   _____

5. Identify the important vocabulary. _____

   _____

6. Did you find the text easy to read or hard to read? _____

   Why? _____

7. Tell your partner what you learned, and whether your prediction was accurate.

Summary

Students must acquire multiple literacies to comprehend the many text forms they will encounter both in and out of school. Comprehension is a strategic process during which readers simultaneously extract and construct meaning through interaction with written language. Readers' comprehension depends on their ability to manage themselves as readers, the text, and the situation or activity. Students use their skills, fluency, stance, social and cultural background, and interest in authentic assignments to read content texts. In addition, vocabulary knowledge, experiences, abilities, motivation, and strategies enable readers to construct meaning.

Readers' language and cognitive competence create students' foundations for acquiring the skills and strategies that they need to understand content texts of various types such as textbooks, novels, magazines, and Internet materials (Bean, 2001). The texts students read provide the knowledge, language, and framework for understanding. Teachers create aspects of the reading situation because they establish time, place, participants, the assignment, and the purposes, and they guide stance or perspective.

Teaching students comprehension strategies gives them the tools for enhancing their content comprehension. Strategies for vocabulary were introduced in Chapter 4. In this chapter, reaction logs, comparison/contrast logs, identifying various text organizations, and using graphic organizers are introduced to help students improve their comprehension of content texts. Struggling readers and English language learners need comprehension instruction and strategies to develop understanding of content materials.

Discussion Questions

1. How could reading comprehension occur without prior knowledge?
2. What are textual schemata? How do they function in reading comprehension?
3. Compare the characteristics of active readers with those of passive readers.
4. How are reading comprehension and content reading related?
5. How can learning academic language help both struggling readers and English language learners?
6. How do you think an active reader would employ metacognition?
7. What do content teachers need to know about teaching English language learners?
8. What do content teachers need to know about teaching struggling readers?

Enrichment Activities

1. Read an article in the local newspaper, and write down all the thinking processes that you use to understand what you are reading.
2. Read a current bestseller, and write a brief paragraph that presents the theme (main idea) of the book. Have a classmate who has read the same book analyze your comprehension.
3. Find examples of paragraphs in content area textbooks that follow organizational patterns illustrated in this chapter. Bring these examples to class to share and discuss.
*4. Choose one of the metacognitive activities presented in this chapter, and plan ways to adapt it to your content area.

5. Observe a class that includes English language learners and identify the adjustments that the teacher makes to enhance learning.
6. Identify a content text that you might use in teaching and plan the adjustment necessary for struggling readers. (This could include locating adapted reading materials and/or Internet sites.)

---

*These activities are designed for in-service teachers, student teachers, and practicum students.

Resources including the TeachSource Video Cases can be found on the website for this book. Cengage Learning's CourseMate brings course concepts to life with interactive learning, study, and exam preparation tools that support the printed textbook. Go to www.cengage.com/login to register your access code.

CHAPTER 6

Strategies for Constructing Meaning in Texts

Overview

Comprehension is "the process of constructing a supportable understanding of a text" (Neufeld, 2005, p. 302). The goal of comprehension is to understand deeply, to retain knowledge and information, and to apply the knowledge and information gained. Strategies are "deliberate, goal-directed attempts to control and modify the reader's efforts to decode text, understand words, and construct text meanings" (Afferbach et al., 2008, p. 364). Instruction and practice help students learn to select and implement strategies for developing their understanding (Afferbach, 2008). According to Pressley (2006), the goal is to teach a small repertoire of comprehension strategies. These strategies "should be explicitly taught and modeled long term at all grade levels" (Dymock, 2007, p. 161). Different comprehension strategies are implemented before reading, during reading, and following reading. This chapter focuses on teaching the strategies that readers can use to build understanding.

Purpose-Setting Questions

As you read this chapter, try to answer these questions:

1. Describe a teacher of strategic reading.
2. How can readers identify appropriate comprehension strategies?
3. How do strategies help students comprehend?
4. What do good readers do?

Good Readers

What cognitive strategies are the most useful?

Good readers use **cognitive strategies**, which are systematic plans that students consciously use to monitor and improve reading comprehension (Beck, 2005). These strategies allow students to gain control of their own comprehension. **Strategic readers** actively interact with the text and the context (reading task and purpose);

they connect information in the text with preexisting knowledge. They have a repertoire of strategies that they know how to use to help them comprehend. They use strategies like those that Neufeld (2008) identified in his analysis of comprehension instruction in content area classrooms and the thinking processes involved in reading comprehension. He outlined the following research supported strategies that will be identified and explained in this chapter:

- Question asking and answering
- Clarifying a purpose for reading
- Activating relevant prior knowledge
- Making predictions about text
- Attending to text structure
- Creating summaries (oral, written, and visual)
- Monitoring comprehension (metacomprehension)
- Using fix-up strategies

What is the teacher's role in developing strategic readers?

The explicit teaching of strategies can enable students to acquire relevant knowledge from text. Explicit strategy instruction includes modeling, scaffolding, think-alouds, and coaching with direct explanations of why strategies are valuable, as well as explanations of how and when to use them (either before, during, or after reading, depending on the strategy). The teacher's role in teaching strategies begins with engaging students in the learning process. Engagement is a key factor in reading comprehension because engaged readers are active readers who are motivated to read and seek to understand (Pflaum and Bishop, 2004).

Scaffolding is a strategy for supporting learning experiences. The most useful form of scaffolding for secondary students is organizing students' engagement with text through prereading activities, during-reading activities, and postreading activities. Prereading, or getting ready to read strategies (Neufeld, 2005), include clarifying a purpose for reading, such as to prepare for class discussion or a test; relating students' experiences to the text; activating background knowledge; developing prereading questions; and predicting text content or story plot.

During-reading strategies include guided reading and summarizing. Postreading activities include discussion, answering questions, responding to text, and writing summaries. The preceding activities are suggestions, but are certainly not exhaustive. Application of scaffolding activities is discussed later in this chapter.

Teachers create contexts for engagement when they develop knowledge goals, real-world connections, and meaningful choices about reading. Teachers should choose interesting texts that are vivid, important, and relevant to students (Pflaum and Bishop, 2004). Teachers should learn what students bring to their reading and create bridges or scaffolds between prior knowledge and new information. Strategic instruction enables students to assume responsibility for independent comprehension gradually. Figure 6.1 illustrates these concepts, summarizing the steps that content teachers can use when teaching comprehension strategies.

FIGURE 6.1

Teaching Process
for Comprehension
Strategies

1. **Teacher engages students.** The teacher motivates students, activates their interests and prior knowledge. The teacher gives the strategy a label and explains its value for reading comprehension.

2. **Teacher models strategy.** The teacher shows students how to use the strategy. The teacher may use a think-aloud to demonstrate. A think-aloud is a process that illustrates ways of thinking about reading content. The teacher reads from a text aloud, stopping periodically to tell his thoughts about the content he has read. Following the demonstration, the students should practice "thinking" aloud.

3. **Teacher monitors guided student practice.** Students practice the strategy until they can apply it in their own reading.

4. **Teacher steps back.** Students independently apply the strategy to comprehend.

Cognitive Processing

The comprehension process is one that calls on both general knowledge and specialized knowledge, as well as thinking strategies. **Cognitive processing** leads to schema development, which facilitates storage of knowledge in memory. Teachers can stimulate students' cognitive processing through a variety of activities such as **rehearsal** (practicing use of information), review, comparing and contrasting, and drawing connections (Rosenshine, 1997).

Thinking and Questioning

Teachers should raise questions about real-world problems, projects, and tasks that relate to students and focus their thinking. Curiosity stimulates students to question. Teachers and/or students can raise questions that pose contradictions to stimulate motivation (Ciardiello, 2007). Follow-up discussion strategies, such as asking for elaboration, influence the degree and quality of classroom discussion. Thinking is more likely to flourish when ideas are valued and varying points of view are encouraged. In a thoughtful environment, students' answers and ideas are accepted, clarified, and expanded, often by the teacher's asking, "Why do you think that?"

Effective Questioning

Questioning can effectively guide and extend comprehension. In addition, asking and answering questions reveals our thoughts and feelings, to ourselves as well as to others (Fordham, 2006). Strategies such as providing relevant questions before students read the selection help them focus on major ideas and concepts. Asking questions that require interpretation and critical thinking stimulates higher levels of cognitive processing. In contrast, focusing on literal questions that require specific correct answers limits thinking, because students can memorize the required answers. Stimulating questions are those that have several appropriate responses; such questions give students opportunities to experience success when expressing

What activities stimulate cognitive processing?

MEETING THE CHALLENGE

SOCIAL STUDIES

After the principal of Woodridge High School censored material in the school newspaper, Jeff Colson's eleventh-grade social studies students began to complain that he had violated their freedom of speech. Jeff asked the students to identify the ways that the principal had violated specific rights encoded in the Bill of Rights. After discussion, the students discovered they could not cite violations because they didn't know anything about the Bill of Rights. Jeff decided to develop a *WebQuest* to explore the topic. WebQuests are inquiry-oriented projects in which the information that students read and study comes from the Internet. Students may e-mail questions to Internet sites and they may use videoconferencing. In this WebQuest students were to work in small groups and individually. Their evaluation would be based on writing and debating.

The students were to study the Bill of Rights and relate that document to the principal's decision concerning the school newspaper. After phase one of the WebQuest, Jeff planned to have the students research challenges to the Bill of Rights and compare those challenges to their school situation. In the final phase of the WebQuest, the students were to study the Fourteenth Amendment to the Constitution and relate it to the Bill of Rights. All of the students started in groups of three to locate copies of the Bill of Rights from the Library of Congress Internet site. After they did that, Jeff identified related Internet sites: ACLU Briefing Papers—The Bill of Rights (http://archive.aclu.org/) and the Bill of Rights Institute (http://www.billofrightsinstitute.org/).

The students then organized into small groups to study the Bill of Rights word by word. After this thorough study, the students discussed their various interpretations of the document in relation to the incident in their school. Then the students wrote position papers in which they explained what they believed and cited portions of the Bill of Rights and related documents to support their positions. They asked the principal to write a position paper regarding the school paper incident. The first part of the study concluded with a debate to which they invited the principal. They challenged his position and wrote a rebuttal. They were pleased that he agreed to listen to them and to discuss their grievances, and they looked forward to his response to their rebuttal. The students were highly motivated by this experience and very interested in studying the challenges to the Bill of Rights.

their own ideas. Good questions require multiple-word answers that foster cognitive growth. When students offer one-word answers, a teacher might ask, "Why do you think that?" or "Can you give me examples of this?" To increase comprehension, teach students to ask themselves and others clarification questions such as these: "Is this what you mean: _____?" "Can you give me a nonexample of _____?" "Would you say more about _____?" "What is the main point?"

What could happen when you allow "wait time" after asking a question?

Giving students ample time to reflect on their answers improves the quality of answers. Allowing three to five seconds of "**wait time**" after asking a question gives students time to process the question and formulate a response. The wait time for questions that focus on stimulating students' higher levels of thinking and those that encourage independent thinking should be longer than the time given for literal-level questions. Thoughtful answers require more processing time. Teachers should expect individual differences in the amount of wait time that students need to formulate thoughtful answers. Some students process quickly and others process slowly, but the answers from both types of students can be of equal quality.

Providing appropriate wait time for students is a challenge for teachers who are concerned about silence in the classroom. Some teachers may feel compelled to ask follow-up questions to encourage students' answers, when waiting would improve the quality of answers.

Questions can be posed before, during, and after reading. Teachers can ask strategic questions (ones that prompt students to use strategies) throughout the reading (Fordham, 2006). Questions asked before reading activate schemata and focus attention on important ideas and concepts. Strategic questions before reading about the topic of erosion might be "Have you ever seen an area that was badly eroded? What do you think caused this erosion? These questions would lead students to activate their prior knowledge on the topic. At this point, students can also generate questions about a topic or concept. During reading, students can ask themselves questions about how well they are comprehending. After reading, teachers can ask questions such as "Did you find the answers to your questions?" "What are they?" "Which questions are still unanswered?" "What did you learn that we didn't ask questions about?" "What did the writer do to make readers feel or think a certain way?" "What evidence to support a particular idea did the writer give?" Students who read a passage and answer questions about it generally learn more than students who only read the passage. Teachers who are preparing questions for a discussion should review the following points:

1. What are the important ideas in this selection?

2. What ideas and concepts do I want the students to remember from this selection?

3. What questions will lead students to understand these ideas and concepts?

4. What thinking abilities have the students in this group already developed?

5. What thinking abilities do the students in this group need to develop?

Student Questions

Self-questioning is a powerful strategy for stimulating content learning. Question generation prompts learners to seek answers that they want to know (Ciardiello, 2007). Teaching unsuccessful readers to raise questions as they read helps them acquire the ability to comprehend complex verbal material. It appears that students who ask themselves questions engage in self-monitoring of their understanding, which leads them to independent comprehension.

What is divergent thinking?

Self-questioning stimulates **divergent thinking** and encourages independent learning. Divergent thinking is "thinking outside the box." It is thinking that follows different paths and moves beyond the original material. Research shows that students need direct strategy instruction to become successful generators of higher-level questions (Duke and Pearson, 2002; Rosenshine, Meister, and Chapman, 1996). The strategy instruction approach introduced in Figure 6.1 can be applied to self-questioning.

Types of Thinking and Reading

Literal Thinking and Reading

What is the focus of literal thinking?

Literal thinking is concerned with directly stated facts and ideas that answer the question "What did the author say?" Readers often quote the text to answer literal questions. The major forms of literal thinking are recognizing and recalling stated main ideas; recognizing and recalling stated details; recognizing and recalling stated sequences; following stated directions; and recognizing stated causes and effects.

ENGLISH/
LANGUAGE
ARTS

Example 6.1 shows some literal-level questions based on two books. *The Wednesday Wars*, by Gary Schmidt, is the story of Holling Hoodhood's seventh-grade school year. Each chapter is a month of the school year. *The Book Thief*, by Markus Zasuk, is the story of Liesel, who lives in Germany during World War II.

Students learn best when teachers model the process of answering questions. For example, the teacher could model answering the first question for *The Wednesday Wars* by sharing his or her thoughts in a think-aloud. The teacher might begin with "I wonder why the author described the two sides of town the way he did? I think he did this to show the contrast between the two sides of town, one side Jewish and the other Catholic, which left Holling as a Presbyterian alone in the middle. The book says that Catholics had to attend Catechism on Wednesday afternoons. The Jewish students had to attend Hebrew School then. The text then says that Mrs. Baker said, "So on Wednesday afternoon you attend neither Hebrew School or Catechism. . . . You are here with me" (p. 4). The reason is found in the direct words of the text. This discussion alerts students to the author's writing style and his organizational patterns. Teachers can provide students with opportunities to demonstrate their own thinking strategies. Questions that lead students to relate the text to their prior knowledge, to support their answers from the text or prior knowledge, or to apply knowledge are

---

EXAMPLE 6.1   Literal Level Questions based on *The Wednesday Wars* and *The Book Thief*

The Wednesday Wars

ENGLISH/
LANGUAGE
ARTS

1. Why does Holling have to spend Wednesday afternoons in Mrs. Baker's classroom?
2. Describe what happened to the first batch of cream puffs.
3. What did Holling think when Mrs. Baker first told him that they would be reading Shakespeare?
4. How do you learn that Holling liked Shakespeare?

The Book Thief

SOCIAL
STUDIES

1. Why is Liesel living with a foster family?
2. What is the title of the first book that Liesel stole?
3. After three weeks of living with foster parents, what did Liesel know about her foster father?
4. Who taught Liesel to read?

especially useful for encouraging them to model thinking processes. When listening to the students present their thinking, the teacher should focus on the cognitive process, as well as the answer. After students have some experience with thinking strategies, they can work in pairs, modeling thinking for each other.

Inferential Thinking and Reading

How does literal thinking contrast with inferential thinking?

Inferential thinking is concerned with deeper meanings that are difficult to define because they involve several types of reasoning. This is further complicated by the fact that inferential questions often have more than one "correct" answer. To make inferences, readers must relate facts, generalizations, definitions, and values. Inferential questions emphasize finding relationships among elements of the written text. Essentially, making inferences involves using one's schemata to fill in information that the author implies, based on background knowledge that the reader is assumed to have. Building on readers' background knowledge is essential, due to space and time limitations. For example, in the sentence "Nancy pulled on her mittens and her parka before opening the door," the reader draws upon personal experience to infer that Nancy is going outdoors into cold weather. Students should always be prepared to support and explain their answers. Two activities that involve making inferences are comparing and contrasting historical figures and forming generalizations from material in their content textbooks.

In making inferences about reading content, readers examine the author's words, reading between the lines for implications that are not explicitly stated. To do this, readers combine information from their own experiences with text information. The main types of inferences include *location* inferences, in which the reader infers the place; *agent* inferences, which require the reader to infer the person acting; *time* inferences, which are concerned with when the action occurs; *action* inferences, which have to do with the action occurring in the text; *instrument* inferences, which are concerned with tools or devices involved in the text; *object* inferences, which require readers to infer objects the author has implied; *cause-and-effect* inferences, referring to implied causes and/or effects; *category* inferences, which require the reader to infer a category to which objects mentioned in the text belong; *problem–solution* inferences, referring to implied problems or solutions implied by the author; and *feeling–attitude* inferences, which are concerned with the characters' feelings and attitudes that are implied by the author.

To demonstrate the inferential reasoning process, teachers can employ the think-aloud strategy by expressing their reflections aloud. For instance, in an inferential question for *The Wednesday Wars* about conflicts that the main character had, the teacher might say Holling had a conflict with Doug Swieteck, and he tripped Doug and sent him flying through the air and injured him, although not seriously. He had a conflict with Mrs. Baker, when she sent him to other teachers to avoid having him in her class on Wednesday.

**ENGLISH/
LANGUAGE
ARTS**

**ENGLISH/
LANGUAGE
ARTS**

In answer to the same type of question about *The Book Thief*, the teacher might say that Liesel perceived a conflict with the mayor's wife, because she was stealing books, but eventually the mayor's wife opened her library to Liesel. After that, the conflict she felt was more internal.

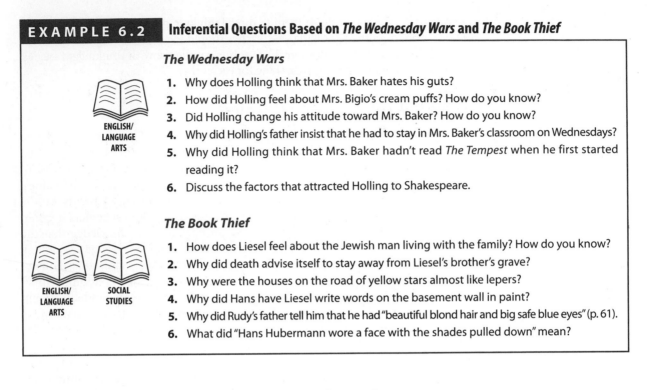

EXAMPLE 6.2 | **Inferential Questions Based on *The Wednesday Wars* and *The Book Thief***

The Wednesday Wars

ENGLISH/ LANGUAGE ARTS

1. Why does Holling think that Mrs. Baker hates his guts?
2. How did Holling feel about Mrs. Bigio's cream puffs? How do you know?
3. Did Holling change his attitude toward Mrs. Baker? How do you know?
4. Why did Holling's father insist that he had to stay in Mrs. Baker's classroom on Wednesdays?
5. Why did Holling think that Mrs. Baker hadn't read *The Tempest* when he first started reading it?
6. Discuss the factors that attracted Holling to Shakespeare.

The Book Thief

ENGLISH/ LANGUAGE ARTS

SOCIAL STUDIES

1. How does Liesel feel about the Jewish man living with the family? How do you know?
2. Why did death advise itself to stay away from Liesel's brother's grave?
3. Why were the houses on the road of yellow stars almost like lepers?
4. Why did Hans have Liesel write words on the basement wall in paint?
5. Why did Rudy's father tell him that he had "beautiful blond hair and big safe blue eyes" (p. 61).
6. What did "Hans Hubermann wore a face with the shades pulled down" mean?

Critical Thinking and Reading

How are literal thinking and inferential thinking related to critical thinking?

Critical thinking is central to the curriculum because schools strive to educate minds rather than to train memories. Critical literacy expands readers' responses and thinking about the texts they read (McLaughlin and DeVoogd, 2004). "Critical reading develops on a continuum in a gradual progression from the superficial to the increasingly complex (Mendelman, 2008). The importance of critical thinking is well established. All readers need to consider critically the information they receive about the world around them. Mendelman (2008) recommends teaching critical thinking in every class. Critical readers recognize that they receive a limited amount of information when they read (or listen). Moreover, the information is usually presented from a particular point of view, filtered through the writer's perceptions. These varying perceptions lead to discrepancies in different accounts of the same incident. To think critically, readers must begin with an understanding of what the author is saying, so both literal and interpretive thinking are necessary to critical thinking skills.

What do critical readers do?

Critical readers question what they read, suspend judgment until all facts are presented, evaluate, and decide. Critical thinking is evaluative thinking (Clarke and Whitney, 2009). To make judgments, the reader compares text with external criteria derived from experience, research, teachers, and experts in the field; therefore, background knowledge is essential to critical reading. Critical readers examine their own beliefs and the ways those beliefs influence their own and others' thinking (Hall and Piazza, 2008). Critical readers recognize the author's purpose and point of view or context, and they distinguish fact from opinion. They test the author's assertions against their own observations, information, and logic. The major facets of critical reading are summarized in the following:

- The reader is open-minded and suspends judgment until adequate data are available, thus avoiding jumping to conclusions.
- The reader constantly questions the content.
- The reader has a problem-solving attitude.
- The reader is knowledgeable regarding the topic.
- The reader discerns the author's purpose.
- The reader evaluates the author's qualifications.
- The reader evaluates the validity of the material.
- The reader evaluates the use of propaganda.
- The reader evaluates the author's logic.
- The reader evaluates the author's use of language.

Critical reading involves three major types of abilities: semantics, logic, and evaluating authenticity (Lewis, 1991). *Semantics* abilities include understanding the denotative and connotative uses of words, the use of vague and precise words, and the use of words in a persuasive manner. *Logic* skills include understanding the reliability of the author's argument and statements, recognizing the use of propaganda, distinguishing fact from opinion, and recognizing the various forms of persuasive writing.

What types of activities are used to evaluate authenticity?

Authenticity skills include determining if adequate information is included, comparing this information with other relevant information, examining the author's qualifications, and using authoritative research sources. Critical reading in the content areas consists of explicit applications of the principles of critical thinking, which are discussed further in Chapters 11 and 12. Suggestions for teaching critical reading procedures are given in later sections of this chapter.

Critical reading questions based on *The Wednesday Wars* and *The Book Thief* are shown in Example 6.3.

EXAMPLE 6.3   **Critical Reading Questions Based on *The Wednesday Wars* and *The Book Thief***

The Wednesday Wars

**ENGLISH/
LANGUAGE
ARTS**

1. What made Holling "almost glad" to be alone with Mrs. Baker?
2. Why did the author reveal the setting, and how is this setting important?
3. Do you think that Holling's attitude toward his classmates changed from the beginning to the end of the story? What made you think it did or didn't change?
4. What caused Holling to change his attitude toward Mrs. Baker?
5. Was Danny a good friend to Holling? What did he do that made you know this?

The Book Thief

**SOCIAL
STUDIES**   **ENGLISH/
LANGUAGE
ARTS**

1. Why does Liesel's foster father trade cigarettes to get a book for her after he asked her to stop stealing books?
2. What is the symbolism of the Book Thief and her family living on Himmel Street?

Note: When modeling critical thinking about this critical reading question, the teacher could say, "I thought about the death that occurred on Himmel Street in several ways. For instance, they lived on *Heaven* Street, and those who died there were near heaven before death."

3. Why did Liesel's foster father slap her after she said that she hated Hitler?
4. Was it really stealing for Liesel to take back the book that had been given to her? Why or why not?
5. Were Rudy and Liesel bad people because they enjoyed stealing the things they took? Why did you answer this way?
6. Why did the Standover man make a book for Liesel? Discuss the pictures and the significance of the words on the pages.
7. How did Liesel's book save her life?

Semantic Learning Activities

1. Since "loaded" words play on readers' emotions, students will benefit from practice in identifying them. Words like *un-American* and *extremist* call forth a negative reaction, whereas words such as *freedom, peace,* and *human rights* stimulate positive feelings. Students can practice identifying "loaded" words in Internet, newspaper, and magazine articles, advertisements, editorials, and letters from readers, as well as in textbooks.

2. Critical readers discover that words used in vague, general ways interfere with content clarity (e.g., the expressions "Everyone is doing it" and "They say"). Students should locate examples of vague word usage in their reading material.

Logic Learning Activities

SOCIAL STUDIES

1. Have students create syllogisms that state an author's premises and conclusions, similar to this one based on a social studies text chapter:

Premises. People with undesirable characteristics were rejected. Some "new" immigrants had undesirable characteristics.

Conclusion. Those "new" immigrants were rejected.

2. Have students verify through research statements found in local newspaper stories.

ENGLISH/ LANGUAGE ARTS

3. Have students examine sentences to identify words that signal the author's opinion, such as these qualifying words: *think, probably, maybe, appear, seem,* and *believe.* The following sentences are examples:
   a. I believe this is the best cake I have ever eaten.
   b. Jane will probably come home for vacation.

4. Making a graphic representation (chart) of the facts and opinions presented by an author will help the reader examine ideas critically. Example 6.4 is a chart based on information taken from a social studies textbook.

EXAMPLE 6.4	Fact and Opinion Chart

SOCIAL STUDIES

Facts	Opinions
"Old" immigrants were from British Isles, Germany, Scandinavia.	"Old" immigrants were acceptable.
"New" immigrants were from Slavic countries, Italy, Greece.	"New" immigrants were unacceptable, ignorant, greedy, diseased, criminal, insane, wild eyed, bad smelling.

ENGLISH/ LANGUAGE ARTS   **SOCIAL STUDIES**

5. Recognizing propaganda is one of the abilities required for critical reading. Discussions of propaganda techniques and methods for analyzing propaganda could be held in class. Make sure that students realize that these propaganda techniques are usually used in combination:

    a. *Bad names.* Disagreeable words are used to arouse distaste for a person or a thing.
    b. *Glad names.* Pleasant words are used to create good feelings about a person or a thing.
    c. *Plain folks.* This kind of propaganda avoids sophistication. Political candidates use this technique when they kiss babies and pet dogs.
    d. *Transfer.* This type of propaganda attempts to transfer to a person or thing the reader's respect for the flag, the cross, or some other valued symbol.
    e. *Testimonial.* This technique is like transfer except that a famous or well-informed person gives a testimonial for a product or a person. Positive feelings for the famous person are supposed to be transferred to the product.
    f. *Bandwagon.* This is an attempt to convince readers that they should accept an idea or purchase an item because "everyone is doing it."
    g. *Card stacking.* This technique utilizes accurate information but omits some data so that only one side of a story is told.

6. After learning to identify propaganda techniques, the reader should analyze the propaganda using the following questions:

    a. What technique is used?
    b. Who composed the propaganda?
    c. Why was the propaganda written?
    d. To what reader interests, emotions, and prejudices does the propaganda appeal?
    e. Will I allow myself to be influenced by this propaganda?

Critical Thinking Activities

1. Writers should support their conclusions in the text; however, readers often need additional data to evaluate the validity of content. Ask students to consult other sources of information to evaluate the validity of the content of an article, book, or chapter.

2. Ask students to evaluate the author's qualifications for writing on the topic at hand. Questions like these will guide them:
   a. Would a lawyer probably be qualified to write a book on writing contracts?
   b. Would a football player probably be qualified to write a book on foreign policy?
   c. Would a chef probably be a qualified author for a book on menu planning?
   d. Would a physician probably be qualified to write a book on music theory?

Creative Thinking and Reading

What is the most important aspect of creative thinking?

MATHEMATICS   **SCIENCE AND HEALTH**

ENGLISH/ LANGUAGE ARTS   **TECHNICAL EDUCATION**

HES/HUMAN ECOLOGY

SOCIAL STUDIES   **ENGLISH/ LANGUAGE ARTS**

Creative thinkers find new ways of viewing ideas, incidents, or characters that stimulate original or novel thinking or production of new materials. They strive for originality and ideas that are fundamental, far-reaching, and powerful. Creative thinkers are able to view their experiences from different perspectives. Good **creative thinking** always involves a measure of critical thinking, or it would be nonsensical (Perkins, 1995). Creative thinkers generate possibilities, then critically sift through and rework them. They need to be knowledgeable about a subject to think more creatively about it.

Creative thinkers and readers may come up with several ways of solving a math problem or of performing an experiment in science class. They may turn a situation from a literature selection into a puppet show, a skit, or a painting. They may make a unique table in wood shop or develop a design in human environmental science that surpasses those suggested in the book. To do these things, creative thinkers translate existing knowledge into new forms. Creativity is stifled when all school activities must be carried out according to the precise specifications of the teacher and when deviations from prescribed forms are always discouraged.

Creative thinking is based on knowledge about the subject and opportunities to solve problems and to respond to authentic situations. Creative thinking and reading activities related to *The Book Thief* and *The Wednesday Wars* are illustrated in the next section.

Creative Thinking and Reading Activities

SOCIAL STUDIES   **ENGLISH/ LANGUAGE ARTS**

ENGLISH/ LANGUAGE ARTS   **ENGLISH/ LANGUAGE ARTS**

ENGLISH/ LANGUAGE ARTS

1. In *The Book Thief*, Death observes children scrambling for coins while the Jewish children cautiously look around. This observation illustrates the difference in life for Jewish and non-Jewish people during World War II in Germany. Write a description of how you believe each of the two groups of children feels during this experience.

2. In *The Book Thief*, Death tells how he/she/it doesn't look. Describe how you think he/she/it does look, and tell why.

3. In *The Book Thief*, where would you have hidden books that you had acquired the way Liesel acquired hers, if you had been in her position?

4. In The Wednesday Wars, what would you have done to ensure getting to the Mickey Mantle signing in time and appropriately dressed, knowing what Holling knew about his father and the length of the play?

5. In *The Wednesday Wars*, what other inexpensive things could Holling have done for Meryl Lee on Valentine's Day?

Figure 6.2 summarizes types of questions and strategies to increase quality thinking.

FIGURE 6.2

Questioning for Quality Thinking

Source: "Cueing Thinking in the Classroom: The Promise of Theory-Embedded Tools," by Jay McTighe and Frank T. Lyman Jr., 1988, *Educational Leadership* 45(7), pp. 18–24, Figure p. 21. (c) 1988 by ASCD. Reprinted with permission. Learn more about ASCD at www.ascd.org.

Front	**Back**
QUESTIONING FOR QUALITY THINKING	STRATEGIES TO EXTEND STUDENT THINKING

Front

QUESTIONING FOR QUALITY THINKING

Knowledge — Identification and recall of information
　　Who, what, when, where, how _____?
　　Describe _____.

Comprehension — Organization and selection of facts and ideas
　　Retell _____ in your own words.
　　What is the main idea of _____?

Application — Use of facts, rules, principles
　　How is _____ an example of _____?
　　How is _____ related to _____?
　　Why is _____ _____ significant?

Analysis — Separation of whole into component parts
　　What are the parts or features of _____?
　　Classify _____ according to _____.
　　Outline/diagram/web _____.
　　How does ___ compare/contrast with__?
　　What evidence can you list for _____?

Synthesis — Combination of ideas to form a new whole
　　What would you predict/infer from ___?
　　What ideas can you add to_____?
　　How would you create/design a new _?
　　What might happen if you combined _ with _____?
　　What solutions would you suggest for _?

Evaluation — Development of opinions, judgments, or decisions
　　Do you agree _____?
　　What do you think about _____?
　　What is the most important _____?
　　Prioritize _____.
　　How would you decide about _____?
　　What criteria would you use to assess _?

Back

STRATEGIES TO EXTEND STUDENT THINKING

- **Remember "wait time I and II"**
  Provide at least three seconds of thinking time after a question and after a response

- **Utilize "think-pair-share"**
  Allow individual thinking time, discussion with a partner, and then open up the class discussion

- **Ask "follow-ups"**
  Why? Do you agree? Can you elaborate? Tell me more. Can you give an example?

- **Withhold judgment**
  Respond to student answers in a non-evaluative fashion

- **Ask for summary (to promote active listening)**
  "Could you please summarize John's point?"

- **Survey the class**
  "How many people agree with the author's point of view?" ("thumbs up, thumbs down")

- **Allow for student calling**
  "Richard, will you please call on someone else to respond?"

- **Play devil's advocate**
  Require students to defend their reasoning against different points of view

- **Ask students to "unpack their thinking"**
  "Describe how you arrived at your answer." ("think aloud")

- **Call on students randomly**
  Not just those with raised hands

- **Student questioning**
  Let the students develop their own questions

- **Cue student responses**
  "There is not a single correct answer for this question. I want you to consider alternatives."

Authentic Reading Tasks

Reading comprehension instruction should link classroom literacy activities with real-world, authentic reading and writing experiences (Duke et al., 2006). These experiences help students connect the use of print with the home or the wider culture. For example, *The Book Thief* fits well with World War II history, and a field trip to the United States Holocaust Memorial Museum could be compared with the movie or the book *The Boy in the Striped Pajamas*.

Thematic units are one approach to developing authentic literacy tasks that integrate the language arts and other curricular areas. The integrated curriculum can be authentic and can provide learning experiences more closely attuned to the way children and adults learn. **Integrated units** promote higher-order thinking, concept development, and transfer of knowledge.

Integrated units make teaching and learning meaningful by interrelating content and process. **Themes** give instruction a focus, create coherence across content and process, and enable students to understand what and why they are learning. Integrated units of study help students transform knowledge into the schemata and tools for learning that will be helpful throughout their lives. Themes also provide a framework for students to discover the connections among literature selections. To capitalize on the merits of integrated, thematic units, teachers need to serve as mediators of comprehension strategies and skills as they guide students who are discovering the connections that are the heart of integrated instruction. The role of themes, topics, and real literature in developing literacy is discussed throughout this book, and Chapter 10 focuses on literature in content classrooms. In the next "Meeting the Challenge" vignette, the integrated unit approach to using literature in the classroom is demonstrated.

MEETING THE CHALLENGE

Kyle Richards overheard his eighth-grade students discussing a news story about skiers who had survived five days without food or shelter following an avalanche. Then another student told the group about people who survived long periods of time in collapsed buildings after an earthquake. These discussions gave him an idea for a thematic unit on survival in various environments. On the basis of the students' discussion, he thought they would recognize the authenticity of this unit. Furthermore, he could integrate it with the science and social studies curriculum. An abridged version of the unit he taught follows.

Major Concepts of the Unit

1. Many survivors do not have special skills; instead, they are people who refuse to give up.
2. Many survivors are ordinary people who are thrust into extraordinary circumstances that force them to find ways to solve their problems and keep on living.

3. Survivors often have to meet basic needs, such as finding food, water, shelter, and protection. People who lack basic knowledge about their environment have greater difficulties in solving their problems.

4. The sources of food, water, shelter, and protection differ with the nature of the environment. For example, a person stranded on a tropical island would face different problems from those faced by one caught in a blizzard.

5. Survivors' lives are changed by the problems they face and overcome.

Unit Initiation

Kyle asked the students to brainstorm the concept of survival as it related to newspaper articles about hurricanes, earthquakes, and floods, as well as stories about individuals who had survived other environmental traumas. Then he had the students map survival situations and create individual definitions of the term *survival*. The map they created is illustrated in Figure 6.3.

Following the brainstorming and semantic mapping of survival, the class studied the book *Hatchet* by Gary Paulsen. They also read newspaper and magazine articles related to survival.

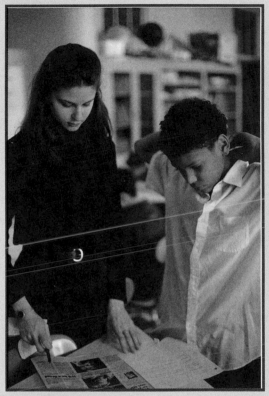

News stories may serve as the basis for thematic units.
Little Blue Wolf Productions/Corbis

FIGURE 6.3

Survival Map Created by Students

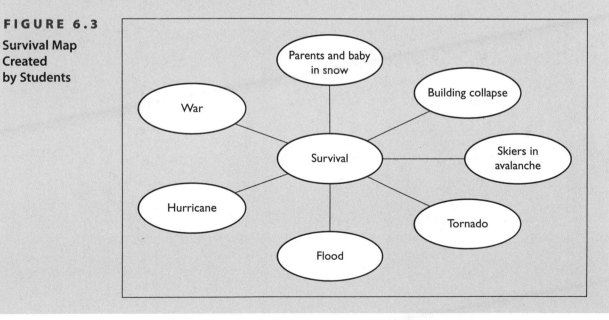

Before Reading

1. The students identified the problems and dangers they would face if they were alone in a Canadian wilderness without assistance or equipment. They discussed the topic, and the teacher recorded their ideas on a transparency. When they finished brainstorming, they fit their ideas into categories of food, shelter, clothing, protection from animals, and so forth. They summarized these ideas in their journals and on a class chart.

2. Students were told they could choose just one piece of equipment to take into the wilderness with them. Then they wrote a paragraph or more about what they chose and why they chose that particular piece of equipment. Many students cited points from newspaper and magazine articles that helped them choose their equipment.

SCIENCE AND
HEALTH

During Reading

1. The students identified the various ways the main character in *Hatchet*, Brian, solved his problems, and they compared his strategies with those discussed in newspaper and magazine articles.

2. The protagonist in *Hatchet* was struggling with several problems throughout the book, so the teacher asked students to identify the words associated with these concepts: *divorce, fire, mistakes,* and the *secret*. They listed these words in their journal for class discussion.

SOCIAL
STUDIES

3. The students identified scientific and geographic knowledge that would have helped Brian survive.

SCIENCE AND
HEALTH

Following Reading

The students discussed the following questions:

1. "Why did Brian call the fire a 'hungry friend,' and 'close and sweet'?"
2. "What was the most valuable thing Brian invented or had in this story? Why did you choose this?"
3. "What did Brian mean when he called himself a city boy in this story? Was he complimenting himself?"
4. "Why did Brian want to tell somebody about his success in building a fire?"
5. "What did Brian learn from his experience? How did he learn this?"
6. "Who taught Brian?"

Students also did the following:

1. They identified additional figurative language that made the writing especially effective. They compared the writing style of the newspaper and magazine stories with that of the novel.

ENGLISH/
LANGUAGE
ARTS

2. They contrasted Brian's character traits at the beginning and at the end of the story and made charts to show the contrasts.
3. They identified and discussed the theme of the book.
4. They identified the three types of conflict in the book and explained each one.
5. They discussed how this experience changed Brian's life.

Extensions

The students chose projects from the following list that could be related to the novel or a newspaper or magazine article:

SCIENCE AND HEALTH

1. Research flora and fauna that might exist in the Canadian wilderness that Brian could have used for food.
2. Identify other kinds of shelters that he could have constructed or found in this setting.
3. Research the concept of light refraction, which played such an important role in this book.
4. Research fire, and find different ways to build fires.
5. Find a map of a similar area. Then create a map of Brian's camp and the lake.
6. Identify ways of measuring time when one lacks the usual means.

Language Arts Extensions

ENGLISH/ LANGUAGE ARTS

1. Write a script in which Brian is interviewed on a television program. The students may role-play this activity.
2. Write about Brian's first meal after returning home.
3. Compare survival situations depicted in various stories and articles. Discuss the elements to be survived, the means of survival, and the aftermaths of the situations.
4. Compare the plot lines in several books.
5. Prepare a television show or play that illustrates the survival theme.

Related Books

The Postcard by Tony Abbott
The Goats by Brock Cole
Julie of the Wolves and *My Side of the Mountain* by Jean George
Slake's Limbo by Felice Holman
Animal Ecology by Mark Lambert and John Williams
No Pretty Pictures by Anita Lobel
Dogsong and *Tracker* by Gary Paulsen
What's Going to Happen to Me? When Parents Separate and Divorce by Eda Le Shan
Megiddo's Shadow by Arthur Slade
The Trap by John Smelcer
Sparrow by Sherri L. Smith
Shelters from Tepee to Igloo by Harvey Weiss

Strategies to Increase Comprehension

Throughout this text, strategies and activities are introduced to improve students' comprehension. These strategies focus on literacy and constructing meaning. Initially, most of the strategies involve direct teacher instruction and guidance, but the universal goal is for students to use the strategies independently. Ultimately, students should internalize and implement appropriate strategies.

Some of the following suggestions should be implemented before reading, some during reading, and others after reading; some strategies are used throughout the reading process.

Scaffolds for Comprehension

Scaffolds are temporary supporting techniques that enable a student to successfully complete a task he or she could not complete without the assistance of the scaffold. Scaffolding connects students to the text and the comprehension task. Scaffolds are instructional frameworks that support students as they develop content literacy (Stephens and Brown, 2005). Scaffolds focus on the task and how to complete it, but the ultimate goal is to help students become independent learners. In reality, all of the strategies in this book are scaffolds because they support the teacher who is giving students the support they need to comprehend.

Scaffolding strategies can be adapted to any content area and they can be structured through various organizational formats. Teachers can work with the entire class, especially when working toward common goals. A small group of students may work with specific goals and tasks. These groups should be flexible, depending on the purposes and tasks. Some students work well with partners who are working to achieve the same goals. In some instances, individual students work well when assigned specific responsibilities (Stephens and Brown, 2005). Moreover, the varied groups enable the teacher to develop a clear picture of individual students' progress.

Think-alouds, which were discussed earlier, are strategies that teachers and students use for scaffolding. Additional strategies are found throughout this text and the following scaffolding strategies are examples:

- Directed reading-thinking activity (DRTA)
- Discussion
- Know–Want to Know–Learned (K-W-L)
- Problem-solving approach
- Reciprocal teaching
- Writing strategies
- Visualization strategies

Directed Reading-Thinking Activity (DRTA)

What is the key activity in a DRTA?

Stauffer (1969) developed the **directed reading–thinking activity (DRTA)** to encourage students' thinking. In a DRTA, students develop their own purposes for reading when the teacher asks them to predict what the material will be about from the title clues and the graphic aids in the text. Predictions may be listed on the board and modified or deleted as the students request. Students may change their ideas about the predictions, and they can explain their predictions during class discussion.

The teacher divides the reading material into portions that provide good prediction points. Students read to a specified point, stop, assess their previous predictions, either confirm or reject the predictions, and make new predictions if they have rejected the old ones. Students discuss the confirmation or rejection of predictions and support their decisions by referring to information gathered from the text. This process is continued until the entire selection has been read. Students' early predictions are likely to be diverse because the reading clues are sparse at that point, but the predictions become more convergent as the reading continues.

The four steps in a content area directed reading-thinking activity are as follows (Haggard, 1986):

1. Activate prior knowledge.

2. Predict the content of the next text portion.

3. Read the selection.

4. Confirm, reject, revise, or elaborate previous predictions.

Example 6.5 illustrates the application of DRTA to an assignment in *Fish & Wildlife: Principles of Zoology and Ecology.*

EXAMPLE 6.5   **Earth Science DRTA**

SCIENCE AND HEALTH

STEP 1 Activate prior knowledge

Teacher: What determines the kind of environment that an animal lives in?
Student A: A place where the animal can obtain food.
Teacher: Do you think that an animal can only live in one place?
Student B: No, because bears move out of the mountains when they can't find food.

STEP 2 Predict

Teacher: What topics do you predict will be covered in the section on Animal behavior and habits?
Student A: I think this section will discuss animal adaptations.
Student B: I think that it will discuss whether there is only one place that some animals can live.
Teacher: That is a thoughtful prediction.
Student C: What happens when the food is not available?
Student D: I think they have to eat a different food or move to a different place.
Teacher: What animals do you predict will be discussed?
Student E: I think bears, birds, and deer.

STEP 3 Read

Teacher: Now read this section to learn whether your predictions are accurate.

STEP 4 Confirm, reject, revise, or elaborate predictions

In Step 4 the students discussed and concluded the following:
a. The book discussed birds, cats, and deer in the first section, not bears.
b. Some birds did adapt to their environment.
c. Some animals, like cats, cannot eat certain kinds of food.

Discussion

What are the major
values of discussion in
the content classroom?

Creating a social environment in the classroom promotes dialogue and discussion, as well as developing a learning community (Wollman-Bonilla, 1994). **Discussion** is a powerful tool for developing higher-order thinking because participants interact as they present multiple points of view and listen to counterarguments. Students who participate in discussions learn to listen to and validate other students' perspectives. Meanings shared in discussion groups are more than a collection of individual ideas; they are part of new sets of meanings developed as members talk and listen to one another.

In a well-planned discussion, students interact with one another as well as with the teacher, and they are encouraged to make comments and to ask questions that are longer than two- or three-word phrases. Such discussions offer students opportunities to enrich and refine knowledge gained from the text.

Know–Want to Know–Learned (K-W-L)

What additional
columns could you add
to the K-W-L chart?

The Know–Want to Know–Learned (**K-W-L**) strategy encourages students to activate prior knowledge and stimulates cognition and metacognition (Carr and Ogle, 1987; Ogle, 1986). Initially, the students brainstorm what they already know about the reading topic. Then they write the brainstormed information in the K (Know) column of a chart like the one shown in Example 6.6. As the students work, the teacher should encourage them to categorize the information and list their categories at the bottom of the column. The students generate questions about the text, which are listed in the W (Want to Know) column. Additional questions may be generated as the students proceed. Finally, information learned from the text is entered in the L (Learned) column. The students map the material and use the map to write a summary.

Problem-Solving Approach

What kinds of thinking
are stimulated in a
problem solving
approach?

A **problem-solving approach** to reading encourages students to spend time understanding a problem before attacking it (McTighe and Lyman, 1988). In this

---

EXAMPLE 6.6   **K-W-L for Eleventh-Grade Government—"Civil Liberties": The First Amendment Freedoms**

SOCIAL
STUDIES

K (Know)	W (Want to Know)	L (Learned)
Freedom of speech	Does the First Amendment mean we	
Personal freedom	can do *anything* we want to? Are we	
Freedom to write	free to do things that will hurt us?	
Language		
Civil liberties		

| EXAMPLE 6.7 | **Problem-Solving Paradigm Based on *Sports Medicine Essentials* by Jim Clover** |

Problem: How to treat a strain.

Solutions	Evaluate Possible Solutions	Support for Expectations
Ice the strain	+	He used ice.
Compress with elastic wrap	+	He used elastic wrap.
Elevate above the heart	+	He elevated the strain.
		The strain improved on following day.

Solution: He used all three solutions to treat the strain.

Evaluate Solution

The solutions worked well. The strain was better the next day.

approach, the teacher introduces various methods of problem solving and poses problem situations for students to analyze. Then students identify a problem and state it in their own words, after which they brainstorm possible solutions. Critical thinking is the next stage because students have to examine the possibilities generated and eliminate the unworkable ones. Students can compare this problem with others that they know about or discuss it with another person to clarify thinking. In addition, students may gather relevant information and find out how other people have solved similar problems. A problem can be broken into parts or restated to expand students' understanding. Finally, writing out a problem often helps students solve it. Completing a guide similar to the one in Example 6.7 is helpful for students who need practice with problem solving.

The following are examples of problems that could be used in problem-solving reading activities:

1. *Social studies.* During a World War II unit give the students contradicting quotations concerning Franklin Delano Roosevelt. Then ask them to research to determine which point of view they espouse.

2. *Science.* Assign students to read news articles related to the tsunami that occurred in South Asia at the end of 2004 and to research the kinds of problems that victims of a tsunami may face.

TECHNICAL EDUCATION

HES/HUMAN ECOLOGY

BUSINESS EDUCATION   **SOCIAL STUDIES**

SCIENCE AND HEALTH   **SOCIAL STUDIES**

3. *Technology education.* During a unit on finishing various types of materials, such as wood, concrete, plastic, and compressed wood, have the students explore the finishes that are most appropriate, most economical, and most durable.

4. *Human environmental science.* Students should use the new food pyramid as a basis for planning the nutritional needs of individuals with various diseases, such as diabetes, or allergies.

Controversial issues provide material for the problem-solving approach to content area reading. In such an approach, teachers may select issues related to assigned reading or from the Internet, newspapers, newsmagazines, and television programs. Controversial issues that may be used follow:

1. The president's economic changes at the beginning of a new term of office. (economics class)

2. The moral and/or scientific issues in genetic engineering. (science class)

3. The role of computers in education and in other facets of life. (social studies class)

For reluctant readers in an eleventh-grade class, Darvin (2006) asked the students to think of personal problems that they could use reading and writing to solve. The students chose very important personal problems and were highly motivated to solve them. Some had impressive solutions.

Reciprocal Teaching

What are the strategies involved in reciprocal teaching?

Reciprocal teaching features "guided practice" in applying simple, concrete strategies to text comprehension (Alfassi, 1998; Palincsar and Brown, 1986; Rosenshine and Meister, 1994). This very successful instructional procedure consists of these four strategies:

1. Summarize the paragraph or assignment in a sentence.

2. Ask one or two higher-level questions.

3. Clarify any difficult parts.

4. Predict what the next paragraph or section will discuss.

The teacher models the process and then gradually turns it over to the students while providing feedback and encouragement. This activity may be done with pairs or triads (three students, or one adult and two students).

Writing Strategies

Educators have recognized for some time that writing improves comprehension. Writing forces students to shape and form their responses to the text—to bring these thoughts to conscious awareness. Chapter 9 has additional information about writing and its relation to reading comprehension and retention.

Visualization Strategies

What is visualization?

Visualization is the process of forming mental images that depict reading content, such as story settings, characters, story action, geographic areas, famous historical figures, scientific experiments, and steps in mathematics problems. Visualization activities like these will benefit students:

SOCIAL STUDIES

1. *Social studies.* Develop a "You Are There" activity. The students could act out the process of approval for judges appointed to the Supreme Court. This will involve a certain amount of research to understand the process. They could discuss the emotions engendered by the occasion.

2. When working with problem-solving activities in any subject, students can be asked to visualize alternative solutions that will help them work through the various ways of solving a problem.

Enhancing Comprehension Before, During, and After Reading

The unit plan in the "Meeting the Challenge" on pages 188–191 integrates strategies for all three phases of reading, as do the following study guide and the directed reading lesson. These plans are used most appropriately after students have acquired strategies for the three phases of reading comprehension.

Study Guides

What value do study guides have?

One of the most valuable strategies for increasing students' comprehension is the **study guide**. A study guide is a set of statements and/or questions designed to direct students' attention to the key ideas in a passage and sometimes to suggest the skills to apply for successful comprehension. A study guide creates a point of contact between the student and the written material, showing readers how to comprehend content.

The instructor's goals and the students' needs determine the composition of a study guide. It may cover a chapter, a larger unit, or merely part of a long chapter. If students are given a study guide to read before they study an assignment, they can respond to the questions and activities as they read the material. Study guides may take a variety of forms. Examples of these forms are found throughout this text.

A single study guide may set purposes for reading, provide aids for interpretation of the material, or do both. Study guides are particularly valuable when the teacher uses grouping in the content class. Each small group of students can sit together, work through their study guide individually, and then discuss their answers with one another, reconciling any differences in their answers. Handling material this way causes the students to think about the material they are reading; critical thinking is necessary as students try to reach a consensus about their answers.

Example 6.8 shows a science selection related to oceanography; a study guide follows.

| EXAMPLE 6.8 | Science Selection and Study Guide |

Oceanography

SCIENCE AND
HEALTH

Throughout history, poets and sailors alike have been awed by the size of the world's oceans. When viewed from space, Earth appears mostly blue, because oceans cover more than 70 percent of its surface. For this reason, Earth is sometimes called the water planet. The immense volume of water on Earth is hard to imagine; the average depth of the oceans is more than four times the average elevation of the continents.

As vast and interesting as they are, the oceans remain largely a mystery. Aided by new technology, scientists are continually discovering and learning about interactions between the oceans and Earth's other environments.

The Beginnings of Oceanography

Oceanography is the scientific study of the ocean using chemistry, biology, physics, geology, and other sciences. In the mid-1800s, a U.S. Navy officer named Matthew F. Maury conducted one of the first modern ocean studies. Maury used the logbooks of U.S. Navy captains to compile charts of ocean currents and winds. In 1855, he published his findings in the book *The Physical Geography of the Sea*.

The first large-scale ocean research project came in 1872, when scientists aboard the British ship *H.M.S. Challenger* used their onboard laboratory equipment to measure ocean depths, take water samples, record temperatures, and study currents. Oceanographers today still use data gathered during this expedition.

World War II brought about the next great advance in oceanography. The military's development of submarines and surface ships led to more accurate ocean charts and new instruments, such as sonar and magnetic recorders. These devices became the basic tools of modern ocean research.

Analysis
Why is oceanography an important science?

Study Guide
Overview question: Since extensive research has been used to explore the oceans, why do they continue to be mysterious?
1. Identify the various scientists involved in oceanography.
2. How does the author illustrate the depth of oceans?
3. Describe the oceanographic research conducted in 1872.
4. Why are scientists studying the interactions between oceans and earth's other environments?
5. How does oceanographic research relate to your life?

Source: From *Earth Science* by Nancy E. Spaulding and Samuel N. Namowitz. Copyright © 2003 by McDougal Littell Inc., a division of Houghton Mifflin Company. All rights reserved. Reprinted by permission of McDougal Littell Inc., a division of Houghton Mifflin Company.

The teacher's instructional intent in the study guide in Example 6.8 is apparent in the overview question, which is designed to focus on the understandings that students are expected to acquire from the selection; moreover, this question focuses the reading while requiring critical or creative reading abilities. The balance of the guide provides a series of questions that relate to the ideas in the text.

This study guide could be used for all students who can read the textbook, with or without teacher assistance; however, if a teacher wanted to reduce the guide's length, some questions could be assigned to all students, and other questions could be divided between those who need assistance from the teacher and those who do not. The teacher may work closely with the instructional-level group members as they discuss their assigned questions and may monitor the independent-level group less intensively. The group that cannot handle the text material should be given another reading assignment in order to learn the content. This group should have its own study guide, geared to its assignment. The whole-class discussion that follows the small-group sessions with the guides will help all the students clarify their concepts and see relationships among the ideas.

**ENGLISH/
LANGUAGE
ARTS**

A three-level study guide directs students toward comprehension at the literal level (directly stated ideas), the interpretive level (implied ideas), and the applied level (using information to solve problems). See Chapter 10, Example 10.1, for an example of a guide designed for the short story "Man without a Country" by Edward Everett Hale.

Directed Reading Lessons

How does a directed reading lesson compare with a directed reading-thinking lesson?

A **directed reading lesson** (DRL) is a method for guiding students' comprehension of a reading selection. Directed reading approaches vary from source to source, but the following components are present in all the plans: motivation and building background, skill-development activities, guided reading, and follow-up activities. The following directed reading lesson is based on a selection from *Houghton Mifflin English* (Haley-James, 1986, p. 417).

Directed Reading Lesson

What are the steps in a directed reading lesson?

**ENGLISH/
LANGUAGE
ARTS**

Motivation and Building Background

1. Ask the students if they know what a *villain* is. After discussing the word's current meaning, tell them that it originally meant "a person from a villa" and that its meaning has changed for the worse.

2. Ask the students if they know what *nice* means. After discussing the word's current meaning, tell them that it once meant "ignorant" and that its meaning has changed for the better.

3. Ask the students if they know any words that have come from place names or names of people. Let them name as many as possible. Be ready to provide some examples for them, such as *pasteurization*.

Skill-Development Activities

4. Remind students that words presented in boldface print are important words for which to know meanings.

5. Review types of context clues that are often found in textbooks. Give special attention to definition clues, since there is a definition clue for the word *etymology* in the assignment.

6. Review the meaning of *-logy* (the study of). Have students name and define words ending in *-logy* (*biology, geology,* and so forth).

7. Review the meaning of the word part *un-* (not). Have students name and define words with this part (*unhappy, unwanted*).

8. Review the meaning of the word part *-able* (able to be). Have students name and define words with this part (*workable, marketable*).

Guided Reading

9. Silent reading—Have students read the selection silently for the following purposes:
   a. Determine the meaning of the word *etymology.*
   b. Find two words that were derived from the names of places.
   c. Determine the meaning of *unpredictable.*
   d. Find a word that had a negative meaning change over the years.
   e. Find a word that had a positive meaning change over the years.

10. Discussion and oral reading—Choose some students to read aloud and discuss the parts related to the silent reading purposes, especially if the students find the purpose questions difficult to answer.

Follow-up Activities

11. Have the students do the two practice activities at the bottom of the selection and discuss their results in class.

12. Have the students list five words that they find that have interesting etymologies. Have a class discussion of the words.

FOCUS ON   *Struggling Readers*

Comprehension Scaffolding

Students who must struggle with decoding text will find it difficult to comprehend; therefore, teachers may need to assign alternative text material on the topic. Students need to know 95 to 99 percent of the words in a text and the concepts they represent in order to comprehend the text. The majority of struggling readers do not know enough of the words or concepts. Many struggling readers lack the necessary schemata to permit them to connect with the text and predict the ideas they will be reading. Many of them lack concepts and world knowledge that more accomplished readers take for granted. Therefore, teachers may have to introduce background information that will build concept knowledge to prepare students to read.

Struggling readers should be guided to realize how the assigned material relates to them and to identify the value of assigned reading. Scaffolding strategies are especially important to support their comprehension efforts. These strategies will help them read with understanding and organize the information so that students increase their ability to remember what they have read. The strategies in Chapters 4, 5, and this chapter will help struggling readers comprehend.

Struggling readers should have a clear understanding of the reading assignment and the teacher's purposes for their reading. After they grow more competent, they should be encouraged to state their own purposes. Moreover, they should write the questions they are seeking to answer prior to reading; after reading, they should write the answers to their questions. Struggling readers should be encouraged to look back at the text to find answers or the information they need to infer answers; otherwise, they will guess rather than using a logical thought process.

Struggling readers will benefit from working with partners or coaches. They tend to achieve more success working in small groups. Multimedia materials, such as are found on the Internet, are motivating for struggling readers and require the same comprehension strategies as do books. A comparison of these media is shown in Figure 6.4.

Strategy	Book	Electronic Media
Activate schemata	Reader relates prior experience to the reading content and purpose.	Reader uses these strategies.
Ask questions	Reader asks questions.	Reader does the same.
Identify main ideas and thesis	Reader uses these strategies.	Reader uses the same strategies.
Use literal, inferential, and critical reading skills	Reader uses these thinking skills.	Reader uses these same skills.
Synthesize information and ideas	Reader synthesizes.	Reader synthesizes.
Monitor understanding and correct as needed	Reader skims, scans, and rereads to correct.	Reader does the same.
Navigate	Readers uses typographical information and index, table of contents, headings, and glossary.	Reader uses typographical information, index, and headings, but also some different navigational skills, including identification of related sites to search, use of hyperlinks, and use of navigation tools, such as back arrows.

Source: Adapted from Schmar-Dobler (2003).

FIGURE 6.4

Comparison of Book and Multimedia Comprehension Strategies

"Repeated Readings" are valuable for both struggling readers and ELLs. The purpose of this strategy is to increase students' automatic recognition of words, which increases their fluency and their comprehension. This technique is developed in several ways. Initially, students can read aloud with the teacher, who reads a little faster than the students, so they are echoing the teacher. Students also do three-minute readings, and, reading the same text, they try to read more words each time they read it. They may read for different purposes each time (e.g., to identify the characters, to determine the setting), to provide some reason for reading again. Additional practice is developed through giving students recordings of books so they can continue practicing.

FOCUS ON   *English Language Learners*

Learning How to Comprehend Written English

English language learners can acquire basic vocabulary and concepts, but teachers cannot assume that ELLs have the comprehension skills necessary to succeed in content classes. ELLs need to be taught comprehension strategies through explicit modeling and scaffolding (Harper and de Jong, 2004). Therefore, the strategies introduced in this chapter are important to ELLs' comprehension.

Teachers who have ELLs in class should be aware that English is a word-order language; many other languages are based on word case, and many Asian languages originated as pictographic languages. These factors are related to the syntactic differences that ELLs experience in functioning with English.

ELLs will experience cultural difficulties with many texts because they are unacquainted with concepts that are common to fluent readers of English. Therefore, teachers need to prepare students to read, particularly in the content areas of history, English, and literature. On the other hand, many math and science concepts transcend culture. While teaching a Korean student, Barbara Stoodt-Hill discovered that some Korean concepts cannot be translated into English and some English concepts cannot be translated directly into Korean. Even students whose first language is English, such as some students originally from India, will exhibit conceptual differences in their understanding of the language in their textbooks. When assessing their oral language and written language, teachers must ask them to explain their ideas. The comprehension of ELLs is enhanced by multimedia materials and bilingual books. This is illustrated in Figure 6.4. Bilingual books are becoming more widely available and teachers will find them useful for both ELLs and the other students in their classes, because they can learn words in the ELLs' language (Ernst-Slavit and Mulhern, 2003). Teachers can obtain information about bilingual books from these sources: American Library Association, *English Journal, Journal of Adolescent and Adult Literacy*, and the Cooperative Children's Book Center of the University of Wisconsin.

Summary

Comprehension is an active, constructive process based on interactions among a reader, a text, and the reading situation or purpose. Readers implement strategies before, during, and after reading text. Effective readers use strategies that are appropriate to the material and the task. Their strategies are plans for using skills to comprehend. Struggling readers and English language learners need to learn the strategies introduced in this chapter in order to become competent comprehenders. Figure 6.5 summarizes comprehension strategies.

FIGURE 6.5

Comprehension
Strategies

1. Develop a positive attitude toward reading
2. Identify important ideas
3. Identify the organizational pattern of the text
4. Identify the sequence of events
5. Monitor understanding
6. Paraphrase
7. Predict
8. Question
9. Relate new knowledge to prior knowledge
10. Reread
11. Search for relationships
12. Summarize

Discussion Questions

1. Why do you think critical reading is so important for today's students?
2. What strategies and activities can a teacher use before having students start a reading assignment to aid their comprehension?
3. How is discussion related to reading comprehension?
4. What is the purpose of a think-aloud exercise?
5. How do strategies function in reading comprehension?
6. What attributes characterize fluent readers?
7. How are struggling readers like their classmates?
8. How do ELLs differ from their classmates?

Enrichment Activities

*1. Visit a secondary school classroom to watch questioning procedures. Identify the type of questioning used most often. Also note how much time the students are allowed for formulating answers.
*2. Select a chapter in a content textbook, and make a plan to help secondary school students comprehend the chapter, using strategies suggested in this chapter.

*3. Adapt one of the strategies suggested in this chapter to your content area.

4. Examine the exercises suggested in this chapter, and identify those that will be most useful in your content area.

*5. Prepare a strategy lesson for an English language learner.

6. Visit a classroom that includes struggling readers and observe the teaching adaptations used.

---

*These activities are designed for in-service teachers, student teachers, and practicum students.

Resources including the TeachSource Video Cases can be found on the website for this book. Cengage Learning's CourseMate brings course concepts to life with interactive learning, study, and exam preparation tools that support the printed textbook. Go to www.cengage.com/login to register your access code.

CHAPTER 7

Location and Organization of Information

Overview

In this chapter we discuss location skills related to use of the library or media center, books, computer databases, and the Internet. Location skills are important to information literacy, which is "the ability to seek out and critically evaluate information across a range of media" (Black, 2009, p. 693.) Technology is often useful for locating information in ways that are similar to those used for traditional print sources (Black, 2009; Lankshear and Knobel, 2007); however, there are some new ways of locating information with technology. We also give attention to the organizational skills of outlining, summarizing, and note taking. These skills are important to students' success with assignments such as written reports, research papers, and class presentations in all content area classes.

Purpose-Setting Questions

As you read this chapter, try to answer these questions:

1. What location skills do secondary school students need in order to use the library or media center effectively?
2. What location skills do students need in order to use books effectively for content area classes?
3. How can students use the Internet and other computer resources effectively to locate information?
4. What organizational skills are helpful to students who are reading material that they will use later in some manner?
5. What are some different ways to annotate text?
6. What special help with location and organization skills do struggling readers and English language learners need?

Location Skills

To take part in many study activities (primarily content area reading and writing assignments), students must be able to locate specific reading materials. Teaching students to use location aids in libraries, media centers, and in books, and to use computer databases and the Internet, will enable them to find the materials they need.

Libraries and Media Centers

A study done by Ross Todd and Carol Kuhlthau showed that learning, in general, and information literacy, in particular, are facilitated by an effective school library with a credentialed librarian. Students indicated that the library helped them learn to find and use information, work out questions for topics they are researching, and learn more about their topics ("New Study Supports Value of School Libraries," 2004).

"In schools, libraries are places where text, technology, and literacy converge in concentrated form" (Kapitzke, 2001, p. 451). Teachers, librarians, and media specialists should work cooperatively to help students develop the skills needed for effective use of the library and media center. Since the library and media center can often be the same entity or serve the same purpose, depending on the institution, the *library* and the *librarian* will, from this point on, also refer to the *media center* and the *media specialist*, respectively, but the expanded role of these facilities and their personnel in dealing with multimedia should not be overlooked.

Libraries connect teachers and students to information through online access and other information sources (Lambeth, 1998). Libraries are now the repositories of electronic media, as well as print media. The librarian can help by showing students the locations of books, periodicals, card catalogs, computer terminals, and reference materials in the library; by explaining the procedures for checking out books and returning them; and by clarifying the rules relating to behavior in the library. The librarian can also demonstrate the use of the card catalog (either manual or computerized) and can explain the arrangement of books in the library. (Dewey decimal classification is the arrangement most commonly used in school libraries in the United States for classifying nonfiction books, although some libraries classify books by Library of Congress numbers.) Posters displayed in the library can remind students of checkout procedures, library rules, and arrangement of books, as well as ways to use card catalogs and the basic procedures involved in computer searches.

The librarian can be extremely helpful to teachers. He or she may:

1. help teachers locate both printed and other materials related to current units of study.

2. help teachers plan a unit on use of reference materials in the library.

3. help teachers discover reading interests of individuals and specific groups of students.

4. alert teachers to professional reading materials in their content areas.

5. give presentations to students on the availability and location of materials for particular content areas.

6. put materials on particular content topics on reserve for a class.

7. let teachers know when new material related to their content areas is added to the library collection.

Locating Information in Books

Secondary teachers tend not to teach textbook use to their students, perhaps thinking that it has been covered previously. Since elementary teachers do not always provide such instruction, possibly because they use trade books rather than textbooks in their classes, secondary school content teachers need to consider adding this component to their classes (Alvermann and Moore, 1991; Dreher, 1992). Some elements of texts that must be understood to locate information include such text characteristics as headings and subheadings, boldface and italic fonts, and use of graphics, as well as the navigation tools, including the table of contents, index, and glossary. Knowledge of skimming and scanning are also important (Brown, 2003).

In a study of the ability of eleventh-grade students to search texts for information, Dreher and Guthrie discovered that many students could locate the appropriate text pages. However, although the students' responses showed that they knew highlighted terms were important in locating information, they did not seem to be able to evaluate the appropriateness of particular terms to the question posed (Dreher, 1992). This indicates a need to pay attention to metacognitive (self-monitoring) skills in classroom instruction.

In a study of college students, Dreher and Brown reported similar findings, with many students locating the correct page, but not evaluating the answers chosen. Some were not able to decide on an appropriate search term and therefore were unsuccessful in their search. Help in deciding on key words when searching for information is important (Dreher, 1992). The need to determine appropriate search terms is also critical in the use of computer databases and the Internet. Teachers should help students locate appropriate key words because some research indicates that teachers and students do not necessarily perceive the same words as being key words in a particular passage.

Students' search skills can be improved with more use of textbooks for varied purposes. Students who are searching texts for information need to have a clear idea of what they are searching for and how it will be used; decide on text sections to examine for the needed information (table of contents, index, etc.); extract the needed information from the text section or sections chosen (choosing only information that fits the search task); integrate that information with prior knowledge; and repeat the procedure until all the needed information has been found.

Most informational books include special features that students can use to locate needed material. Content area teachers will find that explaining the functions of prefaces, tables of contents, indexes, appendixes, glossaries, footnotes, and bibliographies is well worth the effort in increasing students' efficiency as they use books. Some things that teachers may wish to teach about text features are discussed next.

Preface

When a content area teacher presents a new textbook to secondary school students, he or she should ask the students to read the preface and/or introduction to decide why the book was written and to discover the manner in which the material is presented.

Table of Contents

The table of contents of a textbook should also be examined on the day the textbook is distributed. Students can be reminded that the table of contents indicates the topics that the book includes and the pages on which those topics begin. The teacher can ask questions, such as the following, during the text introduction:

1. What topics are covered in this book?

2. What is the first topic that is discussed?

3. On what page does the discussion about _____ begin? (This question can be repeated several times with different topics inserted in the blank.)

Index

Students need to understand that an index is an alphabetical list of the important items and proper names mentioned in a book, with the pages where each item or name appears. Students generally need practice in using index headings and subheadings to locate information in their books.

A preliminary lesson on what an index is and how to use it to locate information can be presented. Afterward, the teacher can use the students' own textbooks to teach index use. The lesson idea shown in Example 7.1 can be modified for use with an actual index in a content area textbook.

EXAMPLE 7.1   **Sample Index and Questions**

MATHEMATICS

Sample Index
Absolute value, 145, 174–175
Addition
    of decimals, 101
    of fractions, 80–83
    of natural numbers, 15–16, 46–48
    of rational numbers, 146–148
    of real numbers, 170
Angles, 203
    measurement of, 206–207
    right, 204

Axiom, 241
Base
   meaning of, 5
   change of, 6–7

Index Questions

1. On what page would you look to find out how to add decimals? Under what main topic and subheading did you have to look to discover this page number?
2. On what pages will you find *base* mentioned?
3. What pages contain information about absolute value?
4. On what pages would you look to find out about measurement of angles? What main heading did you look under to discover this? What subheading did you look under?
5. Where would you look to find information about adding real numbers? Would you expect to find any information about real numbers on page 146? Why or why not?
6. Is there information about addition of natural numbers on pages 46–48? Is information on this topic found on any other pages?
7. Find the meaning for *base,* and read it aloud. Did you look in the index to find the page number? If not, could you have found it more quickly by looking in the index?

Appendix

Students can be shown that the appendixes in textbooks and other books contain helpful information, such as documents, maps, and tables.

Glossary

Glossaries are often found in content area textbooks. Students need to know that glossaries are similar to dictionaries but include only words presented in the books in which they are found or terms related to a specific subject and include only the definitions of multiple-meaning words that are specific to the subject. Glossaries of technical terms can greatly help students in understanding a book's content. The skills needed for proper use of a glossary are the same as those needed for using a dictionary.

Footnotes and Bibliography

Footnotes and bibliographies are extremely valuable aids for students doing assigned research activities. Footnotes often tell the source of information in the text and can guide a student to the original source if further clarification is needed. Sometimes the footnotes directly supply clarifying information. Bibliographies may refer students to other sources of information about the subjects discussed in a book. The chapter bibliographies in textbooks are generally lists of references that the authors consulted when preparing the chapters and references that contain additional information about the subjects.

Special Reference Books

Secondary school students are often called on to find information in reference books such as encyclopedias, dictionaries, almanacs, and atlases, and on the Internet. Unfortunately, many students reach middle school or high school without knowing how to use such tools effectively.

Prerequisites for effective use of reference books include the following:

1. Knowledge of alphabetical order and the fact that information in encyclopedias, dictionaries, and some atlases is arranged in alphabetical order. (Most secondary school students have mastered the principles of alphabetical order, but a few need help, especially with alphabetization beyond the first letters of words.)

2. Ability to use guide words (i.e., knowing the location of guide words on a page and understanding that they represent the first and last entry words on a dictionary or encyclopedia page).

3. Ability to use cross-references (related primarily to use of encyclopedias).

4. Ability to use pronunciation keys (related primarily to use of dictionaries).

5. Ability to choose from several possible word meanings the one that most closely fits the context in which the word was found (related to use of dictionaries).

6. Ability to read maps—interpreting the scale and legends and locating directions on maps (related to use of atlases).

7. Ability to determine which volume of a set will contain the information being sought (related primarily to use of encyclopedias).

8. Ability to determine key words under which related information can be found.

Because encyclopedias, almanacs, and atlases are often difficult to read, teachers should use caution in assigning students work in these reference books. Students will not benefit from attempting to do research in books written on a level they find frustrating. When the material is too difficult, students tend to copy the material word for word instead of extracting the important ideas. Since different sources have different reading difficulty levels, teachers should match the difficulty of the reference books used with the abilities of the students involved.

As mentioned previously, many reference works are available online, including dictionaries, encyclopedias, and collections of maps. Students need to learn to use these sources as well. Keyword search techniques (discussed in Chapter 2 and later in this chapter) are important when using online references. Online references often contain helpful aids to understanding, such as links to pictures, word pronunciations, and definitions.

Encyclopedias

Some secondary school students need help with the use of encyclopedias. They may need to practice locating varied subjects in the encyclopedia. Teachers should lead the students to decide on the key words that will help them find the specified information by first explaining and modeling the procedure. For example, for "Education in Sweden" they should look first under "Sweden" and then find the section on education. Example 7.2 can be used to assess students' ability to locate information in encyclopedias.

SOCIAL STUDIES

A surprising number of junior high school students and a few high school students do not realize that the name of a person in an encyclopedia is alphabetized by the last name, not the first. A student who had to write a report on James Otis came to Betty Roe and announced that James Otis was not in the encyclopedia. Puzzled, Betty asked the student to show her how he had proceeded in looking for the name. He went to the "J" volume of the encyclopedia and began to look for "James." He seemed surprised when he was told that proper names are listed alphabetically by last name and then followed by the first name. The last two items in Example 7.2 can be used to check on or work with students' understanding of this concept.

EXAMPLE 7.2   **Activity for Using an Encyclopedia**

Directions: Look up each of the following topics in the encyclopedia. On the line beside each topic, write the letter(s) of the volume in which you found the topic and the page number on which the topic is discussed.

1. Solar system   _____
2. U.S. Constitution   _____
3. Oleander   _____
4. Education in Sweden   _____
5. Computer use in library systems _____
6. Martin Luther King Jr.   _____
7. John Paul Jones   _____

A number of encyclopedias are available on CD or DVD for use with computers. (See the section "Using Computer Databases" later in this chapter for more detail about electronic encyclopedias.) These references have many hypertext and hypermedia links (see Chapter 2) that help to illuminate the material for students.

Dictionaries

Students frequently lack familiarity with dictionary content and use. A few have some trouble with alphabetical order. A much larger number have trouble with guide words and use of the pronunciation key, and many do not realize the variety of information, such as parts of speech, principal parts of verbs, degrees of adjectives, etymologies, and illustrations, found in a dictionary entry. Spending some time familiarizing students with dictionary use can pay dividends in their future learning.

A particular need for secondary school students is determining which definition of a word fits the context in which it was found. Students have the tendency to try to force the first definition they find to fit all situations.

FOREIGN LANGUAGES

With more and more English language learners in U.S. schools, use of bilingual dictionaries gains importance. Such dictionaries can be useful both to ELLs in dealing with use of words in class and to English speakers in communication with classmates who are ELLs. They also are useful for students enrolled in foreign language classes.

Motivational Activities

Since location skills are presented to students repeatedly during their school careers, they may seem boring, even though they may not be thoroughly learned. The introduction of games, audiovisual presentations, and other motivational activities may enhance interest in the instruction. For example, paper-and-pencil scavenger hunts in the library, like the one described in the next "Meeting the Challenge" vignette, may be fun for students. Teachers can use library scavenger hunts to help students learn to use many types of library resources, including computer-based indexes and the online search catalog. Online scavenger hunts could be similar to the pencil-and-paper one described, with items such as the following:

SCIENCE AND HEALTH   **ENGLISH/ LANGUAGE ARTS**

1. Locate a picture of the moon, taken from space, on the NASA website. Print the picture.

2. Locate a site that has student writing posted. Print a sample page. Write down the URL for the site.

MEETING THE CHALLENGE

Ms. MacMurray wants to check on the reference skills of the inner-city eighth-graders in her English class. She confers with the librarian, Mrs. Freedle, after school the day before she has a library period. Together they pull out a variety of reference books that the students need to know how to use. Then Ms. MacMurray writes a series of questions, such as the following ones, that can be answered using each type of reference book (atlas, encyclopedia, dictionary, and almanac) or by accessing a reference source from the Internet:

1. What is a book by Herman Melville? (Write down its name, call number, and location in the library.)
2. What is a catamaran, according to the *American Heritage Dictionary*?
3. Write the phonetic respelling for the word *catamaran*.
4. What volume and page of the *World Book Encyclopedia* contains a discussion of catamarans?
5. What is the URL of a website that describes catamarans?
6. What states border Colorado?
7. Who is Madame Curie?

Reference skills can be checked by letting teams search for answers to a series of research questions in the library or media center.

Chris Schmidt/
iStockphoto.com

**ENGLISH/
LANGUAGE
ARTS**

After the questions have been constructed, Ms. MacMurray and Mrs. Freedle return the reference books to their accustomed places.

Back in her own room, Ms. MacMurray takes the list of students in the English class and arranges the students in pairs. Then she duplicates her list of questions so that each pair of students will have a copy. Choosing from among several prizes that she has solicited from local businesses, she decides which prize to give the team with the most correct answers within the time limit. (If there is a tie, the first team to finish with the highest number of correct answers wins.)

The next day, Ms. MacMurray assigns the students to their teams, gives a list of questions to each team, and escorts the students to the library. Teammates confer to choose a strategy and then begin their searches. As they work to win the contest, Ms. MacMurray notes the good and poor strategies of library use they exhibit—guidance for future lessons in her class. She later uses explanations and activities such as ones described in this chapter to work on the understanding and use of indexes, tables of contents, glossaries, computer databases, the card catalog, the basic library arrangement, alphabetical order, guide words, and dictionary respellings, if these prove to be problem areas.

Using Computer Databases

What value do computer databases have for students?

**SCIENCE AND
HEALTH**

The location skills that students need in today's schools include the ability to retrieve information stored in **computer databases**, either ones that the students have compiled themselves or others that are available in the school.

A database is an organized collection of information. Conceptually, a database is like a filing cabinet (or several cabinets), with separate file folders for each article in the database. The information may be categorized by subject or by another categorization scheme and is indexed for easy access. Typically, the computer system supporting a database allows the user to construct complicated search requirements, for example, "Find all articles on distortion in optics used for telescopes published after 1980 in Sweden." Databases can be user created (student created) or preexisting, large or small, general or specific.

Finding information has become a computer-oriented task involving databases to a great degree. Many occupations rely on the use of such databases, making the need for information-retrieval skills and an understanding of database maintenance important for today's students. The use of these sources requires knowledge of how to construct search questions for the particular database system, of the organizational scheme of the subject matter, and of search techniques in general.

SCIENCE AND HEALTH

SOCIAL STUDIES

MUSIC

SCIENCE AND HEALTH

The user must be able to phrase complex questions that limit the retrieval process to pertinent information without omitting any desired information.

A computer database can be organized in a wide variety of ways. A limited database might contain the names, symbols, and basic properties of chemical compounds used in the manufacture of paper, or the names, dates of inauguration, and birthplaces of the presidents of the United States. A large database is *Who's Who in America*. The contents are the same as those in the printed volume, but its structure as a database allows searching by such things as birthplace (e.g., what famous people are from Claysville, Idaho), profession, or college of matriculation.

Schools now have access to both local and remote databases. A local database resides on the computer system of the user, whereas a remote database resides on a computer system other than the user's. The most prevalent means of remote access is through the Internet.

A local database in a classroom might range from a small quantity of information collected as part of a class project to a complete encyclopedia. Several encyclopedias are available in computer-readable form, on CDs or DVDs. Examples are *Encyclopedia Britannica* (Britannica) and *World Book Encyclopedia* (World Book). A number of dictionaries are also available on CDs or DVDs.

An entire multivolume encyclopedia can be contained on a single disk. Multimedia encyclopedias contain more than text; they include pictures, maps, animated diagrams, voice recordings, music recordings, and sound effects (such as sounds that animals make). Users might read about Bach, view his picture, and hear a recording of one of his musical compositions. They might also read about grizzly bears, see a video of one, and hear its sound.

Creating small databases in the classroom can give students valuable experience in categorizing and organizing material. For this type of work on the computer, the teacher needs access to database software, which may be a part of a suite of programs. For example, *Microsoft Works* contains database, word-processing, and spreadsheet applications, as well as other productivity tools. Another choice is the OpenOffice suite, which can be downloaded for free from http://www.openoffice.org. After the information for the database has been collected and entered into the computer, the database system can be used for critical analyses, such as comparing similarities and differences (e.g., "What problems do urban areas have in common? How are these problems different from those in rural areas?"), analyzing relationships, examining trends, and testing and refining hypotheses.

One important application of databases for students is the computerized card catalog in many libraries. Such databases replace the traditional card catalogs, providing the traditional indexing plus complex search capabilities. Many libraries also provide access to the card catalogs of other libraries and even Internet sites that contain electronic books and magazines and homepages that have links to a wide variety of types of information, which may include multimedia as well as text.

Using the Internet

What kinds of information can be found by searching Internet sites?

The Internet offers many online resources. These include the encyclopedias, dictionaries, and atlases already discussed; collections of literature, images, animations, and music; opinion and research articles; book, movie, and theater reviews; biographies of historical figures, authors, and other people; government and public policy data; reports of current events; and interactive learning activities. This list is not exhaustive. Some of the material available on the Internet is relevant to class studies, but much is not relevant. Students must be able to decide about the relevance of material that they find. The bounty of available material can lead to problems, such as easy plagiarism, exposure to commercialism or pornography, and wasted instructional time.

ENGLISH/ LANGUAGE ARTS

SOCIAL STUDIES

Teachers must understand both the benefits and the hazards of Internet use. Both primary and secondary sources of information can be found on the Internet. Primary sources include diaries, government documents, photographs, videos, and other types of original materials. Secondary sources include summaries and analyses of information from other sources. Much of the information available on the Internet is not controlled for accuracy, so students must do more than simply locate material on the appropriate topic; they must also evaluate the information they locate. There are some reliable sources that require subscriptions. One of these is *Encyclopedia Britannica Online,* which offers paid subscriptions or a free one-year subscription to people who maintain websites (Gunelius, 2008). Another is *Grolier Online.*

Searching for information on the World Wide Web can be made easier with the use of search engines. Search engines check terms that a user enters into the computer against terms found on webpages that have been indexed by the search service. Popular search engines are Google, Yahoo!, and Dogpile. Because different search engines use different search techniques, they often provide different results based on the same search terms, and some are better at finding particular types of information than others. A site that can help students evaluate their search needs is http://www.noodletools.com/. On the first page under "Free Software Tools," click on the link "Choose the Best Search."

Simple searches on search engines require students to decide on relevant keywords for the search. Often a keyword search will return far more "hits" (matches that indicate potentially useful sites) than the user can realistically check. When this happens, many engines allow users to do advanced searches with quotation marks around phrases to indicate that the entire phrase must be found, Boolean searches (that use Boolean logic), or other refined searches. These techniques are specific to the search engine being used, and teachers and students would do well to familiarize themselves with the search engines they use most often. Search engines frequently have "Help" options that connect to detailed explanations of how to use advanced search techniques.

Organizational Skills

ENGLISH/ LANGUAGE ARTS

When participating in study activities such as writing reports, secondary school students need to organize the ideas they encounter in their reading. Four helpful organizational skills are outlining, summarizing, note taking, and marking text. All require recognition and recording, in an organized form, of important ideas from the materials read. The act of organizing information helps students comprehend and retain it better. According to Friend (2001/2002, p. 321), "[I]n order to organize new information, students must draw on prior knowledge and pay attention to the nature of relationships among ideas. As they organize information by constructing a summary, an outline, or a graphic organizer, students generate links among new ideas they are studying."

Pearson and Santa (1995) found that students recalled terms in categorized lists more readily than those in random order, and they demonstrated this to the students by having class members try to learn lists of terms in each condition. Students then saw the value of organizing material in order to learn it.

Outlining

What different ways can be used to outline material that is read for class?

Teachers should help their students to understand that **outlining** is recording information from reading material in a way that makes clear the relationships between the main ideas and the supporting details. Before students can learn to construct an outline properly, they must know how to identify main ideas and supporting details in reading selections. Information about how to assist students in locating main ideas and recognizing related details is found in Chapter 5.

Readiness for formal outlining tasks may be developed by having students work with *arrays*, which are freeform outlines. When constructing arrays, students are required to arrange key words and phrases in ways that show the relationships set forth by the author. They can use words, lines, and arrows to do this. It is important to use a simple, familiar story or an uncomplicated expository selection for this activity, so that the students can focus on the logical arrangement of the terms rather than worrying about the details of the story or selection. Example 7.3 shows a story array for the familiar story "Johnny Appleseed."

**ENGLISH/
LANGUAGE
ARTS**

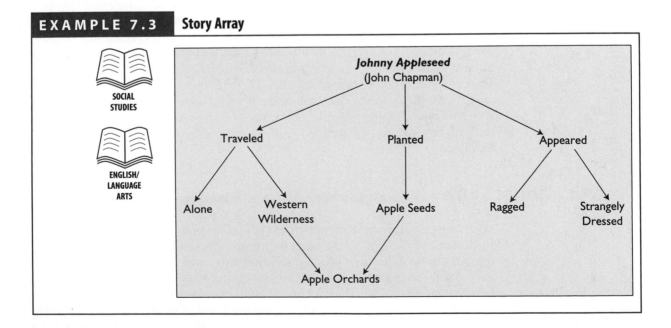

EXAMPLE 7.3   **Story Array**

**SOCIAL
STUDIES**

**ENGLISH/
LANGUAGE
ARTS**

Johnny Appleseed
(John Chapman)

Traveled   Planted   Appeared

Alone   Western   Apple Seeds   Ragged   Strangely
           Wilderness   Dressed

Apple Orchards

Teachers can guide students to learn how to make arrays by supplying the words and phrases and then letting the students work in groups to complete the arrays. First, the students read the selection; then they arrange the words and phrases appropriately, using lines and arrows to indicate relationships. The teacher questions students about the positioning and direction of arrows, asking for reasons for the choices made. In addition, the teacher is available to answer students' questions. Eventually, the students are expected to choose key words and concepts themselves and to arrange them without the teacher's help.

Arthaud and Goracke (2006) described teaching struggling readers to organize information by using structured story webs, first showing them completed webs on chapters that they were reading and then providing them with partially completed webs—with less and less detail—until they could complete entire webs independently. A similar plan was used to teach traditional outlining.

Two types of outlines that students may find useful are the *sentence outline* and the *topic outline*. In a sentence outline, each point is stated in the form of a complete sentence; in a topic outline, the points are written in the form of key words and phrases. The sentence outline is generally easier to master because the topic outline involves an extra task—condensing main ideas, already expressed in sentence form, into key words and phrases.

The first step in making an outline is extracting the main ideas from the material and listing them beside Roman numerals in the order in which they occur. The next step is locating the details that support each of the main ideas and listing them beside capital letters below the main idea that they support. These details are indented to indicate subordination to the main idea. Details that are subordinate to these details are indented still more and preceded by Arabic numerals. The next level of subordination is indicated by lowercase letters. Although other levels of subordination are possible, secondary school students will rarely need such fine divisions.

An important idea about outlining that a teacher may wish to stress is that the degree of importance of ideas in an outline is shown by the numbers and letters used, as well as by the indentation of entries. Points that have equal importance are designated by the same number or letter style and the same degree of indentation.

Teachers can help students see how a textbook chapter would be outlined by showing them how the headings within the chapter can indicate different levels of subordination. For example, in some textbooks the title for the outline would be the title of the chapter. Roman numeral headings would be centered, or major, headings in the chapter, capital letter headings would be side headings, and Arabic numeral headings would be italic or paragraph headings.

Another approach to helping students to learn to outline their reading assignments is for the teacher to supply the students with partially completed outlines of the material and then have them complete the outlines. The teacher can vary the difficulty of the activity by gradually leaving out more and more details until the students create the entire outline alone. Also, many word-processing programs have outlining features that can facilitate the students' outlining activities.

Outlining can be helpful in any subject area. A standard form of outlining, used throughout the school, will decrease confusion among the students.

Summarizing

What should be included in a good summary?

Good summaries of reading assignments can be extremely valuable to students when they are studying for tests. To write a good **summary**, a student must restate what the author has said in a more concise form. The process of stating ideas in a more succinct form improves students' comprehension and retention of the material. Summary writers should preserve the main ideas and essential supporting details of selections in their summaries but should not include illustrative material and statements that merely elaborate on the main ideas. The ability to locate main ideas is therefore a prerequisite for learning how to write good summaries. Summarization also requires making generalizations about the connections among two or more ideas, categorizing information, paraphrasing, proper sequencing of information, and synthesizing the ideas into a coherent presentation. Knowledge of the structure of the text being summarized can help the student connect the ideas coherently (Lanning, 2008). Summarizing involves the incorporation of all of these skills to reach the outcome of a concise, coherent restatement or retelling. (Development of these skills is discussed in Chapter 5.) Lanning (2008, p. 29) points out that "summarizing raises a reader's understanding beyond item level knowledge and moves it to a conceptual level" where it is best remembered and more easily transferred.

If a paragraph is well written, the topic sentence is a good summary of the paragraph. For that reason, practice in finding the topic sentences of paragraphs is also practice in the skill of summarizing paragraphs.

Summaries of longer selections may be constructed by combining the main ideas of the component paragraphs into summary statements. Certain types of paragraphs can generally be disregarded when making summaries. Introductory and illustrative paragraphs do not add new ideas and therefore are not helpful in constructing a concise overview of the material. Students who write summaries of their reading assignments may wish to compare their summaries with the author's concluding or summary paragraphs to make sure that they have not omitted essential details.

When writing summaries, students should try not only to limit the number of sentences they use but also to limit the number of words within sentences. For example:

- *Original sentence.* A match, carelessly discarded by an unsuspecting tourist, can cause the destruction by fire of many acres of trees that will take years of work to replace.

- *Changed sentence.* Carelessly discarded matches can result in extensive destruction of forested areas by fire.

Teachers should show students that they must delete trivial and redundant material to create good summaries by modeling the strategy. They should use superordinate terms to replace lists of similar items or actions (e.g., "animals" for "pigs, dogs, and cats"). A superordinate action can be used to replace steps in an action (e.g., "made spaghetti sauce" for "took tomato sauce, sliced mushrooms, chopped onion, oregano, and salt, . . . and placed on the stove to cook on low heat"). As mentioned previously, each paragraph can be represented by an implied main idea sentence or by a directly stated topic sentence. Paragraphs can then be examined to see which ones are most needed. Only necessary paragraphs should be kept, and some that are kept can be combined (Brown and Day, 1983; Brown, Day, and Jones, 1983; Recht, 1984). Think-alouds followed by guided practice, and then individual practice are effective ways to teach summarization.

Practice in summarizing is most effective if it is based on material in current textbooks or other reading material for classes. The teacher may give students a textbook section to read, along with three or four summaries of the material. Then students can choose the best summary from those presented and explain why it is best. This is good preparation for independent student writing of summaries. A good practice activity is to have students retell sections of material to partners or in small groups (Lanning, 2008).

Précis writing is a special form of summarizing that is discussed in detail in Chapter 9. Teachers can use it with English language learners to develop abstracting and synthesizing skills and to develop vocabulary through use of synonyms. ELLs can begin by writing a précis in a group setting and continue by writing individual ones.

Note Taking

Taking notes on material read for classes can be a helpful memory aid. Well-constructed notes can save students time and effort. To take good notes, students must think about the material they are reading and organize it in a meaningful way; as a result, they will be more likely to remember it. It is also true that the simple act of writing ideas helps fix them in students' memories.

Students should be encouraged to use the form of note taking that helps them the most. Some may use semantic webs, outlines, or mind mapping when taking notes on an assignment in a textbook. Others may write a summary of the textbook materials. Some may use graphics that show description, time/order, cause-and-effect, problem-solution, comparison/contrast, and definition-examples patterns visually through the form in which the notes are taken. For example, the description pattern could have notes taken in a sunburst shape, with the concept being described in the center of the circle and the descriptive details on the rays; and the time/order pattern could have a stair-step numbered listing of events in order. Teachers should teach each pattern and the structure for notes taken in that pattern.

What are the characteristics of the Cornell Note-Taking System?

Pauk and Owens (2005) suggest use of the **Cornell Note-Taking System**, which Pauk developed. With this system, the student draws a vertical line two and a half inches from the left-hand side of each page to create a cue column and a horizontal line two inches from the bottom of the page to create a summary area. Students take notes on the material in the area to the right of the cue column and above the summary area. When the students review the notes, they write questions answered in the notes in the cue column to clarify the information in their minds and to strengthen their memory for the material. In the summary area of the page, they sum up that page of notes in one or two sentences. This summarization helps them look at the main ideas covered instead of a collection of details. Fisher, Frey and Lapp (2008) affirmed the fact that this system increased students' comprehension of text. Example 7.4 shows the Cornell System in use.

EXAMPLE 7.4   **Cornell Note-Taking System**

Psych. 105 – Prof. Martin – Sept. 14 (Mon.)

MEMORY

Memory tricky – Can recall instantly many trivial things of childhood, yet forget things recently worked hard to learn & retain.

Memory Trace
— Fact that we retain information means that some change was made in the brain.
— Change called "memory trace."
— "Trace" probably a molecular arrangement similar to molecular changes in a magnetic recording tape.

Three memory systems: sensory, short term, long term.
— Sensory (lasts one second)
  Ex. Words or numbers sent to brain by sight (visual image) start to disintegrate within a few tenths of a second & gone in one full second, unless quickly transferred to S-T memory by verbal repetition.
— Short-term memory [STM] (lasts 30 seconds)
  • Experiments show: a syllable of 3 letters remembered 50% of the time after 3 seconds.
    Totally forgotten end of 30 seconds.
  • S-T memory — limited capacity — holds average of 7 items.
  • More than 7 items — jettisons some to make room.
  • To hold items in STM, must rehearse — must hear sound of words internally or externally.
— Long-term memory [LTM] (lasts a lifetime or short time).
  • Transfer fact or idea by
    (1) Associating w/information already in LTM.
    (2) Organizing information into meaningful units.
    (3) Understanding by comparing & making relationships.
    (4) Frameworking – fit pieces in like in a jigsaw puzzle.
    (5) Reorganizing – combining new & old into a new unit.
    (6) Rehearsing – aloud to keep memory trace strong.

Questions (left column):

How do psychologists account for remembering?

What's a "memory trace"?

What are the three memory systems?

How long does sensory memory retain information?

How is information transferred to STM?

What are the retention times of STM?

What's the capacity of the STM?

How to hold information in STM?

What are the retention times of LTM?

What are the six ways to transfer information from STM to LTM?

Summary:

Three kinds of memory systems are sensory, which retains information for about 1 second; short-term, which retains for a maximum of 30 seconds; and long-term, which varies from a lifetime of retention to a relatively short time.

The six ways (activities) to transfer information to the long-term memory are associating, organizing, understanding, frameworking, reorganizing, and rehearsing.

Source: Walter Pauk and Ross J. Q. Owens, *How to Study in College*, 8th ed. Copyright © 2005 by Houghton Mifflin Company. Used with permission.

What advantages can
you see in using an
I-Chart for note taking?

Note taking for a research report can also be done in the form of I-Charts (inquiry charts) (Hoffman, 1992; Randall, 1996). An **I-Chart** is composed of a grid that has questions about the subject at the tops of columns and references consulted along the left-hand margin, providing the headings for the rows. There is also a place for other interesting facts that the students know and a summary of the findings. Hoffman (1992) wrote out the references in the right-hand column, but Randall (1996) let the students number the references and make a bibliography, and she used a separate I-Chart for each question, rather than having multiple questions on a page. Students were encouraged to paraphrase the answers to questions on their charts. Example 7.5 on page 222 shows a sample I-Chart.

Before students take notes for a research paper, they must identify the questions that the paper should answer. The questions can be listed under categories important to the topic, and students can go to appropriate reference sources to find out about the categories. For example, "What types of printers exist?" and "What are some advantages of a laser printer?" could be categorized under the topic "Printers." All notes taken on the topic "Printers" could be labeled with this term, to facilitate organization of notes. Other categories might be "Monitors," "CPUs," and "Keyboards," for example.

Notes for a research paper can be especially effective when made on index cards that can later be sorted into topics to be covered in the paper. If note cards are used, each one should include the source of information so that the paper is well documented. Some guidelines for note taking that may be helpful to students follow:

1. Key words and phrases should be used in notes.

2. Enough of the context must be included to make the notes understandable after a period of time has elapsed. Consider using telegraphic sentences, that is, sentences that leave out unnecessary words.

3. The bibliographical reference should be included with each note card or page.

4. Direct quotations should be copied exactly and should be used sparingly.

5. Notes should differentiate clearly between direct quotations and reworded material.

6. Notes should be as brief as possible.

7. Use of abbreviations can make note taking less time-consuming. Examples: w/ for "with" or = for "equals." Only abbreviations that are easy for the writer to remember should be used.

Teachers may be able to help their students learn to take good notes by "thinking through" a textbook assignment with them orally in class, emphasizing the points that should be included in a good set of notes by writing them on an overhead transparency or electronic whiteboard. This provides them with a model of the process of note taking. Students then can be encouraged to take notes on another assignment and compare them with a set of notes the teacher has constructed on the same material.

What must you provide
to students when
teaching them to
annotate reading
material?

Annotating Text

One form of note taking is actually annotating (marking) text. When students are using school-owned textbooks, they are prohibited from marking directly in the

| EXAMPLE 7.5 | Modified I-Chart |

SCIENCE AND
HEALTH

| Name: Mike | Topic: Fly ash Pollution |

Subtopic: What potential impact does fly ash have on our community?

| What I really want to know: | Fly ash from a coal-burning plant will be dumped in our county in an abandoned mine. What problems may that cause? |

| Bibliography Reference # 1 | Created from burning coal in electric-generating plants. Main ingredient is Silicon Dioxide. Some of it is in crystalline form, which is sharp, pointed and hazardous. |

| 2 | Fly ash contains several hazardous materials: toxins in significant amounts include arsenic (43.4 ppm); barium (806 ppm); beryllium (5 ppm); boron (311 ppm); cadmium (3.4 ppm); chromium (136 ppm); chromium VI (90 ppm); cobalt (35.9 ppm); copper (112 ppm); fluorine (29 ppm); lead (56 ppm); manganese (250 ppm); nickel (77.6 ppm); selenium (7.7 ppm); strontium (775 ppm); thallium (9 ppm); vanadium (252 ppm); and zinc (178 ppm). |

| 3 | Many lawsuits for damages have been filed about the fly ash spill at a TVA plant in Tennessee. |

| Interested related facts: | Fly ash can be recycled into concrete. It is not hazardous in this form. The EPA wants to increase the percentage of fly ash that is used this way. |

Key words: pollution, hazardous, toxin, beneficiation

New questions to research: Why isn't more fly ash used in making concrete?

books. When the materials belong to the student, however, marking the text is a good way to facilitate note taking. Teachers can provide handouts of text selections that students can use to learn how to annotate text. Teacher modeling of annotation of text and instruction on each element of annotation is important for the technique to be learned by students (Zywica and Gomez, 2008).

Students may use a highlighter pen to mark the main idea of each paragraph and the key vocabulary words, or they may underline these ideas and circle or box key words. They may mark the main ideas with one color and the supporting details with another color to get the effect of an outline.

Students may write notes in the margins of pages, as well. They may note important ideas, categories for information, questions for the teacher, or personal reactions or connections to the text. Underlined material may be annotated to show connections with other material in the lesson.

Zywica and Gomez (2008) suggest annotations for headings, key content vocabulary, other difficult words, main ideas or important facts, supporting details for main ideas, procedural words, embedded definitions, transition words, inferences and conclusions, formulas and equations, and confusing material. Not all selections will need annotations for all of these elements, and not all of these types of annotations should be taught at once. After an annotation type is taught, it should be reinforced periodically, as other types are added. Teachers must always point out the connection of annotation with the learning of the content of the material being annotated.

Having students annotate important content material on a regular basis is important. When copies of the material are not available for all students, the students can work as a whole group on a projected copy of the material, or the students can work in small groups to annotate the reading or sections of the reading that can be shared with the rest of the class. Discussion of the annotations will give students a better understanding of key concepts in the readings (Gomez, Herman, and Gomez, 2007; Zywica and Gomez, 2008).

FOCUS ON *Struggling Readers*

Location and Organization Skills for Struggling Readers

Location and organization skills are especially important for struggling readers. They often do not know where to find information because they have never used reference books or the Internet for research purposes. Once they are acquainted with sources of information, they have to learn how to locate the information within the source to complete assignments. Once they find the needed information, struggling readers tend to write a word-for-word copy of the material, or they may write details rather than main ideas; therefore, they must learn to sort important ideas from unimportant ideas. Outlining, summarizing, and note-taking skills will help them experience success in the content areas. Direct instruction and application practice can help them develop these skills.

Location and Organization Skills for ELLs

Secondary English language learners can develop location and organization skills after they have a working knowledge of English. They have a strong need to learn about English reference works. If they are fluent readers in their native language and have used reference works in that language, learning how to use those works is likely to be easier to master. Bilingual dictionaries are especially helpful to these learners. Electronic references that provide bilingual options can also help ELLs. English language learners often need instruction on taking notes and writing summaries. Outlining may not present as much of a challenge because it makes use of the existing text. The use of structured story webs, described earlier in this chapter, can be a beneficial technique. Recorded class instructions and lectures are also useful in helping English language learners develop organizational skills.

Adolescent ELLs may learn much about location skills by participating in digital activities related to popular culture. Black (2009) found that the involvement of adolescent female ELLs with online fan fiction sites led them to seek information about technological problems. They did this either by visiting online help sites and forums or by posting questions on personal webpages to elicit help from the readers. They learned to use these techniques because they had a compelling reason to solve their problems: they were contributors to an accepting community with common interests.

Electronic books (described in Chapter 2) make marking text even easier (Larson, 2008). Students can insert comments, mark out text, highlight, underline, or change type to boldface or another color when using many electronic texts, particularly those downloaded from the Internet.

Summary

Students in content area classes must be able to locate information in the library or media center; in textbooks, other informational books, and reference books; in computer databases; and on the Internet, in order to do effective research for class presentations and written reports. To use the library, they often must know how to use the card catalog, computer terminals, and the library's system for book arrangement. To use books successfully, they need to know the parts of a book and the functions of each part. To use reference books, they need to know about alphabetical order, guide words, cross-references, pronunciation keys, map legends, map scales, and other location and interpretation aids. To use computer databases, they must know how to construct search questions for specific systems. Use of the Internet to locate information requires the understanding of keywords and search engines.

Also important to students who are writing reports are the skills of outlining, summarizing, and note taking. All these skills require the ability to recognize main ideas and supporting details. Outlining requires showing relationships among the main ideas and supporting details, whereas summarizing requires stating the important information in a more concise way. Notes may be taken in outline or summary form, in the form of graphic organizers, in split-page format, on I-Charts, or in another form that the student finds useful to organize the information. Notes are frequently taken on note cards when they will be used for a research paper. Another way to take notes is to annotate the text directly. Struggling readers and ELLs may need extra support in learning location and organization skills.

Discussion Questions

1. How can the librarian and the content area teacher cooperate to teach library skills that students need for research activities?
2. What parts of a book must students be able to use effectively if they are to locate needed information efficiently?
3. What types of reference books need special attention from you, if your students are to do effective research for your class?
4. What are necessary skills for locating information on the Internet?
5. How can outlining help students to understand the material in the textbook for your content class?
6. What helpful guidelines for note taking can you share with students?
7. Which technique for teaching note taking discussed in this chapter holds the most promise for your classes? What others do you know of that you could use instead?
8. What computer skills do students need to make use of today's libraries and media centers?
9. What location and organization skills are most likely to be problems for struggling readers and English language learners?

Enrichment Activities

1. Plan a lesson on use of the index of a secondary-level textbook of your choice. Teach the lesson to a group of your classmates. *Teach the lesson in a secondary school classroom, if possible.
2. Take a content area textbook at the secondary level and plan procedures to familiarize students with the parts of the book and with the reading aids the book offers.
3. Plan a lesson on how to use the Internet to locate information. *Teach the lesson in a secondary school classroom, if possible.

4. Visit a secondary school library, and listen to the librarian explain the reference materials and library procedures to the students. Evaluate the presentation, and decide how you might make changes if you were responsible for it.

*5. Make a bulletin board display that would be helpful to use when teaching either outlining or note taking. Display it either in your college classroom or in a secondary school classroom.

6. Make a lesson plan to teach students to annotate content area reading material. Share it with your classmates.

---

*These activities are designed for in-service teachers, student teachers, and practicum students.

Resources including the TeachSource Video Cases can be found on the website for this book. Cengage Learning's CourseMate brings course concepts to life with interactive learning, study, and exam preparation tools that support the printed textbook. Go to www.cengage.com/login to register your access code.

CHAPTER 8

Reading–Study Strategies for Textbook Use

Overview

In this chapter we consider the development of strategies that enhance both comprehension and retention of information in printed material. We describe study methods such as SQ3R, ROWAC, and SQRQCQ and discuss their usefulness in helping students manage content area reading assignments. Teaching procedures such as PSRT are also included.

Ways to help students learn to read to follow directions are suggested. How to help students learn from the graphic aids (maps, graphs, tables, diagrams, and pictures) in their content area reading materials is discussed, as well as how to help them learn to adjust their reading rates to fit their purposes and the materials to be read. The final topics are fluency, retention, and test taking.

Purpose-Setting Questions

As you read this chapter, try to answer these questions:

1. What are some study methods designed for use with content area reading selections, and how do they help?
2. What are some teaching procedures for helping students learn study skills and helping them read with more comprehension, and why are they effective?
3. How can a teacher help students of varying abilities learn to follow written directions accurately?
4. What types of graphic aids are found in textbooks, and what must students know about each one to read it effectively?
5. What are some factors to consider in instruction related to reading rate?
6. Why is flexibility of rate important to secondary school students?
7. What activities can help students retain what they read?
8. How can teachers help students read test questions with understanding?
9. What can teachers do to help struggling readers and English language learners develop needed reading-study skills?

Preparation for Study

Time spent discussing effective study preparation is well spent because it allows students to be more productive when they study. Following are some tips for teachers to pass along:

1. Record assignments in a special notebook and mark your calendar with assignment deadlines.

2. Under each long-term assignment, list component tasks (e.g., brainstorming, library research, organization, rough draft, final paper). Set a deadline for completing each task so that you will finish the assignment on time. Enter dates on your calendar.

3. At the start of every week, make a separate page for each day of that week. On the page for each day, list tasks to be worked on, including both parts of long-term assignments and new assignments for the week.

4. Each day prioritize your tasks (Ellis, 2009) and work on the most important tasks at the times of day when you are most alert and energetic. If tasks are equally important, work on the harder tasks during your most productive times. On days when not much daily work is assigned, try to get ahead on the long-term activities.

5. Study in a place with as few distractions as possible and at the time of day when you are most alert.

6. Gather all your materials before you sit down to study. You will usually need pencils, pens, paper, textbooks, and reference books (especially a dictionary), and specialized materials for some assignments.

7. If you are a visual learner (learn best through seeing), use reading and graphic aids for studying. If you are an auditory learner (learn best through hearing), talk about the material and possibly listen to recordings of lectures. You may even want to read the material aloud to yourself. If you are a kinesthetic learner (learn best through movement), take notes on the material or find a way to use the ideas in a practical manner. In other words, take advantage of your strengths when you study.

8. Do not multitask. Your effectiveness is likely to decrease and your number of errors to increase when you try to do several things simultaneously (Ellis, 2009).

Importance of a Study Method

Secondary school students can often read narrative material effectively, but have difficulty with expository text. They also frequently do not study effectively because they *do not know how*. They have never learned how to focus on the important material, identify the organization of material, make use of graphic aids, vary reading rates and study procedures to fit the material, or connect new learning to things they already know. They often approach all content reading material with the same attention and speed used for pleasure reading of narrative material.

What are metacognitive skills and why are they important?

Many students fail to make use of **metacognitive skills**—that is, they do not monitor their comprehension of the material they read as they are reading it. The topic of metacognition was introduced in Chapter 5. To summarize, metacognition means knowing what is known already, knowing when comprehension of new material has been accomplished, knowing how the understanding was attained, and knowing what to do if comprehension has not been accomplished. Students frequently look at or pronounce the words in a selection and feel that they have read it, without checking to see if they have located important ideas and have understood the content and how it fits in with information that they already know. They fail to ask, "Do I understand this point?" and "Does this make sense?" Even if they ask these questions, when the answers are negative, they may not remedy the situation by choosing and applying appropriate strategies, such as rereading, checking word meanings in a glossary or dictionary, looking for relationships among ideas, and identifying the organizational pattern of the text in order to clear up problems with meaning (Babbs and Moe, 1983). All these activities are part of effective studying. Instruction in how to ask appropriate questions can be beneficial (Ciardiello, 1998).

Teachers must show students the importance of activating prior knowledge about a topic, relating new information to the prior knowledge, and deciding whether the new information makes sense in light of previous knowledge. They must also make students aware of the strategies they can use to help them figure out meanings that are not immediately apparent. Teacher modeling of self-questioning about meaning and deciding on strategies to use when meaning is unclear is a good approach for increasing metacognitive activities among students.

**TeachSource
Video Case**
Metacognition: Helping Students Become Strategic Learners

Having purposes for their reading activities can increase the likelihood that students will apply metacognitive skills. If they have purposes for reading, they can check to see if those purposes were met. If they have no purposes, they may not know what to look for or what questions to ask about the material.

Study methods have been developed to help students approach content area reading in ways that make comprehension and retention of the material more likely. These methods help students to set purposes for reading the material and to monitor their reading to determine if they have understood the concepts. They often cause the student to look at the material more than once for different purposes, thereby making retention of the ideas more likely.

Students need to become aware of the advantages of using a study method. They need to be told how to apply each method and how to decide when to apply it. For example, SQRQCQ is appropriate for use with reading word problems in mathematics, but not appropriate for reading a history text.

MATHEMATICS

Students who do not know a study method to use when reading content area assignments may resort to pronouncing all the words in the selections as they read without actually thinking about the content. They may then rely on rote memorization to get them through tests on the material and, therefore, may never find meaning in the content they are studying because such memorization does not require understanding.

Teaching Procedures

Teachers find certain teaching procedures particularly helpful in enhancing students' study skills. The PSRT strategy and some recitation techniques can be useful approaches.

What does PSRT stand for?

The steps in the **PSRT** strategy are *Prepare*, *Structure*, *Read*, and *Think* (Simons, 1989). The *Prepare* step includes finding out what the students already know about the concepts in the material and, if necessary, supplementing this background information. Brainstorming about the key concepts should take place during this step. The *Structure* step involves helping students understand the text's organization through use of a graphic overview that is partially completed on the board with them. During the *Read* step, the students read the text independently for a purpose and individually complete the overview presented in the previous step. During the *Think* step, a discussion of the text is held, the overview on the board is completed as a class activity, and the students summarize the text and answer higher-order, teacher-developed questions about it. This procedure is effective because of its high levels of teacher-student interactions. It also takes into account the importance of background knowledge and text organization to reading comprehension.

EXAMPLE 8.1   **PSRT Lesson**

SOCIAL STUDIES

The students are being asked to read the selection called "Revolutions in Food Production" from *Modern World History,* which is reproduced in Chapter 5 on pages 162–163. The teaching session might proceed like the following one:

Prepare

SCIENCE AND HEALTH

Teacher:	What do you think a section called "Revolutions in Food Production" will be about?
Student A:	Changes in the way food is produced.
Teacher:	What do you already know about food production from our previous reading and your other experiences?
Student A:	The weather affected crop production. You know, droughts and floods and storms ruined crops.
Student B:	Pests sometimes spoiled crops.
Student C:	Early on, people just produced crops for their own families; then they started having some people produce for others who worked at other jobs. Now there are huge companies who raise and process food for lots of people.
Student D:	The soil can wear out.
Student E:	Bigger populations make it hard to produce enough food for everybody.
Teacher:	What might be considered a revolution in food production?
Student B:	Better ways to protect crops from weather.
Student C:	Better ways to kill pests.
Student F:	Ways to get bigger crops from the same amount of land.

Structure

The teacher puts the following organizer on the board and helps the students see that it can be completed from their reading passage.

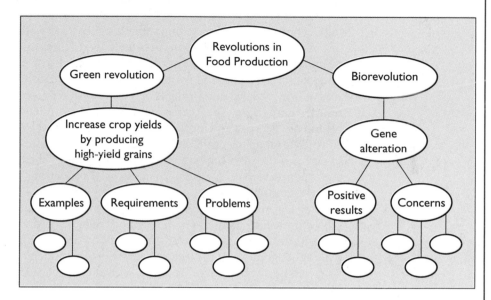

Read

Students read the text to answer the question "What are the results of revolutions in food production?" and to fill in the rest of the graphic organizer on their own papers.

Think

The students and teacher discuss the selection and complete the overview on the board together. Then the students summarize the text. One summary might be "The green revolution has been successful in increasing crop yields by producing high-yield grains, but not all nations can meet the requirements for this technique, and there are potential problems, especially related to use of chemicals. The biorevolution has successfully altered tomato genes, resulting in longer-lasting flavor and freshness, but there are concerns about negative effects related to plant diseases."

   Finally the teacher may ask such questions as the following:

1. What countries would have major problems taking advantage of the green revolution?
2. Should chemicals be used for agriculture? Why, or why not?
3. Why do some people fear eating gene-altered vegetables?
4. Is this fear reasonable?

Classroom recitation techniques can be used to encourage good study practices. Recitation involves saying aloud the information to be remembered. It may serve as a motivational factor for studying material because students feel the need to prepare when they may be required to make presentations in class. It also can strengthen memory for the material, as a student must think about the information, say it, and hear the result. Some forms of recitation include paraphrasing previous contributions to the content discussion, telling something that was learned from the day's lesson, discussing answers to questions presented by teachers or students, and responding simultaneously with the rest of the class to true/false or multiple-choice questions. The total-class response activities allow students to respond without feeling the pressure of being singled out. Students may hold up a "true" or "false" symbol at the same time that others do. The teacher can question the students to discover the thinking behind both correct and incorrect responses when not all students respond correctly.

Teacher modeling of the steps in study skills procedures before students are asked to perform the steps can be a very useful technique. The teacher can move through a procedure, verbalizing the steps being used and letting the students see how each step is accomplished.

Then teachers should provide students with opportunities to practice the methods before asking them to use the methods independently. The teacher should guide students through the use of each study method during a class period, using an actual reading assignment. At the teacher's direction, the students should perform each step in the chosen method. For example, with the use of SQ3R, all students should be asked to survey the material together, reading the chapter title, the introduction to the chapter, the headings, and the chapter summary. At this time they should also be asked to inspect graphic aids within the chapter. Each of the other steps, in turn, should be carried out by all students simultaneously. This technique can be applied to any of the study methods described in this chapter.

Specific Study Methods

With what types of printed materials should SQ3R and ROWAC be used?

Many methods of approaching study reading have been developed. Two methods that are good to use for expository texts, especially for social studies and science selections, are the SQ3R method, developed by Robinson (1961) and ROWAC, developed by Roe. SQRQCQ is a study method appropriate for use with word problems in mathematics. Each of these methods is considered in turn. Each teacher should choose the method or methods that best fit his or her classes' needs.

Study Methods for Expository Texts

SQ3R

When the five steps of the **SQ3R** method are applied to a content area reading selection, a variety of reading activities must be employed (Robinson, 1961). The five steps of SQ3R encourage metacognitive strategies: previewing the text, establishing purposes for reading, monitoring comprehension, summarizing, and reviewing. The steps are as follows:

1. *Survey.* During the survey step, the readers read the chapter title, the introductory paragraph(s), the headings, and the summary paragraph(s). At this time the readers should also inspect any graphic aids, such as maps, graphs, tables, diagrams, and pictures. This survey provides readers with an overview of the material contained in the reading assignment and a framework into which they can organize the facts contained in the selection as they read, enhancing the potential for comprehension. This step gives the readers enough information to generate individual purposes for reading the text.

   Manz (2002) suggests a memory device for carrying out a preview (such as the survey step requires) of a text assignment: THIEVES. As mentioned in the previous paragraph, teachers encourage students to read or examine the *Title,* the *Headings, Every* paragraph's first sentence, *Visuals* and vocabulary, *End-*of-chapter questions, and the *Summary.*

2. *Question.* During this step, readers formulate questions that they expect to find answered in the selection. The author may have provided purpose questions at the beginning of the chapter or follow-up questions at the end. If so, the students may use these questions as purpose questions for the reading. If not, the readers can turn the section headings into questions and read to answer self-constructed questions.

3. *Read.* This is the step in which the students read to answer the purpose questions formulated in the previous step. Notes may be taken during this careful reading.

4. *Recite.* In this step, the students try to answer the purpose questions formulated during the second step without referring to the book or to their notes. This step helps to "set" the information in memory, facilitating later recall. This rehearsal process aids the transfer of information from short-term to long-term memory (Jacobowitz, 1988). This activity gets the students involved and provides feedback on learning (Pauk, 2001).

5. *Review.* At this point the students review the material by rereading portions of the book or by rereading notes taken during the careful reading, to verify the answers given during the previous step. This activity aids the students' retention of the material; immediate reinforcement of ideas helps them overcome the tendency to forget material shortly after reading it.

The SQ3R method, like other study techniques, seems to be learned best when taught in the context of content materials during content classes.

ROWAC

What are the differences in SQ3R and ROWAC?

Another general study method, ROWAC, which was developed by Betty Roe, utilizes the reading–writing connection and emphasizes the importance of passage organization more than SQ3R does. Teachers may want to use this approach especially with their kinesthetic learners. The steps in this method are as follows:

1. *Read.* Read each heading and subheading in the assigned material. (This introduces the student to the nature of the content to be covered and helps to activate his or her background knowledge about the material.)

2. *Organize.* Organize the headings and subheadings in some way (e.g., outline or semantic web). (This gives the student a framework into which to insert the details gained from a careful reading.)

3. *Write.* Write a few paragraphs about what you predict the material will contain, based on the organizer. (This causes the student to engage with the topics to be covered in an active manner, examining connections and sequences and making inferences. This active engagement with the topics should provide motivation and purpose for the reading of the assignment.)

4. *Actively read.* Actively read the material. (This means that the student should constantly be checking the written predictions for accuracy, questioning the reasons for variations between what was expected and what is presented, and filing information in the categories provided by the advance organizer.)

5. *Correct predictions.* Correct your original predictions by revising the paragraphs that you wrote originally. You don't have to rewrite material. Mark out words, phrases, and sentences; use carats to insert ideas; and make marginal notes. The important thing is that the final version, although not neat, is an accurate reflection of the content of the chapter. (This helps the student to integrate the new material into the organizational structure more solidly.)

A Study Method for Mathematics

SQRQCQ

Why is SQRQCQ valuable for reading mathematics materials?

Since mathematics materials present special problems for readers, the **SQRQCQ** study method was developed for use with statement or word problems in mathematics (Fay, 1965). The steps are as follows:

MATHEMATICS

1. *Survey.* The student reads the problem rapidly to obtain an idea of its general nature.

2. *Question.* In this step, the student determines the specific nature of the problem, that is, "What is being asked in this problem?"

3. *Read.* The student reads the problem carefully, paying attention to specific details and relationships.

4. *Question.* At this point, the student must make a decision about the mathematical operations to be carried out and, in some cases, the order in which these operations are to be performed.

5. *Compute.* The student does the computations decided on in the previous step.

6. Question. The student checks the entire process and decides whether or not the answer seems to be correct. He or she asks if the answer is reasonable and if the computations have been performed accurately.

Like SQ3R and ROWAC, this method encourages use of metacognitive skills. Students preview the problem in the survey step, set purposes in the first two question steps, and monitor their success with the problem in the final question step.

Reading to Follow Directions

Another skill that secondary school students need for effective study is the ability to read to follow directions. Students are constantly expected to follow written directions both in the classroom and in everyday life. Teachers write assignments on the board and distribute duplicated materials with directions written on them. Textbooks in different content areas contain printed directions that students are expected to follow. There are also many aspects of everyday activities that require us to follow directions: recipes, assembly and installation instructions, forms to be completed, voting instructions, and registration procedures, to name a few. The activities mentioned involve multiple steps to be followed. Failure to complete the steps properly may result in penalties such as inedible food, nonworking appliances, and receipt of incorrect merchandise.

Many people fail at a task either because they do not know how to follow written directions or because they ignore the directions and try to perform the task without understanding its sequential steps. Almost everyone is familiar with the saying, "When all else fails, read the directions." This tendency to take printed directions lightly may have been fostered in the classroom. Teachers hand out printed directions and then explain them orally. Teachers also often tell students each step to perform as they progress through the task, rather than asking them to read the directions and ask about which parts are unclear. These actions promote a general disregard for reading directions.

Following directions requires two basic comprehension skills: the ability to locate details and the ability to detect sequence. Because each step in a set of directions must be followed exactly and in the appropriate sequence, reading to follow directions is a slow and deliberate task. Rereading is often necessary. The following procedure may prove helpful:

1. Read the directions from beginning to end to get an overview of the task to be performed.

2. Study any accompanying pictorial aids that may help in understanding one or more of the steps or in picturing the desired end result.

3. Reread the directions carefully, visualizing each step to be performed. Read with an open mind, disregarding any preconceived ideas about the procedure involved.

4. Take note of such key words as *first, second, next, last,* and *finally.* Let these words help you picture the order of the activities to be performed.

5. Read each step again, just before you actually perform it.

6. Carry out the steps in the proper order.

Students will learn to follow directions more easily if the presentation of activities is scaled in difficulty from easy to hard. Teachers can start with directions that have few steps and progress to longer sets of directions as the students' proficiency increases.

Some activities for developing skills in following directions are suggested below:

1. Give students a paragraph containing key direction words (*first, next, then, last, finally,* etc.), and ask them to underline the words that help to show the order of events.

ENGLISH/ LANGUAGE ARTS

2. Have students follow directions given in a trade book that is being read in a reading or English class. For example, the young adult novel *If You're Reading This, It's Too Late* by Pseudonymous Bosch has the directions for constructing and performing a magic trick in its Appendix. Students would enjoy this activity and see the need for following the directions exactly.

3. Make it a practice to refer students to written directions instead of telling them orally how to do everything. Ask students to read the directions silently and then tell you in their own words what they should do.

4. Teach the meanings of words commonly encountered in written directions, such as *array, estimate, example, horizontal, phrase,* and *vertical.*

5. Have students follow directions to make something from a kit.

6. Use activities similar to the one in Example 8.2 to make a point about the importance of following directions.

Any exercises designed to improve students' ability to understand details and detect sequence will also help them improve their skills in following directions. Activities in which students must integrate information from graphic aids, such as charts or diagrams, with printed information in the text will also be helpful.

Graphic Aids

How do graphic aids help students to understand content material?

The ability to interpret **graphic aids** requires visual literacy, the ability both to interpret and create nonverbal messages (Forcier and Descy, 2008; Lohr, 2008). Textbooks contain numerous graphic aids—maps, graphs, tables, charts, diagrams, and pictures—that students often disregard because they have had no training in their use. These aids can help students understand the textbook material better if teachers help them learn to extract the information from each type of graphic aid, but the students need to be explicitly directed to use them to find *specific* information. Simply having a reliable approach to each of the types of graphic aids may be all many secondary students need to benefit from the aids in their textbooks.

EXAMPLE 8.2	**Activity on Following Directions**

Questionnaire: Read this entire questionnaire before you begin to fill in the answers. Work as quickly as you can. You have three minutes to finish this activity.

Name _____

Address _____

_____

Phone number _____ Age _____

What is your father's name and occupation? _____

What is your mother's name and occupation? _____

Do you plan to go to college? _____ If so, where? _____

What career are you most interested in? _____

How many years of study past high school will you need for this career? _____

Who is the person that you admire most? _____

What is this person's occupation? _____

After you have completed reading this questionnaire, turn the paper over and write your name on the back. Then give the paper to your teacher. You should have written nothing on this side of the page.

Graphic aids serve different purposes in different textbooks. At times, they include information not discussed in the text, although it is related to the text discussion. Sometimes they contain information stated in the text, but they present it in a more visual form. At other times, they may contain a mixture of information from the text and information not from the text, making connections apparent. Whatever their content, graphic displays have been found to improve students' comprehension. This may be true because graphic aids often allow readers to scan large collections of information to see meaningful patterns and to help them visualize certain kinds of information (Gillespie, 1993).

Maps

SOCIAL STUDIES

Maps are found in many content area materials, although they are most common in social studies textbooks. Since maps are generally included in textbooks to help clarify the narrative material, students need to be able to read them to understand fully the material being presented.

Some students may have been taught map-reading techniques in elementary school, but many have not had any structured preparation for reading maps. Therefore, secondary school students may vary greatly in their abilities to handle assignments containing maps. A survey of map-reading skills should be administered early in the school year by teachers who expect map reading to be a frequent activity throughout the year. A sample map and some useful questions for surveying map-reading skills are shown in Example 8.3.

After administering a survey of map-reading skills and evaluating the results, the teacher should systematically teach any of the following skills that the students have not yet mastered:

1. Locating and comprehending the map title.

2. Determining directions.

3. Interpreting a map's legend.

4. Applying a map's scale.

5. Understanding the concepts of latitude and longitude.

6. Understanding common map terms.

7. Making inferences concerning the material represented on a map.

The first step in map reading should be examining the title of the map to determine the area being represented and the type of information being given about the area. Map titles are not always located at the tops of the maps, as students often expect them to be. Therefore, students may overlook the title of a map unless they have been told to scan the map to find it.

Next, students should locate the directional indicator on the map and orient themselves to the map's layout. They should be aware that north is not always at the top of the map, although most maps are constructed in this manner.

Interpretation of the legend or key is the next step in map reading. The map legend contains an explanation of each of the symbols used. If students do not understand these symbols, the map will be incomprehensible to them.

To determine distances on a map, students must apply the map's scale. Because it would be highly impractical, if not impossible, to draw a map the actual size of the area represented (for example, the United States), maps show areas greatly reduced in size. The relationship of a given distance on a map to the same distance on the earth is shown by the map's scale.

An understanding of latitude and longitude will be helpful in reading some maps. Parallels of latitude are lines on a globe that are parallel to the equator. Meridians of longitude are lines that encircle the globe in a north-south direction, meeting at the poles.

| EXAMPLE 8.3 | **Map of the United States and Latin America** |

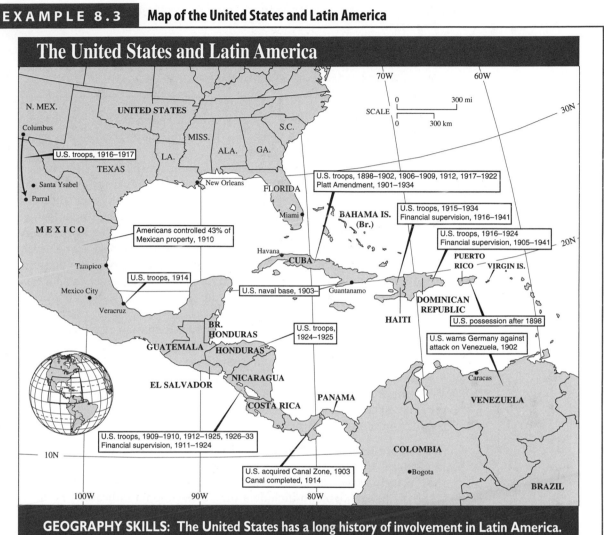

The United States and Latin America

N. MEX.

Columbus

UNITED STATES

S.C.

MISS.

ALA.

GA.

U.S. troops, 1916–1917

LA.

TEXAS

New Orleans

FLORIDA

• Santa Ysabel

• Parral

Miami

BAHAMA IS.
(Br.)

70W

60W

SCALE

0   300 mi

0   300 km

30N

M E X I C O

Americans controlled 43% of
Mexican property, 1910

Havana

CUBA

U.S. troops, 1898–1902, 1906–1909, 1912, 1917–1922
Platt Amendment, 1901–1934

U.S. troops, 1915–1934
Financial supervision, 1916–1941

U.S. troops, 1916–1924
Financial supervision, 1905–1941

PUERTO
RICO   **VIRGIN IS.**

20N

Tampico •

U.S. troops, 1914

Mexico City •

Veracruz •

U.S. naval base, 1903

Guantanamo

DOMINICAN
REPUBLIC

HAITI

U.S. possession after 1898

BR.
HONDURAS

GUATEMALA

HONDURAS

U.S. troops,
1924–1925

U.S. warns Germany against
attack on Venezuela, 1902

EL SALVADOR

NICARAGUA

COSTA RICA

PANAMA

Caracas •

VENEZUELA

U.S. troops, 1909–1910, 1912–1925, 1926–33
Financial supervision, 1911–1924

10N

COLOMBIA

• Bogota

U.S. acquired Canal Zone, 1903
Canal completed, 1914

BRAZIL

100W

90W

80W

GEOGRAPHY SKILLS: The United States has a long history of involvement in Latin America.
Critical Thinking: Why might the Caribbean Sea have been called an "American lake"?

Source: The map is from *America's Past and Promise*, by Lorna Mason, Jesus Garcia, Frances Powell, and C. Frederick Risinger.
Copyright © 1995 by Houghton Mifflin Company, p. 609. All rights reserved.

Questions

SOCIAL
STUDIES

1. What area does this map cover?
2. What information about the area is provided?
3. What is the distance from Havana to Miami in miles? In kilometers?
4. What information does the inset map provide?
5. Which Latin American country has had the most recent U.S. involvement, according
   to this map?

6. Where is a U.S. naval base located on the map? Why would that location be strategically important?
7. Using degrees of latitude and longitude, what is the location of Puerto Rico?
8. In what country is Caracas located?
9. What is a canal? What canal is shown on this map?

Students need to understand many common map terms to comprehend maps fully. In addition to *latitude* and *longitude*, there are *equator, hemisphere, peninsula, continent, isthmus, gulf, bay*, and many others.

Teachers should encourage students to perform more than simple location activities with maps. They should ask students to make inferences about the material represented on maps. For example, for a map showing the physical features of an area (such as mountains, rivers, lakes, deserts, and swamps), the students might be asked to decide what types of transportation would be most appropriate in that area. This kind of activity is extremely important at the secondary school level.

Relating a map of an area they are studying to a map of a larger area that contains the smaller one can help students. For example, a map of Tennessee can be related to a map of the United States. In this way, the position of Tennessee within the United States becomes apparent.

Some educators use interactive whiteboards to teach map-reading skills ("Ideas for Teaching with Interactive Whiteboards," 2005). Whiteboards allow teachers to "project text, data, images, video, and sound from a computer onto a 66-inch screen using whatever programs teachers have running on their computers, including PowerPoint, Excel, AutoCAD, or a standard web browser" (Levin-Epstein, Murray, and Pierce, 2005, p. 22).

Further suggestions for working with map-reading skills follow:

MATHEMATICS

1. Before presenting a chapter in a textbook that requires much map reading, ask students to construct a map of an area of interest to the class. Help students draw the map to scale. (A mathematics teacher may be enlisted to help with this aspect.) Ask students to include a title, a directional indicator, and a legend. This exercise will help prepare students to read the maps in their content textbooks with more understanding.

2. When students encounter a map in a content area textbook, encourage them to use the legend by asking questions such as the following:
   • Where is there a campground on this map?
   • Where do you find a symbol for a state capital?
   • Are there any national parks in this area? If so, where are they located?

ENGLISH/ LANGUAGE ARTS   **SOCIAL STUDIES**

3. Help students with map terminology by first identifying map features with examples and then asking them to point out on a wall map features such as a *gulf* and a *peninsula* when these features are pertinent to the content presentation.

4. Have students map the locations of the events in a novel or the events in a history chapter or nonfiction trade book that does not provide a detailed map. Make sure they include a title, legend, directional indicator, and scale.

MEETING THE CHALLENGE

The seventh-graders in Mr. Kyle's urban classroom have been having trouble learning to read maps. Mr. Kyle has come up with a creative approach to this problem. He takes heavy-grade poster board on which he has drawn an outline map of an area and cuts it up with a knife-blade saw. He gives the puzzle pieces that he has created in this manner to his students. First, the students have to put the pieces of the map back together. Then they have to fill in the details of the area on the map (e.g., cities, rivers, landmarks, etc.). To accomplish this task, they must supply a legend with the appropriate symbols, directional indicators, and map scales, as well as place names. When they finish, they use puzzle glue to hold their production together. It can be displayed for other groups, and class members can refer to it as they study the area. The students take pride in their accomplishment.

Map-reading instruction is important for students in social studies classes.
© Dennis MacDonald / PhotoEdit

SOCIAL STUDIES

Graphs

SOCIAL STUDIES **SCIENCE AND HEALTH**

Graphs often appear in social studies, science, and mathematics books, and sometimes in books for other content areas. Graphs are used to make comparisons among quantitative data.

Types of Graphs

MATHEMATICS

There are four basic types of graphs.

1. *Picture graphs (or pictographs).* Picture graphs use pictures to compare quantities. They aid in visualization of data and are often thought to be the easiest type of graph to read. Readers must realize, however, that only approximate amounts can be indicated by pictographs, making estimation of amounts necessary when interpreting them.

2. *Circle or pie graphs.* Proportional parts of a whole can be shown most easily through use of circle or pie graphs. These graphs show the percentage of the whole represented by each individual part.

3. *Bar graphs.* Bar graphs are useful for comparing the quantities of several items or the quantities of a particular item at different times. These graphs may be either horizontal or vertical.

4. *Line graphs.* Line graphs can depict changes in amounts over a period of time or under different circumstances. They have vertical and horizontal axes. Each point that is plotted on a line graph has a value on both axes.

Representative samples of each of these types of graphs and accompanying sample questions are shown in Examples 8.4, 8.5, 8.6, and 8.7.

EXAMPLE 8.4   Sample Picture Graph and Questions

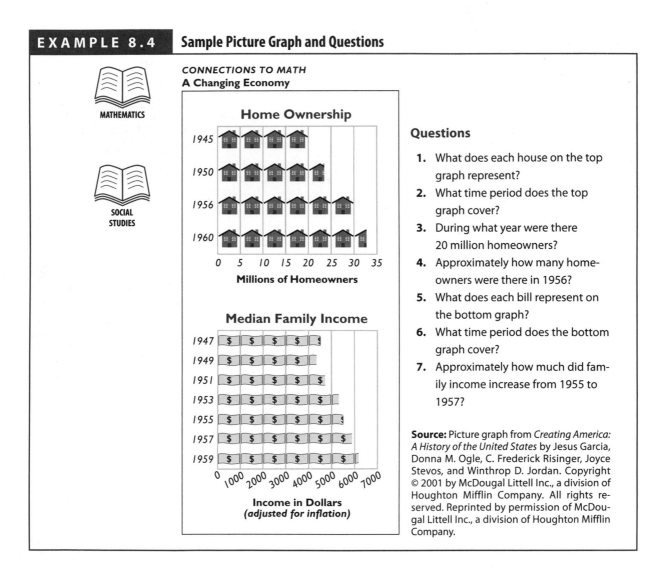

CONNECTIONS TO MATH
A Changing Economy

Home Ownership

Millions of Homeowners

Median Family Income

Income in Dollars
(adjusted for inflation)

Questions

1. What does each house on the top graph represent?
2. What time period does the top graph cover?
3. During what year were there 20 million homeowners?
4. Approximately how many home-owners were there in 1956?
5. What does each bill represent on the bottom graph?
6. What time period does the bottom graph cover?
7. Approximately how much did fam-ily income increase from 1955 to 1957?

Source: Picture graph from *Creating America: A History of the United States* by Jesus Garcia, Donna M. Ogle, C. Frederick Risinger, Joyce Stevos, and Winthrop D. Jordan. Copyright © 2001 by McDougal Littell Inc., a division of Houghton Mifflin Company. All rights re-served. Reprinted by permission of McDou-gal Littell Inc., a division of Houghton Mifflin Company.

EXAMPLE 8.5 **Sample History Text with Circle Graphs and Questions**

SOCIAL
STUDIES

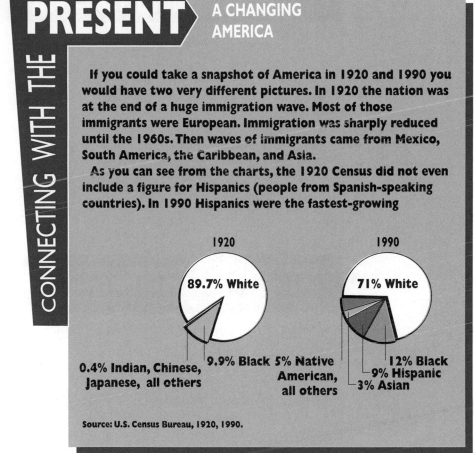

CONNECTING WITH THE

PRESENT

A CHANGING
AMERICA

If you could take a snapshot of America in 1920 and 1990 you would have two very different pictures. In 1920 the nation was at the end of a huge immigration wave. Most of those immigrants were European. Immigration was sharply reduced until the 1960s. Then waves of immigrants came from Mexico, South America, the Caribbean, and Asia.

As you can see from the charts, the 1920 Census did not even include a figure for Hispanics (people from Spanish-speaking countries). In 1990 Hispanics were the fastest-growing

1920

89.7% White

0.4% Indian, Chinese, Japanese, all others

9.9% Black

1990

71% White

5% Native American, all others

12% Black
9% Hispanic
3% Asian

Source: U.S. Census Bureau, 1920, 1990.

Source: Graphs from *America's Past and Promise*, by Lorna Mason, Jesus Garcia, Frances Powell, and C. Frederick Risinger. Copyright © 1995 by Houghton Mifflin Company. All rights reserved.

Questions

1. How did the percentage of whites in the United States change from 1920 to 1990?
2. How did the nonwhite population of the United States change from 1920 to 1990?
3. What are some possible reasons for the changes that occurred between 1920 and 1990?

EXAMPLE 8.6   **Sample Bar Graph and Questions**

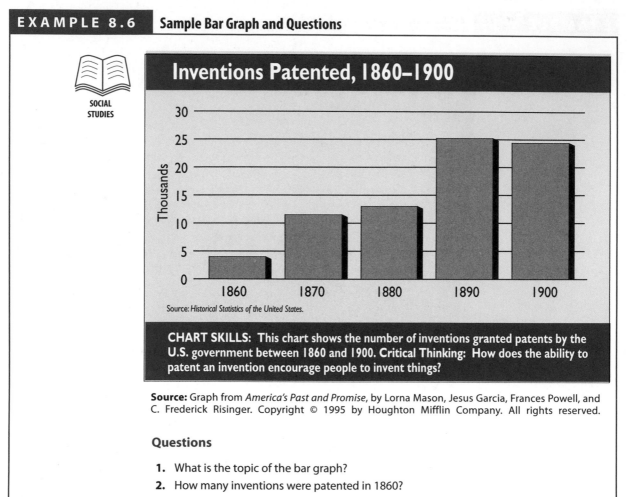

SOCIAL STUDIES

Inventions Patented, 1860–1900

Source: *Historical Statistics of the United States.*

CHART SKILLS: This chart shows the number of inventions granted patents by the U.S. government between 1860 and 1900. **Critical Thinking:** How does the ability to patent an invention encourage people to invent things?

Source: Graph from *America's Past and Promise*, by Lorna Mason, Jesus Garcia, Frances Powell, and C. Frederick Risinger. Copyright © 1995 by Houghton Mifflin Company. All rights reserved.

Questions

1. What is the topic of the bar graph?
2. How many inventions were patented in 1860?
3. In what year shown were the most inventions patented?
4. What is the general trend in the numbers of inventions patented? What might be some reasons for this trend?

Graph-Reading Skills

Students should be taught to check the title of a graph to discover what comparison is being made or what information is being supplied. They must also learn to interpret the legend of a picture graph and to derive needed information from a graph accurately.

Teachers can help students discover the following information about the graphs in their textbooks:

1. The purpose of the graph. (Usually indicated by the title, the purpose becomes more evident when the accompanying narrative is studied.)
2. The scale of measure on bar and line graphs.

EXAMPLE 8.7   **Sample Line Graph and Questions**

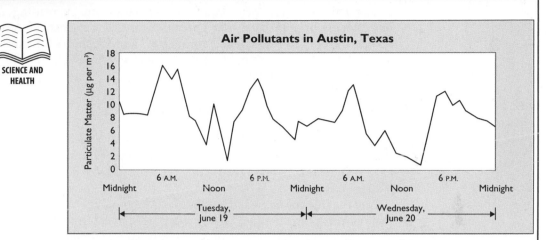

SCIENCE AND
HEALTH

Source: Line graph from *Earth Science* by Nancy E. Spaulding and Samuel N. Namowitz. Copyright © 2003 by McDougal Littell Inc., a division of Houghton Mifflin Company. All rights reserved. Reprinted by permission of McDougal Littell Inc., a division of Houghton Mifflin Company.

Questions

1. How does the concentration of pollutants at 6 a.m. Tuesday compare with the concentration of pollutants at 6 a.m. Wednesday?

2. Air pollution can worsen the health of people with lung disease. According to the graph, when is the best time for such a person to run errands?

3. At what time does the concentration of pollutants peak on both days?

4. What could be the cause of the peaks in the amounts of pollution on the two days?

5. Falling rain tends to clean pollutants from the air. What evidence is there that no rain fell Tuesday morning before 6 a.m.?

6. Assume these trends continue into Thursday, June 21. Predict the time on that day when the amount of pollutants is most likely to be greatest.

3. The legend of picture graphs.

4. The items being compared.

5. The location of specific pieces of information within a graph (e.g., the intersection of the point of interest on the vertical axis with the point of interest on the horizontal axis).

6. The trends indicated by a graph. (For example, does an amount increase or decrease over a period of time?)

7. The application of graphic information to actual life situations. (A graph showing the temperatures for each month in Sydney, Australia, could be used for planning what clothes to take on a trip to Sydney at a particular time of the year.)

The ability to both comprehend and draw graphs is an important communication tool. One of the best ways to help students learn to read graphs is to have them construct their own after the teacher has modeled how to do this. They can graph such things as fund-raising activities, number of students participating in extracurricular activities, time spent on different activities, outside readings done by various students, or quiz scores over a period of time. The teacher can construct graphs such as the ones in Examples 8.4 through 8.7 and ask students to answer questions about them. Questions can also be asked about particular graphs in the students' textbooks or related trade books.

Tables

Tables, which are found in reading materials for all subject areas, contain information arranged in vertical columns and horizontal rows. One problem that students have with reading tables is extracting the needed facts from a large mass of information presented.

Like the titles of maps and graphs, the titles of tables contain information about their content. Also, because tables are arranged in columns and rows, the headings for the columns and rows also provide information. Specific information is obtained by locating the intersection of an appropriate column with an appropriate row. Example 8.8 shows a sample table. The questions that follow the table are presented as models for the types of questions that teachers might ask about the tables in their students' content textbooks.

Charts and Diagrams

SOCIAL STUDIES

Charts and diagrams appear in textbooks for many different content areas. They are designed to help students picture the events, processes, structures, relationships, or sequences described by the text. At times they may be used as summaries of text material. Example 8.9 is a chart from a history book that summarizes text material and shows a process. This chart indicates the direction of flow in the process through use of arrows and numbers.

Students must be made aware of the abstract nature of diagrams and of the fact that they often distort or oversimplify information. Interpretation of the symbols found in diagrams and understanding of the perspectives used in diagrams are not automatic; teachers must provide practice in such activities.

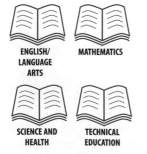

ENGLISH/ LANGUAGE ARTS   **MATHEMATICS**

SCIENCE AND HEALTH   **TECHNICAL EDUCATION**

Numerous types of charts and diagrams are used in the various content areas. Examples include tree diagrams (English), flow charts (mathematics), and process charts (science). Careful instruction in reading such charts and diagrams must be provided for interpretation of content material. Example 8.10 shows a diagram from a woodworking textbook. Such a diagram could also appear in a science textbook.

The teacher needs to help students recognize that this is a labeled diagram of a *cross section* of a tree trunk. Having them look at the labels of the parts and asking where the bark is on this diagram can help them become oriented to the view presented. Students may be asked to label unlabeled diagrams similar to this one as a check on retention of the concepts and terminology presented in the text.

A semantic map, one type of graphic organizer, is a diagram of the relationships among concepts in a text. Having students draw semantic maps of content material

EXAMPLE 8.8	Sample Table and Questions

SCIENCE AND HEALTH

Common Air Pollutants

Air Pollutant	Major Sources	Effects
Carbon monoxide (CO)	Automobile exhaust	Reduces delivery of oxygen to body tissues; impairs vision and reflexes
Nitrogen dioxide (NO_2)	Burning of fossil fuels in power plants and automobiles	Irritates lungs and lowers resistance to respiratory infections; contributes to acid rain and smog
Sulfur dioxide (SO_2)	Burning of fossil fuels in power plants, oil refineries, paper mills, volcanoes	Irritates respiratory system; contributes to acid rain
Particulate matter (dust, smoke, soot, ash)	Factories, power plants, oil refineries, paper mills, volcanoes	Contributes to respiratory problems; linked to some cancers
Lead (Pb)	Smelters, battery plants	Damages nervous and digestive systems
Ozone (O_3)	Reactions of nitrogen oxides and hydrocarbons in the presence of sunlight	Reduces lung function and causes inflammation

Source: Table from *Earth Science* by Nancy E. Spaulding and Samuel N. Namowitz. Copyright © 2003 by McDougal Littell Inc., a division of Houghton Mifflin Company. All rights reserved. Reprinted by permission of McDougal Littell Inc., a division of Houghton Mifflin Company.

Questions

1. What type of information is located in this table?
2. What are the column headings?
3. What does nitrogen dioxide cause?
4. What is a major source of carbon monoxide?
5. What pollutant damages nervous and digestive systems?

can help them comprehend it better. (See Chapter 4 for details on semantic mapping.) Fisher (2001) suggests the use of *graphic organizer notebooks*, collections of blank organizers and webs that are designed by the teacher to fit particular text material. Students are asked to fill in these graphic organizers after they have read the content material.

Diagramming the word problems presented in mathematics textbooks can help students visualize the problems and subsequently solve them. Such approaches to math problem solving are fairly common in elementary schools, but they often are dropped at the secondary level, even though they are still valid.

MATHEMATICS

| EXAMPLE 8.9 | History Chart |

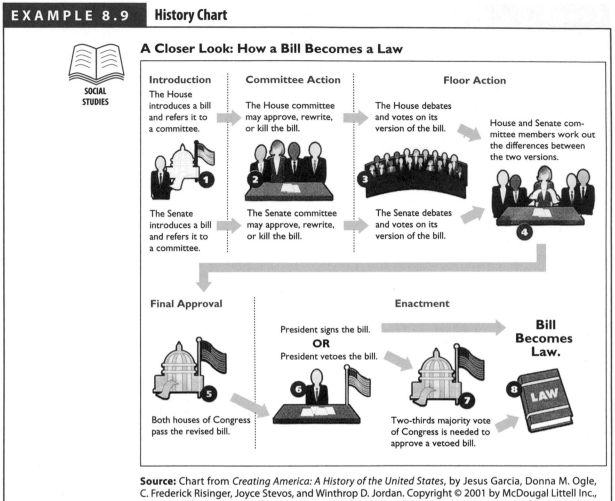

A Closer Look: How a Bill Becomes a Law

SOCIAL STUDIES

Introduction

The House introduces a bill and refers it to a committee.

The Senate introduces a bill and refers it to a committee.

Committee Action

The House committee may approve, rewrite, or kill the bill.

The Senate committee may approve, rewrite, or kill the bill.

Floor Action

The House debates and votes on its version of the bill.

The Senate debates and votes on its version of the bill.

House and Senate committee members work out the differences between the two versions.

Final Approval

Both houses of Congress pass the revised bill.

Enactment

President signs the bill.
OR
President vetoes the bill.

Two-thirds majority vote of Congress is needed to approve a vetoed bill.

Bill Becomes Law.

LAW

Source: Chart from *Creating America: A History of the United States*, by Jesus Garcia, Donna M. Ogle, C. Frederick Risinger, Joyce Stevos, and Winthrop D. Jordan. Copyright © 2001 by McDougal Littell Inc., a division of Houghton Mifflin Company. All rights reserved. Reprinted by permission of McDougal Littell Inc., a division of Houghton Mifflin Company.

Pictures and Cartoons

Content area textbooks contain pictures that are designed to illustrate the material described and to interest students. The illustrations may be photographs offering a realistic representation of concepts, people, and places, or they may be line drawings that are somewhat more abstract in nature.

Students frequently see pictures merely as space fillers, reducing the amount of reading they will have to do on a page. Therefore, they may pay little attention to pictures, although the pictures are often excellent sources of information.

Since pictures are representations of experiences, they may be utilized as vicarious means of adding to a student's store of knowledge. Teachers should help students

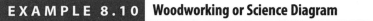

EXAMPLE 8.10 | **Woodworking or Science Diagram**

SCIENCE AND
HEALTH

TECHNICAL
EDUCATION

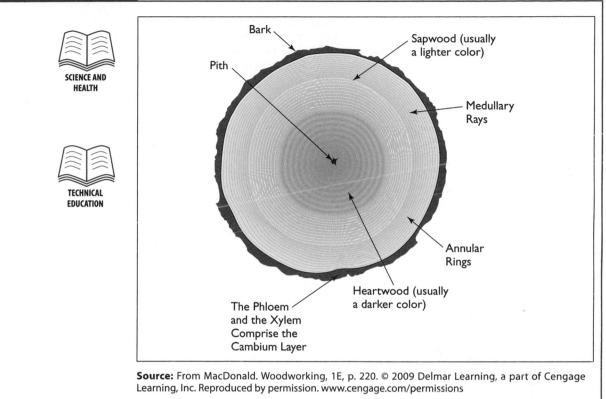

Bark

Sapwood (usually a lighter color)

Pith

Medullary Rays

Annular Rings

Heartwood (usually a darker color)

The Phloem and the Xylem Comprise the Cambium Layer

Source: From MacDonald. Woodworking, 1E, p. 220. © 2009 Delmar Learning, a part of Cengage Learning, Inc. Reproduced by permission. www.cengage.com/permissions

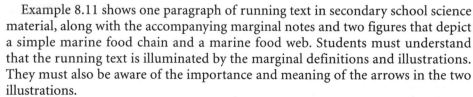

SCIENCE AND
HEALTH

ENGLISH/
LANGUAGE
ARTS

extract information from textbook illustrations and illustrations in other content materials by encouraging them to study the pictures before and after reading the text, looking for the purpose of each picture and its specific details. Studying pictures may help students understand and retain the information illustrated. Visual literacy skills are important to getting the full amount of information from illustrations.

Example 8.11 shows one paragraph of running text in secondary school science material, along with the accompanying marginal notes and two figures that depict a simple marine food chain and a marine food web. Students must understand that the running text is illuminated by the marginal definitions and illustrations. They must also be aware of the importance and meaning of the arrows in the two illustrations.

Cartoons are special types of pictures that contain special symbols. They often distort the things they represent in order to make a point. Students should be encouraged to read cartoons critically. Example 8.12 shows a cartoon that might appear in a literature textbook. This cartoon makes the point that allusions to literature are often used in cartoons, and the cartoons are not funny if the readers are not familiar with the literature. In the case of this cartoon, the teacher could ask,

| EXAMPLE 8.11 | Science Textbook Illustration |

Autotroph—("self-feeder") organism that makes its own food rather then consuming other organisms.

Food chains and more complex *food webs* illustrate feeding relationships among organisms in biological communities. At the base of food chains and webs are *autotrophs*, which produce their own food for growth and reproduction through photosynthesis. In the ocean, the primary autotrophs are *phytoplankton*, microscopic

SCIENCE AND HEALTH

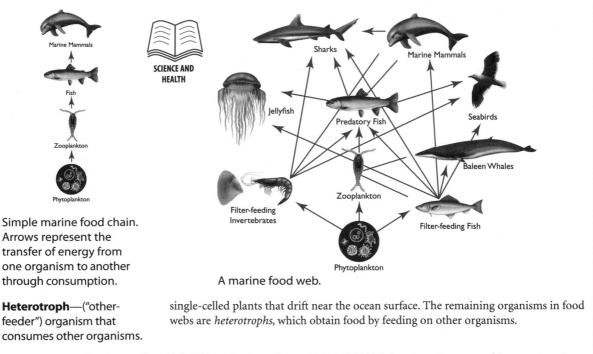

Simple marine food chain. Arrows represent the transfer of energy from one organism to another through consumption.

A marine food web.

Heterotroph—("other-feeder") organism that consumes other organisms.

single-celled plants that drift near the ocean surface. The remaining organisms in food webs are *heterotrophs*, which obtain food by feeding on other organisms.

Source: From Hall. *GIS Investigations*, 1E, pp. 135-136. © 2008 Delmar Learning, a part of Cengage Learning, Inc. Reproduced by permission. www.cengage.com/permissions

SCIENCE AND HEALTH

SCIENCE AND HEALTH

SOCIAL STUDIES

ENGLISH/ LANGUAGE ARTS

"Why is this cartoon funny?" Students would have to know that Mark Twain was the author of a book named *Tom Sawyer* in order to see the humor, especially if they expect letter writing to be a topic in an English class.

The *Six Chix* comic strip in Example 8.13 might be used in an explanation of metamorphosis.

Example 8.14 can be used as an exercise in examining how a cartoon delivers a message. Teachers can have the students in a science class discuss the reasons that the Tennessee Valley Authority (TVA) would build mini-nuclear reactors; in a social studies class discuss the reason for the man's violent reaction and what TVA is; and in an English class discuss the reason for his mistake and the function of word parts in the humor of the cartoon. To read the cartoon, the students need graphic literacy. There are lines that show the motion of the man and the paper, stylized indicators of sweat, speech balloons (the jagged one showing a shaky utterance), and an arrow with a label for the man.

EXAMPLE 8.12 Literature-Related Cartoon

© R. Daniel Proctor/Knoxville News-Sentinel. Reprinted with permission.

EXAMPLE 8.13 Biology-Related Comic Strip

Copyright © SIX CHIX—MARGARET SHULOCK. Reprinted with permission of King Features Syndicate.

Students can illustrate sections of content text with their own pictures or cartoons as they read. This action causes them to process the material more deeply and results in increased comprehension. Students should understand that their artistic ability is not the point and is not being evaluated. Evidence of insight into the content is the focus of the evaluation.

EXAMPLE 8.14   Cartoon for Science, Social Studies, or English

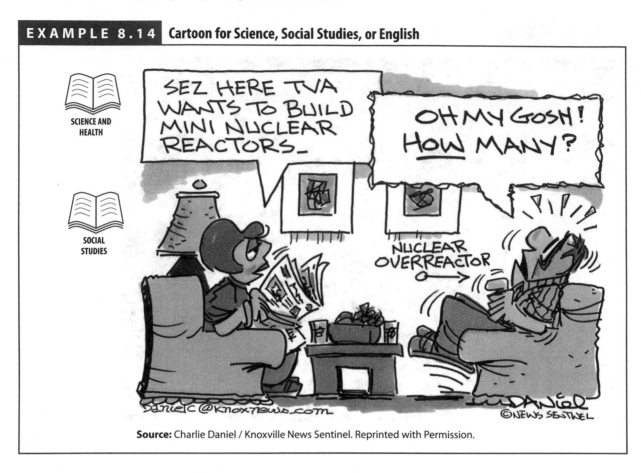

Source: Charlie Daniel / Knoxville News Sentinel. Reprinted with Permission.

Adjusting Rate to Fit Purpose and Materials

What is meant by
flexibility of rate?

Students will use study time most efficiently if they are taught to vary their reading rates to fit their purposes and the materials they are reading. The ability to make these adjustments, which is important for good comprehension, is called **flexibility of rate**. Good readers adjust their rates, thinking, and approaches automatically and are not aware that they make several changes when reading a single page.

Flexible readers can distinguish between important and unimportant ideas, and they read important ideas carefully, giving less attention to the less important ideas. Information about familiar topics is read more quickly than information about new topics because familiarity with a topic allows the reader to anticipate ideas, vocabulary, and phrasing. A selection that has a light vocabulary burden, more concrete concepts, and an easily managed style of writing can be read more rapidly than material with a heavy vocabulary load, many abstract concepts, and a difficult writing style. Light fiction that is read strictly for enjoyment can and should be absorbed much faster than the directions for a science experiment; newspapers and

SCIENCE AND
HEALTH   MATHEMATICS

magazines can be read more rapidly than textbooks; however, theoretical scientific content and statistics must be read more slowly than much social studies content.

Students often think that everything should be read at the same rate. Thus, some of them read light novels as slowly and deliberately as they read mathematics problems. These students will probably never enjoy reading for recreation because they work so hard at reading and it takes them so long. Other students move rapidly through everything they read. In doing so, they usually fail to grasp essential details in content area assignments, although they "finish" reading all of the assigned material. Rate of reading should never be considered apart from comprehension. Therefore, the optimum rate for reading any material is the fastest rate at which an acceptable level of comprehension is obtained. Teachers who wish to concentrate on improving their students' reading rates should include comprehension checks with all rate exercises.

Work on increasing reading rate should not be emphasized until basic word recognition and comprehension skills are thoroughly under control. Improvement in these skills often results in increased rate without any special attention to it. For best results, flexibility of rate should be developed with the content materials that students are expected to read.

Factors Affecting Rate

Many factors influence the rate at which a person can read a particular selection. Some are related to the material, but some are related to the reader. Factors related to the material include size and style of type, format of the pages, use of illustrations, organization, writing style of the author, and abstractness or complexity of ideas in the material. Factors related to the reader include the reader's background of experiences, reading ability, attitudes and interests, and reason for reading the specific material. Obviously, these factors differ with each selection. Therefore, different rates are appropriate for different materials.

Poor reading habits may greatly decrease reading rate. Poor habits include excessive vocalizing (forming each word as it is read); sounding out all words, those familiar and those unfamiliar; excessive regressing (going back and rereading previously read material); and pointing at each word with the index finger. Concentrated attention to the elimination of these problems can yield good results. Often, secondary school students simply need to be made aware of the habits that are slowing them down and need to be given some suggestions for practice in overcoming them.

Techniques for Increasing Rate and Flexibility

Many methods have been devised to help students increase or adjust their rates of reading. The approaches most classroom teachers use are having timed readings, teaching skimming and scanning techniques, and providing flexibility exercises.

Timed Readings

To help students increase their rates of reading in material that does not require intensive study reading, teachers may use timed readings. Like other study skills,

SCIENCE AND
HEALTH

MATHEMATICS

techniques for improving rate may be learned best in situations in which they are actually used. In choosing appropriate selections for rate instruction, the content teacher should avoid material that includes many small details (e.g., a science experiment or a mathematics statement problem). Materials that present general background and recreational reading in the content area are more useful for this activity (e.g., the story of a scientific discovery or the biography of a mathematician).

Timed readings should always be accompanied by comprehension checks. An extremely high rate score is of no use if the student fails to comprehend the material. Teachers should encourage rate increases only if comprehension does not suffer. Some students need help in basic reading skills before they can participate profitably in these rate-building activities.

Graphs can be kept of the results of timed rate exercises over a period of weeks or months. Seeing visible progress can motivate students to continue to work on improving their rates. Comprehension charts should also be kept so rate increases can be viewed in the proper perspective.

Skimming and Scanning Techniques

When might you need to skim text? How is scanning of text accomplished?

Skimming and **scanning** are special types of rapid reading. Skimming refers to reading to obtain a general idea or overview of the material, and scanning means reading to find a specific bit of information. Skimming is faster than rapid reading of most of the words in the material because, when readers skim material, they read selectively. Scanning is faster than skimming because only one piece of information is being sought. When scanning, readers run their eyes rapidly down the page, concentrating on the particular information they seek.

Skimming techniques are used in the survey step of the SQ3R method discussed earlier in this chapter. Teachers can help develop skimming skills as they work to teach this study method.

When teaching students to skim, the teacher should tell them to read all of the first two paragraphs of a chapter or selection to get an overview and then begin to leave out material as they read, reading only key sentences and phrases to get the main ideas. The teacher should point out that, if the final paragraph summarizes the material, students may want to read it more carefully.

Students should try to read as fast as possible when they skim. Students should use skimming when they do not have much time and need to cover the material as fast as possible.

Some skimming activities include the following:

1. Give the students a short time to skim an assigned chapter and write down the main ideas covered.

2. Ask students to skim newspaper articles and match them to headlines written on the board. Have a competition to see who can finish first with no errors.

3. Give students the title of a research topic and have them skim an article to decide whether it is pertinent to the topic.

Scanning activities are easy to design. Some examples follow:

SOCIAL STUDIES

1. Have students scan a history chapter to find the date of a particular event.

2. Have students scan a textbook to find information about a particular person.

Students need to scan for key words related to the specific facts they seek. An exercise in generating key words that are related to a specific topic may be beneficial.

Flexibility Exercises

Since not all materials should be read at the same rate, students need assistance in determining appropriate rates for different materials. The table in Example 8.15 shows three reading rates of a good reader in words per minute (wpm), each of which is appropriate for a particular type of reading material.

One type of flexibility exercise is to ask a series of questions such as the following ones and then discuss students' reasons for their answers:

MATHEMATICS

SCIENCE AND HEALTH

1. What rate would be best for reading a statement problem in your mathematics textbook?

2. Which could you read most quickly and still achieve your purpose—a television schedule, a newspaper article, or a science textbook?

3. Is just skimming an appropriate way to read directions for a science experiment?

4. What reading technique would you use to look up a word in the dictionary?

EXAMPLE 8.15 | **Rate Chart**

Kind of Reading	Rate	Comprehension
Slow: *Study reading* speed is used when material is difficult or when high comprehension is desired.	200 to 300 wpm	80–90%
Average: An *average reading* speed is used for everyday reading of magazines, newspapers, and easier textbooks.	250 to 500 wpm	70%
Fast: *Skimming* is used when the highest rate is desired. Comprehension is intentionally lower.	800+ wpm	50%

Source: Reprinted by permission of Edward Fry.

Fluency

People sometimes equate fluency with rate, but fluency "consists not only of rate, accuracy, and automaticity, but also of phrasing, smoothness, and expressiveness" (Worthy and Broaddus, 2001/2002, p. 334). Fluent reading is important to comprehension. Students beyond the primary grades who are not fluent readers face problems in dealing with classroom reading demands as material becomes more difficult and assignments become longer and require more processing.

ENGLISH/ LANGUAGE ARTS

The method of repeated reading has proven successful in helping students develop fluency. With this method, "students practice rereading a familiar text with teacher guidance and feedback . . . until they reach an appropriate level of accuracy and speed" (Worthy and Broaddus, 2001/2002, p. 336). Worthy and Broaddus use reading performances in Readers' Theater to provide purposeful repeated readings for students. Readers' Theater is reading aloud from scripts in a dramatic, expressive manner. This technique is started by model read-alouds performed by the teacher. Students may follow along in the text. Sometimes they may read chorally with the teacher. Guided practice may take the form of reading in groups with teacher feedback. Independent practice should follow before the Readers' Theater is performed for others (Worthy and Broaddus, 2000/2001).

ENGLISH/ LANGUAGE ARTS

Daily self-selected silent reading in comfortable materials is also important in developing fluency. Thematic units (see Chapter 10) often allow some choice of reading materials. They offer opportunities for students to read materials at their own reading levels and still participate actively in a unit of study. Teachers need to be familiar with the wide variety of trade books available to supplement their units of study. Any genre, from picture books to realistic fiction to science fiction to nonfiction, may be of use.

Retention

Secondary school students are expected to retain much of the material from their content area textbooks. Use of study methods to enhance **retention** has already been discussed extensively in this chapter. Teachers can help students apply these techniques and others that will facilitate retention of material. Concentrating on material as it is read is important to retention. Some suggestions that the teacher may offer include these:

1. Always read study material with a purpose. If the teacher does not supply you with a purpose, set a purpose of your own. Having a purpose for reading will help you extract meaning from a passage, and you will retain material that is meaningful to you longer.

2. Try to grasp the author's organization of the material. This will help you to categorize concepts to be learned under main headings, which are easier to retain than small details and which facilitate recall of the related details. To accomplish this task, outline the material.

3. Try to picture the ideas that the author is attempting to describe. Visualization of the information being presented will help you remember it longer.

4. As you read, take notes on important points in the material. Writing information down can help you to fix it in your memory. (See Chapter 7 for note-taking guidelines.)

5. After you have read the material, summarize it in your own words. If you can do this, you will have recalled the main points, and rewording the material will demonstrate your understanding.

6. When you have read the material, discuss the assignment with a classmate or a group of classmates. Talking about the material facilitates remembering it.

7. Apply the concepts that you read about, if possible. Physical or mental interaction with the material will help you retain it.

8. Read assignments critically. If you question the material as you read, you will be more likely to remember it.

9. If you wish to retain the material over a long period of time, use spaced practice (a number of short practice sessions extended over a period of time) rather than massed practice (one long practice session). Massed practice facilitates immediate recall, but for long-term retention, spaced practice produces the best results.

10. Recite the material to yourself or to another student as soon as possible after reading the material. Always check your accuracy and correct any errors immediately, so that you will not retain inaccurate material.

11. Overlearning facilitates long-term retention. To overlearn something, you must continue to practice it for a period of time after you have initially mastered it.

12. Mnemonic devices can help you retain certain types of information. (For example, remember that there is "a rat" in the middle of "separate.")

13. A variety of types of writing can improve retention of content area reading material. Writing answers to study questions can foster recall of isolated bits of information. Essay writing can produce more long-term and reasoned learning of a smaller amount of material. Note taking can cause students to deal with larger chunks of meaning than does answering study questions, but it does not involve reorganization of material, as does essay writing (Langer, 1986).

14. Relate the material you are reading to things you already know. Making such connections can aid in the acquisition of new concepts and in the retention of material read.

15. Monitor your reading to determine if you understand the material. If not, reread it or take other steps to ensure understanding.

16. Avoid studying in a distracting setting.

17. Study more difficult and less interesting material when you are most alert.

18. Anticipate what is coming next as you read a passage, and read to see if your prediction was accurate.

Teachers can also facilitate student retention of material by offering students ample opportunities to review information and to practice skills learned and by offering positive reinforcement for correct responses given during the practice and review periods. Class discussion of material to be learned tends to aid retention. Emphasis on classifying the ideas found in the reading material under appropriate categories can also help.

Test Taking

Secondary school students sometimes fail to do well on tests, not because they do not know the material, but because they have difficulty reading and comprehending the test. Teachers can help students by suggesting ways to read different types of tests effectively.

Essay tests often contain the terms *compare, contrast, diagram, trace the development, describe, discuss,* and others. Teachers can explain how they expect students to answer questions containing each of these terms and any other terms they plan to use. This will help prevent students from losing points on the test because they "described" instead of "contrasted." Teachers can point out that, if students are asked to compare two things or ideas, both similarities and differences should be mentioned. If students are asked to contrast two things or ideas, differences are the important factors. If students are asked to describe something, they are expected to paint a word picture of it. If they are asked to diagram something, an actual drawing is required. Sample answers to a variety of different test questions utilizing the special vocabulary may be useful in helping students understand what the teacher expects. An example follows:

Question: Contrast extemporaneous speeches and prepared speeches.

Answer: Extemporaneous speeches are given with little advance thought. Prepared speeches are usually preceded by much thought and research. Prepared speeches often contain quotations and paraphrases of the thoughts of many other people about the subject. Extemporaneous speeches can contain such material only if the speaker has previously become very well informed in the particular area involved. Assuming that the speaker has little background in the area, an extemporaneous speech would be likely to have less depth than a prepared speech since it would involve only the speaker's immediate impressions. Prepared speeches tend to be better organized than extemporaneous speeches because the speaker has more time to collect thoughts and arrange them in the best possible sequence.

It is important for the students to know exactly what the test will cover and what type of test will be given, for this information will affect the study procedures used. The teacher should provide this information, but the students should ask about it if the teacher is vague about the content or fails to mention the type of test.

Students need to realize the importance of working carefully when they are taking tests and of following directions exactly. They should examine the test before they begin, to determine if they have questions about what they are to do, the point values of the questions, or the manner of responding to the questions. They should answer the ones they know well first and then allocate the remainder of their time to the harder questions (Strichart and Mangrum, 1993). They should be aware of the time available to complete the test and should avoid spending too much time on items they are not likely to be able to answer. Before they turn in their papers, they should always check to make sure that they have not inadvertently left one or more answers blank. In general, it is wise to answer all questions with a best guess, but this suggestion is invalidated if the teacher imposes a penalty for guessing.

The student must read objective tests carefully. Generally, every word in an item must be considered. Teachers should emphasize the importance of considering the effect of words such as *always*, *never*, and *not*, as well as others of this general nature. Students need to understand that all the parts of a true-false question must be true if the answer is to be true. They must also be taught to read all possible responses for a multiple-choice question before choosing an answer.

Teachers can help students improve their performance on most tests by offering the following useful hints:

1. When studying for essay tests:
   a. Remember that your answers should include main ideas accompanied by supporting details.
   b. Expect questions that cover the topics most emphasized in the course, since only a few questions can be asked within the limited time.
   c. Expect questions that are broad in scope.
   d. Read your class notes and rewrite them more concisely.
   e. Consider the important topics covered, and try to guess some of the questions that the teacher may ask. Prepare good answers for these questions, and try to learn them thoroughly. You will probably be able to use the points you rehearse in your answers on the actual test, even if the questions you formulated are not exactly the same as the ones the teacher asks.

2. When studying for objective tests:
   a. Become familiar with important details.
   b. Consider the types of questions that have been asked on previous tests, and study for those types. If dates have been asked for in the past, learn the dates in the current material.
   c. If listing questions are a possibility, especially sequential listings, try preparing mnemonic devices to help you in recalling the lists.

3. Learning important definitions can be helpful for any kind of test and can be useful in answering many essay questions.

4. Apply the suggestions listed in the earlier section, "Retention."

When teachers construct tests, they should take care to avoid making the test harder to read than the original material. Otherwise, students could know the material required but be unable to comprehend the questions because the readability level of the test was so high. Students might then receive low test scores because of the teacher's inappropriate test preparation rather than because of their own lack of knowledge of the concepts involved.

The preceding discussion focuses primarily on how to take teacher-made tests, because they are the most frequently given tests during the year. Less frequently students are faced with taking standardized tests, although many of these tests are high-stakes governmentally mandated tests, increasing their importance to teachers and students. These tests are given under strictly controlled conditions. Because of the desire for objective assessment, they tend to be objective in nature, and the previously given tips for taking objective tests apply. The strict timing on these tests and the very specific directions for marking answer sheets cause many students problems. Practice with similar answer sheets under timed conditions could familiarize students with the procedures and decrease anxiety about taking the tests.

FOCUS ON   *Struggling Readers*

Study Skills and Struggling Readers

Struggling readers are frequently disorganized, a state that is detrimental to their school progress. For example, a struggling reader named Ethan stumbles into the classroom after class has begun. He bumps into a desk and drops all of his books, along with a variety of crumpled papers. When the teacher asks for his homework, he says that he started it, but he thinks it is at home because he didn't remember that it was due.

Study skills instruction can give struggling readers the essential organizational skills that will enable them to learn from text. First, struggling readers need assistance in learning how to attend to teachers and how to sustain their attention. In addition, they need help in understanding the vocabulary in a spoken presentation or written selection, in recognizing important points, in following a sequence of ideas, and in understanding verbal and nonverbal cues. Teachers can help students by modeling good listening practices and providing them with practice in the listening skills necessary to accomplish these learning tasks as a basis for developing study skills.

Struggling readers often need assistance in organizing and completing assignments. Teachers can help struggling readers by giving them all of their assignments in written form, which may include detailed, step-by-step instructions. For example, students need to know exactly what the assignment is, when it is due, and the sequence of steps involved in completing it. Study methods are very helpful to struggling readers as they learn how to learn from textbooks and how to complete assignments. SQ3R is a good beginning study method because it can be applied effectively to expository texts. However, struggling readers need direct instruction in using this study method and they need teacher-directed practice with SQ3R until they can apply it automatically. Ten teacher-directed practices are usually necessary for them to achieve fluent application of this method.

FOCUS ON	*English Language Learners*

Study Skills and ELLs

English language learners will also benefit from learning study skill strategies because they are learning content from textbooks written in their second language. The teaching strategies described in this chapter are useful for ELLs. However, they should be fluent comprehenders of English in order to learn a study method and apply it to their textbooks. They will especially need to learn the common words that occur in test questions and instructions, such as *compare* and *describe*. A beginning point for ELLs is to learn to use SQ3R and then to add additional methods as they are needed.

Summary

Reading–study skills are skills that enhance comprehension and retention of information contained in printed material. They help students manage their reading in content area classes.

Study methods such as SQ3R and ROWAC are applicable to a number of different subject areas, including social studies and science. SQRQCQ is effective for use with statement or word problems in mathematics. Instructional procedures such as the PSRT strategy and some recitation techniques can be used to enhance the development of study skills.

The ability to follow written directions is vitally important to secondary school students. Teachers should plan activities to help students develop this important skill.

Content area textbooks are filled with graphic visual aids such as maps, graphs, tables, diagrams, and pictures. Teachers should give students guidance in interpreting these helpful text features.

Other areas to which teachers should give attention are adjustment of reading rate to fit the purpose for which the reading is being done and the material to be read, developing fluency, retention of material read, and test-taking skills.

Discussion Questions

1. Which of the study methods listed in this chapter is best for use in your content area? Why?
2. What is a useful procedure for teaching students to read directions with understanding?
3. What graphic aids occur most commonly in your content area? What can you do to help students interpret them effectively?
4. What is the best setting in which to offer students instruction concerning flexibility of rate? Why is this so?

5. What are some techniques for helping students increase reading rate with acceptable comprehension?
6. How can you help your students retain as much of the material that they read in their content textbooks as possible?
7. Should you give attention to helping your students develop test-taking skills? Why, or why not?
8. What can you do to help struggling readers develop needed reading-study strategies?
9. What can you do to help English language learners develop needed reading-study strategies?

Enrichment Activities

*1. Teach one of the study methods described in this chapter to a class of secondary school students. Work through it with them step by step.
2. Collect materials that include directions that secondary-level students often need to read. Discuss with your classmates how you could help the students learn to read the materials more effectively.
3. Collect a variety of types of maps. Decide which features of each map will need the most explanation for students.
4. Collect a variety of types of graphs. Make them into a display that could be used in a unit on reading graphs.
5. Develop a procedure to help secondary school students learn to be flexible in their rates of reading. Use materials of widely varying types.
*6. Examine several of your old tests. Decide what reading difficulties they may present for your students. Isolate special words for which meanings may have to be taught.

*These activities are designed for in-service teachers, student teachers, and practicum students.

Resources including the TeachSource Video Cases can be found on the website for this book. Cengage Learning's CourseMate brings course concepts to life with interactive learning, study, and exam preparation tools that support the printed textbook. Go to www.cengage.com/login to register your access code.

Applying Literacy Instruction in the Content Areas

CHAPTER 9
Writing in the Content Areas

CHAPTER 10
Literature-Based and Thematic Approaches to Content Area Teaching

CHAPTER 11
Reading in the Content Areas: I

CHAPTER 12
Reading in the Content Areas: II

CHAPTER 9

Writing in the Content Areas

Overview

In this chapter we consider the relationships among reading, writing, and thinking in content area classes; the process approach to writing instruction; and types of writing-to-learn strategies that content area teachers may employ. The goal is to help content area teachers learn to use writing to advantage in their classes.

The process approach to writing emphasizes prewriting, drafting, revision, editing, and publication procedures. It requires the student to be concerned with the message and the audience from the beginning, whereas a focus on the product often gives inordinate attention to the mechanics of writing without emphasizing the development of the message. Publication procedures include sharing the products in written or oral form with classmates, the larger audience of the community, or perhaps a global audience on the Internet.

Some genres of content area writing can be categorized as writing-to-display-learning and some as writing-to-learn. Examples of writing-to-display-learning genres are essays (including photo essays), book reports, research papers (including multigenre reports), laboratory reports, essay exams, and formal letters. Examples of writing-to-learn genres are journals (content and dialogue), notes taken on assigned readings, language experience approach, pen pals, Internet writing projects and activities, and freewriting.

The process approach to writing is useful with many types of content area writing, especially research reports, as well as creative writing endeavors. It can be implemented on computers, and the Internet offers sites to help students with writing questions.

Purpose-Setting Questions

As you read this chapter, try to answer these questions:

1. What is the relationship between reading and writing activities in content area classes?
2. What are some types of writing that are useful in the content areas?
3. What are the steps in the process approach to writing instruction?
4. What are some ways to evaluate writing?
5. What writing instructional practices work best with struggling readers and writers?
6. What writing instructional practices work best with English language learners?

The Relationships Among Reading, Writing, and Thinking

The Nature of Writing

Each incidence of writing occurs "at a particular moment in the writer's biography, in particular circumstances, and under particular external and internal pressures. In short, the writer is always transacting with a personal, social, and cultural environment" (Rosenblatt, 1989, p. 163). Writers are also transacting with the texts that they are producing, using the reservoirs of past linguistic experiences at their disposal. Freewriting (discussed later in this chapter) is a way of tapping the individual's linguistic reservoir without concern about organization or form of expression.

A writer necessarily reads what he or she has written as it is being produced. When this happens, the writer is checking to see if the writing is projecting a meaning that meets the purpose for the writing. The writer weighs words against an internal standard to see if they are right. The writer also may attempt to read the material as potential audiences will read it to see if the meaning they will construct is congruent with his or her purpose (Rosenblatt, 1989).

Values of Writing in the Content Areas

Study in the content areas is designed to promote the learning of facts, principles, and procedures related to the disciplines involved. Such learning involves both literal and higher-level thinking skills and retention of material studied.

Writing is a tool for thinking, and it helps develop thinking skills. Its "linear and structured form imposes its own sense of order on our attempts to think about relationships. And, as 'frozen speech,' it makes metalinguistic reflection more easily accomplished" (Glatthorn, 1989, p. 284). Jacobs (2008a) urges content area teachers to integrate writing into their classes to help the students see how the context of the writing affects the genres used.

Writing can help readers explore what they know. Through writing, students come to terms with their own thoughts, solve problems, and discover new ideas; in other words, writing helps them clarify their thinking and leads to an ongoing process of self-knowledge (Britton et al., 1975, Elbow, 1978).

Frequent use of writing activities of various types can help students develop fluency, an aspect of writing that can be achieved only with practice. The advantages of writing as a tool for thinking are more available to fluent writers than to those who are not fluent.

SOCIAL
STUDIES

Students in secondary school content area classes might write individually or form teams to write about historical events or characters, to compose comparison and contrast essays, to create mini-research papers, or to do various other creative projects, sharing findings from research with the rest of the class. This provides authentic audiences for the writing (Rekrut, 1997; Sanacore, 1998).

The Relationship Between Reading and Writing in Content Area Classes

Secondary school students need both reading and writing skills for learning. Teachers of content area classes have generally perceived *reading* as a means of learning, but few have viewed *writing* in this way. Consequently, many content area classes exhibit a noticeable lack of writing activities. This situation is unfortunate, since both reading and writing are valuable learning techniques for students in these classes.

What are the links between reading and writing?

Reading and writing are both concerned with communication: readers consider the biases and expertise of the author, and writers consider the natures and backgrounds of their audiences. Both make use of written words that represent thoughts, and oral language vocabulary development is a key ingredient in successful reading and writing activities.

Another link between reading and writing is that the construction of meaning in reading is related to the organization of written material. Raphael and others (1986) have found that teaching students about expository text structure has a positive effect on both report writing and content area reading. (See Chapter 5 for more on teaching expository text structure.) Learning to write using a particular organizational pattern has the potential to help students understand material that others write in that pattern.

Reading and writing are complementary skills. Written material is necessary for reading to take place, but written material is useless until it is read. A focus on one of these skills naturally involves the other. Fisher and Frey (2003) found that the best writing they got from struggling readers and writers occurred after discussions of readings. Connecting reading and writing in meaningful ways was highly beneficial.

We have previously stated that reading is a thinking process. Elaboration on this idea can be found in Chapter 6. This relationship to thinking is another link between reading and writing.

Techniques of Combining Reading and Writing Effectively

ENGLISH/ LANGUAGE ARTS

Despite the connections between reading and writing, use of random writing activities in a content course may not help students in reading. Ferris and Snyder (1986) found that use of a process approach to writing instruction (discussed extensively later in this chapter) increased writing skills, but not reading skills, for students in eleventh-grade English classes. To be mutually beneficial, assignments must focus on the relationships between the two disciplines. For example, after students read a selection from a text, teachers can discuss its organization in relation to the organization of some of the students' own compositions. Teachers may also have students write paraphrases of difficult texts to help them understand these texts better and to make the students more aware of the depth of their understanding.

Konopak and others (1987) did find, however, that a writing treatment resulted in students' production of higher-level ideas gained from their reading and synthesis

What are some ways students can use writing to activate prior knowledge before reading?

of information from various class activities. The writing treatment included making jot lists to activate prior knowledge, brainstorming and classification of ideas, preliminary writing based on the classifications, reading, and further writing.

Writing before starting the reading assignment can help students retrieve background knowledge that they need in order to comprehend ideas in the written material. Activation of such knowledge can be beneficial to reading achievement. Writing responses to prereading questions can be particularly helpful. Writing can be based on organizational devices, such as feature matrixes, webs, outlines, or timelines, that help students understand relationships among various areas of content knowledge. The students and teacher may cooperatively develop a class organizer containing aspects of a topic, or students may develop individual organizers based upon personal knowledge and research. A teacher may introduce the idea of writing with this approach by directing the development of an organizer from a text chapter, and then may lead the group through the writing of a paragraph based on a portion of the organizer (i.e., an item on a feature matrix, a strand of a web, a main division of an outline). Subsequently, the teacher may let individuals or small groups write on other parts of the organizer, supplementing information from the textbook with information gained from reading in other research materials. Eventually students can completely develop their own organizers and write entire compositions from them.

Example 9.1 shows an organizer both in its early stages of development during the prereading period and in completed form. This organizer was developed for

SCIENCE AND HEALTH

| EXAMPLE 9.1 | **Incomplete and Completed Organizer** |

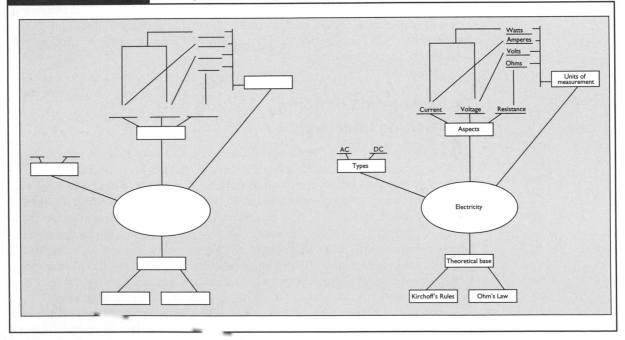

information included in a chapter in a physics text. Notice how the organizer shows the relationships described in the chapter. Types of electricity, aspects of electricity, units of measurement of electricity, and theory related to electricity are all discussed in the chapter. Each of these topics also has subtopics discussed under it. These subtopics are connected by lines in the organizer. Because the subtopics of the major topics, aspects of electricity and units of measurement of electricity, are related, the organizer also shows these subtopics connected with lines; for example, resistance is one aspect of electricity and resistance is measured in ohms.

The Process Approach to Writing in the Content Areas

If teachers are to implement writing across the curriculum, they need to know how to guide students through the writing process, regardless of the type of content. In content classes, writing has often been treated as a two-step process: (1) the writing assignment is given, and (2) the students write a paper and turn it in to the teacher. This is an inadequate and inaccurate picture of what writing in content classes should be. Students are not helped to develop their writing products, but they are graded on their effectiveness, which could have been improved considerably by developmental instruction. Fisher and Frey (2003, p. 404) point out that "often instructional minutes are wasted when students are given independent writing prompts for which they are unprepared."

Research has indicated that a process approach to writing instruction is a good way to support writing development in students (Patthey-Chavez, Matsumura, and Valdes, 2004). When a process approach to writing is used, the development of the written material is guided through various stages, with students receiving feedback from the teacher and from peers at each stage. Students are encouraged to think about their topics, the organization for their writing, and a variety of possible audiences. The papers may be shared with peers, younger students, parents, or the community at large in letters to the editor of the local paper or postings on webpages. Realizing that other people will see their material, students tend to produce papers that are more coherent and have more complete explanations than they do when they assume that the teacher, who knows all about the topic anyway, is the only audience for the paper.

The writing process can be divided into steps in several different ways, but all the systems of division have multiple stages. The system we will discuss divides the process into five basic steps that are *overlapping* and *recursive*: prewriting, writing a draft, revising, editing, and publishing and sharing (Roe and Ross, 2006). Each of these steps is discussed in detail in the following sections.

How can use of mini-lessons in writing enhance teaching in the various content areas?

Literature can be used as a model of quality writing for students. Harvey (2002) points out that using well-crafted nonfiction books and newspaper and magazine articles as models for nonfiction writing results in richer, more compelling nonfiction writing. Possible choices are books by Russell Freedman, Walter Dean Myers, Jim Murphy, Katherine Lasky, Gary Paulsen, or Gary Soto or articles from *National Geographic*. Nonfiction selections serve as models for using headings, boldface and italic print, and captions for photographs and illustrations. Modeling and guided practice with such materials and features are essential to development of skill in writing nonfiction.

ENGLISH/ LANGUAGE ARTS

From these nonfiction models teachers can also point out such techniques as writing beginnings that excite interest, organizing material in logical sequence to aid understanding, and offering concrete details to support main ideas. Broaddus and Ivey (2002) point out the dependence of writers on distinct terms and details. Collecting fascinating information from a variety of sources lends richness to nonfiction writing. Some nonfiction materials have unusual formats, such as letters or diary entries, that can provide opportunities for creative choices in writing. Much nonfiction material today describes practical real-life applications of content concepts through literary devices that involve the same techniques that are used in fiction selections. Other possibilities for lessons on expository writing include choosing topics, techniques for revision, paraphrase writing, feature matrix development, and webbing.

SCIENCE AND HEALTH

SOCIAL STUDIES

Obviously, process writing is easily linked to English classes, but the procedure is equally valuable in other content area classes. Mini-lessons in classes such as science and social studies, for example, would be likely to focus more on choosing and delimiting topics for inquiry, on using a feature matrix for organizing related material, or on webbing ideas than on paraphrase writing or sentence combining. They would emphasize the use of writing to express knowledge, show connections between ideas, and gain new insights into the material through organization of information from multiple sources.

Effective writing lessons include teacher modeling, guided practice, and feedback. High-quality feedback is particularly important (Patthey-Chavez, Matsumura, and Valdes, 2004). Writing and conferences should take place after the mini-lessons. This procedure allows students to apply what they learn from the mini-lessons in authentic writing experiences. Conferences are valuable opportunities for students in any content area to get feedback on the effectiveness and accuracy of their written communication. Encouraging students to attend to the strategic arrangement of words and ideas and to the choice of words that convey unmistakable meaning is an important function for teachers (Romano, 1996).

Teachers should be careful to emphasize the recursive nature of the stages in the writing process. These stages are components among which students move—often in a nonlinear fashion (e.g., returning to prereading activities in the midst of writing a draft)—with different writers approaching the process in different ways.

Prewriting

What activities take place during the prewriting stage?

Prewriting is often neglected in content classes. This stage is used for:

- Selection and delimitation of the topic
- Determination of the audience for the writing
- Decisions about the general approach for the writing
- Activation of the students' prior knowledge of the subject
- Discussion of ideas with classmates
- Organization of ideas

The topic for the writing is sometimes selected by the teacher in a content class, but the other activities can be assumed by the students. In composition classes, and sometimes in other areas, even topic selection is included in the prewriting activities. For example, high school teacher Jessie Singer let her seniors choose something that they were passionate about. They first listed passions, then wrote turning-point essays telling when in their lives their passion was sparked (Singer and Hubbard, 2002/2003). Van Horn (2008) found that having students write about objects of personal significance to them, especially if the objects were produced by them, motivated students to write. Zenkov and Harmon (2009) had a group of culturally, economically, and linguistically diverse students take photographs over an extended period of time in an effort to answer questions about the purposes of school, things that help in school success, and things that obstruct school success. The students met to discuss and write answers to the focus questions that were represented in their pictures. They wrote descriptive paragraphs that were revised during conferences with the researchers. They also titled their photographs. Open-ended questions, discussion, and conferences resulted in engagement.

SOCIAL STUDIES

Secondary students often do not adequately *limit the scope of topics* they choose. Therefore, they face researching an overwhelming amount of material on a broad topic. When they discover the scope of the task ahead of them, their response is often to inquire, "How long does the paper have to be? How many sources do we need to consult?" when they should ask themselves, "What is needed to cover this topic adequately?" A social studies student may decide to write about a topic as broad as "The Civil War" when he or she should be considering something much more specific, such as a single battle or a single theme related to the war. The teacher's modeling of topic delimitation can help students to perform this task effectively.

TeachSource Video Case
Developing Student Self-Esteem: Peer Editing Process

Students need to *practice writing for audiences other than the teacher*. The audience can be their classmates, with peers listening to and/or reading each other's drafts during the development of the drafts. Students also often have access to each other's revised writings in the form of classroom "books" composed of the collected writings of several students or of a single student, bulletin board displays, or oral sharing sessions. During peer conferences, students can learn to ask each other questions that request clarification or expansion of the information given. The peers, therefore, let each other know when the needs of the audience are not being taken into consideration. Students may find it helpful to have an audience response form to guide them in giving feedback to their classmates about the effectiveness of a piece of writing.

Teachers get a limited picture of the capabilities of a student if they are always asked to write for the same audience. Having students write the same information for different audiences provides a broader perspective (Martínez, Orellana, Pacheco, and Carbone, 2008).

Teachers may want to plan lessons that focus on other audiences or *take other approaches*. Letters to the editor of the local newspaper on timely subjects such as water pollution, unfairness of restrictions on youth gatherings, or the drug problem in the schools give students the larger community as an audience. Students may also be asked to write simplified explanations of concepts they are studying for students in lower grades who need the information to enrich their study units, or

SCIENCE AND HEALTH   **SOCIAL STUDIES**

**ENGLISH/
LANGUAGE
ARTS**

composition students may write books or short stories designed for younger read-ers and share them with classroom teachers of lower grades. Students may write directions for carrying out procedures for their classmates to follow in class or explanations of steps in scientific experiments that other students may be curious about or want to duplicate.

To prepare students for writing position papers on topics of high interest, Mayer (2007) has the students participate in a student-run symposium on the topics before they write. The research necessary for the three-minute presentations, the actual presentations, and the contributions from classmates provide prewriting preparation for their written position papers.

Deciding on an approach to the writing may include choosing a format, such as a letter, a short story, a poem, a memorandum, or an essay. It also can include choosing the manner of presenting expository information, such as comparison/contrast, chronological order, problem/solution, cause-and-effect, or some other organiza-tional pattern.

Writing in Different Genres

Students need to explore a variety of forms of discourse in order to discover their strengths and interests. To come up with other ideas for assignments for journals or other forms of writing, teachers may wish to consider some of the discourse forms for content writing presented in Example 9.2.

The student's *prior knowledge about the topic can be activated* through activities such as class discussion, brainstorming, webbing, freewriting, and making compar-ison charts or feature matrixes. Students *listen to the contributions of others* in class activities and remember related items to contribute. Interaction among students at this stage is extremely desirable.

Ideas may be organized through a web or map, a feature matrix, a timeline, or an outline. Students should be taught all of these techniques and be allowed to choose the one that appears to fit the task best for each assignment.

Writing a Draft

What takes place during the stage of writing a draft?

The stage of **writing a draft** is designed to allow the writer to put his or her ideas on paper without worrying about mechanics or neatness. Ideally, the writing time should be in an uninterrupted block so that intervening activities do not break the student's train of thought. Noskin (2000) points out that writing a draft is not continuous writing, but is writing interrupted with pauses to rethink their purposes or audiences, do more brainstorming, or discuss problems with the writing. This illustrates the recursive nature of the writing process.

Some sharing of ideas with classmates may take place during this period in the form of spontaneous conversation among students seated close together. This should be allowed if it is not disruptive to the other students. This conversation is essentially a continued rehearsal of students' writing ideas and, as such, represents a return to the prewriting stage—more evidence of the recursive nature of the writing process. Peer responses may help to shape the writing in some cases, and the interaction may

EXAMPLE 9.2	A Sample of Discourse Forms for Content Writing

- Multigenre reports on readings, areas of research, historical figures, etc.
- Blogs, wikis, or webpages on class assignments
- E-mail messages
- Journals/diaries/logs for real or fictional characters
- Biographical sketches of historical characters or living people
- Descriptions of real people, places, or events or fictional characters, places and events
- Letters to newspapers, government officials, resource people, school personnel, and other actual people to state an opinion or request information about a topic of study
- Letters to historical or fictional characters or letters that historical or fictional characters might have written
- Job applications for jobs related to the content area or topic of study
- Summaries of assigned readings
- Advertisements for books, events, or products
- Poems related to the topic of study or created for an English assignment
- Plays that make a point about a topic of study or are created for an English assignment
- Creative writing in a variety of genres
- Children's books that present information on a topic of study or fit a particular genre under study
- Newspaper articles, editorials, features, or fillers
- Songs related to a content area or topic
- Reviews of books, articles, videos, television programs, music, or art
- Science observations or lab reports
- Math word problems and solutions
- Predictions about or responses to literature
- Real or imaginary interviews
- Directions to a location or to tell how to do something
- Dictionaries of content area terms
- Written arguments for or against a position
- Radio or television scripts
- Cartoons and comic strips
- Graphic novels
- Electronic presentations (*PowerPoint*, etc.)
- Puzzles or games
- Captions for photos

make a sense of audience easier to attain. Certainly if the paper is to be a collaborative effort, the collaborators need to converse as the draft progresses.

Although the production stage may primarily be an individual effort, there is value in students' discussion of their projects with each other. The relationship of talking to writing is a central one; good talk encourages good writing; and talk encourages writers to express tentative conclusions and opinions.

Teachers may need to help students overcome their reluctance to take risks related to spelling and punctuation and their reluctance to produce messy first drafts by bringing in examples of their own first drafts, which are double-spaced to allow for changes, with words, phrases, and sentences struck out and others inserted between lines or in margins and with some incorrectly spelled words circled to be looked up later. Students often have the impression that the draft has to be perfect from the beginning. Thus, to avoid imperfection, they substitute less exact words for ones they cannot spell without using the dictionary and substitute shorter, less complex sentences for ones they cannot punctuate without additional thought and time.

In the midst of drafting a paper, peer and teacher conferences about the writing may take place. Quick, informal teacher conferences may occur as the teacher circulates among the students to see how work is progressing. The teacher may ask students how their writing is going and, when problems are revealed, ask pertinent questions to help the writers think through the problem areas effectively. For example, if a student says, "I'm not sure what order to use to tell about these events," the teacher might say, "What order did the author of your history book use to tell about the events that came just before those events?" The student may answer, "Time order," and the teacher may ask, "Is that an appropriate order for you to use here, or do you have a reason to want to use another order? What would be the value of chronological order or some other order to your presentation?" These conferences are brief but help productive writing to continue. The teacher does not tell the student what to do with the writing but leads him or her to think in channels appropriate for the task.

In some areas, conferences between secondary student writers and university methods students are taking place online. Prospective teachers learn about the characteristics of the students that they will be teaching as they help them craft their writing through e-mail conversations (Robbins and Fischer, 1996). More about such e-mail partnerships, including writing and other aspects, is found in Chapter 2 of this book.

Students may request peer conferences for the purpose of asking for help with some part of the writing that is giving them trouble. They may read their writing to one or more peers and say something to this effect: "I'm having trouble with this ending. What can I do to improve it?"

The peers should first respond to the piece by indicating their understanding of what it says; then they should offer positive comments on good points. Finally, they should give suggestions that they may have for improvement or ask questions such as, "Would it help if you left out the last paragraph? How would it sound if you referred to the beginning statement here?" When a student has an entire first draft finished, he or she may wish to read it to a peer or several peers for further response. At this point in development, the student should read the work to his or her peers rather than having them read it. This procedure keeps the mechanical problems of the draft from interfering with a content analysis by the other students. Peers need to offer specific revision suggestions, or their comments will not be as helpful as they should be. They should tell the writer what they believe is good about the piece and why they think so, what parts need clarification, and what specific ways they believe the piece can be improved. Teachers may need to give some instruction in generating more specific, helpful comments, perhaps by telling the students why certain responses to a piece would or would not be effective.

Revising

Why is revision unnecessary for some types of student writing?

For pieces that others will read, **revision** is a necessary step, although it is not necessary for everything students write. Revision should not be expected, for example, in journals or class notes unless the student does it spontaneously.

The first step in the revision process is for the student to read his or her own piece carefully, considering the criteria for writing that have been established in the class. Students should realize that revision is not just **editing** for spelling, grammar, and punctuation. It involves reorganizing the material, clarifying ideas, and adding and deleting information as needed. Although revision is listed here as the third step in the writing process, it is important to realize that revision is recursive and can occur at any point in the writing process. For example, revision may happen during planning, as ideas are clarified in the writer's mind, or while writers review material that they have written.

How do revision and editing differ?

A list of criteria to use in judging students' written work may be cooperatively developed by the teacher and students, or the teacher may provide it. A set of criteria that a group might develop is as follows:

1. *Beginning.* Does it arouse the reader's interest from the start? It should get the reader "hooked" right away.

2. *Middle.* Is the information or action presented in a logical order? Is the organizational pattern evident to the reader? The organizational pattern should fit your information.

3. *Ending.* Does the ending tie up the piece satisfactorily? It should not leave the reader "hanging."

4. *Sentence structure.* Have you used complete sentences? Do your sentences make sense? Sentence fragments should be avoided, except in special cases, such as dialogue.

5. *Vocabulary.* Have you used words that say exactly what you want to say? Consider the precise meanings of the words that you used, and make sure they fit the context.

6. *Point of view.* Did you maintain a single point of view in the story? Make sure that you have not shifted from third person to second person or first person, for example.

7. *Focus.* Does your piece stay on the main topic? Delete portions that stray from the main point.

8. *Audience.* Is your story appropriate for the intended audience? Read the piece with your audience in mind, and make sure that you have taken their backgrounds into consideration.

EXAMPLE 9.3	Revision Guide

1. As you listen to your classmate read the material, write notes about positive points, such as precise and vivid word usage, good ideas, coherent organization, good transitions, attention-getting beginnings, and satisfying endings.
2. Write down any questions you have when the writer has finished.
3. Identify for the writer any section that was confusing, and suggest what would make it clearer. You may suggest that the writer add more information in specific places or clarify parts, start the piece with an attention-getting statement, change the order of the ideas presented, add signal words or transitions, or add personal reflections on the material or conclusions the writer has drawn based on the information collected. Be sure to point out factual errors or explanations that are incomplete.

A revision guide, such as the one in Example 9.3, could be used by a peer who is participating in a peer conference activity with the writer. It can prompt the peer to provide specific suggestions for revision.

Students can make their paper and pencil revisions by using carets and writing additional material between lines, marking out or erasing unwanted material, using circles and arrows to move material around, or even cutting and pasting. Their markings need to be clear, but the paper does not necessarily need to look neat. If the piece has been written electronically, the revision activity is much easier, and the final copy will be cleaner. A few clicks of the mouse can delete, insert, and move material around. Papers revised in this manner never need to look messy.

Editing

Editing involves polishing the writing for consumption by others. It includes checking for grammar, punctuation, and spelling. A computer's spell checker can highlight suspicious words for the student to check, and grammar checkers are available to check for incomplete sentences, incorrect punctuation, redundancies, wordiness, and other problems. These tools just alert students to potential problems and force them to look closely at their writing; they do not make changes for the students. The students must take responsibility for making judgments about the flagged material. Many flagged parts may be perfectly acceptable, whereas some errors will not be flagged. Computers cannot consider meaning in their analyses, and therefore they are inaccurate at times when a human editor would understand the situation. If students write their pieces on the computer, they should run the grammar and spell check programs to help them detect errors, but this should be in addition to proofreading in the usual manner.

Students can be taught strategies to help them use spell checkers more effectively. They can alter words that are identified as misspelled, but for which alternative spellings are not suggested, until the checker is able to offer alternatives. Different spellings for sounds must be tried in order to accomplish this. Students can also check dictionary definitions of alternatives that are offered to be sure which one fits their context. Teachers should point out that some words, especially technical terms, may not be in the spell checker's dictionary.

After students have read and revised their papers to the best of their abilities, they may submit their work for peer editing. They may have regular partners for peer editing or they may choose different peer editors at different times. Peer editors read and mark their classmates' papers with the class writing criteria in mind, write positive comments about the material, and make suggestions for changes or ask for clarification about parts of the writing. This process should be modeled by the teacher before the students are expected to use it. Teacher analysis and feedback on the finished product will enhance the learning.

Internet Assistance in Revision and Editing

**ENGLISH/
LANGUAGE
ARTS**

Help with revision and editing can also be found on the Internet. Online writing labs (OWLs) offer such services as writing aids, online tutoring, grammar and style guides, reference works, and links to writing and research aids. OWLs may offer interaction with other writers and critiques of writing samples as well. Additionally, students may find the Good Grammar, Good Style™ pages (http://www.protrainco.com/grammar.htm) and The Index to the Guide to Grammar and Writing (http://grammar.ccc.commnet.edu/grammar/index2.htm) useful.

Publishing

In what ways may student writing be "published"?

**HES/HUMAN
ECOLOGY**   **ENGLISH/
LANGUAGE
ARTS**

**TECHNICAL
EDUCATION**   **SCIENCE AND
HEALTH**

The pieces that students carefully revise for sharing with others, as just described, are "**published**" in one of a number of ways. They may simply be shared orally by the student author, or they may be posted on bulletin boards, bound into a book to be placed in the classroom library or school library, or published in a school magazine or newspaper. Many types of writings may be "published" in various classes. Members of a shop class could develop directions for assembly of various items. Students in a health or human environmental science class could produce meal plans for family members with special dietary needs, such as low-cholesterol diets or low-calorie diets. Literature students could turn a short story into a play for presentation in class or to a wider audience, and science students could write descriptions of science fair exhibits or class experiments.

Although the books students write may be bound simply with staples, brads, or spiral bindings at the school, there are ways to have students produce more professional-looking materials. In the "Meeting the Challenge" on page 278, Barbara Bridges tells how she allowed her students to produce impressive books.

Adolescent writers are particularly attracted to zines as publications. According to Jacobi (2007, p. 44), "Zines are typically single-authored, handmade, do-it-yourself, creative publications centered on themes and issues that explore the personal and the political, the extraordinary and the mundane."

Bott (2002) and several other teachers in her school have their students develop zines to publish personal writing for English classes. The teachers developed their own personal zines first to familiarize themselves with the process. Then they decided on guidelines for the zines that their students would develop. The idea was

MEETING THE CHALLENGE

ENGLISH/ LANGUAGE ARTS

Barbara Bridges, a teacher in Cumberland County, Tennessee, tells about her experience in publishing student writing in professionally bound books, as follows:

Last year was my first year to teach sixth-grade writing. A colleague of mine introduced me to Student Treasures, Inc., a company that offers a school-wide program for publishing student writing in professionally bound books. I found two example books written by student teachers while in college methods courses. I read these books to my students and polled whether they wanted to commit to this project. Their answer was unanimous: "Yes!"

Four classrooms participated. For our classroom books two classes chose to write poetry and two classes chose to write stories. Classes chose illustrators for the book covers from interested students by drawing names. Each student contributed one piece of writing and one illustration. We discussed possible topics, and I let them pick their own topics.

The students began the writing process by writing rough drafts of their work. After revision and editing for mechanics, we progressed to the computer lab where students worked with choosing fonts, sizes, and spacing for their papers. The final step was running the papers through spell check. With finished papers in hand, the students then considered illustrations to correspond with their poems or stories. The students could draw their own pictures, have other students help them (giving those students credit under their pictures), bring pictures from home, or work in the computer lab using clip art. Students, parents, other teachers, our computer assistant and technician, and I compiled the books. Then the books were sent to the publisher to be bound. After about two weeks, we received the bound books.

The students showed their books to everyone. A coach mentioned in a story was truly honored with the mention of his name. I shared the excitement of the finished project with the colleague who introduced me to this project and worked hand in hand with me during computer time and compiling of the books. The sparkle in the students' eyes was truly worth all the work. This is one of the best projects in my fifteen years of teaching. The books will be treasured for years to come. I had nothing but positive reviews from the parents.

to have students produce poems, stories, memoirs, lists, puzzles, reviews, graphics, drawings, cartoons, word plays, advice columns, or collections of writings on themes. They all had to have a cover with an appropriate title, an introduction to the zine, a table of contents, and at least nine personally created pages of the student's writing. Students were allowed to use pseudonyms if they wanted to protect their identities, since the zines would be "published" at the school and copies would be placed in the library. One day a week, for seven weeks, the students worked on their zines at their computers. Some zines were autobiographical; and some were about students' interest areas, such as music. The zines were graded on mechanics, originality, creativity, and completeness of thought and execution. Some students participated in public readings of their work, and the students read one another's zines.

Publishing on school, class, or personal webpages has also become common. This type of publishing can give students a worldwide audience. As a way to display understanding of a character, Comer (2009) suggests letting students design a webpage for a character from literature as if the character had designed the page. Example 9.4 shows a sample webpage that she developed for Bella, a character in

ENGLISH/ LANGUAGE ARTS

EXAMPLE 9.4 | **Sample Character Home Page**

Dr. Melissa Comer | **TTU**

www.BellaLovesEdward.com

Plowing through life as a vampire. . . one century at a time.

HOME | CONFESSIONS | LOVE | VAMPIRISM | LIFE

EDWARD

ISABELLA

My name is Isabella, Bella to most, Bells to my dad Charlie. I'm a recent newborn; life, at the least the life I knew, has ceased. I'm now a Cullen, a vampire, an un-dead. Click here for the whole story. . .

MY LIFE AS A VAMPIRE. . . THE BEGINNING

EDWARD, MY LOVE

Source: Dr. Melissa Comer, Tennessee Technological University–Cookeville, 2009.

EXAMPLE 9.5	Sample Twitter Sequence

1. Meeting Romeo last night was amazing!!! 3 days ago from web
2. Romeo, Romeo wherefore art thou Romeo? 3 days ago from web
3. My parents won't like me seeing Romeo because he's a Montague. 2.5 days ago from web
4. Romeo is my love, my life. Not sure what to do . . . 44 hours ago from web
5. Making plans to run away with Romeo. I know I'm only 13 but still . . . 42 hours ago from web
6. Thanks to Friar Laurence! He wed Romeo and me and even thinks that our union will help heal the rift between our families. 40 hours ago from web
7. Oh no, Romeo is banished by the Prince of Verona for killing Tybalt. 38 hours ago from web
8. Romeo and I spent our first night together. 30 hours ago from web
9. Friar Laurence helps me out with a drink that will make me seem dead for "2 and 40 hours" 29 hours ago from web
10. This can't be! Romeo believed me to be dead and drank poison. 15 minutes ago from web
11. I cannot live without him. Where's the dagger? 10 minutes ago from web
12. My Romeo! I'll be with you in death. 5 seconds ago from web.

Source: © Melissa Comer. Reproduced by permission.

Twilight and other books in that series. Comer also suggests having each student choose a character from a book under study and develop a series of tweets (Twitter posts) that this character might have written in this day and time. A sample series of tweets that she developed is shown in Example 9.5.

Students see the reason for careful crafting of their writing when others are going to read it for information or entertainment. They get much satisfaction from seeing others reading their work, and they appreciate the opportunities to read the work of their peers. An avenue of writing for an audience that has gained popularity with adolescents is blogging (Littrell, 2005). If blogs are to be used to help students become better writers and thinkers, teachers need to be involved with the students by talking about what is posted to their blogs ("Best of the Blogs," 2005). Chapter 2 has a detailed discussion of blogging.

Types of Writing-to-Learn Activities in the Content Areas

Many types of writing are used in content area classes to enhance learning. The types discussed here are some of the more common ones with which teachers have reported positive results. Knowledge of the steps in the process approach to writing can help teachers to implement some of these writing-to-learn strategies more effectively.

Writing-to-learn activities cause students to be more active learners as they express their understanding of the content materials. They also require a response from every student (Knipper and Duggan, 2006).

Language Experience Writings

How can language experience materials be used in a content area classroom?

Language experience writings are materials written in the students' own words. In the secondary school, **language experience materials** may be written by a group of students who have read about a common topic and wish to summarize their findings. The teacher can record all significant contributions on the board as they are offered. At the conclusion of the discussion, the teacher and students together can organize the contributions in a logical order (e.g., chronological or cause-and-effect). The teacher can then duplicate the group-composed material and distribute it to the class members. This approach works well with struggling readers and writers and English language learners (Fisher and Frey, 2003; Furr, 2003).

Students who can handle the textbook with ease may file the experience material to use for review for tests. A group that is unable to handle the textbook presentation may use the material more extensively. For example, the teacher may meet with this group and guide the members through the reading of the material by using purpose questions. The students are likely to succeed in reading this material because they have seen the content written on the board and because it is in the words of fellow students. Having heard a discussion of the content, the students will find it easier to apply context clues as they read. Any technical vocabulary or multiple-meaning words can be located and discussed thoroughly. These words may be written in a special notebook with accompanying pronunciations and definitions and a reference to the experience material in which they occurred. A booklet made up of experience material can serve as a reference source for these words when they are encountered again and can be used in studying for tests. English language learners and other at-risk students may especially benefit from such notebooks.

SCIENCE AND HEALTH

Experience materials may also be developed by individuals and groups who wish to record the results of scientific experiments or the periodic observation of some natural phenomena. These materials may be shared with the rest of the class in oral or written form. Such activities are extremely valuable for students who are not able to gain much information from a textbook that is too difficult for them. McMillan and Wilhelm (2007) had seventh-grade students observe the moon at a self-chosen time every day over a five-week period, sketch the sky, and write at least a two-sentence observation. Readings and other moon-related activities, such as study of moon craters and causes of the Earth's seasons, also took place in classes during this time period. The final project was production of five poems and a piece modeled on the legends of natural phenomena that they had read. They found "that the practice of experiential learning had a hand in students' identity and literacy development" (p. 375).

MATHEMATICS

Wood (1992) found the language experience approach to be effective for use with content instruction in math classes. Wood suggested having mathematics problems assigned to small groups of students, with each student solving the problems and writing the processes involved in the solutions. Then the students would share their solutions with the rest of the group. This type of language experience

SOCIAL STUDIES

SCIENCE AND HEALTH

activity could be extended by having the group as a whole revise a written solution to make it clearer, more accurate, or less wordy, if necessary.

Many others have found the language experience approach to work well in social studies and science classes. This approach motivates struggling readers and English language learners, builds their self-esteem, provides them with concepts that allow participation in content classes, builds reading vocabulary (including technical vocabulary), and activates and organizes the students' prior knowledge in the content areas.

Poetry

Students in English classes often need direction in writing poetry. Certainly writing of poetry of different types should be modeled by the teacher before the students are asked to write their own. Each poetry type should be introduced separately. It may help to have the students write group poems before writing individual ones (Roe and Ross, 2006). Young (2007) suggests generative writing groups, that involve a group of four students working together to generate poetry by having each student perform a specific role. Students need to know the poetry-related vocabulary (e.g., *metaphor, simile, alliteration,* etc.) and agree upon a genre of poetry to pursue. The teacher provides many examples of the genres. Then each group chooses a topic; and in each group, one student provides two or more concrete images for the poem, one provides five intriguing words for it, one supplies two metaphors or similes that correlate with the images, and one supplies five words that go with the other chosen words to provide pleasing sounds through alliteration, assonance, rhyme, etc. The group takes all of these elements and puts them together into a poem. Shanklin (2009) suggests pretesting students to find out which ones already understand figurative language (and its labels) and teaching needed concepts to small groups who need them, avoiding repetition of the same material every year.

Because students often have negative feelings toward poetry, it is extremely important to include a prewriting phase to poetry instruction in which the students hear many high-quality poems read well. Most poetry, except for concrete poetry, is written for the ear, not the eye (Roe and Ross, 2006). If the teacher cannot read poetry well, recordings of poems being read by someone who understands and loves them may be used. After extensive exposure to oral poetry, students should be asked to read accessible poetry for themselves. Use of figurative language is common in poetry writing, and in English classes students may be led to use metaphors, similes, personification, and other figures of speech discussed in Chapter 4 as they begin to write poems of various types.

Tarasiuk (2009) had students read poems and then listen "to the same poems as podcasts on the Internet" (p. 50). That allowed the students to discuss the difference in the two experiences with the poems. Tarasiuk then created a model podcast of a poem, with words, images, and music included to form what she referred to as "Extreme Poetry." Then the students worked in centers to prepare images and choose music to go with their interpretations of the poems that had been read in class. Finally they produced podcasts of their original poetry with words, images, and music, using Apple GarageBand software. The teacher converted these podcasts to Apple QuickTime files, published them on her class website and burned them onto CDs for the students. After students chose and observed a particular tree in a study of environmental changes, one teacher had students use Microsoft Photo Story or Microsoft Movie Maker software to combine text, sound, and images to provide digital poetry (Hughes and John, 2009).

SOCIAL STUDIES

Writing poetry is a natural part of an English class, but there are many ways to use poetry in the content areas. As Heard (2009) points out, poems can be about anything of concern, including war, gangs, and extreme weather. Friese and Nixon (2009) combined poetry and social studies in one unit. The students were led to write *list poems* and *two-voice poems* about the historical content that was being studied. They made use of photographs and objects or artifacts to inform and motivate the students to write their poems. Writing two-voice poems was done to help students synthesize their understanding of conflicting points of view of the people involved in the time period. Much interactive modeling was done to help the students understand how to produce two-voice poems. Paul Fleischman's *Joyful Noise* and *I Am Phoenix* both are books of poems for two voices.

Biopoems can help students more deeply understand a historical figure or person currently in the news. Prompts for each line of the poem are given to the students, and they research the person to complete the poem. Knipper and Duggan (2006) suggest an eleven-line poem with prompts for the various lines. Example 9.6 on page 284 shows a modified version of a biopoem.

Content Journals

What are some of the benefits of using content journals?

Content journals, or learning logs, allow students to keep a written record of content area learning activities that is personal and informal. They help students to clarify their thoughts and feelings about topics under study. Students usually choose what to write in these journals, although teachers may suggest general areas of consideration and types of things they may wish to record, if appropriate. For example, the teacher may ask that the students record any questions that occur to them as they read a content chapter or listen to a class lecture and discussion, new ideas that they have gained, confusion about a topic or procedure, feelings about the subject area, predictions about the assigned reading, explanations of a recently taught concept, or some other general category—such as the answers to some broad content-related questions—at specific times. For example, Bachman-Williams (2001) uses daily journal writing in her science classes. She provides some prompts that are specific content questions, but other prompts ask for personal knowledge, reflection, or pattern poetry related to the class. When the teacher makes a request or notes a specific thing to be recorded, journal entries may be shared by volunteers. The teacher should give prior warning that sharing will be encouraged. At other times the students may choose among the many possibilities that arise in the classroom for their daily entries.

Commander and Smith (1996) have used learning logs to promote students' metacognitive awareness. They asked questions about students' learning behaviors to which the students responded in log entries, helping them achieve insight about their learning and begin to assume responsibility for it.

EXAMPLE 9.6   **Biopoem**

George
Patriotic, brave, dignified, commanding
Husband of Martha Custis
Lover of his country
Who felt passionate about—
Independence from Great Britain
Strong defense for the country
A unified nation
Who wanted—
To maintain a good reputation
To maintain discipline
To be needed by his country
Who feared—
Not being equal to service as commander in chief
Failure as a leader
Mutiny in the troops over inadequate provisions
Who gave—
His service as commander without salary
Advice to his grandchildren and nephews
His slaves their freedom after his death
Who wanted to see—
America as an independent nation
A strong well-provisioned army
Slavery abolished through legislation
Resident of Mount Vernon
Washington

The student who is doing the writing is the primary audience for the content journal, although the teacher may periodically collect the journals and read them. However, content journals are not graded in the ordinary sense; spelling and grammatical errors are not marked, for example.

When teachers take up journals, they may occasionally make encouraging comments to students in response to their entries. These comments should focus on the message that the student was trying to convey and ignore problems with punctuation, spelling, and grammar. This frees students from the fear of writing something that is not mechanically perfect and results in more comprehensive, creative, and revealing journal entries.

Teacher comments should always be written in correctly spelled and punctuated standard English, which will serve as a model to the student for future writing. If a word has been repeatedly misspelled by the student, the teacher may write a comment in the journal that uses the word spelled correctly, without referring to spelling. The example can be more potent than the admonition would have been.

Teachers usually designate times in class for students to write in their journals. At the beginning of a class, students may write summaries of what they learned on the previous day, or at the end of class they may write summaries of what they learned that day. They may write predictions about the lesson that they are about to begin, list everything that they think they already know about the topic, or do both. They may explain how they will apply the day's lesson in everyday life. They may record the progress of a laboratory experiment or observational study.

SCIENCE AND HEALTH

ART   **SCIENCE AND HEALTH**

Franks (2001) collaborated with an art teacher and a science teacher to bring writing across the curriculum to her classroom. She had students make daily weather observations, focusing first on cloud types. As part of the observation, the students were asked to sketch the cloud formations. Then they responded daily to one of five writing prompts concerning their observations, questions that came to mind, reflections about personal memories, associations of things observed with other things or with moods, or forecasting. Before sketching the cloud types, very few of the students recalled how to draw and describe them in writing on a quiz. After they sketched and wrote about the types, 90 percent did well on the quiz.

Some teachers set aside the same time period each day for journal writing, and students are asked to write for the entire five or ten minutes about the class or observations related to the class. Andrasick (1990) recommends at least ten minutes. Teachers can use the journals to discover gaps in understanding and any confusion that the students have about the topics.

MATHEMATICS

Gordon and MacInnis (1993) provided prompts to guide students' journal writing about decimals but allowed the students to write open-ended entries about any mathematics topic that concerned them. The prompts were much like essay questions (e.g., asking how decimals are similar to and different from fractions), but the open-ended responses were simply a type of freewriting. Gordon and MacInnis made these journals into dialogue journals (discussed later in this chapter) as well, responding to all of the entries by the following week. They used information discovered from the journal entries to provide more individualized instruction (Gordon and MacInnis, 1993, p. 42). The journals also encouraged students to reflect upon their mathematical understandings.

Freewriting

What is freewriting, and what purposes does it serve?

ENGLISH/ LANGUAGE ARTS

Some teachers have students use content journals for true **freewriting**—that is, writing that has no teacher restrictions on content. Students simply write in a sustained manner for a specified period of time without stopping to correct mistakes or ponder the content. In content classes, the teacher often specifies that the journal entries focus on a specific topic, even though the writing will not be graded. This writing may be in response to something that they have read. Freewriting is good for encouraging interpretation and evaluation of the material read. It may result in the discovery of alternative interpretations of the text as students strive to continue to write without pauses for correction or reflection (Andrasick, 1990). Language teachers may obtain more direct benefit from true freewriting than other content teachers do because part of their curriculum centers on self-expression. Elbow (1978, p. 67) believes, "If you are really interested in good quality writing, then you must make it your immediate goal that people write copiously, not well. Only when people begin to use writing on other occasions than when it is required—only when they have written for diverse purposes over a period of years—will they eventually come to produce good writing." Writing consistently in journals on a daily basis is valuable to the development of ease in writing.

Reading Response Journals

What types of entries are included in reading response journals?

ENGLISH/ LANGUAGE ARTS

Reading response journals are a type of learning log for literature classes. With these journals, typically the students read or listen to a chapter of a book and then write about it for about five minutes immediately afterward. They comment about the characters, setting, plot, author's writing style and devices, and their personal reactions. The teacher writes while the students are writing and shares his or her entries frequently as a model for the students. Students also may volunteer to share their material. The sharing can be followed by discussion. The teacher can read the journals and comment on entries, clarifying points of confusion for the students and giving positive reinforcement to those who show that they have gained insight into the story.

Kletzien and Hushion (1992) used graphic thinking symbols, such as an arrow to indicate a prediction or a scale to indicate a judgment or an evaluation, to mark examples of particular response types in the students' journals. Recalling information, giving ideas and examples, indicating causes and effects, indicating similarities and differences, making inferences, making personal identifications, using analogies, using metacognitive strategies, and analyzing authors' techniques were among the types of responses recognized and marked by the teachers. This approach resulted in responses that went beyond summaries, ones that were more varied and thoughtful.

Some teachers use reading response journals more like learning logs and have students write before, during, and after reading. Prereading writing prompts are given to arouse curiosity about the topic, activate prior knowledge and experiences that are related, encourage personal connections with the material, and generate hypotheses about the characters and action. During-reading writing prompts may ask students to react to such features of the text as character and setting, respond personally to events or people, draw conclusions and make further predictions, or adjust previous predictions. Postreading writing prompts may lead students to apply themes to current situations; to consider the contributions of particular literary elements to the effect of the whole piece; to show changes that took place in people, places, and things over the course of the story; or to compare the work to similar works or works by the same author.

Andrasick (1990) discusses a type of journal in which students write quotations, paraphrases, or summaries of the ideas in the book on the left-hand pages of a notebook. The students use the corresponding right-hand pages to respond to the entries on the left-hand side. They may both ask questions and make comments about the material. The important thing is that they reflect on the content. Andrasick says the students are having a dialogue with the author of the text about the material. Example 9.7 shows an excerpt from such a journal (Alfred, 1991).

EXAMPLE 9.7	Student's Journal Entries

Dialogue Journal

Chapter Three

Andrasick, K. D. (1990). *Opening Texts: Using Writing to Teach Literature*. Portsmouth, NH: Heinemann.

What the Text Says	What I Say
p. 40 "... shouldn't be concerned so much with particular data as with student's ability to use data."	I'm not sure if I agree ... The way kids are tested, e.g., ACT, other standardized tests, they must know factual data. If we can change this, then I *might* agree.
p. 40 "Many students deny the value of their experiences with texts, dismissing them prematurely."	This really bothers me. Sure, some teachers listen to students' ideas, but that's it. They say, "That's nice," and then continue with their lecture. How else can kids be expected to react?
p. 41 "When we focus on text content by asking students to respond ... to a series of short answer questions, we deflect attention from larger textual elements and may actually interfere with students' abilities to approach thematic issues."	No way! When I read a novel, for example, I always look for specific elements that may tie into a theme. Answering ... questions [is] a good way to increase knowledge about themes that are prevalent throughout a work.
p. 41 "Learning to discriminate between the solidity of the visible surface structure and the fluctuating, invisible text world the pages potentially contain requires practice" (Andrasick, pp. 40–41).	What a yucky sentence! Engfish! Engfish! Engfish!

Source: Suellen Alfred, "Dialogue Journal," *Tennessee Reading Teacher* 19 (Fall 1991): 14. Reproduced by permission of the author.

Character Journals

In what content areas would character journals be most useful?

ENGLISH/ LANGUAGE ARTS

Character journals are diaries in which students assume the role of one of the main characters in a book. In them, each student makes first-person journal entries for a chosen character on episodes throughout the book. These entries help the students attain insight into the characters and their actions. They can try to convey behavior, feelings, and goals of the characters through their entries. The characters that readers remember best are those that they know the most about. Knowledge of the plot of a story is advanced by knowing what the major character wants most as the story progresses (Roser, Martinez, Fuhrken, and McDonnold, 2007). This journaling process also helps students examine their own beliefs, actions, and values.

Responses to Thought Questions

How can teachers prepare students to answer essay questions?

Thought questions resemble the essay questions that teachers use on tests. Writing responses to essay questions is probably the most traditional writing task that teachers expect of students. Teachers often assign study questions to classes for homework as study aids. Unfortunately, they may not prepare students to respond effectively to such questions, as was pointed out in Chapter 6. If the students do not know the meanings of the terms used in the questions, they will not understand what is being asked of them. Teachers should use the procedures suggested in Chapter 6 for helping students learn to answer essay questions before asking them to respond in their journals. Teachers should define terms (such as *compare*, *contrast*, and *discuss*), model answers that fit questions with each of the important terms, and provide students with practice questions for writing and discussion in class. Since the journal activity is ungraded, this practice in answering such questions is not threatening to the students, and they can be free to experiment with the technique without fear of failure.

One study showed that use of study questions did not increase students' topic knowledge as much as use of written essays or note taking on the topic. The study questions seemed to cause the students to focus on specific ideas chosen by the teacher and, therefore, "may best be used to invoke quick recall of isolated items of information" (Langer, 1986, p. 406). Teachers who use study questions as a part of journal writing should be aware that they may cause the students to focus on details of the content rather than on the overall picture.

Creative Applications

SOCIAL STUDIES

ENGLISH/ LANGUAGE ARTS

BUSINESS EDUCATION

MATHEMATICS

SCIENCE AND HEALTH

TECHNICAL EDUCATION

Some teachers have students use either their journals or other formats for a variety of creative applications of writing in the subject area or across the curriculum. The students may be asked to write stories about a historical period that they are studying in social studies class, making sure that they construct characters, settings, dialogues, and plots that fit the time that has been chosen. They may also write fictional interviews with historical characters or characters from novels, news stories about historical events, letters to historical figures or from one historical figure to another, advertisements that would be appropriate to the time period, picture books for younger students (See the "Meeting the Challenge" on page 289.), and poetry about historical events. In a career education class, students might write résumés, business letters, or technical articles. Teachers should model each type of writing and give examples before asking their students to write in this genre. Ray (2006) gathers examples of the chosen genre; has the students examine and read these examples, making notes about the way they are written; discusses the texts with the students; and has the students write texts of that genre as she writes one.

Students in math classes may write their own statement problems. In a class on electronics, students can write imaginative accounts of things such as what life would be like without electron flow. Students in an industrial technology class can write sets of instructions for performing a specific type of task that classmates will be asked to follow. In science class, students can write observations of weather

MEETING THE CHALLENGE

Dick Heyler, writing teacher in Athens, Pennsylvania, has found a way to get all of his students involved in writing-to-learn across the curriculum. Here is his account of his approach, using the writing of children's books as the focus.

SOCIAL STUDIES

MATHEMATICS

SCIENCE AND HEALTH

ENGLISH/ LANGUAGE ARTS

For the past several years my ninth-grade creative writing students found creative ways to complain about their history, math, and science courses. When they entered ninth grade, the science, math, and history all became more difficult and many of them struggled with it. This elective is open to all students, and I find creativity in ALL of them, including struggling readers.

This year I wanted to help them in their classes, but still have them devise and carry out the writing deemed necessary by the curriculum. This is what I tried:

First, I told them to bring in two concepts from science class, two from history class, and two from math class that they were having a difficult time understanding.

On that first day I read *The Lorax* by Dr. Seuss. The students were familiar with Dr. Seuss, but few had read this book. *The Lorax* is about caring for the environment and would fit in any course about current environmental problems. I then led them into a conversation in which they brought up the theme of environmentalism on their own.

Next, I brought in many children's books from the nearby elementary library. I heard, "Ohhh, I remember that book," and "That is my favorite book ever." We then talked about how the illustrations worked with the story and how the story followed the narrative conventions: plot, setting, character, theme, etc. At this point, they were charged to write their own stories, using for the theme one of the concepts from their content classes they were having difficulty understanding.

Their choices were pretty evenly spread across the three disciplines. Students could work with partners, or they could work alone.

They spent two days researching their concepts; they did this online, in the library, and by asking their content teachers. Then the major work came. They needed a rough draft of the story and rough illustrations. Most partnerships included an artist, but the students were assured that the story was the main focus of the class. Our librarian furnished the class with blank, hard covered books, but we could have made our own out of copier paper.

Students collaborated, wrote, sketched, researched, and asked others for help in defining mathematical and science terms they struggled with for about six days of in-class and out-of-class work. They produced children's books about such concepts as pi, algebra, phases of the moon, the hydrologic cycle, Andrew Jackson, the War of 1812, and, one of my favorites, the declassifying of Pluto from status as a planet.

Once the books were finished, the students clamored to be able to read them to others. Off we went to the elementary school where some students read their work to younger students.

I even "twisted the arms" of some colleagues to give extra credit to those who completed a book in that content area. All colleagues agreed and one even wanted the books sent to his wife's fifth grade classroom.

It was successful on many levels. The students spent time with a troublesome concept from a content area and found it easy to write about. They then explained that concept to another audience. So they read, wrote, researched, organized, spoke, and listened their way through a creative writing project that began with student grumbling, and ended in their applying literacy skills both in the writing class and in the content class.

ENGLISH/
LANGUAGE
ARTS

patterns, types of pollution found in a particular locality, or the effects of certain types of soil on plant growth.

Cruz (2001) uses sent and unsent letters about the things the class is studying. For example, students might write letters to friends explaining the topic under study. Partners in the class may listen to the letters and give feedback about the clarity of the explanations. Then Cruz may have the students write about the topic in a different genre, perhaps an analysis paper or a research report. This process helps them make the transition from informal to formal writing. Sometimes the students may role-play the part of someone else—a homeless person, an underpaid police officer, or a city official—and write a letter on a current area of study from that person's perspective.

Translating Literature into Comic Book Form

ENGLISH/
LANGUAGE
ARTS

One of the more creative approaches to literature response outside of journaling is the creation of a comic book based on the selection. In one middle school class, Costello (2008) observed students in a ninth-grade English class producing a classic comic book based on *Romeo and Juliet*. The class was divided into small groups, each of which worked to illustrate one of the five acts of the play. The teacher assured the students that artistic ability was not necessary for success in this endeavor. The emphasis was on creating a visual representation of the play that conveyed understanding of the action and emotion. In each group the students performed self-selected roles. Some were script or narrative writers, artistic directors, or production managers. Their work followed the reading of the play. They examined comic books to determine how the illustrators depicted characters and their emotions and how dialogue balloons and narrative captions were used with the pictures. Much critical thinking and collaborative discussion was necessary to decide upon the content of each frame of the comic. At the end of the work, all five acts were combined to form a complete classic comic book.

Oral History Project

SCIENCE AND
HEALTH

ENGLISH/
LANGUAGE
ARTS

TECHNICAL
EDUCATION

SOCIAL
STUDIES

In Pennsylvania, teachers participate in an oral history project that incorporates state language arts, science and technology, and social studies standards as students learn a research technique. The students choose a person as a subject for the project. When elderly subjects are chosen, the project often turns into a gripping history lesson, covering political and social movements, historical periods, or a study of careers. Students in some classes may be allowed to choose community members or even classmates. They interview their subjects and research the subjects' history and interests. They generally present their results to others through a "triptych"—a tri-fold presentation board to display the material gleaned from the interview and research (Dickson et al., 2002). For this oral history project, triptychs may include pictures of the people; artifacts important to their stories; news articles about them, real or composed from information in the interview; memoirs written or dictated by the people about their life experiences; and other materials that help convey the people's stories (Dickson et al., 2002). Teachers model each component for the

| EXAMPLE 9.8 | Rubric for Writing Assessment |

Pennsylvania Writing Assessment Domain Scoring Guide

	Focus	Content	Organization	Style	Conventions
	The single controlling point made with an awareness of task (mode) about a specific topic.	*The presence of ideas developed through facts, examples, anecdotes, details, opinions, statistics, reasons, and/or explanations.*	*The order developed and sustained within and across paragraphs using transitional devices including introduction and conclusion.*	*The choice, use and arrangement of words and sentence structures that create tone and voice.*	*The use of grammar, mechanics, spelling, usage and sentence formation.*
4	Sharp, distinct controlling point made about a single topic with evident awareness of task (mode)	Substantial, specific and/or illustrative content demonstrating strong development and sophisticated ideas	Sophisticated arrangement of content with evident and/or subtle transitions	Precise, illustrative use of a variety of words and sentence structures to create consistent writer's voice and tone appropriate to audience	Evident control of grammar, mechanics, spelling, usage and sentence formation
3	Apparent point made about a single topic with sufficient awareness of task (mode)	Sufficiently developed content with adequate elaboration or explanation	Functional arrangement of content that sustains a logical order with some evidence of transitions	Generic use of a variety of words and sentence structures that may or may not create writer's voice and tone appropriate to audience	Sufficient control of grammar, mechanics, spelling, usage and sentence formation
2	No apparent point but evidence of a specific topic	Limited content with inadequate elaboration or explanation	Confused or inconsistent arrangement of content with or without attempts at transition	Limited word choice and control of sentence structures that inhibit voice and tone	Limited control of grammar, mechanics, spelling, usage and sentence formation
1	Minimal evidence of a specific topic	Superficial and/or minimal content	Minimal control of content arrangement	Minimal variety in word choice and minimal control of sentence structures	Minimal control of grammar, mechanics, spelling, usage and sentence formation

Non-scorable			Off-prompt	

0 • Is illegible; i.e., includes so many indecipherable words that no sense can be made of the response
• Is incoherent; i.e., words are legible but syntax is so garbled that response makes no sense
• Is insufficient; i.e., does not include enough to assess domains adequately.
• Is a blank paper

• Is readable but did not respond to prompt

Source: Pennsylvania Department of Education.

students before the students are expected to implement it. Rubrics are used to evaluate each step of the project and the final result. An example of a rubric is shown in Example 9.8.

Multigenre Books

ENGLISH/ LANGUAGE ARTS

Dean and Grierson (2005) have students write multigenre books to look at a topic from different perspectives. The use of multiple genres allows students to produce richer and more insightful texts. Students also learn to use the structures of different genres in their writing. Dean and Grierson have students first study the texts of multigenre books to analyze their structure as a model for their own writing.

SCIENCE AND
HEALTH

SOCIAL
STUDIES

Lessons that involve modeling of the required tasks and guided practice are taught, culminating in the writing of such books by the students. Avi's *Nothing But the Truth* and Michael Ondaatje's *The Collected Works of Billy the Kid* are examples of multigenre writing. Pictures, diagrams, lists, brief reports, memos, diary entries, letters, transcripts, newspaper articles, telegrams, timelines, and poems are some of the possible genres in multigenre books (Dornan, Rosen, and Wilson, 2003). The information presented in this way can make an informational book more interesting and informative to readers.

When students study the use of pictures and varying text patterns and their contributions to the model books, they are encouraged to activate their prior knowledge; skim, scan, and underline as they read; and analyze new vocabulary terms. The students can construct Venn diagrams to show how the same and different ideas are presented in different genres. The actual writing may be done in groups or individually. Students are guided in generating ideas for the writing, researching the topics, writing drafts, revising drafts, and preparing bibliographies.

SOCIAL
STUDIES

Grierson, Anson, and Baird (2002) had sixth-grade students use multigenre writing to explore and honor the past. The students used multigenre writing to create original works based on their own heritages, after researching personal ancestors and developing artifacts to create a paper about their lives. The use of varied genres helped them bring facts to life. Jane Yolen's *The Devil's Arithmetic* was used as a stimulus to write about the past in order for it to be remembered.

Paraphrasing and Summarizing

What are paraphrasing and summarizing?

Paraphrasing and **summarizing** material learned in content area classes and from content area textbooks provide material for content journals. A surprising number of secondary school students do not know how to paraphrase the text material in their content subjects. In fact, when asked to paraphrase, many do not realize that they are simply expected to put the material into their own words. This process can just be rewording, or new forms may be used to represent the meaning of the text. For example, material from expository text may be described in tabular or graphic form. Dictionaries and thesauruses are helpful tools for paraphrasing. Paraphrase writing can result in improved listening, speaking, reading, and writing vocabularies and increased comprehension and recall. Therefore, paraphrase writing in content journals can be a fruitful activity.

To teach paraphrasing, teachers should define the concept, demonstrate it for the students first with short paraphrases, offer the students guided practice in providing short paraphrases, and then provide planned independent practice. Instruction in paraphrases of longer passages can follow.

Practice in paraphrasing can be enjoyable. The teacher can present students with statements such as "A fowl in the palm is of the same value as a pair in the shrub." Students can be asked to paraphrase this sentence to produce a familiar saying. Students are permitted to refer to dictionaries and thesauruses for the activity. Later, the students may be asked to locate familiar expressions, paraphrase them, and present the paraphrases to the class for decoding. Eventually, the students can be asked to locate key sentences in the textbook assignment for the day and write paraphrases in clear language.

MATHEMATICS   SOCIAL
STUDIES

TECHNICAL
EDUCATION

Judging the clarity and accuracy of the paraphrases can be done in small groups, with all group members presenting their own paraphrases and participating in the evaluation of those of other students. Both paraphrasers and evaluators have to examine the text material closely in order to complete this activity. Students in math classes can paraphrase statement problems; those in social studies classes can paraphrase news articles, campaign literature, and advertisements; those in shop class can paraphrase instructions for a project; and so on for any subject area.

A form of summarizing is précis writing. Précis are abstracts of materials that retain the point of view of the original materials. Précis writing has been credited with improving both writing and research skills and with enhancing comprehension and recall of content material (D'Angelo, 1983; Bromley and McKeveny, 1986). The teacher should demonstrate the process to the students, showing them how to analyze the original material, select main ideas for inclusion in the précis, reject nonessential material, and paraphrase the ideas through the use of synonyms and the restructuring of sentences. Taking such a close look at the content makes learning and remembering the material much more likely than if the material were processed less actively. Models of acceptable précis should be provided for students to help them understand the task and to help them evaluate and revise their own products. Students can study their précis to help them review for tests.

Group composition of a précis is a good beginning step. This can be done by having the students dictate as the teacher or one of the students records the précis. This is an application of the language experience technique described earlier in this chapter.

Students definitely need direct instruction in summary writing, which is not offered by many teachers. One technique is to have students write a summary of a long piece in several paragraphs, then reduce that summary to two paragraphs, and then one paragraph (Jones, 2006). More information on summarizing is found in Chapter 7.

Dialogue Journals

What is the distinctive feature of dialogue journals?

Although dialogue journals *could* be content journals, they need not be. The distinctive feature of **dialogue journals** is that they set up a two-way written conversation between the teacher and each student. Their primary purpose is to open lines of communication. Students write about anything they choose, including both in-class and out-of-class experiences and concerns. They may offer their opinions, state grievances, provide information, make predictions, ask questions, answer questions, apologize, make promises, offer thanks, make evaluations, or give directions, among other possibilities. The written statements, questions, or observations are not evaluated by the teachers; the teachers respond to them as personal communications.

Each day, time is made available for the students to write in their journals. The teachers read all the entries and respond to them. The responses may include recognition of what the students are saying, clarification of things about which the students are confused, answers to students' questions, questions for students to answer related to the writing or to some common interest, and sharing of personal thoughts and feelings. Grammatical and spelling errors in journal entries are not marked. The next day the students read the teachers' responses and continue the written dialogue with another entry. If classes are large, the teacher may read only a portion of the journals each day, making sure that all are read within a reasonable time period.

Written Conversations

ENGLISH/
LANGUAGE
ARTS

SOCIAL
STUDIES

Similar to dialogue journals, but involving communication between two students, written conversations have been used by Karen Shelton to integrate reading, writing, and social studies in middle school language arts classes. Her students work in pairs and hold a conversation through writing, much as they do when they pass notes in class. They pass the same booklet or paper back and forth, writing comments and responses each time. She had students hold written conversations about the Japanese internment camps of World War II. Partners wrote notes to one another about their reactions to a book on this topic at several key points in the action.

Students respond positively to this approach when they can choose their own partners. Connecting fun with learning tends to engender active involvement in the lessons. Written conversations were personally meaningful for many students in Shelton's classes. They acknowledged the ideas of their partners and indicated that they gained new perspectives on the material by doing so (Bintz and Shelton, 2004).

ENGLISH/
LANGUAGE
ARTS

Bloem (2004) paired university students with public school students to correspond through dialogue journals. At the beginning of the project, university students read polished stories written by their partners, and then wrote their initial letters to their partners in notebooks. Each of the partners wrote seven letters during the exchange, and the university students read and commented on two polished drafts written by their partners. The university students became both audiences and mentors for their younger partners. This project was an opportunity for reflection and productive discussions that benefited both partners.

RAFT Assignments

How can RAFT assignments be beneficial to content area learning?

RAFT is an acronym for Role, Audience, Format, and Topic (Santa, Havens, and Harrison, 2007). **RAFT assignments** are explicit as to each of these factors: the student is told who the writer is, who the audience is, what form the writing will take, and the topic for the writing. Student roles may vary widely; they can be scientists, blood cells, trees, animals, or other animate or inanimate objects. The audiences can be classmates, younger children, or the general public. Formats can include letters, editorials, memoranda, and poems. A sample assignment might be as follows: You are the brother of a boy who is considering experimenting with cocaine (role). Through a letter (format) to your brother (audience), try to persuade him not to do this, backing up your arguments with facts about this drug (topic).

Research Reports

Research reports involve organizing and outlining numerous facts. Writers must also synthesize information from various sources. Research papers can promote critical thinking about topics under study. They also offer practical applications of various study skills, such as library use, reference book use, note taking, outlining, and summarizing. Research papers should not be assigned without careful assessment of students' prerequisite skills, so that appropriate instruction can be offered if necessary skills are not in evidence. These skills should be taught as needed and connections made between the skills and the current task of answering the research questions that have been raised. Students may be allowed to choose note taking, footnoting, and bibliographic forms; or the teacher may specify forms that are required.

When content area teachers assign reports to be written for their classes, they sometimes allow students to choose their own topics. In other instances, a teacher may ask each student to write on a predetermined topic. Some educators feel that students should have a great deal of control over what they write. Britton and others (1975, p. 23) say, "however controlled the situation, the writer is *selecting* from what he knows and thinks . . . and embodying that knowledge and thought in words which he produces, no matter how much he draws on the language of a book or of the teacher's notes." Therefore, from the perspective of Britton and others, having the teacher assign topics and guide students in writing procedures does not negate the ownership of the writing.

SOCIAL STUDIES

ENGLISH/ LANGUAGE ARTS

Gifted students can research the accuracy of historical novels as a project that can result in research papers that solve real problems. Anachronisms and other inaccuracies can be located by consulting reference books about the period. The students thus can have a choice of the novel to write about and a choice of focus for the paper, but they also have a well-defined task.

The process that follows can be used to help students prepare good reports. The first step listed obviously is not applicable if the teacher chooses the topic.

> **Step 1.** *Select a topic.* The topic selected must be pertinent to the content area material being studied. It should be chosen because of its interest value for both the reporter and the rest of the class, if the reports are going to be shared. Ordinarily, students tend to choose topics that are much too broad for adequate coverage. The teacher needs to help students narrow their topics so that the task of preparing the report is more manageable.
>
> **Step 2.** *Collect information on the topic.* Students should use the location skills discussed in Chapter 7 to collect information from a variety of sources. The organizational skill of note taking, covered in Chapter 7, is also essential for use at this point.
>
> **Step 3.** *Organize the material.* Outlining or webbing the information collected is the main activity in this step. Material from the different sources used must be fused together. The sequence and relationship of main ideas and details are important considerations in forming the outline or web.
>
> **Step 4.** *Write a first draft.* Utilizing the outline or web just formulated and the notes compiled, the students write an initial draft of the report.
>
> **Step 5.** *Read the first draft for revision and editing.* The students read the first draft and check for organization, sentence and paragraph sense, cohesiveness of the information, appropriate usage, correct spelling, and proper punctuation. They also confirm that all material is properly documented. At this point,

peer editing may be utilized. With this approach, a peer editor carefully reads the report of his or her classmate, answering questions provided by the teacher. Some sample questions are as follows: "Does the report have a title that accurately reflects its contents? Does the report have a good beginning that sparks interest in the topic? Is the sequence in which the information is presented logical? If not, what do you think is wrong with it? Is enough information included? In your opinion, what questions remain to be answered by the report? Does the report have errors in mechanics (e.g., spelling, capitalization, punctuation)? If so, mark them for the author. Does the report have a conclusion that sums up the material adequately? Do you have any questions or suggestions for the author?" After answering these questions, the peer editor returns the report and comments to the author, who revises it for submission to the teacher, carefully considering the editor's comments. Often two students work together, each acting as peer editor for the other.

Step 6. *Revise the report.* The students make needed changes in the initial draft and rewrite the report in a form acceptable for submission to the teacher. Revision is easier if the report has been written using word-processing software on a computer.

The teacher can do much to help prepare students to perform effectively on an assigned written report. A procedure that a teacher might follow is described next.

1. *Name a broad topic related to the course of study.* Ask students for suggestions as to how the topic could be narrowed to make it more manageable. Consider a number of acceptable topics that might be derived from the original topic.

2. *Choose one of the acceptable narrowed topics.* Take the students to the library and have them locate sources of information on the topic. Ask each of them to take notes from at least one source and to record bibliographical information. Remind them to make use of skimming and scanning techniques as they search for information. (See Chapter 8 for information on skimming and scanning.) Encourage use of computer databases and electronic encyclopedias, if they are available. (See Chapter 7 for a discussion of these resources.) Point out the risks of using Wikipedia as an electronic encyclopedia (as discussed in Chapter 2).

3. *Return to the classroom.* As a class, synthesize the notes into a single outline. (Use a chalkboard, dry-erase board, computer-controlled projector, or overhead projector.)

4. Write the report from the outline as a whole-class or small-group activity, with the teacher working as the scribe or assigning a student to be the scribe. The scribe may be writing manually or on a computer.

5. Have the students read the draft for content, organization, and mechanics.

6. Make needed changes in organization, spelling, and expression on the basis of the proofreading.

The teacher who follows this procedure has essentially walked the students through the steps of report writing before asking them to attempt it on their own.

Thereafter, the students will know what to expect when they are assigned individual reports to write.

In addition to preparing students for report writing, the content area teacher should contact the school's librarian before assigning a research report. The librarian can help students locate relevant resources.

Students can work in teams on research reports, following steps similar to those just enumerated. Working with partners or small groups may be less threatening to many students than working alone would be, and greater learning appears to result from team reports than from individually produced reports. Teachers must monitor the teams' work regularly and should also encourage self-monitoring of progress by team members (Rekrut, 1997).

Expository Writing Program

Raphael and others (1988) developed the Expository Writing Program (EWP) to help students learn how to write well-organized reports with data collected from a number of sources. The EWP is designed around "think sheets" that stimulate strategy use for planning the report, gathering data, drafting, editing, and revising. The EWP Prewriting Think Sheet focuses on planning concerns, such as considering the topic, things the students already know about the topic, and the audience for the paper. The Organizing Think Sheet focuses students' attention on different sets of questions that fit different text structures, such as comparison/contrast, problem/solution, and explanation. Students use the sheet that is appropriate for their chosen organizational pattern. A lined sheet of colored paper forms the think sheet for writing the first draft. Edit and Peer Editor Think Sheets provide the framework for first self-editing and then peer editing. These sheets focus on the content and organization of the paper and on planning the next step of the writing. A Revision Think Sheet encourages the students to integrate the feedback from others into a revision plan.

MEETING THE CHALLENGE

**ENGLISH/
LANGUAGE
ARTS**

Teaching students to do research papers can be approached in a number of ways. The following is the procedure that a first-year teacher in a rural high school, Katherine Dooley, used:

1. Kathy held a class-long brainstorming session to answer two questions: "What are you an expert at?" and "What do you want to know more about?" For the purposes of this assignment, she specified that they were *expert* at anything they had ever done themselves. She gave examples of things they might be expert at and of what she would want to know more about. Her students listed many interesting habits, hobbies, and ideas.

2. Kathy read their lists, circling interesting topics and writing her own brainstorming in the margins.

If the piece has been written electronically, the revision activity is much easier.

© Muntz/Taxi Collection/ Getty Images

SCIENCE AND HEALTH

3. Then she took her class to the library, returned their papers, and held individual writing conferences to discuss ideas. An "expert gum chewer" chose to write about gum. As he searched for information, the student learned how to use a variety of types of technology, sharpened his problem-solving skills, and actually enjoyed the experience. He came to Kathy daily and said things like "Yuck! Did you know gum contains . . . ?" or "Wow! Look at this, Ms. Dooley." An "expert reader of children's books" listed sexism as something she would like to know more about. Kathy had circled both of the ideas, and during the conference they decided that she could write about the portrayal of women in ten Caldecott-winning books from several decades. For this topic the vast majority of the information came, not from copying directly from another source, but from the student's own evaluation. The student's connection to the topic led her to show Kathy illustrations that particularly angered her. Her feeling about the research topic was evident from her paper.

With this method, Kathy received interesting, unusual papers. "When I allowed them to choose topics that were meaningful to them, they actually enjoyed learning about their topics," she said.

Kathy Dooley met the challenge of getting the students to write research papers by giving them some personal choice that led to motivation. Teachers in areas other than English could offer structured choices. For example, a science teacher might ask, "Which of these scientific breakthroughs or procedures has the most impact on *your* life? About which one do you have the most background knowledge? In which one do you have the most interest?" With the answers to these questions as a starter, each student could be led to choose a topic that would provide some personal motivation.

Different Formats for Reports

Beyersdorfer and Schauer (1992) use a special type of research report—the personality profile. First they have students read about interesting people and select subjects to profile. Then the students learn interviewing and note-taking techniques, write scripts for their interviews, and carry out the interviews. Finally, they make decisions based on the data collected, write the profiles, and present the profiles orally to their classmates.

**ENGLISH/
LANGUAGE
ARTS**

**SOCIAL
STUDIES**

To give research reports an audience other than the teacher, Roessing (2007) has her students write a *South Africa for the Dummy* guide for the class to use as they read the book *Waiting for the Rain*. The guide covers topics that are important to understanding the story, such as geography of Africa, the Boer War, discriminatory laws, and Nelson Mandela. Students choose and research different topics, and the sections are combined to form the guide. Each student receives a copy to read as the topics become important to understanding the novel. Roessing also has her students write *You Are There* books, in which they write second person accounts of events, places, or people involved in the Holocaust. Students collaborate with research-writing partners to produce these books that include details about sounds, sights, feelings, and utterances that put the reader right into the action.

Some educators offer other variations to enhance students' motivation to write. Moulton (1999) recommends using Romano's (1995; 2000) multigenre approach to writing research papers, having students include many research tools (for example, the Internet) in the data collection and then vary the form of presentation of information. Instead of having students meld their findings into a traditional paper format, the teacher has them write several pieces based on their research, presenting their information through different genres. "For instance rather than stating that someone was born in a particular year and place, the student might create a birth certificate, the flyleaf of a Bible, a birth announcement, a hospital invoice, or a letter to or from the new parents" (Moulton, 1999, p. 529). Events might be related through personal letters, journal entries, or newspaper articles. Such a presentation requires students to interpret the material from another person's point of view, and it requires them to understand multiple genres. A formal bibliography is included with such research writing, but internal citations are not. Students may use endnotes to explain why they chose particular genres and to cite the sources for their information. Many of Moulton's students used computer technology to prepare realistic-looking documents—a natural integration of technology and writing.

Allen (2001) has suggested an approach to multigenre research papers for middle school students, also based on Romano's writing. Romano wrote in the foreword to Allen's book, "*Multigenre* simply means 'composed of many kinds of writing.' Multigenre papers are many-voiced and rhetorically diverse" (p. vii). Allen describes multigenre papers in this way: "each piece in the paper utilizes a different genre, reveals one facet of the topic, and makes its own point. Conventional devices do not connect the pieces in a multigenre paper, nor are the pieces always in chronological order. The paper is instead a collage of writing and artistic expression with an overarching theme that engulfs and informs the reader" (p. 2). Allen's students often used the Internet, videos, personal interviews, other primary sources, and field trips, as well as books from the library, for some references. As the students prepared their papers, Allen provided instruction related to research skills, writing in a variety of genres, and planning and organizational skills. The students cooperatively developed a rubric to evaluate the presentations based on their papers. A sample multigenre report is shown in Example 9.9.

EXAMPLE 9.9   Multigenre Report

Haiku
Water gently flows
Freshly cleaned and purified
Free from pollutants

Example 1

Poem
I was lost in a flood of trash
My beauty not seen
Animals steered clear
Because my water was green

Example 2

WANTED
Water Quality Specialist
Temporary position for an experienced scientist

Benefits:
Office located in town square
Flexible hours
Vacation package

Salary is negotiable

Minimum of Doctor's Degree
in Biology or related field

Interview required
Applications available at Cookeville City Hall
or call 555–9562

Equal Opportunity Employer

Example 3

Example 4

Don't Drink That Water Research Report
By Meagan Jasitt

Problem

If a community's public water supply is contaminated, what is the most effective way to purify water from local sources (streams, lakes, rivers, or wells) to make it potable?

Hypotheses

1. I believe that by using materials that are available in the home, people can make natural sources of water drinkable.
2. I think that of the different methods, distillation will be the most effective way to purify water.

Materials

Coliscan Easygel (20 ml) in sterile bottle
Aquachek 5-in-1 Water Quality Test Strips for Chlorine, Hardness, Alkalinity, and pH
Aquachek 5-in-1 Water Quality Test Strips for Nitrate and Nitrite
Iodine solution (2%)
Clorox Ultra bleach (6.00% sodium hypochlorite)
Sterile, pretreated Petri dishes with lids
Sterile collection bottles
3 ml sterile droppers
Plastic cups
1-gallon plastic collection bottle

Pots for boiling and collecting water
Glass cover
Coffee filters and large funnel
Sand
Ice
Timer
Digital camera
Safety glasses
Disposable gloves

Procedure

1. Collect water samples from a local stream
2. Test these water samples for nitrite level, nitrate level, pH, hardness, alkalinity, chloride level, and free chlorine using chemical test strips.
   a. Tap water
   b. Untreated stream water
   c. 500 ml stream water treated with 2 drops of 6.00% sodium hypochlorite (Clorox Ultra)
   d. 500 ml stream water treated with 3 drops of 2% Iodine
   e. Untreated stream water filtered through a coffee filter
   f. Untreated stream water filtered through sand and a coffee filter
   g. Untreated stream water boiled for 20 minutes in an aluminum pot
   h. Untreated stream water vapor that was condensed

3. Steps for bacteria testing
   a. Place 5 ml of each water sample (2.a-2.h) into a bottle of Coliscan Easygel
   b. Pour solution into sterile Petri dish
   c. Cover and turn each dish over after 45 minutes
   d. Count colonies formed after 48 hours
   e. Determine kinds of bacteria found in Petri dishes and bacteria count

Results

In drinking water, any bacteria can cause illness, especially fecal coliform bacteria. If the fecal coliform bacteria are plentiful, it can cause typhoid fever, hepatitis, dysentery, and ear infections. By using Coliscan Easygel, both fecal and non-fecal bacteria can be identified by the colors of their colonies after letting samples set for at least 30 hours.

My water samples came from a local stream that contained mostly non-fecal bacteria. Chemically treating this water with small amounts of sodium hypochlorite and iodine killed the bacteria. Treating the water with these household chemicals was easy and effective, though there may be some health problems for some people. Boiling is effective in killing bacteria, but the container may help to contaminate the water. Distillation is a slow process that requires boiling and condensation, but pure water is the result.

Conclusions

1. By using household materials, people can make natural sources of water potable.
2. Distilled water was the purest water produced in this experiment, but making it consumed much time and energy.
3. Water treated with iodine most closely resembled tap water, but iodine can be hazardous to some people.

References

Curtis, R. (1998). Outdoor action guide to water purification. Retrieved February 23, 2005, from http://www.princeton.edu/~oa/manual/water.shtml.

Jarrett, D. (2005, March 10). Monterey water system water quality report 2004. *Cookeville Herald-Citizen*, p. 8.

LaMotte Company. (2004). *ColiQuant EZ* (Code 3–0034). Chestertown, MD: LaMotte Company. Pacific Crest Trail Association. (n.d.). Water sources and purification. Retrieved February 23, 2005, from http://www.pcta.org/planning/before_trip/health/water.asp.

Thompson, G., & Turk, J. (1992). *Earth and its environment*. Fort Worth, TX: Saunders College Publishing.

University of Missouri Extension. (2005). *Bacteria in drinking water* (WQ102). Retrieved March 7, 2005, from http://muextension.missouri.edu/xplor/envqual/wq0102.htm.

Photo Essay

Multigenre Science Project

Meagan Jasitt
Cookeville High School
Cookeville, TN
March 2005

Hypotheses

1. I believe that by using materials that are available in the home, people can make natural sources of water drinkable.
2. I think that of the different methods, distillation will be the most effective way to purify water.

Materials
Meagan Jasitt

Local stream
Meagan Jasitt

Collecting water sample
Meagan Jasitt

Treating sample with 2% iodine
Meagan Jasitt

Treating sample with
2% iodine

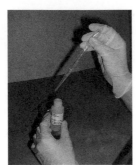

Adding 5 ml sample to
Coliscan Easygel

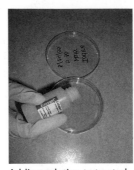

Adding solution to treated
Petri dish

Chemical analysis with test
strips

Chemical analysis with test
strips

Water samples after
48-hour treatment

Counting colonies
of bacteria

Counting colonies
of bacteria

Tap water sample

Untreated stream water
bacteria colonies

Coffee filter method

Sand filter method

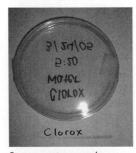

Stream water sample
treated with 6% sodium
hypochlorite

2% iodine treated sample

Distilled water sample

Boiled water sample

Meagan Jasitt

Conclusions

1. By using household materials, people can make natural sources of water potable.
2. Distilled water was the purest water produced in this experiment, but making it consumed much time and energy.
3. Water treated with iodine most closely resembled tap water, but iodine can be hazardous to some people.

Meagan Jasitt

Example 5

Homeland Security Chief Discusses Emergency Water Supply Awareness
By Meagan Jasitt
Associated Press Reporter

COOKEVILLE (TN) - In case of a disaster, when tap water is not available, citizens should have some of the following supplies available to purify local water sources: iodine, bleach, and an assortment of cooking pots for distillation.

The Secretary of Homeland Security stated that adding 2–3 drops of iodine or Clorox to a quart of water and letting it sit for 30 minutes can purify contaminated water. However, there may be some risks to pregnant women and people with thyroid disease. The Secretary also said that distillation and boiling are probably the most effective methods but not always the most convenient. For more information you can go to http://www.fema.gov/rrr/waterf.shtm.

Example 6

(Letter to the editor of the Cookeville Herald-Citizen)

Editor:

"Hello, I was sent by the city to test your water." This is the greeting that many residents of my Cookeville neighborhood have been receiving when they open their front doors.

Unfortunately, after hearing from the "city employee" that their water is contaminated, some citizens have been convinced or conned into buying hundreds of dollars worth of water filtering equipment.

I'm concerned and ask your assistance to help us determine if the water in our community is potable and safe to use. Do these "employees" work for the city or are they part of a new scam that is spreading across Cookeville?

M. Jasitt
Concerned Citizen

Example 7

(Chief of Police response to the letter to the editor)

Editor:

This letter is a response to the letter by the Concerned Citizen about a possible water testing scam. My office has received quite a few calls about fraudulent water testing, and we are currently investigating the problem.

The Director of the Cookeville Water Department told me that the water supplied by Cookeville meets all of the health requirements of the state of Tennessee. City workers are not going to homes and asking to conduct water tests. If you are concerned about the cleanliness of your water, you may call the Water Department and discuss the problem.

If anyone has any information about possible crimes, please phone the police headquarters. Report anyone who comes to check the water quality at homes in your neighborhood.

J. Smith
Cookeville Chief of Police

End Notes

Examples 1 and 2, *Haiku* and *Poem*—These poems were created after reviewing examples of short poems. *Haiku* is a haiku. *Poem* is a quatrain (abcb). Both are about water quality, which was the topic of my science fair project.

Example 3, *Wanted: Water Quality Specialist*—After thinking about the qualifications for someone who could be hired by the city to test water, I wrote this advertisement. I used actual newspaper employment advertisements as examples.

Example 4, *Don't Drink That Water*—This is my actual research project for tenth-grade Honors Chemistry at Cookeville High School. Most of the work on the project was done during my two weeks of spring break in March 2005. I started my research in February and followed the scientific method. I tested my hypothesis, collected data, and developed conclusions. My project won third place at the Cookeville High School Science Fair and was an honorable mention at the Upper Cumberland Regional Science Fair at Tennessee Tech University.

Example 5, *Homeland Security Newspaper Article*—While looking for information about water purification, I read about preparing for emergencies on the Department of Homeland Security and Federal Emergency Management Agency websites. This letter is important because I think that people should be prepared for any catastrophes that may occur.

Examples 6 and 7, *Letters to the Editor*—Letters to the editor and responses are good ways for people to get action and to have their questions answered. Having public officials publish responses is also good because many citizens can be informed with just one short letter. The *Cookeville Herald-Citizen* newspaper publishes a lot of letters to the editor and I used some of them as examples.

Source: Reprinted by permission of Meagan and Lance Jasitt.

Laboratory Reports

Secondary science classes often have laboratory components for which laboratory reports must be written. Lab reports should include the problem being investigated, the student's hypothesis, needed materials, the procedure followed, the results of the study or experiment, conclusions that may be drawn from the data, and references that were consulted. Example 9.9 has a lab report as a part of the multigenre report shown.

The writing of a laboratory report can be modeled by doing an experiment and writing a cooperative laboratory report on the board or on a transparency. The teacher can lead the students through each step in the process; then the students can use their lab guides to write reports independently.

Photo Essays

ART

Use of photo essays and various types of semantic maps can be effective for building background knowledge of culturally diverse students and for helping them to organize their thoughts into writing. In one study the students worked in pairs initially to develop photo essays with meaningful conceptual frameworks and then reconstructed the photos on storyboards, using semantic mapping formats. The images in the photos helped to bridge the language differences of the student population and to provide a common base for communication.

ENGLISH/
LANGUAGE
ARTS

The procedure was to plan topics or themes, take photos to illustrate the topics, organize the pictures on a storyboard, and then write a composition on the topic with the storyboard in view. Students brainstormed ideas for photos before actually taking the pictures. When the pictures had been processed, the student pairs worked together on the arrangement on the storyboards. The assignments elicited sequential, thematic, and classification writing styles (Sinatra et al., 1990). An example of a photo essay is included as a part of Example 9.9.

Pen Pals

ENGLISH/ LANGUAGE ARTS

Writing to pen pals is a way to provide students with authentic reading and writing experiences because it involves real communication activities. A number of teachers have discovered the advantages of e-mail pen pals for motivating students to do meaningful reading and writing. E-mail applications were addressed in Chapter 2. Garcia-Vazquez and Vazquez (1994) paired Latino/a high school students with Latino/a university students with great success. The high school students carefully drafted their messages to their pen pals and often edited them several times before mailing them. McDermott and Setoguchi (1999) have had college methods students converse with seventh-graders about literature in pen-pal letters in a program much like the one Betty Roe conducted through e-mail. (See Chapter 2 for details.)

Internet Writing Projects and Activities

ENGLISH/ LANGUAGE ARTS

Internet writing projects can be motivational for secondary school students. After discovering that some of her reluctant writers in class were active, engaged writers on blogs, Witte (2007) decided to develop a collaborative journal activity between her middle school students and university preservice teachers. The Talkback Project made use of a blog for literature conversations about novels that the middle schoolers were reading in literature circles. The preservice teachers were encouraged to ask the middle school students questions that helped them make connections between the text and other texts, the text and the world, and the text and themselves. The two groups had face-to-face meetings, as well as their blog postings. At the end, the students made videos about the reading they had done. Although privacy concerns caused the school district to cancel the project, the participants protested, because they felt their voices were being heard when they participated. The students and teachers who had participated believed that the cancellation of the project in the future was unfortunate.

Instant messaging (IM) is an activity engaged in by a large segment of adolescents. Teachers, however have often been concerned that instant messaging will cause a decline in students' conventional writing skills, including spelling, grammar, and punctuation. Jacobs (2008a) did not find evidence that IM causes writing skills to deteriorate, however, and some educators believe that use of IM increases the possibilities for adolescents to become involved in literacy activities (Jacobs, 2008b). Although IM expressions occasionally find their way into school assignments, Jacobs's findings may have occurred because many adolescents do not view their IM activities as writing, but as talking, and they view IM as using different conventions from formal writing (Jacobs, 2008a; Lenhart, Arafeh, Smith, and Macgill, 2008).

Middle school students have been asked to write reports of their research on particular topics as PowerPoint presentations. First, the students were exposed to a number of alphabet books on different topics and to the teacher's own PowerPoint text to use as literature models. Then they used pictures and information from Internet sites. Some even incorporated music and animation. Bilingual students were allowed to use text in multiple languages (Evers, Lang, and Smith, 2009).

Mentoring Projects

ENGLISH/
LANGUAGE
ARTS

To help middle school students improve their writing skills through writing work-shops and to help university students learn about writers' workshops, university students were paired with sixth- or seventh-grade students (Smith-D'Arezzo and Kennedy, 2004). Both groups were taught about the six traits of writing from the Northwest Regional Educational Laboratory (n.d.): ideas, organization, voice, word choice, sentence fluency, and conventions. The partners critiqued each other's writing, using a rubric based on the six traits. The students in both groups completed three writing projects. There were two or three face-to-face conferences about writing for the partners. In the last meeting, the students gave partners their scores on the pieces and explained how they derived the scores.

Evaluation of Writing

Not all of the writing that students do in content area classrooms is formally eval-uated. Journal writing, for example, is done for its learning value and is not for-mally evaluated for a grade. Language experience writing is usually evaluated by the students who develop it as it is produced. Generally this kind of writing is not graded by the teacher but is used as a learning aid in the classroom.

If the process approach to writing is used, there is much ongoing evaluation as a written piece is developed. Students elicit feedback about their writing from their peers, they proofread their own work with revision checklists in mind, and they receive feedback from their teachers during student–teacher conferences. In addi-tion to the evaluative efforts that have gone on as materials are written, there are times when teachers must formally evaluate a final draft of a written assignment. The grading procedures may be holistic or analytic in nature.

When *holistic grading* is used, the teacher evaluates the written material as a whole. The paper is read for general impression and overall effect. It may be compared with pieces that have already been graded or scored for the inclusion of features important to the particular type of writing involved. Kirby and Liner (1988, p. 221) point out that holistic grading "focuses on the piece of writing as a whole and on those features most important to the success of the piece. . . . The rating is quick because the rater does not take time to circle errors or make marginal notations." Kirby and Liner suggest that teachers may use a list of criteria related to the impact of the writing, the inventiveness of the approach, and the individual flavor of the writing as a guide for their holistic grading. They refer to this type of grading as *impression marking*.

Rubrics are often used to help teachers evaluate students' writing. Rubrics are discussed in Chapter 3, and a sample rubric is found in Example 9.8.

Analytic scales not only focus readers' attention on the features that are needed for the writing to be effective but also attach point values to each feature. The reader sums the scores for each feature in determining the overall grade. The Diederich Scale is an example of an analytic scale. It leads the scorer to assign a score of 1 (poor), 2 (weak), 3 (average), 4 (good), or 5 (excellent) to quality and development of ideas *and* organization, relevance, and movement (both of which are weighted heavier than the other considerations); style, flavor, and individuality and wording and phrasing (both of which are given intermediate weights); and grammar and sentence structure, punctuation, spelling, and manuscript form and legibility (all of which receive the lowest weights). Content and organization represent 50 percent of the grade; aspects of style, 30 percent; and mechanics, 20 percent. Scales such as this keep raters focused on the carefully defined criteria and keep them from being unduly influenced by surface features rather than considering all the factors contributing to the effectiveness of a piece of writing (Kirby and Liner, 1988; Dornan, Rosen, and Wilson, 2003). If students are asked to keep folders of written work over the course of a semester or year, their progress can be noted by comparing the earlier pieces with the latest ones. Students may gain more satisfaction from this type of final evaluation than from many other methods because they can see the differences in the writing and often can see that early teacher comments led to improvements in later products.

More on assessment, especially portfolio assessment, can be found in Chapter 3.

FOCUS ON *Struggling Readers*

Writing Instruction for Struggling Readers and Writers

Furr (2003) uses a modified writing workshop with students who read three to four years below their current grade level. These students need procedures to help them decide such things as how to begin and what to do next. They are more comfortable beginning with expository prose on topics that have been covered in school because they have more control of the vocabulary and syntax they need to use when they have had guided reading experiences with the subject matter. In sustained silent reading time, nonfiction texts with little reading difficulty are popular with these students.

Before beginning writing workshop, Furr has his students participate in guided reading of a variety of nonfiction texts. These books are discussed, important vocabulary is clarified, and the words are used in meaningful written sentences. The information in these texts is supplemented by teacher read-alouds and other books on the same topics for independent reading by the students.

The first expository piece is developed through shared writing, similar to the language experience approach. The class cooperatively begins a web on the chosen topic after the teacher explains and models the webbing process. Students then complete the web individually. The teacher next explains the need for and the development of a hook and a general statement about the topic for the report, as a way to begin. This process is modeled and some brainstorming by the students follows.

The class composes part of the draft of the body of the report together. Each box on the web is used as the focus of a paragraph. Furr circulates and holds conferences with the students as they finish the report independently. Students are allowed to consult one another as they write, as well. They finish by editing their material for mechanics, checking for capitals, agreement, punctuation, and spelling.

They are encouraged to read through their report four times, focusing on a different element each time. Finished reports are illustrated and displayed.

Fisher and Frey (2003) used a gradual release model for writing instruction with ninth-grade struggling readers. With this model control of the writing gradually shifts from the teacher to the student. The instruction began with a language experience approach in which the teacher acted as a scribe and wrote the students' thoughts about a topic on a dry-erase board. The topic chosen was often based on a shared reading experience. As the teacher wrote, various aspects of the writing were discussed, such as mechanics, spelling, grammatical constructions, or vocabulary. The students had interesting thoughts to share in the writing, even though their independent writing was a struggle. The language experience approach was followed by interactive writing in which the students did the actual writing of the class's ideas. Fisher had different students write single words from each chosen sentence, until the students had written the entire sentence in their combined effort at the board.

Fisher also used published writing to provide patterns that the students could emulate in their own individual writing. The patterns offered a scaffold for these students. For example, in Shelley Moore Thomas's book *Somewhere Today: A Book of Peace*, each page starts with "Somewhere today" in the first sentence. After discussion of newspaper articles and lectures on a topic, students wrote their own sentences beginning with "Somewhere today," typed them on the classroom computer, and illustrated them. These were printed and then bound into a class book.

Generative sentences beginning with single words were turned into topic sentences for paragraphs by Fisher and Frey (2003). The topic sentences were developed under supervision in class, and the paragraphs were assigned to be completed as homework—homework that had a high probability of being completed because it was off to a good beginning. Freewriting that had as its focus the production of as many words on a given topic as quickly as possible was used to provide the students with written material that they could take through the revision process. This procedure culminated in independent writing to prompts based on reading that had been done in class. The entire procedure resulted in improved reading and writing skills for the students in the class.

In other settings, less-motivated and "difficult" students were actively engaged by multigenre writing (Grierson, Anson, and Baird, 2002). They often turned in assignments early and indicated that they really cared about their writing projects.

Harvey (2002) suggests using more short nonfiction to teach reading and writing skills to struggling readers and writers. The length is less intimidating to these students; there are usually eye-catching illustrations; they can be reread easily and quickly; and they are short enough for read-alouds of complete, well-crafted pieces that provide writing models.

Learning clubs, in which struggling readers are involved in choosing reading materials and participating in motivational activities that involve reading and writing, can engage struggling adolescent readers and writers (Casey, 2008/2009).

Students share responsibility for learning from the chosen material and participate in such activities as developing Venn Diagrams to compare stories or characters, preparing posters with pictures and explanatory paragraphs, or writing new chapters for stories. Struggling students need to have these clubs provide a safe environment for expressing opinions and explaining ideas. This means that the teacher has to be accepting of the students' contributions.

Independence in strategy use is important. Struggling readers may be led to self-regulate their strategy use by having a list of steps they should follow, along with reminders on how to stay on task, that the teacher helps them develop (Helsel and Greenberg, 2007).

FOCUS ON *English Language Learners*

Writing Instruction for ELLs

Fisher and Frey's (2003) gradual release model for writing instruction (see the previous "Focus on Struggling Readers") also worked extremely well with the English language learners in the class. One good example was Mubarak, who was from Somalia. He was able to write fewer than five words a minute when the rapid freewrites were started, but in four months he was averaging 40 words a minute. The language experience approach that was used in the gradual release model has also been suggested by many educators as a good procedure for English language learners (Fisher and Frey, 2003).

Dialogue journals can work well with ELLs. Such journals ensure that this reading material will be somewhat adjusted to the students' individual reading abilities because teachers can modify their writing to fit the language proficiency of the students (Dolly, 1990).

To help ELLs understand how audience affects the grammar, intonation, and vocabulary, as well as the language (English, Spanish, etc.) used, Martínez, Orellana, Pacheco, and Carbone (2008) had students participate in reenacting translation situations that they had participated in or observed. They presented the reenactments to the class, and the class discussed word choices and other aspects of the change in the material translated, in order to fit the particular audience. They pointed out that these changes were shifts in voice. Then the students were given a writing assignment about a social issue that they had chosen from a list formed by brainstorming. After choosing an issue, the students brainstormed to develop a list of audiences for their arguments about these issues. The students were helped to practice by playing a game in which they chose an issue and an index card with an audience for an argument about the issue. The researchers modeled the process first and then let the students play it in pairs. Discussion of the differences in arguments on the same issue for different audiences helped the students see how audience affects the writing process. In their writing assignment, the students chose an issue and two different audiences and wrote their arguments in a writing workshop process with peer editing. This activity also helped the students see how their translating skills could be used to accomplish school tasks.

Espinosa (2006) worked with bilingual students to help them do autobiographical writing. She slowed down the teaching process to adapt to the bilingual students' needs. She also challenged the students to think about details that make memories come alive. This activity gave the students high interest, meaningful experiences in reading and writing.

Yi (2008) discovered that many adolescent ELLs found a satisfying literacy experience with a website that was developed by adolescent Korean ELLs as a place that they could converse, write poems and stories, and upload pictures. The students wrote in a mixture of Korean and English. They reacted positively to an activity called "relay writing," in which one person writes a section of a novel and posts it, and another person adds a section, and so on. The contributors may comment on their sections to let the next writers know why they included or omitted particular things. Other readers/writers may comment on each episode in a review section. These comments tend to be brief and encouraging. Yi also found that some of the participants were reluctant to participate and participated sparingly for a variety of reasons. When interest in the relay novel writing waned, the ELLs participated in "relay compliments," in which a student wrote about another participant, including vignettes about the person and complimenting him or her. Then that person chose another student to compliment. These activities might well be adapted to use in a classroom, allowing ELLs to share their ideas and cultures with other students and one another.

Summary

Writing is valuable in content area classes because it is a tool for thinking and for attaining self-knowledge and because it enhances retention of the material studied. As these benefits are gained, fluency in writing is also promoted.

Reading and writing are closely related written language skills. Both are concerned with communication, involve construction of meaning, and make use of vocabulary. Writing assignments can foster reading progress, if they focus on the relationships between reading and writing. Writing before reading can help students activate their background knowledge about a topic, enhancing reading comprehension.

A process approach to writing tends to produce superior writing products and a better understanding of the writing process than an approach in which the teacher assigns a paper and the students write it and turn it in without process guidance. The writing process can be broken down into five overlapping and recursive steps: prewriting, writing a draft, revising, editing, and publishing. Many types of writing-to-learn activities have been used in content classes. They include language experience writings, content journals, dialogue journals, RAFT assignments, research reports, laboratory reports, photo essays, pen pals, Internet writing projects, and multigenre projects.

Not all writing done in class needs to be evaluated. Journal writing is a prime example of this. Writing that is developed through a process approach is subject to ongoing evaluation as the writing progresses. Sometimes teachers need to evaluate a final draft of a piece of writing for grading purposes. When this is the case, they may use either holistic or analytic grading procedures.

A modified writing workshop preceded by guided reading and teacher read-alouds of nonfiction texts is effective with struggling readers and writers. A gradual release model for writing instruction is also helpful with these students and with English language learners. Use of short nonfiction is beneficial in this process. Multigenre writing is motivational for students who are not generally eager to write. English language learners benefit from the use of dialogue journals and the language experience approach.

Discussion Questions

1. In what ways is writing valuable in content area instruction?
2. What in your subject area would lend itself to language experience writing?
3. Which types of writing-to-learn activities would be most helpful in your content area? Can you see applications for such activities as blogs, webpages, or even tweets in your subject area? Why, or why not?
4. Why is the prewriting stage so important to the writing program?
5. What are some advantages to publishing and sharing students' writing?
6. What method of evaluation of final drafts seems most appropriate to you? Why?
7. What are the values of Internet writing projects?
8. What procedures are most helpful to struggling readers and writers and to English language learners?

Enrichment Activities

*1. Observe one period of a content area class. List the types of writing that the students are asked to do and the length of time spent on each writing activity.
*2. Try using content journals, or learning logs, in your classroom for a three-week period. Report your reaction to this technique to your classmates.
3. List creative applications of writing to your subject area.
*4. Have your students develop a zine or a creative writing webpage.
*5. Guide a group of secondary school students through the process of writing a group report. Let the students blog about their group research papers as they go through the writing process.
*6. Have your students blog about literature selections or textbook assignments that they have read.
7. With a partner from this class, role-play the use of dialogue journals for a specific type of class (e.g., a tenth-grade biology class). One of you write as the teacher and one as the student. Be prepared to discuss with the class your reactions to the technique.

8. Write a multigenre report on a topic in your subject area to use as an example for your students.

9. Develop a photo essay on a topic in your subject area to use as an example for your students.

10. List Internet sites that are good resources for secondary school writing instruction.

---

*These activities are designed for in-service teachers, student teachers, and practicum students.

Resources including the TeachSource Video Cases can be found on the website for this book. Cengage Learning's CourseMate brings course concepts to life with interactive learning, study, and exam preparation tools that support the printed textbook. Go to www.cengage.com/login to register your access code.

CHAPTER 10

Literature-Based and Thematic Approaches to Content Area Teaching

Overview

Literature has many values in the secondary curriculum, not only in English classes, but also in other content areas, where it can illuminate events and issues that are treated only briefly in textbooks. It is also beneficial because it offers material on various subjects at different difficulty levels. Literature is often incorporated into thematic units in a variety of content areas. Thematic units also include resources other than literature and require much planning on the part of the teacher.

Students need instruction on reading strategies needed to approach literature and strategies related to literary elements. Teachers can use a number of activities to encourage deeper responses to literature.

Purpose-Setting Questions

As you read this chapter, try to answer these questions:

1. How can literature enhance secondary school instruction?
2. How can teachers approach use of literature in content area instruction?
3. What activities can be used to encourage student response to literature?
4. What four basic types of activities are part of a teaching unit?
5. How can use of literature and thematic units benefit struggling readers and English language learners?

Values and Uses of Literature in the Secondary School Curriculum

Secondary school instruction is often highly textbook oriented. However, the need to cover a wide range of topics in a single textbook often leads to superficial coverage of each topic, often reducing it to dry facts that have little interest for students. Trade books can help to remedy this situation. Since a single trade book covers a limited amount of material—a single process, a short time period, or a single individual, for example—it has the room to elaborate on the material and to use detail that brings the situations to life for the readers.

Another problem with textbooks is that, generally, all of the textbooks in a class are on a single reading level. Many students do not have the reading skill to access the information in these texts. Teachers may use alternate textbooks for some of their students, but if such materials are unavailable, teachers can use trade books. Of course, any book intended for use to develop content concepts *must* be examined for accuracy before it is used. Donovan and Smolkin (2002, p. 508) point out that "many books suggested for science instruction deliver incorrect information."

Trade books with various difficulty levels are available for almost any topic in the school curriculum. Some publishers supply information about readability and interest levels of many of the trade books they produce and so do some large online bookstores. Teachers can apply readability measures to other books of interest. However, since many factors outside the text itself influence readability, teacher judgment may work as well as a formula in deciding what to use for particular students.

Young Adult Literature

ENGLISH/
LANGUAGE
ARTS

Young adult literature selections can be used to introduce students to the various literary genres before more difficult traditional classics are tackled. Joan Lowery Nixon's excellent young adult mysteries can be used to help secondary students become familiar with the mystery genre, for example. Her writing can introduce the students to "the form of the narrative, chapters, rising action, climax, and resolution," as well as "foreshadowing, flashbacks, and point of view" (Pavonetti, 1996, p. 454). She presents a variety of characterizations, from flat to well-rounded ones, typical of the variety that students will encounter later. She thereby allows them to build the needed schemata for the genre (Pavonetti, 1996).

ENGLISH/
LANGUAGE
ARTS

There are a number of young adult novels written in verse. Some examples are Creech's *Love That Dog*, Grimes's *Dark Sons*, Hesse's *Out of the Dust* and *Witness*, and Woodson's *Locomotion*. Using such books in middle-school classrooms can help students become aware of imagery and language use (Napoli and Ritholz, 2009).

ENGLISH/
LANGUAGE
ARTS

By pairing adolescent novels with adult novels that have related themes, styles, or other literary traits, teachers help students make a step up to more sophisticated reading and learn how to recognize connections between the works. Pairing themes is a good beginning technique. Gallagher (1995) suggests several such pairings, including the teaching of Harper Lee's *To Kill a Mockingbird* along with Nathaniel Hawthorne's *The House of the Seven Gables* for the theme of the power of love and the study of historical settings, and the teaching of S. E. Hinton's *The Outsiders* along with Herman Melville's *Billy Budd* for the theme of loneliness and isolation and the study of character development. Joan Lowery Nixon's *The Name of the Game Was Murder* can be paired with Agatha Christie's *And Then There Were None* (Pavonetti, 1996) to explore the mystery genre. John Steinbeck's *The Grapes of Wrath* can be paired with Karen Hesse's *Out of the Dust* to identify similarities of themes and motifs (Knickerbocker and Rycik, 2002). Han Nolan's *If I Should Die*

Before I Wake can be paired with Elie Wiesel's *Night* to help students examine similar struggles of protagonists who face the horrible experiences associated with the Holocaust, and Art Spiegelman's graphic novel *Maus: A Survivor's Tale* addresses such an experience, as well (Schwarz, 2002).

ENGLISH/
LANGUAGE
ARTS

Young adult literature can also be used to address literacy concerns directly. Jerry Spinelli's *Maniac Magee*, Elizabeth Speare's *Sign of the Beaver*, and Cynthia Voigt's *Dicey's Song* all deal with characters who read well and ones who are struggling to learn to read. Additionally, Brozo and Schmelzer (1997) believe that exposing boys to literature with positive male role models can lead to increased motivation to read and can enhance literacy growth.

Literature can serve other functions, as well. For example, Andrews (1998) feels that literature can increase students' sensitivity to diversity. Landrum (1998/1999; 2001) has compiled annotated bibliographies of novels that feature characters with disabilities and has provided criteria for evaluating novels that feature characters with disabilities. Patricia Hermes's *I Hate Being Gifted* allows students to see problems faced by gifted students.

ENGLISH/
LANGUAGE
ARTS   MATHEMATICS

Daisey and Jose-Kampfner (2002) encourage the use of biographical storytelling about successful Latinos by language arts and mathematics teachers. Latino students "respond positively to knowledge that is presented in a humanized or story format" (Daisey and Jose-Kampfner, 2002, p. 581). An example of such a biography is that of Cleopatria Martinez, who grew up in a housing project, but earned a Ph.D. in mathematics. Teachers need to act as cultural mediators when students are reading and discussing multicultural books, or "there is the potential for a pooling of misinformation" (Lehr and Thompson, 2000, p. 484), but for monocultural teachers and students good multicultural literature can be extremely informative.

Literature must be chosen carefully to meet the needs and abilities of the students. The Newbery Award books are excellent sources of young adult novels that may meet curricular needs. One study showed that the majority of Newbery Award books have secondary readability levels (Leal and Chamberlain-Solecki, 1998), so the frequent use of these books in upper elementary grades does not mean that they are necessarily going to be "easy reading" for secondary students. Teachers should be aware of the varying difficulty levels of the books being used and should offer scaffolding as needed.

ENGLISH/
LANGUAGE
ARTS

One good way to help struggling readers and aliterate students enjoy reading is to have them view and discuss theatrical performances based on young adult literature. Brinda (2008) organized a field trip to a performance of L'Engle's *A Wrinkle in Time* with adolescent reluctant readers after they read the book, and found that the students were enthusiastic about the book because they understood the performance. Some wanted to reread parts of the book. In the process, they learned more about comprehension and visualization. Theatrically based techniques that Brinda used included letting students in small groups take on self-selected roles of a production team (director; set, lighting, sound, and costume designers; and actor). They used sketches, models, and readings of the text to bring their book to life. They discussed "wow" moments and confusing sections in the book. Guest experts came into the class and discussed the students' concepts for production with them.

Even students who are effective in reading and interpreting literature need to read some relatively easy material with content that is relevant to their daily lives.

This reading helps maintain motivation to read (Knickerbocker and Rycik, 2002). Lynch (2008/2009) suggests having students reread children's books that they have enjoyed after writing what they remember about the books and their reading of them in as much detail as they can manage, including the setting of the reading and their feelings during it. Rereading books that remind teenagers of pleasurable reading experiences may help to rekindle their confidence in and enjoyment of reading.

Picture Books

What are the benefits of using picture books in secondary content area classes?

Motivation to read is a problem with many students, and trade books often offer more motivation than do textbooks. Picture books can serve as motivators for reading with junior high students (Danielson, 1992). They also can be used to develop critical thinking skills, to make a connection between reading and writing, and to develop vocabulary, even for high school students. They add spice to content classes. Some picture books that are good for young children, such as *Jumanji* by Chris Van Allsburg (good for inferential reasoning), can be used with secondary students, but there are also some picture books that have themes especially appropriate for older readers, such as *My Hiroshima* by Jinko Morimoto and *Hiroshima No Pika* by Toshi Maruki, both of which make a good accompaniment to a study of World War II. These books allow students to apply critical reading skills and serve as stimuli for discussion and writing. Some coffee table picture books designed for adults are also elaborately illustrated, usually with photography, and often cover information that is related to social studies and science topics.

SOCIAL STUDIES

Books like Graeme Base's *Animalia* and *The Eleventh Hour* could be used for vocabulary and concept development and for critical thinking, respectively. Middle school English teachers might find books by Ruth Heller useful when discussing parts of speech, a traditionally low-interest topic for older students.

ENGLISH/ LANGUAGE ARTS

Picture books work well in middle school classrooms partly because the texts are brief, the artwork is appealing, and the language is accessible. They are good to use as parts of thematic units or as prompts for creative writing activities (Miller, 1998). Wordless picture books "have been shown to be valuable for developing reading, writing, and oral language with virtually all students who have the proper guidance and encouragement" (Cassady, 1998, p. 432).

SCIENCE AND HEALTH

SOCIAL STUDIES

Guided reading of combined text-picture books works well with middle and high school students. Examples of such books that teachers may choose to help students gain more from their reading include Jacqueline Briggs Martin's *Snowflake Bentley* and Peter Sis's *Starry Messenger*. "Picture walks" through the illustrations in such books provide good prereading activities. Students can examine the pictures for themes and details and tie them into prior knowledge through discussion. Instruction related to comprehension of the printed text can follow (Dean and Grierson, 2005).

SOCIAL STUDIES

Some books are not strictly picture books, but have pictures embedded that add depth to the understanding of the story or informational material. One such book, *George Washington—The Writer—A Treasury of Letters, Diaries, and Public Documents*, compiled and edited by Carolyn Yoder, uses photographs and illustrations of the content and from the time period that enrich the impact of the written documents.

SOCIAL
STUDIES

These pictures should be discussed as thoroughly as the text. Ann Bausum's *Denied Detained Deported: Stories from the Dark Side of American Immigration* is another book that uses photographs and illustrations to enrich the readers' understanding of the text.

Comic Books and Graphic Novels

What are the benefits of using comic books and graphic novels in secondary content area classes?

SOCIAL
STUDIES

ENGLISH/
LANGUAGE
ARTS

Many teachers and librarians have come to recognize the value of comics and graphic novels in enticing adolescents to read and for instructional purposes. Most people are familiar with comic books from their childhood, but they may be unaware of the broad range of types of comic books now being published. In addition to having fast-paced action and strong plots, many graphic novels deal with prejudice, coming of age, social injustice, and other areas of interest to adolescents, while exploring historical events, mythology, and classic stories. *Spider-Girl* comics, for example, sometimes deal with difficult topics like domestic abuse and with many moral dilemmas. They are classroom friendly in that they are profanity free (Blassingame, 2006). Comic strips may be used for many of the purposes that comic books are used. They have the advantage of brevity, but they tell a story with print and graphics, as do picture books (McVicker, 2007).

A way to distinguish comic books from graphic novels is length of text and type of binding, for comic books are shorter and generally stapled, rather than bound like other books (Schwarz, 2006). Although many graphic novels are arranged in the same page order as traditional English novels, some require reading from back to front, as is typical in Japan, definitely a process that must be learned by American readers.

ENGLISH/
LANGUAGE
ARTS

SOCIAL
STUDIES

ART

SCIENCE AND
HEALTH

MATHEMATICS

Graphic novels are fully illustrated stories made of boxed pictures and text, usually more than 32 pages long, in which the storytelling is dependent on the artwork, just as it is in comic books. Bucher and Manning (2006, p. 14) point out that they "contain the same visual impact and clipped, pared-down writing style that adolescents have grown accustomed to." Even though they are illustrated, they must be read to be understood, the pictures and text are both integral to the stories, requiring sophisticated reading strategies. Because students are more likely to be familiar with graphic novels than are teachers, Cat Turner, a secondary English teacher, and Liz Spittal, a teaching specialist, actually asked eleventh and twelfth graders to develop guidebooks designed to help teachers understand graphic novels (NCTE, 2005).

Some graphic novels are science fiction or fantasy novels, but others include realistic fiction, historical fiction, humor, and nonfiction, and the same is true of comic books. Adaptations of literary classics are available in both comic book and graphic novel form and may be useful to English teachers in teaching literary terms and techniques and serving as a bridge to classics, although many English teachers feel that use of such adaptations is inappropriate because the students do not get the full impact of the original works. Some graphic novels relate to content classes such as history, art, science, and math, and some relate primarily to English classes. They can be used in English class to teach about use of dialogue and the way dialogue shows characterization, as well as to teach general story structure elements. *Batman*

ENGLISH/
LANGUAGE
ARTS

SOCIAL
STUDIES

SCIENCE AND
HEALTH

MATHEMATICS

has been used by some in a study of mythology. A graphic novel such as *Satchel Paige: Striking Out Jim Crow* might be used in a study of biography. Additionally, these novels offer the opportunity to teach such visual literacy skills as interpreting facial expressions and body language (Bucher and Manning, 2006; Schwarz, 2002). Years ago, Betty Roe found that *Spiderman* comics not only interested her sixth-grade reluctant readers, but provided good vocabulary development activities for even the gifted readers. Cleaver (2008) points out the value of action comics for teaching onomatopoeia (words that sound like their meaning). Spiegelman's *Maus* books have been used in history instruction about the Holocaust. Some schools in Maryland are using the comic *Dignifying Science* to study the lives of women scientists, and *Clan Apis* has been used in other places to study the honeybee's life. *Fallout* could be used in studying about the atomic bomb (Bucher and Manning, 2006). Acknowledging the educational potential of comics, Yang (2008) even drew comics lectures for his substitute teacher to hand out to his algebra class when he had to miss class. Many teachers have found that use of comics and graphic novels has been successful with struggling readers and ELLs.

In one special after-school program, conducted at Columbia University, students were given the opportunity to write and publish their own comics on a variety of issues. The students created storylines with themes such as the evils of racism, environmental awareness, and conflict resolution; and struggling readers and students with behavior problems became highly engaged and productive. Some of the students learned collaboration skills (Bucher and Manning, 2006; Cleaver, 2008; Strauss, 2004; Toppo, 2005). Cleaver (2008) tells how Kathy Campbell used this model for a class in Arizona. Her students wrote about what they would do if they were superheroes and then transformed their writing into their own comic books. This required developing visual images and dialogue. The experience resulted in richer word choices, as they became more aware of the visualization involved in writing. Such an activity emphasizes sequence, inferences, and characterization.

Read-Alouds

What types of materials may teachers best use for read-alouds?

Read-alouds by the teacher from literature that would cause reading difficulty for some students can enhance content area studies and can entice students to read other sources. Middle school teachers find value in reading to their students daily (Albright and Ariail, 2005; Ivey 2003). Read-alouds can broaden students' horizons, encourage listening skills, model fluent and expressive reading, engender pleasure in reading, spark writing and discussion, and invite listeners to read. The National Commission on Reading (Anderson, Hiebert, Scott, and Wilkinson, 1985) encouraged reading aloud to students throughout the grades, including secondary school. Read-alouds may be used to introduce topics, to make situations in texts that students read for themselves more comprehensible, and to show how content area material applies to real life. Read-alouds also serve to introduce students to more types (or genres) of books than they might otherwise encounter. These read-alouds have been found to provide motivation for middle school students and catalysts for their learning.

MATHEMATICS   SCIENCE AND
HEALTH

ENGLISH/
LANGUAGE
ARTS

Many award-winning adolescent-literature selections are related to content area studies, and they make excellent read-aloud choices, as do some books that are written primarily for younger audiences or adults. Other choices include picture books that delve into complex issues and newspaper and magazine articles that are related to class content (Albright and Ariail, 2005). *The Phantom Tollbooth* by Norton Juster has a good explanation of infinity that may enlighten middle school math students and E. Annie Proulx's *Postcards* has a description of a ground blizzard that could be used in a science class. Richard Lederer's *Anguished English* and *More Anguished English*, both popular with high school students, are good materials for alerting students to such problems as dangling modifiers and words that are not quite appropriate for the context (Nilsen and Nilsen, 1999). Some examples were drawn from statements made by high school students in essays, adding to the interest factor.

Teachers must prepare for read-alouds and make their purpose obvious to the students. Material to be read aloud must be previewed to ensure appropriate content and fluent presentation. Teachers can model their thinking processes while reading through think-alouds. They should hold class discussions before, during, and after read-alouds (Albright and Ariail, 2005). Selecting related books for students to read independently can be a good technique (Fisher, Flood, Lapp, and Frey, 2004).

What are the advantages of using audiobooks in a secondary school classroom?

An extension of the idea of read-alouds is the use of **audiobooks**. Listening to audiobooks can add the dimension of hearing authentic accents, phrasing, and emphasis for characters in stories. Dialects become more manageable than they are on the printed page. Correct pronunciations of proper names are heard. Good timing, emphasis, pause, and stress make humor more understandable for some readers. Poetry, especially, can be presented with a model of expert phrasing, accent, rhythm, and pronunciation that can enhance comprehension (Baskin and Harris, 1995). Students, especially those who cannot read at the level necessary to perform adequately in a secondary class, can read along with unabridged, single narrator audiobooks. This can help students sense text subtleties. Many selections are available on recordings read by the authors. Some examples are Madeleine L'Engle's *A Wrinkle in Time* and Sir William Golding's *Lord of the Flies*. Elizabeth George Speare's *The Witch of Blackbird Pond;* Markus Zusak's *The Book Thief;* Mildred D. Taylor's *Roll of Thunder, Hear My Cry;* Pam Muñoz Ryan's *Esperanza Rising,* and many other selections are available in recordings by people other than the authors. Abridgments should be used with caution.

ENGLISH/
LANGUAGE
ARTS

The temptation to ease the reading burden on students by using videos in place of the books from which they were made should be resisted in many cases. Video versions of books often have simplified vocabulary, dialogue, plots, settings, themes, and characterizations. They may sometimes be used, however, to prompt an interest in reading the books. For example, teachers may have students read a book that will soon be released as a video. They may ask students to write and perhaps perform their own screenplays based on these books or to create multimedia presentations based on the literature. After the students see the videos, they can compare the videos with the books or write traditional reviews (Baines, 1996). They can also compare the videos with the screenplays that they wrote.

Literature Instruction

ENGLISH/
LANGUAGE
ARTS

Literature instruction is designed to turn students into lifelong readers who enjoy good literature. Incorporating interesting literary selections into secondary classes helps teachers achieve this goal. These selections may be presented in a literature anthology or as trade books, and they should include a variety of genres. Students need some direct instruction in literary analysis and guided experiences with reading required literature selections, especially classics that may have unfamiliar settings and characters. Learning about authors also can help students analyze their writing. Good choices for instruction may be Walter Dean Myers's *Bad Boy*, Gary Paulsen's *Guts*, and Bruce Brooks's *What Hearts* (Knickerbocker and Rycik, 2002; Ernst-Slavit, Moore, and Maloney, 2002; and Louie, 2005).

Offering choices in student reading results in higher motivation to read. Teachers can provide a theme or question to which the reading must be related and then allow the students to choose reading material from a number of types of texts that the teachers identify, including materials that represent multiple genres. Book club discussions on books related to the theme or question allow the students to share insights into the selections and enlarge their engagement and understanding (Lapp and Fisher, 2009).

Teaching students to use a preview technique called *Chapter Glancing* can help students read a book thoughtfully. With this procedure, the students are shown a sheet with two columns: one is for the chapter title or number, and the second is for the first paragraph of the chapter. Room is left between chapters for notes. As each beginning paragraph is read, the teacher asks the students for their thoughts about it and uses comments to extend their thinking. As subsequent paragraphs are discussed, the students may discuss how the chapters are connected. The information in the discussions serves as a scaffold for the subsequent reading of the book (Morgan and Williams, 2007).

Mini-Lessons

Teachers may teach mini-lessons on literary topics or reading strategies before the students begin reading, when a reading workshop approach is used in which students read, write in response journals, meet in literature circles to discuss their reading, and develop projects from the reading to share with their classmates. Modeling a strategy through a think-aloud is a good technique to use for a mini-lesson. When teaching a difficult piece, such as *Romeo and Juliet*, for example, the teacher may use a think-aloud based on the beginning of the work to demonstrate paraphrasing, using background knowledge, predicting, visualizing, and using metacognitive strategies when readers do not understand (Adams, 1995). (Think-alouds are discussed in detail in Chapter 6. Paraphrasing is discussed in Chapter 9, and the other strategies mentioned are covered in Chapters 5 and 6.)

To prepare students to work with characterization, Manyak (2007) has students brainstorm about characters' traits. Then he presents them with a set of new terms that could be applied to the characters being discussed, introducing one new word at a time with a definition and example. He asks which characters the word could be used to describe and why the word would fit those characters. This builds new vocabulary and encourages students to look more analytically at the characters in a story. Students should be encouraged to consider both the outer and inner aspects of the characters, including their appearance, behavior, feelings, and goals (Roser, Martinez, Fuhrken, and McDonnold, 2007).

Use of Reading Guides

If the selections are related to students' schemata, they will be easier to comprehend. Reading guides, such as anticipation guides and three-level study guides, can help many students comprehend literature selections better. Study guides are described in more detail in Chapter 6.

A three-level guide can be especially useful with literature selections. The guide in Example 10.1 is designed for use with the short story "The Man without a Country" by Edward Everett Hale.

The main value of reading guides is the discussion that follows their completion. Students should share their answers and their reasons for the answers.

EXAMPLE 10.1   **Three-Level Study Guide**

ENGLISH/ LANGUAGE ARTS

Directions: Check the statement or statements under each level that answer the question.

Literal—What Did the Author Say About Philip Nolan?

_____ **1.** Philip Nolan said, "I wish I may never hear of the United States again!"

_____ **2.** Philip Nolan never actually met Aaron Burr.

_____ **3.** The court decided that Nolan should never hear the name of the United States again.

_____ **4.** Nolan was placed on board a ship and never allowed to return to the United States.

_____ **5.** Nolan was often permitted to go on shore.

_____ **6.** Nolan did not intentionally make it difficult for the people who were supposed to keep him from knowing about his country.

Interpretive—What Did the Author Mean by His Story?

_____ **1.** Nolan never seriously regretted having denied his country.

_____ **2.** Nolan spoke against his country without realizing how much it had meant to him.

_____ **3.** Nolan never really missed hearing about his country.

Applied—How Can the Meaning Be Applied to Our Lives?

_____ **1.** People should consider the consequences of their actions before they act.

_____ **2.** People can live comfortably away from home.

_____ **3.** Punishment is not always physical; it may be mental.

Electronic Discussions

The use of a networked computer lab equipped with collaboration software allows students to discuss literary works by keying in responses to their classmates' comments, using a simple word-processing program. This technique often encourages shy students to respond more. The discussions can be controlled through the choice of questions presented to the students. The discussions work best with only one question per conference. There can be several conferences in a fifty-minute class, covering different questions.

Internet discussion groups that are password protected, to allow only students from designated classes to participate, are another option. Additionally, there are Internet sites where writers can post their work to be critiqued.

SOCIAL STUDIES

Eighth-grade students read Ellis's *The Breadwinner*, discussed it in groups, and then wrote about it on an online discussion board. The procedure resulted in increased engagement with the text and helped them to connect the text to their own knowledge base (Grisham and Wolsey, 2006). Larson (2009) had students respond to teacher prompts and then read and reply to their classmates' comments on novels they were reading to connect with study of U.S. History. Later, after some instruction in how to write good prompts, the students were allowed to start new threads in the discussion with their own prompts. These prompts helped the students to connect the novels with their experiences, eliciting feelings about the texts; to think about the material critically and creatively; and to clarify confusing parts.

E-mail discussions of literature can be shared by placing all students and the teacher on a class mailing list. "Reply to all" responses allow all class members to see the comments made by each individual.

Whole-Class Novel Study

What is a social constructivist perspective of learning?

Unrau and Ruddell (1995) present a Text and Classroom Context model "designed with a **social constructivist perspective** of learning in which the teacher fosters a learning environment that engages students in a meaning negotiation process" (p. 21). Meanings evolve from interactions among the reader, the text, the classroom community, the teacher, and the context. Readers must confirm that the constructed interpretations of the text are grounded in the text, reasonably supportable by reference to the content of the text, for, as Rosenblatt (1983) has pointed out, to understand a work, the reader must recreate the ideas that the author presents and assimilate them with his or her own knowledge.

When applying this model to class study of a novel, the students can first read the novel and then write summaries or interpretations in their learning logs. Then they can discuss the novel in groups of three. Each member of the group is given a responsibility—recorder, reporter, or prompter (who keeps the group on task). Interpretations voiced during discussion are not seen as final but are revised as the dialogue continues. The text is fixed, but its meanings for readers change over time. Whole-class discussions can follow small-group meetings or can be guided by use of a directed reading-thinking activity (DRTA) or other strategies that encourage individual responses and group sharing (Unrau and Ruddell, 1995). (See Chapter 6 for a discussion of the DRTA.)

Casey (2008/2009) recommends book clubs or learning clubs that are based on the students' interests. The literacy activities are not just tied to single literature selections, but "may include magazines, fiction, the Internet, videos, photographs, and conversations with 'experts'" (p. 285). Students may help one another with difficult vocabulary, do comparisons and contrasts between themselves and characters in a story being studied, and create character storyboards, among other learning activities they may choose or be assigned.

Literature Response Groups (Literature Circles)

What are the benefits of literature response groups?

In **literature response groups,** or literature circles, several students who have chosen to read the same novel read a specific number of chapters each week and meet in a group each week to discuss the reading. Students choose novels from several for which the teacher has multiple copies (preferably six to eight copies). Students can indicate their top three choices, and the teacher can form groups to read the top choices, taking preferences into account. Each time the groups complete their novels, new groups may be formed for different selections. Students who did not get their first choices for the first books read should be given preference in getting their first choices for the next books.

As students read, they can make notes on "sticky notes" or strips of paper shaped like bookmarks and place them on the appropriate pages. These notes can be used as a basis for the small-group discussion and for a written response to the reading that the teacher may require them to do either before or after the discussion. These responses can be read aloud as a review to begin the next week's discussion.

Alternatively, students may write responses in reading response journals. They may include changes in a character, things they questioned, things they felt about the characters or the plot, and/or things that they can relate to personal experiences or other books they have read. The teacher can respond to these journals periodically, and the entries can be shared aloud in class and discussed.

The teacher may meet with the groups, or they may meet independently. The teacher should only intervene in the discussion when the students have strayed from the topic or missed important points (Simpson, 1994/1995). It may help for the teacher to participate in a group to model appropriate behavior. For example, the teacher can model active listening, asking for other opinions to be offered, building on points that another person has made, finding evidence in the book, and making connections (Clarke and Holwadel, 2007).

Sustained Silent Reading (SSR)

What are the benefits of sustained silent reading in a content area class?

Readers become more fluent in reading by actually reading. In a **sustained silent reading** (SSR) program, students are given a block of time to read self-selected materials for pleasure. Secondary students may be given from fifteen to thirty minutes to read without interruption and without the threat of testing or reporting that inhibits some readers. The teacher also reads self-selected material during this time. Nobody is allowed to interrupt the reading of the others. There must be a plentiful supply of appropriate and interesting texts available, teacher encouragement, a regularly scheduled time, and a lack of testing (Clausen-Grace and Kelley, 2007). Offering students time in class for self-selected reading shows that teachers value it.

Simpson (1994/1995) points out that students can be allowed to discuss the books read during SSR, but we feel that discussion should not be required. DeBenedictis (2007) lets her students read and write or draw about what they are reading for twenty to twenty-five minutes and then discuss the reading, writing, and drawing for ten to twenty minutes. The students are invited to share if they want to do so. If they request permission to do so, they are allowed to work quietly with a partner during the initial period.

Hartley (2008) was not having success in getting students to read self-selected books until she got her students involved in choosing the reading materials for the classroom library. She found them more ready to read magazines, graphic novels, nonfiction, and fiction selections based on television shows than they had been to read her original classroom selections.

Readers' Theater

Readers' theater is the expressive interpretation of a story through oral reading by a cast of readers who use a script developed from the story. Different students read characters' dialogue and narration. As a response to a literature selection that is read, small groups or individual students can be asked to prepare readers' theater scripts to be performed for the class. If an individual develops the script, he or she can assign classmates to the different parts. If a small group develops the script, the members may perform the reading themselves.

Students who take the parts practice reading their parts until they are reading fluently with good expression. Then they perform the readers' theater for the class. The performance consists of sitting or standing before the class and reading the script, as a cast would read a play.

Quinn, Barone, Kearns, Stackhouse, and Zimmerman (2003) found that developing and performing readers' theater scripts was motivational for reluctant readers. They expanded the activity to have the students role-play the scripts, and they found that the students were more successful when they acted out the story than when they simply read it. The "Meeting the Challenge" vignette on page 326 shows how a readers' theater presentation can be used to motivate students to read a literature selection.

Directed Reading Lessons

A directed reading lesson such as that in Example 10.2 is another way for teachers to help students read and understand books. Directed reading lessons are discussed in detail in Chapter 6.

EXAMPLE 10.2   **Directed Reading Lesson: Literature**

Motivation and Building Background

**ENGLISH/
LANGUAGE
ARTS**

1. Ask the students these questions: Do you know any good ghost stories? Have you ever sat around with a group of friends telling ghost stories? How did you feel later, particularly if you had to go some place alone? You probably felt the way Ichabod Crane felt in this story after he listened to some ghost stories and rode home alone over country roads.

2. Tell the students that the story they are going to read is a ghost story. The characters in this story include a pedagogue; a hero; a rosy-cheeked maiden; and a contented farmer. After they read the story, they should try to name each of the characters listed.

Skill Development Activities

3. Have the students match a number of words from the story with their definitions.

Words	Definitions
continual reverie	German soldiers
Hessian troopers	singing of psalms
spectre	constant daydream
psalmody	ghost

Guided Reading

4. Silent—Have the students read the story silently. Tell them to think about these purpose questions as they read: What factors created an atmosphere for the ghost to appear? What happened to Ichabod?

5. Discussion—After the students have read the selection, use these questions for further discussion:
   a. How would you characterize the residents of Sleepy Hollow?
   b. Is the setting important in this story? Why?
   c. Do you think Katrina was really interested in Ichabod? Why?
   d. How are Brom Bones and Ichabod Crane alike? How are they different?
   e. What was the point of view of this story?
   f. Do you agree with the old man about the purpose of this story? What do you think the purpose was?

Follow-Up Activities

6. Have students write a paragraph telling what they would have done if they were Ichabod.
7. Ask students to read another story written by Washington Irving and compare it with "The Legend of Sleepy Hollow."
8. Have students draw a picture of the way they visualize Ichabod.

MEETING THE CHALLENGE

ENGLISH/
LANGUAGE
ARTS

As a way to motivate students to read *Macbeth* and build their background for reading it, Cindy McCloud made use of a readers' theater activity. Before class, she gave a readers' theater script of the witches' scene in Macbeth to a selected group of students, who would take the parts of the witches and Macbeth. These students were asked to practice and polish the reading of their parts. The other students in the class were not told about this activity ahead of time.

When class started, Ms. McCloud told the class to close their eyes. Then she said, "Imagine a fantastical cave filled with fog. In the entrance of the cave you see lights flickering. These lights grow dim and get brighter, then dimmer, then brighter. This piques your curiosity: you must know what these strange lights are. You walk further into the cave and spot three of the strangest looking women you have ever seen. Of course, their very appearance gives you a terrible scare, and you hide behind a rock and peer over it just enough to see what they are doing. These three cloaked, bearded figures are conjuring up a powerful spell."

Interesting introductions can motivate students to read literature selections.

Dana White/PhotoEdit

As the rest of the class continued to imagine the scene, Ms. McCloud cued the designated students to take the parts they had been assigned and begin to read the scene in character. The other students were allowed to open their eyes as the selected students read the scene, acting out with appropriate gestures the part in which the witches conjure up their potion.

This interest-grabbing introduction to the play prepared the students for the subsequent reading. Students who previously had no interest in the play now saw that it had possibilities and were willing to give it a chance.

Activities to Encourage Students' Response to Literature

ENGLISH/
LANGUAGE
ARTS

Whether literature is used as the focus of study in an English class or literature selections are used as tools for study in other content areas, students need to be led to respond to the content of the selections.

Written Responses

Written responses are valuable tools. Reading response journals, character journals, dialogue journals, learning logs, freewriting in response to reading, paraphrasing and summarizing, and creative responses (e.g., writing letters to story characters, news stories about characters, or even fan fiction) are all written responses that have been covered in detail in Chapter 9 or in this chapter. Wolk (2009, p. 671) says, "Most of the writing students do in response to books should be authentic: essays, letters, speeches, poetry and monologues are examples of authentic writing that can be done to connect young adult fiction to issues of social responsibility and the larger world around us."

Lehr and Thompson (2000) suggest the use of assigned journal writing activities (for example, letters supposedly written by a character in the book to someone, explaining the character's problems or feelings). Assigned writing could be a good way to help students see things from the perspective of others who are different from them in culture, race, age, gender, or some other aspect. Other written responses could include writing letters to the author for clarification of information, comparing and contrasting the work with other works, making timelines for the stories, or mapping the story's literary elements (setting, characters, plot, etc.).

In out-of-school situations, teenagers often write fan fiction, which creates new story episodes for the characters in a novel. They may respond to the chance to write fan fiction about a novel that is read for class. As Cherland (2008/2009, p. 280) says, "It requires the ability to read and write critically, against the grain, and to think beyond what we already know, abilities we would like to foster in all teens."

Oral Responses

The most valuable oral responses to literature are the small-group and whole-class discussions that have been mentioned repeatedly as important learning tools in the classroom. Group members share insights that individuals might not achieve alone (Knickerbocker and Rycik, 2002). Another type of oral response is the conversion of the material into a readers' theater presentation, with students dividing the material into speaking parts along content or character lines and reading the material orally with good oral expression.

**TeachSource
Video Case**
Performance
Assessment: Student
Presentations in a High
School English Class

Perhaps the most difficult oral response option is dramatization of the material. This dramatization can range from a spontaneous reenactment of an event or scene, without written script, costumes, properties, scenery, or audience beyond the class members, to a carefully planned presentation, with a student-developed script, memorized lines, costumes, properties, scenery, and an outside audience. Drama can evoke an aesthetic response to the literature. In addition, interpretation of literature is expanded through drama because it takes the students into the events to experience them vicariously. This immersion in the experience helps the students to see the points of view of the people involved in the events (Fennessey, 1995). For example, Leslie Kahn encouraged students to use drama to help them reflect on prejudice expressed in *We Remember the Holocaust* by David Adler (Short, Kauffman, and Kahn, 2000).

Developing Thematic Teaching Units

What is a thematic teaching unit?

A **thematic teaching unit** is a series of interrelated lessons or class activities organized around a theme, a literary form, or a skill. Sometimes a single book or a cluster of literature selections form the basis for the unit. More often, the textbook, supplementary literature, Internet sites, and other supplementary material are included. Such a unit allows holistic study of the topic. Meaningful units incorporate the types of situations and activities through which people learn outside of school (Barton and Smith, 2000). Because unit activities are varied in terms of the amount of reading skill and the levels of thinking required, they offer excellent opportunities to adjust reading assignments to fit all students. Different students may complete different activities, such as reading, listening to, and/or viewing different resource materials, and share the results of these varied activities with their classmates.

What are the steps in creating a thematic unit?

Use of teaching units takes a great deal of teacher planning. The teacher must develop objectives for a unit that are in keeping with the curriculum and standards for the discipline, must decide on skills to be developed, and must plan appropriate activities. The students may be involved in deciding on objectives and activities within the framework of the curriculum requirements. Parents may also become involved in unit activities if teachers send home memos about the themes that the class is studying and suggestions on how the parents can help the learning process by sharing personal knowledge about the topic with their children or with the entire class.

The web shown in Figure 10.1 depicts the parts of a unit graphically. A unit generally involves four basic types of activities:

1. Introduction of the unit

2. Development of the unit

3. Organization of findings

4. Culmination activities

Introduction of the Unit

The students are introduced to the unit's theme or central idea, the literary form to be explored, or the skills to be developed. Through class discussion and/or pretests, the teacher determines the extent to which the students' backgrounds of experience in the area can contribute to the unit activities. The teacher helps students develop questions that they need to answer about the unit theme. During this discussion, the teacher assists the students in relating the area of study to their own personal experiences or needs. Doing brainstorming or using semantic webs of concepts or terms related to the unit theme may be effective in activating the students' background knowledge and in facilitating the discussion. The teacher may supply motivation for participating in the unit activities by playing audio or video recordings related to the subject. Some units can start with a book that the students form a question or set of inquiry questions about (Wolk, 2009). One teacher started a unit on World War II with the students writing about a "day that will live in infamy" from their own lives, which elicited memories of September 11, 2001, from some and memories of family upheavals from others. For other units she developed DVDs with video clips, music, and photos that she had collected

SOCIAL STUDIES

FIGURE 10.1

Unit Development Web

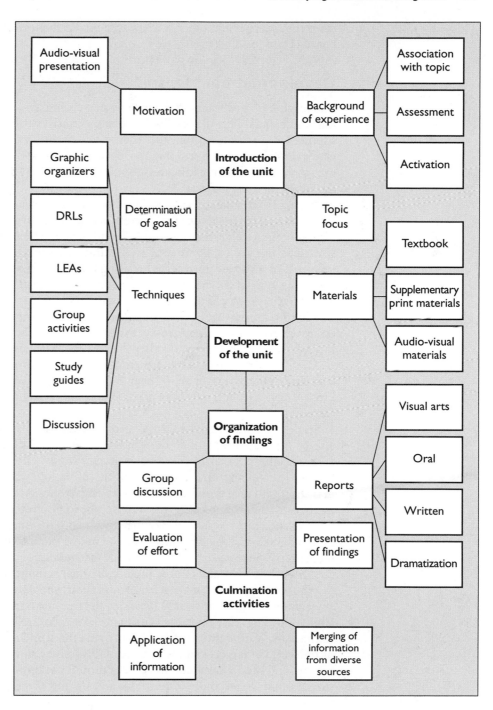

from the Internet and other sources and shared them using an interactive white-board (Hansen, 2009, p. 602).

Development of the Unit

The teacher begins teaching the unit by presenting core instructional material to the whole class. This material will probably consist of the textbook material and supplementary material that the teacher has carefully chosen for those students who cannot benefit from reading the text because of its difficulty level. The teacher may develop directed reading lessons (DRLs) for both the textbook material and the supplementary material.

During the first step of some of the directed reading lessons, the teacher may use structured overviews to develop needed background for reading. Next, using techniques presented in Chapters 4, 5, 6, 7, and 8, he or she may teach needed reading strategies and skills that are vital to the understanding of the particular passages involved. As a part of the directed reading lesson, the teacher may guide the actual student reading of the material by means of a study guide. The students can combine what they have learned through class discussion and language experience activities. The follow-up activities will be included among the independent assignments for research groups or interest groups formed by the teacher or by student choice or for individual student activities after the core material has been read.

After the core instructional presentation, the teacher may either assign areas of concern to the students or allow them to choose areas in which they have a particular interest. Self-selection may have the advantage of providing internal motivation for the unit study.

Students then form several small groups (research groups that may or may not also be interest groups) that attempt to answer specific questions, clarify specific areas of concern, or analyze particular literary works. These research groups may be formed to capitalize on the special abilities of various class members. The teacher may meet with each group to discuss the possible reference sources that are available: textbooks, library books (fiction and nonfiction), encyclopedias, other reference books, magazines, newspapers, original documents, the Internet, videos, and a variety of other audio-visual aids. Many units, including inquiry units, would benefit from inclusion of poetry, a genre that content teachers sometimes overlook (Wilhelm, 2009). Students may also choose to do individual activities.

Whenever applicable, the teacher should choose books that reflect a multicultural environment, and there should be access to large-print books, Braille materials, or audio recordings that cover the class material if there are visually impaired students in the class. Multicultural resources provide the students with a realistic picture of the world at large, even if the cultural diversity within the particular school is narrow, and they allow students whose cultural backgrounds vary from the main-stream culture to feel more comfortable and see how their culture fits into the overall picture.

The teacher must make available books and reference aids on a number of different levels. Students then can choose books, articles, and poems for their thematic study that are appropriate to their own reading abilities. A review of study skills, such as using the library, using reference books, outlining, taking notes, skimming, and scanning, may be helpful for some students. (See Chapters 7 and 8 for a discussion of these skills.) In addition, nonprint resources, such as audio and video recordings may be used for some less able readers.

Each member of each research group is responsible for collecting data. Differentiated assignments within the groups may be developed by the teacher or by group leaders guided by the teacher.

Organization of Findings

The research groups meet after ample time has been allowed for individual members to collect data. Each group then reviews the information collected from the various sources, discusses and attempts to resolve differences of opinion, and forms the findings into a coherent report. The discussion allows the students to share the information they have discovered and to find out what others have learned. The report may be accompanied by audiovisual aids, such as charts, tables, maps, graphs, pictures, or videos. It may be in one of a number of forms, including an oral or written report, a panel discussion, a dramatization, a mural, or a multimedia presentation. Some students may also present the results of individual research.

Culmination Activities

At the end of the unit study, the different research groups and individuals present their reports to the whole class. The class critically examines the information that is presented, merges it with the core of information learned from the textbook and supplementary materials, and determines whether the purposes of the unit have been met or the students need to regroup to finish the task.

SOCIAL
STUDIES

At the end of a World War II unit, eleventh-grade students each took on the identity of a person who had lived through the war, and, based on research done on the person or the group to which that person belonged, developed a scrapbook of mementos this person might have collected, then shared their "memories" with their classmates, all of whom acted in character (Hansen, 2009).

The teacher should help the students relate the findings to events in their own lives. An activity that immediately applies the findings to real situations is beneficial because it emphasizes the relevance of the unit.

Table 10.1 presents the steps in unit development.

Sample Unit Ideas

ENGLISH/
LANGUAGE
ARTS

A unit in literature might be developed around a type of literature, such as "Tall Tales of the United States." The opening discussion could include an attempt to define "tall tales" and could provide opportunities for the students to name tall tales with which they are familiar. The teacher might use a video during the introductory stage to clarify the nature of tall tales. Different groups could be formed to read

TABLE 10.1

Unit Development

Introduction	Development	Organization of Findings	Culmination
1. Build background and motivation 2. Connect unit to students' experiences	1. Core lessons presented through a directed reading approach, use of structured overviews, teaching of needed skills, study guides, language experience approach 2. Research groups 3. Needs groups	1. Discussion 2. Oral or written reports	1. Merging of Information from diverse Sources 2. Evaluation of effort 3. Application of Information

tall tales about different superhuman individuals, for example, Old Stormalong, Paul Bunyan, Mike Fink, and Pecos Bill. Other groups could concentrate on tall tales of other types, such as Washington Irving's "Rip Van Winkle" and "The Legend of Sleepy Hollow" or Mark Twain's "The Celebrated Jumping Frog of Calaveras County." As a culminating activity, each student could write a tall tale of the type that he or she has read. The tales could be shared in oral or written form with the rest of the class.

**ENGLISH/
LANGUAGE
ARTS**

In a poetry unit for tenth-graders, Meeks (1999) first immerses her students in poetry by having them read poems and choose favorites to copy for their portfolios and to share with the class on charts. She also shares her favorite poetry and her own poetry. She demonstrates the reading and writing of poetry to the students and then lets the students try. She makes clear her expectations for the students' poetry reading, writing, and collection, but she gives the students the responsibility for choosing group members, poets to study, topics for written assignments, and presentation formats. After developing their poems through a process writing approach, the students share their poems in real-world situations, such as reading them to senior citizens or posting them on the Internet. Meeks responds to the students' poetry writing by using stickers or by highlighting interesting parts.

**ENGLISH/
LANGUAGE
ARTS**

A unit on Shakespeare could include one or more of these introductory activities: a whole class reading and discussion of Gary D. Schmidt's *The Wednesday Wars*, Caroline B. Cooney's *Enter Three Witches: A Story of Macbeth*, or Lisa Fiedler's *Dating Hamlet: Ophelia's Story*; literature circles on Gary Blackwood's books, *The Shakespeare Stealer*, *Shakespeare's Scribe*, and *Shakespeare's Spy* or Susan Cooper's *King of Shadows*, with each group doing an oral report detailing the information that they learned about Shakespeare's times and the lives of the actors; a whole class viewing of a video or a live presentation of a Shakespearean play. The class could then read one or more of the plays. Several are available as graphic novels, and there may be more than one graphic novel available for a particular play, so the teacher can match the version chosen to the students' needs. Some of the reading could be done in the form of reader's theater in class. Class activities could include having students develop webpages for particular characters in the plays or tweets that a character might write, write character pro-files for characters, do research on the dispute about who wrote Shakespeare's plays, compare *Romeo and Juliet* to *West Side Story* or compare any Shakespearean play to a contemporary book or movie. Books for individual reading and report-ing could include Avi's *Romeo and Juliet Together (and Alive!) At Last*; Jennifer Lee Carrell's *Interred with Their Bones*; and J. B. Cheaney's *The Playmaker* and *The True Prince*. A culminating activity could be for the class to enact one of the plays or a portion of the play, with or without costumes or props, or for small groups to enact favorite scenes for the rest of the class. (See Davis, 2009, for more ideas of books to use with such a unit.)

SOCIAL
STUDIES

Hansen (2009) describes a unit on slavery that involved the use of websites, paintings, poetry, and literature selections, in addition to the textbook. The non-textbook materials provided specific details that made the topic real and personal to the students. One African-American student wrote to the textbook publisher, complaining that the lack of detail and emotion in the text was inadequate to inform the students about the institution of slavery. Students learn history more effectively when they are allowed to examine it critically and relate to it emotionally.

SOCIAL
STUDIES

In a study of the American Revolution and its aftermath, the students dramatized actions that took place in the colonies, such as riots and town meetings. They wrote speeches to convince their fellow colonists of the injustices of the British. They took key vocabulary words, such as *confederation, tariff,* and *sovereign* and both defined and illustrated the meanings. Their drawings often connected the meanings to their current lives. Cartoons and photographs were used to enrich the study, as well (Hansen, 2009).

SOCIAL
STUDIES

The "Meeting the Challenge" in this section includes excerpts from a unit on the Holocaust. The detailed planning that precedes the teaching of this unit makes it likely to be successful with students. Any unit on a content subject needs stated concepts to be learned, resources to be used, and instructional activities that are planned before the unit begins. Other resources and activities may be located and used as a result of student–teacher interactions as the unit progresses. Possible unit resources include textbooks, fiction and nonfiction trade books, electronic media (such as CDs and DVDs), and Internet sites.

SOCIAL
STUDIES

Because textbook presentations are by necessity brief and condensed, good units provide much supplementary material that fills in gaps and fleshes out the infor-mation for students. The "Meeting the Challenge" is part of a unit developed by a student in a graduate-level methods course who realized the limited viewpoint offered to students by a single textbook presentation. This unit originally had additional information for student use and teacher resources, but space does not allow their inclusion. The author of the unit found bountiful reading material that provided high levels of student interest and was pertinent to the topic.

Developing a unit similar to the one in this vignette would be possible in almost any content area. Both nonfiction and fiction trade books are available on a wide variety of subjects. Librarians and media specialists are generally happy to work with classroom teachers in locating appropriate trade books to complement unit studies.

MEETING THE CHALLENGE

SOCIAL STUDIES

In an attempt to incorporate her knowledge of the values of student involvement in learning, multiple readings of various types, and integration of literature into content area study into a practical teaching plan, Jill Ramsey developed a unit plan for the study of the Holocaust.

Literature-Based Unit on the Holocaust

BEGINNING HOLOCAUST STUDIES

OVERALL OBJECTIVES OF THE UNIT

Through the reading of literature related to the Holocaust it is the hope that students:

- Gain an understanding of the concepts of diversity, culture, community, prejudice, human rights, acting morally, and taking a stand.
- Share a vision of a world where people are embraced for their similarities and appreciated for their differences.
- Gain an understanding of the harm caused by prejudice and an ability to confront prejudice individually and as part of a community.
- Demonstrate an ability to think critically about human behavior.
- Demonstrate a desire to act morally.

PROCEDURES

I.   Literature Books to Be Used:
  A. Read Aloud: *Number the Stars*
  B. Historical fiction: *The Upstairs Room*
  C. Historical nonfiction: *Anne Frank: The Diary of a Young Girl*, *Anne Frank: Beyond the Diary*, *Tell Them We Remember*, *The Hidden Children*, and *Surviving Hitler: A Boy in the Nazi Death Camp*
  D. Picture books: *The Butterfly*, *I Never Saw Another Butterfly*, *October '45: Childhood Memories of War*, *The Children of Topaz*, and *Terrible Things*

II. Oral testimony

III. Photographs

IV. PowerPoint presentation

V.   History (textbooks, websites, trade books, timelines)

VI. Narrow problem/question/issue/project unit
  A. How did children and adolescents make the best of the worst times in the history of mankind? In what ways were they resourceful, creative, and willing to make sacrifices that affected their entire lives?
  B. What happens when prejudice causes people to lose everything that they had, and then to start all over in a new place, where they are still not wanted?
  C. What are the lessons of this horrible time in history called the Holocaust? Why do we study them today?

VII. Connections to the Holocaust
  A. People, regardless of perceived or real differences, are fundamentally alike.
  B. Communities contain the potential for both acceptance and rejection of their members.

C. Families in communities performed important functions that helped many.

D. The Holocaust provides a context for exploring the dangers of remaining silent, apathetic, and indifferent in the face of others' oppression.

E. Students must think about use and abuse of power and the roles and responsibilities of individuals, organizations, and nations when confronted with civil rights violations and/or policies of genocide.

F. During the Holocaust, people had roles that were assumed or thrust upon them, such as victim, perpetrator, bystander, and rescuer.

G. Students need to confront prejudice, deal with moral issues, and gain a deeper respect for human decency.

H. Students can empathize with people who have survived hardship by listening to the stories of those who survived the Holocaust.

I. Bystanders during the Holocaust closed their hearts and minds to the suffering of others; bystanders exist today; students need to learn values so that they are able to reason morally and take appropriate action; students can learn about the risks and rewards of taking action against injustice.

J. Knowledge gives students the power to learn from the past and take action in the future.

VIII. Activities

A. Student self-learning activities:
   1. Literature circles (reading, discussion, journaling, researching)
   2. Connecting other curricular areas with centers that incorporate the following: social studies, writing, science, geography, art, and music as appropriate to this subject matter

B. Research of a topic

C. Peer learning activities: Discussion; creation of timelines, tiles, bulletin boards; oral history interviews; use of research materials to locate answers to complex questions; study pair activities; small group shared reading/writing

D. Teacher-directed or teacher-guided activities: Focus lessons; read aloud with overheads and text discussion; KWL; semantic mapping, story mapping, concept maps; shared writing; lecture; shared reading; discussion

IX. Outcomes

Children learn prejudice early in their lives. But, just as prejudice and hate can be taught, so can the opposite values of tolerance, acceptance, and love. Schools are one of the best hopes for instilling this in students, reducing the possibility of future genocide. Students must understand that without knowledge and understanding history does repeat. Never Again!

X. Additional Ideas for Student Introduction

A. Use a KWL about what is known about this time in history, and what students want to learn.

B. Give historical time frame and background information. (Historical background not included for space considerations.)

C. Begin a double timeline on adding machine tape with historical dates on the top, students to complete literature dates and activities on the bottom. This helps them put their books in accurate time frames of history.

D. Show what resources may be used as references during readings in literature circles.

E. Introduce vocabulary for literature of the Holocaust.

BUILDING A CONTEXT TO STUDY THE HOLOCAUST

TERRIBLE THINGS: AN ALLEGORY OF THE HOLOCAUST

OVERVIEW

Terrible Things is an award-winning picture book illustrated with black-and-white drawings. The "Terrible Things" of the title are never distinctly shown. They always appear as swirling dark clouds that sometimes suggest human shapes and at other times suggest huge, menacing animals.

An allegory is a picture or story that has a meaning beyond the one conveyed in the obvious story line. *Terrible Things* is a good starting point for trying to help students understand what happened during the Holocaust.

Together, read the book *Terrible Things* (have copies for every two students to share). Have students take turns reading the roles of Little Rabbit, Big Rabbit, and the other animals.

After the class has had a chance to reflect on what they've just read, spend time on the discussion questions.

Then ask students to list on the board some of the questions Little Rabbit asks about the Terrible Things and the answers Big Rabbit gives.

LITTLE RABBIT'S QUESTIONS

- "Why did the Terrible Things want the birds?"
- "What's wrong with feathers?"
- "But why did the Terrible Things take them away?"
- "Do the Terrible Things want the clearing for themselves?"

BIG RABBIT'S RESPONSES

- "We mustn't ask."
- "The Terrible Things don't need a reason."
- "Be glad it wasn't us."
- "Just mind your own business."
- "We don't want them to get mad at us."

ASK STUDENTS

What is Big Rabbit trying to tell Little Rabbit? Do the answers satisfy Little Rabbit? How can you tell? What answers would you give to Little Rabbit's questions? What other questions would you ask? What does the story imply about non-Jews' reactions to the fate of the Jews and others during the Holocaust?

PROJECTS

Have students work individually or in groups to:
- Retell the story as a poem.
- Adapt the story as a play or readers' theater.

- Write the next chapter and answer these questions:
  Where does Little Rabbit go?
  How does he "tell other forest creatures"? What happens then?

CLASS DISCUSSION

1. Why do you think the author told the story of the Holocaust in this symbolic way? Who is this story directed to?
2. Why do you think the Terrible Things take away the animals one group at a time?
3. In an allegory, people, places, and events are used as symbols. What can the clearing in the woods stand for? What about the different animals? The Terrible Things?
4. What kinds of excuses do the other animals offer to explain the fate of each group as it is taken away? How do these reactions help the Terrible Things?
5. How are the Terrible Things described? What verbs are used to describe their actions? How do the descriptions affect your feelings about the Terrible Things?
6. During the Holocaust, terrible things were done by real people, people with faces, names, and life histories. Why do you think the author shows the Terrible Things as anonymous?
7. What choices do the animals in the clearing have when the Terrible Things come?
8. What would you say to Big Rabbit's statement, "We are the White Rabbits. It couldn't happen to us"?
9. When the Terrible Things come for the rabbits, what do the rabbits do? What choice does Little Rabbit make? Why? What does this tell you about the Terrible Things?
10. Little Rabbit hopes someone will listen to him. Why might no one listen? Read Martin Niemoller's poem "First They Came for the Jews" and discuss its relationship with *Terrible Things*. (Activity details omitted for length considerations.)

BOOK TALK

GRADE LEVELS: MIDDLE AND HIGH SCHOOL

OBJECTIVES
- To create a journal reflecting upon a Holocaust-themed book.
- To discuss a Holocaust-themed book and a personal response to it with others using e-mail.

MATERIALS
1. Sign-up sheet, directions worksheet, computer(s), paper, pens
2. Class collection of young adult books related to the Holocaust: *Anne Frank: The Diary of a Young Girl; Surviving Hitler: A Boy in the Nazi Death Camps; Tell Them We Remember; The Hidden Children; The Upstairs Room*

PROCEDURES
Prior to initiating this activity with your class, establish a relationship with a remote classroom, preferably outside of your school. You may consider posting a message on an Internet message board for teachers interested in being involved in this project.

When you have a partner class established, explain to students that they will be engaged in a unit-long reading/writing project via e-mail, corresponding with a remote classroom. Every student will be paired with a student from the participating class, based on the book they choose to read.

Pass around a sign-up sheet, where students may write their names and the names of the Holocaust books they have chosen to read. E-mail the participating teacher with the list of students and books so that students may be paired.

As students read their selected books, have them keep response journals about what they are reading. Instead of summarizing the material, they are to reflect upon it and relate what they have read to their own lives: Responses might begin with a brief summary, or the statement, "The themes of this book are . . .," but the main portion of the responses states, "This reminded me of a time in my life when . . ." or "These themes are relevant today because . . . ."

Students are to write in their journals and correspond with their remote reading partners once a week, sharing portions of their journals, questions they might have, new words, dilemmas, and issues brought up by the novel that left them puzzled. The mission is to create open book talks between the student pairs. E-mail correspondences are to be printed and kept within the journals. These will be collected at the end of the project.

After reading the book, each student is to complete one of the following projects:

- Write a letter through one character's perspective to another character in the book.
- Write a poem based on the book.
- Create a dictionary of terms that would help someone reading this book.
- Write a short story about the Holocaust.
- Write a one-act play based on the book; include appropriate stage directions.
- Any other ideas that are approved by the teacher.

Students may share their final projects with their e-mail partners as well as with their class.

ASSESSMENT

Evaluation will be based on the students' journals and projects they have completed.

MATERIALS
Multiple copies of *Anne Frank: Beyond the Diary* by Ruud van der Rol and Rian Verhoeven

LESSON 1
Assign students to read pages 3–36. Discuss these elements in this section of the book: the birthday present, the move from Frankfurt to Amsterdam, the map showing where Anne lived during her brief life (pp. 12, 13), the segment on Hitler coming to power, fleeing to another country, and German occupation of the Netherlands.

LESSON 2
Assign students to read pages 37–86.

Activity: The Nazis passed and implemented many anti-Jewish laws such as these—Jews may use only Jewish barbers; Jews must be indoors from 8:00 p.m. to 6:00 a.m., and so on. List at least six of these laws you have read about, pretend these laws were passed against your culture, and explain how the enforcement of such laws would change your life.

Discuss these elements of the book: Dear Kitty, actual pictures of Anne's diary and house, deportation of Jews, street map of Amsterdam, sister Margot and cutaway view of the house, and going into hiding.

LESSON 3

Assign students to read pages 87–107.

Activity: Discuss with the students the following hypothetical situation: If Anne Frank were alive today and coming to speak to their school or community, what do they think her message would be? Ask the students to create a poster advertising her presentation.

Discuss these elements in this section of the book: the diary is left behind; pictures from the concentration camps; and map of major concentration camps (pp. 91, 95), containing information on estimated number of Jews killed in various countries during the war.

LESSON 4

Discuss the quotation from Anne Frank's diary that appears on page 106 of the book: "You've known for a long time that my greatest wish is to become . . . a famous writer" (May 11, 1944).

• How has her wish come true?
• Why is this considered ironic?
• Would her wish have come true if she had lived?
• Why?

LITERATURE-RELATED ACTIVITIES

The following are some suggestions that Jill included for possible literature-related activities. Others have been omitted for space considerations.

1. Read *Number the Stars* by Lois Lowry.

In this story, a Christian family in Denmark risks their own lives to save the lives of a Jewish family. Discuss with the students that throughout history, there have been individuals or groups of people who have risked their lives in an effort to save others (e.g., the Underground Railroad to help free slaves in the United States). As a group, select one such effort, research it, and then create a full-page newspaper advertisement to let the world know about it. Finally, compare this effort with the efforts made to save the Jews during World War II.

In addition to *Number the Stars*, the following books related to the Jewish resistance might be used:
Rescue: The Story of How Gentiles Saved Jews in the Holocaust by Milton Meltzer
Raoul Wallenberg by Michael Nicholson and David Winner

2. Read some of the poems and share the drawings in *I Never Saw Another Butterfly* by Hana Volavkova.

After students have had the opportunity to peruse the book, ask them to create a poem with an illustration that will pay tribute to the children of Terezin and will demonstrate that they will always be remembered.

3. Read *Tell Them We Remember: The Story of the Holocaust* by Susan D. Bachrach.

Read the Afterword on page 86. The last paragraph states that the most pressing question on one of the tiles in the Holocaust Memorial Museum in Washington, D.C., is "Why?" Discuss the "Why?" with your students—why and how could something as atrocious as the Holocaust happen?

Two other books that Jill could have used are Markus Zusak's *The Book Thief* (discussed in Chapter 6) and John Boyne's *The Boy in the Striped Pajamas*.

FOCUS ON   *Struggling Readers*

Literature-Based and Thematic Approaches for Struggling Readers

Use of wordless picture books is beneficial in helping struggling readers develop oral and written language skills (Cassady, 1998). Students can discuss the pictures and then write about the content based upon the information that they have gained.

Comics offer a visual element that can help the struggling readers comprehend the text (McVicker, 2007). Graphic novels can also have this benefit.

Read-alouds allow struggling readers to be exposed to content from books that are beyond their reading levels. Class discussion of these read-alouds builds background for the struggling readers to use as they read related material. Varied literature selections allow teachers to offer struggling readers trade books on the content topics that are within their reading capabilities. Heterogeneous group discussions let all students share the different content that they have learned from the trade books.

Thematic unit studies generally have hands-on activities, a wide variety of materials, and information sources in addition to print materials. This combination offers struggling readers a number of avenues for learning the content concepts. The activities that do not include reading and writing provide these students with needed background and scaffolding to approach the content reading.

FOCUS ON   *English Language Learners*

Literature-Based and Thematic Approaches for ELLs

When English language learners first begin learning a second language, they learn a great deal from listening to others speak and read aloud (Pinnell and Jaggar, 2003; Fisher, Flood, Lapp, and Frey, 2004).

ENGLISH/
LANGUAGE
ARTS

SOCIAL
STUDIES

ELLs learn best through meaningful talk, and literature discussions are good examples of meaningful talk. Listening to recordings of literature selections, viewing videos related to literature, such as *Hamlet, Shakespeare in Love,* or *10 Things I Hate About You* (a high school movie loosely based on *The Taming of the Shrew*); viewing pictures of historical situations, such as conditions during the 1930s, when the class is reading *The Grapes of Wrath*; as well as lectures and discussions can help ELLs comprehend literature selections. It is preferable for all of the students to read the same book and discuss sections of the book as they read. Discussions only after an entire book has been read may not work well for these students (Wolfe, 2004).

Wordless picture books can be used as vehicles to develop oral language and writing skills with linguistically and culturally diverse students (Cassady, 1998). Picture books may make some content studies more comprehensible to ELLs

(Ernst-Slavit, Moore, and Maloney, 2002). Comic books and graphic novels may serve this purpose also. Narrative material is often good for introducing abstract concepts. Informational picture books have provided a good way to introduce content information and expository writing in a secondary, English as a second language (ESL) classroom (Hadaway and Mundy, 1999).

Anticipation guides as prereading activities (see Chapter 5) let students think about their prior knowledge before reading a selection. Preteaching of vocabulary and use of graphic organizers are also beneficial for these students. Teaching of study skills (see Chapters 7 and 8) is also important.

SOCIAL STUDIES

Including a wide variety of literature from diverse cultures in the secondary school curriculum can help students better understand people from other countries and cultural groups. These books must be chosen carefully to avoid unacceptable use of stereotypes and to ensure authenticity of content and images (Nilsson, 2005; Louie, 2006). Knoester (2009, p. 684) says, "Teaching strategies may include developing thematic units that focus on cultural minority literary figures and making available ample books and other publications featuring cultural minority characters and written by authors from many cultural backgrounds." Prereading instruction can help students acquire cultural, historical, and political background that affects the actions of characters from other cultures. This instruction may include such activities as participation in simulations and discussions, viewing videos, listening to lectures, and doing Internet research (Louie, 2005). Some cultural groups are represented in fewer books than are others. Hispanic characters, for example, are underrepresented, although books with Hispanic characters are increasing in number (Nilsson, 2005).

Thematic-unit activities offer hands-on activities and video resources to help ELLs develop concepts. These materials also provide preparation for reading content materials. Teachers should include texts of different types, such as magazines, posters, and photographs for ELLs' instructional needs because multimodal texts can enhance language and literacy learning for these students (Ajayi, 2009).

A study of the reading habits of urban adolescents indicated that many of the students could read best in Spanish. If the teacher's intent is to build a love of reading, providing books in the students' first languages may be helpful (Hughes-Hassell and Rodge, 2007).

Summary

Literature is valuable for study in itself and as a tool to enhance learning in other content areas. In addition to including a variety of genres in literature instruction, teachers should consider using picture books, comic books, and graphic novels, as well as text-only materials. Teachers can use mini-lessons on reading strategies and literary elements, reading guides, electronic discussions, whole-class novel study, literature response groups, sustained silent reading, and directed reading lessons to help students learn more from and about the literature that they read. Teachers can encourage students to respond to literature through both written and oral responses.

Literature is an extremely important resource in thematic units in the content areas. The topics that are covered briefly in text materials are enlarged upon, and the situations depicted allow the students to experience the material vicariously.

Discussion Questions

1. How can trade books enhance content area instruction?
2. What are the advantages of using graphic novels and comic books in secondary classes?
3. What are the values of literature response groups?
4. Which instructional techniques seem most useful for your teaching situation?
5. What types of literature could you use in your particular curricular area?
6. What types of activities could you use in your content area to encourage student response to literature?
7. What are some valuable uses of technology in thematic units?
8. How does unit teaching lend itself to differentiation of assignments?
9. How can struggling readers and English language learners benefit from use of literature and thematic units in content area classes?

Enrichment Activities

*1. Write out a plan for a directed reading lesson for a literature selection that you are currently using. Try it with your students, and report to the class concerning the results.
*2. Develop a mini-lesson for a reading strategy or literary element. Use a think-aloud as a part of your lesson. Try it with your students, and report to the class concerning the results.
3. Choose a topic, and locate trade books on a variety of difficulty levels that students could use when studying this topic.
*4. Plan a unit from your chosen subject area. Try it with students in your class. Decide how you could improve the unit if you were to teach it again. Don't forget to include some activities that make use of technology, especially Internet applications.
5. Develop special literature activities to assist struggling readers and ELLs in learning content concepts. Include picture books, graphic novels and comic books, where appropriate.
6. Choose a short story from a literature textbook. Choose prediction points for the selection that would allow you to use it for a DRTA. Discuss the stopping points that you have chosen with your college classmates.

---

*These activities are designed for in-service teachers, student teachers, and practicum students.

Resources including the TeachSource Video Cases can be found on the website for this book. Cengage Learning's CourseMate brings course concepts to life with interactive learning, study, and exam preparation tools that support the printed textbook. Go to www.cengage.com/login to register your access code.

CHAPTER 11

Reading in the Content Areas: I

Overview

Literacy is central to learning content area material, including science and mathematics (Olson and Truxaw, 2009). The content teachers' role is relating literacy skills to subject matter. Meaningful interactions with content area texts require cognitive strategies such as asking questions and self-questioning (Wilson et al., 2009). Students are not merely reading, but they are learning content. The students need cognitive strategies and multiple literacies, including academic literacies, to negotiate the demands of content reading. Content teachers have to understand the discourse and literacy demands, as well as curriculum goals and expectations of particular content areas, in order to implement instruction that students need to engage with both texts and multimedia materials. Understanding, interpreting, and using knowledge are basic learning processes in content subjects.

Concern for content reading has increased significantly because data reveals that students lack needed skills. For example, in 2004, 1.2 million high school graduates took the ACT Assessment, but only 22 percent achieved scores that indicated they were ready for college in three academic areas: English, math, and science (Lewis, 2007). The Alliance for Excellent Education reports that about six million middle and high school students read below grade level (Wise, 2008). Such data show the need for content reading instruction.

In this chapter, we focus on guiding students in learning content and in effectively using content-related materials in social studies, science, mathematics, English, and foreign languages.

Purpose-Setting Questions

As you read this chapter, try to answer these questions:

1. How can teachers facilitate learning in each of these content areas: social studies, science, mathematics, English, and foreign languages?
2. What common writing patterns appear in each of the content areas discussed in this chapter?
3. How are multimedia materials, especially computer-based ones, changing content area studies and teaching in these areas?
4. Why do deficiencies in academic literacy cause major problems for learning in many content areas?

Introduction to Reading Content Material

How are the goals of content reading different from those for other types of reading?

The goals of content reading are different from those for reading literature and from those of elementary school reading instruction. Content textbooks in the middle and secondary school differ from elementary school content textbooks that are often written in narrative style rather than the expository style and the academic language of secondary content textbooks.

In middle school and high school content area reading, students are expected to understand, retain, and apply information they acquire. Instruction and support enables students to understand academic language and to comprehend, analyze, synthesize, and apply complex information. They can learn to recognize and apply knowledge of the major text structures (Bertelsen and Fischer, 2003/2004).

Discourse

How does content discourse differ from other forms of discourse?

Discourse in content textbooks and related materials is written to impart and explain information with patterns of organization that vary from subject to subject. The discourse in textbooks tends to be longer and more laden with facts than that found in magazines, newspapers, many multimedia sources, and many online materials. It is written in academic language that adolescents usually do not experience in their out-of-school language communities. As a result, middle school and high school students' command of academic language is not as well developed as their other literacy skills (Lewis, 2007). However, the culture of schooling requires academic literacy, which includes special skills, knowledge, vocabulary, and linguistic patterns.

Zwiers (2008) states that classroom talk is a tool for developing academic literacy. Classroom discussion is a means of working with information so that it becomes knowledge and understanding. He recommends that teachers allow for repetition of content terms and thinking processes during the course of classroom discussion.

Content Teaching and Learning that Works

What are the most effective types of content reading Instruction?

Wilson and others (2009) studied QARs (question–answer relationships) in a two-year study with secondary content teachers. The teachers prepared explicit lesson plans for open-ended questions and modeled think-aloud activities when teaching QARs. The study showed that participants learned QARs through the think-aloud activities. (QARs are explained in Chapter 5.)

Neufeld (2005) found that question asking and answering and clarifying a purpose for reading were techniques supported by research. An extensive body of research confirms that teaching students to generate their own questions about texts can significantly improve their comprehension. Reciprocal teaching, QAR, and questioning the author, as well as self-questioning based on Bloom's taxonomy are recommended approaches to developing questioning skill. (Reciprocal teaching is explained in Chapter 6.) Questioning the author guides students to ask such questions as "What is the author telling me?" or "Why is the author telling me this (referring to a fact and/or statement)?" (Beck et al., 1991). Bloom's Taxonomy (Bloom, 1976) is frequently used as a basis for developing questions on different cognitive levels. This taxonomy includes the following levels in ascending order: Knowledge, Understanding, Application, Analysis, Synthesis, and Evaluation.

Ogle (2009) recommends the **K-W-L** procedure for content area reading. **K** refers to "What do I **K**now about the topic?" **W** refers to "What do I need to know?" **L** refers to "What did I **L**earn?" The **K** step provides the activation of schemata. The **W** step provides purposes for reading, and the **L** step should answer the purpose questions and provide other information.

Lewis (2007) identifies a set of guiding principles for developing academic literacy. Among these principles are developing critical thinking and using process-oriented instructional approaches that encourage development of self-monitoring and metacognitive habits. Students need learning opportunities that allow them to assume responsibility for their own learning. Kelley and Clausen-Grace (2007) stress metacognition, as well as predicting, questioning, and summarizing in their suggested yearly plan for teaching.

These studies and expert opinion underscore the importance of asking and answering questions when guiding students' learning in content area subjects. These views of comprehension and content learning focus on the importance of discussion of content after reading.

Reading and Critical Literacy

What makes critical literacy important in content reading?

The array of content-related multimedia, print sources, and Internet sites requires both teachers and students to analyze the quality and veracity of the content. Readers must consider the sources of all material they read. Even textbooks should be read from a critical stance. For example, a study of secondary social studies textbooks revealed a surprising number of inaccuracies (Grady, 2002). Chapter 6 discusses critical reading and includes critical reading activities.

Critical literacy goes beyond critical reading because it invites readers to ask vital questions about content. These questions are appropriate to printed text literacy and media literacy. Guided analysis of print and visual information, whether from a content textbook or a television program, fosters student awareness of critical thinking about point of view, organization, fact versus opinion, bias, omission, argument, and rhetorical devices (McKeown et al., 2009). Such analysis encourages students to think deeply about the subject at hand. Certainly, many secondary students are not ready to discuss all of these dimensions of an assignment at the same time, but they can gradually work through these thinking processes to achieve content goals.

Content Strategies and Assignments

What type of content reading instruction is most effective?

The most effective content reading instruction occurs when teachers guide students in learning content as they acquire reading strategies (Rhoder, 2002). Content teachers have the expertise to identify the important ideas and concepts of the subject matter for the students. When planning lessons, teachers should ask themselves,

SOCIAL
STUDIES

"What do I want my students to know when they finish this chapter, unit, or lesson?" For example, in a unit or lesson in geography, the content learning objective might be for students to understand how geographic features are formed, which would involve reading and understanding sequence and cause-and-effect relationships.

To plan content reading instruction, teachers also should think through the learning task from the students' perspective, identifying the skills and instructional approach that will enable them to achieve the objectives, incorporating the skills and approach in the lesson. Instructional examples are included in Chapters 5, 6, 7, and 8, as well as this chapter.

Teaching strategies for the broad array of materials used in content reading include prereading strategies, during-reading strategies, and after-reading strategies that were introduced in Chapters 5 and 6. Writing has proven to be a very helpful process in developing content comprehension. The suggestions in Chapters 9 and 10 will help teachers integrate writing and literature with content learning.

Authentic Reading Assignments

What are authentic reading assignments?

Authentic reading assignments involve activities concerned with actual problems and inquiries or simulations, which may include taking oral histories, solving community problems such as selecting toxic waste sites, or addressing other local political or school problems. These activities lead students into authentic experiences with reading, learning, and the application of ideas. Each section of this chapter introduces purposeful teaching strategies that can be adapted to various types of content, although the space constraints prohibit demonstrating every strategy with each type of content. Students who learn to use these strategies can apply them to printed materials and electronic media in their content studies.

Content Text Structures

How is content text structured?

Secondary teachers see their disciplines as organized bodies of knowledge with defined methods of inquiry. However, many students do not recognize the connections among the facts and ideas they study. Instead, they attempt to learn each detail or idea as a separate entity. They overlook main ideas and their relationships to details. These students recall content as a series of memorized fragments. The "Meeting the Challenge" on page 347 illustrates the fallacies in this approach to comprehension. Although this instance occurred in a biology class, it illustrates that students who understand the way knowledge is structured in any subject can better understand it.

Organizational Patterns in Content Texts

What are the most common organizational patterns in content texts?

Six major patterns or organizational structures occur most frequently in content materials: chronological order, list structure, comparison/contrast, cause-and-effect, problem–solution, and definition or explanation pattern. These structures are found in all subjects, sometimes alone, but often in combination. Among these patterns, chronological order and list structure are easiest to learn; therefore, students should

MEETING THE CHALLENGE

SCIENCE AND HEALTH

Matthew Smith was a diligent student who read and reread his textbooks until he knew the material thoroughly. However, Matthew encountered a major challenge in tenth-grade biology. First, he found that no amount of rereading made the content sink into his memory. He did not have the time to read and reread his biology text and to read his other assignments as well. At the end of the first grading period, Matthew's grades were on a downward spiral, and he was deeply frustrated.

Matthew made an appointment with his guidance counselor, who set up a three-way conference with Matthew, the biology teacher, and himself. After some discussion, they asked the reading teacher to join them. She asked Matthew to demonstrate his reading and study strategies through a think-aloud and discovered that he was simply reading and rereading each sentence without grasping the overall concept of the unit and the chapter, which in this instance was "Genetics."

The reading teacher arranged four sessions with Matthew. During these sessions he learned how to use the table of contents as an overview and advance organizer. He learned to seek connections among the ideas he was reading and to connect them to his own experiences. As a result, Matthew began to grasp main ideas and supporting details, as well as the connections among ideas and concepts. He became a successful student whose grades improved throughout the school year. He finished the year with a B average in biology.

Professional educators meet to formulate plans for helping to alleviate their students' problems.

Chris Schmidt/iStockphoto.com

examine these first. Identifying these patterns in different subjects helps students achieve broader understanding and gives them a feeling of greater control over complex subject matter. After examining the easier structures, students can move on to the more challenging ones. Instruction about structure should focus on the actual materials students will read in each subject area. A number of strategies have proved successful in developing students' awareness of text patterns including:

What strategies are most successful for teaching students text patterns?

- Providing examples across topics and texts.

- Relating text patterns to real-life experiences.

- Having students identify signal words and make notes in the margins.

- Making visual representations of text patterns.

- Having students practice writing text patterns.

Social Studies Content

What disciplines are included in social studies?

SOCIAL STUDIES

Social studies classes encompass many academic disciplines, including history, anthropology, geography, economics, political science, psychology, philosophy, and sociology. Multicultural education is an overarching theme in curriculum development. The primary objective of multicultural education is to help all students reach their potential through exploring cultural pluralism. Students learn that many cultures have contributed to the culture of the United States. The Internet is an excellent source of materials for cultural studies.

Critical Thinking in Social Studies

Why is critical thinking significant in the social studies?

SOCIAL STUDIES

Critical thinking has particular significance in the social sciences because understanding cause-and-effect relationships, distinguishing fact from opinion, separating relevant information from irrelevant information, and identifying and evaluating propaganda are essential skills for learning social studies. At the center of critical thinking is the understanding that we receive a limited amount of information about a particular event from one source; that is, content is presented from a particular point of view. For example, consider the terrorist attacks on the World Trade Center in New York and the Pentagon in Washington, D.C., on September 11, 2001, and think of the different perspectives of victims, victims' families, firefighters, police officers, Americans of the Muslim faith, and Arabs living in this country. These people no doubt shared feelings of horror, but each had different perspectives on the disaster. When learning about unfamiliar cultures, students need schemata that enable them to understand human behaviors outside of their experiences. Teachers find that anticipation guides, study guides, and advance organizers enhance critical thinking.

How can comprehension of social studies content be enhanced?

Comprehension of social studies content is enhanced when readers are prepared to:

1. Understand the ideas and viewpoints of others.

2. Acquire and retain a body of relevant concepts and information.

3. Think critically and creatively, thus developing new attitudes and values and the ability to make decisions.

4. Consult a variety of sources to develop more than one perspective regarding a topic.

5. Read critically about what has happened and why these events occurred.

How is social studies content written?

SOCIAL STUDIES

Social studies materials are written in a precise, factual, expository style that presents comprehension problems for a significant proportion of students. However, a student must comprehend 75 percent of the ideas and 90 percent of the vocabulary of a selection in order to learn effectively from these materials. Through activities like those described in Chapter 4 and the activities that follow, word meanings are reinforced, and recall is enhanced.

EXAMPLE 11.1   Social Studies Study Guide

SOCIAL STUDIES

Directions: Pay attention to the terms in Column A—they are important for understanding of this selection. After reading the selection, draw a line from the term in Column A to its meaning in Column B.

Column A	Column B
Trade association	An organization designed to advance economic, social action, or other concerns of its members.
Interest group	An organization of competing companies in one industry that sets industry standards and influences policies.
Gross national product	The value of goods and services produced by a country for a given year.

Comprehension

Directions: Write short answers to the following questions:
1. What do economic interest groups try to influence?
2. What are four major categories of economic interest groups?
3. Why do economic interest groups focus on the government?
4. How do interest groups affect your life?
5. What are the positive qualities and the negative qualities of interest groups?

Directions: Write a short essay to answer this question:
6. What do interest groups for dentists and clothing manufacturers have in common?

What is the purpose of study guides?

Study guides are maps to cognitive processing. A study guide may cover a chapter, a larger unit, a part of a chapter, or multiple materials on a topic. Students should have the study guide prior to reading an assignment, so they can reflect about the content while they read. Students should be encouraged to read critically in order to accomplish this. Example 11.1 illustrates a social studies study guide.

A **concept guide** is a form of study guide that is concerned with developing students' understanding of an important content concept. Concept guides may be developed in a number of different ways. Example 11.2 on page 350 is a concept guide based on a government text chapter on civil rights. A student would complete this guide after reading the chapter. Concept guides are also discussed in Chapter 4.

Writing Patterns

SOCIAL STUDIES

Social studies materials are dense with ideas and facts, but they are organized around writing patterns that help readers understand the cognitive relationships of key ideas, concepts, and information. When students recognize these patterns, they are better prepared to comprehend social studies content.

| **EXAMPLE 11.2** | **Social Studies Concept Guide** |

SOCIAL
STUDIES

Directions: Write a + (plus sign) before each term that is associated with civil rights, according to the information in your social studies textbook. Write a − (minus sign) before each word that is unrelated to the concept of civil rights. Be prepared to explain and support your answers by using your textbook.

_____ restrictive covenant	_____ affirmative action
_____ treason	_____ equality
_____ reverse discrimination	_____ private education
_____ segregation	_____ equal opportunity
_____ integration	_____ people's vote
_____ suspect classification	_____ open housing
_____ socialist government	_____ goods and services

Cause-and-Effect Pattern

Each area of social studies is concerned with chains of causes and effects: one cause results in certain effects that become causes of other effects. The passage in Example 11.3 is written in the **cause-and-effect writing pattern**. Example 11.4 is a cause and effect chart based on the text in Example 11.3.

Definition or Explanation Pattern

What is the purpose of the definition/ explanation pattern?

The **definition or explanation pattern** is used to define or explain important concepts. The concept is the main idea, and the supporting details constitute the elements of the definition or explanation. To comprehend this pattern of writing, the student must identify both the concept and the author's definition or explanation. This pattern is important to the reader because the knowledge included in the definition or explanation frequently serves as a basis for learning subsequent information on the topic.

Chronological Order (Time Order) Pattern

What is the purpose of the chronological order pattern?

In the **chronological order pattern**, events are arranged in order of occurrence. The teacher can help students develop a concept of time periods by having them consider time in relation to their own lives and the lifetimes of their parents and ancestors. For example, the Vietnam War probably occurred in the lifetime of the grandparents of present-day students.

Understanding time is necessary for comprehending social studies material, but reflecting on what one has read is more valuable than memorizing dates. Indefinite time references, such as "in the early days" or "in ancient times," may confuse

EXAMPLE 11.3   Cause-and-Effect Pattern in a Text about Government

SOCIAL
STUDIES

Private Interest Groups

Private interest groups seek economic benefits for their members or clients. Examples include business, labor, and agriculture groups.

Business

Business organizations are the most numerous and among the most powerful interest groups in Washington (see Figure 1). Much of politics is essentially the interaction—some would say the confrontation—between business and government.[21] Business seeks to maximize profit, whereas government, at least sometimes, works to protect workers and consumers from the unfettered effects of profit-seeking businesses through regulation of employees' wages and working conditions, products' safety, and monopolistic practices.

Today, however, there is less confrontation between business and government than during other eras. The Republican Party has long favored business, and since the 1990s the Democratic Party, anxious to compete for campaign contributions, has often favored business too.[22] In a capitalist economy, there are powerful incentives and pressures for politicians of all political persuasions to accede to, rather than antagonize, business, which is so important to the nation's economic success.[23] If the economy falters, the politicians get blamed. So business usually does well, regardless of which party occupies the White House or dominates Congress.

Source: *Understanding American Government: The Essentials* by Susan Welch, John Gruhl, John Comer, Susan Rigdon, p. 219. Wadsworth Cengage Learning, 2009.

EXAMPLE 11.4   A Cause and Effect Chart for Text in Example 11.3

SOCIAL
STUDIES

Cause	Effect
Business organizations are numerous.	Become powerful interest groups
Business seeks to maximize profit and government protects citizens.	Confrontation between business and government.
Both parties favor business.	No matter which party is in power, business does well.

readers; therefore, the teacher needs to clarify these terms. The chronological order pattern is presented in Example 11.5 on page 352.

Comparison and/or Contrast Pattern

What is the purpose of the comparison/ contrast pattern?

When using the **comparison and/or contrast pattern,** an author explains social studies ideas by using likenesses and differences to develop understanding. Example 11.6 shows this writing pattern.

| EXAMPLE 11.5 | Chronological Order or Time Order Pattern (Social Studies) |

SOCIAL
STUDIES

Remaining Neutral

Britain made it hard for the United States to remain neutral. Late in 1792, the British began seizing the cargoes of American ships carrying goods from the French West Indies.

Washington sent Chief Justice John Jay to England for talks about the seizure of U.S. ships. Jay also hoped to persuade the British to give up their forts on the Northwest frontier. During the talks in 1794, news came of the U.S. victory at the Battle of Fallen Timbers. Fearing another entanglement, the British agreed to leave the Ohio Valley by 1796. In **Jay's Treaty,** the British also agreed to pay damages for U.S. vessels they had seized. Jay failed, however, to open up the profitable British West Indies trade to Americans. Because of this, Jay's Treaty was unpopular.

Like Jay, Thomas Pinckney helped the United States reduce tensions along the frontier. In 1795, **Pinckney's Treaty** with Spain gave Americans the right to travel freely on the Mississippi River. It also gave them the right to store goods at the port of New Orleans without paying customs duties. In addition, Spain accepted the 31st parallel as the northern boundary of Florida and the southern boundary of the United States.

Meanwhile, more American settlers moved west. As you will read in the next sections, change was coming back east as Washington stepped down.

Source: Jesus Garcia, Donna M. Ogle, C. Frederick Risinger, Joyce Stevos, and Winthrop D. Jordan, *Creating America: A History of the United States.* Copyright © 2001 by McDougal Littell Inc., a division of Houghton Mifflin Company, p. 302. All rights reserved. Reprinted by permission of McDougal Littell Inc., a division of Houghton Mifflin Company.

| EXAMPLE 11.6 | Comparison and/or Contrast Pattern (Social Studies) |

Who Does Not Vote?

Voting is related to education, income, and occupation—that is, to socioeconomic class. Those who are more educated, have more money, and have higher-status jobs vote more often. If you are a college graduate, the chances are about 70 percent that you will vote; if you have less than a high school education, the chances are less than half that.[36] Differences between higher- and lower-income people are also quite large and growing. Although voting among all groups of Americans has declined in the past forty years, the proportion of college-educated persons who participated fell by less than 10 percent, while that of high school-educated persons dropped by nearly 20 percent. Education apparently is linked to voting because those with more years of education are more interested in, and knowledgeable about, politics.

Source: Jesus Garcia, Donna M. Ogle, C. Frederick Risinger, Joyce Stevos, and Winthrop D. Jordan, *Creating America: A History of the United States.* Copyright © 2001 by McDougal Littell Inc., a division of Houghton Mifflin Company, p. 302. All rights reserved. Reprinted by permission of McDougal Littell Inc., a division of Houghton Mifflin Company.

The teacher and students may develop a chart to show comparisons and contrasts. Example 11.7 compares citizens who vote with those who do not vote.

EXAMPLE 11.7	Comparison Chart for Social Studies

Frequent Voters	Frequent Nonvoters
More educated	Less educated
More affluent	Below average income
Higher-status jobs	Lower-status jobs

Question-and-Answer Pattern

Authors sometimes use a **question-and-answer pattern** to organize social studies materials. In this pattern, the author asks a question and then answers it. Readers should be able to recall the author's questions and identify his or her answers. Example 11.8 combines the question–answer pattern and the comparison and or contrast pattern.

EXAMPLE 11.8	Question-and-Answer Writing Pattern (Social Studies)

SOCIAL
STUDIES

Slaves Ride the Underground Railroad

Antislavery forces did more than protect and rescue runaway slaves. In fact, they helped many slaves escape. A secret network known as the **Underground Railroad** guided some 100,000 fugitive slaves to freedom between 1780 and 1865.

What was the Underground Railroad? It was not a railroad, and it did not move underground. The Underground Railroad was a complex system of about 3,000 people—both blacks and whites—who helped transport escaped slaves. Under the cover of night, "conductors" led runaways to freedom, providing food and safe hiding places. They risked great danger in aiding slaves.

Source: Beverly J. Armento, Gary B. Nash, Christopher L. Salter, and Karen K. Wixson, *A More Perfect Union*, p. 333. Copyright © 1993 Houghton Mifflin Company. Reprinted by permission of Houghton Mifflin Company. All rights reserved.

Exercises for Social Studies Instruction

Give students practice exercises such as the following to enhance learning in social studies:

1. From the list of words and phrases below, choose a word or phrase from List A that is associated with each of the terms in List B.

List A: *Words and Phrases*

Rules of conduct   Control behavior
Power to interpret and apply law   Self-government
People's vote   Rights of the people

List B: *Word List*

1. Jurisdiction   3. Autonomy
2. Plebiscite   4. Civil rights

2. An activity called "Possible Sentences" encourages students to learn word meanings and to predict ideas they will encounter when reading content (Tierney, Readence, and Dishner, 1990). For this activity, use the following steps:

    a. Identify important vocabulary in the reading selection and write the words on the board. Pronounce each word as you write it. The terms below are taken from a social studies text chapter that discusses democracy and socialism.

    Democracy   Civil rights
    Socialism   Laws

    b. Ask each student to construct sentences using at least two of the terms. Record these sentences on the board, underlining the important words. Continue eliciting sentences from the students as long as the sentences are presenting new ideas.

    In a <u>democracy</u>, <u>laws</u> are made by elected officials.

    c. Have students read their textbooks to verify the accuracy of the sentences they constructed.

    d. After they read the text, have the students evaluate each sentence using the text as a reference. Students may also use glossaries, dictionaries, and thesauruses. Have students modify the sentences if necessary.

3. The List-Group-Label lesson uses categorization to help students develop and refine concepts. This activity also encourages students to relate content to past experiences. It includes the following steps:

    a. Give students a topic drawn from the materials they are studying. An appropriate topic could be "The Geography of Georgia."

    b. Have students develop a list of words or expressions they associate with the topic. Record these words on the board until the list totals approximately twenty-five words.

    Appalachian Mountains   Blue Ridge Mountains   Stone Mountain
    Peanuts   Savannah River
    Altamaha River   Cotton

    c. Have students group words from the large list, providing a label for each group.

Mountains	*Waterways*	*Products*
Blue Ridge Mountains	Savannah River	Peanuts
Stone Mountain	Altamaha River	Cotton
Appalachian Mountains		

4. Critical reading in social studies materials can be guided with questions like these:

   a. What was the author's purpose in writing this selection?

   b. Is the author knowledgeable and current about the subject?

   c. Is the author biased in his or her presentation? Why do you think so? An author's biases are likely to appear when causes of events are explained. The author's point of view may be affected by factors such as his or her age, nationality, religion, political views, race, family history, sex, and audience for the writing.

   d. Is the material well written and interesting?

   e. Does the author employ propaganda? If so, does the propaganda influence you?

   f. Does the author imply anything that is not directly stated? What is implied? What does the author say that leads you to this conclusion? (Hickey, 1990)

5. Technology, literature, newspapers, magazines, and field trips to museums and exhibits provide students with experiences to help build understandings of people, places, and events.

   a. A textbook chapter or unit on the western migration could be explored with a software program such as *Oregon Trail* (Riverdeep). This classic pioneer simulation software lets students experience history as they play the roles of emigrants traveling by covered wagon to Oregon and California on the Overland trails. Literature such as *Pioneer Women: The Lives of Women on the Frontier* (Peavy and Smith, 1996) and the *Western Historical Quarterly* would enrich this study. Copies of original documents and newspapers can be obtained from state historical societies.

   b. To study Vietnam, teachers could use software such as *Passage to Vietnam* (Against All Odds Prod.), a stunningly beautiful and very informative journey through Vietnam that could be used in conjunction with *Vietnam: Why We Fought—An Illustrated History* (Hoobler and Hoobler, 1990), *Portrait of a Tragedy: America and the Vietnam War* (Warren, 1990), and *Fallen Angels* (Myers, 1988). Newspapers from this period are available in most public libraries or in newspaper archives.

   c. The Internet enables students to visit national parks vicariously and see sites within the parks, which helps students develop geographic concepts.

Science and Health Content

What are the levels of science writing?

SCIENCE AND HEALTH

The language of science is a unique hybrid (Lemke, 2004). There are at least four levels of science writing that require different reading approaches: (1) articles in the popular press (newspapers and magazines); (2) articles in popular scientific journals (for example, *Scientific American*); (3) science textbooks; and (4) articles in scientific research journals. In addition, there is a different medium for acquiring scientific information that requires still another approach—the Internet. Websites such as the *Science Daily* site that includes Top Science Headlines and the *U.S. News & World Report* site are two examples.

Middle school science teachers report that science textbooks do not follow standards-based principles for concept learning and student reading achievement (Radcliffe et al., 2008). Fleming and Billman (2005) found that the unfamiliar vocabulary and confusing text structures in science texts make science texts challenging for middle school students.

What makes science content complex?

Lemke (2004) examined science texts and found such text features as diagrams included in footnotes and lengthy and complex research reports accompanied by complex diagrams. Experimental reports were presented in graphs and tables, but the written text referred to and commented on the information without explaining it. The complexity of science writing is increased by the fact that students encounter multimodal science texts (Wilson, 2008). Students encounter digital media that present multiple representations in various communication media.

The importance of understanding scientific discourse in content reading was revealed in Olson and Truxaw's (2009) research. They studied teachers' applications of literacy in mathematics and science and learned that teachers needed to understand the discourse forms in order to interpret meaning.

What challenges do students encounter in understanding scientific content?

Lemke (2004) studied students' challenges with understanding scientific discourse. He videotaped one student during his chemistry lesson and found that the student had to interpret the following:

MATHEMATICS

- A stream of rapid verbal English from his teacher.
- Text and layout information presented on an overhead transparency.
- Text, layout, diagrams, chemical symbols, and mathematical formulas in the open textbook in front of him.
- The display on his hand-held calculator.
- Text, layout, diagrams, symbolic notations, and mathematics in his personal notebook.
- The teacher's gestures, blackboard diagrams, and writing.
- The actions and speech of other students, including their manipulation of demonstration apparatus.
- The running commentary of his next-seat neighbor.

The process for reading a science text is the same as that used by professional scientists for reading research articles. Readers of scientific texts must follow scientific thinking, the terse scientific writing style, and the dense content. They have to read slowly and more than once, with pencil and paper in hand, considering each new idea.

What approaches help students understand health materials?

Written materials in health are similar to scientific materials and include a similar range of writing. Therefore, the same approaches will help students understand health materials. Health has become an important field of study as people take more responsibility for their own health and well-being. Health education seeks to help students understand both their physical bodies and their emotional growth and development.

SCIENCE AND HEALTH

Authentic Learning Experiences

What are authentic learning experiences?

The emphasis on authentic learning experiences increases students' need for interactive reading, which means they should relate questions, experiments, and problem solving to the text. Science and health students need study guides and strategies that will help them perceive connections and relationships. The following strategies and activities will help teachers develop students' understanding of scientific reading and writing.

Scientific terminology can be developed using the Frayer Model, which was introduced in Chapter 4. Example 11.9 illustrates this strategy.

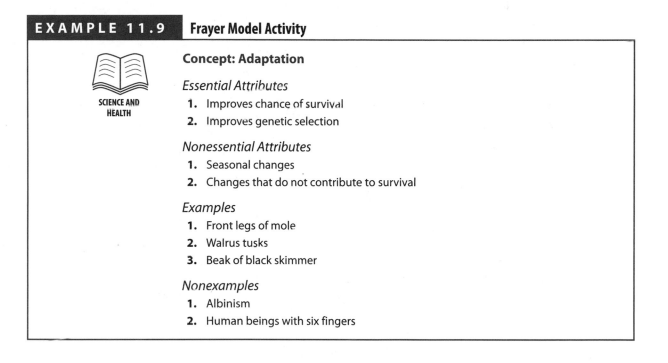

EXAMPLE 11.9   **Frayer Model Activity**

SCIENCE AND HEALTH

Concept: Adaptation

Essential Attributes

1. Improves chance of survival
2. Improves genetic selection

Nonessential Attributes

1. Seasonal changes
2. Changes that do not contribute to survival

Examples

1. Front legs of mole
2. Walrus tusks
3. Beak of black skimmer

Nonexamples

1. Albinism
2. Human beings with six fingers

Writing Patterns

The main ideas and supporting details in scientific materials are frequently organized into classification patterns, definitions or explanations of technical processes, cause-and-effect patterns, and problem-solution patterns. Other patterns used to structure scientific content are the experimental pattern and the comparison pattern. These patterns and related strategies are illustrated in the following section.

Classification Pattern

How is information organized in the classification pattern?

In the **classification pattern**, information is ordered under common headings and subheadings. The information sorted in this way may relate to living things, objects, or general ideas. This pattern is a type of outlining that shows a classification, the distinguishing characteristics of the members of the class, and examples (see Examples 11.10 and 11.11). The classification represents a main idea, and the distinguishing characteristics and examples are treated as details.

| EXAMPLE 11.10 | **Classification Pattern (Science)** |

The Geologic Timetable

SCIENCE AND HEALTH

A geologist studying the rocks in a particular area can use the rules discussed in Topic 2 to determine the relative ages of the rocks in that area. If these rocks can be matched with the rocks in another area, their relative ages can also be determined. By matching rocks over large areas, geologists have determined the relative ages of most of the rocks on Earth's surface. Over many years, geologists have worked out a timetable that subdivides geologic time into units based on the formation of certain rocks.

The **geologic timetable**, shown in Figure 32.3 on pages 600–601, is a summary of the major events of Earth's history preserved in the rock record. Fossils are an important part of that history. In fact, many of the rock layers have been identified and matched based on the fossils in them.

The longest segments of geologic time are called **eras.** The oldest era is the **Archean Era**. The Archean Era began when Earth was formed between 4 and 5 billion years ago. The earliest known rocks formed during the Archean Era.

The **Proterozoic Era** began about 2.5 billion years ago. The difference between Archean and Proterozoic rocks is that Proterozoic rocks contain fossils of simple plants and worms that lived in the oceans. No evidence of life on land has been found in Proterozoic rocks.

The **Paleozoic Era** is marked by a more abundant fossil record. The rocks formed during the Paleozoic Era contain fossils of both land and ocean plants and animals. The Paleozoic Era began about 570 million years ago.

The **Mesozoic Era** began about 250 million years ago. Dinosaurs thrived during most of Mesozoic time.

Source: From *Earth Science* by Nancy Spaulding and Samuel Namowitz. Copyright © 2003 by McDougal Littell Inc., a division of Houghton Mifflin Company. All rights reserved. Reprinted by permission of McDougal Littell Inc., a division of Houghton Mifflin Company.

Outline of Text

I. The Geologic Timetable
    A. Major events of Earth's history
        1. As preserved in the rock record
        2. As preserved in fossils
    B. The longest segments of geologic time are eras.
        1. Archean Era
        2. Proterozoic Era
        3. Paleozoic Era
        4. Mesozoic Era

Definition or Explanation Pattern

SCIENCE AND
HEALTH

The definition or explanation pattern occurs frequently in scientific content and health-related materials (see Example 11.11). This pattern may explain processes that are biological (the digestive process) or mechanical (the operation of an engine). It also may provide definitions for scientific terms, such as *atmosphere*. Diagrams often accompany this kind of pattern, so the reader must integrate written content information with the diagrams.

EXAMPLE 11.11   **Explanation Pattern (Science)**

SCIENCE AND
HEALTH

What is Observation?

Every single moment, we are gathering information about what is around us, through our senses—sight, taste, hearing, smell, and touch. We do this largely without thinking, and it is very important to our survival. Why are we not aware of all the information our senses are gathering at any time? The simple answer is that we cannot pay attention to everything at once. Instead of a constant flow of data cluttering up our thoughts, our brains select what information they take in; we unconsciously apply a filter (Figure 1–2). We simply pay attention to things that are more likely to be important. What is important is decided by various factors, including whether the environment changes. For example, if you are sitting in a room and everything is still, you are unlikely to be filled with thoughts about the color of the sofa, the shade of the light, or the size and shape of the walls. But if a cat walks in, or you hear a loud bang, you will perceive these changes in your environment. Paying attention to the details of your surroundings requires a conscious effort.

Source: *Forensic Science Fundamentals & Investigations* by Anthony J. Bertino and Patricia Nolan Bertino, page 4. South-Western Cengage Learning, 2008.

The following exercises can help students comprehend the explanation of a process:

1. Have students attempt to restate an explanation in their own words.

2. Have students reread the explanation to check their comprehension.

3. Have students study the sequence of steps in a process and attempt to explain the process by recalling the steps in sequence.

4. Mask the labels in a diagram that accompanies a process explanation, and have students insert appropriate labels.

Cause-and-Effect Pattern

SCIENCE AND
HEALTH

The cause-and-effect pattern often occurs in scientific or health-related materials. Example 11.12 shows the cause and effect pattern. Study guides can be developed to help students read this pattern. Example 11.13 presents an earth science passage and a study guide in the form of a cause-and-effect map built on the passage.

EXAMPLE 11.12 **Science Cause-and-Effect Passage**

SCIENCE AND
HEALTH

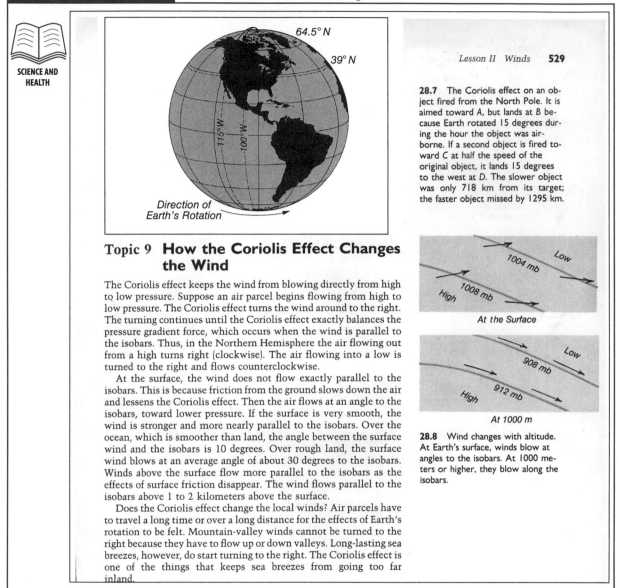

*Direction of
Earth's Rotation*

Lesson II Winds **529**

28.7 The Coriolis effect on an object fired from the North Pole. It is aimed toward *A*, but lands at *B* because Earth rotated 15 degrees during the hour the object was airborne. If a second object is fired toward *C* at half the speed of the original object, it lands 15 degrees to the west at *D*. The slower object was only 718 km from its target; the faster object missed by 1295 km.

28.8 Wind changes with altitude. At Earth's surface, winds blow at angles to the isobars. At 1000 meters or higher, they blow along the isobars.

Topic 9 How the Coriolis Effect Changes the Wind

The Coriolis effect keeps the wind from blowing directly from high to low pressure. Suppose an air parcel begins flowing from high to low pressure. The Coriolis effect turns the wind around to the right. The turning continues until the Coriolis effect exactly balances the pressure gradient force, which occurs when the wind is parallel to the isobars. Thus, in the Northern Hemisphere the air flowing out from a high turns right (clockwise). The air flowing into a low is turned to the right and flows counterclockwise.

At the surface, the wind does not flow exactly parallel to the isobars. This is because friction from the ground slows down the air and lessens the Coriolis effect. Then the air flows at an angle to the isobars, toward lower pressure. If the surface is very smooth, the wind is stronger and more nearly parallel to the isobars. Over the ocean, which is smoother than land, the angle between the surface wind and the isobars is 10 degrees. Over rough land, the surface wind blows at an average angle of about 30 degrees to the isobars. Winds above the surface flow more parallel to the isobars as the effects of surface friction disappear. The wind flows parallel to the isobars above 1 to 2 kilometers above the surface.

Does the Coriolis effect change the local winds? Air parcels have to travel a long time or over a long distance for the effects of Earth's rotation to be felt. Mountain-valley winds cannot be turned to the right because they have to flow up or down valleys. Long-lasting sea breezes, however, do start turning to the right. The Coriolis effect is one of the things that keeps sea breezes from going too far inland.

| EXAMPLE 11.13 | Cause-and-Effect Pattern and Map (Science) |

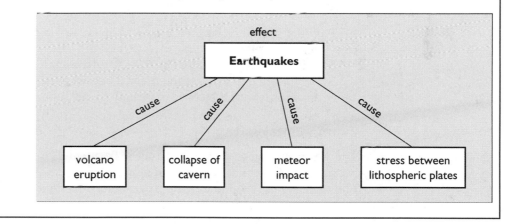

SCIENCE AND
HEALTH

Earthquakes can occur for many reasons. The ground can shake from the eruption of a volcano, the collapse of a cavern, or even from the impact of a meteor. However, the major cause of earthquakes is the stress that builds up between two lithospheric plates.

Most of the time, friction between plates prevents movement along the plate boundary. Instead, the stresses cause the plates to deform, or change shape. Eventually, the stresses become great enough to overcome the frictional forces, and the plates suddenly move. This movement causes an earthquake. The plates then snap back to the shapes they had before they were deformed but at new locations relative to each other. This explanation for the cause of an earthquake is called the **elastic-rebound theory** and is fundamental to an understanding of earthquakes.

Source: From *Earth Science* by Nancy Spaulding and Samuel Namowitz. Copyright © 2003 by McDougal Littell Inc., a division of Houghton Mifflin Company. All rights reserved. Reprinted by permission of McDougal Littell Inc., a division of Houghton Mifflin Company.

Cause-and-Effect Map

Directions: Read the assigned selection and identify all of the causes in the selection. Label each of the boxes connected to the arrows that lead to "earthquakes," which is the effect in this reading. A completed map is shown.

effect

Earthquakes

cause   cause   cause   cause

| volcano eruption | collapse of cavern | meteor impact | stress between lithospheric plates |

The following exercises can be used to provide practice with the cause-and-effect pattern and other writing patterns:

1. Writing (composition) can be used to reinforce reading comprehension in any content area or of any writing pattern. In the following paragraph, the student writer connected the earth science content he read to his own experiences.

The climate is the average pattern of weather in a place. The climate affects the habitat, which includes the water, rocks, soil, and air that all living things need. Since the plants and animals need certain things to live, they exist in places where the habitat provides these things. The kinds of water, rocks, soil, and air that are available make a difference in the kinds of plants and animals that live in that place. Woodpeckers and sapsuckers live in North Carolina forests because they eat the insects that live in the pine trees growing in this state.

2. Ask students to write questions about the content they read. For example,
    a. Why do some animals become extinct?
    b. If Guilford County became a desert, what animals would become extinct?

For additional teaching suggestions, see the social studies section.

**TeachSource
Video Case**
Integrating Technology
to Improve Student
Learning: A High
School Science
Simulation

Problem-Solution Pattern

The **problem-solution pattern** of writing is used in scientific and health-related materials to describe a real or hypothetical problem and its actual or suggested solution. For example, a writer might use this style of writing to explain how a vaccine was developed for polio.

To teach students to read and understand the problem-solution style of writing, the teacher may use the following techniques:

1. Ask students to identify the problem presented in a passage and to state it in their own words.

2. Ask students to locate the solution or solutions that the author suggests.

3. Ask students to prepare a problem and solution statement similar to the following:

    Problem: Why don't bacteria grow and divide in the region surrounding bread mold?
    Solution: Fleming found that mold gave off a chemical that killed the bacteria. He isolated the chemical and tested it against bacteria. He tested the chemical on animals with bacterial disease and on sick human volunteers.

Experimental Pattern

What does the student have to do when reading the experimental pattern?

SCIENCE AND
HEALTH

The **experimental pattern** of writing is frequently used in scientific materials because experiments are the basis of much scientific knowledge and advancement. The reader must be able to read experiment directions and translate them into action. The reader must carry out the directions precisely and observe the outcomes carefully. The purpose of an experiment is comparable to a main idea, and experimental directions are comparable to details.

Following are the steps a reader should use when reading and conducting an experiment:

1. Ask the following questions:
    a. What am I to find out?
    b. What materials are needed?
    c. What processes are used?
    d. What is the order of the steps in the experiment?
    e. What do I expect to happen?

2. Perform the experiment.

3. Observe the experiment.

4. Compare the actual outcomes with predicted outcomes. (Success or failure of an experiment is determined by the learning that takes place.)

5. Ask: How is this experiment related to the topic I am studying?

SCIENCE AND HEALTH

Comparison Pattern

The comparison writing pattern also appears in science materials. In some content, writers use comparisons in the form of analogies to help readers understand scientific content.

Additional Knowledge Needed for Reading Scientific Materials

What additional knowledge is important for students reading scientific materials?

In addition to understanding technical terminology and the organizational patterns featured in scientific materials, the reader of science must have mathematical understandings and knowledge. He or she must know and be able to apply the abbreviations, equations, and symbols that appear in scientific content.

Mathematics Content

MATHEMATICS

The importance of technology in our society leads to greater emphasis on mathematics and science. The scientific and mathematical knowledge that citizens and experts need has increased immensely in the past decade (Draper and Siebert, 2009). Mathematics requires a style of thinking involving modeling and abstraction. Mathematics has important applications in many areas of work and study, and students should explore these applications. Literacy is critical to mathematical reasoning and to exploring applications of mathematics.

Literacy in Mathematics

How have literacy demands in mathematics changed?

Students have calculators, computers, and access to the Internet, so there is not a strong need for them to become storehouses of facts or to be quick at complex computations (Draper and Siebert, 2009). However, students need many opportunities to listen to, read about, write about, speak about, reflect on, and demonstrate mathematical ideas. Literacy in mathematics should focus on fluency with mathematics texts, because literacy skills developed separately from the subject matter do not transfer well (Alvermann, 2004). Mathematics teachers must strive to engage a diverse student population in a variety of interesting and meaningful activities that are structured to develop critical thinking and problem solving.

Students need to develop extensive applications of mathematics concepts, including connections to everyday life. Today's mathematics instruction emphasizes the use of "real-world" mathematics problems and materials and of computer capabilities to develop conceptual understanding (National Council of Teachers of Mathematics, 1989). Current textbooks acquaint students with people who use math in their professions and businesses. Moreover, mathematics instruction builds connections with other subjects, and many teachers are striving to develop a broad, integrated mathematics curriculum in the middle school.

Mathematics is a highly compressed system of language in which a single symbol may represent several words. For example, the symbol > represents the words *is greater than*. In addition, some words, such as *odd* and *power,* have meanings that are quite different from their meanings in everyday conversation. Students may benefit from keeping mathematics journals in which they list special symbols and words and their meanings.

Reading Mathematics

The following procedures are recommended for guiding mathematics comprehension.

What are the components of a directed reading lesson in mathematics?

A directed reading lesson gives students a guide that can help them understand mathematics texts. The following set of steps can be used for directing the reading of a mathematics chapter:

1. *Introduce the new terms, using them in sentences.* Sentences from the text may be used. Give students an activity such as constructing a mathematics dictionary. Students may use their texts to help work out the meanings of the words.

2. *Ask students to preview the chapter and identify the topic.*

3. *Provide students with two or three silent reading purposes.* This step may be varied. If students have some background knowledge about the topic, they can help formulate silent reading purposes.

4. *Have students read the text silently.* Students should take notes on the content and formulate questions while reading.

5. *Work through examples and ask questions to clarify understanding.*

6. *Discuss the silent reading purposes and the questions students formulated in Step 4.*

Study guides such as the one in Example 11.14 can also be helpful.

EXAMPLE 11.14   **Three-Level Study Guide for Mathematics**

MATHEMATICS

Directions: Put a checkmark by the statements that are correct, according to the text.
Literal: What did the text say about adding and subtracting integers?

_____ **1.** When adding integers with different signs, subtract the lesser absolute value from the greater absolute value. Give the result the same sign as the addend with the lesser absolute value.

_____ **2.** When adding integers with different signs, subtract the lesser absolute value from the greater absolute value. Give the result the same sign as the addend with the greater absolute value.

_____ **3.** For every number a, $a + (-a) = 0$.

———— **4.** To subtract a number, add its additive inverse. For any numbers *a* and *b*, $a - b = a + (-b)$.

———— **5.** To add integers with the same sign, add their absolute values. Give the result the opposite sign as the addends.

Interpretive: How exactly do the addition and subtraction laws apply to numbers?

———— **1.** $-5 + (-7) = -12$

———— **2.** $2 + (-3) = 1$

———— **3.** $-2 + 1 = -1$

———— **4.** The additive inverse of 5 is -5.

———— **5.** The additive inverse of -7 is $-\frac{1}{7}$.

———— **6.** $3 \quad (-1) = 3 + 1$

———— **7.** $-1 - (-7) = -1 + 7$

Applied: How can the use of adding and subtracting numbers (using positive and negative numbers) be applied to real life?

———— **1.** It might be useful in temperature scales.

———— **2.** It can be applied to telling time.

———— **3.** It could be applied to money situations, like balancing a checkbook.

Source: Developed by Stephanie Dykes, Jennifer Brown, and Keith Shakleford to be used with material from Alan G. Foster, Joan M. Gell, and Berchie W. Gordon, *Algebra 1: Applications and Connections*, pp. 55–57. Lake Forest, Ill.: Glencoe, 1992.

Writing Patterns

What writing patterns are found in mathematics?

The writing patterns that occur most frequently in mathematics are the problem pattern and the demonstration pattern. In addition, graphs and charts are often used in math content reading.

Verbal Problems

MATHEMATICS

Solving **word problems** (**verbal problems**) is a very sophisticated task. According to Miller and Koesling (2009, p. 65), "Rich word problems provide the teacher with in-depth assessment of a student's skills." This assessment helps teachers determine what additional instruction students need.

Many readers have significant difficulties reading and understanding word problems, which are mathematical situations stated in words and symbols. Even when they can read the words and sentences with facility, they have difficulty choosing the correct process (operation) to solve the problem.

MATHEMATICS

The following steps are a guided reading procedure for students to use with word problems:

1. *Survey.* Read the problem out loud. Try to visualize the situation.

2. *Question.* What is the problem asking you to find? This step gives students a purpose for reading the problem. It helps them know why they are reading.

3. *Question.* What is (are) the correct process (or processes) (e.g., addition, subtraction, division, or a combination) to use in solving the problem?

4. *Read.* Read the problem again to locate pertinent information needed to solve the problem and to decide the order in which the mathematical operations should be performed.

5. *Work.* Work the problem and check your answer.

EXAMPLE 11.15　**Math of Money—Problem–Solution Pattern**

MATHEMATICS

Math of Money

Ted owes $720 on his credit card. He plans to make the minimum required payment of $20 this month. His interest rate is 18 percent per year. What is his monthly interest rate? How much of his payment will be interest? If he doesn't charge anything else, how much will his $20 payment reduce his debt?

Solution

0.18 per year ÷ 12 months = 0.015 = 1.5 percent per month

Ted pays 1.5 percent interest each month.

$720.000 × 0.015 = $10.80

The monthly interest rate is applied to Ted's unpaid balance of $720.00, so the monthly interest is $10.80.

$20.00 − $10.80 = $9.20

Ted's minimum payment this month reduces his debt by only $9.20. Since interest is charged on and added to the unpaid balance, his debt will decrease by a little more than this amount in following months. At this rate, it will take him more than five years to pay off his debt. If he charges anything else in those five years, it will take even longer to pay off the debt. From these numbers, you can see that Ted could get into debt trouble easily by making only the minimum payment each month.

Source: *Economic Education for Consumers* by Roger Miller and Alan Stafford, p. 341. South-Western Cengage 2010.

EXAMPLE 11.16　**Verbal Problem (Mathematics)**

MATHEMATICS

Converting Customary Units to Metric Units

Objective: To convert customary units to metric units. Because most other countries use the metric system, many United States companies convert the customary measurements of their products into metric units before exporting them. You can do this type of conversion using a chart like the one below.

When You Know	Multiply By	To Find
Inches	2.54	Centimeters
Feet	0.3	Meters
Yards	0.91	Meters
Miles	1.61	Kilometers
Ounces	28.35	Grams
Pounds	0.454	Kilograms
Fluid ounces	29.573	Milliliters
Pints	0.473	Liters
Quarts	0.946	Liters
Gallons	3.785	Liters

Example: Anderson Architects designs buildings worldwide. They recently designed a house that might be built in both the United States and Canada. The United States plans show that the length of the house is 57 ft and the width of the house is 33 ft. What are the length and width in meters that should be shown on the Canadian plans?

Source: Francis J. Gardella, Patricia R. Fraze, Joanne E. Meldon, et al., *Mathematical Connections*, p. 84. Copyright © 1992 by Houghton Mifflin Company. Reprinted by permission of Houghton Mifflin Company. All rights reserved.

MATHEMATICS

What is the demonstration pattern in mathematics?

Demonstration Pattern

The **demonstration pattern** is usually accompanied by an example that illustrates operations and concepts. This writing pattern is important in mathematics materials because it shows students how to work problems. Following are exercises to help students understand the strategies that they can use while reading the demonstration pattern.

1. The student should work through the example to determine whether he or she understands the process. If the student does not compute the same answer as shown in the example, he or she should work slowly through the example again, rereading each step carefully to determine the point in the process at which he or she erred.

2. The student should paraphrase the process in his or her own words.

3. The student should apply the process to other situations.

MATHEMATICS

Graphs and Charts

Graphs and charts are often used to represent mathematical concepts in math materials as well as in other content textbooks, in newspapers, and in magazines. Example 11.17 shows the use of graphs in mathematics textbooks.

EXAMPLE 11.17 | Graphing Equations (Mathematics)

MATHEMATICS

SECTION

7.1

Using Linear Equations in Standard Form

Learn how to...

• write and graph equations in standard form

So you can...

• solve problems with two variables, such as nutritional planning or telecommunications problems

Nancy Clark recommends that runners replace their muscles' energy stores after a marathon. A runner should eat at least 0.5 g of foods containing carbohydrates for each pound of body weight within 2 h after the race. The athlete should eat at least this amount again 2 h later.

EXAMPLE 1 | **Interview: Nancy Clark**

Leon should eat at least 70 g of carbohydrates after running a marathon. One cup of apple juice contains **30 g** of carbohydrates, and 1 oz of pretzels contains **23 g**. Write and graph an equation showing combinations of pretzels and juice that provide 70 g of carbohydrates.

SOLUTION

Step 1 Write an equation.

Let j = number of cups of juice.

Let p = number of ounces of pretzels.

$$\begin{array}{ccc} \text{Carbohydrates} & + & \text{Carbohydrates} \\ \text{from juice} & & \text{from pretzels} \end{array} = 70$$

$$30j \quad + \quad 23p \quad = 70$$

Step 2 Graph the equation.

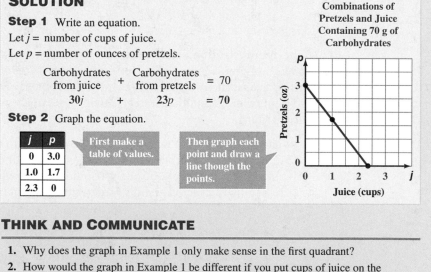

Combinations of Pretzels and Juice Containing 70 g of Carbohydrates

j	p
0	3.0
1.0	1.7
2.3	0

First make a table of values.

Then graph each point and draw a line though the points.

BY THE WAY

After the Boston Marathon, runners eat snacks such as pretzels and bread supplied by their sponsors. Ten small pretzels weigh about one ounce.

THINK AND COMMUNICATE

1. Why does the graph in Example 1 only make sense in the first quadrant?
2. How would the graph in Example 1 be different if you put cups of juice on the vertical axis?

Source: Miriam A. Leiva and Richard G. Brown, *Algebra I: Explorations and Applications* (Evanston, Ill.: McDougal Littell, 1997), p. 281. Reprinted by permission.

Symbols, Signs, and Formulas

Students of mathematics must learn to read and use the special symbols, signs, and formulas found in mathematics textbooks. This is illustrated in Examples 11.14–11.17. First, they need to realize the importance of knowing symbols, signs, and formulas. Then they must focus on the meaning of each and learn each in relationship to its meaning and application.

Teaching Mathematics Content

MATHEMATICS

Teachers can use vocabulary strategies to introduce the important terms and concepts in meaningful contexts. Brainstorming will help students associate mathematics terms with previous experiences. Comprehension of mathematics content is facilitated with advance organizers, structured overviews, study guides, concept guides, and directed reading lessons to focus attention on understanding while reading. Example 11.18 illustrates a mathematics reading guide based on the textbook selection in Example 11.16.

EXAMPLE 11.18   **Mathematics Reading Guide (based on Example 11.16)**

MATHEMATICS

Part I: Facts of the Problem

Directions: Read the problem. Then in Column A, check the statements that contain the important facts of the problem. You may refer to the problem to verify your responses. In Column B, check the statements that will help you solve the problem.

A	B	
_____	_____	**1.** Anderson Architects designs buildings worldwide.
_____	_____	**2.** These architects have been in business for five years.
_____	_____	**3.** They recently designed a house for construction in the United States.
_____	_____	**4.** This house can also be built in Canada.
_____	_____	**5.** The United States plans show the length of the house is 57 feet.
_____	_____	**6.** The United States plans show the width of the house is 33 feet.

Part II: Mathematical Ideas and Interpretations

Directions: Check the statements that contain mathematical concepts related to the problem. You may go back to Part I to review your responses.

_____ **1.** Canadians measure in meters.

_____ **2.** In the United States, measurement is generally stated in feet.

_____ **3.** Canadians could convert meters to feet in order to interpret the house plans.

_____ **4.** To convert feet to meters, multiply the measurements in feet by 0.3.

_____ **5.** People in the United States are using metric measurement more frequently now than 25 years ago.

Part III: Computation

Directions: Below are possible mathematical calculations. Check those that apply to this problem. You may refer to Part I and Part II to verify your responses.

_____ **1.** 57 ft + 33 ft = 90 ft

_____ **2.** 57 ft – 33 ft = 24 ft

_____ **3.** 57 ft (0.3 m per ft) = 17.1 m

_____ **4.** 33 ft (0.3 m per ft) = 9.9 m

_____ **5.** 57 ft ÷ 0.3 m per ft =

English (Language Arts) Content

What are the components of the language arts?

**ENGLISH/
LANGUAGE
ARTS**

The language arts are listening, speaking, reading, writing, viewing, visually representing, and thinking. A command of English is essential to effective communication; therefore, study of the language arts focuses on effective use and appreciation of the English language. English has the most varied subject matter of all the content subjects. Study of English requires readers to work with grammar, composition, and many forms of literature—novels, short stories, poetry, biographies, and autobiographies, for example.

Vocabulary Development

Vocabulary development is an important aspect of English instruction because students who have a large store of word meanings at their command are better communicators. Exploring changes in word meanings is one way to expand students' vocabularies.

Changes in Word Meanings

Studying etymology shows students that meanings of certain words have changed over time. For example, the word *marshal* once meant "one who held horses," a meaning not quite as impressive as its present-day meaning. Daily use of words over the years leads to gradual change in their meanings, which can be systematically analyzed as illustrated in the following list of types of changes:

**ENGLISH/
LANGUAGE
ARTS**

1. *Amelioration.* The meaning of the word has changed so that the word means something better than it once did. For example, a person who was called *enthusiastic* was once considered a fanatic. Currently, enthusiasm is considered a desirable quality.

2. *Pejoration.* Pejoration indicates that the word has _____ than it did earlier in its history. For example, a *villa*_____ servant from a villa. Currently, a villain is considere_____

3. *Generalization.* Some words become more gene_____ generalization operates, the meaning of words is b_____ *picture* meant painting, but now *picture* may mea_____ drawing. In fact, a picture may not be representat_____ picture may not have a distinct form.

4. *Specialization.* The opposite of generalization is _____ word meanings become more specific than they were in the past. At one time, *meat* meant any food, not just lamb, pork, or beef.

5. *Euphemism.* This term indicates the use of an affectation to convey elegance or the use of a more pleasant word for an unpleasant one. For example, a *janitor* is often called a "custodian" or a "maintenance engineer," and a person does not *die* but rather "passes away."

6. *Hyperbole.* This is an extreme exaggeration. For example, a man who is tired might say that he could "sleep for a year." Exaggeration is being used to make the point of extreme fatigue. Many people currently use the word *fantastic* to describe almost anything unusual, although *fantastic* means strange, wonderful, unreal, and illusory.

Activities such as the following can be used to develop word meanings through etymology:

1. Give students a list of words with instructions to determine the origin of each term and the types of changes that have occurred in its meaning. Words such as the following could be used in this activity: *city, ghetto, manuscript, lord, stench.*

2. Ask students to identify the origins of the names of the months or the days of the week. For example, *October* is from the Latin *Octo* (eight), because it was the eighth month of the Roman calendar. *Monday* means "day of the moon."

3. Encourage students to determine the origins and meanings of their first names and surnames. For example, *Susan* means "lily." Many surnames are related to occupation or geographic origin. The surname *Butler* means a bottle maker; the surname *Hatfield* refers to a wooded field.

Types of Words

How can the unique characteristics of words be used to increase word knowledge?

Word knowledge can be increased by exploring some of the unique characteristics of different types of words. Activities that involve acronyms, oxymorons, and homonyms, for example, will develop students' vocabularies. Following are definitions of some special types of words:

1. *Acronym.* A word composed of the first letters or syllables of longer terms, such as MADD, which means "*Mothers Against Drunk Driving.*"

2. *Oxymoron.* Two incongruous words used together, such as *cruel kindness.*

3. *Homonyms*, or *homophones*. Words that sound alike but have different meanings, such as *to, too, two; pare, pair; sum, some*.

4. *Heteronyms*. Words that have different pronunciations and meanings, although they are spelled exactly the same, such as:
   - Don't *subject* me to that experience.
   - What is the *subject* of your book?

5. *Coined word*. A word invented to meet specific needs. Words are often coined by using previously existing words and word parts. *Gerrymander, curfew, motel,* and *astronaut* are examples of coined words. Many product names are coined words, for example, *Jell-O* and *Bisquick*.

A book that students may enjoy reading, as they learn more about the English language in general and aspects of vocabulary in particular, is *The Word Snoop* by Ursula Duborsarsky.

Denotative and Connotative Meanings of Words

What are the denotative and connotative meanings of words?

ENGLISH/ LANGUAGE ARTS

The denotative and connotative meanings of words can be introduced through literature. **Denotation** is the literal definition of a word as defined by the dictionary. **Connotation** refers to the ideas and associations that are suggested by a term, including emotional reactions. For instance, the word *home* denotes the place where one lives, whereas it may connote warmth, love, and family. Readers must learn to recognize the connotations of words in order to comprehend a selection. By definition, *cunning* and *astute* are very similar, but when the word *cunning* is used to describe a person, it usually implies a negative quality, while describing a person as *astute* is complimentary.

Students can look for examples of both connotative and denotative uses of words in the literary selections they read. In addition, the following activities will increase their understanding of denotation and connotation:

1. In each pair, select the word that you would prefer to use for describing yourself. Tell why you chose the word.
   a. *creative* or *screwball*
   b. *stolid* or *easygoing*
   c. *conceited* or *proud*

2. Provide students with a list of words similar to the preceding list, and ask them to write a plus (+) beside each positive word, a minus (−) beside each negative word, and a zero (0) beside each neutral word.

Figurative language is connotative use of language. The author implies ideas through figurative language, and this expressive application of language makes written language more interesting to readers. Refer to Chapter 4 for suggestions to aid in instruction related to figurative language.

Literature

ENGLISH/
LANGUAGE
ARTS

The goal of teaching literature is to develop in readers a lifelong interest in and appreciation for literature. Having students read and respond to interesting literary selections helps teachers achieve these goals. When students read material that is related to their interests and background experience, their schemata will enable them to read with greater comprehension. Many students need guides that will help them comprehend literature, such as anticipation guides, advance organizers, and three-level study guides.

Novels and Short Stories

ENGLISH/
LANGUAGE
ARTS

Reading novels and short stories is basic to the study of literature. These types of literature are imaginative expressions of writers' ideas: the authors share experiences with the readers by relating incidents through stories. The longer form of the novel permits an author to develop literary elements, such as characterization, in greater depth than is possible within the form of the short story.

Response is the readers' reactions and feelings about reading content. Researchers have identified eight processes that are involved in a student's response to literature (Cooper and Purves, 1973). These processes are as follows:

1. *Description.* Students can restate in their own words what they have read.

2. *Discrimination.* Students can discriminate among different writings on the basis of type, author, theme, and so forth.

3. *Relation.* Students can relate several aspects of a piece of literature to each other. For example, students can discuss the relationship between a story's setting and plot or can compare the plots of two different stories.

4. *Interpretation.* Students can interpret the author's ideas and can support these interpretations.

5. *Generalization.* Students can use what they have learned in one piece of literature to understand another one.

6. *Evaluation.* Students can apply criteria to evaluate a piece of literature. For example, they might evaluate the quality of the element of characterization.

7. *Valuing.* Students can relate literature to their own lives.

8. *Creation.* Students can respond to literature by creating their own art, music, writing, drama, or dance.

How are schemata related to the study of literature?

When teaching novels or short stories, teachers activate students' schemata. Then they have students read through the story, although the reading may extend over several class sessions. Reading the entire selection enables students to understand the entire plot, character development, setting, and theme. If the reading of a selection is limited to chapters or smaller parts, the reader may not grasp the entire selection or the way the components of the selection fit together.

In addition to using the eight processes of responding to literature to guide instruction, the teacher asks students to support answers to questions with material from the selections they have read. Students may be asked to diagram story structure in the following manner:

Title			
Setting	*Theme*	*Plot*	*Characters*
Place Time	Symbols Incidents	Episode #1 Episode #2 Episode #3	Main character Supporting character

Poetry

ENGLISH/
LANGUAGE
ARTS

Poetry is a condensed form of writing that expresses in a succinct fashion the writer's thoughts and emotions and stimulates the reader's imagination. Frequently, a poet can inspire a reader to perceive familiar things and ideas in a new way. Poets use rhythm, rhyme, imagery, and many other devices to make a reader see or feel what they are expressing.

Teachers may use the following techniques with poetry:

1. Poems should be read aloud.

2. Poems should be read in their entirety for full appreciation.

3. Poems should usually be read twice for full appreciation.

4. Prose and poetry on the same topic may be compared in order to understand the succinctness of poetry.

More on poetry instruction and its uses across the curriculum is found in Chapters 9 and 10.

Drama

What type of literature is drama?

ENGLISH/
LANGUAGE
ARTS

Drama is literature that is written to be acted. In drama, the characters tell the story. Scripts include stage directions needed to understand the plot. The reader should pay attention to all information in parentheses and italics. The name of the speaker is printed before his or her lines, and the reader must be alert to the names of the speakers in order to determine who is speaking and how the action unfolds.

The following teaching procedures help students understand drama when they read it:

1. Ask the students to visualize story action.

2. Have the students read the speeches aloud to aid comprehension.

3. Have the students act out described actions to arrive at a better understanding of the action.

4. Have the students write a play and act it out as described.

Essays and Editorials

ENGLISH/
LANGUAGE
ARTS

Essays, editorials, and position papers are expository forms of writing. **Exposition** is used to explain information from a particular point of view. The author is usually trying to convince readers to accept his or her argument. Exposition contains a greater amount of information than fiction does. The strategies suggested in this chapter (and in Chapters 5, 6, 7, 8, and 12) for guiding the reading of content materials aid the teacher in teaching exposition. Following are activities that teachers can use to help students comprehend expository materials:

1. Identify the author's purpose.

2. Identify the author's argument.

3. Identify the details the author uses to support his or her argument and the sequence in which the author presents these details.

4. Identify the author's organizational pattern.

5. Identify the author's biases related to the topic and the audience.

The preceding activities can be used for discussions and study guides.

Genre and Multigenre Studies

ENGLISH/
LANGUAGE
ARTS

Genre studies are those that include reading and writing a variety of materials reflecting a specific type of discourse (genre). These activities direct students' attention to the type of discourse they are reading, which is important for today's students, as diverse materials and multiple literacies become increasingly important to learning.

Multigenre reading and writing (reading and writing of many genres) are valuable instructional activities for projects, units, inquiry, and research papers. Moulton (1999) reports multigenre papers that included newspaper articles, lists, narrative stories, letters, journals, photos, documents, stream-of-consciousness writing, and maps. Students could also use Internet materials, videos, photo essays, and magazine articles. See Chapter 9 for more on multigenre writing.

Grammar and Composition

ENGLISH/
LANGUAGE
ARTS

Textbooks and electronic media are used in many language arts classes to teach grammar and composition. They use technical vocabulary words such as *complex sentences*, *interrogative*, and *adjective*. These textbooks and handbooks usually follow an expository pattern: a concept or idea is explained and illustrated, a definition or generalization is developed, and application exercises are provided. Many details are packed into a page, and students need to skim and scan when they need to find specific information. Frequently the material is almost in outline form, requiring readers to identify supporting details and main ideas. Some of the models and examples used in language arts textbooks are written in a narrative style, so that the reader must switch from expository to narrative style. Example 11.19 shows content from a grammar and composition text that is written in a definition or explanation pattern.

| **EXAMPLE 11.19** | **Content from a Grammar and Composition Text** |

ENGLISH/
LANGUAGE
ARTS

Lesson 6 ***Placement of Phrases***

I   Here's the Idea

A common mistake that writers make is putting phrases in the wrong positions in sentences. This mistake usually involves phrases used as adjectives or adverbs.

Misplaced Phrases

A **misplaced phrase** is a phrase that is placed so far away from the word it modifies that the meaning of the sentence is unclear or incorrect. The types of phrases that are most often misplaced are prepositional phrases and participial phrases.

Draft

> *Misplaced prepositional phrase*
>
> The U.S. team in men's indoor volleyball won the most
> Olympic gold medals during the 1980s.

The sentence above says that the U.S. men's indoor volleyball team won more Olympic gold medals than any other team in any sport. This is not true.

Revision

> The U.S. team won the most Olympic gold medals
> in men's indoor volleyball during the 1980s.

Dangling Phrases

When the word or words that a phrase should modify are missing from a sentence, the phrase is called a **dangling phrase.** Most dangling phrases are participial phrases or infinitive phrases.

Draft

> *Dangling participial phrase*
>
> Failing to win a gold medal in the 1900s, the Olympic women's
> indoor volleyball competition has been disappointing.

The sentence above says that a competition won a gold medal.

Revision

> *Words modified*
>
> Failing to win a gold medal in the 1900s, the U.S. women's
> indoor volleyball team was disappointing at the Olympics.

Source: Mary Newton Bruder, Rebekah Caplan, Sharon Sicinski Skeans, and Richard Vinson, *Language Network, Grade 9*, p. 78. Copyright © 2001 by McDougal Littell Inc., a division of Houghton Mifflin Company. All rights reserved. Reprinted by permission of McDougal Littell Inc., a division of Houghton Mifflin Company.

Many teachers use their text as a handbook or have students obtain handbooks to use as a reference. Students find handbooks such as Andrea Lunsford's *Easy Writer* (2006) helpful.

Focusing on paraphrasing and finding applications for grammar, spelling, punctuation, and capitalization instruction helps students retain the information. Advance organizers, study guides, and concept guides are especially useful for teaching the conventions of language. The Internet offers websites for grammar, spelling, and punctuation.

Foreign Languages

Why is foreign language study so valuable?

FOREIGN LANGUAGE

The ability to read and speak foreign languages is a valuable skill in today's world because of increased travel and communication among the people of the world. Current approaches to foreign language study include meaning-centered activities with a cultural focus that emphasizes functional language use. See Example 11.20.

Learning to read a foreign language is very similar to learning to read one's native language. The teacher exposes students to oral language to develop their readiness for learning the new language. Listening comprehension of language precedes reading comprehension; and foreign language tapes, computer programs, and foreign language broadcasts on radio and television develop listening comprehension.

Prior to reading, students need to learn about the concepts and hear the vocabulary used in the assigned selections. Discussion and practice of common phrases and expressions are useful in developing readiness to read, as is using the context to understand words and expressions. In addition, the teacher should provide questions to guide the students' silent reading.

Reading for global meaning in a foreign language is more effective than translating a page or passage word by word. Stopping several times on each line to check English equivalents keeps students from effectively accessing the ideas from the written language. Students should have opportunities to listen to, speak, read, and write the language. These activities will help them learn both the semantics and the syntax of the language. Teachers can use the same methods in teaching students to read a foreign language that they use in teaching them to read English.

The following are some specific activities useful for helping students develop comprehension of a foreign language:

1. Teach students to use a foreign language dictionary.

2. Encourage students to write their own ideas in the language being studied.

3. List words in English that are derived from the language studied.

4. Ask students to describe a basketball, football, or soccer game in the language they are studying.

5. Provide students with direction cards written in English. Have them state the directions in the foreign language. For example, directions for finding the sporting goods department in a department store could be provided.

EXAMPLE 11.20 **Teacher's Edition of a Spanish Text**

FOREIGN
LANGUAGE

UNIDAD 1 Etapa 3
Vocabulary/Grammar

Teaching Resource Options

Print

Más práctica Workbook PE,
pp. 25–28, 32
Cuaderno para hispanohablantes PE,
pp. 25–26, 30
Block Scheduling Copymasters
Unit 1 Resource Book
Más práctica Workbook TE, pp. 154–
157, 161
Cuaderno para hispanohablantes TE,
pp. 162–163, 167
Information Gap Activities, pp. 171–172
Audioscript, pp. 182–184

Audiovisual

OHT 33 (Quick Start)
Audio Program Cassettes 3A, 3B / CD 3;
(*Para hispanohablantes* Cassette 3B /
CD 3)

Technology

Intrigas y aventuras CD-ROM, Disc 1

Quick Start Review

♻ Numbers

Use OHT 33 or write on the board:
Write out the missing numbers in words:

1. $10 + 10 = ?$ 6. $16 + 1 = ?$
2. $95 - 80 = ?$ 7. $80 - 15 = ?$
3. $14 \times 2 = ?$ 8. $12 \times 3 = ?$
4. $100 \div 20 = ?$ 9. $100 \div 2 = ?$
5. $? - 52 = 18$ 10. $? - 34 = 15$

Answers *See p. 67B.*

Teaching Suggestions
Giving Dates: Day and Month

• Have students read the **Gramática**
box and look at the vocabulary.
• Model the months.
• Ask simple yes/no questions until you
are sure students understand the
concept and structure. For example:
pointing to calendar: ¿Es el (seis de
octubre) hoy? (Sí.) ¿Mañana, es el
(siete de octubre)? (Sí.) etc.
• Use the TPR activity for additional
practice.

ACTIVIDAD 16 Objective: Transitional practice
Saying how many there is/are

Answers will vary.

ACTIVIDAD 16

En la clase

Hablar/Escribir Explica cuántas
personas de cada tipo hay en
la clase. (*Hint: Explain how many of
each type of person there are in the class.*)

Nota

The word **hay** is used to mean *there is*
or *there are.*

Hay muchos murales en la ciudad
de Los Ángeles.
*There are many murals in the city of
Los Angeles.*

Hay un concurso muy interesante.
There is a very interesting contest.

To say that there are none, use
No hay...

1. chicas castañas
2. chicos castaños
3. chicos rubios
4. chicas rubias
5. chicos morenos
6. chicas morenas
7. chicos pelirrojos
8. chicas pelirrojas
9. chicos
10. maestros

NOTA CULTURAL

In Spanish-speaking countries,
the date is written with the
number of the day first, then the
number of the month.
el dos de mayo = 2/5

82 ochenta y dos
Unidad 1

GRAMÁTICA

Giving Dates: Day and Month

When you want to give the date, use the following phrase:

Es el + number + de + month.

—¿Cuál es la fecha de hoy?
What is the date today?

—Hoy es el **once** de noviembre.
Today is the eleventh of November.

In Spanish, the only date that does not follow
this pattern is the first of the month.

Es el primero de noviembre.
It is November first.

Notice that the
names of months are not
capitalized in Spanish.

Vocabulario

Los meses del año

enero	febrero	marzo	abril
mayo	**junio**	**julio**	**agosto**
septiembre	**octubre**	**noviembre**	**diciembre**

¿Cuál es tu mes favorito?

Classroom Community

Group Activity Have students create a wall-sized
calendar for the upcoming month. They should
decorate the days with special holidays, school sporting
or academic events, and birthdays.

TPR Write the months of the year across the board.
As you say a month, students born in that month go up
and stand under it. When all months have been called
out, each student says the date of his/her birthday.
Students in each month then line up according to
dates.

La familia de Francisco

Escribir Explica cuándo son los cumpleaños. *(Hint: Explain when their birthdays are.)*

modelo

Francisco: 15/3

*El cumpleaños de **Francisco** es el **quince de marzo**.*

1. Alma: 4/1
2. Verónica: 22/10
3. Andrés: 5/5
4. la abuela: 23/7
5. yo: ¿?
6. mi madre: ¿?
7. mi padre: ¿?
8. mi amigo(a): ¿?

■ **MÁS PRÁCTICA** *cuaderno p. 32*
■ **PARA HISPANOHABLANTES**
   cuaderno p. 30

¿Cuál es la fecha de tu cumpleaños?

Hablar Pregúntales a otros estudiantes la fecha de su cumpleaños. ¿Cuántos cumpleaños hay en cada mes? *(Hint: Ask other students their birthdays. How many are in each month?)*

Nombre	Su cumpleaños es
Ramón	el 13 de junio

¿Cuál es la respuesta?

Escuchar Escoge la respuesta correcta. *(Hint: Choose the correct answer.)*

1. a. Tiene cinco años.
   b. Tiene setenta años.
   c. Tiene veinte años.

2. a. Son viejas.
   b. Son grandes.
   c. Son jóvenes.

3. a. Soy policía.
   b. Soy estudiante.
   c. Soy maestro.

4. a. Llevo un suéter.
   b. Llevo una camiseta.
   c. Llevo una chaqueta.

Mi madre

Escribir Describe a un miembro de tu familia. *(Hint: Describe a family member.)*

modelo

Mi madre se llama Elena. Es alta y castaña. Tiene los ojos verdes. Le gusta cantar y leer. Es muy inteligente. Tiene cuarenta años. Su cumpleaños es el cuatro de mayo.

■ **MÁS COMUNICACIÓN** *p. R3*

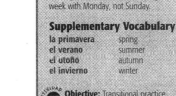

Pronunciación

Trabalenguas

Pronunciación de la *m* y la *n* The letters m and n are pronounced in Spanish just as they are in English. Try the following tongue twisters.

Nueve nenes nadan.   **Mi mamá me mima.**

ochenta y tres
Etapa 3   83

Teaching All Students

Extra Help Have students list 5 friends or family members with their birthdays, first as a number, then written out in Spanish.

Multiple Intelligences

Kinesthetic Have students make small placards with the months of the year on them. They should decorate them according to the season. Send 12 students, each with a different month in hand, to the front of the class. Have them quickly organize themselves from January to December. The cards can be used for spelling practice.

Source: Estella Gahala, Patricia Hamilton Carlin, Audrey L. Heining-Boynton, Ricardo Otheguy, and Barbara J. Rupert, *¡En Español!, Uno,* pages 82–83. Copyright © 2000 by McDougal Littell Inc., a division of Houghton Mifflin Company. All rights reserved. Reprinted by permission of McDougal Littell Inc., a division of Houghton Mifflin Company.

Cross Cultural Connections

Remind students that many calendars from Spain and Latin America begin the week with Monday, not Sunday.

Supplementary Vocabulary

la primavera	spring
el verano	summer
el otoño	autumn
el invierno	winter

Objective: Transitional practice
Day and month

Answers
1. El cumpleaños de Alma es el cuatro de enero.
2. El cumpleaños de Verónica es el veintidós de octubre.
3. El cumpleaños de Andrés es el cinco de mayo.
4. El cumpleaños de la abuela es el veintitrés de julio.
5. Mi cumpleaños es el...
6. El cumpleaños de mi madre es el...
7. El cumpleaños de mi padre es el...
8. El cumpleaños de mi amigo(a) es el...

Objective: Transitional practice
Day and date in conversation

Answers will vary.
Alternate: Have students ask you your birthday.

Objective: Transitional practice
Listening comprehension/vocabulary

Answers *(See script p. 67B.)*
1. b   3. b
2. c   4. b

Objective: Open-ended practice
Describing family, telling ages, talking about birthdays in writing

Answers will vary.

Dictation

After students have read the tongue twisters in the **Pronunciación**, have them close their books. Dictate the tongue twisters in segments while students write them.

■ Block Schedule

Retention Have students write a description of a friend or a famous person, modeled after **Actividad 20**. (For additional activities, see **Block Scheduling Copymasters**.)

6. The preceding activity can be reversed, with the directions printed in a foreign language and the students stating them in English.

7. Have students write, in a foreign language, an advertisement to sell an automobile.

8. Provide students with grocery advertisements, and ask them to write the foreign word for each item in the advertisement.

9. Provide students with objects to categorize by form, function, color, or texture in the foreign language.

10. Demonstrate a think-aloud for a foreign language reading selection, then have the students create their own think-alouds for content they are reading in the foreign language.

11. Access foreign language sites on the Internet.

12. List cognates and false cognates.

FOCUS ON *Struggling Readers*

Struggling Readers in Content Area Reading

One of the greatest content literacy problems facing struggling readers is their lack of concepts and vocabulary relating to the subject matter at hand (Grady, 2002). The extent to which readers are able to understand texts depends on prior knowledge and their ability to implement comprehension strategies. Struggling readers read infrequently, so they have not acquired the requisite background knowledge, skills, and vocabulary needed for comprehending content materials. Teachers need to build background for understanding and to illustrate the relationships between students' existing knowledge and the texts they are reading. Various kinds of reading support and scaffolding help these readers.

Reading coaches are a form of support that has been successful in helping struggling readers in the content areas. Bacon (2005) used a one-on-one peer coaching system wherein students acted as reading coaches for one another and learned to prompt, question, and probe their peers' thinking, in much the same way that a reading specialist does.

A reading apprenticeship was developed as part of an academic literacy course in a San Francisco high school (Greenleaf et al., 2001). In this program, students were mentored as they read subject area texts. The mentors helped students understand how and why readers need vocabulary and concepts related to different texts. One of the questions addressed in this program was, "What do I need to know to be able to understand these different kinds of texts?" The author reports that the struggling readers in the program demonstrated significant gains on standardized reading comprehension measures. Moreover, the students indicated that they believed the mentoring approach affected them in positive ways.

Self-questioning is a highly effective strategy (Stoodt-Hill, 2005). Students require modeling prior to developing their own questions about the topic under study. Generating questions to find the answers through study encourages active reading. This helps students grasp the important ideas. After reading they remember more of the vital information and are better able to analyze and synthesize. Alverman (2004) analyzed the research on self-questioning and found that self-questioning would serve science learning well.

Explicitly teaching strategies for understanding text and monitoring comprehension helps struggling readers understand content textbooks. The most valuable strategies for helping struggling readers are K-W-L, self-questioning, visual imagery, ReQuest (Reciprocal questioning), retelling, and question-answer relationships (Dole et al., 1996; Quatroche, 1999). All of these valuable strategies have been discussed previously in this text except ReQuest. Reciprocal questioning (ReQuest) improves comprehension and helps students develop questioning skills. This strategy is used most effectively in the classroom when the teacher models the process with a student and then pairs students to follow the procedure. The basic steps in ReQuest follow:

1. Both student and teacher (or paired student) silently read the first sentence of the selection. Then the student asks the partner as many questions as possible about the sentence—with the book closed. The student attempts to ask the kinds of questions that the teacher would routinely pose for the class.

2. The teacher (or paired student) answers all the student's questions, asking the student to restate any question that was poorly stated. The teacher or partner restates any answers that the student does not fully understand.

3. After all the questions have been answered, the second sentence is read—and the teacher or second student now asks thought-provoking questions to ensure comprehension of the content. The teacher acts as a questioning model for the student and goes on to pose questions that require evaluation of prior student responses.

4. ReQuest continues until the student can confidently answer the questions, "What do you think is going to happen in the rest of this selection?" And "What have you read that causes you to make this prediction?" The student reads to the end of the selection to determine if the prediction was correct.

FOCUS ON *English Language Learners*

English Language Learners and Content Area Reading

The rapid growth in the number of English language learners (ELLs) (Willner et al., 2009) exacerbates the difficulty of addressing the needs of this population. ELLs need cultural background to develop the fund of everyday knowledge needed to understand content textbooks (Moje et al., 2004). They need resources to help them make sense of the United States. They also need a sense of both oral and written language as they exist in the United States. Effective instruction for ELLs requires teacher-planned scaffolding (Graves and Fitzgerald, 2003). Activating or building background knowledge is necessary, as is specific text knowledge. Graves and Fitzgerald (2003) suggest that ELLs write a list of what they know about a topic before reading. The goal is to prepare students to read the selection.

The following guidelines for improving content instruction for ELLs are based on recommendations by Willner, Rivera, and Acosta (2009):

1. Students need to learn content.

2. When assessing student progress, help ELLs access the language of the test.

3. Students have individual needs. To meet these needs teachers can provide dictionaries or dual language texts. Some students may require oral tests.

4. A team approach can be helpful because the team can provide multiple perspectives regarding individual ELLs.

Summary

This chapter focuses on content literacy both in printed texts and other media. Secondary students read content materials in social studies, science and health, mathematics, English (language arts), and foreign languages. Written materials and media in each of these content areas have characteristic patterns of language and organization that students can use to increase comprehension. Examples of content texts and strategies to increase understanding are presented throughout the chapter. Content literacy presents particular problems for struggling readers and for English language learners. These students tend to lack the background knowledge and concepts needed for successful content reading.

Discussion Questions

1. How are social studies content and mathematics content alike in their demands? How are they different?
2. Why is critical reading important in all content areas?
3. How do multiple literacies relate to content reading?
4. How can teachers help students comprehend mathematics content?
5. What are the characteristics of science materials?
6. How can reading coaches help both struggling readers and English language learners?

Enrichment Activities

*1. Prepare a study guide for a chapter in a social studies or science textbook. Use it with a secondary class.

*2. Prepare a study guide for a verbal problem in a mathematics textbook. Use it with a secondary class.

*3. Develop a bibliography of trade books that could be used to enrich a textbook chapter. Let secondary students use books from this list as they read the chapter.

*4. Prepare a multigenre assignment for your content area.

5. Check professional journals such as *Social Education*, *Science Teacher*, *Mathematics Teacher*, and *English Journal* for articles dealing with reading of content material. Share your findings with the class.

6. Check the readability level of a textbook and/or supplementary material used for one of the subjects treated in this chapter. See Chapter 3 for details.

7. Review computer software that could be used to teach one of the content subjects in this chapter.

*8. Identify Internet sites to use with your content area.

*These activities are designed for in-service teachers, student teachers, and practicum students.

Resources including the TeachSource Video Cases can be found on the website for this book. Cengage Learning's CourseMate brings course concepts to life with interactive learning, study, and exam preparation tools that support the printed textbook. Go to www.cengage.com/login to register your access code.

CHAPTER 12

Reading in the Content Areas: II

Overview

The focus of this chapter is reading in career-oriented and performance-based content areas. This curriculum is changing due to increasing interest in vocational and technical education. Many students are concerned with preparing for employment when they graduate from high school, while other students enroll in these courses to prepare for further vocational education. Courses in forensic science, woodworking, and landscaping are courses now included in vocational high school curricula and many of these courses are taught in secondary schools that are not identified as vocational high schools.

The lines between academic and career-oriented education have become increasingly blurred as educators have recognized that all students need active involvement in constructing meaning and connecting learning to the world outside of school (Wonacott, 2002). Further major changes are taking place in workplace education as the curriculum becomes more demanding due to an upgraded core of academic courses. The content study and achievement required of **tech-prep students** are comparable to that required of college-prep students (Bottoms and Presson, 2000; Wonacott, 2002). Programs for these students are founded on the belief that blending the content of traditional college-preparatory studies in mathematics, science, and language arts with quality vocational and technical studies will provide a high-quality education for career-oriented students (Plank, 2001; Roberson et al., 2001).

Educators in career-oriented and technical classes teach with textbooks to complement and enhance the understanding and execution of hands-on work which is very important in career-oriented and technical classes (Darvin, 2006). "The relationship between reading and performance is of particular importance considering the large population of adolescents and adults in the United States who work in the trades and use trade-related texts in their daily lives" (Darvin, 2006, p. 10). Literacy skills are necessary for use of technology in every occupational category (Smith, 2000; Sumner, 2001; Wonacott, 2001). Therefore, teachers need to prepare students to communicate with technology in the workplace and to continuously update their knowledge in order to keep pace with technology.

Purpose-Setting Questions

As you read this chapter, try to answer these questions:

1. Identify some ways that technology communication skills are necessary for students in career studies.
2. What reading skills increase comprehension of content information in physical education?
3. What reading skills are required in music and art?
4. What strategies are useful for helping students comprehend the content and applications of vocational and technical materials?
5. Why are traditional college-preparatory studies important to preparing career-related education students?

Literacy for Career-Related Education

Work-based learning is a key factor in current models of career-related education (Hoyt, 2001). Today's students need basic skills and opportunities for practical applications of these skills as well as higher-order thinking skills in order to deal with the changes in work and the workplace (Hoyt and Wickwire, 2001). The instructional practices in these programs should help students recognize the importance of literacy learning in career-oriented education. The classroom environment should be supportive and encouraging, so that students experience success as they read, study, and relate text to hands-on experiences (Parris and Taliaferro, 2009).

Why is "work based" literacy important to the global community?

Career technical education contributes to our country's ability to compete in the global community. Its curriculum, standards, and organizing principles are drawn from the workplace (National Association of State Directors of Career Technical Education Consortium, 2001). An organized, comprehensive approach is needed to address changes in the work force and in national priorities and policies. However, the history of vocational education in this country shows that the programs also must keep the four-year college option open to students in a high school vocational curriculum; otherwise it will be difficult to attract ambitious students and to avoid acquiring a second-rate image. The Carl D. Perkins Career and Technical Education Act of 2006 (Public Law 109-270) concentrated attention on the academic achievement of career and technical education students and on strengthening connections between secondary and post-secondary education (U.S. Department of Education, 2006).

Why are literacy demands in vocational and technical education more complex in today's world?

Students who are preparing for career-oriented areas face more complex literacy demands than their predecessors did. Preparation for work now demands that students engage in the process of making meaning out of complex and layered combinations of messages that use video, audio, and print representations. This task requires comprehension, analysis, synthesis, and evaluation of the messages from which they gather information. Both workers and job seekers must transform information by writing and speaking about it and by visually representing it.

Finally, they must transmit information through publishing or otherwise disseminating it (Kibby, 2000).

What kinds of writing do students use in career-related education?

In **career-related education**, students reflect as they write about what they have seen and done in the workplace, and they discuss their writing in class. This process allows them to see how the problems they have confronted at work may relate to the subjects they have studied in school. Students also need writing skills to report observations and data collected, to fill in job cards, and to complete projects.

Hobbs and Frost (2003) conducted media-literacy skill research with eleventh-grade students. One research group was instructed in media literacy skills for a year. This group achieved a higher level of comprehension skills than a second group which did not receive instruction in media literacy skills. This study illustrates that media-literacy skills can be taught. Computer literacy skills instruction is necessary. Students may appear to be computer literate because they have computers at home and are adept at playing games on them, but these students do not fare as well when they need to use computers for work-related purposes.

Why is literacy important in technical and managerial jobs?

TECHNICAL EDUCATION

Literacy is an integral part of technical and managerial jobs. People in these positions read to analyze problems, propose solutions, and carry out research. Managers and supervisors read to review, advise, assign, and develop organizational procedures and policies. They write materials such as letters, memos, policies, and training materials. Managers may have to create training programs when new equipment or material, such as a new type of cash register or a new version of accounting software, is installed. Business software must often be updated, and business files of customers, clients, and patients have to be systematically examined to ensure that they are current.

Aspects of Vocational Literacy

Why are students less fluent when reading vocational materials than when reading narrative materials?

TECHNICAL EDUCATION

Since the amount of written material used in vocational subjects appears to be less than that required in other subjects, students and teachers may misjudge the difficulty of these materials. Many vocational materials are written in a concise expository style with technical vocabulary and are dense with information. Even brief vocational reading selections demand precise, careful reading. Many students will be less fluent when reading vocational materials, because they often have to read and reread since they are reading for application of information (Darvin, p, 2006). Students must be able to follow directions and to apply ideas and words to actual situations; misreading could be costly. See Figure 12.1 for a text illustrating the communication skills needed in the building trades.

Technical and Specialized Terminology

BUSINESS EDUCATION

Each career-related subject includes a great deal of specialized vocabulary that represents essential concepts. For example, the word *credit* has a special meaning in bookkeeping, where it refers to a bookkeeping entry that shows money paid on an account. ("You should place this entry on the *credit* side of the ledger.") In

FIGURE 12.1

Text Illustration of the Communication Skills Needed in the Building Trades

Source: John L. Feirer, Gilbert R. Hutchings, and Mark D. Feirer, *Carpentry and Building Construction*, 5th ed. (New York: Glencoe McGraw-Hill, 1997), p. 939. Reprinted by permission of Glencoe McGraw-Hill.

Appendix E: Communication Skills

Good communication skills are needed in almost every job. Good communication skills are especially important in the building trades. Here, an error in communicating or understanding information can have serious consequences.

The Need to Communicate

It is the rare individual who works without the need to communicate with others. Almost everyone has to communicate with his or her fellow workers several times a day. Such communication can, of course, involve relatively unimportant information. It can also relate to serious matters. Communication with your coworkers is a necessary part of every job in the building trades. Because of this, it is important that you have good communication skills.

Verbal Skills

All who work in the building trades need the same general communication skills. They need to be able to communicate clearly. They need to be able to listen well. Some individuals, however, will need these skills in a greater degree than others. This is because they will have a greater need to rely on such skills in their jobs. The need for communication skills can depend on job responsibilities. For example, a worksite supervisor would generally have a need for a greater range of communication skills.

Regardless of your job, you must be able to tell your coworkers the information they need to do their jobs. If necessary, you must also be able to offer them clear instruction on work procedures.

Writing Skills

Depending on your job, you may need to prepare written instructions or reports for others. Work of this sort is usually done by those immediately supervising a worksite. For very large construction projects, the preparation of such reports may be done by those overseeing the general project. Small builders and contractors have to communicate with clients by means of written bids.

Ability to Read Plans

You may need to refer to plans, such as building plans. The number and type of plans you will need to refer to will depend on your job. In any case, you must be able to read and understand the plans that you work with. This will require that you have a knowledge of the symbols and conventions used in technical drawing.

Listening Skills

Having good communication skills also means that you must be a good listener. As well as being able to communicate clearly with others, you must be able to understand what they are telling you. This means that you must be able to listen well. It also means that you must be able to read and understand written instructions (such as those on plans and drawings). You must also be able to ask clearly worded questions when you do not understand something.

HES/HUMAN ECOLOGY

Why is vocabulary instruction needed for vocational subjects?

career-related subjects, technical terms usually represent concrete concepts. For example, in human environmental science (human ecology), *sauté* represents a particular way of cooking food that can be observed.

The precise meaning of a technical word usually cannot be derived from context clues or a dictionary definition. Technical material often does not provide the necessary clues to help a reader define a term, and many dictionaries do not include the technical definitions of vocational terms. Therefore, vocabulary instruction is especially important in vocational subjects, and teachers need to develop word meanings as they teach these subjects. Teaching vocational and performance-based terminology means pointing out and defining new terms before assigning reading materials. Instructors can demonstrate the concrete meanings of many technical terms by showing students the objects or activities the words represent. Students can develop dictionaries of technical terms by writing vocabulary in notebooks. This activity will help them learn word meanings and spellings. Pictures or drawings can be added to the terms to vary this activity. The teacher should give the students quizzes on these words every other week to check vocabulary development. Additional suggestions for developing word meanings are presented in Chapter 4.

Following Directions

Why are direction-following skills particularly important to career-oriented students?

TECHNICAL EDUCATION   **BUSINESS EDUCATION**

Every technical and career-oriented subject requires the student to read directions and to translate them into action. For example, students in technological education must read directions for operating and repairing various pieces of equipment. In business education, students read directions for operating computers and other business machines and for setting up bookkeeping systems. Example 12.1 illustrates following directions in the building trades.

Reading directions is a slow, precise process. Students often need to reread and apply strategies such as SQ3R to achieve complete understanding. They will find the following questions useful for building comprehension:

1. What am I trying to do? (What is the task?)

2. What materials are required?

3. Do I understand all of the terms (words) used in these directions?

4. What is the sequence of steps?

5. Have I omitted anything?

6. Am I ready to perform the task?

7. Was I successful in accomplishing the task?

These questions can be incorporated into study guides. Additional suggestions for developing study guides are included later in this chapter and in Chapters 6 and 11. Suggestions for following directions are found in Chapter 8.

EXAMPLE 12.1 | **Following Directions in Building Trades**

TECHNICAL EDUCATION

PROCEDURE 6-2

Squaring Up an Assembly

Step 1: Check a glued assembly to see if it is square by measuring diagonals. If they are the same, it is square. This is shown in Figure A.

Step 2: If the assembly is out of square, place a clamp across the long diagonal. Corners can be protected by using blocks, as shown in Figure B.

Step 3: Slowly tighten the clamp, and check the diagonal measurements again. Continue until the assembly is square, as shown in Figure C.

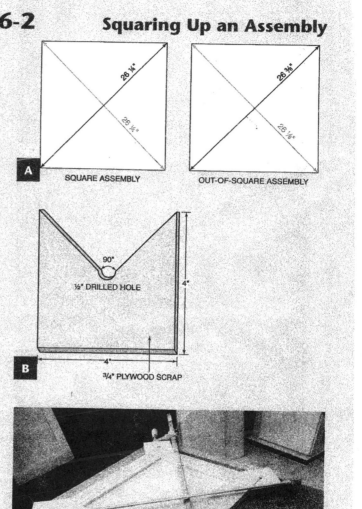

A SQUARE ASSEMBLY — 26 ¼" — 26 ¼"

OUT-OF-SQUARE ASSEMBLY — 26 ⅜" — 26 ⅛"

B 90° — ½" DRILLED HOLE — 4" — 4" — ¾" PLYWOOD SCRAP

C

Source: *Woodworking* by Nancy MacDonald, p. 154. Delmar Cengage Learning, 2009.

Technology

How is technology related to vocational and technical fields?

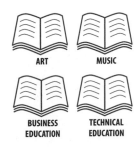

ART

MUSIC

BUSINESS EDUCATION

TECHNICAL EDUCATION

There are many important computer applications in vocational and performance-based fields, including ones for securing up-to-date information and for solving problems. For example, in performance-based fields, students of dance can choreograph on computers; art students can explore art on the Internet and create art on a computer; and musicians can compose on computers.

Likewise, computers are used in vocational fields—for example, to diagnose automotive problems or to provide support in the business arena. The use of computers and the Internet are nearly universal today. Therefore, students in all of these content areas will need to learn the computer applications and the Internet sites that are relevant to their work. Users need to apply critical reading skills to the materials they access.

Teachers and prospective teachers will find the Internet enormously helpful in their work. The Education Resources Information Center website (http://www.eric.ed.gov/) includes lists of journals and lesson plans for specific subjects and grade levels. The site also has links to electronic newsletters that help teachers stay up-to-date. (See Chapter 2 for more about computer use.)

Graphic Materials

Why are graphic materials so important to career-oriented studies?

Career-oriented students have to read a variety of **graphic materials**, such as blueprints, drawings, cutaways, patterns, pictures, and sketches. They must be able to visualize to and interpret the scales and legends that accompany many graphic materials in order to understand both the illustrations and the textual materials.

Teachers should give students many opportunities to convert written directions, drawings, and blueprints into models and actual objects. Students must coordinate the text with any illustrations and perform such tasks as matching blueprints and diagrams with pictures of the finished products. These activities help students develop the ability to visualize written ideas. Having students prepare directions, diagrams, and blueprints for classmates to follow will help them to become more adept at understanding these written materials themselves.

Example 12.2 shows graphic material intermingled with text from a physical education textbook.

Reading Rate

Readers of vocational and technical materials must adjust their reading rates according to purpose, type of content, and familiarity with the subject, as is true of all readers. Vocational materials are often problem oriented and include many directions that require students to adjust their reading rates to accommodate variations in reading content. In vocational studies, students read a wide variety of materials that require frequent rate adjustments. Teachers can facilitate rate adjustment by having students identify appropriate rates for each type of content.

| EXAMPLE 12.2 | Physical Education |

The Game of Volleyball

In 1895 William C. Morgan, a YMCA director in Holyoke, Massachusetts, invented a game called *mintonette* in an attempt to meet the needs of local businessmen who found the game of basketball to be too strenuous. The new game caught on quickly because it required only a few basic skills, easily mastered in limited practice time and by players of varying fitness levels. The original game was played with a rubber bladder from a basketball. Early rules allowed any number of players on a side. In 1896 the name was changed by Alfred T. Halstead, who, after viewing a game, felt that *volleyball* would be a more suitable name due to the volleying characteristic of play.

As the game has progressed, many changes in play have occurred. For example, the Filipinos are credited with adding the spike.

The game's status has changed from its being a recreational activity to being recognized as a strenuous sport as well. The Japanese added the sport to the Olympic Games program in 1964; this contributed to the fast growth of volleyball in the last 25 years.

The exciting aspect of volleyball is that it attracts all types of players —recreational to competitive, little skilled to highly skilled—and all ages. The game has great appeal because it requires few basic skills, few rules, few players (from two to six players on a side), and limited equipment, and it can be played on a variety of surfaces, from a hardwood floor to a sandy beach.

Playing a Game

The game of volleyball is played by two teams each having two to six players on a 30-foot square (9-meter square) court, the two courts separated by a net. The primary objective of each team is to try to hit the ball to the opponent's side in

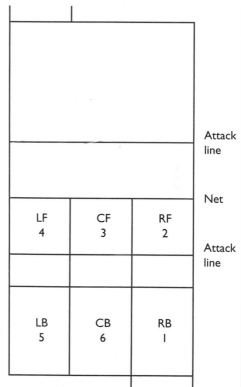

FIGURE A

Players arranged in proper rotational positions

such a manner as to prevent the opponent from returning the ball. This is usually accomplished by using a three-hit combination of a forearm pass to a setter, followed by a set to an attacker, who spikes the ball into the opponent's court.

When there are six players on a side, three are called *forwards*, and three are called *backs*. The three players in the front row are called *left forward* (LF), *center forward* (CF), and *right forward* (RF). The three players in the back row are called *left back* (LB), *center back* (CB), and *right back* (RB). Players need to be in their correct *rotational positions* until the serve is executed. This means that players cannot overlap positions from front to back or from side to side (see Figure A). After the serve, players are allowed to play in any position on or off the court, with one restriction: back row players cannot leave the floor to hit the ball when in front of the attack line.

Source: Barbara L. Viera and Bonnie Jill Ferguson, *Volleyball Steps to Success* (Champaign, Ill.: Leisure Press, 1989), p. 1. Copyright © 1989 by Leisure Press. Reprinted by permission of Human Kinetics Publishers.

Problem Solving

What are some career-oriented and performance-based materials that require problem solving?

In vocational and performance-based subjects, the teachers' goals are to increase the students' ability to think on the job and to perform job-related tasks. Meeting these goals is facilitated when students bring real-life problems to class discussion and to reading. Students who have opportunities for work-based learning have an advantage because they can contribute actual experiences and problems to class discussions and problem solving.

A problem-solving approach and student questions create a mental context for reading and thinking. The following problems were selected from problems posed by or for students in various content areas:

1. List the financial records and documents necessary for a businessperson who operates one of the following: a restaurant, a computer repair shop, or an electronic sales company. The business could be designated as a small business with fewer than ten employees or a larger business with the number of employees specified.

2. Detail the materials and equipment needed to take a corn crop from planting to harvest.

3. List the tools you need to build a chair.

4. Identify the materials needed to build a specific item or machine.

5. Prepare menus for nutritionally balanced meals for a week for a family of three, based on a specified budget.

6. Set up an office mailing system for a company.

The problem-solution writing pattern is common in career-related materials. These materials also include presentations of factual information and how-to-do-it directions. Reading instruction should focus on these types of content materials.

Writing

Writing is an asset in understanding and retaining content materials. Through writing activities, students expand their understanding of technical and vocational language and their ability to express ideas effectively. Writing activities also develop students' knowledge of technical vocabulary, sentence structure, paragraph organization, and sequencing. Vocational and technical teachers need to model writing, provide guided practice, and give students feedback to guide their applications of writing in vocational subjects. In Chapter 9, suggestions for content area writing activities are given.

Utilizing Motivation

What are some techniques to motivate students to learn in career-oriented and technical education classes?

TECHNICAL EDUCATION

Many students are personally motivated to learn about vocational and technical subjects, so their interest can stimulate them to read. However, vocational and technical education teachers should stimulate their students to do further reading. The classroom library should include trade periodicals and Internet access, which provide information about new products, materials, and techniques. These periodicals also include general information about the various trades and careers. One issue of *Career World* discussed agribusiness, political careers, chefs, and physicians, as well as career guidance and interviewing strategies. Teachers can use trade- and career-related materials to develop their students' reading interests and understanding of the content area, thereby increasing students' ability to predict content and, consequently, to comprehend content materials. Following are some suggestions for using motivational strategies to increase comprehension of content materials:

1. Display subject area books, magazines, and related materials appropriate to student interest and reading levels.

2. Suggest additional readings in magazines, newspapers, periodicals, books, and Internet sites.

3. Review and refer to relevant books.

4. Use learning activities such as field trips, movies, audio and video recordings, computer programs, and radio and television programs to build background and to stimulate a desire for further information.

5. Provide time in class for reading materials related to class topics.

6. Have students compare and contrast the way two or more authors have treated a topic.

7. Encourage students to discuss their readings with each other in pairs or in cooperative learning groups.

8. Permit students to work together so that good readers can help less able ones.

The Textbook as a Reference

Teachers should make a particular effort to explain and demonstrate the use of textbooks and real-life printed materials as reference works, since vocational teachers use a wide variety of materials in a problem-solving format and students often are not acquainted with this approach. Instruction that familiarizes the students with the wealth of information provided in printed materials will help them to use these materials for acquiring knowledge and solving problems.

Reading Strategies

What is the difference between reading-to-learn and reading-to-do?

Teachers need to prepare students to read vocational materials prior to reading, support them during reading, and follow up after reading. Reading-to-learn and reading-to-do are both kinds of reading that vocational and technical students are often required to do. **Reading-to-learn** is a task in which an individual reads with the intention of understanding and remembering textual information. **Reading-to-do** is a task in which an individual uses the material as an aid to doing a specific task. In the latter situation, the materials often serve as "external memories" because the individual may refer to them to check information rather than to specifically learn the content. The most common on-the-job reading is reading-to-do, which may demand the following reading strategies:

1. *Read/rehearse,* which involves repeating the information or reading it again.

2. *Problem solve/question,* which involves answering questions posed by the text or searching for the information necessary to solve a specific problem.

3. *Relate/associate,* which is associating new information with the individual's existing store of information.

4. *Focus attention,* which involves reducing the amount of information to be remembered in some way, such as by underlining, outlining, or taking notes.

Directed reading lessons are useful in helping vocational students learn to read textual materials. Example 12.3 is a directed reading lesson based on human environmental science (human ecology) content.

Example 12.4 explains the factors that interfere with the quality of landscaping materials.

EXAMPLE 12.3   **Directed Reading Lesson (Human Environmental Science/Human Ecology)**

HES/HUMAN ECOLOGY

Motivation and Building Background

1. Ask students the following questions: What kind of fabric is used in the clothing you are wearing today? What is your favorite kind of fabric? Here is a box of various types of fabric. Look at each piece, and try to determine the contents of each piece of fabric.

Skill-Development Activities

2. Discuss and pronounce each of the following vocabulary words. Be certain students have a concept for each type of fabric by giving them labeled samples of each to examine.

wool	brocade	satin	velvet
synthetic fabric	lamé	cotton	

Guided Reading

3. *Silent*—Provide students with *silent reading purposes* such as the following: How do you choose a suitable fabric to make a dress? How are synthetic fabrics different from natural fabrics? Have the students read the lesson silently.

4. *Discussion*—Discuss the silent reading purposes, and ask discussion questions such as the following: Do you prefer natural or synthetic fabrics? Why? What are the advantages of natural fabrics? What kind of dress pattern would you choose for a brocade fabric?

Follow-Up Activities

5. Have students reread as necessary to solve the problem of selecting an appropriate fabric for their next garment.

EXAMPLE 12.4   Landscape Design

Grading Standards

None of the selection factors described previously will be of much significance if the plants are not grown and harvested in a manner that enables them to be transplanted successfully. Though the preparation of the transplant site is the responsibility of the landscape company, the production of the plants and their proper preparation for sale is the responsibility of the nursery that grew them. It is possible for plants to be unsuitable for several different reasons.

- The root system could be too small and/or severely damaged by faulty digging techniques.
- The root ball of B&B stock could be unnecessarily large, making the plant unduly heavy and more costly to handle and install.
- The plant may not have been prepared in advance of being dug to promote a vigorous root system within the soil ball.
- The root system may have been permitted to dry out after harvest and is partially or completely dead.
- The soil ball of B&B stock may have broken during harvest and then have been falsely recreated with filler soil stuffed inside the burlap wrap.
- Containerized plants may be too long in the container and have become root bound.
- The plant may be infected or infested with insects or pathogens, many of which are not apparent at the time of purchase.
- There may be harvest scars (injuries from digging or other causes) that will make the plant susceptible to insects or diseases later in the season.
- The plant may not be true to type. It may look similar to the species ordered, but not be the actual species, which can be especially difficult to determine when the plant is young.

Source: *Landscaping Principles & Practices*, 7th ed., by Jack E. Ingels,. p. 119. Delmar Cengage Learning, 2009.

Applications of Literacy Strategies

The sections that follow discuss how specific literacy skills and strategies can be applied to particular subject areas. However, the skills and strategies that are demonstrated can be used interchangeably in the various subject areas. In addition, the activities included in Chapter 11 can be used with the content areas discussed in this chapter.

Technical Education

TECHNICAL EDUCATION

Technical content includes materials written about machine operation, woodworking, auto mechanics, drafting, electronics repair, and so forth. Obviously, these areas have large technical vocabularies that students must understand. Example 12.5 shows a selection from a carpentry text.

Readers must understand the following essential words in order to understand the selection in Example 12.5: *pulley, lever, triangulation, pivot, load, effort, movement, force, distance.*

Many of the terms that are used in technical education classes are related to tools and equipment. Demonstrating and labeling tools and equipment clearly in the classroom can help students learn to recognize these terms when they appear in textbooks.

Many reading tasks in technical education involve the students' ability to read and carry out directions. For example, students must know how to follow step-by-step directions for operating equipment, constructing furniture, or performing maintenance on an engine's fuel injection system. They must learn to follow the directions on "job sheets," which are used in technology education classes to assign daily work. Teachers should prepare study guides to help students comprehend and carry out complicated written instructions.

Safety rules are very important reading content for technology education. In the workplace, employees will also need to be able to read and understand material safety data sheets (MSDS) to handle potentially hazardous materials properly.

Business Education

What subjects are included in business education?

BUSINESS EDUCATION

Business education encompasses a wide variety of studies, including keyboarding, accounting, computer applications, general business concepts and procedures, business mathematics, business law, management, economics, and business communications. Each of the courses in business education has considerable written content. Courses in business rely heavily on reading as an important part of instruction. Many people in business face an increasing volume of transactions and the accompanying paperwork that both require the heavy use of computers and facsimile machines.

Many of the written materials used in business and industry are complex and have a high readability level. These materials are often filled with specialized concepts and loaded with information. However, business education textbooks probably do not reflect the diversity apparent in business reading materials. Generally, these textbooks fall into two categories: how-to manuals and informational books. Students must acquire the reading skills, not only to read the textbooks that are

EXAMPLE 12.5   Technical Content

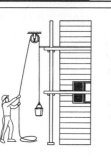

TECHNICAL
EDUCATION

By using more than one pulley you can create a mechanical advantage. A greater advantage is created by using more pulleys. By counting the number of ropes between the top and bottom sets of pulleys you can determine the mechanical advantage.

Triangles are used frequently in carpentry. Used together, triangulation can make a structure very strong and rigid.

Note the number of triangles in this roof structure.

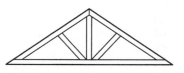

Note that a wall becomes much more stable by adding triangulation.

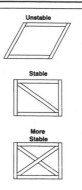

LEVERS

The lever is the most commonly used mechanism in carpentry. It can be used to move a heavy load with little effort or to increase or amplify movement. There are three classes (types) of levers. The class is determined by the location of the pivot in relation to the load.

First-Class Lever

Person moving rock with a Pry Bar.

Second-Class Lever

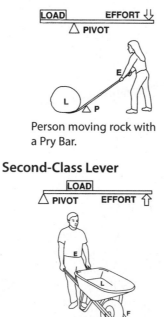

Third-Class Lever

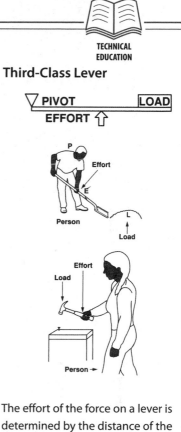

The effort of the force on a lever is determined by the distance of the force from the pivot. It is written as:

Movement = Force x Distance from Pivot

The mechanical advantage of this lever is determined by dividing the load by the effort.

MA = load/effort
MA = 120/40 = 3/1
MA = 3 to 1

Source: John L. Feirer, Gilbert R. Hutchings, and Mark D. Feirer, *Carpentry and Building Construction*, 5th ed. (New York: Glencoe McGraw-Hill, 1997), p. 934. Reprinted by permission of Glencoe McGraw-Hill.

often the basis of classroom instruction, but also to read the other business materials that will be important to their careers.

What literacy skills do business education students need?

Business education students and people who work in business commonly apply literacy skills such as the following:

1. Reading directions or instructions and implementing them. Workers who have to stop others to ask for instructions or who complete tasks incorrectly slow down others and themselves.

2. Skimming and/or scanning to locate needed information. These skills may be used to locate materials needed in problem solving and report writing.

3. Reading and identifying main ideas and details in newspapers, magazines, and professional journals to learn about current trends in the business world.

4. Reading memos. Memos are organized differently from other types of written communication, and they often inform employees of changes in existing practices or policies in a business situation; therefore, the receiver must read these communications and remember the details.

5. Reading and responding to business letters. Business letters are organized differently, use more technical vocabulary, and often use different syntax from social correspondence. Thus they require different reading skills.

6. Reading invoices to check their accuracy.

7. Reading computer printouts to locate needed information. These printouts may be used for problem solving or as a basis for planning programs to meet specific needs.

8. Reading reference materials such as interest tables, financial handbooks, and handbooks of business mathematics. Students must interpret and apply this information.

9. Reading and interpreting textbooks in order to complete class assignments that enable students to learn business skills.

10. Reading materials that contain much technical vocabulary. There are specific terms for each course.

Example 12.6 contains a selection from a business education textbook. It illustrates the steps for entering journaling data. Note the technical terminology, including *vendor, debit, credit, accounts payable,* and *contra amount.*

Business students need to combine skimming and scanning with close reading after they locate the text they need to examine carefully. First, they should *skim* for the main idea or *scan* for specific information that they need to solve a problem, to compose a letter or memo, or to write a report. Then they should carefully and analytically read (*close reading*) the section or sections of content containing the information they need. Close reading for details and main ideas is important because in many situations even a small error can have serious consequences. For example, an accounting error can make a company appear profitable when it is actually losing money; a secretary's error in keyboarding and proofreading a business

EXAMPLE 12.6   **Accounting Content**

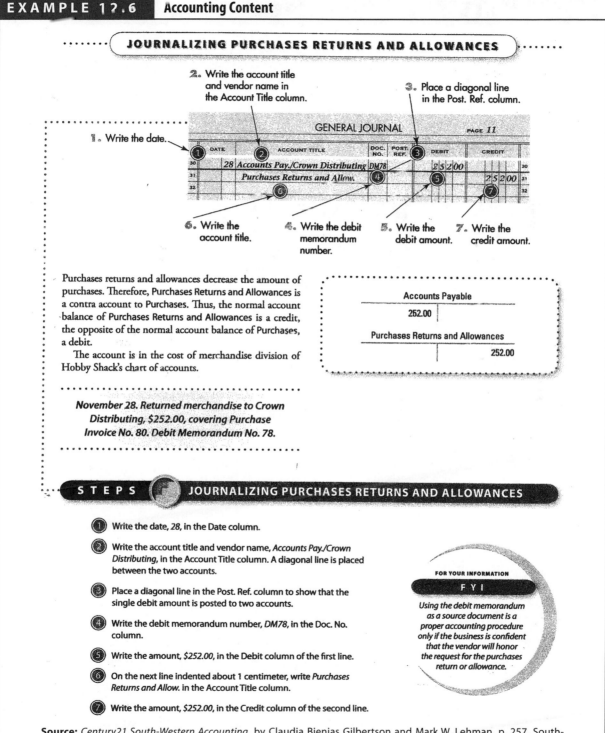

Purchases returns and allowances decrease the amount of purchases. Therefore, Purchases Returns and Allowances is a contra account to Purchases. Thus, the normal account balance of Purchases Returns and Allowances is a credit, the opposite of the normal account balance of Purchases, a debit.

The account is in the cost of merchandise division of Hobby Shack's chart of accounts.

November 28. Returned merchandise to Crown Distributing, $252.00, covering Purchase Invoice No. 80. Debit Memorandum No. 78.

S T E P S   **JOURNALIZING PURCHASES RETURNS AND ALLOWANCES**

1. Write the date, *28*, in the Date column.

2. Write the account title and vendor name, *Accounts Pay./Crown Distributing*, in the Account Title column. A diagonal line is placed between the two accounts.

3. Place a diagonal line in the Post. Ref. column to show that the single debit amount is posted to two accounts.

4. Write the debit memorandum number, *DM78*, in the Doc. No. column.

5. Write the amount, *$252.00*, in the Debit column of the first line.

6. On the next line indented about 1 centimeter, write *Purchases Returns and Allow.* in the Account Title column.

7. Write the amount, *$252.00*, in the Credit column of the second line.

FOR YOUR INFORMATION

F Y I

Using the debit memorandum as a source document is a proper accounting procedure only if the business is confident that the vendor will honor the request for the purchases return or allowance.

Source: *Century21 South-Western Accounting*, by Claudia Bienias Gilbertson and Mark W. Lehman, p. 257. South-Western Cengage Learning, 2008.

MEETING THE CHALLENGE

BUSINESS EDUCATION

Lori Carruthers teaches business education courses in a large high school. Many of her students are employed in after-school and weekend jobs while enrolled in her classes. Although these students have opportunities to apply what they are learning in class, Lori has found that they do not relate their jobs to textbook assignments. When she asks questions in class discussion that should lead them to reflect on these relationships, the students look blank.

She decided to develop an application/reading guide that would lead them to apply the text to their experiences. The following guide is the first one she developed.

Teachers can help students apply text materials to real-world experiences.

Application Guide

1. How are the accounts receivable in your place of business similar to those described in this chapter? How are they different?
2. Does every business have to have financial records? Why or why not?
3. Does the business where you work have financial records? What kinds of records are kept?
4. Does the business where you are employed have computerized financial records? What are the advantages of computerized financial records? What are the disadvantages of computerized records?
5. What source documents are used for the financial records in your place of employment? How are the source documents similar to those discussed in this chapter?
6. How will understanding the process of recording charge sales, payments, and returns help you in other jobs that you might have in the future?

letter can change the entire meaning of an important communication or a contract; and a tiny error in a computer program may result in a program that will not run or gives incorrect results.

Chapters 4, 5, and 6 include suggestions for teaching students how to read for meaning. Teaching strategies such as preview guides, study guides, and directed reading lessons can help business education students refine vital comprehension skills. Each of these strategies can be applied to a specific area of business education.

Business education teachers need to link their classroom activities to real-world requirements. The "Meeting the Challenge" in this section shows how one teacher did this. The guide that Ms. Carruthers developed was effective in helping the students link new information from the class to real-life needs.

BUSINESS EDUCATION

A Reading Strategy for Business Education Materials

Students who must read the many kinds of materials identified earlier in this section can improve their reading comprehension by using a strategy like **PRC**. Its three phases are *prereading, reading,* and *consolidation.*

Prereading.   The prereading phase of the business reading process is the limbering up part. The readers survey the reading material to identify the type of content (e.g., memo, letter, report, text) and to set the stage for remembering it. During this phase, the readers identify topics around which they can cluster the ideas that are in the selection. They also identify the author's organization; knowing how the material is organized will help them pinpoint the main ideas when reading. During the prereading phase, the readers establish questions that will guide their reading, such as:

1. What new information does this selection tell me?

2. What is the main point?

3. What are the important details?

4. What questions will I be asked about this reading?

Reading.   The students read carefully if close reading is necessary or scan if that is adequate. If they are reading to gather data to write an important report, some close reading is in order. However, if the students are reading to locate specific pieces of information and those details are all that is needed from the content, then scanning is appropriate.

Consolidation.   During this phase, readers consolidate the information acquired from reading. Processing the information helps them organize it for long-term memory and for implementing the ideas presented when that is necessary. Readers may take notes to aid remembering and should ask themselves questions similar to the following:

1. What is it that I don't understand?

2. How does this information relate to what I already know?

3. What other examples can I think of?

4. How does this information change or alter what I already know?

5. How can I implement this information?

Human Environmental Science (Human Ecology)

Why is human environmental science considered a multidisciplinary field?

Human environmental science (human ecology) is a multidisciplinary field that emphasizes a synthesis of knowledge in the social and behavioral sciences. This content area focuses on child and family behavior, technological innovations, health, foods and nutrition, clothing and textiles, design, management, housing,

HES/HUMAN ECOLOGY

home furnishings, and personal growth and development. Secondary students pursue these studies for both vocational and avocational purposes.

These students find that literacy plays an important role in studying the complex materials used in human environmental science (human ecology). Effective teaching strategies include guided reading lessons, study guides, and preview guides. Students learn best from their reading when teachers guide them as they read a passage.

Human environmental science (human ecology) content includes many technical terms, for example, *developmental stages*, *teachable moment*, *top sirloin*, *kinship networks*, and *French seam*. Example 12.7 presents a selection from a textbook in this area. Notice that the reader must understand the following terms: *hue, primary colors, tint, value,*

EXAMPLE 12.7   **Selection on Color (Human Environmental Science/Human Ecology)**

HES/HUMAN ECOLOGY

ART

Color

Color, the fifth element of clothing design, has many visual effects. Special terms—such as *hue, value, shade, tint*, and *intensity*—are used to describe the effects of color.

Hue is a *specific color* name. Green, red, and blue-violet are examples of hues. A color wheel is an arrangement of basic hues. It shows how the colors are related to each other. Although there are hundreds of hues, they are all blends of three primary colors: red, yellow, and blue, as shown in the color wheel on page 554.

When two primary colors are equally mixed, a secondary color results. The secondary colors are orange, green, and purple. Orange is a mixture of red and yellow and appears on the color wheel halfway between these hues. Green is a mixture of blue and yellow, and purple is a mixture of red and blue.

It is possible to create an infinite number of hues on the color wheel simply by mixing the primary colors in different amounts. For example, by adding more blue to a blue-yellow mixture you will obtain a bluish green commonly known as turquoise. By adding more yellow, you will get a bright yellow-green color often called chartreuse (shahr-TROOS).

White, black, and gray are considered neutrals. They are not included on the color wheel, but they are used to create different values of a hue. **Value** is the *lightness or darkness of a color*. Adding black to a color results in a *darker value,* or **shade,** of that color. Burgundy is a shade of red, for example. Adding white to a color results in a *lighter value,* or **tint,** of that color. Pink is an example of a tint of red.

Intensity is the *brightness or dullness of a color*. Hot pink and lemon yellow are bright. They are high in intensity. Navy blue and rust are examples of subdued colors that are low in intensity.

Source: Linda R. Glosson, Janis P. Meek, and Linda Smock, *Creative Living*, 7th ed. (New York: Glencoe McGraw-Hill, 2000), p. 553. Reprinted by permission of Glencoe McGraw-Hill.

EXAMPLE 12.8	**Study Guide for Selection on Color**

HES/HUMAN ECOLOGY

ART

Introduction

This selection discusses color and terms to describe the effects of color, color classifications, and the relationships among colors. The terms include *primary colors, secondary colors, hues, value, shade, tint,* and *intensity.* Some of the relationships consist of shades and tints of colors, intensity, and complementary relationships.

Vocabulary

Find an example for each of the following terms:

primary colors	hue
secondary colors	intensity
shade	tint

Comprehension

Directions: Place a + (plus sign) beside each statement that is supported by the reading selection and a – (minus sign) beside each item that is not supported by the selection.

Literal

___ **1.** Intensity refers to brightness.

___ **2.** Colors are sorted into two basic groups.

___ **3.** All secondary colors are made by combining primary colors.

Interpretive

___ **4.** Special effects in dress can be created by individuals who understand the effect that colors have on people.

___ **5.** Short people would probably want to wear solid color outfits.

___ **6.** Green would appear on the color wheel between red and blue.

Applied

Directions: Write short answers for the following questions:

7. Identify three ways in which you can use the ideas in this article for planning your wardrobe.

8. Should you dress in solid colors or complementary colors? Why?

9. How can you form the color pink?

shade, and *intensity.* The study guide in Example 12.8, which follows the selection, will help students check their understanding of these terms and of the content.

Human environmental science (human ecology) students need to learn to read **graphic aids,** such as diagrams, patterns, drawings, graphs, and charts.

Example 12.9 illustrates a chart from a human environmental science textbook.

| EXAMPLE 12.9 | **Human Environmental Science (Human Ecology) Chart** |

**HES/HUMAN
ECOLOGY**

Strategies for Letting Off Steam

These strategies help control angry feelings.

Strategies That Work: Ten Ways to Let Off Steam

Everyone feels angry at times. You can't prevent it—but you can learn to deal with it effectively. Doing so can help prevent arguments from becoming violent.

Taking time to think before you react is a good idea. Take time to calm down and make a good decision about what approach to take. Think about how to communicate your feelings in acceptable ways.

Here are 10 ideas to help you calm down:

- Count to 10. Better yet, count to 20. You could even say the alphabet out loud.
- Breathe deeply, concentrating on your breathing until you feel calmer.
- Call a time-out. Go into another room or outside until you cool off.
- Get a pencil and paper, and write down what caused the anger and why.
- Listen to music.
- Phone a friend. If you can't reach a friend, phone for the weather.
- Be physically active. Do some sit-ups, go for a run, or ride a bike.
- Splash some cold water on your face, or take a warm bath.
- Hug a pillow.
- Lie down on the floor, and concentrate on a spot on the ceiling.

Making the Strategy Work
Think . . .

1. When people routinely blow up in anger, what effect does this have on those around them?
2. How does the saying "Think before you speak" apply to what you just read about anger?
3. On a scale of 1 to 10 (where 1 is poor and 10 is excellent), rate your own ability to manage anger. Explain your reasoning.

Try . . .
Which technique would be most effective for you when you are angry? Make a pledge to yourself to try using that technique when the need arises. Write your pledge, and place it where it can serve as a reminder to you.

Source: Linda R. Glosson, Janis P. Meek, and Linda Smock, *Creative Living*, 7th ed. (New York: Glencoe McGraw-Hill, 2000), p. 39. Reprinted by permission of Glencoe McGraw-Hill.

Human environmental science (human ecology) students should know how to interpret labels for specific information, such as the labels on foods, fabrics, and cleaning products that tell exactly how much of each item or ingredient is contained in the package. They also should know how to interpret directions for use of products. Teachers can prepare students for reading directions through directed reading lessons, study guides, and other instructional strategies suggested in Chapters 6, 8, and 11.

Agriculture

Why are business and managerial education a part of agricultural education?

AGRICULTURE

Agriculture is a complex, multidisciplinary field, and agricultural literacy courses introduce students to the depth, breadth, and diversity of agriculture in our world today, including its impact on our daily lives. Some topics of study in this field include:

- Agriculture science/production management
- Agriculture processing/food and fiber
- Agriculture supplies and services
- Agriculture mechanization/engineering and technical support services
- Agriculture resources management
- Careers in agriculture
- Animal science
- Agriculture business management

This wide variety of subject matter creates a literacy challenge for students. Each of these content areas involves a different technical vocabulary and has its own characteristic patterns of organizing content. These patterns include cause and effect, problem solving, comparison, experiment, directions, and chronological order. In addition, authors often use graphs, charts, diagrams, and pictures. Example 12.10 on page 406 illustrates animal science content.

Physical Education

How is literacy related to physical education instruction?

PHYSICAL EDUCATION

Physical education is an important area of study today. The content of physical education classes can be used to motivate reluctant readers; students who may not be interested in reading other materials often willingly read physical education materials.

Reading serves five purposes in physical education:

1. Physical education topics can motivate students to read, and reading can motivate students to become involved in athletics.

2. Students can learn game rules and signals by reading.

3. Reading can be used to increase and refine students' skills.

4. Reading can increase understanding of a sport and thus can enhance the spectators' or participants' enjoyment.

5. Reading increases students' understanding that mind and body are not separate. Therefore, physical education contributes to mental function (Marlett and Gordon, 2004).

EXAMPLE 12.10   **Animal Science Selection**

Introduction to Animal Science

AGRICULTURE

SCIENCE AND HEALTH

Animals are a vital part of our culture and society, and have been for thousands of years. Animals are sources of food and fiber for homes and for the table, as well as integral parts of our households and recreational activities (see Table 1-1). In the United States, two out of three households have a pet in residence. Millions of people participate in exhibiting animals for pleasure and recreation. A common misconception is that animal science is only for those interested in cattle, sheep, pigs, poultry, and horses. However, the field of animal science developed into the study of the biology and management of all domestic animals. In the last decades, animal scientists have become more and more concerned with issues relevant to not only animals that provide food and fiber, but also those that provide pleasure and companionship in our lives, such as dogs, cats, and companion birds.

The production of animals for human use, whether as food or as companions, is a multibillion-dollar annual industry in the United States, and is a vital part of our national economy. According to the United States Department of Agriculture (USDA), more than $70 billion of meat animals were produced in the United States in 2005. The value of animals raised for meat has risen significantly over the last 40 years.

TABLE 1.1

Census of domestic animals in the United States

Birds (pet-type)[4]	10,100,000
Cattle and calves[1]	95,497,994
Cats[2]	77,600,000
Chickens (egg-laying)[1]	429,317,605
Chickens (meat-type)[1]	1,389,279,047
Dogs[2]	65,000,000
Ducks, Geese, Other[1]	Not available
Emus[1]	48,221
Horses[3]	9,200,000
Ostriches[1]	20,550
Pigs[1]	62,458,647
Turkeys[1]	93,028,191

[1]2002 National Agricultural Statistics Service survey.
[2]American Pet Products Manufacturers Association 2003–2004 survey.
[3]American Horse Council survey.
[4]U.S. Pet Ownership and Demographics Sourcebook, 2001, American Veterinary Medical Association.

Source: *An Illustrated Guide to Animal Science Terminology*, by Colleen Brady, p. 1. Thomson Delmar Learning, 2008.

Sports and games present opportunities to develop thinking and reasoning skills (Landers et al., 2001). Physical education is taught in various ways; instructional material can be in the form of anything from a video to a piece of sculpture, to a magazine article or a computer game (Marlett and Gordon, 2004). Students also have reading tasks that include reading rules and directions for playing games and reading books and magazines to improve their techniques in various sports. For example, many books and magazine articles are available to help people improve their golf swings and tennis strokes.

Reading physical education material requires a number of reading skills. There is extensive specialized vocabulary in this reading content. Each sport has a separate set of terms to be learned (e.g., *love, touchdown, foul,* and *guard*). Notice that the word *love* from tennis and the terms *foul* and *guard*, which apply to several sports, are multiple-meaning terms for which students have other uses in their everyday vocabularies. Students must learn to translate physical education terms into action.

The team and individual sports taught in physical education classes require much special equipment. To learn the names and functions of the various pieces of equipment, students could illustrate each piece of equipment, label it, and describe its function. They could maintain a notebook for this purpose, in which the equipment for each sport is categorized and alphabetized. Teachers may wish to develop *inventories of terminology* related to each sport studied.

These inventories can be used both as preparation to introduce the sport and, after study, as a means to review students' understanding of this vocabulary. Students can supply synonyms or define terms in their own words and may develop an illustrated dictionary of sports terms. Examples of inventories of sports terms are shown in Example 12.11.

EXAMPLE 12.11   **Sports Term Inventories**

PHYSICAL EDUCATION

Directions: Define the following terms in your own words.

Tennis	Basketball	Volleyball
overhead smash	dribble	court
backhand	field goal	forearm pass
forehand	foul	setter
love	free throw	set
serve	pass	attacker
net	pivot	spike
game point	press	forwards
deuce	rebound	backs
match	shoot	rotational positions
fault	traveling	net
double fault	charge	attack line
volley	backboard	serve
lob	basket	dink
slice	drive	
chop	dunk	

Critical (evaluative) reading is also important in physical education materials. Critical thinking is developed in sports activities when students evaluate the strategies or equipment suggested by different authors. This is a good thinking activity, since various authorities suggest widely different approaches to a sport. Critical thinking also comes into play when students evaluate exercises and equipment for physical fitness. For example, recent television commercials recommend some equipment for exercising specific parts of the body, although many physical fitness authorities consider the equipment useless.

Example 12.12 is a partial guide for planning an effective conditioning program. A trainer needs to understand this information in order to plan appropriate fitness activities.

EXAMPLE 12.12 | **Sports Medicine Material**

Existing Habits and Preferences

An effective conditioning program must also work within the parameters of the client's existing habits and preferences. If a client hates running, then a running program is not likely to provide motivation—a swimming program might be a better choice but not if a client is afraid of the water or doesn't have access to a pool. Similarly if a client likes to sleep late a workout schedule that requires getting up at 5:30 in the morning isn't likely to be successful. The client must have a decent shot at following through with the program. Goals alone are not motivation enough. Other factors must also work in the client's favor in order to succeed. The job of the SCS is to stack the deck in the client's favor: Think of ways to make the program fun and inviting. Be innovative. Suggest to clients with long commutes to and from work that they avoid wasting time on the road by exercising at the office until rush hour is over. They can run up and down the stairs, jump on the mini trampoline, jump rope, and find other fun pieces of equipment that can be used to safely get them into shape. Clients who rely on public transit or a carpool for transportation can also put the time spent waiting for their ride to good use by exercising while they wait.

Source: *Sports Medicine Essentials: Core Concepts in Athletic Training* & Fitness Instruction 2nd ed., by Jim Clover, p. 188. Delmar Cengage Learning, 2007.

Art

ART

Art students use and study the media of artistic expression more frequently than they use and study textbooks. The study of art often does not involve as much textbook reading as many other content areas. Nevertheless, art students need to have well-developed reading skills because they read many types of written content for a variety of purposes. For example, they read to acquire information about artistic techniques, art history, and the lives of important artists. Following is a summary of the reading strategies art students commonly use:

1. *Reading for information in materials such as reference books, art history books, biographies, and magazines.* Art students often read about exhibitions, artists, and techniques. They read to identify art styles or movements. They read such magazines as *Arts and Activities, School Arts, Popular Photography, Digital Camera, PC Photo, Art in America, The Artist's Magazine,* and *American Artist* for information on current ideas, trends, and techniques. Reading for information involves identifying main ideas and supporting details.

2. *Reading to follow directions.* Art students must read and follow steps in sequential order. This kind of reading would occur when they read about topics such as new media and new techniques or how to make a woodcut.

3. *Reading to interpret charts and diagrams.* For example, art students need to use a color wheel to learn about complementary colors.

4. *Reading critically.* The art student uses this skill when evaluating reviews of art shows or the impact of a medium or a style.

5. *Reading to implement information or directions.* After reading about a particular medium or style, an art student may experiment with it.

6. *Reading and organizing information for reports.* Art students may be required to write reports on the lives of artists, styles of art, or ways of interpreting moods and feelings in art. This reading task requires that the reader identify main ideas and details.

7. *Reading to understand technical vocabulary related to art.* This vocabulary includes words like *linear, hue,* and *perspective.*

Study guides, preview guides, and vocabulary activities are particularly helpful to art students. In addition, many of the other strategies presented in Chapters 4, 5, 6, 9, and 11 can be used to help art students develop appropriate literacy skills. Examples of art reading activities follow, including a vocabulary activity, a preview guide, and a study guide.

Example 12.13 on page 410 includes material from a textbook used for teaching art. As you read this brief selection, note the many technical words and expressions used (e.g., *linear perspective, diminishing contrasts, hue, value, intensity of color, texture, two-dimensional surface, infinite concept, atmospheric perspective, pictorial composition, theme, picture plane, volume of deep space, softening edges of objects, scale,* and *middle ground*). Following the selection are two reading guides that are based on the passage (Examples 12.14 and 12.15).

MUSIC

Music

Written music is a form of language, and learning to read music is comparable to learning to read prose or poetry selections. Both reading music and reading other

EXAMPLE 12.13   Art Content

ART

Problem 1

In conjunction with linear perspective, artists of the past frequently used diminishing contrasts of hue, value, and intensity of color and texture to achieve deep penetration of space on a two-dimensional surface. This is known as the infinite concept of space or atmospheric perspective.

Create a pictorial composition based on the theme "Objects in Space." Conceive of the picture plane as the near side of a volume of deep space. Use the indications of space suggested in the opening paragraph, plus softening edges of objects as they are set back in depth. The human figure may be used to help suggest the scale of objects in space. Foreground, middle ground, and deep space may be indicated by the size of similar objects.

Source: Otto Ocvirk, Robert Bone, Robert Stinson, and Philip Wigg, *Art Fundamentals: Theory and Practice* (Dubuque, Iowa: William C. Brown Company, 1975), p. 114.

EXAMPLE 12.14   Preview Guide

ART

Directions: Check *Yes* if you believe the reading selection will support the statement; check *No* if you believe the selection will not support the statement.

Yes	*No*	
_____	_____	**1.** The infinite concept of space and atmospheric perspective are the same thing.
_____	_____	**2.** Artists of the past used diminishing contrasts of hue, value, and intensity of color to achieve atmospheric perspective.
_____	_____	**3.** Students should conceive of the picture plane as the far side of a volume of deep space.
_____	_____	**4.** Trees are used to suggest scale.

selections rely on the student's ability to recognize likenesses and differences in sounds, shapes, and symbols. Each piece of music can be considered a text. In studying music, students must be able to read the words, the music, and the technical language, as well as the accompanying expository and narrative text. Music instruction usually requires a high level of reading ability, including knowledge of notes, lyrics, and music theory. For example, music students read and interpret a large number of musical terms, such as *sonatina*, *spiritoso*, *andante*, and *allegretto*. In addition, special symbols are used in music books and scores. These symbols aid the student in interpreting the music. Students must be able to recognize symbols for elements such as treble clef, bass clef, notes (whole, half, quarter, etc.), rests (varying values corresponding to note values), sharps, flats, crescendo, and diminuendo. The teacher must frequently demonstrate musical terms, concepts, and technology

EXAMPLE 12.15 **Study Guide**

ART

Introduction

This selection poses a problem for art students to solve. If you have questions after you have read the problem, refer to books and articles in the bibliography on linear perspective.

Vocabulary

Provide an example for each of the following words: *linear perspective, diminishing contrasts, hue, value, intensity, texture, two-dimensional surface, infinite concept of space, atmospheric perspective, pictorial composition, theme,* and *picture plane.*

Comprehension

Directions: Write a short answer to each question.

Literal
1. What does this selection ask you to do?
2. What concept is explained in the first paragraph?
3. What is the theme of the pictorial composition that you are to create?

Interpretive
4. Why does the author suggest that a human figure be used to suggest scale?
5. Will color play an important role in this composition?
6. What similar objects might be used to indicate foreground, middle ground, and deep space?

Applied
7. What materials will you need to complete this problem?
8. Can you create another composition that has the same title but uses a different object to show scale? If so, what could you use?

using instruments and/or recorded music. Example 12.16 on page 412 illustrates how a music teacher may demonstrate musical concepts.

Students must be able to understand material that is written about music in order to interpret the music. Instruction in music classes often is based on students' ability to read and understand the following types of content (Tanner, 1983):

- Expository and narrative materials about composers

- Critiques, reviews, and descriptions of performances

- Exposition—music history

- Reporting—current events related to music

- References—research, reviews

- Types of media—books, magazines, newspapers, scores

EXAMPLE 12.16   **Demonstrating Musical Concepts**

MUSIC

TECHNICAL
EDUCATION

Electronic Timbres

Electronically generated sounds are all around us. The invention of new sound technology, particularly the extraordinary developments of the last quarter of the twentieth century, has enabled us to extend the range of musical timbres. The expressive potential of these sounds is infinite and only awaits the imagination of new composers to probe their possibilities. Already there are literally thousands of new musical compositions that owe their existence to this technology.

ACTIVITY   Realize the Potential

Listen to a demonstration of some samples of sounds and expressive effects that can be created on a synthesizer.

Listen to American composer Wendy Carlos (b. 1939) explain and demonstrate how she made the public conscious of the Moog synthesizer with her recording *Switched-On Bach*, the first classical album to go platinum.

What feats are required to make electronic music expressive and musical in a way similar to music made with acoustic instruments? Discuss such matters as vibrato, the need for overdubbing, touch sensitivity, and the need for taste.

Why is a perfect automated rhythm less exciting than a human's imperfectly performed rhythm?

Technology Option

Music with MIDI   Use a MIDI program to create a composition featuring unique and original sounds from your MIDI gear.

Most of us are so accustomed to electronic sounds in television commercials, on pop recordings, and in film scores that we may not be able to distinguish these sounds from the more traditional acoustic sources (musical instruments, voices). Although electronic technology has produced hundreds of new timbres, we do not yet have a common language or vocabulary to describe these new sounds. Quite often, however, sounds that are generated electronically deliberately mimic acoustic instruments or human voices and can be labeled accordingly. Often, instruments are electrified—the organ and guitar are common examples. The trick is to get our ears to distinguish sounds that are produced acoustically from those that are produced electronically.

Source: Charles Fowler, Timothy Gerber, and Vincent Lawrence, *Music! Its Role and Importance in Our Lives* (New York: Glencoe McGraw-Hill, 2000), p. 342. Reprinted by permission of Glencoe McGraw-Hill.

To help secondary students with the task of reading music and textbooks used in music classes, teachers may use the following strategies:

1. Anticipate students' problems before they read. Standardized reading tests and teacher-made inventories can provide data regarding students' reading skills. Observing students' performance in reading music is very helpful in isolating their strengths and weaknesses.

2. Teach the necessary vocabulary before students read a selection.

3. Develop and use illustrated dictionaries of musical terms.

4. Teach students how to study and prepare assignments (see Chapter 8). Demonstrating these techniques with music content can be helpful.

5. Use strategies such as study guides, directed reading lessons, structured overviews, preview guides, and vocabulary study to help students read and understand music content.

Example 12.17 on page 414 is taken from a music text that provides students with guidance to help them read music-related text. The authors have identified the major objectives of the chapter, the vocabulary, and the specific names of artists that students are expected to learn. Such guidance gives students comprehension purposes and sets their expectations to learn the content that the teacher expects.

Hicks (1980) points out that for music, the reading process involves recognizing the notes, which represent pitch; the meter symbols, which indicate time; and various other interpretive and expressive markings. At the same time, an instrumentalist must physically manipulate valves, bows, slides, or keys. Hicks suggests that teachers present the early stages of music reading as a problem-solving activity involving simple duple and triple meters. He suggests presenting all songs in the same key, emphasizing continuity and repetition and using materials that have repeated patterns and a narrow range. He also recommends including familiar elements in each new activity. This activity could include such elements as the following:

1. Provide background information about the song.

2. Present the words of the song in poem form on a duplicated sheet (to avoid confusion that may result from all the accompanying signs and symbols on a music sheet).

3. Discuss any words that students may not recognize or comprehend, as well as the overall meaning of the lyrics.

4. The teacher and students should divide the words into syllables cooperatively. A duplicated sheet may again be prepared with words in this form.

After the musical aspects of the song are taught, the students can use the duplicated sheet (with divided words) to sing from. Later, they may use the music books that contain syllabicated words along with the notes and other symbols.

EXAMPLE 12.17   **Music Text**

MUSIC

Jazz

Jazz is America's musical gift to the world. This unique invention, born in New Orleans and bred largely in Memphis, St. Louis, Chicago, and New York, is still alive and kicking and going into its second century of high status. Without a doubt, it is the most original and influential music to emerge from the American continent—so far.

Objectives

By completing this chapter, you will:

• Learn about the beginnings of jazz.
• Become acquainted with the early contributions of Jelly Roll Morton, Fletcher Henderson, and Louis Armstrong.
• Be able to distinguish between the many styles of jazz, such as Dixieland, small band jazz, swing, bebop, and fusion.
• Learn some examples of classic jazz.
• Find out about the contributions of other jazz performers, such as Charlie Parker and Dizzy Gillespie, and learn what made them so great.

Vocabulary

| bop | Dorian mode | scat singing |
| break | fusion | swing |

Musicians to meet

| Benny Goodman | Charlie Parker |

Source: Charles Fowler, Timothy Gerber, and Vincent Lawrence, *Music! Its Role and Importance in Our Lives* (New York: Glencoe McGraw-Hill, 2000), p. 507. Reprinted by permission of Glencoe McGraw-Hill.

When preparing to perform a composition, music students must ask themselves a number of questions regarding the composition and their performance. The following questions may be included:

1. What skills do I need to learn or develop to play this piece?

2. What mood should be conveyed?

3. What are the key signature and the time signature?

4. What rhythms does the composer use?

5. What intervals are used?

6. How long are the phrases?

7. How did the composer want the piece played?

8. What dynamic markings are shown, and why?

9. Would it help me if I heard the song played by someone else?

10. Would it help me if I heard the lyrics?

FOCUS ON | *Struggling Readers*

Helping Struggling Readers Read Vocational Content

Many times struggling readers are guided into vocational studies, but they lack the required skills to succeed. They have often spent much time outside of their classrooms for developmental instruction, which deprives them of the content exposure they need (Pisha and Coyne, 2001). Isolated skills instruction does not prepare them for content area learning (NCTE, 2004). Prior knowledge is necessary for building interest and desire to learn (NCTE, 2004; Tobias, 1994). Existing knowledge of the subject matter is the single most influential factor in determining what students will learn from reading a text about that subject matter (Grady, 2002). Struggling readers usually need to develop background for the materials they will read and review. Vocabulary related to the subject they are studying will help them read with understanding. Chapter 4 includes suggestions for vocabulary development. Teachers of vocational and perform-ance subjects have special problems, because students must translate reading content to actual practice. However, computer programs and the Internet can help students understand (Grady, 2002).

Internet sites such as these are helpful for vocational subjects: Knowledge Network Explorer (http://www.kn.pacbell.com/) provides educational sites in vocational, technology, business, and many other areas. This site also con-nects to Blue Web'n, which is an online library of outstanding Internet sites cat-egorized by subject, grade level, and format. The School House: School to Work website (http://teacherpathfinder.org/School/SchWork/schworkprogs.html) features links to school-to-work program resources.

Discussions with classmates will help students view topics from different perspectives; moreover, students can work together to construct meaning (Lloyd, 2004). Discussion of readings and classroom experiences encourage students to continue exploration of content subjects. After reading texts and exploring Internet sites, students should participate in discussion to clarify their understandings.

FOCUS ON *English Language Learners*

Helping English Language Learners Read Vocational Content

Hernandez (2003) identified four key instructional dimensions for English language learners (ELLs).

1. Prior knowledge

2. Variety of instructional materials

3. Cognitive development

4. Study skills

Initially, ELLs may lack the prior knowledge necessary to comprehend content materials (Harper and de Jong, 2004). Teachers can relate the subject matter to students by asking questions regarding what they have learned about the content and eliciting what students know about the topic from their own life experiences. Vocational teachers can use communication-based instruction to develop students' readiness, as well as their vocabulary for studying the content subject. Reading and discussing texts with classmates in a cooperative learning experience helps students (Jacobs and Gallo, 2002). ELLs benefit from peer tutoring or coaching from students who are fluent users of English. These students and the teachers model English for ELLs.

Vocational teachers may need to broaden their notions of text. They should present basic foundations of subject matter through visuals, hands-on experiences, guest speakers, field trips, and related readings (Hernandez, 2003). ELLs benefit from experience with workplace materials that expose them to the level of English they will need in the future (Wade and Moje, 2000). Using simple syntax when discussing examples, differences, and similarities helps students develop oral fluency and comprehension. Lessons may need to be sequenced, so that students can be systematically exposed to information needed as readiness for another subject.

ELLs need the cognitive development that will enable them to comprehend content materials (Hernandez, 2003). Texts can be used as references when students discuss points of view or main ideas and support them with examples. ELLs can summarize information, sequence events, infer conclusions, and compare and contrast. Text materials can be read to ELLs or recorded text can be played for them, so they can increase their comprehension and participation in reading and writing. In this manner, students can develop important comprehension skills (see Chapters 5 and 6).

ELLs also need study skills (Hernandez, 2003). They should learn the parts of a book and how to access information quickly. They also have to learn how to research information that will further their studies in content areas. Chapters 7 and 8 of this text will help teachers teach these skills.

Summary

Efficient literacy is a prerequisite for successful learning. Although many people believe that the literacy demands of vocational subjects are less rigorous than those of academic programs, literacy is equally important in these fields of study. Transferable skills and work-related learning that incorporates writing tasks and implementation of technology are important elements of these programs.

Vocational and performance materials are written and organized to impart information, give directions, and provide solutions to problems. Teachers should use vocabulary strategies, advance organizers, study guides, preview guides, directed reading materials, mapping, and study methods to help students comprehend these materials. Systematic literacy instruction as a part of content instruction will improve students' learning in these courses. Struggling readers and English language learners need the same skills as other students, but they need to be taught in ways that will help them to succeed in vocational subjects.

Discussion Questions

1. How are literacy demands of work-related education changing?
2. How and why is vocational education changing?
3. What kinds of literacy tasks do students encounter in vocational and technical studies?
4. What strategies can teachers use to help students comprehend vocational materials?
5. Discuss the increased integration of vocational education and academic education.
6. How can teachers effectively teach the variety of content in human environmental science and agriculture?
7. Why is literacy increasing in importance for contemporary students?
8. What adjustments should vocational teachers make for struggling readers and English language learners?
9. How does instruction for English language learners differ from instruction for struggling readers?
10. Why are vocational and technical studies important for secondary students?

Enrichment Activities

*1. Select a set of directions from a subject treated in this chapter, and rewrite the directions in simpler language for struggling readers.
2. Develop an annotated bibliography of materials that could constitute a classroom library in one of the subjects treated in this chapter. Indicate readability levels whenever possible.
3. Make a dictionary of terms for use in one of the areas treated in this chapter. You can use drawings and pictures from magazines, catalogs, and newspapers to illustrate the dictionary.

4. Collect pamphlets, magazines, newspapers, and library books that could be used to develop understanding of vocabulary and concepts in a subject treated in this chapter. Use them with secondary school students.

5. Select a section in a textbook on a subject treated in this chapter, and make a reading lesson plan for it.

6. Prepare a presentation, describing how you would help teach a student to read one of the following: (a) an invoice or balance sheet; (b) a contract; (c) a tax form; (d) a physical education activity or game; (e) a critical review of art or music; (f) a specialized handbook; or (g) a reference source.

7. Examine materials from technology education, business education, and human environmental science (human ecology) textbooks. Locate examples of the common difficulties in reading these texts.

*8. Prepare a vocabulary activity to teach new terms in a textbook chapter. Use it with a group of secondary school career-education students.

*9. Prepare a study guide for a selection from one of the subjects discussed in this chapter. Use it with a group of secondary school career-education students.

10. Use a readability formula to compute the readability level of a textbook for one of the content areas discussed in this chapter. (See Chapter 3 for a discussion of readability formulas.)

11. Identify new applications of technology in your chosen field of study.

---

*These activities are designed for in-service teachers, student teachers, and practicum students.

Resources including the TeachSource Video Cases can be found on the website for this book. Cengage Learning's CourseMate brings course concepts to life with interactive learning, study, and exam preparation tools that support the printed textbook. Go to www.cengage.com/login to register your access code.

GLOSSARY

aesthetic response: Readers' personal feelings about a story or text that may be expressed in relation to art, music, drama, or composition.

analogies: Comparisons of two similar relationships; using similarities of ideas for the sake of comparison.

assimilation: The process that occurs when a reader integrates new ideas with existing ideas stored in long-term memory.

attribute relations: A network of related characteristics.

audiobooks: Recordings of books that students can listen to as they read along in the text or listen to in order to understand better the dialect or style of the writing.

authentic purposes: The reasons for reading that relate to real life.

authentic reading tasks: Assignments and activities that are based on actual experiences that students may encounter.

blog: See Web log.

career-related education: A program that prepares students for employment.

cause-and-effect writing pattern: A common writing pattern in social studies and science that is concerned with the chains of causes and effects. This pattern recognizes that a cause results in effects that become causes of other effects.

CD: Compact disc; a digital data storage device from which information can be accessed in nonlinear fashion.

character journals: Diaries in which students assume the role of one of the main characters in a book.

chronological order pattern: This writing pattern is concerned with the time order of events.

classification pattern: A writing pattern that groups items into categories by types (objects, animals, ideas, rocks, soil, historical periods, etc.).

cloze test: An alternative method of determining students' reading levels in which the students are asked to read selections of increasing levels of difficulty and supply words that have been deleted from the passage; a method for matching students with reading materials.

cognitive flexibility: The ability to examine text from various perspectives or points of view.

cognitive processing: Thinking about content. It involves rehearsal (repeating information), review, comparing and contrasting, and drawing conclusions.

cognitive strategies: Approaches to understanding based on mental activities.

coherence (of text): Text that is organized in a cohesive manner to convey meaning.

college-prep students: Students who are enrolled in a high school curriculum that prepares them for a college education.

comparison and/or contrast pattern: A writing pattern that explains ideas through describing likenesses and differences.

computer-assisted instructional programs: Computer programs that present instructional material.

computer databases: Electronically searchable organized bodies of information.

concept: A mental construct derived from categories of experiences and related webs of ideas. For example, *cat* is a concept.

concept guide: A form of study guide that focuses on basic ideas in the content areas.

conceptual learning: Learning based on understanding relationships among ideas rather than lists of independent facts.

conceptual relationships: Connections among ideas; networks of words that are connected hierarchically or as examples or nonexamples.

connotation: The ideas and associations suggested by a term, including emotional reactions.

content area teachers: Teachers of classes in specific disciplines, for example, mathematics, science, or history.

content journals: Written records of content area learning activities that are personal and informal; learning logs.

content schemata: A reader's prior knowledge that permits him or her to comprehend content texts.

context: The words and phrases that surround a specific word.

context clues: The meaning clues in the text surrounding a word.

Cornell Note-Taking System: A type of split-page note taking that includes notes, questions answered in the notes, and a summary of each page of notes.

creative thinking: Cognitive activity that focuses on novel ways of viewing ideas, incidents, or characters.

criterion-referenced tests: Tests that check the test taker against a performance criterion, which is a predetermined standard.

critical readers: Individuals who question what they read, suspend final judgment until all facts are presented, evaluate, and decide.

critical thinking: Cognitive activity that requires evaluating information and ideas. The reader has to decide whether or not to believe content.

database programs: Computer programs that facilitate the development and searching of databases, organized bodies of information that can be sorted and searched electronically.

definition or explanation pattern: This writing pattern tells the meaning of a concept and/or explains a concept.

demonstration pattern: This writing pattern is usually accompanied by an example that illustrates operations and concepts.

denotation: The literal definition of a word as defined by the dictionary.

desktop-publishing programs: Computer programs that combine text and graphics for publishing newsletters, reports, brochures, and other documents.

diagnostic tests: Tests that help to locate specific strengths and weaknesses of readers.

dialogue journals: Journals in which a two-way written conversation is carried on between the teacher and each student.

digital literacy: The ability to understand, evaluate, and integrate information in multiple formats delivered by the computer.

direct instruction: Systematic, teacher-led instruction on targeted objectives.

directed reading lessons (DRL): A method for guiding students' comprehension of a reading selection.

directed reading-thinking activity (DRTA): A guided comprehension strategy involving predicting, reading, and confirming or rejecting predictions.

discourse: A major unit of language that is longer than a sentence.

DVD: A digital storage device that offers high-quality images and sound.

divergent thinking: Cognitive activity that follows different paths, that extends in different directions.

editing: Correcting spelling, grammar, and punctuation to polish the writing.

efferent response: Responses to content that focus on knowledge, information, and facts.

elaboration: Increasing complexity, adding detail to an idea or a word.

electronic mailing lists: Electronic distributors of messages on specific topics to groups of readers who have subscribed to the lists.

e-mail: Electronic mail; messages sent electronically from one computer user to another.

English language learners (ELLs): Students whose first language is not English.

experimental pattern: This pattern is often used in scientific materials. In this pattern, the steps for a hands-on exploration of a problem or discovery are described, so the reader can perform the steps involved.

exposition: Written or spoken language that explains.

expressive vocabulary: The words that an individual knows well enough to use in speaking and writing.

figurative language: Words that are used in a non-literal manner. Figurative language includes personification, similes, metaphors, hyperbole, euphemisms, and allusions.

flexibility of rate: The ability to vary rate according to purpose and difficulty of material.

fluency: Reading with speed, accuracy, automaticity, good phrasing, smoothness, and expression.

Frayer Model: A model of concept learning that includes examples and nonexamples.

freewriting: Writing that has no teacher restrictions on content.

full inclusion: This term refers to the practice of serving students with disabilities and other special needs entirely within the general classroom. In full inclusion settings, students spend the entire day in the general classroom.

graphic aids: Visual aids, such as maps, graphs, tables, charts, diagrams, and pictures.

graphic materials: Drawings such as blueprints, cutaways, patterns, pictures, and sketches.

graphic organizers: Visual representations or structured overviews that illustrate hierarchical and/or linear relationships among key concepts.

group reading inventory: A teacher-made test, based on the textbooks that the students are actually expected to use, designed to determine if the material is suitable for instructional purposes with the students.

homepage: The introductory page for a website.

hypermedia: Nonsequentially linked text, graphics, motions, and sounds that allow computer users to access information from different media in the order that they choose.

hypertext: Nonsequential text links that allow computers users to access text in the order that they choose.

I-Chart: A procedure for note taking for a research report, composed of a grid that has questions about the subject at the tops of columns and references consulted along the left-hand margin to form the row headings.

inclusion: This term describes the practice of including students with disabilities in general education classes.

in-depth word study: Exercises that increase vocabulary knowledge through association.

individualized education plan (IEP): An instructional plan to meet the needs of individual students who qualify for special education services.

Individuals with Disabilities Education Act (IDEA): This act provides that all children, including students with disabilities, are entitled to a free, appropriate public education.

inferential thinking: Cognitive activity that is concerned with deeper meanings that require reading between the lines rather than meanings that are directly stated.

informal reading inventory: A compilation of graded reading selections, accompanied by questions prepared to test the reader's comprehension, that is designed to determine students' reading levels and reading strengths and weaknesses.

integrated curriculum: A curriculum that blends subjects together based on overlapping skills, concepts, attitudes, and content identified for each subject. Subjects such as math, science, social studies, fine arts, and language arts are often integrated, although integration is not limited to these subjects.

integrated unit: A unit focused on a specific topic that is studied from the perspective of more than one content area.

Internet: An international "network of networks" that links a multitude of computers.

intertextuality: The links between the ideas gleaned from one text and those discovered in another text or texts.

K-W-L: A reading strategy that stands for Know–Want to Know–Learned.

language experience materials: Accounts that are written by individuals or groups of students of actual experiences that they have had.

literacy: The ability to read and write.

literal thinking: The cognitive activity of recognizing directly stated facts and ideas.

literature response groups: Also known as literature circles; several students who have chosen to read the same novel read a certain amount each week and meet in a group each week to discuss the reading.

media literacy: The ability to comprehend and produce material for media other than print.

metacognition: Thinking about one's own thinking and controlling one's own learning; comprehension monitoring.

metacognitive skills: Skills in comprehension monitoring.

mind mapping: Visual note taking that shows connections among ideas. Based on a central image, key words, colors, codes, and symbols.

morphological analysis: Word identification strategy based on identification of a root that carries the base meaning of the word and affixes that modify the base meaning.

multimedia: The use of a number of different media (graphics, text, moving images, sounds, etc.) in the same application.

multiple intelligences: Types of learning avenues, including verbal, logical, body, visual, musical, interpersonal, intrapersonal, naturalist, and existentialist.

multiple literacies: Reading and writing skills necessary for comprehension of content that vary according to the type of content.

newsgroups: Sometimes called electronic bulletin boards; network locations to which messages are posted so that interested computer users can read the messages electronically.

norm-referenced tests: Tests that compare students' performance with the performance of a norm group, a sampling of students in the same grade or of the same age.

organizational patterns: The structures used to organize texts. The common text patterns include sequential, comparison/contrast, cause/effect, definition or explanation, and enumeration.

outlining: Recording information from reading material in a way that makes clear the relationships between the main ideas and the supporting details.

paraphrasing: Putting material that one has read into one's own words.

PORPE: A technique to help students study for essay examinations: Predict, Organize, Rehearse, Practice, Evaluate.

portfolio: A collection of student-produced materials that teachers use to evaluate progress and achievement.

PRC: A study strategy that has three phases: prereading, reading, and consolidation.

preview guide: A guide completed prior to reading that helps the student relate prior knowledge to the topic.

prewriting: The initial stage in the writing process, used for selection and delimitation of topic, determination of audience, decisions about general writing approach, activation of prior knowledge of the topic, discussion of ideas with classmates, and organization of ideas.

print literacy: The ability to read printed language.

problem-solution pattern: A writing pattern that is often found in scientific and health-related content. In this pattern the writer identifies a difficulty and explains how to solve it.

problem-solving approach: This approach to comprehension encourages students to understand the question they need to answer, to state it in their own words, and then to brainstorm possible solutions. Finally, they need to evaluate the solutions.

PSRT: A teaching procedure that is helpful in enhancing students' study skills: Prepare, Structure, Read, Think.

publishing: Sharing writing with others in oral or written form.

question-and-answer pattern: This writing pattern is based on queries posed by the author and his or her response to these queries.

question/answer relationships (QARs): A strategy for increasing comprehension that focuses on the processes for generating answers to questions and on the relationships between questions and answers.

questions: Inquiries that call for replies. These inquiries are classified by various schemes such as literal, inferential, critical, and creative.

RAFT assignments: Writing assignments that include the Role of the writer, Audience for the writing, Format of the writing, and Topic to be written about.

read-alouds: Selections that the teacher reads aloud to the students because the students do not have the reading proficiency or motivation to read them for themselves.

readability: Reading difficulty level of texts that can be computed using statistical formulas.

reading: An active process in which the reader calls on experience, language, and schemata to anticipate and understand the author's written language.

reading comprehension: The process of understanding material that is read; a strategic process during which readers simultaneously extract and construct meaning. Reading comprehension is the product of vocabulary and language comprehension.

reading guide: A written guide that helps students comprehend and organize the material that they are reading.

reading response journals: A type of learning log for literature classes in which students comment on characters, setting, plot, author's writing style and devices, personal reactions, and other items related to a selection that has been read.

reader-response theory: This theory explains students' emotional and functional responses to written text.

reading-to-do: Tasks in which an individual uses the material read as an aid to doing something else.

reading-to-learn: Tasks in which an individual uses the material read with the intention of remembering and applying textual information.

receptive vocabulary: The words that readers recognize when they hear them and/or see them.

reciprocal teaching: A form of guided practice for comprehension. Readers apply simple, concrete strategies to achieve text comprehension.

rehearsal: A cognitive processing strategy that involves repeating information to oneself.

reliability: The degree to which a test gives consistent results.

response: See aesthetic response and efferent response.

retellings: Oral or written reconstructions of material that is read.

retention: The ability to remember what has been read.

revision: The stage in the writing process in which material is reexamined, reorganized, clarified, expanded, or in some other way changed to improve the presentation.

ROWAC: A general study method: Read, Organize, Write, Actively read, Correct predictions.

rubric: A set of criteria used to describe and evaluate a student's level of proficiency in a particular subject area.

scanning: Rapid reading to find a specific bit of information.

schema theory: Schemata (plural of schema) are abstract networks of knowledge, information, and experiences stored in long-term memory.

self-questioning: Inquiries that an individual poses to himself or herself.

semantic feature analysis: Comparing the attributes of related concepts.

semantic maps: Figures illustrating conceptual relationships.

semantics: Linguistic term referring to word meaning.

situational context: The setting in which one reads a text.

skimming: Reading to obtain a general idea or overview of material.

social constructivist perspective: A perspective in which the teacher provides a learning environment designed to engage students in a process of negotiating meaning through interaction of the reader, the text, the classroom community, the teacher, and the context.

social justice notebooks: Notebooks in which students write their stands on controversial human rights issues that they have read about in news articles or editorials.

socioeconomic status: Position in society based on such factors as social class, income, education level, and job held.

spreadsheets: Grids of rows and columns used to organize data into patterns, often used to store and manipulate numerical data.

SQ3R: A general study method: Survey, Question, Read, Recite, Review.

SQRC: A general study method: State, Question, Read, Conclude.

SQRQCQ: A study method for mathematics: Survey, Question, Read, Question, Compute, Question.

stance: The point of view or perspective that integrates the text and the situational context. The two major stances are aesthetic and efferent.

strategic reading: Actively reading the text by connecting text information with preexisting knowledge and using learned procedures to interact with the text.

study guides: A set of questions and/or suggestions designed to direct students' attention to the key ideas in a passage and sometimes to suggest the skills to apply for successful comprehension.

study skills: Techniques and strategies that aid readers in learning from written materials.

summarizing: Concisely restating what the author has said in a work or a section of a work.

summary: A concise restatement of what the author has said in a work or a section of a work.

survey tests: Tests that measure general achievement in reading.

sustained silent reading: A technique in which students are given a block of time to read self-selected materials for pleasure, without fear of testing or reporting being required.

symbols: Compressed language that may represent one or more words.

syntax: A linguistic term referring to word order in sentences and paragraphs.

tech-prep students: Students who are enrolled in a high school curriculum that prepares them for careers or employment in industry or applied science.

text coherence: A quality of text that moves from one idea to the next without confusing or losing the reader.

text organization: The way authors arrange text; the order of presentation in a text. Content authors organize text using these forms: comparison-contrast, sequential, cause-and-effect, definition or explanation, and question-answer.

textual context: The quality and difficulty of writing and organization found in texts.

textual schemata: Readers' organized knowledge of and experience with different forms of written discourse that prepare them to read a variety of content.

thematic teaching unit: A series of interrelated lessons or class activities organized around a theme, a literary form, or a skill.

themes: topics or major ideas.

validity: The extent to which a test measures what it is intended to measure.

vicarious experience: Experience acquired through using the imagination with a picture, film, model, etc., rather than firsthand experience.

videoconferencing: Holding conferences over the Internet with others who can be seen on the computer monitors and heard through speakers.

visualization: The process of forming mental images that depict reading content.

vocational literacy: The reading and writing skills that people need in order to perform the work in their careers or vocations.

wait time: The period of time a teacher waits between asking a question and expecting an answer.

web log (blog): A Web-based journal.

word identification skills and strategies: Skills and strategies used by students to decode unfamiliar words.

word problems (verbal problems): Mathematics problems that are presented in words and symbols.

word-processing programs: Computer programs designed to allow entry, manipulation, and storage of text.

work-based learning: Instruction that involves apprenticeship at a work site.

writing a draft: The second stage in the writing process, in which the writer puts ideas on paper without worrying about mechanics or neatness.

REFERENCES

Aaron, Ira E., Jeanne S. Chall, Dolores Durkin, Kenneth Goodman, and Dorothy S. Strickland. "The Past, Present, and Future of Literacy Education: Comments from a Panel of Distinguished Educators, Part II." *The Reading Teacher* 43 (February 1990): 370–380.

Adams, Pamela E. "Teaching *Romeo and Juliet* in the Non-tracked English Classroom." *Journal of Reading* 38 (March 1995): 424–432.

Afflerbach, Peter, P. David Pearson, and Scott G. Paris. "Clarifying Differences between Reading Skills and Reading Strategies." *The Reading Teacher* (February 2008): 364–373.

Ajayi, Lasisi. "English as a Second Language Learners' Exploration of Multimodal Texts in a Junior High School." *Journal of Adolescent & Adult Literacy* 52 (April 2009): 583–595.

Albright, Lettie K., and Mary Ariail. "Tapping the Potential of Teacher Read-Alouds in Middle Schools." *Journal of Adolescent & Adult Literacy* 48 (April 2005): 582–591.

Alexander, J. Estill, and Jeanne Cobb. "Assessing Attitudes in Middle and Secondary Schools and Community Colleges." *Journal of Reading* 36 (October 1992): 146–149.

Alfred, Suellen. "Dialogue Journal." *Tennessee Reading Teacher* 19 (Fall 1991): 12–15.

Allen, Camille A. *The Multigenre Research Paper*. Portsmouth, N.H.: Heineman, 2001.

Allington, Richard. *What Really Matters for Struggling Readers: Designing Research-Based Programs*. New York: Addison-Wesley, 2001.

Alvermann, Donna E. "Multiliteracies and Self-Questioning in the Service of Science Learning." In E. Wendy Saul (ed.) *Crossing Borders in Literacy and Science Instruction: Perspectives on Theory and Practice*. Newark, Del.: International Reading Association, 2004, pp. 226–238.

Alvermann, Donna E. "Why Bother Theorizing Adolescents' Online Literacies for Classroom Practice and Research?" *Journal of Adolescent & Adult Literacy* 52 (September 2008): 8–19.

Alvermann, Donna E., and David W. Moore. "Secondary School Reading." In R. Barr, M. L. Kamil, P. Mosenthal, and P. D. Pearson (eds.), *Handbook of Reading Research*, vol. 2, pp. 951–983. New York: Longman, 1991.

Alvermann, Donna E., Andrew Huddleston, and Margaret C. Hagood. "What Could Professional Wrestling and School Literacy Practices Possibly Have in Common?" *Journal of Adolescent & Adult Literacy* 47 (April 2004): 532–540.

Amrein, Audrey L., and David C. Berliner. "High Stakes Testing, Uncertainty, and Student Learning." *Education Policy Analysis Archives* 10, no. 18 (2002). Retrieved from http://epaa.asu.edu/epaa/v1On18/.

Anderson, Rebecca, and Ernest Balajthy. "Stories about Struggling Readers and Technology." *The Reading Teacher* 62 (March 2009): 540–542.

Anderson, Richard C., Elfrieda H. Hiebert, Judith A. Scott, and Ian A. G. Wilkinson, *Becoming a Nation of Readers: The Report of the Commission on Reading*. Washington, D.C.: National Institute of Education, 1985.

Andrade, Heidi. "Self-Assessment Through Rubrics." *Educational Leadership* 65 (December 2007/January 2008): 60–63.

Andrasick, Kathleen Dudden. *Opening Texts: Using Writing to Teach Literature*. Portsmouth, N.H.: Heinemann, 1990.

Andrews, Sharon E. "Using Inclusion Literature to Promote Positive Attitudes toward Disabilities." *Journal of Adolescent & Adult Literacy* 41 (March 1998): 420–426.

Applegate, Anthony, Mary DeKonty Applegate, Catherine M. McGeehan, Catherine M. Pinto, and Ailing Kong. "The Assessment of Thoughtful Literacy in NAEP: Why the States Aren't Measuring Up." *The Reading Teacher* 62 (February 2009): 372–381.

Applegate, Mary, Anthony Applegate, and Virginia Modla. "'She's My Best Reader; She Just Can't Comprehend';

Studying the Relationship between Fluency and Comprehension." *The Reading Teacher* 62 (March 2009): 512–521.

Armbruster, Bonnie B., and Thomas H. Anderson. *Content Area Textbooks*. Reading Education Report No. 23. Champaign: University of Illinois, July 1981.

Armon, Joan, and Tony Ortega. "Autobiographical Snapshots: Constructing Self in Letras y Arte." *Language Arts* 86 (November 2008): 108–119.

Arreola, Daniel, Marci Deal, James Petersen, and Rickie Sanders. *World Geography*. Evanston, ILL: McDougal Littell, 2003.

Arthaud, Tamara J., and Teresa Goracke. "Teaching Tips: Implementing a Structured Story Web and Outline Strategy to Assist Struggling Readers." *The Reading Teacher* 59 (March 2006): 581–586.

Ash, Gwynne. "Teaching Readers Who Struggle: A Pragmatic Middle School Framework." *Reading Online* 5, no. 7 (2002). Retrieved from http://www.readingonline.org/articles/art_indexasp?HREF=ash/index.html.

Ausubel, David. *Educational Psychology: A Cognitive View*. 2nd ed. New York: Holt Rinehart Winston, 1978, pp. 523–526.

Azzam, Amy M. "Engaged and On Track." *Educational Leadership* 65 (March 2008): 93–94.

Babbs, Patricia J., and Alden J. Moe. "Metacognition: A Key for Independent Learning from Text." *The Reading Teacher* 36 (January 1983): 422–426.

Bachman-Williams, Paula. "Promoting Literacy in Science Class." In Harriet Arzu Scarborough (ed.), *Writing Across the Curriculum in Secondary Classrooms*, pp. 7–15. Upper Saddle River, N.J.: Merrill/Prentice Hall, 2001.

Bacon, Stephanie. "Reading Coaches: Adapting an Intervention Model for Upper Elementary and Middle School Readers." *Journal of Adolescent & Adult Literacy* 48 (February 2005): 416–427.

Bader, Lois A., and Katherine D. Wiesendanger. "Realizing the Potential of Informal Reading Inventories." *Journal of Reading* 32 (February 1989): 402–408.

Badke, William. "Stepping Beyond Wikipedia." *Educational Leadership* 66 (March 2009): 54–58.

Baines, Lawrence. "From Page to Screen: When a Novel Is Interpreted for Film, What Gets Lost in the Translation." *Journal of Adolescent & Adult Literacy* 39 (May 1996): 612–622.

Baines, Lawrence. "Reading & Happiness." *Phi Delta Kappan* 90 (May 2009): 686–688.

Balajthy, Ernest. "Text-to-Speech Software for Helping Struggling Readers." *Reading Online* 8 (January/February 2005). Retrieved from http://www.readingonline.org.

Balajthy, Ernest. "Technology and Current Reading/Literacy Assessment Strategies." *The Reading Teacher* 61 (November 2007): 240–247.

Barab, S., S. Zuiker, S. Warren, D. Hickey, A. Ingram-Goble, et al. "Situationally Embodied Curriculum: Relating Formalisms and Contexts." *Science Education* 91 (2007): 750–782.

Barbetta, Patricia M., and Linda A. Spears-Bunton. "Learning to Write: Technology for Students with Disabilities in Secondary Inclusive Classrooms." *English Journal* 96 (March 2007): 86–93.

Barrett, Helen C. "Researching Electronic Portfolios and Learner Engagement: The REFLECT Initiative." *Journal of Adolescent & Adult Literacy* 50 (March 2007): 436–448.

Barron, Robert. "The Use of Vocabulary as an Advance Organizer." In H. Herber and P. Sanders (eds.) *Research in Reading in the Content Areas: First Year Report*. Syracuse, N.Y.: Syracuse University Press, 1969, pp. 29–39.

Bartholomew, Barbara. "Sustaining the Fire." *Educational Leadership* 65 (March 2008): 55–60.

Barton, Keith C., and Lynne A. Smith. "Themes or Motifs? Aiming for Coherence through Interdisciplinary Outlines." *The Reading Teacher* 55 (September 2000): 54–63.

Baskin, Barbara H., and Karen Harris. "Heard Any Good Books Lately? The Case for Audiobooks in the Secondary Classroom." *Journal of Reading* 38 (February 1995): 372–376.

Bauman, James, Donna Ware, and Elizabeth Edwards. "Bumping Into Spicy, Tasty Words that Catch your Tongue: A Formative Experiment on Vocabulary Instruction." *The Reading Teacher* 61 (October 2007): 108–122.

Baumann, James F., Edward J. Kame'enui, and George Ash. "Research on Vocabulary Instruction: 'Voltaire Redux.'" In J. Flood, D. Lapp, J. R. Squire, and J. M. Jensen (eds.), *Handbook of Research on Teaching the English Language Arts*, pp. 604–632. New York: Macmillan Publishing Company, 2003.

Beach, Richard, and Candance Doerr-Stevens. "Learning Argument Practices Through Online Role-Play: Toward a Rhetoric of Significance and Transformation." *Journal of Adolescent & Adult Literacy* 52 (March 2009): 460–468.

Bean, Thomas W. "An Update on Reading in the Content Areas: Social Constructionist Dimensions." *Reading Online* 5, no. 5. Retrieved from http://www.readingonline.org (December 2000/January 2001).

Beck, Ann. "A Place for Critical Literacy." *Journal of Adolescent & Adult Literacy* 48 (February 2005): 392–400.

Berne, Jennifer, and Blachowicz, Camille. "What Reading Teachers Say about Vocabulary Instruction: Voices from the Classsroom." *The Reading Teacher* 62 (April, 2009): 314–323.

Bertelsen, C. D., and J. M. Fischer. "Mediating Expository Text: Scaffolding and the Use of Multimedia Curricula." *Reading Online* 6 (December 2002/January 2003). Retrieved from http://www.readingonline.org/articles/Oakley.html.

"Best of the Blogs." *eSchool News* 8 (August 2005): 8.

Beyersdorfer, Janet M., and David K. Schauer. "Writing Personality Profiles: Conversations Across the Generation Gap." *Journal of Reading* 35 (May 1992): 612–616.

Biemiller, Andrew. "Vocabulary: Needed If More Children Are to Read Well." *Reading Psychology* 24 (October/December 2003): 323–335.

Bintz, William P., and Karen S. Shelton. "Using Written Conversation in Middle School: Lessons from a Teacher Researcher Project." *Journal of Adolescent & Adult Literacy* 47 (March 2004): 492–507.

Blachowicz, Camille, L. Z. and Donna Ogle. *Reading Comprehension: Strategies for Independent Learners*. New York: Guilford Press, 2008.

Blachowicz, Camille, and Peter Fisher. *Teaching Vocabulary in All Classrooms*. Upper Saddle River, N.J.: Pearson, 2006.

Black, Rebecca W. "Access and Affiliation: The Literacy and Composition Practices of English-language Learners in an Online Fanfiction Community." *Journal of Adolescent & Adult Literacy* 49 (October 2005): 118–128.

Black, Rebecca W. "English-Language Learners, Fan Communities, and 21st-Century Skills." *Journal of Adolescent & Adult Literacy* 52 (May 2009): 688–697.

Blassingame, James. "Books for Adolescents." *Journal of Adolescent & Adult Literacy* 50 (September 2006): 74–84.

Bloem, Patricia. "Correspondence Journals: Talk That Matters." *The Reading Teacher* 58 (September 2004): 54–62.

Bloom, B. S. *Human Characteristics and School Learning.* New York: McGraw-Hill, 1976.

Bormuth, John. "The Cloze Readability Procedure." *Elementary English* 45 (April 1968a): 429–436.

Bormuth, John. "Cloze Test Readability: Criterion Reference Scores." *Journal of Educational Measurement* 5 (Fall 1968b): 189–196.

Bott, Christie "C. J." "Zines—The Ultimate Creative Writing Project." *English Journal* 92 (November 2002): 327–333.

Brabham, E. J., and S. K. Villaume. "Vocabulary Instruction Concerns and Visions." *The Reading Teacher* 56 (March, 2004): 264–268.

Brady, Coleen. *An Illustrated Guide to Animal Science Terminology.* Clifton Park, N.Y.: Thomson Delmar Learning, 2008.

Brinda, Wayne. "Engaging Aliterate Students: A Literacy/Theatre Project Helps Students Comprehend, Visualize, and Enjoy Literature." *Journal of Adolescent & Adult Literacy* 51 (March 2008): 488–497.

Britton, James, Tony Burgess, Nancy Martin, Alex McLeod, and Harold Rosen. *The Development of Writing Abilities (11–18).* London: Macmillan Education, 1975.

Broaddus, Karen, and Gay Ivey. "Surprising the Writer: Discovering Details through Research and Reading." *Language Arts* 80 (September 2002): 23–30.

Bromley, Karen. "Vocabulary in the Secondary Classroom ." In S. R. Parris, D. Fisher, and K. Headley (eds.), *Adolescent Literacy Field Tested for Every Classroom,* pp. 58–60. Newark, Del.: International Reading Association, 2009.

Bromley, Karen D'Angelo, and Laurie McKeveny. "Précis Writing: Suggestions for Instruction in Summarizing." *Journal of Reading* 29 (February 1986): 392–395.

Brookhart, Susan M. "Feedback That Fits." *Educational Leadership* 65 (December 2007/January 2008): 54–59.

Brookhart, Susan, Connie Moss, and Beverly Long. "Formative Assessment That Empowers." *Educational Leadership* 66 (November 2008): 52–57.

Brooks, Bruce. *Midnight Hour Encores.* New York: Harper & Row, Junior Books, 1986.

Brown, A. L., and J. D. Day. "Macrorules for Summarizing Texts: The Development of Expertise." *Journal of Verbal Learning and Verbal Behavior* 22 (1) (1983): 1–14.

Brown, A. L., J. D. Day, and R. Jones. "The Development of Plans for Summarizing Texts." *Child Development* 54 (1983): 968–979.

Brown, Gavin T. L. "Searching Informational Texts: Text and Task Characteristics That Affect Performance." *Reading Online* 7 (September/October 2003).Retrieved July 26, 2009 from http://www.readingonline.org/articles/art_index.asp?HREF=brown/index.html.

Brozo, William G. "Learning How At-Risk Readers Learn Best: A Case for Interactive Assessment." *Journal of Reading* 33 (April 1990): 522–527.

Brozo, William G., and Ronald V. Schmelzer. "Wildmen, Warriors, and Lovers." *Journal of Adolescent & Adult Literacy* 41 (September 1997): 4–11.

Bruce, Bertram C. "Constructing a Once-and-Future History of Learning Technologies." *Journal of Adolescent & Adult Literacy* 44 (May 2001): 730–736.

Brumfield, Robert. "Computer Simulation for Students Is 'Making History.'" *eSchool News* 8 (October 2005): 28.

Bucher, Katherine, and M. Lee Manning. *Young Adult Literature: Exploration, Evaluation, and Appreciation.* Upper Saddle River, N.J.: Pearson/Merrill/Prentice Hall, 2006.

Buehl, Doug. "Self-Questioning Taxonomy." In *Classroom Strategies for Interactive Learning*, 3rd ed., p. 13. New York: Scholastic, 2003.

Buehl, Doug. "Self-Questioning Taxonomy." In *Classroom Strategies for Interactive Learning*. Newark, Del.: International Reading Association (2009): 157–161.

Bureau of Labor Statistics. *American Time Use Survey*. United States Department of Labor, 2008. Retrieved from www.bls.gov/news.release/pdf/atus.htm.

Burron, Arnold, and Amos L. Claybaugh. *Using Reading to Teach Subject Matter: Fundamentals for Content Teachers*. Columbus, Oh.: Merrill, 1974.

Burton, L. DeVere. *Fish & Wildlife: Principles of Zoology and Ecology*, 2nd ed. Albany, N.Y.: Delmar Thomson Learning, 2001.

Burton, L. DeVere. *Fish & Wildlife: Principles and Ecology*, 2nd ed. Albany, N.Y.: Delmar Thomson, 2003.

Carnine, Douglas, Carlos Cortes, Kenneth Curtis, and Anita Robinson. *World History*. Evanston, Ill.: McDougal Littell, 2006.

Carr, M., and G. Claxton. "Tracking the Development of Learning Dispositions." *Assessment in Education* 9 (1) (2002): 9–37.

Casey, Heather K. "Engaging the Disengaged: Using Learning Clubs to Motivate Struggling Adolescent Readers and Writers." *Journal of Adolescent & Adult Literacy* 52 (December 2008/January 2009): 284–294.

Cassady, Judith K. "Wordless Books: No-Risk Tools for Inclusive Middle-Grade Classrooms." *Journal of Adolescent & Adult Literacy* 41 (March 1998): 428–432.

Cassidy, Jack, Sherrye D. Garrett, and Estanislado Barrera. "What's Hot in Adolescent Literacy?" *Journal of Adolescent and Adult Literacy* 50 (December 2005/January 2006): 30–36.

Chance, Larry. "Use Cloze Encounters of the Readability Kind for Secondary School Students." *Journal of Reading* 28 (May 1985): 690–693.

Chandler-Olcott, Kelly, and Donna Mahar. "Adolescents' *Anime*-Inspired 'Fanfictions': An Exploration of Multiliteracies." *Journal of Adolescent & Adult Literacy* 46 (April 2003): 556–566.

Chappuis, Stephen, and Jan Chappuis. "The Best Value in Formative Assessment." *Educational Leadership* 65 (December 2007/January 2008): 14–18.

Chase, A., and F. Duffelmeyer. "VOCAB-LIT: Integrating Vocabulary Study and Literature Study." *Journal of Reading* 34 (November 1990): 188–193.

Cherland, Meredith. "Harry's Girls: Harry Potter and the Discourse of Gender." *Journal of Adolescent & Adult Literacy* 52 (December 2008/January 2009): 273–282.

Ciardiello, Angela V. "Did You Ask a Good Question Today? Alternative Cognitive and Metacognitive Strategies." *Journal of Adolescent & Adult Literacy* 42 (November 1998): 210–219.

Ciardiello, Vincent A. *First! Motivating Adolescent Readers with Question Finding*. Newark, Del.: International Reading Association, 2007.

Clarke, Lane W., and Erin Whitney. "Walking in Their Shoes: Using Multiple-Perspectives Texts as a Bridge to Critical Literacy. *The Reading Teacher* 62: (March, 2009): 530–534.

Clarke, Lane W., and Jennifer Holwadel. " 'Help! What Is Wrong With These Literature Circles and How Can We Fix Them.' " *The Reading Teacher* 61 (September 2007): 20–29.

Clausen-Grace, Nicki, and Michelle Kelley. "You Can't Hide in R⁵: Restructuring Independent Reading to Be More Strategic and Engaging." *Voices from the Middle* 14 (March 2007): 38–49.

Cleaver, Samantha. "Comics & Graphic Novels." *Instructor* (May/June, 2008): 28–30, 34.

Clover, Jim. *Sports Medicine Essentials*, 2nd ed. Clifton Park, N.Y.: Delmar Cengage Learning, 2007.

Coencas, Joseph. "How Movies Work for Secondary School Students with Special Needs." *English Journal* 96 (March 2007): 67–72.

Coiro, Julie. "Reading Comprehension on the Internet: Expanding Our Understanding of Reading Comprehension to Encompass New Literacies." *The Reading Teacher* 56 (February 2003): 458–464.

Coiro, Julie. "Rethinking Online Reading Assessment." *Educational Leadership* 66 (March 2009): 59–63.

Comer, Melissa. "2 Txt or Nt 2 Txt: An Exploration of Strategies That Capitalize on Digital Literacy." Presentation at Tennessee Tech Council of Tennessee Reading Association Summer Conference, June 2009.

Commander, Nannette Evans, and Brenda D. Smith. "Learning Logs: A Tool for Cognitive Monitoring." *Journal of Adolescent & Adult Literacy* 39 (March 1996): 446–453.

Conley, Mark W., and Kathleen A. Hinchman. "No Child Left Behind: What It Means for U.S. Adolescents and What We Can Do About It." *Journal of Adolescent & Adult Literacy* 48 (September 2004): 42–50.

Considine, David, Julie Horton, and Gary Moorman. "Teaching and Reading the Millenial Generation through Media Literacy." *Journal of Adolescent and Adult Literacy* 52 (March 2009): 471–481.

Cooper, Charles, and Ann Purves. *A Guide to Evaluation*. Lexington, Mass.: Ginn, 1973.

Copeland, Matt, and Chris Goering. "Blues You Can Use: Teaching the Faust Theme Through Music, Literature, and Film." *Journal of Adolescent & Adult Literacy* 48 (February 2003): 436–441.

Coppola, Julie. "Meeting the Needs of English Learners in All English Classrooms: Sharing the Responsibility." In G.G. Garcia (ed.), *English Learners: Reading the Highest Level of English Literacy.* Newark, Del.:International Reading Association, 2003, 182–196.

Cormier, Robert. *The Choclate War.* New York: Laurel Leaf Books, 1974. Cote Parra, Gabriel Eduardo. "Learning English Through Online Discussion Groups." *Journal of Adolescent & Adult Literacy* 44 (September 2000): 36–38.

Costello, Adrienne M. "A Marvel in the Making: Composing a Shakespearean Comic Book in a High School Class." *Talking Points* 20 (October 2008): 2–9.

Cruz, MaryCarmen E. "Writing to Learn as a Way of Making Sense of the World." In Harriet Arzu Scarborough (ed.), *Writing Across the Curriculum in Secondary Classrooms.* Upper Saddle River, N.J.: Merrill/Prentice Hall, 2001, pp. 71–89.

Curry, Adam, and Peter Ford. "What Are Schoolblogs?" January 2002. Retrieved from http://www.schoolblogs. com/stories/storyReader$265, July 28, 2005.

Curtis, Mary, and Ann Longo. *When Adolescents Can't Read: Methods and Materials That Work.* Brookline, Mass: Brookline Books, 1999.

Cutler, Carrie S., and Eula E. Monroe. "Sixth Graders' Oral Retellings of *Compare* Word Problems." *FOCUS—On Learning Problems in Mathematics* 28, no. 2 (2006), 37–55.

Dale, Edgar, and Joseph O'Rourke. *The Living Word Vocabulary.* Elgin, Ill.: Dome, 1976.

D'Angelo, Karen. "Précis Writing: Promoting Vocabulary Development and Comprehension." *Journal of Reading* 26 (March 1983): 534–539.

Darvin, Jacqueline. "Real World Cognition Doesn't End When the Bell Rings: Literacy Instruction Derived from Cognition Research." *Journal of Adolescent & Adult Literacy* 49 (February 2006): 398–407.

Darvin, Jacqueline. "On Reading Recipes and Racing Forms: The Literacy Practices and Perceptions of Vocational Educators. *Journal of Adolescent & Adult Literacy* 50 (September 2006): 10–18.

David, Jane L. "Teaching Media Literacy." *Educational Leadership* 66 (March 2009): 84–86.

Davis, Anne P., and Ewa McGrail. "The Joy of Blogging." *Educational Leadership* 66 (March 2009): 74–77.

Davis, Julie A. "Shakespeare Reads for Teens." *VOYA* (June 2009): 99–101. Retrieved August 5, 2009 from www. voya.com.

Davis, Michelle R. "Wiki Wisdom: Lessons for Educators." *Digital Directions* 1 (Fall 2007): 16–18.

Dean, Deborah, and Sirpa Grierson. "Re-envisioning Reading and Writing through Combined-Text Picture Books." *Journal of Adolescent & Adult Literacy* 48 (March 2005): 456–468.

DeBenedictis, Deb. "Sustained Silent Reading: Making Adaptations." *Voices from the Middle* 14 (March 2007): 29–37.

DelliCarpini, Margo. "Success with ELLs: Use Music, Arts, and Newspapers." *English Journal* 98 (November 2008): 98–101.

DelliCarpini, Margo, and Amanda N. Gulla. "Success with ELLs: "Creating Space for Collaboration." *English Journal* 98 (March 2009): 127–132.

Deschenes, C., D. Ebeling, and J. Sprague. *Adapting Curriculum and Instruction in Inclusive Classrooms: A Teacher's Desk Reference.* Bloomington, Ind.: Institute for the Study of Developmental Disabilities, Indiana University, 1994.

Deubel, Patricia. "Podcasts: Where's the Learning?" *T.H.E. Journal* (June 2007). Retrieved from http://www.thejournal. com/articles/20764.

Developmental Disabilities, Indiana University, 1994.

Dickson, Diane Skiffington, Dick Heyler, Linda G. Reilly, Stephanie Romano, and Bob DiLullo. "The Oral History Project." Handout, 47th Annual Convention of the International Reading Association, San Francisco, Calif., April 29, 2002.

Dodge, Bernie. "Webquest.Org." 2007. Retrieved from http://webquest.org/index.php.

Dolly, Martha R. "Integrating ESL Reading and Writing Through Authentic Discourse." *Journal of Reading* 33 (February 1990): 360–365.

Donovan, Carol A., and Laura B. Smolkin. "Considering Genre, Content and Visual Features in the Selection of Trade Books for Science Instruction." *The Reading Teacher* 55 (March 2002): 502–520.

Dornan, Reade W., Lois Matz Rosen, and Marilyn Wilson. *Within and Beyond the Writing Process in the Secondary Classroom.* Boston: Pearson Education Allyn and Bacon, 2003.

Draper, Roni, and Daniel Siebert. "Content Area Literacy in Mathematics and Science Classrooms." In *Field Tested: Effective Solutions for Every Classroom.* Newark, DE: International Reading Association (2009): 105–116.

Dreher, Mariam Jean. "Searching for Information in Textbooks." *Journal of Reading* 35 (February 1992): 364–371.

Duke, Nell K., and P. David Pearson. "Effective Practices for Developing Reading Comprehension." In A. Farstrup and S. J. Samuels (eds.) *What Research Has to Say About Reading Instruction.* Newark, Del.: International Reading Association, 2002, pp. 205–242.

Dymock, Susan. "Comprehension Strategy Instruction: Teaching Narrative Text Structure Awareness." *The Reading Teacher* 61 (October, 2007): 161–167.

Echevarría, Jana, MaryEllen Vogt, and Deborah J. Short. *Making Content Comprehensible for English Learners: The SIOP® Model.* Boston: Pearson Allyn and Bacon, 2008.

Eckert, Lisa, "Bridging the Pedagogical Gap: Intersections between Literacy and Reading Theories in Secondary and Post Secondary Literacy Instruction." *Journal of Adolescent & Adult Literacy* 52 (October, 2008): 110–118.

Edwards, Patricia A., Jennifer D. Turner, and Kouider Mokhtari. "Balancing Assessment *of* Learning and *for* Learning in Support of Student Literacy Achievement." *The Reading Teacher* 61 (May 2008): 682–684.

Elbow, Peter. "Why Teach Writing?" In Philip L. Brady (ed.), *The Why's of Teaching Product.* Portsmouth, N.H.: Boynton/Cook, 1991, pp. 3–16.

Elbow, Peter, and Pat Belanoff. "State University of New York at Stony Brook Portfolio-Based Evaluation Program." In Pat Belanoff and Marcia Dickson (eds.), *Portfolios: Process and Composition,* pp. 57–69. Washington State Council of Teachers of English, 1978.

Ellis, Dave. *Becoming a Master Student: Concise.* Boston: Cengage Learning, 2009.

Ernst-Slavit, Gisela, and Margaret Mulhern. "Bilingual Books: Promoting Literacy and Biliteracy in the Second-Language and Mainstream Class." *Reading Online 7* (September/October 2003). Retrieved from http://www.readingonline.org/articles/art_index.asp? HREF=/articles/ernstslavit/index.html.

Ernst-Slavit, Gisela, Monica Moore, and Carol Maloney. "Changing Lives: Teaching English and Literature to ESL Students." *Journal of Adolescent & Adult Literacy* 48 (October 2002): 118–128.

Espinosa, Cecilia M. "Finding Memorable Moments: Images and Identities in Autobiographical Writing." *Language Arts* 84 (November 2006): 136–144.

Evers, Amy J., Lisa F. Lang, and Sharon V. Smith. "An ABC Literacy Journey: Anchoring in Texts, Bridging Language, and Creating Stories." *The Reading Teacher* 62 (March 2009): 461–470.

Fahey, Kevin, Joshua Lawrence, and Jeanne Paratore. "Using Electronic Portfolios to Make Learning Public." *Journal of Adolescent & Adult Literacy* 50 (March 2007): 460–471.

Faust, Mark A., and Ronald D. Kieffer. "Challenging Expectations: Why We Ought to Stand by the IRA/NCTE Standards for the English Language Arts." *Journal of Adolescent & Adult Literacy* 41 (April 1998): 540–547.

Fay, Leo. "Reading Study Skills: Math and Science." In J. Allen Figurel (ed.), *Reading and Inquiry,* pp. 93–94. Newark, Del.: International Reading Association, 1965.

Fennessey, Sharon. "Living History through Drama and Literature." *The Reading Teacher* 49 (September 1995): 16–19.

Ferris, Judith Ann, and Gerry Snyder. "Writing as an Influence on Reading." *Journal of Reading* 29 (May 1986): 751–756.

Fisher, Douglas. "'We're Moving On Up': Creating a School wide Literacy Effort in an Urban High School." *Journal of Adolescent & Adult Literacy* 45 (October 2001): 92–101.

Fisher, Douglas, and Nancy Frey. "Writing Instruction for Struggling Adolescent Readers: A Gradual Release Model." *Journal of Adolescent & Adult Literacy* 46 (February 2003): 396–405.

Fisher, Douglas, Nancy Frey, and Diane Lapp. "Meeting AYP in a High-Need School: A Formative Experiment." *Journal of Adolescent & Adult Literacy* 52 (February 2009): 386–396.

Fisher, Douglas, James Flood, Diane Lapp, and Nancy Frey. "Interactive Read-Alouds: Is There a Common Set of Implementation Practices?" *The Reading Teacher* 58 (September 2004): 8–17.

Flanigan, Kevin, and Scott Greenwood. "Effective Content Vocabulary Instruction in the Middle: Matching Purposes, Words, and Strategies." *Journal of Adolescent and Adult Literacy* 51 (March 2007): 226–228.

Flynt, E. Sutton and William Brozo. "Developing Academic Language: Got Words?" *The Reading Teacher* 61 (May 2008): 500–502.

Forbes, Leighann S. "Using Web-Based Bookmarks in K–8 Settings: Linking the Internet to Instruction." *The Reading Teacher* 58 (October 2004): 148–153.

Forcier, Richard C., and Don E. Descy. *The Computer as an Educational Tool.* Upper Saddle River, N.J.: Pearson Education, 2008.

Fordham, Nancy W. "Crafting Questions that Address Comprehension Strategies in Content Reading." *Journal of Adolescent & Adult Literacy* 49 (February 2006): 390–396.

Franks, Leslie. "Charcoal Clouds and Weather Writing: Inviting Science to a Middle School Language Arts Classroom." *Language Arts* 78 (March 2001): 319–324.

Frayer, D. A., W. C. Frederick, and H. J. Klausmeier. *A Schema For Testing the Level of Concept Mastery.* Technical Report No. 16. Madison, Wis.: University of Wisconsin, R&D Center for Cognitive Learning, 1969.

Friese, Elizabeth E. G., and Jenna Nixon. "Poetry and World War II: Creating Community through Content-Area Writing." *Voices from the Middle* 16 (March 2009): 23–30.

Fry, Edward. *Reading Instruction for Classroom and Clinic.* New York: McGraw-Hill, 1972.

Fry, Edward. "A Readability Formula for Short Passages." *Journal of Reading* 33 (May 1990): 594–597.

Fryar, R. "Students Assess Their Own Reporting and Presentation Skills." In H. Fehring (ed.), *Literacy Assessment.*

Newark, Del.: International Reading Association, 2003, pp. 36–39.

Furr, Derek. "Struggling Readers Get Hooked on Writing." *The Reading Teacher* 56 (March 2003): 518–525.

Gallagher, Janice Mori. "Pairing Adolescent Fiction with Books from the Canon." *Journal of Adolescent & Adult Literacy* 39 (September 1995): 8–14.

Garcia, Eugene. *Student Cultural Diversity*. Boston: Houghton Mifflin, 2002.

Garcia-Vazquez, Enedina, and Luis A. Vazquez. "In a Pen Pals Program: Latinos/as Supporting Latinos/as." *Journal of Reading* 38 (November 1994): 172–178.

Gee, J. P. *What Video Games Have to Teach Us About Learning and Literacy*. New York: Palgrave Macmillan, 2003.

Gee, James. "Reading as Situated Language: A Sociocognitive Perspective." *Journal of Adolescent & Adult Literacy* 44 (February 2004): 714–725.

Gee, James Paul, and Michael H. Levine. "Welcome to Our Virtual Worlds." *Educational Leadership* 66 (March 2009): 48–52.

Geisert, Paul G., and Mynga K. Futrell. *Teachers, Computers, and Curriculum: Microcomputers in the Classroom*. 3rd ed. Boston: Allyn & Bacon, 2000.

Gerber, Susan, and Jeremy D. Finn. "Learning Document Skills at School and at Work." *Journal of Adolescent & Adult Literacy* 42 (September 1998): 32–44.

Gibbons, Pauline. *Scaffolding Language, Scaffolding Learning: Teaching Second Language Learners in the Mainstream Classroom*. Portsmouth, N.H.: Heinemann, 2002.

Gill, Sharon. "The Comprehension Matrix: A Tool for Designing Comprehension Instruction." *The Reading Teacher* 62 (October 2008): 106–113.

Gillespie, Cindy S. "Reading Graphic Displays: What Teachers Should Know." *Journal of Reading* 36 (February 1993): 350–354.

Glasgow, Jacqueline N. "Motivating the Tech Prep Reader Through Learning Styles and Adolescent Literature." *Journal of Adolescent & Adult Literacy* 39 (February 1996): 358–367.

Glatthorn, Allen. "Thinking, Writing, and Reading: Making Connections." In Diane Lapp, James Flood, and Nancy Farnan (eds.), *Content Area Reading and Learning: Instructional Strategies*, Englewood Cliffs, N.J.: Prentice Hall, 1989.

Glazer, Susan Mandel, and Carol Smullen Brown. *Portfolios and Beyond: Collaborative Assessment in Reading and Writing*. Norwood, Mass.: Christopher-Gordon, 1993.

Gollnick, Donna M., and Philip C. Chinn. *Multicultural Education in a Pluralistic Society*. Columbus, Ohio: Merrill, 2002.

Gomez, L., P. Herman, and K. Gomez. "Integrating Text in Content-Area Classes: Better Supports for Teachers and Students." *Voices in Urban Education*, 14 (2007): 22–29.

Goodson, E. Todd. "The Electronic Portfolio: Shaping an Emerging Genre." *Journal of Adolescent & Adult Literacy* 50 (March 2007): 482–484.

Gordon, Christine J., and Dorothy MacInnis. "Using Journals as a Window on Students' Thinking in Mathematics." *Language Arts* 70 (January 1993): 37–43.

Grabe, Mark, and Cindy Grabe. *Integrating the Internet for Meaningful Learning*, 5th ed. Boston: Houghton Mifflin, 2007.

Grace, Marsha. "Implementing a Portfolio System in Your Classroom." *Reading Today* 10 (June–July 1993): 27.

Grady, Karen. *Adolescent Literacy and Content Reading*. ERIC #176. Bloomington, Ind: ERIC: Clearinghouse on Adult, Career, and Vocational Education, December 2002.

Grant, Rachel, and Shelley Wong. "Barriers to Literacy for Language-Minority Learners: An Argument for Change in the Literacy Education Profession." *Journal of Adolescent & Adult Literacy* 46 (February 2003): 386–394.

Graves, Donald. "What I've Learned from Teachers of Writing." *Language Arts* 82 (November 2004): 88–94.

Graves, Donald H. "Help Students Learn to Read Their Portfolios." In Donald H. Graves and Bonnie S. Sunstein (eds.), *Portfolio Portraits*. Portsmouth, N.H.: Heinemann, 1992a, pp. 85–95.

Graves, Donald H. "Portfolios: Keep a Good Idea Growing." In Donald H. Graves and Bonnie S. Sunstein (eds.), *Portfolio Portraits*. Portsmouth, N.H.: Heinemann, 1992b, pp. 1–12.

Graves, Donald, and Jill Fitzgerald. "Scaffolding Reading Experiences for Multilingual Classrooms." In Gilbert G. Garcia (ed.) *English Language Learners: Reaching for the Highest Level of English Literacy*. Newark, Del: International Reading Association, 2003, pp. 96–124.

Graves, Michael F., and Jill Fitzgerald. "Scaffolding Reading Experiences for Multilingual Classrooms." In Gilbert G. Garcia (ed.) *English Language Learners: Teaching the Highest Level of English Literacy*. Newark, Del.: International Reading Association, 2003, pp. 96–124.

Graves, Michael. *The Vocabulary Book: Learning and Instruction*. New York: Teachers College Press, 2006.

Graves, Michael (ed.) *Essential Reading on Vocabulary Instruction*. Newark, Del.: International Reading Association, 2009.

Greenleaf, Cynthia, Ruth Schoenbach, Christine Cziko, and Faye Mueller, "Apprenticing Adolescent Readers to Academic Literacy." *Harvard Educational Review* 71 (2001): 70–129.

Greenwood, Scott, and Kevin Flanigan. "Overlapping Vocabulary and Comprehension: Context Clues Complement Semantic Gradients." *The Reading Teacher* 61 (March 2007): 249–254.

Grierson, Sirpa T., Amy Anson, and Jacoy Baird. "Exploring the Past through Multigenre Writing." *Language Arts* 80 (September 2002): 51–59.

Griffith, Lorraine, and Timothy Rasinski."A Focus on Fluency: How One Teacher Incorporated Fluency with Her Reading Curriculum." *The Reading Teacher* 58 (October 2004): 126–137.

Grigg, Wendy, Patricia L. Donahue, and Gloria Dion. *The Nation's Report Card: 12th-Grade Reading and Mathematics.* Washington, D.C.: National Center for Educational Statistics, 2007.

Grisham, Dana L., and Thomas D. Wolsey. "Recentering the Middle School Classroom as a Vibrant Learning Community: Students, Literacy, and Technology Intersect." *Journal of Adolescent & Adult Literacy* 48 (May 2006): 648–660.

Groenke, Susan L. "Missed Opportunities in Cyberspace: Preparing Preservice Teachers to Facilitate Critical Talk about Literature Through Computer-Mediated Communication." *Journal of Adolescent & Adult Literacy* 52 (November 2008): 224–233.

Gunelius, Susan. "Web Logs Blog: Sign Up for Free Access to Encyclopedia Britannica Online." *About.com Guide to WebLogs*, April 30, 2008. Retrieved from http://weblogs. about.com/b/2008/04/30/sign-up-for-free-access-to-encyclopediabritannica-online.htm.

Guskey, Thomas R. "How Classroom Assessments Improve Learning." *Educational Leadership* 60 (February 2003): 7–11.

Guskey, Thomas R. "The Rest of the Story." *Educational Leadership* 65 (December 2007/January 2008): 28–35.

Hadaway, Nancy L., and JaNae Mundy. "Children's Informational Picture Books Visit a Secondary ESL Classroom." *Journal of Adolescent & Adult Literacy* 42 (March 1999): 464–475.

Haggard, Michael. "An Interactive Strategies Approach to Content Reading." *Journal of Reading* 29 (1986): 204–210.

Haley-James, Shirley. *Houghton Mifflin English,* Boston: Houghton Mifflin, 1986, p. 417.

Hall, Leigh. "Anything but Lazy: New Understandings about Readers, Teaching and Text." *Reading Research Quarterly* 41 (2006): 424–426.

Hall, Leigh A., and Susan V. Piazza. "Critically Reading Texts: What Students Do and How Teachers Can Help. *The Reading Teacher* 62 (September 2008): 32–41.

Hansen, Jane. "Multiple Literacies in the Content Classroom: High School Students' Connections to U.S. History." *Journal of Adolescent & Adult Literacy* 52 (April 2009): 597–606.

Hansen, Jill. " 'Tell Me a Story': Developmentally Appropriate Retelling Strategies." Newark, Del.: International Reading Association, 2004.

Hardman, Michael L., Clifford J. Drew, and M. Winston Egan. *Human Exceptionality: School, Community, and Family.* Boston: Houghton Mifflin Company, 2008.

Harmon, Janis M., Karen D. Wood, Wanda B. Hedrick, Jean Vintinner, and Terri Willeford. "Interactive Word Walls: More Than Just Reading the Writing on the Walls." *Journal of Adolescent and Adult Literacy* 52 (February 2009): 398–408.

Harper, Candace, and Ester de Jong. "Misconceptions About Teaching English-Language Learners." *Journal of Adolescent & Adult Literacy* 48 (October 2004): 152–162.

Hartley, Jennifer. " 'You Should Read This Book!' " *Educational Leadership* 65 (March 2008): 73–75.

Harvey, Stephanie. "Nonfiction Inquiry: Using Real Reading and Writing to Explore the World." *Language Arts* 80 (September 2002): 12–22.

Hasselbring, Ted S., and Margaret E. Bausch. "Assistive Technologies for Reading." *Educational Leadership* 63 (December 2005/January 2006): 72–75.

Heard, Georgia. "Celestino: A Tribute to the Healing Power of Poetry." *Voices from the Middle,* 16 (March 2009): 9–13.

Helsel, Lisa, and Daphne Greenberg. "Helping Struggling Writers Succeed: A Self-Regulated Instruction Program." *The Reading Teacher* 60 (May 2007): 752–760.

Henwood, Geraldine F. "A New Role for the Reading Specialist: Contributing Toward a High School's Collaborative Educational Culture." *Journal of Adolescent & Adult Literacy* 43 (December 1999/January 2000): 316–325.

Hernandez, Ana. "Making Content Instruction Accessible for English Language Learners." In Gilbert G. Garcia (ed.) *English Learners: Reaching the Highest Level of English Literacy.* Newark, Del.: International Reading Association, 2003, pp. 125–149.

Hibbing, Anne Nielsen, and Joan L. Rankin-Erickson. "A Picture Is Worth a Thousand Words: Using Visual Images to Improve Comprehension for Middle School Struggling Readers." *The Reading Teacher* 56 (May 2003): 758–770.

Hiebert, Elfrieda, and Michael Kamil (eds.) *Teaching and Learning Vocabulary: Bringing Research to Practice.* Mahwah, N.J.: Erlbaum, 2004.

Higgins, Betty, Melinda Miller, and Susan Wegmann. "Teaching to the Test . . . Not! Balancing Best Practice and Testing Requirements in Writing." *The Reading Teacher* 60 (December 2006): 310–319.

Hobbs, Renee, and Richard Frost. "Measuring the Acquisition of Media-Literacy Skills." *Reading Research Quarterly* 38 (July/August/September 2003): 330–355.

Hornof, Michelle. "Reading Tests as a Genre Study." *The Reading Teacher* 62 (September 2008): 69–73.

Hoyt, Kenneth. "Career Education and Education Reform: Time for a Rebirth." *Phi Delta Kappan* 83 (December 2001): 327–331.

Hoyt, Kenneth, and Pat Wickwire. "Knowledge-Information-Service Era Changes in Work and Education and the Changing Role of the School Counselor in Career Education." *Career Development Quarterly* 49 (March 2001): 238.

Hughes-Hassell, Sandra, and Pradnya Rodge. "The Leisure Reading Habits of Urban Adolescents." *Journal of Adolescent & Adult Literacy* 51 (September 2007): 22–33.

Hughes, Janette, and Amy John. "From Page to Digital Stage: Creating Digital Performances of Poetry." *Voices from the Middle* 16 (March 2009): 15–22.

Hutchison, Amy C. "Internet Reciprocal Teaching (IRT): A Research-Based Model for Teaching the New Literacies of Online Reading Comprehension." Presentation at the 54th International Reading Association Annual Convention, North Central, May 5, 2009.

"Ideas for Teaching with Interactive Whiteboards." *eSchool News* 8 (February 2005): 24.

Ikpeze, Chinwe H., and Fenice B. Boyd. "Web-Based Inquiry Learning: Facilitating Thoughtful Literacy with Web Quests." *The Reading Teacher* 60 (April 2007): 644–654.

Invernizzi, Marcia A., Timothy J. Landrum, Jennifer L. Howell, and Heather P. Warley. "Toward the Peaceful Coexistence of Test Developers, Policymakers, and Teachers in an Era of Accountability." *The Reading Teacher* 58 (April 2005): 610–616.

Irwin, Judith Westphal, and Carol A. Davis. "Assessing Readability: The Checklist Approach." *Journal of Reading* 24 (November 1980): 124–130.

Israel, Susan E. *Using Metacognitive Assessments to Create Individualized Reading Instruction.* Newark, Del.: International Reading Association, 2007.

Ivey, Gay. "'The Teacher Makes It More Explainable': And Other Reasons to Read Aloud in the Intermediate Grades." *The Reading Teacher* 56 (May 2003): 812–814.

Jacobi, Tobi. "The Zine Project: Innovation or Oxymoron." *English Journal,* 96 (March 2007): 43–49.

Jacobowitz, Tina. "Using Theory to Modify Practice: An Illustration with SQ3R." *Journal of Reading* 32 (November 1988): 126–131.

Jacobs, George, and Patrick Gallo. "Reading Alone Together: Enhancing Extensive Reading via Student-Student Cooperation." *Reading Online* 5 (February 2002). Retrieved from http://www.readingonline.org/articles/art_index.asp?HREF=/articles/jacobs/index.html.

Jacobs, Gloria. "People, Purposes, and Practices: Insights from Cross-Disciplinary Research into Instant Messaging." In J. Coiro, M. Knobel, C. Lankshear, and D. J. Leu (eds.), *Handbook of Research on New Literacies,* pp. 469–493. New York: Routledge, 2008a.

Jacobs, Gloria E. "We Learn What We Do: Developing a Repertoire of Writing Practices in an Instant Messaging World." *Journal of Adolescent & Adult Literacy* 52 (November 2008b): 203–211.

Jacobs, Vickie. "Adolescent Literacy Field Tested: Effective Solutions for Every Classroom." In Shari Parris, Douglas Fisher, and Kathy Headly (eds.), *The Landscape of Adolescent Literacy,* pp. 5–20. Newark, Del.: International Reading Association, 2009.

Jetton, Tamara L., and Patricia A. Alexander. "Learning from Text: A Multidimensional and Developmental Perspective." *Reading Online* 5, no.1: http://www.readingonline.org (July/August, 2001).

Johnson, Andrew, and Jay Rasmussen. "Classifying and Super Word Web: Two Strategies to Improve Productive Vocabulary." *Journal of Adolescent & Adult Literacy* 43 (November 1998): 204–207.

Johnson, Denise. "Web Watch: Internet Resources to Assist Teachers with Struggling Readers." *Reading Online* 4 (April 2001). Retrieved from http://www.readingonline.org/electronic/elec_index.asp? HREF=/electronic/webmatch/ struggling/index.html.

Johnson, M. S., R. A. Kress, and J. J. Pikulski. *Informal Reading Inventories.* 2nd ed. Newark, Del.: International Reading Association, 1987.

Johnston, Peter, and Paula Costello. "Principles for Literacy Assessment." *Reading Research Quarterly* 40 (April/May/June 2005): 256–267.

Johnston, Peter H. *Choice Words: How Our Language Affects Children's Learning.* York, Maine: Stenhouse, 2004.

Johnston, Peter. "Literacy Assessment and the Future." *The Reading Teacher* 58 (April 2005): 684–686.

Jones, Raymond. "Strategies for Reading Comprehension: Summarizing," 2006. Retrieved July 17, 2009 from http://www.readingquest.org/strat/summarize.html.

Joseph, Laurice M. "Teaching Tips: Incremental Rehearsal: A Flashcard Drill Technique for Increasing Retention of Teaching Words." *The Reading Teacher* 59 (May 2006): 803–807.

Kapitzke, Cushla. "Information Literacy: The Changing Library." *Journal of Adolescent & Adult Literacy* 44 (February 2001): 450–456.

Kapitzke, Cushla, Samuela Bogitini, Min Chen, Greg MacNeill, Diane Mayer, Bruce Muirhead, and Peter Renshaw. "Weaving Words with the Dreamweaver: Literacy, Indigeneity, and Technology." *Journal of Adolescent & Adult Literacy* 44 (December 2000/January 2001): 336–345.

Kelley, Michelle, and Nikki Clausen-Grace. "Laying the Foundation for the Metacognitive Teaching Framework." In *Comprehension Shouldn't be Silent*. Newark, DE: International Reading Association (2007): 22–41.

Kibby, Michael W. "What Will Be the Demands of Literacy in the Workplace in the Next Millennium?" *Reading Research Quarterly* 35 (July/August/September 2000): 380–381.

Kieffer, Michael, and Nonie Lesaux. "Breaking Down Words to Build Meaning: Morphology, Vocabulary, and Reading Comprehension in the Urban Classroom." *The Reading Teacher* 61 (October 2007): 134–144.

Kirby, Dan, and Tom Liner, with Ruth Vinz. *Inside Out: Developmental Strategies for Teaching Writing*. 2nd ed. Portsmouth, N.H.: Heinemann, 1988.

Kirk, Samuel A., James J. Gallagher, and Nicholas J. Anastasiow. *Educating Exceptional Children*. 10th ed. Boston: Houghton Mifflin, 2003.

Kist, William. "Finding 'New Literacy' in Action: An Interdisciplinary High School Western Civilization Class." *Journal of Adolescent & Adult Literacy* 45 (February 2002): 368–377.

Kletzien, Sharon B. "Strategy Use by Good and Poor Comprehenders Reading Expository Text of Differing Reading Levels." *Reading Research Quarterly* 26 (1991): 67–86.

Kletzien, Sharon, and B. Hushion. "Reading Workshop: Reading, Writing, Thinking." *Journal of Reading* 35 (March 1992): 444–450.

Kletzien, Sharon B., and Maryanne R. Bednar. "Dynamic Assessment for At-Risk Readers." *Journal of Reading* 33 (April 1990): 528–533.

Knickerbocker, Joan L., and James Rycik. "Growing into Literature: Adolescents' Literary Interpretation and Appreciation." *Journal of Adolescent & Adult Literacy* 46 (November 2002): 196–208.

Knipper, Kathy J., and Timothy J. Duggan. "Writing to Learn Across the Curriculum: Tools for Comprehension in Content Area Classes." *The Reading Teacher* 59 (February 2006): 462–470.

Knobel, Michele, and Colin Lankshear. "Remix: The Art and Craft of Endless Hybridization." *Journal of Adolescent & Adult Literacy* 52 (September 2008): 22–33.

Knobel, Michele, and Dana Wilber. "Let's Talk 2.0." *Educational Leadership* 66 (March 2009): 20–24.

Knoester, Matthew. "Inquiry Into Urban Adolescent Independent Reading Habits: Can Gee's Theory of Discourses Provide Insight?" *Journal of Adolescent & Adult Literacy* 52 (May 2009): 676–685.

Konopak, Bonnie C., Michael A. Martin, and Sarah H. Martin. "Reading and Writing: Aids to Learning in the Content Areas." *Journal of Reading* 31 (November 1987): 109–115.

Kuhn, M.E., and S. Stahl. *Fluency: A Review of Development and Remedial Practices* (CIERA Rep. No. 2-008). Ann Arbor Center for the Study of Reading Achievement, 2000.

Kymes, Angel. "Teaching Online Comprehension Strategies Using Think-Alouds." *Journal of Adolescent & Adult Literacy* 48 (March 2005): 492–500.

Lambeth, William. "Remaking Schools for the Information Age: What Media Centers Can and Must Do." *T.H.E. Journal* 25 (June 1998): 78–79.

Landrum, Judith E. "Adolescent Novels That Feature Characters with Disabilities: An Annotated Bibliography." *Journal of Adolescent & Adult Literacy* 42 (December 1998/January 1999): 284–290.

Langer, Judith A. "From Theory to Practice: A Prereading Plan." *Journal of Reading* 25 (November 1981): 152–156.

Langer, Judith A. "Learning Through Writing: Study Skills in the Content Areas." *Journal of Reading* 29 (February 1986): 400–406.

Lankshear, C. and M. Knobel. "Sampling 'the New' in New Literacies." In M. Knobel and C. Lankshear (eds.), *A New Literacies Sampler*, pp. 1–24. New York: Peter Lang, 2007.

Lanning, Lois A. "Putting the Strategies into Practice: Summarizing." In *Four Powerful Strategies for Struggling Readers, Grades 3–8*, pp. 25–48. Newark, Del.: Corwin Press/International Reading Association, 2008.

Lapp, Diane, and Douglas Fisher. "It's All About the Book: Motivating Teens to Read." *Journal of Adolescent & Adult Literacy* 52 (April 2009): 556–561.

Lapp, Diane, James Flood, and Douglas Fisher. "Intermediality: How the Use of Multiple Media Enhances Learning." *The Reading Teacher* 52 (April 1999): 776–780.

Larson, R., L. Boswell, T. Kanold, and I. Stiff. *Course 2 Math*. Evanston, Ill.: McDougal Littell, 2005.

Larson, Lotta. "Reader Response Meets New Literacies: Empowering Readers in Online Learning Communities." *The Reading Teacher*, 62 (May 2009): 638–648.

Larson, Lotta C. "Electronic Reading Workshop: Beyond Books with New Literacies and Instructional Technologies." *Journal of Adolescent & Adult Literacy* 52 (October 2008): 121–131.

Lave, J. "Situated Learning: Legitimate Peripheral Participation." Cambridge University Press, Cambridge, 1991. Retrieved from http://www.infed.org/biblio/b-learn.htm

Lawrence, Salika A., Kelly McNeal, and Melda N. Yildiz. "Summer Program Helps Adolescents Merge Technology, Popular Culture, Reading, and Writing for Academic Purposes." *Journal of Adolescent & Adult Literacy* 52 (March 2009): 483–494.

Leal, Dorothy J., and Julia Chamberlain-Solecki. "A Newbery Medal-Winning Combination: High Student Interest Plus

Appropriate Reading Levels." *The Reading Teacher* 51 (May 1998): 712–715.

Lee, Jihyun, Wendy S. Grigg, and Patricia L. Donahue. *The Nation's Report Card: Reading 2007*. Washington, D.C.: National Center for Educational Statistics, 2007.

Lehr, Susan, and Deborah L. Thompson. "The Dynamic Nature of Response: Children Reading and Responding to *Maniac Magee* and *The Friendship*." *The Reading Teacher* 53 (March 2000): 480–493.

Lemke, Jay L. "The Literacies of Science." In E. Wendy Saul (ed.), *Crossing Borders in Literacy and Science Instruction Perspectives on Theory and Practice*. Newark, Del.: International Reading Association, 2004, pp. 33–47.

Lenhart, Amanda, Mary Madden, and Paul Hitlin. *Teens and Technology*. Washington, D. C.: Pew Internet and American Life Project, 2005.

Lenhart, A., M. Madden, and P. Hitlin. *Teens and Technology: Youth Are Learning the Transition to a Fully Wired and Mobile Nation*. Washington, D.C.: Pew Internet & American Life Project, 2008.

Lenhart, A., M. Madden, A. Rankin McGill, and A. Smith. *Teens and Social Media*. Washington, D. C.: Pew Internet and American Life Project, December 19, 2007. Retrieved from http://www.pewinternet.org/Reports/2007/Teens-and-Social-Media.aspx, April 2, 2009.

Lever-Duffy, Judy, and Jean B. McDonald. *Teaching and Learning with Technology* Boston: Pearson Education Allyn & Bacon, 2008.

Levin-Epstein, Michael, Corey Murray, and Dennis Pierce. "Across-the-Board Instruction." *eSchool News* 8 (February 2005): 21–26.

Lewis, J. "Redefining Critical Reading for College Critical Thinking Courses." *Journal of Reading* 34 (March 1991): 420–423.

Lewis, Jill. "Academic Literacy: Principles and Learning Opportunities for Adolescent Readers." In J. Lewis and G. Moorman (eds.) *Adolescent Literacy Instruction*. Newark, Del.: International Reading Association, 2007, 143–166.

Littrell, Annette B. *"My Space": Using Blogs as Literature Journals with Adolescents*. Dissertation, Tennessee Technological University–Cookeville, 2005.

Lloyd, Carol V. "Engaging Students at the Top (Without Leaving the Rest Behind)." *Journal of Adolescent & Adult Literacy* 42 (November 1998): 184–191.

Lloyd, Susan. "Using Comprehension Strategies as a Springboard for Student Talk." *Journal of Adolescent & Adult Literacy* 48 (October 2004): 114–124.

Lohr, Linda L. *Creating Graphics for Learning and Performance*. Upper Saddle River, N. J.: Pearson Education, 2008.

Louie, Belinda. "Development of Empathetic Responses with Multicultural Literature." *Journal of Adolescent & Adult Literacy* 48 (April 2005): 566–578.

Louie, Belinda Y. "Guiding Principles for Teaching Multicultural Literature." *The Reading Teacher* 59 (February 2006): 438–448.

Love, Kristina. "Mapping Online Discussion in Senior English." *Journal of Adolescent & Adult Literacy* 45 (February 2002): 382–396.

Love, Mary Susan. "Multimodality of Learning Through Anchored Instruction." *Journal of Adolescent & Adult Literacy* 48 (December 2004/January 2005): 300–310.

Lowe, Ross E., Charles A. Malouf, and Annette R. Jacobson. *Consumer Education and Economics* 4th ed. New York: Glencoe McGraw-Hill, 1997.

Lunsford, Andrea, *Easy Writer*. New York: St. Martin's Press, 2006.

Lynch, Tom Liam. "Readings and Literacy: How Students' Second Readings Might Open Third Spaces." *Journal of Adolescent & Adult Literacy* 52 (December 2008/January 2009): 334–341.

MacDonald, Nancy. *Woodworking*. Clifton Park, N.Y.: Delmar Cengage Learning, 2009.

MacGinitie, Walter H. "Some Limits of Assessment." *Journal of Reading* 36 (April 1993): 556–560.

Manyak, Patrick. "Character Trait Vocabulary: A Schoolwide Approach." *The Reading Teacher* 60 (March 2007): 574–577.

Manz, Suzanne Liff. "A Strategy for Previewing Textbooks: Teaching Readers to Become THIEVES." *The Reading Teacher* 55 (February 2002): 434–435.

Maring, Gerald H. "Video Conferencing." International Reading Association Convention, San Francisco, California, May 1, 2002.

Martiínez, Ramón Antonio, Marjorie Faulstich Orellana, Mariana Pacheco, and Paula Carbone. "Found in Translation: Connecting Translating Experiences to Academic Writing." *Language Arts* 85 (July 2008): 421–431.

Mastropieri, Margo M., and Thomas E. Scruggs. *The Inclusive Classroom: Strategies for Effective Instruction*. Columbus, Ohio: Prentice Hall/Merrill, 2000.

Matthews, Michael. "Electronic Literacy and the Limited English Proficient Student." *Reading Online* 3 (May 2000). Retrieved from http://www.readingonline.org/electronic/elec_index.asp?HREF=/electronic/matthews/index.html.

Mayer, James C. "Persuasive Writing and the Student-Run Symposium." *English Journal* 96 (March 2007): 39–42.

McDermott, J. Cynthia, and Sharon Setoguchi. "Collaborations That Create Real-World Literacy Experiences." *Journal of Adolescent & Adult Literacy* 42 (February 1999): 396–397.

McGrath, Beth. "Partners in Learning: Twelve Ways Technology Changes the Teacher-Student Relationship." *T.H.E. Journal* 25 (April 1998): 58–61.

McKenna, Michael C., and Katherine A. Dougherty Stahl. *Assessment for Reading Instruction*, New York: Guilford Press, 2008.

McKeown, Margaret, Isabel Beck, Ronette G. K. Blake. "Rethinking Reading Comprehension Instruction for Strategies and Content Approaches." *Reading Research Quarterly* 44 (2009): 218–253.

McLaughlin, Maureen, and Glenn DeVoogd. "Critical Literacy as Comprehension: Expanding Reader Response." *Journal of Adolescent & Adult Literacy* 48 (September, 2004): 52–62.

McLaughlin, Maureen, and Mary Beth Allen. *Guided Comprehension: A Teaching Model for Grades 3-8.* Newark, Del.: International Reading Association, 2002.

McMillan, Sally, and Jennifer Wilhelm. "Students' Stories: Adolescents Constructing Multiple Literacies through Nature Journaling." *Journal of Adolescent & Adult Literacy* 50 (February 2007): 370–377.

McNabb, Mary "Navigating the Maze of Hypertext." *Educational Leadership* 63 (December 2005/January 2006): 76–79.

McTighe, J., and F. Lyman, Jr. "Cueing Thinking in the Classroom: The Promise of Theory-Embedded Tools." *Educational Leadership* 45 (April 1988): 18–24.

McVicker, Claudia J. "Comic Strips as a Text Structure for Learning to Read." *The Reading Teacher* 61 (September 2007): 85–88.

Mealey, D. L., B. C. Konopak, M. A. Duchein, D. W. Frazier, T. R. Host, and C. Nobles. "Student, Teacher, and Expert Differences in Identifying Important Content Area Vocabulary." In N. D. Padak, T. V. Rasinski, and J. Logan (eds.), *Literary Research and Practice: Foundations for the Year 2000*, Fourteenth Yearbook of the College Reading Association, pp. 117–123. Pittsburg, Kans.: College Reading Association, 1992.

Meeks, Lynn Langer. "Making English Classrooms Happier Places to Learn." *English Journal* 88 (March 1999): 73–80.

Mendelman, Lisa. "Critical Thinking and Reading." *Journal of Adolescent & Adult Literacy* 51 (December 2007/January 2008): 300–301.

Miller, George, and P. Gildea. "How Children Learn Words." *Scientific American* 257 (1987): 94–99.

Miller, Paula, and Dagmar Koesling. "Mathematics Teaching for Understanding Reasoning, Reading and Formative Assessment." In S. Plaut, ed., *The Right to Literacy in Secondary Schools: Creating a Culture of Thinking.* New York: Teachers College, Columbia University. (2009): 65–79.

Miller, Roger, and Alan Stafford. *Economic Education for Consumers.* South-Western Cengage: Mason Ohio, 2010.

Miller, Roger LeRoy, and Alan D. Stafford. *Economic Education*, 4th edition. Mason, Ohio: South-Western Cengage Learning, 2010.

Miller, Terry. "The Place of Picture Books in Middle-Level Classrooms." *Journal of Adolescent & Adult Literacy* 41 (February 1998): 376–381.

Milliken, Mark. "A Fifth-Grade Class Uses Portfolios." In Donald H. Graves and Bonnie S. Sunstein (eds.), *Portfolio Portraits.* Portsmouth, N.H.: Heinemann, 1992, pp. 34–44.

Moje, Elizabeth Birr. "Foregrounding the Disciplines in Secondary Literacy Teaching and Learning: A Call for Change." *Journal of Adolescent & Adult Literacy* 52 (October 2008): 96–107.

Moje, Elizabeth, Kathryn Ciechnowski, Katherine Kramer, Lindsay Ellis, Rosario Carrillo, and Tehani Collazo. "Working Toward Third Space in Content Area Literacy: An Examination of Everyday Funds of Knowledge and Discourse." *Reading Research Quarterly* 39 (2004): 38–70.

Mokhtari, Kouider, Angel Kymes, and Patricia Edwards. "Assessing the New Literacies of Online Reading Comprehension: An Informative Interview with W. Ian O'Byrne, Lisa Zawilinski, J. Greg McVerry, and Donald J. Leu at the University of Connecticut." *The Reading Teacher* 62 (December 2008/January 2009): 354–357.

Monroe, Eula Ewing, Sharon S. Black, and Amanda J. Buhler. "Oral Retellings: Their Nature and Use in Solving Word Problems Among Third Graders." In T. Lamberg and L. R. Wiest (eds.), *Proceedings of the 29th Annual Meeting of the North American Chapter of the International Group for the Psychology of Mathematics Education.* Stateline (Lake Tahoe), Nev.: University of Nevada–Reno, 2007.

Morgan, Brian, and Richard D. Smith. "A Wiki for Classroom Writing." *The Reading Teacher* 62 (September 2008): 80–82.

Morgan, Denise N., and Jeffery L. Williams. "Chapter Glancing: Noticing and Naming Chapter Openings." *The Reading Teacher* 61 (October 2007): 168–172.

Morrow, Lesley Mandel. "Retelling Stories as a Diagnostic Tool." In Susan Mandel Glazer, Lyndon W. Searfoss, and Lance H. Gentile (eds.), *Reexamining Reading Diagnosis:*

New Trends and Procedures. Newark, Del.: International Reading Association, 1989, pp. 128–149.

Moulton, Margaret R. "The Multigenre Paper: Increasing Interest, Motivation, and Functionality in Research." *Journal of Adolescent & Adult Literacy* 42 (April 1999): 528–539.

Mountain, Lee. "Rooting Out Meaning: More Morphemic Analysis for Primary Pupils." *The Reading Teacher* 58 (May 2005): 742–749.

Mountain, Lee. "Synonym Success—Thanks to the Thesaurus." *Journal of Adolescent and Adult Literacy* 51 (December 2007/January 2008): 318–324.

Mustacchi, Johanna. "What's Relevant for YouTubers?" *Educational Leadership* 65 (March 2008): 67–70.

Napoli, Mary, and Emily Rose Ritholz. "Using Jacqueline Woodson's *Locomotion* with Middle School Readers." *Voices from the Middle* 16 (March 2009): 31–39.

National Assessment of Educational Progress (NAEP). *The Nation's Report Card: Frequently Asked Questions*, 2009. Retrieved from http://nationsreportcard.gov/faq.asp.

National Association of State Directors of Career Technical Education Consortium. *Career Technical: An Essential Component of the Total Educational System.* Washington D.C., 2001.

National Council of Teachers of English (NCTE). "Using Comics and Graphic Novels in the Classroom." *Council Chronicle*, September 2005. Retrieved from http://www.ncte.org/magazine/archives/122031.

National Council of Teachers of English and International Reading Association. *Standards for the English Language Arts.* Urbana, Ill.: 1996.

National Council of Teachers of English's James Squire Office of Policy Research. "Reading and Writing Differently." *The Council Chronicle* (November 2008): 15–21.

Neufeld, P. "Comprehension Instruction in Content Area Classes." *The Reading Teacher* 59 (December 2005): 302–312.

"New Study Supports Value of School Libraries." *Reading Online* 21 (April/May 2004), 25.

Nichols, Sharon L., and David C. Berliner. "Testing the Joy Out of Learning." *Educational Leadership* 65 (March 2008): 14–18.

Nilsen, Alleen Pace, and Don L. F. Nilsen. "The Straw Man Meets His Match: Six Arguments for Studying Humor in English Classes." *English Journal* 88 (March 1999): 34–42.

Nilsson, Nina. "How Does Hispanic Portrayal in Children's Books Measure Up after 40 Years? The Answer Is 'It Depends.'" *The Reading Teacher* 58 (March 2005): 534–548.

Northwest Regional Educational Laboratory. *6+1 Trait Writing*, n.d. Retrieved December 20, 2009 from http://educationnorthwest.org/webfm.send/140.

Norton-Meier, Lori. "Joining the Video-Game Literacy Club: A Reluctant Mother Tries to Join the 'Flow'." *Journal of Adolescent & Adult Literacy* 48 (February 2005): 428–432.

Noskin, David Peter. "Teaching Writing in the High School: Fifteen Years in the Making." *English Journal* 90 (September 2000): 34–38.

Office of Innovation and Improvement, U.S. Department of Education. "Individuals with Disabilities Education Improvement Act of 2004," 2004. Retrieved from http://www.ed.gov/about/offices/list/oii/nonpublic/programs2.html.

Ogle, Donna. "A Teaching Model That Develops Active Reading of Expository Text." *The Reading Teacher* 39 (May 1986): 564–570.

Ogle, Donna. "Reading Comprehension Across the Disciplines: Commonalities and Content Challenges." In *Adolescent Literacy, Field Tested: Effective Solutions for Every Classroom.* (eds.) S. Parris, D. Fisher, and K. Headley. Newark, DE: International Reading Association (2009): 34–46.

Ohler, Jason. "Orchestrating the Media Collage." *Educational Leadership* 66 (March 2009): 9–13.

Olson, Mark, and Mary Truxaw. "Preservice Science and Mathematics Teachers and Discursive Metaknowledge of Text." *Journal of Adolescent and Adult Literacy* 52 (February 2009): 422–431.

Ostensen, Jonathon. "Skeptics on the Internet: Teaching Students to Read Critically." *English Journal.* 98 (2009): 54–59.

Palincsar, AnnMarie, and Ann Brown. "Interactive Teaching to Promote Independent Learning from Text." *The Reading Teacher* 39 (May 1986): 771–777.

Parris, Sheri R., and Taliaferro, Cheryl. "Successful Secondary Teachers Share Their Most Effective Teaching Practices." In S. R. Parris, D. Fisher, and K. Headley (eds.), *Adolescent Literacy, Field Tested: Effective Solutions for Every Classroom*, pp. 219–227. Newark, Del.: International Reading Association, 2009.

Paterson, Katherine. *Bridge to Terabithia.* New York: Crowell, 1987.

Patthey-Chavez, G. Genevieve, Lindsay Clare Matsumura, and Rosa Valdes. "Investigating the Process Approach to Writing Instruction in Urban Middle Schools." *Journal of Adolescent & Adult Literacy* 47 (March 2004): 462–477.

Pauk, Walter. *How to Study in College*, 7th ed. Boston: Houghton Mifflin, 2001.

Pauk, Walter, and Ross J. Q. Owens. *How to Study in College*, 8th ed. Boston: Houghton Mifflin, 2005.

Pavonetti, Linda M. "Joan Lowery Nixon: The Grand Dame of Young Adult Mystery." *Journal of Adolescent & Adult Literacy* 39 (March 1996): 454–461.

Pearson, Jenny Watson, and Carol M. Santa. "Students as Researchers of Their Own Learning." *Journal of Reading* 38 (March 1995): 462–469.

Pennock-Roman, M., and Charlene Rivera. *The Differential Effects of Time on Accommodated vs. Unaccommodated Content Assessments for English-language Learners.* Dover, N.H.: Center for Assessment Reidy Interactive Lecture Series, 2007.

Perkins, David. *Outsmarting: The Emerging Science of Learnable Intelligence.* New York: Free Press, 1995.

Pinnell, Gay S., and M. M. Jaggar. "Oral Language: Speaking and Listening in Elementary Classrooms." In James Flood, Diane Lapp, J. Squire, and J. Jensen (eds.), *Handbook of Research on Teaching the English Language Arts,* pp. 881–913. Mahwah, N.J.: Erlbaum, 2003.

Pisha, Bart, and Peggy Coyne. "Jumping Off the Page: Content Area Curriculum for the Internet Age." *Reading Online* 5 (November 2001): 1–18. Retrieved from http://www.readingonline.org.

Pitcher, Sharon M., Lettie K. Albright, Carol J. DeLaney, Nancy T. Walker, Krishna Seunarinesingh, Stephen Mogge, Kathy N. Headley, Victoria Gentry Ridgeway, Sharon Peck, Rebecca Hunt, and Pamela J. Dunston. "Assessing Adolescents' Motivation to Read." *Journal of Adolescent & Adult Literacy* 50 (February 2007): 378–396.

Plank, Stephen B. "A Question of Balance: CTE, Academic Courses: High School Perspective and Student Achievement." *Journal of Vocation Research* 26, no. 3, 2001.

Polloway, Edward A., James R. Patton, and Loretta Serna. *Strategies for Teaching Learners with Special Needs.* Englewood Cliffs, N.J.: Prentice-Hall, 2001.

Popham, W. James. "A Process—Not a Test." *Educational Leadership* 66 (April 2009): 85–86.

Prabhu, Maya T. "Virtual Environment Boosts Reading Skills." *eSchool News* 11 (October 2008), p. 18.

Prensky, Marc. "Listen to the Natives." *Educational Leadership* 63 (December 2005/January 2006), 8–13.

Prensky, Marc. "Turning on the Lights." *Educational Leadership* 65 (March 2008): 40–45.

Pressley, Michael, Irene W. Gaskins, and Lauren Fingeret. "Instruction and Development of Reading Fluency in Struggling Readers. In S. J. Samuels and A. E. Farstrup (eds.) *What Research Has to Say About Fluency Instruction,* pp. 47–69. Newark, Del.: International Reading Association, 2002.

Quatroche, Diana. "Helping the Underachiever in Reading." ERIC Digest 141. Bloomington, Ind.: ERIC Clearinghouse on Reading, English and Communication, 1999.

Quatroche, Diana J., Rita M. Bean, and Rebecca L. Hamilton. "The Role of the Reading Specialist: A Review of Research." *The Reading Teacher* 55 (November 2001): 282–294.

Quinn, Kathleen Benson, Bernadette Barone, Janine Kearns, Susan A. Stackhouse, and Marie Ellen Zimmerman. "Using a Novel Unit to Help Understand and Prevent Bullying in Schools." *Journal of Adolescent & Adult Literacy* 46 (April 2003): 582–591.

Radcliffe, Rich, David Caverly, James Hand, and Deanna Franke. "Improving Reading in a Middle School Science Classroom." *Journal of Adolescent & Adult Literacy* (February 2008): 398–408.

Randall, Sally N. "Information Charts: A Strategy for Organizing Student Research." *Journal of Adolescent & Adult Literacy* 39 (April 1996): 536–542.

Ranker, Jason. "Making Meaning on the Screen: Digital Video Production about the Dominican Republic." *Journal of Adolescent & Adult Literacy* 51 (February 2008): 410–422.

Raphael, Taffy, Carol Sue Englert, and Becky Kirschner. *The Impact of Text Structure Instruction and Social Context on Students' Comprehension and Production of Expository Text.* Research Series No. 177. East Lansing, Mich.: Institute for Research on Teaching, 1986.

Raphael, Taffy E., and Carol Sue Englert. "Writing and Reading: Partners in Constructing Meaning." *The Reading Teacher* 43 (February 1990): 388–400.

Rasinski, Timothy V., and James V. Hoffman. "Oral Reading in the School Literacy Curriculum." *Reading Research Quarterly* 38 (October/November 2003): 510–522.

Raymond, Margaret E., and Eric A. Hanushek. "High Stakes Research." *Education Next* (Spring 2003). Retrieved from http://www.educationnext.org/20033/48.html.

Recesso, Arthur, and Chandra Orrill. *Integrating Technology into Teaching.* Boston: Houghton Mifflin, 2008.

Recht, Donna. "Teaching Summarizing Skills." *The Reading Teacher* 37 (March 1984): 675–677.

Reilley, Mary Ann. "Finding the Right Words: Art Conversations and Poetry." *Language Arts* 86 (November 2008): 99–107.

Reiss, Jody. *102 Content Strategies for English Language Learners.* Upper Saddle River, N.J.: Pearson Merrill Prentice Hall, 2008.

Rekrut, Martha D. "Collaborative Research." *Journal of Adolescent & Adult Literacy* 41 (September 1997): 26–34.

Renaissance Learning. *Accelerated Reader: Understanding Reliability and Validity.* Wisconsin Rapids, Wisc.: Renaissance Learning, 2006.

Rhodes, Carol. "Mindful Reading: Strategy Training That Facilitates Transfer." *Journal of Adolescent & Adult Literacy* 45 (March 2002): 498–512.

Richardson, Will. "Metablognition." *Weblogg-Ed,* April 27, 2004. Retrieved from http://weblogg-ed.com/2004/04/27, July 28, 2005.

Richardson, Will. "Becoming Network-Wise." *Educational Leadership* 66 (March 2009): 26–31.

Richek, Margaret. "Words are Wonderful: Interactive, Time Efficient Strategies to Teach Meaning Vocabulary." *The Reading Teacher* 58 (May 2005): 414–423.

Richek, Margaret Ann, Lynne K. List, and Janet W. Lerner. *Reading Problems: Assessment and Teaching Strategies.* Englewood Cliffs, N.J.: Prentice-Hall, 1989.

Rief, Linda. "Eighth Grade: Finding the Value in Evaluation." In Donald H. Graves and Bonnie S. Sunstein (eds.), *Portfolio Portraits.* Portsmouth, N.H.: Heinemann, 1992, pp. 45–60.

Robbins, Bruce, and Kris Fischer. "Vaporizing Classroom Walls: The Writing Workshop Goes Electric." *Voices from the Middle* 3 (April 1996): 25–30.

Roberson, Dana L., Jim Flowers, and Gary E. Moore. "The Status of Academic and Agricultural Education in North Carolina." *Journal of Career and Technical Education* 17 (Spring 2001): 51–59.

Robinson, Francis P. Chapter 2. In *Effective Study*, rev. ed. New York: Harper and Row, 1961.

Roe, Betty D., and Elinor P. Ross. *Integrating Language Arts through Literature and Thematic Units.* Boston: Pearson Allyn & Bacon, 2006.

Roe, Betty D., and Sandy Smith. "TALK: Talking About Literature with Kids." Unpublished project description. Cookeville, Tenn.: Tennessee Technological University, 1996.

Roe, Betty D., and Sandy Smith. "University/Public Schools Keypals Project: A Collaborative Effort for Electronic Literature Conversations." In *Rethinking Technology and Learning Through Technology.* Proceedings of the Mid-South Instructional Technology Conference. Murfreesboro, Tenn.: Mid-South Technology Conference, 1997.

Roe, Betty D., Sandy H. Smith, and Paul C. Burns. *Teaching Reading in Today's Elementary Schools.* Boston: Houghton Mifflin Harcourt, 2009.

Roessing, Lesley. "Making Research Matter." *English Journal* 96 (March 2007): 50–55.

Romano, Tom. *Writing with Passion: Life Stories, Multiple Genres.* Portsmouth, N.H.: Boynton/Cook, 1995.

Romano, Tom. "Crafting Authentic Voice." *Voices from the Middle* 3 (April 1996): 5–9.

Romano, Tom. *Blending Genre, Altering Style.* Portsmouth, N.H.: Boynton/Cook, 2000.

Rosenblatt, Louise. *Literature as Exploration.* New York: Noble and Noble, 1983.

Rosenblatt, Louise M. "Writing and Reading: The Transactional Theory." In Jana M. Mason (ed.), *Reading and Writing Connections.* Boston: Allyn & Bacon, 1989, pp. 153–176.

Rosenshine, Barak. "Advances in Research on Instruction." In E.J. Kameenui and D. Chard (eds.) *Issues in Educating Students with Disabilities.* Mahwah, N.J.: Erlbaum, 1997, pp. 197–221.

Rosenshine, Barak, Carol Meister, and Susan Chapman. "Teaching Students to Generate Questions: A Review of the Intervention Studies." *Review of Educational Research* 66 (1996): 181–221.

Roser, Nancy, Miriam Martinez, Charles Fuhrken, and Kathleen McDonnold. "Characters as Guides to Meaning." *The Reading Teacher* 60 (March 2007): 548–559.

Ruddell, Martha R., and Brenda Shearer. "'Extraordinary,' 'Tremendous,' 'Exhilarating,' 'Magnificient,': Middle School At-Risk Students Become Avid Word Learners with the Vocabulary Self-Collection Strategy (VSS)." *Journal of Adolescent & Adult Literacy* 45 (February 2002): 353–363.

Rue, Leslie W. and Lloyd Byars, *Business Management* (New York: Glencoe McGraw-Hill (2001).

Ryan, Mary. "Engaging Middle Years Students: Literacy Projects That Matter." *Journal of Adolescent & Adult Literacy* 52 (November 2008): 190–201.

Ryan, Mary E. *The Trouble with Perfect.* New York: Simon & Schuster, 1995.

Salahu-Din, Deborah, Hillary Persky, and Jessica Miller. *The Nation's Report Card: Writing 2007.* Washington, D.C.: National Center for Educational Statistics, 2008.

Salvia, John, and James E. Ysseldyke. *Assessment in Special and Inclusive Education.* Boston: Houghton Mifflin, 2004.

Samuels, S. Jay. "Toward a Theory of Automatic Information Processing in Reading, Revisited." In Robert Ruddell and Norman Unrau (eds.) *Theoretical Models and Processes of Reading.* 5th ed. Newark, Del.: International Reading Association, 2004, pp. 1127–1148.

Sanacore, Joseph. "Promoting the Lifelong Love of Writing." *Journal of Adolescent & Adult Literacy* 41 (February 1998): 392–396.

Sanacore, Joseph. "Genuine Caring and Literacy Learning for African American Children." *The Reading Teacher* 57 (May 2004): 744–753.

Santa, Carol, Lynn Havens, and Shirley Harrison. "Teaching Secondary Science Through Reading, Writing, Studying, and Problem Solving." In Diane Lapp, James Flood, and Nancy Farnan (eds.), *Content Area Reading and Learning: Instructional Strategies,* New York.: Routledge, 2007, pp. 165–180.

Scharber, Cassandra. "Digital Literacies." *Journal of Adolescent & Adult Literacy* 52 (February 2009): 433–437.

Scharrer, Erica. "Making a Case for Media Literacy in the Curriculum: Outcomes and Assessment." *Journal of Adolescent & Adult Literacy* 48 (December 2002/January 2003): 354–358.

Schmar-Dobler, Elizabeth. "Reading on the Internet: The Link between Literacy and Technology." *Journal of Adolescent & Adult Literacy* 47 (September 2003): 80–85.

Schmidt, Gary. *The Wednesday Wars.* New York: Clarion, 2007.

Schmidt, Renita. "Really Reading: What Does Accelerated Reading Teach Adults and Children?" *Language Arts*, 85 (January 2008): 202–211.

Schumm, Jeanne Shay. "Identifying the Most Important Terms: It's Not That Easy." *Journal of Reading* 36 (May 1993): 679.

Schwarz, Gretchen. "Expanding Literacies through Graphic Novels." *English Journal* 95 (July 2006): 58–64.

Schwarz, Gretchen E. "Graphic Novels for Multiple Literacies." *Journal of Adolescent & Adult Literacy* 46 (November 2002): 262–265.

Seal, Kathy. "Transforming Teaching and Learning Through Technology." *Carnegie Reporter* 2 (Spring 2003): 1–4.

Sefton-Green, Julian. "Computers, Creativity, and the Curriculum: The Challenge for Schools, Literacy, and Learning." *Journal of Adolescent & Adult Literacy* 44 (May 2001): 726–728.

Seltz, Judy. "A Focus on Assessment." *Educational Leadership* 66 (September 2008): 92–93.

Serafini, Frank. "Three Paradigms of Assessment: Measurement, Procedure, and Inquiry." *The Reading Teacher* 54 (December 2000/January 2001): 384–393.

Shanklin, Nancy. "Exploring Poetry: How Does a Middle School Teacher Begin?" *Voices from the Middle* 16 (March 2009): 46–47.

Short, Kathy G., Gloria Kauffman, and Leslie Kahn. "'I Just *Need* to Draw': Responding to Literature Across Multiple Sign Systems." *The Reading Teacher* 54 (October 2000): 160–171.

Showers, Beverly, Bruce Joyce, Mary Scanlon, and Carol Schnaubelt. "A Second Chance to Learn to Read." *Educational Leadership* 55 (March 1998): 27–30.

Simmons, Jay. "Portfolios for Large-Scale Assessment." In Donald H. Graves and Bonnie S. Sunstein (eds.), *Portfolio Portraits*. Portsmouth, N.H.: Heinemann, 1992, pp. 96–113.

Simons, Sandra McCandless. "PSRT—A Reading Comprehension Strategy." *Journal of Reading* 32 (February 1989): 419–427.

Simpson, Anne. "Not the Class Novel: A Different Reading Program." *Journal of Reading* 38 (December 1994/January 1995): 290–294.

Sinatra, Richard. "Integrating Whole Language with the Learning of Text Structure." *Journal of Reading* 34 (March 1991): 424–433.

Singer, Jessie, and Ruth Shagoury Hubbard. "Teaching from the Heart: Guiding Adolescent Writers to Literate Lives." *Journal of Adolescent & Adult Literacy* 46 (December 2002/January 2003): 328–336.

Silva, Elena. "Measuring Skills for 21st Century Learning." *Phi Delta Kappan* 90 (May 2009): 630–634.

Slavin, Robert. "A Cooperative Learning Approach to Content Areas: Jigsaw Teaching." In Diane Lapp, James Flood, and Nancy Farnan (eds.), *Content Area Reading and Learning: Instructional Strategies*. Englewood Cliffs, N.J.: Prentice-Hall, 1989, pp. 330–45.

Smagorinsky, Peter. "Standards Revisited: The Importance of Being There." *English Journal* 88, no. 4 (March 1999): 82–88.

Smith, M. Cecil. "What Will Be the Demands of Literacy in the Workplace in the Next Millennium?" *Reading Research Quarterly* 35 (July/August/September 2000): 378–379.

Smith-D'Arezzo, Wendy M., and Brenda J. Kennedy. "Seeing Double: Piecing Writing Together with Cross-Age Partners." *Journal of Adolescent & Adult Literacy* 47 (February 2004): 390–401.

Smith, Michael, and Jeffrey D. Wilhelm. "I Just Like Being Good at It: The Importance of Competence in the Literate Lives of Young Men." *Journal of Adolescent & Adult Literacy* 47 (March 2004): 454–461.

Smolin, Louanne Ione, and Kimberly A. Lawless. "Becoming Literate in the Technological Age: New Responsibilities and Tools for Teachers." *The Reading Teacher* 56 (March 2003): 570–577.

Snow, Catherine. "Ch. 2, Defining Comprehension." In *Reading for Understanding*. Santa Monica, Cal.: RAND Corporation, 2007.

Standards for the English Language Arts. Urbana, Ill.: National Council of Teachers of English/International Reading Association, 1996.

Stansberry, Susan L. and Angel D. Kymes. "Transformative Learning Through 'Teaching with Technology' Electronic Portfolios." *Journal of Adolescent & Adult Literacy* 50 (March 2007): 488–496.

Stoodt-Hill, Barbara. "Classroom Observations of Successful Strategies for Struggling Readers." John Tyler Community College. A Paper presented to the Virginia Association of Developmental Education (October 2005).

Spaulding, Nancy, and Samuel Namowitz. *Earth Science.* Evanston, Ill.: McDougal Littell, 2005.

Spear-Swerling, Louise. "A Road Map for Understanding Reading Disability and Other Reading Problems: Origins, Prevention, and Intervention." *Theoretical Models and Processes of Reading.* 5th ed. Newark, Del.: International Reading Association, 2004, pp. 517–573.

Spencer, Brenda and Andrea Guillaume. "Integrating Curriculum through the Learning Cycle: Content Based." *The Reading Teacher* 60 (November 2006): 206–219.

Stahl, Steven A., and B. Kapinus. "Possible Sentences: Predicting Word Meanings to Teach Content Area Vocabulary." *The Reading Teacher* 45 (September 1991): 65–70.

Stiggins, R. J. *Student-Involved Classroom Assessment for Learning.* Upper Saddle River, New Jersey: Pearson/Merrill/Prentice Hall, 2005.

Stiggins, Rick. "New Assessment Beliefs for a New School Mission." *Phi Delta Kappan* 86 (September 2004): 22–27.

Stiggins, Rick, and Rick DuFour. "Maximizing the Power of Formative Assessments." *Phi Delta Kappan* 90 (May 2009): 640–644.

Stivers, Jan. "The Writing Partners Project." *Phi Delta Kappan* 77 (June 1996): 694–695.

Strauss, Valerie. "Thinking Outside the Box, Inside the Panel by Giving Them the Pen." *The Washington Post* (June 15, 2004): A10.

Strassman, Barbara K., and Trisha O'Connell. "Authoring with Video." *The Reading Teacher* 61 (December 2007/January 2008): 330–333.

Strichart, Stephen S., and Charles T. Mangrum II. *Teaching Study Strategies to Students with Learning Disabilities.* Needham Heights, Mass.: Allyn & Bacon, 1993.

Sullivan, Jane. "The Electronic Journal: Combining Literacy and Technology." *The Reading Teacher* 52 (September 1998): 90–92.

Summer, Ann. "Implementing the Standards: A Classroom Teacher's Viewpoint." *Technology Teacher* 60 (February 2001): 38–40.

Tarasiuk, Tracy. "Extreme Poetry: Making Meaning through Words, Images, and Music." *Voices from the Middle* 16 (March 2009): 50–51.

Thompson, Gail, Marga Madhuri, and Deborah Taylor. "How the Accelerated Reader Program Can Become Counterproductive for High School Students." *Journal of Adolescent & Adult Literacy* 51 (April 2008): 550–560.

Tierney, Robert J. "Literacy Assessment Reform: Shifting Beliefs, Principled Possibilities, and Emerging Practices." *The Reading Teacher* 51 (February 1998): 374–390.

Tierney, Robert J., John E. Readence, and Ernest K. Dishner. *Reading Strategies and Practices.* Boston: Allyn & Bacon, 1990.

Tobias, Sigmund. "Interest, Prior Knowledge, 64 (Spring 1994): 37–54.

Tombari, Martin, and Gary Borich. *Authentic Assessment in the Classroom.* Columbus, Ohio: Merrill, 1999.

Tomlinson, Carol Ann. "Learning to Love Assessment." *Educational Leadership* 65 (December 2007/January 2008): 8–13.

Toppo, Greg. "Teachers Are Getting Graphic." *USA Today* (May 4, 2005): 1D–2D.

Unrau, Norman J., and Robert B. Ruddell. "Interpreting Texts in Classroom Contexts." *Journal of Adolescent & Adult Literacy* 39 (September 1995): 16–27.

Valmont, William J. *Technology for Literacy Teaching and Learning.* Boston: Houghton Mifflin, 2003.

Van Horn, Leigh. *Reading Photographs to Write with Meaning and Purpose: Grades 4–12.* Newark, Del.: International Reading Association, 2008.

Van Kraayenoord, C. "Toward Self-Assessment of Literacy Learning." In H. Fehring (ed.), *Literacy Assessment.* Newark, Del.: International Reading Association, 2003, pp. 44–54.

Wade, S., and B. Adams. "Effects of Importance and Interest on Recall of Biographical Text." *Journal of Literacy* 22 (1990): 331–353.

Wade, Suzanne, and Elizabeth Moje. "The Role of Text in Classroom Learning: Beginning an Online Dialogue." *Reading Online* 5 (November 2001). Retrieved from http://readingonline.org.

Wade, S., G. Schraw, W. Buxton, and M. Hayes. "Seduction of the Strategic Reader: Effects of Interest on Strategies and Recall." *Reading Research Quarterly* 28 (Spring 1993): 93–114.

Warren, John Robert, and Eric Grodosky. "Exit Exams Harm Students Who Fail Them—and Don't Benefit Students Who Pass Them." *Phi Delta Kappan* 90 (May 2009): 645–649.

Watson, Sue. "IDEA—What You Need to Know," n.d. Retrieved from http://specialed.about.com/od/idea/a/Idea Defined.htm, September 17, 2009.

Watts Pailliotet, Ann, Ladislaus Semali, Rita K. Rodenberg, Jackie K. Giles, and Sherry L. Macaul. "Intermediality: Bridge to Critical Media Literacy." *The Reading Teacher* 54 (October 2000): 208–219.

Weigel, Margaret, and Howard Gardner. "The Best of Both Literacies." *Educational Leadership* 66 (March 2009): 38–41.

West, Kathleen C. "Weblogs and Literary Response: Socially Situated Identities and Hybrid Social Languages in English Blogs." *Journal of Adolescent & Adult Literacy* 51 (April 2008): 588–598.

Wilhelm, Jeffrey D. "Poetry as a 21st Century Problem-Solving Pursuit!" *Voices from the Middle* 16 (March 2009): 40–41.

Williams, Bronwyn T. "What They See Is What We Get: Television and Middle School Writers." *Journal of Adolescent & Adult Literacy* 48 (April 2003): 546–554.

Williams, Bronwyn T. "I'm Ready for My Close-up Now: Electronic Portfolios and How We Read Identity." *Journal of Adolescent & Adult Literacy* 50 (March 2007): 500–504.

Wilner, Lynn S., Charlene Rivera, and Barbara D. Acosta. "Ensuring Accommodations Used in Content Assessments are Responsive to English Language-Learners." *The Reading Teacher* 62 (May 2009): 696–698.

Wilson, Maja. "Why I Won't Be Using Rubrics to Respond to Students' Writing." *English Journal* 96 (March 2007): 62–66.

Wilson, Nance S., Dana L. Grisham, and Linda Smetana. "Investigating Content Area Teachers Understanding of a Content Literacy Framework: A Yearlong Professional Development Initiative." *Journal of Adolescent & Adult Literacy*, 52 (May 2009): 708–375.

Winer, Dave. "The History of Weblogs." *Weblogs.Com News* (2002). Retrieved from http://newhome.weblogs.com/historyofweblogs, July 28, 2005.

Wise, Bob, "Adolescent Literacy: The Cornerstone of Student Success." *Journal of Adolescent & Adult Literacy* 52 (February 2009): 369–275.

Witte, Shelbie. "'That's Online Writing, Not Boring School Writing': Writing with Blogs and the Talkback Project." *Journal of Adolescent & Adult Literacy* 51 (October 2007): 92–96.

Wittrock, Merlin C. "Process Oriented Measures of Comprehension." *The Reading Teacher* 40 (April 1987): 734–737.

Wolf, Kenneth, and Yvonne Siu-Runyan. "Portfolio Purposes and Possibilities." *Journal of Adolescent & Adult Literacy* 40 (September 1996): 30–37.

Wolf, Maryanne, and Mirit Barzillai. "The Importance of Deep Reading." *Educational Leadership* 66 (March 2009): 32–37.

Wolfe, Paula. "'The Owl Cried': Reading Abstract Literary Concepts with Adolescent ESL Students." *Journal of Adolescent & Adult Literacy* 47 (February 2004): 402–413.

Wolk, Steven. "Joy in School." *Educational Leadership* 66 (September 2008): 8–14.

Wolk, Steven. "Reading for a Better World: Teaching for Social Responsibility with Young Adult Literature." *Journal of Adolescent & Adult Literacy* 52 (May 2009): 664–673.

Wollman-Bonilla, J. "Why Don't They 'Just Speak'? Attempting Literature Discussion with More and Less Able Readers." *Research in the Teaching of English* 28 (October 1994): 231–258.

Wonacott, Michael E. "Technological Literacy." ERIC Digest no. 233 (2001).

Wonacott, Michael E. *High Schools That Work: Best Practices for CTE*. Research Triangle Park, N.C. Research Triangle Institute, 2002.

Wood, Karen D. "Fostering Collaborative Reading and Writing Experiences in Mathematics." *Journal of Reading* 36 (October 1992): 96–103.

Worthy, Jo, and Karen Broaddus. "Fluency Beyond the Primary Grades: From Group Performance to Silent, Independent Reading." *The Reading Teacher* 55 (December 2001/January 2002): 334–343.

Yang, Gene. "Graphic Novels in the Classroom." *Language Arts* 85 (January 2008): 185–192.

Yi, Youngjoo. "Relay Writing in An Adolescent Online Community." *Journal of Adolescent & Adult Literacy* 51 (May 2008): 670–680.

Yopp, Ruth, and Hallie Yopp. "Ten Important Words Plus: A Strategy for Building Word Knowledge." *The Reading Teacher* 61 (February 2007): 157–160.

Young, Linda. "Portals into Poetry: Using Generative Writing Groups to Facilitate Student Engagement with Word Art." *Journal of Adolescent & Adult Literacy* 51 (September 2007): 50–55.

Zawlinski, Lisa. "HOT Blogging: A Framework for Blogging to Promote Higher Order Thinking." *The Reading Teacher*, 62 (May 2009): 650–661.

Zenkov, Kristien, and James Harmon. "Picturing a Writing Process: Photovoice and Teaching Writing to Urban Youth." *Journal of Adolescent & Adult Literacy* 52 (April 2009): 575–584.

Zusak, Markus. *The Book Thief*. New York: Knopf, 2006.

Zywica, Jolene, and Kimberley Gomez. "Annotating to Support Learning in the Content Areas: Teaching and Learning Science." *Journal of Adolescent & Adult Literacy* 52 (October 2008): 155–165.

NAME INDEX

Abbot, T., 191
Acosta, B. D., 382
Adams, B., 90
Adler, D., 327
Allen, C. A., 299
Alvermann, D. E., 7, 381
Andrasick, K. D., 285, 286, 287
Andrews, S. E., 315
Anson, A., 292, 308
Applegate, A., 148
Armon, J., 23
Armstrong, L., 414
Arthaud, T., 217
Ausubel, D., 134
Avi, 292, 333
Bach, J.S., 214
Bachman-Williams, P., 283
Bachrach, S. D., 339
Bacon, S., 171, 380
Bader, L. A., 81
Badke, W., 38
Baird, J., 292, 308
Balajthy, E., 31
Barbetta, P. M., 53
Barone, B., 324
Barrett, H. C., 91
Barron, R., 134
Barzillai, M., 29
Base, G., 316
Bausum, A., 317
Bean, R. M., 12
Beaty, M., 40
Bednar, M. R., 100
Berne, J., 111
Beyersdorfer, J. M., 298
Billings, H., 15
Billman, 356
Bishop, W., 38
Blachowicz, C., 111, 120
Black, R., 31, 224
Black, S. S., 89
Blackwood, G., 332
Bloem, P., 294

Bloom, B., 344, 345
Bosch, P., 236
Bott, C., 277
Boyne, J., 339
Bridges, B., 277, 278
Brinda, W., 315
Britton, J., 295
Broaddus, K., 256, 270
Brooks, B., 121, 320
Brozo, W. G., 100, 315
Bruce, B., 49
Bucher, K., 317
Buhler, A. J., 89
Burns, P. C., 55
Burron, A., 85
Campbell, K., 318
Carbone, P., 309
Carlos, W., 412
Carrell, J. L., 333
Carruthers, L., 400
Casey, H. K., 323
Chance, L., 100
Chandler-Olcott, K., 41
Chase, A., 115
Cheaney, J. B., 333
Cherland, M., 327
Christie, A., 314
Clarke, L. W., 148
Clausen-Grace, N., 345
Claybaugh, A. L., 85
Cleaver, S., 318
Coencas, J., 54
Coiro, J. 98
Cole, B., 191
Colson, J., 178
Comer, M., 278, 279, 280
Commander, N. E., 283
Considene, D., 44, 48
Cooney, C. B., 332
Cooper, S., 332
Copeland, M., 48, 49
Cormier, R., 115
Costello, A. M., 290

Costello, P., 86
Crane, I., 325
Creech, S., 314
Cruz, M. E., 290
Curie, M., 212
Custis, M., 284
Cutler, C. S., 89
Daisey, P., 315
Daniel, C., 252
Daniels, C., 49
Darvin, J., 196
Davis, V., 39
Dean, D., 291
DeBenedictis, D., 324
DelliCarpini, M., 171
Dodge, B., 39
Donovan, C. A., 314
Dooley, K., 70, 71, 297, 298
Dreher, M. J., 207
Duborsarsky, U., 372
Duffelmeyer, F., 115
Duggan, T. J., 283
Duncan, L., 15
Elbow, P., 286
Ellis, D., 322
Espinoza, C. M., 310
Ferris, J. A., 267
Fiedler, L., 332
Fisher, D., 219, 247, 267, 269, 308, 309
Fisher, P., 120
Flanigan, K., 118, 120
Fleischman, P., 283
Fleming, 356
Frank, A., 334, 337, 338, 339
Franklin, B., 156
Franks, L., 285
Frayer, D. A., 127, 357
Freedman, R., 269
Frey, N., 219, 267, 269, 308, 309
Friend, R., 215, 216
Friese, E. G., 283
Frost, R., 385
Fry, E., 99, 100

Furr, D., 307
Gallagher, J., 314
Gantos, J., 48
Garcia-Vazquez, E., 305
Gee, J. P., 145
George, J., 191
Giblin, J.C., 148
Gillespie, D., 414
Goering, G., 48, 49
Goethe, J. W., 48
Golding,W., 319
Gomez, K., 223
Goodman, B. 414
Goodman, K., 8
Goracke, T., 217
Gordon, C., 285
Gounod, C., 49
Graves, D. H., 12, 93
Graves, M. F., 382
Greenwood, S., 118, 120
Grierson, S., 291, 292
Griffith-Ross, D. A., 148
Grimes, N., 314
Grodosky, E., 66
Groenke, S., 44
Gulla, A. M., 171
Guthrie, J., 207
Hagood,M. C., 7
Hale, E. E., 199, 321
Hamilton, R. L., 12
Hansen, J., 333
Harmon, J., 271
Hartley, J., 324
Harvey, S., 267, 308
Hawthorne, N., 314
Heard, G., 283
Heller, R., 316
Henderson, F., 414
Hermes, P., 315
Hernandez, A., 171, 416
Hesse, K., 48, 314
Heyler, D., 289
Hicks, C., 413
Hiebert, E., 114
Hinton, S. E., 314
Hobbs, R., 386
Hoffman, J.V., 9, 221
Holman, F., 191
Hornof, M., 66
Horton, J., 44, 48
Huddleston, A., 7
Hushion, B., 286
Hutchison, A., 48
Irving, W., 325, 332
Ivey, G., 270
Jacobi, T., 277
Jacobs, G., 266

Jasitt, L., 22, 23,
Jasitt, M., 300, 301, 302, 303, 304
Johnson, M. S., 81
Johnson, N., 168
Johnson, R., 49
Johnston, P., 86
Jose-Kampfner, C., 315
Juster, N., 319
Kahn, L., 327
Kamil, M., 114
Kapinus, B., 120
Kearns, J., 324
Keat, N., 15
Kelley, M., 345
Kendall, M. E., 15
Kirby, D., 306
Kletzien, S., 100, 286
Knipper, K. J., 283
Knoester, M., 341
Koesling, D., 365
Konopak, B. C., 267
Kress, R. A., 81
Kuhlthau, C., 206
Kymes, A., 91
Lambert, M., 191
Landrum, J. E., 315
Langer, J. A., 71
Lanning, L., 218
Lapp, D., 219
Larson, L., 322
Lasky, K., 269
Lave, J., 147
Lawrence, S., 28
Lederer, R., 319
Lee, H., 314
Lehr, S., 327
Lemke, J. L., 356
L'Engle, M., 315, 319
Lenhart, A., 27
Lewis, J., 116, 345
Liner, T., 306
Liszt, F., 48
Littrell, A. B., 43
Lloyd, C.V., 158
Loebel, A., 191
Love, M. S., 27, 28
Lowry, L., 339
Lunsford, A., 377
Lynch, T. L., 316
Lynn, L., 37
Madden, M., 27
Madhuri, M., 46
Mahar, D., 41
Mandela, N., 299
Mandler, J., 168
Manning, M. L., 317
Manyak, P., 320

Manz, S. L., 233
Maring, G., 45
Martin, J. B., 316
Martinez, C., 315
Martinez, R. A., 309
Maruki, T., 316
Maury, M. T., 198
Mayer, J., 272
McCloud, C., 326
McDermott, J. C., 305
McGrath, B., 56
McMillan, S., 281
McNeal, K., 28
Meeks, L. L., 332
Melville, H., 314
Meltzer, M., 339
Miller, P., 365
Moje, E., 5, 11
Monroe, E. E., 89
Moorman, G., 44, 48
Morgan,W. C., 391
Morimoto, J., 316
Morrow, L. M., 89
Morton, J. R., 414
Moulton,M. R., 299, 375
Mountain, L., 137
Murphy, J., 269
Myers,W. D., 269, 320
Neufeld, P., 176, 344
Newbery, J., 315
Nicholson, M., 339
Nixon, J., 283, 314
Nolan, H., 48, 314
Nolan, P., 321
Noskin, D. P., 272
O'Connell, T., 53
Ogle, D., 345
Ohler, J., 29
Olson, M., 356
Ondaatje, M., 292
Orellana, M. F., 309
Orrill, C., 39
Ortega, T., 23
Otis, J., 211
Owens, 219
Pacheo, M., 309
Park, L. S., 169
Parker, C., 414
Paterson, K., 120, 121
Pauk,W., 219
Paulsen, G., 189, 191, 269, 320
Pearson, J.W., 216
Perkins, C. D., 385
Pikulski, J. J., 81
Popham,W. J., 63
Pressley, M., 175
Proctor, R. D., 251

Proulx, E. A., 319
Quatroche, D., 12
Quinn, K. B., 324
Ramsey, J., 334
Randall, S. N., 219
Rankin McGill, A., 27
Raphael, T., 128, 267, 297
Rasinski, T., 9
Recesso, A., 39
Reilley, M., 23, 24
Richards, K., 188, 189
Rivera, C., 383
Robinson, F. P., 232
Roe, B. D., 40, 55, 232, 233, 318
Roessing, L., 299
Romano, T., 299
Rosenblatt, L., 8, 322
Ruddell, R. B., 322
Ryan, M. E., 121
Ryan, P. M., 319
Santa, C., 216
Scharber, C., 45
Schauer, D. K., 298
Schmelzer, R.V., 315
Schmidt, G., 180, 332
Schmidt, R., 46
Schwartz, R. M., 128
Setoguchi, S., 305
Le Shan, E., 191
Shanklin, N., 282
Shelton, K., 294
Shulock, M., 251
Simpson, A., 324
Singer, J., 271
Sis, P., 316
Slade, A., 191
Smelcer, J., 191
Smith, A., 27

Smith, B. D., 283
Smith, M., 7, 347
Smith, S., 40, 55
Smith, S.L., 191
Smolkin, L. B., 314
Snow, C., 146
Snyder, G., 267
Soto, G., 169
Speare, E., 315, 319
Spears-Bunion, L. A., 53
Spiegelman, A., 315, 318
Spinelli, J., 315
Spittal, L., 317
Stackhouse, S. A., 324
Stahl, S. A., 120
Stansberry, 91
Stauffer, R., 192
Steinbeck, J., 314
Stoodt-Hill, B., 124, 202
Strassman, B., 53
Swieteck, D., 181
Tarasiuk, T., 282
Taylor, D., 46
Taylor, M. D., 14, 319
Thomas, S. M., 308
Thompson, D. L., 327
Thompson, G., 46
Tierney, R. J., 67
Todd, R., 206
Truxaw, M., 356
Turner, C. 317
Twain, M., 250, 332
Unrau, N. J., 322
Valmont,W. J., 33
Van Allsburg, C., 316
Van Horn, L., 271
Vaughn, B., 40
Vazquez, L. A., 305

Venn, J., 309
Voigt, C., 315
Volavkova, H., 339
Wade, S., 90
Walczyk, J.J., 148
Warren, J. R., 66
Washington, G., 316
Washington, T., 125
Weiss, H., 191
Wenger, E., 147
Whitney, E., 148
Wiesel, E., 315
Wiesendanger, K. D., 81
Wilhelm, J., 7, 281
Williams, J., 15, 191
Wilson, M., 87
Wilson, N. S., 344
Wilner, L., 383
Witte, S., 305
Wolf, M., 29
Wolk, S., 327
Wood, K. D., 281
Woodson, J., 314
Worthy, J., 256
Yang, G., 318
Yi, Y., 310
Yildiz, M. N., 28
Yoder, C., 316
Yolen, J., 292
Yopp, H., 112
Yopp, R., 112
Young, L., 282
Yung, S., 149
Zasuk, M., 180
Zenkov, K., 271
Zimmerman, M. E., 324
Zusak, M., 319, 339
Zwiers, 344
Zywica, J., 223

SUBJECT INDEX

academic vocabulary, 123
Accelerated Reader, 46
acronyms, 371
active readers, 148–151
  context for, 148
  question/answer relationships for, 150–151
  self-questioning for, 150, 178
Advancement of Computing Education
  (AACE), 57
administrator, role in reading instruction, 12–13
advance organizers, 234, 347–348, 369, 373,
  377, 417
aesthetic response, 157–158, 327
affixes, 117
agricultural education, 405
All Down the Valley (Billings), 15
allusion, 121
almanacs, 210
alphabetical order, 210–211
amelioration, 370
analogy activities, 132–133
analytic scales, 306–307
And Then There Were None (Christie), 314
Anguished English (Lederer), 319
Animalia (Base), 316
anticipation guides, 156–157, 321, 341
antonyms, 72, 112, 120, 122, 142
appendix, 209
application guides, 245, 270
application questions, 186
applications, creative, 288–289
arrays, 134, 216–217
art instruction, 408–409
assessment, 61–107
  analytic scales, 306–307
  attitude measures, 95
  classroom-based assessments, 68–90
  computer applications for, 96–98
  criterion-referenced tests, 67–68
  for English language learners, 104–105
  high-stakes testing, 66–67
  holistic grading, 306
  informal tests, 68–90

interest assessment, 95–96
literacy performance standards, 17–21
National Assessment of Educational
  Progress (NAEP), 18, 66
norm-referenced tests, 64–67
portfolio assessment, 90–93
of material readability, 98–105
rubrics, 87–88, 94, 97, 291, 306
self-assessment, 94–95
standardized testing (concerns about), 66–67
Standards for the English Language Arts,
  19–20
for struggling readers, 103–104
of writing, 306–307
See also classroom-based assessments;
  norm-referenced tests; standardized
  reading tests
association, in vocabulary development, 70–72
Association for the Advancement of
  Computing Education (AACE), 57
atlases, 210
at-risk students, 23, 25, 281. See also diverse
  students; English language learners;
  struggling readers
attitude measures, 95
attribute relations, 129
audience, writing for, 266–273, 275
audiobooks, 319
audiotapes, 47
authentic learning experiences, 356–357
authentic purposes, 154
authentic reading assignments, 188–191, 305
Authoring with Video (AWV), 53
authors
  evaluating qualifications of, 35–36, 183
  online conferences with, 45
Autobiography (Franklin), 156

background knowledge. See prior knowledge
Bad Boy (Myers), 320
bad names propaganda, 185
bandwagon propaganda, 185
bar graphs, 241, 244

bibliography, 209, 221–222
bilingual books, 202, 212, 224
Billy Budd (Melville), 314
biology-related comic strip, 251
biopoem, 284
blogs, 42–44, 280, 305
Blue Web'n, 415
boldface words, 200, 207, 269
Boolean searches, 215
brainstorming, 49–50, 70–71, 194–195, 328
Bridge to Terabithia (Paterson), 40–41
business education, 396–401
  applying text to experience, 400
  business concepts, 129–130
  content concept development for business
    management, 140
  reading strategy for, 401
  See also vocational literacy

Cable in the Classroom, 51
capacity reading level, 24, 32, 67, 103–104
card catalogs, 206, 214
card stacking propaganda, 185
career-related education, 385–386. See also
  vocational literacy
Career World, 393
Carl D. Perkins Career and Technical
  Education Act of 2006, 385
cartoons, 248–252
categorization activities, 161, 167, 213
cause-and-effect pattern, 10, 20, 47
  and content strategies, 345–346
  defined, 160–161
  and inferences, 181
  and language-experience writing, 281
  and main ideas, 166
  and note taking, 219
  as organizational pattern, 346–347
  and prewriting, 272
  in science content, 359–361
  in social studies content, 348–349, 350–351
  as a writing pattern, 357
CDs, 32, 45, 47, 50, 75

Chapters: My Growth as a Writer (Duncan), 15
character journals, 287
charts, 35
    cause and effect chart, 351
    computer software for, 35
    fact and opinion chart, 185
    flow charts, 246
    as graphic aid, 246–248
    for human environmental science, 403–404
    I-Charts, 221–222
    K-W-L charts, 50, 194
    for mathematics, 242, 367–368
    process charts, 246
    skill inventory for, 78
chat rooms, 44
checklists, for assessing readability, 102
Chocolate War, The (Cormier), 114
chronological order pattern, 93, 350–351
    defined, 160
    in content materials, 346, 350–351
    and selection and evaluation, 93
    and writing, 272, 274, 299
    in social studies content, 352
circle graphs, 241, 243
class relations, 126
classification activities, for vocabulary
    development, 76–77, 79, 94, 102
classification pattern, 357–358
classroom-based assessments, 68–90
    attitude measures, 95
    background knowledge assessment, 69–72
    cloze procedure, 83–85, 90
    gamelike activities, 85
    group reading inventories, 72–76
    group reading inventory sample, 73–76
    informal reading inventories, 80–83
    interest assessments, 95–96
    interviews and conferences, 87
    observation, 85–87
    performance samples, 87–90
    portfolio assessment, 90–93
    retellings, 88–89
    rubrics, 87–88
    self-assessment, 94–95
    written skill inventories, 69, 76–80
    See also assessment
cloze passage, sample, 83–84
cloze procedures, 90, 103–105, 141
cloze tests, 4, 69, 83–85, 102–103
cognitive components, of comprehension, 29,
    151–155
cognitive flexibility, 153
cognitive processing, stimulating, 177–178
cognitive strategies, 175–177. *See also*
    comprehension strategies
coherence, of text, 158–159
coined words, 372

collaboration
    software, 34
    for web-based activities, 38, 42–43
college, literacy demands of, 6
College Bowl, 85
college-prep students, 384
comics, 317–318
comparison/contrast pattern, 160
    as context clue, 120
    and critical readers, 182
    defined, 160
    guides for, 162–165
    organizational pattern, 160
    in science content, 162
    in social studies content, 351–352
    and text comprehension, 160
composition instruction, 269–270, 307–311
comprehension process, 172
    active readers and, 146–155
    cognitive flexibility and, 153
    content area instruction and, 8–11
    defined, 146
    linguistic and cognitive components of,
        151–155
    multiple literacies and, 146
    and the reader, 147
    reader-response theory, 157–158
    reading rate and, 253, 255
    schema theory and, 155–157
    situational context in, 154–155
    stages of, 8–9
    textual context in, 158–172
    in vocabulary development, 115
comprehension strategies, 175–202
    authentic reading tasks, 188–191
    before, during, and after reading, 176, 179,
        190, 197–202
    cognitive components of, 29, 151–155
    and cognitive processing, 177
    cognitive strategies for, 175–177
    creative thinking, 186
    creative understanding, 8–9
    critical comprehension, 8–9
    critical thinking, 152, 177, 183–183, 186
    directed reading lesson, 192–193
    directed reading-thinking activity, 192–193
    discussion, 194
    for English language learners, 202
    and good readers, 175–177
    graphic organizer for, 247
    inferential thinking, 8, 181–182
    K-W-L strategy, 194
    literal thinking, 180–181
    PRC strategy, 401
    problem-solving approach, 194–195
    questioning strategies, 177–179
    reciprocal teaching, 196

    scaffolding, 192
    stimulating cognitive processing, 177–178
    for struggling readers, 15, 200–202
    study guides, 197–202
    summary of, 175–177
    teacher's role in cultivating, 177
    visualization activities for, 197
    writing strategies for, 196
    See also study skills
computer-assisted instruction (CAI), 46–47
computer technology, 33–47
    CDs and DVDs, 32, 45, 47, 50, 75
    computer-assisted instruction (CAI), 46–47
    conference and collaboration software, 34
    databases and spreadsheets, 35, 213–214
    desktop-publishing programs, 33
    digital literacy, 33
    electronic communications, 39–45
    electronic reference works, 45–46, 213–215
    evaluating literacy applications of, 54–56
    Internet, 35–46
    multimedia applications, 47–49
    questions for critical media literacy, 49
    for vocabulary development, 141–142
    in vocational and performance-based
        education, 386, 390
    word-processing programs, 33, 232
    writing development software, 34
    See also Internet; multimedia technology;
        Technology
computer software and the internet, 141–142
concept(s), 113
concept guide, 349
concept load, and readability, 98
concept map, 34
conceptual knowledge, 113–114
conceptual relationships, 126–128
    defined, 126–128
    four mental operations in, 127
    reinforcement activities for, 127
    vocabulary development and, 128
conference and collaboration software, 34
conferences
    electronic, 42
    for assessment, 67, 69, 87, 91
    peer, 94
    portfolio, 93
    and structured interview, 94
    on technology, 57
    videoconferencing, 45
    in writing instruction, 270–271
connotation, 372
considerate text, 159
consolidation, 401
constructing meaning. *See* comprehension
    process; comprehension
    strategies

content area curriculum
  multimedia applications for, 44, 47–49
  and professional organizations, 18
  and reading instruction, 8–14
  strategies and assignments, 345–346
  and student motivation, 7
  and Wikis, 38
content area discourse, 344–345
content area reading, 343–382
  authentic reading tasks for, 346
  content strategies and assignments,
    345–346
  content text structures, 346–347
  diverse student instruction, 21–25
  encouraging recreational reading, 14
  for English (Language Arts), 370–377
  for English language learners, 381–382
  for foreign languages, 377–382
  genre and multigenre studies, 375
  grammar and composition, 375–377
  for mathematics, 363–370
  organizational patterns in, 346–347
  reading and critical literacy, 345
  reading instruction and, 8–17
  for science and health, 355–363
  for social studies, 348–355
  for struggling readers, 380–381
  teaching strategies for, 344–345
  value of using literature in, 373–375
  vocabulary development, 370–372
  See also comprehension process;
    comprehension strategies; reading
    instruction; specific content areas
content area teachers
  context for active reading and, 148–149
  librarian as resource for, 13, 233
  as part of team, 13, 15
  role in literacy instruction, 11–12
  teaching comprehension strategies,
    176–177
  teaching methods for, 344–345
content journals, 283–285
  character journals, 287
  dialogue journals, 293–294
  freewriting in, 285–286
  for literature instruction, 286
  paraphrasing and summarizing in, 292–293
  reading response journals, 286–287
  responses to thought questions, 288
content schemata, 155
content strategies and assignments, 345–346
content text structures, 346–347
context
  reader, 148
  situational, 153–155
  textual, 158–172
  word meanings and, 9, 111, 117–118, 210

context clues, 117–121, 200
  and affixes, 117
  cloze test for, 85
  defined, 118
  and figurative language, 120
  kinds of, 85, 120–121
  morphological analysis and, 117
  and semantics and syntax, 151
  strategies for using, 118–120
  for vocabulary development, 4, 83–84
contextual analysis, 9
contrast. See comparison/contrast pattern
controversial issues, and problem solving, 196
Cornell Note-Taking System, 219–220
corrective reading instruction, 16
creative thinking, 8–9, 152, 186
creative understanding, 8–9
criterion-referenced tests (CRTs), 67–68
critical readers, 182
critical thinking, 8–9, 182–186
  activities for, 185–186
  book questions, 183–184
  logic learning activities for, 184–185
  in mathematics, 186, 363
  media literacy and, 29
  with multiple sources, 183, 185
  for physical education content, 408
  picture books for, 316–317
  and reading, 182–183
  semantic learning activities for, 184
  in social studies, 348–349
cross-references, 79, 210
cultural diversity
  in classroom, 21–25
  in curriculum development, 330
  and language, 21–24
  photo essays for bridging, 304
  See also diverse students; English language
    learners
curriculum. See content area curriculum;
    integrated curriculum
Cyber Mentoring projects, 45
Cyber Patrol, 36

dance instruction, 373, 390
databases, computer, 23, 35, 207, 211, 213–214
definition (or explanation) pattern, 350
  defined, 161, 350
  in science content, 359
  in social studies content, 349–350
definitions
  as context clues, 118–121
  expanding word, 112–113, 121–122
demonstration pattern, 367
denotation, 372
description pattern, 219
desktop-publishing programs, 33

details, supporting, 16–17, 88–89, 149, 159,
    166–167
developmental reading, 14, 16
Devil's Arithmetic, The (Yolen), 291
diagnostic tests, 65
diagrams, 246–248
  and art students, 409
  and assessment, 77
  with definition patterns, 359
  and essay tests, 258
  as graphic aid, 246–248, 390
  and main idea activity, 167
  and science texts, 356, 359
  software for developing, 34
  story structure, 374
  Venn, 292, 309
  woodworking or science, 249
dialogue journals, 285, 287, 293–294, 309–311
Dicey's Song (Voigt), 315
dictionaries
  and assessment, 77, 79, 104–105
  and context and word knowledge, 117–118
  and direct systematic instruction, 114
  electronic, 33, 46
  learning to use, 211–212
  online resources for, 32
  use of respellings, 10
  for vocabulary development, 117–118, 131,
    136–138
  and word identification, 9–10
  for word pronunciation, 10
Diederich Scale, 306
digital literacy, 33
digital natives, 27
Dignifying Science, 318
directed reading lesson (DRL), 199, 330
  follow-up activities, 200
  guided reading, 200
  motivated and building background,
    199–200
  skill-development activities, 200
directed reading-thinking activity (DRTA),
    192–193, 322–323
direct instruction, 114–118
  context and word knowledge, 117–118
  and literature, 320
  morphemic analysis, 116–117
  selecting words for, 116
  for vocabulary development, 115–116
  in summary writing, 293
  and writing, 17
direct systematic instruction, 114–118
  context and word knowledge, 117–118
  defined, 114
  morphemic analysis, 116–117
  selecting words for, 116
  and vocabulary, 115–116

directions, following, 388–389
  activity on, 237
  in building trades, 389
  reading to, 235–236
  and struggling readers, 123–124
  for test taking, 258
  in vocational education, 388–389
disabled students. *See* students with disabilities
discourse, content area, 344–345
discussion
  and audio recordings, 51–52
  and blogs, 43
  for developing comprehension, 10
  electronic, 37–39, 42, 43, 322
  interactive, 69
  informal, 70
  for literature, 45
  PreReading Plan, 71–72, 400
  for self-assessment, 94
  and video recordings, 52, 90–91
divergent thinking, 179
diverse students
  at-risk students, 25
  and computers, 56
  cultural diversity, 21–25
  educationally challenged students, 24
  and photo essays, 304
  picture books, 340–341
  and writing topics, 271
  and reading instruction, 21–25
  See also cultural diversity; English language
    learners; struggling readers; students
    with disabilities
Dogpile, 36, 215
drafting stage, 34, 39, 91, 97, 228, 270–275
  writing a draft, 272–275
drama, 373–374. *See also* Readers' Theater
Dreamweaver, 38
drill-and-practice programs, 46
DRL. *See* directed reading lesson
DRTA. *See* directed reading-thinking activity
DVDs, 47
dynamic assessment, 104

EasyWriter (Lunsford, Connors), 377
editing, 276–277. *See* revision and editing
editorials, 375
ED-MEDIA:World Conference on
  Educational Media and Hypermedia, 57
Education for All Handicapped Children Act
  (EHA), 24
efferent response, 154, 157–158
elaboration, in vocabulary development, 121
electronic books (e-books), 32, 45–46
electronic bulletin borads, 42
electronic communications, 39–45
  blogs, 42–43
  chat rooms, 44–45

discussion groups, 39, 42, 43, 322
  e-mail, 40–41
  forums, 42
  mailing lists, 39, 41–42
  newsgroups, 39, 42
  online book clubs, 45
  podcasts, 44
  social networking sites, 44
  videoconferencing, 39, 45
  See also e-mail; Internet
electronic discussions, 322
electronic reference works, 45–46
electronic threaded discussion group, 42
elementary school reading programs, 16–17
Eleventh Hour, The (Base), 316
ELL. *See* English language learners
e-mail, 40–41
  discussion groups, 42, 43, 273
  mailing lists, 41–42
  mentoring programs, 45, 306
  pen pals, 305
Encarta, 63
encyclopedias, 211
  electronic, 23, 38, 46, 126, 211, 214–215
  learning to use, 210–211
  multimedia, 48
  and word meanings, 136
engagement, in learning process, 176, 234
English
  content area reading in, 370–377
  denotative and connotative meanings, 372
  changes in word meanings, 370–371
  essays and editorials in, 375
  genre and multigenre studies, 375
  grammar and composition instruction,
    375–377
  and literature, 373–374
  types of words, 371–372
  vocabulary development in, 370
  See also literature; vocabulary development
English language learners (ELLs), 21
  assessment for, 104–105
  challenges for, 21–25
  comprehension strategies for, 171–172
  content area reading instruction for,
    381–382
  and cultural diversity, 21–24
  language and cultural diversity, 21–24
  learning how to comprehend written
    English, 202
  literature-based and thematic approaches
    for, 340–341
  location and organization skills for, 224
  media use to help, 30–31
  and read-alouds, 23–24
  and science and social studies, 22
  study skills for, 261
  technology tools for, 30–31

  thematic approaches for, 340–341
  vocabulary development for, 122–123
  vocational content, 416
  writing instruction for, 309–310
  See also diverse students
English teachers, responsibilities of, 17
enumeration pattern, 161, 168
episodic story, 169
essays
  and editorials, 375
  photo essays, 304
  and reading retention, 257
  and rubrics, 87
  and social networking sites, 44
  teaching activities for, 70
  and test taking, 258–259
  and text structures, 169
  and thought questions, 288
  writing-to-display-learning genres, 265
essay tests, 258–259
essay writing, and retention, 257
etymology, 200, 370–371
euphemism, 371
evaluation. *See* assessment
evaluation questions, for website, 56
examples and nonexamples, in conceptual
  learning, 127
experimental pattern, 362–363
explanation pattern, 350
  defined, 161, 350
  in science content, 359
  in social studies content, 349–350
exposition, 375
expository text, 10
  comprehension activities for, 267
  and grammar and composition, 275
  on Internet, 35
  and outlining, 216
  selection organization of, 168
  study methods for, 232–233, 260
  See also textbooks
Expository Writing Program (EWP), 297
  expressive vocabularies, 114
*Eyes on the Prize: America's Civil Rights
  Years* (Williams), 15

fact and opinion chart, 185
Fallen Angels (Myers), 355
"fanfiction" communities, 31, 41
Faustian theme unit, 48
feature matrix, 268, 270, 272
feedback, in writing instruction, 269–271, 277
figurative language, 120–121, 282
films, 23–24, 48–49, 53–54
flexibility of rate, 252–255. *See also* reading
  rate flexibility
flow charts, 246
fluency, 9, 81, 87, 147–148, 170, 201, 255, 265

focus
    in reading process, 394
    in writing process, 275
footnotes, 209–210
foreign languages, 377–382
formative assessment, 63
formulas, mathematical, 369
forums, 42
Frayer Model, 127
freewriting, 266, 272, 285–286, 308, 326–327
frustration level, 76, 81, 84
Fry Readability Graph, 99–100
full inclusion, 24

gamelike activities, for assessment, 69, 85
games
    educational, 46
    See video games
generalization, of word meanings, 371
general vocabulary, 86, 115
generative processing, in vocabulary
        development, 120
generative sentences, 308
genre studies, 375
glad names propaganda, 185
glossary, 77
Golf, 407
Good Grammar, Good Style site, 277
Google, 36, 38, 42, 214
grammar checkers, 33
grammar instruction, 375–377
Grapes of Wrath, The (Steinbeck), 313
graphic aids, 236–252
    activity on following directions, 237
    charts and diagrams, 246–248
    and competency test, 20
    graphs, 241–246
    for human environmental science, 403–404
    maps, 238–241
    for mathematics, 242, 367–368
    pictures and cartoons, 248–252
    for science, 241, 244–247, 249
    in self-assessment, 94
    skill inventory for, 78–79
    for social studies, 135, 243
    tables, 246
    in vocational education, 6, 390
    for web, 136
graphical literacy, 250
graphic novels, 273, 315, 317–318
Graphic Organizer Notebooks, 247
graphic organizers
    for comprehension, 121–122
    and English language learners, 341
    incomplete and complete, 268
    notebook for, 247
    semantic map, 246–247
    for social studies, 135

for strategic reading, 247
for struggling readers, 124
for text organizational patterns, 161,
        163–164
and visual organizers, 134
for vocabulary development, 124, 130,
        134–135
web graphic organizer, 136
and writing development software, 34
graphs, 241–246
    computer software for, 35
    for mathematics content, 242, 367–368
    reading, 78
    skill inventory for, 78–79
    skills for reading, 244–246
    types of, 241–244
group reading inventory (GRI), 73–76, 103, 105
guided practice
    for comprehension, 196
    and fluency, 256
    for writing activities, 270, 292
guided reading, 170, 176, 199, 200, 307, 316
    directions for, 200
    for literature, 325
    for human ecology, 394–395
    and picture books, 316
    and struggling readers, 307
    and word problems, 365–366
guide words, 79, 210–211
Guts (Paulsen), 320

Hatchet (Paulsen), 189
headings, textbook, 156, 168, 207, 217
heteronyms, 372
high-stakes testing, 66–67
Hiroshima No Pika (Maruki), 316
history. *See* social studies
holistic grading, 306
Holocaust thematic unit, 334–339
homepages, 38
homonyms, 372
homophones, 372
Houghton Mifflin English (Haley-James), 199
House of the Seven Gables, The
        (Hawthorne), 314
human environmental science (human
        ecology), 401–405
    classification activity for, 134
    close-ended sort for, 134
    and creative thinking, 186
    directed reading lesson for, 394
    graphic aids for, 403–404
    literacy instruction in, 401–405
    problem-solving reading activity for, 196
    and publishing, 277
    reaction log for, 158
    study guide for, 403
    and technical terms, 388, 402

hyperbole, 121, 371
hypermedia, 35
hypertext, 35
hypertext markup language (HTML), 35, 38,
        49, 97–8

I-Charts, 221–222
If I Should Die Before I Wake (Nolan),
        314–315
I Hate Being Gifted (Hermes), 315
impression marking, 306
inclusion, 24
incomplete and competed organizer, 268
inconsiderate text, 159
independent reading level, 4, 46, 72, 76, 81,
        83–84, 104, 199
in-depth word study, 124, 130–132
index, 208–209
individualized education plan (IEP), 24
Individuals with Disabilities Education Act
        (IDEA), 24
inferential questions, 150, 181–182
inferential thinking, 8, 181–182
informal achievement tests, 68–90
    classroom-based assessments, 68–72
    cloze procedures, 83–85, 90, 103–105, 141
    gamelike activities, 85
    informal reading inventories, 80–82
    observation, 85–86
    performance samples, 87–90
    and struggling readers, 32
    See also classroom-based assessments
informal reading inventories (IRI), 80–83
information communication technology
        (ICT), 27
Inspiration, 34
instructional reading level, 72, 76–77, 81,
        84–85
integrated curriculum
    authentic learning in, 188–191
    content area reading and, 283–285
    oral history project, 290–291
    See also thematic units
integrated units, 188
IntelliTalk3, 31
interactive assessment, 103
interactive reading, 356–357
interest assessments, 95–96
International Reading Association (IRA),
        56–57, 122
International Society for Technology in
        Education (ISTE), 28, 57
International Telecomputing Consortium, 37
Internet, 35–46
    blogs, 42–44, 280, 305
    chat rooms, 44–45
    classroom projects using, 43–44
    computer-assisted instruction, 46–47

Internet *(continued)*
  computer software and, 141–142
  conferences, 42, 45
  e-mail, 40–41
  electronic books, 45–46
  electronic bulletin boards, 42
  electronic communications, 39
  electronic mailing lists, 41–42
  forums, 42
  homepages, 38
  multimedia applications, 47–49
  online book clubs, 45
  online think-alouds, 39
  newsgroups, 42
  and past technology, 50–53
  podcasts, 44
  reference works on, 45–46
  social networking sites, 44
  for text-to-speech software, 31–32, 53
  videoconferencing, 45
  web logs, (blogs), 42–44, 280, 305
  web pages, 35–39
  WebQuests, 39
  Wikis, 38
  for writing instruction, 277, 305
  See also electronic communications; e-mail
interpretive comprehension, 8. *See also*
    inferential thinking
intertexuality, 35
interviews, for assessment, 87, 94
introduction, text, 328–330, 332
inventories. *See* reading skill inventories

JASON Project, 48
Jeopardy!, 85
journals
  content, 383–384
  dialogue, 293–294
  freewriting in, 285–286
  literature response, 43, 286
  paraphrasing and summarizing in, 292–293
  reading response, 286–287
  responses to thought questions, 288
Jumanji (Van Allsburg), 316

key words
  alerting students to, 115
  and direct instruction, 115
  generating, 255
  and I-Charts, 221–222
  and mind mapping, 127
  and mnemonics, 140
  in notes, 221
  and the PReP, 71
  in outlines, 216–217
  for searching reference materials, 210–211
  for searching textbooks, 207
  and students with special needs, 53

  and vocabulary, 115
  and word walls, 140
kinesthetic learning, 228, 234
Knol, 38
Knowledge Network Explorer, 415
K-W-L (Know-Want to Know-Learned)
  charts, 50, 194
  strategy, 36, 50, 194, 345

labels, reading, 405
laboratory reports, 304
Land, The (Taylor), 14–15
language arts. *See* English
language experience writings, 281–282
learning disabilities, 21, 32, 53–54
learning logs, 94, 283–287, 321, 325. *See also*
    content journals
legislation related to secondary school
    literacy, 7–8
letters, business, 398
librarian, 13, 206, 212, 297
libraries, locating information in, 212–213
Library of Congress, 31, 36, 54, 178, 206
line graphs, 242, 245
linguistic diversity, 21–24. *See also* cultural
    diversity; English language learners
List-Group-Label lesson, 354
listing pattern, 161, 168
listservs, 39
literacy
  defined, 5
  digital, 33
  media, 29
  outside school activities requiring, 5
  secondary school demands for, 5–7,
  visual, 236
  vocational, 384–416
  workplace demands for, 6
literacy instruction
  classroom diversity and, 21–25
  components of secondary school prgram,
    14–15
  evaluating use of technology in, 54–56
  faulty assumptions about teaching, 15–16
  personnel responsible for, 11–14, 17
  See also reading instruction; writing
literacy performance standards, 17–21
literal-level questions, 178–179
literal thinking, 8, 180–181
literature, 373–377
  and active readers, 148
  and attribute relations, 129
  bilingual children's literature, 23
  blog responses to, 43
  cartoons, 249, 251
  and character journals, 287
  comic books, 317–318
  and content areas, 15

  and content journals, 286
  and creative thinking, 186
  culmination activities, 331
  and databases, 35
  development of the unit, 330–331
  and direct instruction, 320
  eight process involved in response to,
    373–374
  electronic discussions, 40, 42–44
  and English language learners, 340–341
  and e-mail, 40
  for English language learners, 202
  essays and editorials, 375
  graphic novels, 317–318
  graphic thinking symbols, 286
  guided reading, 325
  and the Holocaust, 336–339
  instruction, 320–326
  introduction of the unit, 328–330
  and the Internet, 40–46, 214
  literature response groups, 305, 320, 323,
    332, 335
  and making subject matter real, 14
  mini-lessons for, 320–321
  movie, 51
  novels and short stories, 373–374
  oral responses to, 327
  organization of findings, 331
  paired readings, 314
  picture books, 316–217
  poetry, 282–283
  and publishing, 278–279
  readability of, 98–99
  Readers' Theater, 256, 324, 326–327
  reading aloud, 156, 318–319
  reading guides for, 321
  reading instruction, 16–17
  reading response journals for, 286–287
  relevance of, 148
  response journals, 43
  sample unit ideas, 331
  and schemata, 156
  and semantic mapping, 327
  and standards, 19
  for struggling readers, 340
  student response activities, 326–327
  study guides, 321, 373
  sustained silent reading, 323–324
  teaching, 16–17
  thematic teaching units, 327–333
  translating into comic book form, 290
  value and uses of, 313–314
  video and audio versions of, 51–52
  vocabulary development for, 115
  whole-class novel study, 322–323
  and writing, 269
  writing-to-learn activities, 269, 277–278,
    286-287, 290

written responses to, 91
young adult, 314–316
See also English; narrative writing
literature response groups (literature circles), 323
literature response journals, 43
"loaded" words, 184
location skills, 206–215
    for Internet, 214–215
    motivational activities for, 212
    for research reports, 294–297
    and scanning, 207
    for textbooks, 207–210
    using computer databases, 213–214
    using libraries, 212–213
    using reference books, 210–212
logic skills, 183
Lord of the Flies (Golding), 319

Macbeth, 70–71
magazines, 190–191
mailing lists, 39, 41–42, 322
main ideas, 166–167
    cause and effect pattern, 166
    and details, 159
    identifying, 16–17, 20, 67, 149
    and organizing, 166–167
    and point of view, 154
    and self-assessment, 94
    and struggling readers, 124
Making History: The Calm and the Storm, 47
managerial job skills, 386
Maniac Magee (Spinelli), 315
"Man Without a Country, The" (Hale), 199
map-reading skills, 238, 240–241
"matching" cloze, 103–104
mathematics, 363–370
    and analogy, 132
    and assessments, 89
    and business concepts, 129, 396
    content area reading in, 364–365
    and creative thinking, 186
    critical thinking in, 363
    and databases, 35
    demonstration pattern for, 367
    and diagrams, 246–247
    and English language learners, 202
    graphing equations, 368
    graphs and charts for, 241–242, 367–368
    literacy in, 363–364
    and maps, 240
    and prereading, 152–153
    problem-solution method, 366
    question/answer relationships for, 151
    and readability, 99
    reading, 364–365
    reading guide, 369–370
    sample index, 208–209

simulation programs, 47
SQRQCQ, 229
strategies for verbal problems, 365–366
study methods for, 234–235
symbols, signs, and formulas in, 140, 369
teaching strategies for, 369–370
three-level study guide, 364–365
verbal problems, 365–366
and videoconferencing, 45
and visualization, 197
vocabulary development for, 115, 126, 132, 135, 369
word web, 137
writing patterns, 365
Math Shop Series, 47
Maus: A Survivor's Tale (Spiegelman), 315
meaning, constructing. *See* comprehension process; comprehension strategies
media center. *See* librarian; libraries, locating information in media literacy
    content area learning and, 345
    defined, 29
    digital literacy, 33
    guiding questions for, 49
    research on, 386
memorization, rote, 229
mentoring programs
    and struggling readers, 380
    using e-mail, 45, 306
    videoconferencing, 45
mentoring projects, 306
metacognition, 152
metacognitive skills
    and active readers, 148
    in comprehension process, 148, 229
    and content journals, 383–384
    definition of, 152
    and good readers, 9
    and K-W-L, 194
    for locating information, 207
    portfolios and, 90–92, 97
    self-assessment and, 95, 152, 207, 229
    study strategies and, 232–233
    and think-aloud, 90
metaphor, 121
metasearch engines, 36
Microsoft FrontPage, 38
Microsoft Internet Explorer, 36
Microsoft PowerPoint, 30, 50
Microsoft Word, 33–34
Midnight Hour Encores (Brooks), 121
mind mapping, 127–128
mini-lessons, 11, 269–270, 320–321
MMORPGs, 34
mnemonic devices, 140–141
modeling activities
    critical thinking, 184
    and English language learners, 202

listening practices, 260
and meaning, 229
and netiquette, 42
reciprocal teaching, 191
and research, 211
for strategic reading, 175–176
for study strategies, 232
and summarizing, 218
and text annotation, 223
think-aloud strategy, 39
and topic delimitation, 271
for writing activities, 183, 218, 269–271
More Anguished English (Lederer), 319
morphemic analysis, 9, 116–117
morphological analysis, 116–117
motivational strategies
    for locating information, 212
    in vocational education, 393
movies, 52, 54, 75, 395
Mozilla Firefox, 36
multicultural education
    computer-assisted instruction, 46
    and literature, 315, 330
    schemata, 156
    and social studies content, 348
    See also cultural diversity
multigenre books, 291–292
multigenre writing, 375
    for reports, 299–301, 304
    and struggling readers, 308
muligenre studies, 375
multimedia applications, 47–49
multimedia literacy, 29
multimedia technology, 29–49
    applications for, 47–49
    classroom advantages of, 56
    computers, 33–47
    in content area curriculum, 44, 47–49
    evaluating literacy applications of, 54–56
    and past technology, 50–53
    for special needs and disabled students, 53–54
    and tomorrow, 57
    See also computer technology
multiple literacies, 29–30
multiple perspectives, 153, 382
music instruction, 410–411
My Hiroshima (Morimoto), 316
mystery genre, 314

Name of the Game Was Murder, The (Nixon), 314
narrative writing, 10, 53, 344. *See also* literature
NASA's Online Interactive Projects, 38
National Assessment of Educational Progress (NAEP), 18, 66
National Association of State Directors of Career

Technical Education Consortium, 385
National Commission on Reading, 318
National Council of Teachers of English
    (NCTE), 19, 57
National Council of Teachers of
    Mathematics, 363
National Educational Technology Standards
    for Students (NETS), 28
National Geographic site, 36, 48
netiquette, 42
Newbery Award books, 315
newsgroups, 39, 42
newspapers, 189–191, 252–253
news stories, 187, 189, 288, 326–327
Night (Wiesel), 315
No Child Left Behind legislation, 7, 104
norm-referenced tests, 64–67
    concerns about, 66–67
    criteria for choosing, 65
    diagnostic reading tests, 65
    diagnostic tests, 65
    of reading achievement, 65–66
    survey tests, 65
    and validity and reliability, 65
    See also assessment
note-taking skills, 219–221
    guidelines for, 221
    for research papers, 220, 294
    retention and, 219
    and television programs, 51
    and videoconferencing, 45
Nothing But the Truth (Avi), 292
novels, 373–374. *See also* literature

objective tests, 70, 259–260
observation, 359
office procedures, open-sort for, 134
online book clubs, 45
online think-alouds, 39
open and closed word sorts, 121, 134
Operation Frog, 47
opinions, words signaling, 184
Oral History Project, 290–291
oral reading/reports
    and fluency, 9
    and guided reading, 200
    observing, 86
    and portfolios, 91
    Readers' Theater, 324
    and schemata, 156
    and TTS software, 31
oral responses, to literature, 327
oral retellings, 88–89
Oregon Trail, 355
organizational patterns, 160–172
    cause-and-effect, 160
    comparison/contrast, 160
    comparison/contrast guide, 162

in content area texts, 346–347
definition or explanation, 161
and English language learners, 171–172
enumeration or listing, 161
and essays and editorials, 375
and expository writing, 168, 296
graphic organizers for text organizers, 164
instructional activities for, 161–72
and literal thinking, 180
main ideas and details activities,
    166–167
and revising, 275
in science content, 363
selection organization of expository
    text, 168
selection organization of narrative texts,
    168–169
sequential or chronological order, 160
story grammar, 169
structured overview, 166
and struggling learners, 169–171
and study skills, 229
and writing, 267, 272
See also specific patterns
organizational skills, 215–224
    annotating text, 221–223
    arrays, 216
    for English language learners,
        219, 224
    note taking, 219–224
    outlining, 216–217
    for research papers, 295
    and story array, 216
    for struggling readers, 223, 260
    and study skills, 260
    as study strategy, 215–216
    summarizing, 218–219
organizer, class, 268
outlining, 216–217
    computer software for, 34, 217
    for writing activities, 215–216
OutLoud, 31
Out of the Dust (Hesse), 314
Outsiders, The (Hinton), 314
overhead projectors, 50
overlearning, 257
OWLs (online writing labs), 277
oxymoron, 371

paraphrasing, 170, 203, 218, 292–293,
    335, 377
Passage to Vietnam, 355
peer conferences, 94, 271, 274, 276
peer tutoring
    for English language learners, 171, 416,
        309–310, 416
    and formative assessment, 69
    and reading, 380

for struggling readers, 380
for writing activities, 295–297, 306
pejoration, 371
pen pals, 305
performance-based education
    art, 408–409
    music, 409–415
    physical education, 405–408
    problem solving in, 392
    technology in, 390
performance samples, 87–90
    cloze procedure, 90
    retellings, 88–89
    rubrics, 87–88
    think-alouds, 89–90
    videotape analysis, 90
personality profile, 298
personification, 120
Phantom Tollbooth, The (Juster), 319
phonic analysis, 10
photo essays, 304
physical education, 14, 195, 405, 407–408
    problem-solving paradigm, 195
    sports medicine material, 408
    sports term inventories, 407
    and vocabulary, 126
picture books, 316–317
picture graphs, 241–242
"picture walks," 316
pictures, 248–252
pie graphs, 241
Pioneer Women: The Lives of Women on the
    Frontier (Peavy, Smith), 355
plagiarism, 215
plain folks propaganda, 185
podcasts, 44
poetry, 282–283
point of view
    critical thinking and, 187
    précis writing, 293
    and problem solving, 195
    in writing process, 275
point-of-view guide, 154
Poor Richard's Almanac (Franklin), 156
portfolio assessment, 90–93
    contents of, 91–92
    purpose of, 92
    selection and evaluation for, 93
*Portrait of a Tragedy: America and the Vietnam
    War* (Warren), 355
"Possible Sentences" activity, 116, 120,
    123–124, 354
Postcards (Proulx), 319
post reading activities, 72, 90, 257, 286, 338,
    345–346, 349, 381, 394, 409
practice, massed vs. spaced, 257
PRC reading strategy, 401
précis writing, 293

prediction
    in DRTA, 192–193
    and reading comprehension, 155, 169, 172, 176
    and ReQuest, 381
    as study strategy, 234
preface, 208
prefixes, 72, 115
preliminary questioning, 70
PreReading Plan (PReP), 71–72
prereading strategies, 176, 346
    and anticipation, 341
    association activities, 130, 134
    for business education materials, 401
    questions, 152–153, 268
    and illustrations, 316
    writing activities, 286
    and struggling readers, 170–171
    visual organizers, 134
    See PreReading Plan (PReP); scaffolding
preview guides, 156–157
    for activating schemata, 156
    as anticipation guides, 156–157, 321
    for art education, 409–410
    and literature education, 373
    for music education, 413
    and reading education, 321, 341
    social science education, 157
    and social studies education, 348
    and struggling readers, 103
    as teaching strategy, 161, 400, 402
    and vocabulary, 5
prewriting, 270–272
principal, role in reading instruction, 12–13, 14
prior knowledge
    and anticipation, 341
    assessment of, 69–72
    comprehension process and, 176–178, 203
    in DRTA, 193
    and English language learners, 416
    and K-W-L, 194
    and literal thinking, 180–181
    and locating information, 207
    and metacognition, 152
    and organizing information, 215–216
    and picture books, 316
    preview guides for, 50
    and prewriting, 270
    and professional judgment, 81
    readability and, 102
    and reading comprehension, 146
    reading response journals, 286
    and reference books, 136–137
    and scaffolds, 176
    and schemata, 155
    and struggling students, 103, 380, 415
    and study methods, 229

textual context and, 158
    for vocabulary development, 115, 135–136
    writing to activate, 268, 272, 282
problem-solution pattern, 181, 219, 346, 357, 362, 366
    and math problems, 366
    and writing, 357, 392
problem-solving approach, 194–197, 392–393
process charts, 246
Project LITT: Literacy Instruction through Technology, 32
pronunciation
    and dictionaries, 10, 211
    and discussion, 126
    and English language learners, 123
    and heteronyms, 372
    and language experience writing, 281
    online resources, 210
    and oral reports, 86
    and poetry, 319
    and self-assessment, 94
    and vocabulary, 130
    and word knowledge, 113
propaganda techniques, 185
PSRT strategy, 230–232
publishing stage, 277–280
purposes, in reading
    comprehension and, 8
    and critical readers, 182–183
    and higher-level thinking, 5
    and online reading, 29
    and reading rate, 10–11
    metacognitive skills and, 152
    retention and, 256
    and study guides, 197

quality thinking, questions for, 187
question-and-answer pattern, 353
question/answer relationships (QARs), 148, 150–151, 344
questions
    and chat rooms, 44
    for critical media literacy, 49
    critical reading, 183–184
    for developing comprehension, 177–179
    and email, 40
    for evaluating computer software, 55–56
    flexibility exercise, 255
    and group reading inventories, 72–76
    guide for generating, 150
    inferential, 150, 181–182
    and informal reading inventories, 80–82
    and literacy demands, 5
    literal-level, 178–179
    and online book clubs, 45
    preliminary, 70
    for quality thinking, 187
    question/answer relationships, 150–151

question-and-answer writing pattern, 353–355
reciprocal, 381
and retention, 257
as study strategy, 257
student, 187
test taking, 258–259
thought question, 288
wait time after, 178–179, 187
See also self-questioning strategies

RAFT assignments, 294
reaction guides, 156
reaction log, 158
readability assessment, 98–105
    autions and controversies with, 101
    checklist approach to, 102
    and ELL, 104–105
    formulas, 99–100
    methods, 101–102
    reading levels and, 98–99, 103, 106
    and struggling readers, 103–104
    user involvement techniques for, 102–103
read-alouds
    for literature, 156, 318–319
    for struggling readers and English language learners, 307
reader context, 148
reader-response theory, 157–158
Readers' Theater, 9, 91, 256, 324, 326–327, 336
reading, defined, 8–9
reading beyond the lines, 8
reading coaches, 379
reading comprehension, 10–11, 146. See also comprehension process; comprehension strategies
reading consultant, 12–13
reading fluency, 9, 147, 171
reading guides, 156, 321
    for literature, 341
    use of, 321
    See also preview guides; study guides
reading instruction
    administrator's role in, 12–13
    classroom diversity and, 21–25
    comprehension skills, 10–11
    in content area curriculum, 8–17
    content area reading, 14
    content area teacher's role in, 11–12
    defining reading, 8–9
    developmental reading, 14, 16
    group reading inventories, 72–76
    literacy performance standards and, 17–25
    misconceptions about, 15–16
    oral reading fluency, 9
    personnel responsible for, 11–14, 17
    principal's role in, 12–13
    reading consultant's role in, 12

reading instruction *(continued)*
  reading, defined, 8–9
  reading orally, 9
  reading specialist's role in, 12
  recreational reading, 14
  and schema theory, 152
  special reading teacher, 12
  for struggling readers, 15–16, 18
  study skills, 11
  vs. subject matter instruction, 16
  teaching literature and, 16–17
  teamwork approach to, 13–14
  word identification skills, 9–10
  See also content area reading; literacy
    instruction
reading interests inventory, 96
reading logs, 91
reading rate flexibility, 252–255
  factors affecting, 253
  flexibility exercises for, 255
  skimming and scanning techniques,
    254–255
  techniques for increasing, 253
  timed readings for, 253–254
  in vocational education, 390
reading response journals, 286–287, 323, 326
reading skill inventories
  group reading, 73–76, 103, 105
  informal reading, 80–83
  reading interest, 95–96
  written skill, 69, 76–80
reading specialists, 4, 12, 14, 16, 65, 81, 380
reading-study skills. *See* study skills
reading-to-do, 394
reading to follow directions, 94, 235–236
reading-to-learn, 394
reading survey, 65
reading transaction, 148–149
reading workshop approach, 320
receptive vocabularies, 114
reciprocal teaching, 196
recitation techniques, 230–232
recreational reading, 14
reference books, 210–212
reference works, 45–46
  electronic, 45–46, 213–215
  and libraries, 13
  locating information in, 207–209
  and prior knowledge, 136–137
  special reference books, 210–212
  skill inventory for, 79
  for vocabulary development, 136–138
Regular Education Initiative (REI), 24
rehearsal, 177
reliability, assessment, 65
remedial reading instruction, 16. *See also*
    struggling readers
repeated readings, 9, 202

ReQuest (Reciprocal Questioning), 381
research groups, in thematic units, 330–331
research reports, 293–297
  Expository Writing Program for, 297–298
  first draft, 295
  multigenre approach to, 299
  multigenre report, 300–304
  note taking for, 219–220
  organizing information for, 295
  personality profile, 298
  student guidelines for, 295–296
  teacher guidelines for, 296
retelling technique, 88–89
retention, 256–258
review, as study strategy, 233
revision and editing
  computer software for, 33–34
  Internet assistance for, 277
  of research paper, 295
  in writing process, 275–277
Romeo and Juliet, 290
ROWAC study method, 232–235
rubrics, 87–88, 94, 97, 291, 306

scaffolding, 176, 192
  and assessment, 69, 76, 83, 104
  comprehension, 192, 200–202
  and constructing meaning, 170
  definition of, 76, 176
  examples of, 192
  as explicit strategy instruction, 176
  and literature, 315, 340
  and think-alouds, 192
scanning techniques, 254–255
scavenger hunts, 212
schema theory, 152, 155–157
  building and activating activities, 156
  conceptual knowledge and, 113
  and cognitive flexibility, 153
  types and relationships in, 155–156
  See also comprehension process
School-to-Work Opportunities Act (1994), 415
science and health
  analogy exercise, 132
  association activity for, 131
  cartoon, 252
  charts, 246
  classification activity, 133
  comic strip, 251
  close-ended sort, 134
  and cognitive flexibility, 153
  comic strip, 251
  comparison/contrast, 162–163
  computer databases, 213–214
  content area reading in, 14
  content journals, 283
  creative approaches to teaching, 285,
    288–289

and creative thinkers, 186
  diagrams, 249
  and discussion, 127
  DRTA for, 193
  and English language learners, 22, 202
  explanation pattern, 359
  graphs, 241, 244–245
  graphic aides, 241, 244–247, 249
  integrating with other disciplines,
    188–191, 290
  I-Chart, 222
  incomplete and completed organizer,
    268–269
  and the Internet, 37–39, 51, 146
  and the JASON project, 48
  laboratory reports for, 304
  language experience approach for, 281
  mind map for, 128
  and morphological analysis, 117
  and motivational activities, 212
  and multigenre report, 300–304
  multiple perspectives, 153
  organizational patterns, 160
  picture books, 316–318
  preview guide, 157
  problem-solving reading activity for,
    195–196
  and process writing, 270
  PSRT Lesson, 230
  publishing, 277
  reaction log, 158
  and read-alouds, 319
  and reading rate 252–255
  research papers, 298
  sample cloze passage for, 83–84
  self-questioning example, 150
  and simulation programs, 47
  situational context, 154
  and spreadsheets, 35
  structured overview, 166
  study guides for, 197–198
  and study skills, 347
  and taking another approach, 271–272
  textbook illustration, 250
  and video recordings, 52
  and vocabulary, 5, 79, 115, 117, 121, 125,
    127–128, 138
  and writing, 17
  and written skill inventories, 76–77
search strategies
  for databases, 35
  for Internet, 35–38
  and media center specialists, 13
  and struggling readers, 32
  See also location skills
secondary school
  literacy demands of, 5–7, 298–299
  legislation related to, and literacy, 7–8

self-assessment, 94–95
self-questioning strategies, 9
   for active reading, 146
   for comprehension, 152
   and content learning, 179, 344
   defined, 150
   and divergent thinking, 179
   question/answer relationships, 150–151
   strategies, 94–95
   and teacher modeling, 229
   for struggling readers, 381
self-rating checklist, 94
semantic context clues, 151
semantic feature analysis, 5, 10, 129
semantic learning activities, 184
semantic mapping, 127
   and brainstorming, 189
   computer software for, 34
   and graphic organizer notebooks, 247
   and literature, 327
   and note taking, 219
   and organizing stories, 168
   and photo essays, 304
   and struggling readers, 103
   See mind mapping
semantics, 151
semantics abilities, 183
semantic webs, 5, 10, 219, 234, 328
sentence outline, 217
sentence structure, 275
   and oral reports, 86
   readability and, 102
   revising, 275
   and secondary school, 17
   writing assessment, 291
sequential pattern, 160
setting, story, 168–169
short stories, 373–374. See also literature
sight-word recognition, 9
Sign of the Beaver (Speare), 315
SimCity, 47
simile, 120
simulation programs, 46–47, 97, 355, 362
situational context, 153–155
skill inventories, 76–80. See also reading skill
   inventories
skimming, 254–255
Smithsonian site, 31
Snowflake Bentley (Martin), 316
social constructivist perspective, 322
social networking sites, 44
social studies
   cause and effect chart, 351
   cause-and-effect pattern, 350–351
   chronological order, 350–352
   comparison/contrast guide for, 351–352
   comparison chart for, 353
   concept guide, 350

content area reading in, 348–355
critical thinking in, 348–349
definition or explanation pattern, 350
direct instruction, 116
exercises for, 353–355
graphic aids for, 135, 243
informal reading inventory selection, 82
K-W-L activity for, 194
question-and-answer writing pattern,
   353–355
reading graphs, 78
study guides for, 349
understanding writing patterns, 349–350
and video recordings, 52–54
visualization strategy for, 197
vocabulary, 47, 79–80, 101, 112, 115
writing patterns, 349
socioeconomic status, and reading
   achievement, 25
Somewhere Today: A Book of Peace
   (Thomas), 306
sorts, for vocabulary development, 10, 122, 133
sources
   consulting, in critical thinking, 183
   primary and secondary, 51, 215, 299
specialization, of word meaning, 371
specialized vocabulary, 371
special needs students. See diverse students
special reading classes, 11
special reading teacher. See reading specialists
spelling checkers, 28, 276–277
sports medicine material, 408
sports term inventories, 407
spreadsheets, 35
SQ3R study method, 232–233, 254,
   260–261, 388
SQRQCQ study method, 232, 234–235
stance, reader, 154
standardized tests, 64–67
   concerns about, 66–67
   for English language learners, 380–381
   negative impact of, 260
standards for literacy performance, 17–25
   National Assessment of Educational
      Progress (NAEP), 9, 18, 66
   Standards for the English Language Arts,
      19–20
   state-level standards, 20
   technology standards and, 28
   See also assessment
Standards for the English Language Arts,
   19–20
Starry Messenger (Sis), 316
storyboards, 303, 323
story grammars, 10, 168–169
strategic reading, 175–176
strategies, 9
structural analysis, 9–10, 92

structured interview or conference, for
   self-assessment, 94
structured overviews, 134
   in directed reading lessons, 163
   for text organizational patterns, 163, 166
   for vocabulary development, 134–135
struggling readers
   assessment for, 103
   and audio book recordings, 52
   comprehension scaffolding, 200–202
   comprehension strategies for, 169–171
   content area reading instruction for,
      380–381
   language experience approach for, 281–282
   and key words, 140
   literature instruction for, 340
   location and organization skills for, 223
   and meaning, 136
   media use to help, 32
   percentages of, in secondary school, 18
   and prefixes, 117
   reading instruction for, 15–16
   and recorded voice, 46, 52
   and retellings, 88
   and scaffolding, 200–202
   study skills for, 259
   technology tools for, 46, 52
   vocabulary development for, 16, 17, 123
   and vocational content, 415
   and word cards, 116
   writing instruction for, 307–309
   and young adult literature, 315
   See also English language learners
student questioning, 187. See also
   self-questioning strategies
students with disabilities, 24
   and audio recordings, 51–52
   technology tools for, 53–54
   See also diverse students
study guides, 197–202
   for art education, 411
   and cause and effect, 359
   and color, 403
   for health, 356
   for human environmental science,
      402–403
   for literature, 373
   for mathematics, 346
   and purpose, 197
   reading, 321
   for science, 198, 356
   for social studies, 349
   technical education, 396
   three-level, 321, 364, 373
   See also preview guides
study methods, 232–235
study questions, and retention, 256–258
study reading speed, 253–255

study skills, 226–260
    and charts and diagrams, 246–248
    for English language learners, 261
    flexibility of reading rate, 252–255
    and fluency, 256
    and following directions, 237
    graph-reading skills, 241–246
    graphic aids, 236–252
    importance of study methods, 228–229
    interpreting graphic aids, 244–246
    map-reading skills, 238–241
    for mathematics, 234–235
    metacognitive skills and, 229
    pictures and cartons, 248–249
    preparation for study, 228–229
    PSRT strategy, 230–232
    reading to follow directions, 235–236
    reading rate and purpose, 252–255
    and retention, 229, 233, 246, 256–258
    and review, 233
    ROWAC study method, 233–234
    specific study methods, 232–235
    SQ3R study method, 232–233
    SQRQCQ study method, 232, 234–235
    for struggling readers, 260
    table-reading skills, 246
    teaching procedures, 230–232
    and test taking, 258–260
    understanding charts and diagrams,
      246–248
    See also comprehension strategies
suffixes, 116–117
summaries
    modeling, 218
    and paraphrasing, 292–293
    and précis writing, 219
    and skimming, 254
summarizing, 218–219
summary, 66
summary paragraphs, in expository text,
    218–219, 232–233, 292
summative assessment, 63
superordinate terms, 134–135, 218
Super Word Web (SWW), 121–122, 134
surveys
    class, 98, 187
    and map reading, 238
    and prereading, 401
    reading survey tests, 65
    and SQ3R, 233
    and SQRQCQ, 234
    and verbal problems, 365
Survey Monkey, 98
survey tests, 65
sustained silent reading (SSR), 323–324
syllogisms, 184
symbols, 369
    and cartoons, 249

    and diagrams, 246
    and literature, 374
    graphic thinking, 286
    mathematical, 140, 364–365, 369
    musical, 410, 413
synonyms, 122, 137, 139–140, 142, 219, 293
syntactic context clues, 151
syntax, 151

table of contents, 208
tables, 246
teachers. *See* content area teachers
teaching procedures, 230–232
teamwork, in reading instruction, 13–14
technical education, 396
technical vocabulary, 115, 281–282, 375, 386,
    393, 396.
technology, 33–47
    advantages of using, 56
    audiotapes, 47–48
    CDs and DVDs, 32, 45, 47, 50, 75
    computer technology, 33–47
    for English language learners, 30–32
    evaluating literacy applications of, 54–56
    future applications for, 57
    integrating into curriculum, 54–57
    media literacy, 29
    multimedia applications, 47–49
    multiple literacies and, 98, 298–299
    overhead projectors, 50
    standards for students, 28
    for students with special needs or
      disabilities, 53–56
    for struggling readers, 32, 46
    television, 50–52
    video recordings, 52–53
    See also computer technology; Internet
tech-prep students, 384. *See also* vocational
    literacy
television, for literacy instruction, 50–51
Tennessee Technological University, 22
testimonial propaganda, 185
testing. *See* assessment; standards for literacy
    performance
test taking, 258–260
Text and Classroom Context model, 322
textbooks, 207–210
    appendix, 209
    bibliography, 209
    footnotes, 209
    glossary, 209
    index, 208
    locating information in, 207–210
    preface, 206
    readability of, 99–100
    table of contents, 208
    See also expository text; textual context
text coherence, 158–159

text organization, 158–159
text-to-speech (TTS) software, 31–32, 53
textual context, 158–172
    considerate vs. inconsiderate text, 159
    main ideas and details, 166–167
    organizational patterns, 160
    organization and coherence, 161
    selection organization, 168
    story grammars, 10, 168–169
textual schemata, 155
thematic units, 327–341
    for authentic learning, 188–189
    culmination activities, 331
    defined, 327–328
    development activities, 330–331
    for English language learners, 340–341
    and fluency, 256
    introduction activities, 328–329
    for literature, 327–333
    news stories as basis for, 189
    organization of findings in, 331
    and picture books, 316
    sample ideas for, 331–333
    steps in unit development, 328
    for struggling readers, 340
    and WebQuests, 39
    See also integrated curriculum
themes, 188
thesaurus, 33, 46, 79, 114
THIEVES memory device, 233
think-aloud strategy, 15, 89–90
    for assessment, 89–90
    and foreign language, 379
    online, 39
    for struggling readers, 15, 104, 347
    teacher modeling of, 39, 318–319, 344
thinking
    creative, 8–9, 152, 186
    critical, 8–9, 182–186
    divergent, 179
    inferential (interpretive), 8, 181–182
    literal, 8, 181–182
    See also comprehension process; compre-
      hension strategies; metacognitive skills
"think-pair-share," 187
think sheets, 297
thought questions, 288
three-level study guides, 199, 321, 364, 373
    for literature, 321, 373
    for math, 364
timed readings, 253–254
timelines, for writing activities, 272, 292
time order pattern. *See* chronological order
    pattern
To Kill a Mockingbird (Lee), 314
Tom Sawyer (Twain), 250
topic outline, 217
topic selection, 271, 295

topic sentence, 218
total-class response activities, 232
trade books, 126, 143–144
transfer propaganda, 185
transparencies, 50
tree diagrams, 246
Trouble with Perfect, The (Ryan), 121

Uniform Resource Locators (URLS), 36
use of the dictionary's respellings, 10

validity, assessment, 65
Venn diagram, 292, 309
verbal problems, mathematical, 365–366
videoconferencing, 39, 45
video games, 27, 30, 34, 41, 47, 85
videotapes
    for assessment, 70–71, 356
    for enhancing learning, 52–53
*Vietnam: Why We Fought—An Illustrated
    History* (Hoobler, Hoobler), 355
virtual classrooms, 37
visual aids. *See* graphic aids
visualization strategies, 197
    for comprehension, 197
    and picture graphs, 241
    for retention, 256
visual literacy, 51, 236, 318
visual organizers. *See* graphic organizers
VOCAB-LIT strategy, 115
vocabulary.com, 142
vocabulary development, 111–144
    academic vocabulary, 123
    additional strategies for, 135–136
    analogy activities for, 132
    assessing progress in, 121–126
    and association, 70–72
    and attribute relations, 129
    books on CD for, 32
    building background for, 126
    and classification activities, 76–77, 79,
        94, 102
    and comprehension, 115
    computer software and the internet,
        141–142
    and conceptual knowledge, 113–114
    conceptual reinforcement activities for,
        129–136
    conceptual relationships and, 126–128
    and content area reading, 370–372
    and context clues, 83–84, 117–121
    context and word knowledge, 117–118
    denotation and connotation, 372
    and dictionaries, 117–118, 131, 136–138
    direct instruction for, 116–118
    direct systematic instruction, 113–118
    discussion, 126–128
    and elaboration, 121

for English language learners, 113, 122–123
expanding meaning, 138–142
expressive vocabularies, 114
Frayer Model, 127–128
general vocabulary, 86, 115
and graphic organizers, 124, 130, 134–135
identifying categories of vocabulary,
    115–116
in-depth word study for, 131
kinds of context clues, 120–121
learning meanings and concepts, 114
for literature, 115
for mathematics, 115, 126, 132, 135, 369
mind mapping for, 127–128
mnemonic strategies, 140–141
morphological analysis for, 116–117
offer opportunities to develop and expand
    meanings, 121–122
for physical education, 126
picture books for, 316–317
reading comprehension and, 10
receptive vs. expressive vocabularies, 114
for science, 131–134
selecting words for direct instruction, 116
semantic feature analysis, 129
sight-word recognition, 9
for social studies, 348, 254
super word web, 122
for struggling readers, 16–17, 123–124
targeted vocabulary instruction, 115
types of taxes, 128
using reference books for, 136–138
visual organizers for, 134–135
in vocational education, 386, 388, 393–394,
    398, 403, 405, 407, 409, 411–416
web graphic organizer, 136
word identification skills, 9–10
and word knowledge, 112–113
and word sorts, 134
and word walls, 139–140
vocational literacy, 384–416
    accounting content, 309
    in agricultural education, 405
    applications of literacy strategies, 396–416
    art, 408–409
    aspects of, 386–395
    in business education, 396–401
    communication skills, 387
    for English language learners, 416
    following directions, 388–389
    graphic materials in, 390
    in human environmental science, 401–405
    literacy for career-related education,
        385–386
    music, 409–415
    physical education, 405–408
    problem solving in, 392–393
    reading rate, 390

reading strategies for, 394
for struggling readers, 415
technical content, 397
technical and specialized vocabulary,
    386–388
in technical education, 396
technology and, 390
using motivational strategies in, 393
using textbooks in, 393–394
vocabulary development, 386, 388,
    393–394, 398, 403, 405, 407, 409,
    411–416
writing in, 386–387

wait time, in effective questioning,
    178–179, 187
Washington State University, 45
web logs (blogs), 42–44, 280, 305
web pages, 35–39. *See also* Internet
webquests, 39, 178
We Remember the Holocaust (Adler), 327
Western Historical Quarterly, 355
What Hearts (Brooks), 320
When My Name Was Keoko (Park), 169
whiteboards, interactive, 239
whole-class novel study, 322–323
Who's Who in America, 214
Wikis (Wikipedia), 38–39, 296
woodworking or science diagram, 249
word association, 70
word cards, 116, 124
word identification skills, 9–10
word knowledge, 112–113
    depth and breadth of, 112
    and pronunciation, 113
    reading comprehension and, 10
    two dimensions of, 112
    types of words, 371–372
    See also vocabulary development
word maps, 124, 128
word problems, mathematical, 89, 229, 232,
    234, 247
    as verbal problems, 365–367
word-processing programs, 33–34, 54, 99.
    See also computer technology
words
    identification of, 9–10
    "loaded," 184
    types of, 371–372
    vague usage of, 183–184
    word knowledge, 112–113
    word walls, 139–140
    See key words
word sorts, 10, 121
word walls, 139–140
word webs, 10, 121–122, 134–135, 137
work-based learning, 385–386. *See also*
vocational literacy

workplace, literacy demands of, 6, 386-395
World Class project, 37
World Wide Web (WWW), 31, 33, *See also* Internet
World Wide Web Virtual Library, 33
Wrinkle in Time, A (L'Engle), 315, 319
Writer's Studio, 34
Write It Right, 34
writing, 266–310
   combining with reading activities, 266–269
   computer technology for, 33–34
   content journals, 283–284
   in different genres, 272
   drafting stage, 272–275
   editing, 276–277
   evaluation of, 306–307
   internet assistance in revision and editing, 277
   language experience, 281–282
   in literacy program, 15
   instruction, 15, 17
   mentoring projects, 306–309
   mini-lessons in 269–270
   misconceptions about teaching, 17
   nature of, 266
   online resources for, 277
   peer tutoring, 295–297, 306
   and prereading, 286
   prewriting stage, 270–272
   and prior knowledge, 268, 272, 282
   problem-solution pattern and, 357, 392
   process approach to, 269–280
   publishing, 277–278

   question and answer, 353–355
   recursive nature of, 269
   relationships among reading, writing, and thinking, 266–269
   revising, 275–277
   sample character home page, 279
   sample twitter sequence, 280sample form for content writing, 273
   strategies, 196
   types of writing-to-learn activities, 280–310
   value to content area instruction, 266–267
   in vocational education, 386–387
   See also literacy instruction; writing-to-learn strategies
writing a draft, 272–275
writing development software, 34
writing labs, 14
writing strategies, 196
writing to display learning genres, 265
writing-to-learn genres, 280–281
writing-to-learn activities, 280–310
   character journals, 287
   children's books, 289–290
   content journals, 283–285
   creative applications, 288–290
   dialogue journals, 293–294
   different formats for reports, 298–299
   discourse forms for, 344, 356, 375
   for English language learners, 309–310
   evaluation of writing, 306–307
   expository writing program, 297–298
   freewriting, 285–286
   Internet writing projects, 305

   laboratory reports, 304
   language experience writings, 281–282
   for literature, 269, 277–278, 286–287, 290
   mentoring programs, 306
   multigenre books, 291–292
   multigenre report, 300–304
   multigenre writing, 291–292, 300–304
   oral history project, 290–291
   paraphrasing and summarizing, 292–293
   pen pals, 305
   photo essays, 304
   poetry, 282–283
   RAFT assignments, 294
   reading response journals, 286–287
   research reports, 294–297
   responses to thought questions, 288
   rubric for writing assessment, 291
   for struggling readers, 307–309
   translating literature into comic book form, 290
   written conversations, 294
   See also writing
written reflections about work, 94
written retellings, 88–89
written skill inventories, 69, 76–80

Yahoo, 36, 215
You Are There activities, 197, 299
young adult literature, 314–316. *See also* literature

zines, 277–278